The Handbook of Negotiation and Culture

The Handbook of Negotiation
and Culture

Edited by
MICHELE J. GELFAND
and JEANNE M. BRETT

Stanford Business Books
An imprint of Stanford University Press
Stanford, California

Printed in the United States of America on acid-free, archival-quality paper

Library of Congress Cataloging-in-Publication Data

The handbook of negotiation and culture /
    edited by Michele J. Gelfand and Jeanne M. Brett.
        p.   cm.
    Includes bibliographical references and index.
    ISBN 0-8047-4586-2 (cloth : alk. paper)
        1. Negotiation.   2. Conflict management.
    3. Negotiation—Cross-cultural studies.   4. Conflict
    management—Cross-cultural studies.   I. Gelfand, Michele J.
    II. Brett, Jeanne M.
    BF637.N4 H365   2004
    302.3—dc22   2003025169

Typeset by TechBooks in 10.5/12 Bembo
Original printing 2004
Last figure below indicates year of this printing:
13   12   11   10   09   08   07

Contents

Tables and Figures

THIS BOOK IS A MUST read for anyone who studies negotiation or its close cousin, mediation. (Theoretically inclined practitioners will also find it quite interesting.) One reason for this is that it contains an up-to-date summary of most of the research in this field. A second reason is that it contains many theory-driven ideas for new research. There are scores of dissertation leads in these pages. The third and most important reason is that it shows clearly that an understanding of the impact of culture is central to an understanding of negotiation. With this volume, the study of culture and negotiation comes of age.

The book is organized into pairs of chapters, one chapter on negotiation theory and research in a particular realm (cognition, emotion, motivation, communication, dispute resolution, social context, justice, mediation, technology, social dilemmas) and the other on the impact of culture on that realm. One thing we learn is that there are some big cultural differences in negotiation behavior and the variables that affect that behavior. For example, negotiators from individualistic cultures tend to take a more competitive approach to managing conflict, while those from collectivistic cultures are more concerned about maintaining positive relationships. Indeed, it turns out that some of the most central findings about negotiation in our society are totally wrong when we move to more collectivistic societies. Thus the usual finding that accountability to constituents enhances competitive intentions and behavior is reversed for collectivists, who are more cooperative under high accountability.

We also learn a lot about the processes that produce these cultural differences. The study of culture has become quite theoretical in recent years, and theory permeates this book. This means that it is now possible to make predictions about which behavior will show cultural differences and which will be invariant across all societies. It also means that we can identify conditions under which culturally dominant tendencies will be strengthened. For instance, theory tells us that when there is high need for closure (for rapid decision making), people tend to think and act in accustomed ways. This implies that high need for closure will tend to accentuate competitiveness in individualistic societies and cooperativeness in collectivistic societies. Research supports this implication.

One of the main messages of this volume is that most cultural differences are relative rather than absolute. In other words, people across the world are *capable* of behaving in almost any fashion, but their *preferences* for one kind of behavior over another differ from culture to culture. Characteristics that are dominant in one culture tend to be recessive in another, and vice versa.

What this means is that it is important to study other societies in order to learn about our own. Social scientists tend to notice first the characteristics that stand out in their society. Hence, they are likely to miss more subtle features that may, nevertheless, be important. By studying other societies where these features are dominant, they can develop concepts and theories that will eventually be useful for understanding their own. An example of this comes from a comparison between societies that emphasize low-context versus high-context communication. In low-context societies (e.g., the United States), people usually say what they mean. In high-context societies (e.g., Japan), a speaker's meaning will often be only hinted at in what is said and requires familiarity with the culture in order to be clearly understood. This has implications for negotiation. Research in the United States has shown that negotiators tend to learn about the adversary's priorities among the issues from what the adversary says about these priorities. By contrast, in high-context societies, it has been found that negotiators often make inferences about these priorities by looking for patterns across the adversary's concessions. My point is that it seems quite likely that the latter kind of inference also takes place in the United States, *but we have not yet noticed it.* Somebody should do that study!

To put this point in a broader context, consider what would have happened if social science had started elsewhere in the world, for example, in China or Japan, rather than in the West. Social science theory would certainly have been different from what it is today, emphasizing the dominant patterns in the culture where it originated. That theory would certainly not be a perfect fit to Western society, but it would help us understand a lot, including aspects of Western society that are now overlooked. If that had happened, we would be calling for a massive research effort in the West to correct that theory's deficiencies. And when that research effort had taken place, we would know more about China or Japan as well as about the West.

All of this is to say, "Bravo!" The search for a broader and deeper negotiation theory—and a broader and deeper social science—is off and running with the publication of this book. As cross-cultural research proliferates, we will learn ever more about our own society, whatever it may be.

Dean G. Pruitt
George Mason University
Institute for Conflict Analysis and Resolution

Preface

RESEARCH ON NEGOTIATION is thriving. Over the last two decades, scholars have advanced our understanding of fundamental psychological processes in negotiation, such as cognition, emotion, and motivation; complex social processes in negotiation, including communication, power, and influence; and effects of the negotiation context, such as teams, third parties, and technology. This research has not only greatly expanded our understanding of the psychology of negotiation, but it has also generated important insights into training managers and others on how to manage and negotiate conflict. Indeed, few areas in organizational behavior can claim to have developed as rapidly, and with as much depth and breadth, as the field of negotiation (Kramer and Messick, 1995).

With such rapid progress, it is important to "take stock" of the field—to identify key theoretical and empirical contributions, as well as to critically reflect on issues that need attention. Thus the first purpose of this book is to provide a comprehensive review of current knowledge about negotiation. Scholars whose own research has framed current knowledge of the basic psychological processes, social processes, and negotiation context review key theoretical and empirical advances in the field of negotiation and identify critical directions for future research.

The second purpose of this book is to place negotiation theory and research in a cultural context. In today's global marketplace, negotiations occur across as well as within cultural borders. Yet research on negotiation and conflict has largely been derived from research participants from Western cultures, which represent roughly 30 percent of humankind (Triandis, 1994). The field largely remains culture-bound—having its roots in Euro-American thought and traditions, and culture-blind—tending to ignore culture in its theories and research. Importantly, this is not due to a lack of existing culture theory or research. In the last few decades, there has been a rapid proliferation of theory and research on culture in social psychology and organizational behavior. This book expands current thinking in negotiation to include cross-cultural perspectives and thus begins to bridge the gap between what we know about negotiation and what we know about culture. Scholars who have conducted cross-cultural negotiation research on basic psychological processes, social processes, and negotiation context review current key theoretical and empirical advances in the study of culture and negotiation, and they develop extensions of negotiation theory that embrace a distinctly cultural perspective.

We selected the topics and chose a structure for this book to serve both of these purposes and to encourage synergy between the fields of negotiation and culture. The content of the book reflects the diversity of theoretical perspectives that have been developed in the field of negotiation: Cognition, emotion, motivation, communication, power and disputing, intergroup relationships, third parties, justice, technology, and social dilemmas. Following chapters on each of these topics, culture scholars provided their perspectives on the same topics. In this way, both negotiation and culture "lenses" have been focused on a variety of topics that are essential to the study of negotiation. We note that there is not a strict one-to-one correspondence between pairs of chapters. This reflects both the gap between research on negotiation and research on negotiation and culture. It also reflects the fact that adding culture often requires questioning assumptions and raising different questions that are not visible when working within one culture.

The book is organized in three sections. Section 1 focuses on psychological processes and emphasizes cognition, how negotiators think and their deviations from rationality; emotion, how moods, affect, and flashes of emotion influence negotiators; and motivation, why negotiators act as they do and what affects their goals. Chapters in this section include cognition and biases (Chapter 1, Thompson, Neale, and Sinaceur), culture and cognition (Chapter 2, Morris and Gelfand), emotion (Chapter 3, Barry, Fulmer, and Van Kleef), culture and emotion (Chapter 4, Kumar), and motivation (Chapter 5, De Dreu). Section 2 focuses on social process and emphasizes the dynamic negotiation process—how negotiators coordinate their behavior and why. Chapters in this section include communication processes (Chapter 6, Weingart and Olekalns), culture and communication processes (Chapter 7, Adair and Brett), power and disputing (Chapter 8, Shapiro and Kulik), and culture and disputing (Chapter 9, Tinsley). Section 3 focuses on the negotiation context—the social and environmental conditions in which negotiations are embedded. Chapters in this section include intergroup relationships (Chapter 10, Kramer), culture and intergroup relationships (Chapter 11, Gelfand and Cai), third parties (Chapter 12, Conlon and Meyer), culture and third parties (Chapter 13, Carnevale, Cha, Wan, and Fraidin), justice and negotiation (Chapter 14, Tyler and Blader), culture and justice (Chapter 15, Lueng and Tong), the technological context of negotiations (Chapter 16, McGinn and Crosen), culture and technology in negotiations (Chapter 17, Barsness and Bhappu), social dilemmas (Chapter 18, Weber and Messick), and culture and social dilemmas (Chapter 19, Brett and Kopelman). In the final chapter, we review themes that cut across the chapters, discussing lessons learned about culture as it relates to negotiation and offering further ways to capitalize on the synergy between culture and negotiation research on the road ahead.

Our goals in designing this book were to compile an up-to-date review of current knowledge of negotiation, to challenge negotiation theorists to more inclusive of all humankind, and to challenge cultural theorists to provide an explanation for patterns of thought and action in an important area of social interaction. Chapters identify numerous knowledge lacuna—opportunities for research for decades to come. The culture chapters also identify the limits of the Western culture-based findings and provide new insights into those findings.

The book will be useful to scholars who are teaching courses on negotiation, courses on culture, or both. It provides a reference for information about the fundamental theoretical approaches to negotiation research and the state of current knowledge about negotiation. It also provides information about the new directions that are shaping both the fields of negotiation and culture research, and provides a resource for research ideas for students and scholars who are interested in studying negotiation or negotiation and culture.

The book is also designed for practicing negotiators and conflict managers who want an understanding of negotiation that is deeper than what is available in most standard textbooks and who also want to understand the cultural limits and extensions of negotiation before theory and research. The paired-chapter organization of the book makes it easy for a practitioner to use it as a reference and as a specific resource. The presentation within chapters that emphasizes a review and explanation of research findings also makes the book particularly accessible to practicing negotiators and conflict managers.

We extend our gratitude to numerous people who have made this book possible. We thank all of the contributors to the volume, the Kellogg School of Management, the Dispute Resolution Research Center (DRRC), and the Department of Psychology at the University of Maryland. We thank Nancy McLaughlin and Toni Betton for helping to get the book ready for publication. We also thank our spouses and children for their support and patience while we worked on the book. Finally, we thank Bill Hicks and his outstanding staff at Stanford University Press for their support and patience, and for helping to make this book a reality.

Michele J. Gelfand
College Park, Maryland

Jeanne M. Brett
Evanston, Illinois

Works Cited

Kramer, R. M., and D. Messick. (1995). *Negotiation as a social process*. Thousand Oaks, CA: Sage.

Triandis, H. C. (1994). *Culture and social behavior*. New York: McGraw-Hill.

The Handbook of Negotiation and Culture

PART ONE

Basic Psychological Processes

Introduction

THE FIVE CHAPTERS that comprise Part 1 all focus on basic psychological processes in negotiation. Included in this section are pairs of chapters that focus on negotiator cognition and pairs of chapters that focus on emotion in negotiations. The last chapter analyzes motivation in negotiation and also highlights the role of culture in motivation. Collectively, these chapters provide insight into the basic psychological processes underlying negotiation and how they are shaped by culture.

In Chapter 1, Thompson, Neale, and Sinaceur trace the evolution of the cognitive tradition in negotiation. Using an archeological metaphor, they uncover distinct historical periods of scholarly research on different negotiation biases. The first period they identify is "cognitive biases," which have their roots in behavioral decision theory and were a direct outgrowth of the cognitive revolution in psychology. They include, for example, negotiator framing, overconfidence, and anchoring. The next period they identify includes biases that have their roots in the perception of social situations, including the fixed pie bias, reactive devaluation, ignoring the cognitions of others, and the fundamental attribution error. This period of biases, through its ties to social psychology, ultimately made the study of cognition in negotiation more social in nature. They divide more recent periods of scholarly activity into motivational biases—biases that stem from negotiators' goals and needs, and emotional biases—biases stemming from inaccuracy of judging and reading emotions in the self and another, faulty beliefs about the duration of emotions, and faulty beliefs about the causal impact that emotions have on behavior. These latter two eras are recent additions to the fossils that predate them and provide a much needed view of the negotiator as a "goal-directed, hotblooded, driven creature." Thompson et al. conclude their chapter with speculations on the next era of research on negotiator cognition, arguing that

3

research should depart from the traditional approach, wherein cognition is only studied at the individual level, and instead should adopt a situated approach to cognition—that focuses on how biases are created and sustained in particular contexts.

In Chapter 2, Morris and Gelfand analyze the cognitive tradition from a cultural perspective. They point out that the evidence for negotiator biases comes almost exclusively from studies using U.S. or other Western samples. This raises a number of questions for negotiation research: Are the biases that have been identified reflective of only "Western" or "individualistic" negotiators, rather than the fundamental aspects of human nature? Has negotiation research ignored other biases that appear only in other cultural settings? The authors reject the polar positions of universalism (that all negotiation biases are found in all cultures) and relativism (that thinking and its biases differ incommensurably across cultures), and instead present a middle range theory that highlights the role of cultural knowledge structures in guiding judgments in negotiation. Grounded in the classic French anthropological tradition of Levi-Strauss (1966), their theory addresses three fundamental issues: Which negotiation biases are most likely culturally variable, and which are likely culturally invariant? Through what pathways does culture influence negotiators' thinking? Furthermore, what are the factors at the negotiation table that trigger the influence of culture? Above all, their analysis illustrates that cross-cultural perspectives can both deepen the study of cognitive processes in negotiation as well as broaden them to be inclusive of more macro culture-level factors.

In Chapter 3, Barry, Fulmer, and Van Kleef begin with the premise that negotiation is fundamentally an emotional social interaction. After defining the constructs of affect, mood, and emotion, the authors review recent conceptual developments on this topic, including emotions at different stages of negotiation, emotional contagion among negotiators, the social functions of emotions, and the interplay between emotion and cognitive appraisals and attributions. They also integrate recent empirical research that has examined emotions as a predictor of negotiation processes and outcomes, emotions as a consequence of negotiation outcomes, and the strategic use of emotions as a negotiation tactic. In the latter part of their chapter Barry et al. suggest areas that are ripe for theoretical development and empirical investigation. They invite us to think about how individual differences, such as personality, gender, self-monitoring, and emotional intelligence, are implicated in emotional experience and expression, and they offer some intriguing propositions. They also call for research on emotion at the group level of analysis, including the development of positive affective tone and its relationship to individual personality traits, such as extroversion. And they urge us to consider the interpersonal effects of emotions in negotiations. For example, what role does one's negative and positive affect play in regulating other negotiators' actions? Can anger produce cooperation, and happiness produce competition? Seeking to broaden researchers' vistas, they remind us that research has thus far been focused on a very narrow range of emotions and that studies of fear, contempt, and anxiety are sorely needed in negotiation research.

In Chapter 4, Kumar underscores the importance of emotion in understanding the dynamics of intercultural negotiations. Integrating insights from cultural psychology (Markus and Kitayama, 1991) and research on emotion in negotiation (Barry and Oliver, 1996), Kumar illustrates how cultural differences can influence emotional dynamics within intercultural negotiations. He points out that because culture can influence the types of goals that are pursued in negotiation, intercultural negotiations are ripe for "emotional conflict." He further argues that even if the same emotions are experienced by people from different cultures, they can produce different behaviors in intercultural negotiations. Kumar concludes that intercultural negotiations are likely to be fraught with behavioral incongruence, which may heighten attributional biases and cause further negative affective states to arise. He cautions that even when negotiators do come to agreement in intercultural contexts, cultural differences in perceptions of fair outcomes may cause further negative affective states to arise after negotiations (see also Leung and Tong, Chapter 15, this volume). Kumar concludes with a discussion of a number of moderating conditions, ranging from individual differences to situational conditions, which may help alleviate emotional conflict in intercultural negotiations.

In the last chapter of this section, De Dreu focuses on motivation in negotiation. He discusses three classes of motives in negotiation: (1) social motivation, the need to attain particular outcome distributions; (2) epistemic motivation, the need to develop an accurate view of the world; and (3) impression motivation, the need to maintain or induce a particular impression. He marshals considerable empirical evidence showing that these motives have an impact on strategic choice in negotiation—the use of distributive or integrative behaviors—and ultimately affect negotiation outcomes. He also reviews evidence showing that these motives have important effects on information processing. For example, theses motives drive the encoding, storage, and retrieval of information, which can bias what is selectively attended to during negotiations. They also drive the amount and depth of information processing, which can lead to the use of suboptimal decision heuristics and ultimately impede negotiation agreements. In discussing the future, De Dreu urges us to take a dynamic view of motivation to uncover the possible correlations between motives, to consider how motives may change over time during negotiations, and to integrate research on motivation and emotion. Finally, echoing Kumar's sentiments, De Dreu calls for cross-cultural research on motivation, arguing that culture may not only affect dominant motives in negotiation, but also may affect the behavioral manifestations of motives as well.

CHAPTER 1

The Evolution of Cognition and Biases in Negotiation Research

AN EXAMINATION OF COGNITION, SOCIAL PERCEPTION, MOTIVATION, AND EMOTION

Leigh Thompson, Margaret Neale, and Marwan Sinaceur

BAZERMAN AND NEALE's (1983) chapter on heuristics in negotiating initiated a new era of negotiation research. Prior to that time, the study of negotiation as led by Pruitt (1981), Kelley (1966), Deutsch (1973), Druckman (1968), Morley and Stephenson (1977), Siegel and Fouraker (1960), and others focused on the bargaining process, the study of moves and countermoves, aspirations and goals, and, to some extent, expectations. The birth of the cognitive negotiation theory was fueled by three events in the social sciences. First, Amos Tversky and Daniel Kahneman's empirical studies and their seminal 1982 book with Paul Slovic, *Judgment Under Uncertainty: Heuristics and Biases,* created a new field of behavioral science: behavioral decision theory. Richard Nisbett and Lee Ross's empirical studies and their book *Human Inference: Strategies and Shortcoming of Social Judgment* (1980) further catalyzed the field of behavioral decision theory. Second, the social cognition movement in social psychology (cf. Taylor and Fiske, 1975) focused researchers on the mental shortcomings of the social actor. Finally, Howard Raiffa, in his book *The Art and Science of Negotiation* (1982), provided a conceptual perspective on negotiation—the asymmetrical prescriptive–descriptive approach—arguing that the best advice (or prescriptions) to negotiators included an understanding not only of what negotiators should do (the rational perspective) but also of what they are likely to do (the behavioral perspective). Raiffa's perspective

The research reported in this chapter and the writing of the chapter was in large part supported by a grant to the first author from the National Science Foundation, Decision, Risk, and Management Science Program, No. 9870892.

provided a structure for thinking rationally in a less than rational world. In the ensuing twenty years, there has been considerable research on negotiation from this cognitive perspective.

In this chapter, we have organized the cognitive negotiation research into four categories of biases: cognitive biases, social perception biases, motivational biases and, most recently, emotional biases. Our choice of categories was based on induction: We began by searching the literature on negotiation and bias from 1990 to 2000, using the key words *negotiation* and *conflict resolution* on the one hand, and *judgment, cognitive, bias, heuristic,* and *attributions* on the other hand. This search yielded 554 citations. We eliminated studies that did not use a negotiation task per se. This eliminated group judgment tasks and scenario-based studies, prisoner's dilemma studies, and computer simulations.[1] We also eliminated studies that did not use some kind of quantitative measure of outcome, without which it is impossible to draw conclusions about the quality of the negotiated agreement; studies that did not have the individual, dyad, or group as the unit of analysis (mainly, this excluded studies from the clinical literature); reports that were not original empirical research articles (e.g., chapters and review reports); studies that focused on culture per se, as this is the focus of several other articles in this volume; and studies that did not focus on one of the four major areas of bias that we identified at the outset. Applying these criteria reduced the citations to 127. After classifying the empirical articles into one of the four major areas of bias, we looked for major themes and organizing principles within each. Our goal was to examine how the landmark studies in each of these areas have shaped the science and practice of negotiation. In the final section of the chapter, we explore the mechanisms by which negotiators can reduce the impact of biases in negotiation.

COGNITIVE BIASES

Cognitive biases are systematic deviations from normative models that prescribe rational behavior, as articulated by game theory and other normative principles. Cognitive biases presumably result from information-processing heuristics, such as framing, anchoring, and overconfidence (Neale and Bazerman, 1991). Cognitive heuristics emanate from faulty information processing. Two approaches have characterized the research on cognitive biases in negotiation (and in decision making as well). The fundamental argument is that decision makers (and negotiators) suffer from fundamental misperceptions when judging the risk, the value (or utility) of gambles and other objects. This approach identifies the well-known economic model of utility maximization and related principles of rationality (cf. von Neumann and Morgenstern, 1947) as the appropriate normative model. The observation that individuals systematically depart from the predictions of economic models largely led to the development of behavioral decision theory as a field of study and the modern conceptualization of negotiation theory as a topic of empirical inquiry. The research literature on cognitive bias in negotiation has been built on straightforward extensions of individual information processing to the (at least) dyadic, interdependent interaction of negotiation. For example, Neale and Bazerman (1991) referred to these biases as "individual biases in negotiations." Only later did scholars (including Bazerman and Neale) begin to study how these biases might socially interact (Arrow, Mnookin, Ross, Tversky, and Wilson, 1995).

The second approach derives from the concept of cognitive schemas or cognitive maps (e.g., Abelson, 1981; Gilovich, 1981; Higgins, Rholes, and Jones, 1977) and, more recently, cognitive mental models as developed by cognitive psychologists (Evans, 1993; Johnson-Laird, 1983; Tabossi, Bell, and Johnson-Laird, 1999). The key assumption is that people attempt to make sense out of novel situations by using previously developed knowledge structures. These knowledge structures (schema, maps, and models) operate in a top-down fashion to direct information processing, including attention, categorization, and retrieval. It is important that the biases that result from the use of such heuristics are not biases that reflect departure from economic models of behavior, but rather biases that indicate departures from social norms or standards.

Table 1.1 reviews these two key principles and identifies the biases that have been identified by each and the empirical studies related to that bias. Next, we review the two organizing principles in greater detail.

Misperceptions of Risk and Value

Much of the research on the misperceptions of risk and value is derived from the work of Kahneman and Tversky (1979) on prospect theory. The fundamental prediction of prospect theory is that people's evaluations of a given prospect are largely a function of people's reference points, defining gain and loss, as opposed to the expected utility of the gamble (Kahneman and Tversky, 1979). Accordingly, a "framing effect" refers to the observation that people typically prefer gains for certain rather than a lottery of equal or greater expected value, but when contemplating losses, people prefer a gamble rather than a certain outcome of something of equal or greater expected value. Neale and Bazerman and their colleagues (Bazerman, Magliozzi, and Neale, 1985; Neale and Bazerman, 1985; Neale, Huber, and Northcraft 1987; Northcraft and Neale, 1986) extended the theory of framing to a negotiation context. In their original study, negotiators were either given a payoff schedule that was positively framed (e.g., indicated profits) or negatively framed (e.g., indicated losses). Whereas the payoff schedules were objectively identical, they led to very different behaviors. Positively framed

TABLE 1.1

Cognitive Biases in Negotiation

Theory	Cognitive Bias	Reasearch Findings
Prospect theory and BDT	Framing	Bazerman, Magliozzi, and Neale (1985); Neale and Bazerman (1985): Positively framed negotiators show greater risk aversion than negatively framed negotiators.
		Bottom and Studt (1993): Positive frames can be a liability when they are not shared by all the parties.
		De Dreu, Emans, and van de Vliert (1992): Negotiators are influenced not only by their own frames, but also by others' communicated frames.
	Anchoring	Northcraft and Neale (1987): Tendency for decision makers to fail to sufficiently adjust a judgment away from an initial starting value.
		Kristensen and Gaerling (1997a): Initial offer, not only market price and reservation price, shapes the adoption of reference point.
		Galinsky, Seiden, Kim, and Medvec (2002): Initial offers affect negotiators' satisfaction with their outcome, more than does objective success.
		Kristensen and Gaerling (1997b): Estimated market price affects both one's aspiration price and one's estimate of the other party's reservation price.
		Korhonen, Oretskin, Teich, and Wallenius (1995): A biased starting position impacts the outcome of negotiations.
		Ritov (1996): Initial offer values, for both the initiator and the noninitiator, affect final profit.
		Galinsky and Mussweiler (2001): The effect of initial offers on outcomes is moderated by perspective taking.
		White et al. (1994): Reservation price seems a dominant reference point.
		Blount, Thomas-Hunt, and Neale (1996): Effect of reservation price upon negotiation outcome is more dominant than market information when negotiators perceive high price variance.
		Whyte and Sebenius (1997): Anchoring effects are as large for groups as they are for individuals; this is because groups tend to adopt either majority rule or consensus rule.

TABLE 1.1

(continued)

Theory	Cognitive Bias	Reasearch Findings
	Availability	Northcraft and Neale (1986): More concrete information is more likely to affect decision making during negotiations.
		Borgida and Nisbett (1977): Vivid, concrete, and emotionally rich information is more impactful than abstract, pallid, and emotionally poor information.
		Taylor and Thompson (1982): Vivid information does not have more impact than equally informative, but pallid, information.
		Neale (1984): Negotiators to whom negotiating costs are highly salient behave in a less concessionary manner.
	Overconfidence	Bazerman and Neale (1982): Tendency for negotiators to overestimate the probability that a neutral arbitrator will choose their own offer.
		Neale and Bazerman (1985): Overconfident negotiators are less concessionary and achieve lower performance than realistically confident negotiators.
Information processing theory	Utility	Simons (1993): When dyads conceptualize utility as a subjective preference, they tend to reach more integrative agreements.
	Perceptual frames	Pinkley (1990): Negotiators may have one of three different cognitive frames: relationship–task, emotional–intellectual, and compromise–win.
		Pinkley and Northcraft (1994): Cognitive frames affect both the content of agreements and negotiation outcomes.
	Task perception	Ross and Samuels (1993): A prisoner's dilemma labeled as the "Community Game," rather than the "Wall Street Game," induced players to cooperate more.
		Thompson and DeHarpport (1998): When both parties share similar perceptions of their interaction, whether communal or exchange, the negotiation is smoother.

negotiators adopted less risky bargaining strategies, preferring an agreement to holding out for a better, but more uncertain, settlement. As a result, they were more concessionary and reached more agreements than negatively framed negotiators. Also, they perceived the negotiated outcomes as more fair than negotiators who had negative frames. The larger number of transactions achieved by positively framed negotiators resulted in higher overall profitability for them, although negatively framed negotiators completed transactions of greater average profit (Neale, Huber, and Northcraft, 1987). Thus a positive frame led to more successful performances over a small number of transactions. However, negotiators who had a positive frame were more likely to agree to less favorable terms than were negotiators who had a negative frame. If negotiators had different frames, the negotiator with the negative frame would be expected to gain a greater share of the available surplus as compared to his or her positively framed counterpart. Indeed, Bottom and Studt (1993) showed that negatively framed negotiators received significantly better outcomes than their positively framed counterparts not only in distributive but also in integrative negotiations. Hence, positive frames can be a liability in distributive and integrative bargaining when they are not shared by all negotiating parties (Bottom and Studt, 1993).

The influence of frames does not mean that one is only influenced by one's own frames. In a negotiation, parties may be influenced not only by their own frames, but also by others' communicated frames (De Dreu, Emans, and van de Vliert, 1992). In particular, negotiators may learn about their counterpart's frame through information exchange during the negotiation process. As a result, negotiators' own frames may change as a function of their counterpart's communicated frame. Relying on such arguments, De Dreu and his colleagues showed that people may be especially affected by the other's loss frame as opposed to his or her gain frame. Specifically, when two negotiators have different frames, the gain-framed negotiator adopts the other's loss frame more readily than vice versa.

Another bias that garnered scholarly attention in negotiation research is anchoring and insufficient adjustment. According to Kahneman and Tversky, an anchoring-and-insufficient adjustment effect (referred to in this chapter as anchoring) occurs when an individual's judgment is weighted by an initial datum and the individual fails to adjust his or her assessment of value sufficiently, given that initial anchor. Tversky and Kahneman's (1974) famous wheel-of-fortune study, where participants were asked to estimate the number of African countries in the United Nations after being given a random starting value, led to similar studies in negotiation.[2] Northcraft and Neale (1987) demonstrated that real estate agents were susceptible to the influence of an anchor, in the form of a listing price previously provided, when they estimated the appraised value of residential properties and made pricing decisions about them. When the real estate agents were asked to identify the factors that influenced their decisions, they denied using the listing price provided as a consideration in their decision. More recent research has used the anchoring principle to examine the weight accorded to first offers in negotiation (Galinsky, Seiden, Kim, and Medvec, 2002; Kristensen and Gaerling, 1997a; also Weingart, Thompson, Bazerman, and Carroll, 1990). Initial offers influence the adoption of a reference point, even in the presence of an estimated market price or of a reservation price (Kristensen and Gaerling, 1997a). They also influence people's satisfaction with and subsequent attitude toward negotiation, such as the amount of preparation for a subsequent negotiation, more than does objective success (Galinsky et al., 2002). Indeed, negotiators whose first offers are immediately accepted are less satisfied with their outcome than negotiators whose first offers are not immediately accepted, even when their objective outcome is actually better. Galinsky et al. (in press) showed that this is because such negotiators engage more in counterfactual thinking: Having one's first offer immediately accepted is more likely to produce thoughts of how one "could have done better."

Not only do anchors affect negotiators' reference points and satisfaction, but they also affect their estimates of their counterparts' reservation prices. For instance, Kristensen and Gaerling (1997b) documented that an estimated market price affected buyers' estimates of sellers' reservation prices. White (Blount) and Neale (1994) showed that initial offers influenced negotiators' perceptions of their counterparts' reservation prices. Anchors also affect negotiated outcomes (e.g., Korhonen, Oretskin, Teich, and Wallenius, 1995; White (Blount) Valley, Bazerman, Neale, and Peck, 1994). In particular, initial offers affect final profit, both for the initiator and the noninitiator (Galinsky and Mussweiler, 2001; Galinsky et al., 2002; Ritov, 1996). According to Ritov, the impact of initial offers endures even when negotiators gain experience. Galinsky and Mussweiler (2001) found that whichever party made the first offer obtained a better outcome. In addition, they demonstrated that the effect of first offers on final settlement was moderated by perspective taking. Specifically, when the negotiator who received the first offer focused on information that was inconsistent with it—that is, she or he thought about the alternatives or the reservation price of the person making the first offer, or about his or her own targets—the advantageous effect of making the first offer was eliminated. This research suggests that some anchors are more powerful than others. Own aspirations or estimates of another's aspirations may be stronger than another's first offer.

This latter result, in turn, poses the more general problem of the relative weight of simultaneous, competing anchors. White (Blount) and associates (Blount, Thomas-Hunt, and Neale, 1996; White and Neale, 1994) assessed the relative importance of different kinds of anchors for actual outcomes.

They found that individual reservation prices influenced bargaining outcomes more strongly than prevailing market prices or negotiator aspirations. In particular, when perceptions of high price variance were present among negotiators, reservation prices were more dominant in determining outcomes than was market information (Blount, Thomas-Hunt, and Neale, 1996). In other research, Galinsky, Mussweiler, and Medvec (2001) examined whether the level of reference points resulted in differentiated outcomes and satisfaction for negotiators. In their experiments, negotiators focused on either a low reference point (reservation prices) or a high reference point (targets). Negotiators who focused on their target prices achieved objectively superior outcomes than negotiators who focused on either their reservation prices or their alternatives to the negotiation. The effect on subjective satisfaction was the opposite. Paradoxically, those negotiators who focused on their higher bound were less satisfied with their objectively superior outcomes than those who focused on their lower bound. Finally, it seems plausible, in general, to argue that the various anchoring effects previously discussed may be extended to intergroup negotiations.

Availability and overconfidence have also held a prominent position in the cognitive bias research in negotiation. The availability of past and present information affects how negotiators evaluate their alternatives (Tversky and Kahneman, 1973): not all of the pieces of information that are relevant to decisions are recalled in an equivalent manner. When information is less concrete, such as opportunity costs, as opposed to out-of-pocket–sunk costs, it is less likely to be included in financial decision making during negotiations (Northcraft and Neale, 1986). Accordingly, manipulating the relative salience of negotiation-related costs produces systematic changes in negotiator behavior (Neale, 1984). Neale showed that when the personal costs of reaching a settlement are made salient, negotiators are less likely to settle. On the other hand, the way one's counterpart presents information may have an a impact on a negotiator's capacity to be persuaded. Research in social psychology demonstrates that people are more easily affected by vivid, concrete, and emotionally rich information, rather than abstract, pallid, and emotionally poor information (e.g., Borgida and Nisbett, 1977; Nisbett, Borgida, Crandall, and Reed, 1982). Vivid information does not necessarily need to be emotion arousing or concrete to be more easily recalled and be more persuasive than nonvivid information (Wilson, Northcraft, and Neale, 1989).

Overconfidence refers to people's unwarranted confidence in their judgment of abilities and the occurrence of positive events and underestimation of the likelihood of negative events. As an example, negotiators in final–offer arbitration consistently overestimate the probability that their side's final offer will be accepted (Bazerman and Neale, 1982; Neale and Bazerman, 1983).

Overconfident negotiators are less concessionary and reach fewer agreements than realistically confident negotiators (Neale and Bazerman, 1985).

Perceptual Frames, Maps, and Schema

Just as negotiation researchers embraced the cognitive models developed by behavioral decision theorists, they also embraced the information-processing models developed by cognitive psychologists. The concept of schemata and information processing took hold in psychology and related fields in the 1980s. The basic idea of information-processing theory is that cognitive activity may be analyzed in terms of a series of stages during which information is transformed or recoded via particular mental processes (see Thompson and Hastie, 1990; Thompson, Peterson, and Kray, 1995). Information processing is largely affected by existing theories, also known as naive theories. To this end, two modes of information processing exist: theory based (also known as top-down information processing) and data driven (also known as bottom-up information processing). The presence of existing theories affects attention, encoding, and retrieval.

Pinkley (1990) concluded that negotiators use one of three different "frames" (these frames refer to perceptual frames rather than cognitive frames; the same use of framing terminology does not imply consistency with prospect theory ideas, as previously discussed)—relationship versus task, emotional versus intellectual, and compromise versus win—to represent conflict situations. Such framing influences negotiator behavior. For instance, when negotiators perceive a dispute in emotional terms, they make apologies or statements about how the negative feelings should be handled (Pinkley, 1990; Pinkley and Northcraft, 1990). Perceptual framing also affects negotiation outcomes. Disputants achieve higher individual and joint outcomes when both they and their negotiating partners adopt task frames rather than relationship frames or cooperation rather than winning frames (Pinkley and Northcraft, 1994). Similarly, Simons (1993) found that negotiation dyads that conceptualized utility as a subjective preference reached more integrative agreements than dyads that conceptualized utility as an objective attribute or as an interpersonal relationship.

Perceptual frames are not only the result of negotiators' a priori representations that are exogenous to the situation, but are also the result of subjective interpretation of situations. How the situation is labeled or construed can have striking consequences on people's behavior (Nisbett and Ross, 1980; Ross and Nisbett, 1991). Indeed, Ross and Samuels (1993) found dramatically different behavior resulted when describing a prisoner's dilemma game as either the "Wall Street Game" or the "Community Game." Thompson and DeHarpport (1998) found similar results when they described the identical negotiation situation as either a "problem solving" situation or a "bargaining" situation.

Both decision heuristics and perceptual frames influence negotiators' behavior and outcomes. Shortcomings in negotiators' information processing may occur either because people rely on a number of simplifying strategies to cope with the complexity of their (information) environment or because they fail to realize the implicit weight of their own cognitive structures, or internal representations, when relying on these simplifying assumptions. Whereas the decision heuristic approach mainly focuses on individual deviations from rationality, research on perceptual frames suggests that the congruence of representations between the parties, or whether people share the same representations, is also important. The research on perceptual frames highlights an important, underrepresented perspective in the cognitive approach—that negotiation is an interdependent process and that the social implications of this interaction must be considered.

Summary

Cognitive bias is one of the most pervasive theoretical lenses for the study of negotiator behavior. There are several advantages of this theoretical approach, most notably, that the judgment and decision-making literature is closely connected to this approach and that cognitive biases can be readily manipulated and assessed in a laboratory or classroom setting. However, in large measure, the cognitive approach is an individualistic approach to an inherently social situation. Studies such as the one by De Dreu, Emans, and van de Vliert (1992), which explored the way frames are communicated during the negotiation interaction, remain relatively scarce. As both Raiffa (1982) and Neale and Bazerman (1991) suggested, rationality in negotiation and decision making requires the individual to consider not only his or her own perspective, biases, and motivations, but also to incorporate the perspective, bias, and motivations of his or her counterpart. We turn next to the social perception bias research that emphasizes the social, rather than cognitive, aspect of the interaction.

SOCIAL PERCEPTION BIASES

Social perception biases differ from cognitive biases in that the nature of bias is centered upon the perception of social objects, events, and people (Thompson and Hastie, 1990; Thompson, Peterson and Kray, 1995). Unlike cognitive biases, social perception biases are inherently interpersonal and have their roots in the perception of social entities and social situations. Table 1.2 reviews key biases in social perception. The table is organized into self-perception biases and other-perception biases. Self-perception biases are

TABLE 1.2

Social Perception Biases

Focus of Perception	Bias	Research
Self	Illusion of transparency	Gilovich, Savitsky, and Medvec (1998): Tendency for people to overestimate the extent to which others can discern their internal states.
		Keysar, Ginzel, and Bazerman (1995): Tendency for negotiators to behave as if others have access to their states of mind.
		Vorauer and Claude (1998): Tendency for negotiators to overestimate the transparency of their objectives, especially when communication with others is less constrained.
	Perspective taking	Kronzon and Darley (1999): People who identified with perpetrators, versus victims, are more likely to exhibit biased evaluation of ethical behavior.
		Neale and Bazerman (1983): High-perspective-taking negotiators were more successful in creating integrative agreements than were low-perspective-taking negotiators.
Other	Fixed-pie perception; reactive devaluation	Bazerman and Neale (1983): Most negotiators tend to think the other party's interests are directly opposed to their own.
		Thompson and Hastie (1990): Fixed-pie perceptions lead to lower individual and joint profits.
		Pinkley, Griffith, and Northcraft (1995): Fixed-pie perceptions occur through both biased information search and biased information processing.
		Oskamp (1965); Ross and Stillinger (1991): Negotiators devalue concessions made by the other party merely as a function of who is offering them.
	Extremism	Robinson, Keltner, Ward, and Ross (1995): Tendency for partisan perceivers to believe that their own perceptions map onto objective reality.
	Fundamental attribution error	Morris, Larrick, and Su (1999): Tendency to see other party's behavior in dispositional terms rather than as the effect of the situation.

TABLE 1.2

(continued)

Focus of Perception	Bias	Research
	Knowledge of other party (e.g., position), ignoring cognitions of others	Neale and Bazerman (1991): Tendency to ignore the cognitions of others.
		Carroll, Bazerman, and Maury, (1988): Tendency to ignore contingencies when negotiators are faced with uncertainty.
		Blount and Larrick (2000): Inability to accurately predict the effect of bargaining procedures on one's opponent.
		Bottom and Paese (1998): Tendency to think that one's counterpart can concede more than she or he really could; this leads to greater negotiation outcomes.
	Coercion bias	Rothbart and Hallmark (1988): Tendency to believe that coercion works effectively on enemies but not the self.

beliefs and judgments about oneself or one's behavior that deviate from what an objective observer would report. Other-perception biases are beliefs and judgments about another party that also deviate from those made by an objective observer.

Self-perception Biases

One of the most well-documented self-perception biases is the tendency for people's own position or point of view to affect their ability to process information in an objective and even-handed fashion. For example, Kronzon and Darley (1999) showed people a film of a dyadic negotiation after which participants made judgments about perpetrators and victims with regard to the use of ethically ambiguous negotiation tactics. Some people were told to take the perspective of the victim; others were told to take the perspective of the perpetrator. Even though the films were identical, the differences in perception led to differential evaluations of behavior, with perpetrator-focused participants more favorable of the perpetrator's actions. Galinsky and Moskowitz's (2000; also Galinsky, 1999; Jones and Nisbett, 1987) studies of perspective taking also found that the ability to entertain the position of the other affects attributional thinking and evaluations of others. They showed that perspective-taking decreases out-group stereotyping and improves out-group evaluations in comparison to the stereotype suppression strategy. They suggested this is because the perspective taker's thoughts about the target are projections of himself or herself. The representation of the target constructed by the perspective taker comes to resemble the perspective taker's own self-representation. Further, negotiators with greater perspective-taking ability are more successful in achieving integrative agreements than negotiators with less perspective-taking ability (Neale and Bazerman, 1983).

One of the consequences of self-focus is that one's beliefs, attitudes, and physical appearance are highly salient to the self. Moreover, people tend to overestimate the extent to which others can discern their internal states. Gilovich, Savitsky, and Medvec (1998) provided evidence for such an "illusion of transparency." They showed, in different contexts, that people often mistakenly believe that their internal states are more apparent than they actually are; for instance, liars tended to overestimate the detectability of their lies. Compelling evidence indicates that the illusion of transparency occurs in negotiations. Keysar, Ginzel and Bazerman (1995) demonstrated that negotiators tend to behave as if their negotiating counterparts had access to the negotiator's privileged information about a given state of affairs. Vorauer and Claude (1998) showed that negotiators overestimated the transparency of their objectives: they presumed that their objectives were more readily apparent to others than was, in fact, the case.

Biased Perceptions of Others

There has been a great deal of research on the biased views that individuals hold about others (Fiske, 1993). Perhaps the most well-known bias in negotiation is the fixed-pie perception (Bazerman, 1983; Bazerman and Neale, 1983; Thompson and Hastie, 1990). The fixed-pie perception is the erroneous belief that the other party's interests are directly opposed to one's own interests when, in fact, they are often not completely opposed. Such a belief may be caused by the same judgment process that creates false consensus. Specifically, bargainers' reliance on their own preferences as a cue to others' preferences should lead them to anticipate a fixed-sum conflict (Bottom and Paese, 1997). Thompson and Hastie (1990) explored the consequences for outcomes. They measured individual fixed-pie perceptions after just five minutes of negotiation and found they predicted individual and joint negotiation payoffs such that fixed-pie perceptions were associated with lower individual and joint profits. Negotiators with strong fixed-pie perceptions failed to identify interests that could be profitably logrolled or that were completely compatible. Pinkley, Griffith, and Northcraft (1995) suggested that this effect occurs through two different, independent mechanisms: biased information search (negotiators' faulty search for necessary information) and biased information processing (negotiators' faulty processing of available information).

A close cousin of the fixed-pie perception is extremism (Robinson, Keltner, Ward, and Ross, 1995). According to Robinson et al. (1995), partisan perceivers believe that their own perceptions map onto objective reality. When they realize that the other side's views differ from their own, they first attempt to "straighten out" the other side; when this does not work, they regard the other side as extremist. That is, partisan perceivers tend to view the other side as having interests that are more opposed to their own than is actually the case. In the context of face-to-face negotiations, this overestimate of the differences in construal between partisan perceivers and the other side has two consequences. First, it exacerbates conflict, as partisan perceivers ascribe more negative traits to their negotiating partner even when partisanship has been randomly assigned right before the negotiation (Keltner and Robinson, 1993; Robinson and Kray, 2001). Second, it reduces the likelihood of reaching comprehensive integrative agreements during face-to-face negotiations (Keltner and Robinson, 1993).

Another relation of the fixed-pie perception is the reactive devaluation bias (Oskamp, 1965; Ross and Stillinger, 1991), in which negotiators discount or dismiss concessions made by the other party merely as a function of who is offering them. This was first demonstrated by Oskamp (1965), who asked participants to evaluate the utility of various options concerning U.S.–Soviet disarmament. All participants evaluated identical options, with the only difference being who ostensibly was the author of the option (the U.S. or the Soviet Union). Evaluations were strongly determined by the author regardless of the actual contents of the proposal. Stillinger, Epelbaum, Kelter, and Ross (1990) extended this idea to face-to-face negotiation. In their experiment, participants negotiated with a confederate over the policy of their university regarding a political issue. The antagonism of the negotiating confederate was held constant. During the negotiation, the confederate for a time adopted a stubborn position. In two experimental conditions, however, the confederate ultimately made a concession; in the third (control) condition, no concession at all was made. Subsequently, participants rated the attractiveness and significance of a number of different proposals, including the ones that had been offered in their negotiation session. Nonoffered concessions were rated as more attractive and significant than offered concessions: The very fact that their counterpart offered them a concession diminished its value in the eyes of the participants.

The fixed-pie perception and extremism bias are also closely related to the fundamental attribution error (Ross, 1977), which states that people tend to view their own behavior as largely determined by the situation but regard other's behavior as driven by chronic dispositions. Recently, Morris, Larrick and Su (1999) demonstrated this bias operated in negotiation. In their studies, negotiators erroneously attributed tough bargaining behaviors to difficult personalities rather than to situational factors. They determined that this fundamental attribution error often results from lack of sufficient information about the opponent's situation.

The research on differential attributions is closely tied to the coercion bias, identified by Rothbart and Hallmark (1988), in which people erroneously believe that coercive tactics will be effective in generating concessions when dealing with opponents, but believe that these same tactics, when applied to the self, will have the opposite effect—that is, to increase their resolve not to concede. Rothbart and Hallmark (1988) found that in-group and out-group members differed in the judged efficacy of coercion and conciliation as social influence strategies. Out-group members perceived coercion as more effective than conciliation when applied to others, while in-group members perceived coercion as less effective than conciliation when applied to their own social or categorical group members.

Another line of research suggests that individuals are largely unable or un-willing to take the perspective of others. Neale and Bazerman (1991) referred to these asymmetries as "ignoring the cognitions of others." Samuelson and Bazerman's (1985) study on the "winner's curse" demonstrated that nego-tiators fail to incorporate valuable information about the decisions made by their opponents, due to their development of strategies to simplify compet-itive decisions (Carroll, Bazerman, and Maury, 1988). Carroll and his col-leagues (1988) suggested that this tendency to ignore the cognitions of others may actually be just one manifestation of a more general bias that consists of ignoring contingencies. Individuals may have a general tendency to make simplifying assumptions when faced with a task that requires incorporating knowledge about future contingent events. That is, when individuals are faced with contingencies, they will make simplifying assumptions to make decision making under uncertainty more manageable. More recently, Blount and Larrick (2000) examined the factors that led people to choose between two alternative ways of playing the ultimatum bargaining game with another party (e.g., subject proposes a division to the other and the other accepts or rejects it vs. subject makes a claim from a common pool and the other makes a counterclaim). Subjects failed to select the version of the ultimatum bar-gaining game that maximized their monetary outcomes (the latter version). This was partially due to their cognitive inability to accurately predict the effect of the alternative versions on their opponents' responses.

Summary

The social perception approach to the study of negotiator bias has been fed by the rich stream of person perception research in social psychology (cf. Asch, 1946; Heider, 1958; Kelley, 1967). This social perception approach is grounded in the psychological principles of cognition, but it moves away from the cognitive focus on payoff schedules and risk to perceptions of the other party, the self, and the relationship. The research on attributional processes is the keystone of the social perception approach, perhaps as a result of its grounding in the psychological principles of cognition. Still, this approach does not provide a meaningful account of the goals and motivations that drive negotiators, a factor that is critical for what Raiffa referred to as the "mixed motive" nature of negotiation. This shortcoming has encouraged the study of "motivational" biases in negotiation.

MOTIVATIONAL BIASES

Motivational biases arise from the activation of particular needs and goals. Whereas social perception biases are thought to be chronically present, motivational biases can be "turned on" with the presence of particular social goals. Obviously, there is a myriad of possible goal states that affect judgment, behavior, and outcomes. Our review of the literature surfaced four key motivational goals: self-enhancement, closure and consistency, cooperation (maximization of shared goals), and accountability (or constituency pressure); (see Table 1.3). Whereas some of these motivations may appear on the surface to be quite cool as they pertain to the organization of cognition, they are commonly viewed as tension and drive states that spur cognitive action.

Self-enhancement as a Motivational Goal

One of the most fundamental goals of human life is the preservation and maintenance of self-identity. Identity enhancement is thought to be extremely important for mental health (Taylor and Brown, 1988), with the general finding being that self-serving behavior increases well-being. Self-enhancement, while related to egocentrism, is not quite the same. Egocentrism is the tendency for people to take credit for behaviors, both good and bad. Self-enhancement is one theoretical explanation for egocentrism. In a mixed-motive situation, self-enhancement may lead to more problematic negotiations. Indeed, in a series of three studies, De Dreu, Nauta, and van de Vliert (1995) found that negotiators tend to make self-serving evaluations of conflict behavior. Disputants viewed their own conflict behaviors as more constructive and as less destructive than those of their opponents. Besides, self-serving evaluation of conflict behavior was associated with increased frustration, reduced problem solving, and enhanced likelihood of future conflict. Thus, self-enhancement may be a central motivational antecedent of conflict escalation.

In social dilemmas, egocentrism leads negotiators to perceive fairness in a biased manner (Wade-Benzoni, Tenbrunsel, and Bazerman, 1996, 1997; cf. Thompson and Loewenstein, 1992). Specifically, the egocentric bias tends to make parties believe that it is fair for them to have more of the negotiated

TABLE I.3

Motivational Biases

Nature of Motivational Bias	Bias	Research Findings
Self-enhancement	Egocentrism and self-serving	De Dreu, Nauta, and van de Vliert (1995): Self-serving evaluation of conflict behavior leads to reduced problem solving and greater likelihood of future conflict.
	Self-identity and affirmation	Bastardi (1999): Negotiators have a need to preserve self-identity, which can be attenuated if they have recently affirmed the self.
Closure, consistency, and balance	Bittersweet effect	Thompson, Valley, and Kramer (1995): Tendency to feel bad if you think the opponent has succeeded.
	Need for closure	De Dreu, Koole, and Oldersma (1999): Negotiators with high (vs. low) NFC are more influenced by focal points when setting limits and making concessions.
		de Grada, Kruglanski, Mannetti, and Pierro (1999): Greater conformity pressures and less egalitarian participation in collective negotiations when high (vs. low) NFC groups.
Cooperation	Future interaction	Axelrod (1984): Indefinite time horizon creates an incentive to cooperate.
		Heide and Miner (1992): Anticipated open-ended future interaction and frequency of contact increase the chances that cooperation emerges.
	Social value orientation	De Dreu and Boles (1998): Social value orientation influences choice and recall of heuristics in individuals preparing for negotiation.
	Communal orientation	Thompson and DeHarpport (1998): Ability to capitalize on joint interests decreases heavily when only one of the parties has a communal orientation.
Accountability	Accountability	Ben-Yoav and Pruitt (1984a): Accountability reduces (or increases) joint benefit when expectation of cooperative future interaction is absent (or present).
		Kramer, Pommerenke, and Newton (1993): Shared social identity leads to greater equality; high accountability leads to greater equality of outcomes.

TABLE 1.3

(continued)

Nature of Motivational Bias	Bias	Research Findings
		De Dreu, Koole, and Steinel (2000): Accountability decreases fixed-pie perception and leads to more integrative agreements.
		Wilson (1992): Wanting to save face leads to negotiators being more aggressive and uncompromising. (This is also a self-enhancement process.)

resource than an independent advisor would judge: Negotiators claim what they want and, at the same time, believe that their claim is fair. In addition, egocentrism leads parties to anticipate that others will make overharvesting decisions and deplete common goods (Wade-Benzoni et al., 1996). As Wade-Benzoni and her colleagues demonstrated, this, in turn, leads all parties to engage in overharvesting. Another problematic consequence of self-enhancement is that the motivation to maintain high self-esteem contributes to negotiator overconfidence and overly positive self-evaluation (Kramer, Newton, and Pommerenke, 1993). Negotiators' overconfidence may vary with the tactics they use. Some findings by Barry (1999) suggested that negotiators might be more likely to consider themselves efficient and be prone to self-enhancement biases when using emotional tactics (such as strategic expression of surprise, disappointment, or nervousness) than when using cognitive tactics (such as misrepresentation and false promises).

Self-affirmation theory (Steele, 1988) argues that when people experience a threat to their self-esteem, they need to affirm the self. For example, when people are given feedback indicating that they have not performed well on a task, they are more likely to promote themselves, and this may have negative consequences for interpersonal and intergroup relations. In particular, self-image maintenance processes may play an important role in stereotyping and prejudice. When people evaluate a member of a stereotyped group, they are more likely to evaluate that person stereotypically if their self-images have been threatened by negative feedback (Fein and Spencer, 1997). Besides, as Fein and Spencer documented, derogating a stereotyped target increases the self-esteem of people whose self-image has been threatened. Bastardi (1999) examined self-affirmation processes in interpersonal negotiation. First, he either made "prochoice" negotiators' identity salient or not. Then, he had them negotiate over abortion laws with an ostensibly "prolife" confederate. Among negotiators whose identity was made salient prior to the negotiation, those who had previously affirmed a valued aspect of identity unrelated to abortion made more concessions and evaluated the confederate more favorably than did those who had experienced threat to an unrelated aspect of identity. Among negotiators whose identity was not made salient, the affirmation versus threat manipulation was not significant. Overall, this suggests that negotiators' need to preserve their identity can be attenuated if they have recently affirmed the self or if their identity was not made salient. At the intergroup bargaining level, however, some research suggests that the effect of self-affirmation on the unwillingness to make concessions may not only be limited to negative evaluation but occurs whenever identity is made salient (cf. Tjosvold, 1977). Tjosvold reported that representatives who received a strong affirmation of personal effectiveness (a positive evaluation) from their group resisted compromising when negotiating with the bargaining representative of an out-group, thereby maintaining their image of competence.

There is evidence that goals can affect negotiator behavior and outcomes at a level below a person's awareness. Kray, Thompson, and Galinsky (2001) found that whereas men outperform women in a mixed-gender negotiation, when women are "primed" with classic gender stereotypes (i.e., explicitly told that gender differences exist), women actually outperform men by a large margin. According to Kray and her colleagues (Kray, Galinsky, and Thompson, 2002; Kray, Thompson, and Galinsky, 2001), "stereotype reactance" occurs when members of traditionally disadvantaged groups (in this case, women) are reminded of the stereotype. Moreover, the key mechanism by which stereotype activation affects behavior is negotiators' aspirations, or goals (Kray et al., 2001).

Cooperation as a Goal

Several theoretical treatments of negotiation have examined the nature of cooperative, competitive, and individualistic goals on negotiation behavior (for a review, see Polzer and Neale, 1995; and De Dreu, Chapter 5, this volume). In general, this research has consistently found that negotiators who anticipate future interaction with another party (e.g., see Axelrod, 1984; Ben-Yoav and Pruitt, 1984b; Heide and Miner, 1992; Mannix, 1994) or adopt a communal or a social value orientation (e.g., De Dreu and Boles, 1998; Dittloff and Harris, 1996; Halpern, 1994, 1996; Shah and Jehn, 1993; Thompson and DeHarport, 1998) are more likely to behave more cooperatively and attain outcomes of higher joint value.

Closure as a Motivational Goal

Webster and Kruglanski (1994) identified need for closure as a key social-information-processing goal. Need for closure (NFC) refers to the notion that some situations elicit an epistemic state of wanting a quick solution through, for instance, time pressure and proximity to decision deadline. NFC is also a property on which persons vary dispositionally: some individuals have a chronic tendency to terminate hypothesis testing and information searches prematurely (Webster and Kruglanski, 1994). Overall, people are more likely to engage in thoughtful or novel information processing when their NFC is low. Research on need for closure in negotiation reports that negotiators rely more on the use of heuristics in negotiation when they have a high dispositional need for closure (De Dreu, Koole, and Oldersma, 1999; see De Dreu, Chapter 5, this volume, for a full review). Need for closure also affects behaviors in group negotiation. Both dispositional and situational needs for closure are positively related to the preponderance of task-oriented behaviors and negatively related to the preponderance of positive social–emotional behaviors (de Grada, Kruglanski, Mannetti, and Pierro, 1999). In fact, both types of NFC elicit conformity pressures and egalitarian participation in collective negotiations.

Accountability as a Goal

In his model of the social perceiver as an intuitive politician, Tetlock (1985) proposed that accountability to constituents is a key goal. Negotiators who are accountable to their constituents make higher demands and are less willing to compromise than those not accountable to constituents (Ben-Yoav and Pruitt, 1984a; Carnevale, Pruitt, and Britton, 1979; O'Connor, 1994). Two motivational processes may explain this finding: decision-making vigilance and evaluation apprehension. Decision makers who are accountable for their actions are vigilant in that they consider relevant information and alternatives more carefully than those who are not accountable (Tetlock, 1985, 1992). Evaluation apprehension refers to the tendency for accountable negotiators to be concerned with how they are viewed by others and, consequently, to use face-saving strategies. Research suggests that wanting to save face leads to negotiators being more aggressive and uncompromising in negotiation (Neale, 1984; Wilson, 1992). While the general effect of accountability on the unwillingness of a negotiator to compromise has been well documented, this effect may be somewhat moderated by the nature of the accountability considered. Indeed, Tetlock, Skitka, and Boettger (1989) showed that people use different motivational strategies when dealing with different kinds of accountability to audiences. Specifically, when people know the views of the audience and are unconstrained by past commitments, they shift their views toward those of the audience. Also, when people are accountable for positions to which they feel committed, they devote the majority of their mental effort to justifying those positions (defensive bolstering). However, when people do not know the views of the audience and are unconstrained by past commitments, they are motivated to think in relatively flexible, multidimensional ways (preemptive self-criticism).

Summary

The motivational perspective on biases provides a compelling account of the conditions under which certain cognitive processes—including the use of thoughtful information processing—will be engaged. Further, the motivational perspective also provides a theoretical framework for the activation of nonconscious goals. The most commonly investigated motivational processes are cooperation and competition. Only recently has the motivational net been stretched to examine other, more complex, goals, such as accountability. Still, motives may not be sufficient to understand the complexity of affect in negotiation. Research on emotions in negotiation has only recently begun to gain momentum. Much like motivational biases, emotions direct our attention to certain aspects of the negotiation. As a measure of their complexity (and perhaps also a partial explanation for why negotiation scholars have ignored this "hot" aspect of the "hot" side of negotiation), emotions and mood states are viewed both as causes, as well as consequences, of negotiation.

EMOTIONAL BIASES

Misperceptions of Affect

Emotional biases can first deal with misperceptions of one's or others' affect. Emotional misperceptions may refer to any of several inconsistencies or reversals between feeling and actions, feelings and the judgments made about them, and feelings at different times of the negotiation (for a review, see Thompson, Medvec, Seiden, and Kopelman, 2001; Thompson, Nadler, and Kim, 1999). Thompson et al. (2001) suggested that emotional biases may center on three misperceptions: (1) inaccuracy in terms of judging and reading emotions in others and oneself; (2) faulty beliefs about the duration of emotional states; and (3) faulty beliefs about the causal effects of emotion on behavior. Evidence suggests that negotiators exhibit biases in each of these areas (see Table 1.4).

Reading Emotions in the Self and Others

People have limited access to their own emotions (Loewenstein and Schkade, 1999), let alone the emotions of others around them. Moreover, people often mispredict why others feel the way they do (Ekman, 1985). In addition, people misjudge the intensity of their feelings (Keltner and Robinson, 1993) and are overconfident in their ability to predict others' emotions (Dunning, Griffin, Miljokovic, and Ross, 1990). Moreover, negotiators often fall prey to the illusion of transparency, such that they believe that others can read their emotions (Gilovich et al., 1998).

TABLE 1.4

Emotional Biases

Nature of Emotion	Bias	Research
Positive affect	Positive affect	Carnevale and Isen (1986): Happy people are more likely to exchange information and be creative in negotiations.
		Barry and Oliver (1996): Argue that affect influences decisions to negotiate, selection of opponent, formation of offers, tactics, concession making, economic outcomes, satisfaction with the outcomes, desire for future interaction, and respect of the agreement terms.
		Forgas (1998a): Positive mood produces less critical reactions and more compliance than negative mood.
		Forgas (1998b): Happy people more are likely to be cooperative and successful in both bilateral and intergroup negotiation.
		Kramer, Newton, and Pommerenke (1993): Positive mood and motivation to maintain these lead to overconfidence and positive self-evaluation.
Negative affect	Anger	Pillutla and Murnighan (1996): Wounded pride or spite leads to feelings of unfairness and rejection of offers that are objectively higher than alternatives.
		Allred, Mallozzi, Matsui, and Raia (1997): Angry negotiators achieved fewer joint gains, without successfully claiming more value for themselves.
		Allred (1999): Anger provokes a sequence of retaliatory impulses and behaviors.

Biases About the Duration of Emotional States

Most people assume that emotional states last longer than they actually do. For example, people assume that positive events, such as winning the lottery, getting a raise, and so on, will have long-lasting effects on their overall happiness. People also assume that intensely negative events, such as getting fired or being in an accident, will leave them unhappy forever. However, the emotional effects of extremely positive or negative events do not last nearly so long as negotiators might think (Gilbert, Pinel, Wilson, Blumberg, and Wheatley, 1998). According to the durability bias, people do not adequately account for the ability of their psychological immune system to adapt (Gilbert et al., 1998).

Biases About Emotion Predicting Behavior

Most negotiators believe that emotions predict behavior. However, because access to emotional states is limited (Wilson, 1985), people often err in assessing what they are feeling, which leads to errors in predicting their subsequent behavior. Furthermore, when people try to introspect and monitor their feelings, it often leads to inconsistent behavior (Wilson and Dunn, 1986). Thompson et al. (2001) suggested, but did not provide empirical evidence, that faulty beliefs about emotion in negotiation are passed on as prescriptive advice.

Consequences of Affect

In addition to the emotional biases that result from misperceiving affect, emotional biases may also arise from the very affect that people experience in negotiations. In general, negotiation researchers have essentially explored the consequences of two kinds of affect: (1) the consequences of diffuse affect or mood on negotiators' information processing; and (2) the consequences of intense emotional feelings, such as anger, on negotiators' judgment and behavior. Because this literature is discussed in depth in Chapter 3 by Barry, Fulmer, and Van Kleef, we only briefly discuss it here.

Consequences of Diffuse Affect

Emotional biases may arise from the influence of mood and diffuse emotional states on cognition. Specifically, emotional biases result when mood or diffuse affective states influence the quality and depth of information processing. One of the best-known perspectives on diffuse affect and information processing is state-dependent theory (Bower, 1981). According to state-dependent theory, people show enhanced information-processing ability when the information being processed or the experience being thought of is affectively congruent with the mood they are in (e.g., recall for items that were encoded in a similar affective state). There are few studies applying this theory to negotiation, although it had many applications to cooperative behavior in general. More prosocial behaviors occur when people experience positive mood, and more antisocial behaviors occur when people experience negative mood (e.g., Bower, 1981, 1991; Isen, 1993; Isen and Levin, 1972). In negotiation, good mood enhances, and bad mood reduces, the tendency to select a cooperative strategy in both bilateral and intergroup negotiation (Forgas, 1998b, Experiments 1 and 3). In parallel to this, positive diffuse affect increases creativity and, consequently, the discovery of innovative negotiation agreements (Carnevale and Isen, 1986; see also Isen, Daubman, and Nowicki, 1987; however, see Schwarz, 1990). Negotiators in a good mood also tend to make more concessions during face-to-face negotiations (Baron, 1990), but this general concessionary tendency may not always be in the best interest of negotiators, as negotiations are not necessarily purely integrative. Moreover, Kramer, Newton and Pommerenke's (1993) research pointed out that positive mood may enhance negotiators' positive illusions—that is, inaccurate perceptions of the self, the world, and the future that one entertains to enhance and protect one's self-esteem (Taylor and Brown, 1988). Thus, positive mood may not only have positive consequences for negotiators.

Consequences of Intense Emotional Feelings

Other research has examined the impact of intense emotions, as opposed to mood. Whereas mood refers to low intensity, diffuse affect (Fiske and Taylor, 1991) that may be exogenous to the negotiation process and need not be directed toward a person, emotion in negotiations implies intense feelings (e.g., anger) that may arise from interacting with the counterpart during the negotiation process and be directed toward her or him. Allred, Mallozzi, Matsui, and Raia (1997) found that negotiators who were angry with each other achieved fewer joint gains and had less desire to work with each other in the future than did negotiators who had more positive emotional regard for each other (see also Pillutla and Murnighan, 1996).

Overall, at least three mechanisms may explain the negative impact of feelings of anger on negotiations. First, angry negotiators are less accurate in judging the interests of opponent negotiators (Allred et al., 1997). Second, negative emotions arising from a negative relationship make negotiators more self-centered in their preferences (Loewenstein, Thompson, and Bazerman, 1989), and being self-centered increases the difficulty of coming to an agreement with others (Thompson and Loewenstein, 1992). Third, anger may provoke a sequence of retaliatory impulses and behaviors (Allred, 1999). Specifically, people may become angry and act in a retaliatory way when they judge that the other party is responsible for some harm that was caused to them (Allred, 1995; Allred, Chiongbian, and Parlamis, 1998; Weiner, 1985, 1996). When harm is attributed to others' disposition, anger may lead negotiators to fail to take into account the devastating consequences of retaliation and to dismiss the others' perspective.

Finally, writing generally about emotions in negotiations, Thompson and her colleagues (Thompson et al., 1999, 2001) argued that emotions can influence negotiations in terms of how they are expressed, how they are experienced, and how they are used strategically. They argued that emotions are contagious in the sense that others are inclined to express similar emotions. Investigating this empirically, Thompson and Kim (2000) found that emotions can even affect the judgment of neutral, third-party observers; indeed, third parties are more effective when negotiators' emotions are positive, holding constant the actual content of the dispute situation.

Summary

Emotional biases are the newest foray into negotiator bias. This perspective emerging in social psychology as well as negotiation focuses on the "hot" aspect of cognition. Emotional biases have two distinct processes: initial states that result in particular behaviors and outcomes for the negotiators and end states that can be attributed to the use of certain behaviors and outcomes. Thus, emotions serve as both independent and dependent variables in research investigations (see Barry, Fulmer, and Van Kleef, Chapter 3, this volume).

Conclusion

Our review of bias in negotiation has several theoretical as well as practical implications.

THEORETICAL IMPLICATIONS

If we take an archeological point of view, there are distinct historical periods that provide compelling clues as to the theoretical developments of the field. The earliest papers on negotiator bias were direct descendants of the cognitive revolution. Even a cursory scan of the abstracts and key words reveals the zeitgeist of cognitive psychology's heyday, for example, heuristics, bias, error, framing, and schemas. We refer to this as the cognitive era. The next era of research ushered in a flurry of research papers on social perception, attribution, and Gestalt processing. This era came closely on the heels of the cognitive era, and indeed in some aspects predated the cognitive era. The next era of research papers on negotiation revealed the fires of motivation, drive, and goals. The negotiator of this era was a goal-directed, hot-blooded, driven creature. The most recent era is that of the emotional negotiator, also a hot-blooded social actor. No doubt the current research focus in social psychology on "emotional intelligence" and emotional informational processing largely shaped this research tradition. Our analysis of the theoretical and empirical research on bias in negotiation reveals important assumptions about negotiation, its actors, and the very process of negotiation. Yet, in the end, it is clear that we are studying—in all its variety—the ways in which negotiators think about the negotiation process and, as a result of this thinking (or lack thereof), how they behave in the context of the mixed-motive, socially interdependent process that is negotiation. It is worth speculating on what might be the next era of research on negotiation and, in particular, negotiator bias. A look at the recent research in related fields of social psychology and cognitive psychology provide some important clues. Here we outline three new directions in the study of negotiator bias, expressed as metaphors: the preconscious negotiator, the situated negotiator, and the learning organism.

Preconscious Negotiator

This metaphor describes the behavior of an actor who is largely influenced by the operation of mental processes and states for which the actor has little or no direct awareness. This new research tradition in social psychology is largely heralded by three independent streams of research—Bargh's research (Bargh, Chen, and Burrows, 1996; Bargh, Lombardi, and Higgins, 1988) on "automotive" behavior, in which he primes constructs at a level below people's awareness and finds dramatic effects on judgment, perception, and behavior; Greenwald and Banaji's work (1995) on implicit stereotyping; and Wegner's work (1989) on control and automaticity in social life (e.g., studies in which people asked not to think of a white bear could not get the vivid image out of their mind). One can easily imagine how negotiation behavior might be affected by the activation of constructs and processes at a level below the negotiator's awareness. Kray, Thompson, and Galinsky's (2001) research on male and female behavior and performance in negotiation revealed that the subtle activation of gender-relevant stereotypes can dramatically affect behavior.

Situated Negotiator

This metaphor represents a distinct departure—even a backlash—against traditional information-processing theory, which largely forms the basis of the cognitive approach. According to the situated cognition approach, cognition, and consequently its products (such as bias), are situated in particular contexts and encounters and cannot be reduced to individual cognitions, as is often done in social psychology wherein mood states are manipulated or measured at the individual level (Argote, 1999; Wegner, 1987, 1995). Research in negotiation (Thompson and DeHarpport, 1994, 1998) and group decision making (Gruenfeld, Mannix, Williams, and Neale, 1996; Phillips, Mannix, Neale, and Gruenfeld, 2001) illustrates the situated nature of the social interaction. For example, rather than measuring or manipulating mood states at an individual level, the situated approach might focus on how the emotion is experienced or expressed by the dyad or group as a whole. The situated negotiator point of view suggests that the proper level of analysis is that of the dyad, group, or organization. Indeed, the very nature of integrative potential in a negotiation is situated: it requires a particular constellation of interests that extends beyond the individual perspective of the focal negotiator.

Negotiator as Learner

Any discussion of negotiator bias naturally raises the question of how to eliminate it. Consequently, a large research literature has focused on ways to reduce the impact of biases on negotiator behavior. In recent years, the focus of learning has received attention at all levels (individual, group, and organization) and from a variety of theoretical approaches (psychology, sociology, education, and operations research). In this tradition, the negotiator is viewed as a learning organism.

One promising approach is the recent work by Thompson and her colleagues (2000) on analogical learning. The basic idea of learning via analogy is this: participants are given an opportunity to solve a problem. Later, they are challenged with a different, novel problem to solve that is from a different domain, thus appearing on the surface to have little or nothing to do with the first problem. However, the underlying or "deep" structure of the two problems is quite similar. The critical question is: Under what conditions will the negotiator "recognize" the applicability of the old problem in this new domain? Research suggests that practice comparing the structure of different cases is superior to deeply analyzing one case at a time (e.g., Thompson et al., 2000).

PRACTICAL IMPLICATIONS

The most immediate practical question raised by our review is how best to eliminate cognitive, social, motivational, and emotional biases. This question is obviously relevant to our previous discussion of learning. The research on learning points to three critical findings that make the elimination of biases particularly challenging: first, most people severely overestimate their ability to learn from experience (Dawes, 1988; Thompson, 1990a, 1990b); second, learning is highly context specific, such that people are often unable to apply a principle or concept learned in one context to another equally relevant but different situation (cf. Thompson et al., 2000); finally, feedback is an especially important aspect of learning (Neale and Northcraft, 1990).

Another important implication of our research review is that to be a successful negotiator, one does not have to be perfect; just noticeably better than his or her counterpart. Although our review of the four types of biases may make any negotiator feel somewhat discouraged, we largely agree with Raiffa's description of the truly rational negotiator—someone who understands not only how the self and the counterpart should behave but also how the self and counterpart actually behave, in terms of emotions, motivations, and cognitions. Thus, understanding what triggers these biases and how they influence negotiators' behaviors and developing ways to reduce their impact are challenging goals for both scholars and practitioners of negotiation.

Notes

1. We did not adhere religiously to this particular caveat. For example, given the relative paucity of empirical research on emotions in negotiations, we chose to include empirical studies that, while not specifically involving a negotiation, shed light on the impact that emotions have on actors in multimotive social situations.

2. There is an ongoing debate about the relation between anchoring and adjustment. Recent research indicates that anchoring may not need necessarily to involve some kind of adjustment process to occur in individual, estimate tasks (e.g., see Epley and Gilovich, 2001). Specifically, anchoring without adjustment would occur when anchors are irrelevant to the task, as this was the case in the original study by Tversky and Kahneman. Then, anchoring may be nothing else than a special case of priming (Mussweiler and Strack, 1999; Strack and Mussweiler, 1997). In negotiation research, however, the anchors that have been empirically examined always deal with the negotiation, either directly (e.g., alternatives) or indirectly (e.g., market information). Thus, they are relevant, and it seems plausible to argue that adjustment does indeed occur in negotiation context.

Works Cited

Allred, K. G. (1995). *Judgment, anger, and retaliation: A new perspective on non-cooperation in organizations.* Unpublished doctoral dissertation, University of California, Los Angeles.

———. (1999). Anger and retaliation: Toward an understanding of impassioned conflict in organizations. In R. J. Bies, R. J. Lewicki, and B. H. Sheppard (Eds.), *Research on negotiation in organizations* (Vol. 7, pp. 27–58). Greenwich, CT: JAI.

Allred, K. G., Mallozzi, J. S., Matsui, F., and C. P. Raia. (1997). The influence of anger and compassion on negotiation performance. *Organizational Behavior and Human Decision Processes, 70*(3), 175–187.

Argote, L. (1999). *Organizational learning: Creating, retaining and transferring knowledge.* Boston: Kluwer.

Arrow, K. J., Mnookin, R. H., Ross, L., Tversky, A., and R. Wilson, Eds. (1995). *Barriers to conflict resolution.* New York: Norton.

Asch, S. E. (1946). Forming impressions of personality. *Journal of Abnormal and Social Psychology, 41,* 1230–1240.

Axelrod, R. (1984). *The evolution of cooperation.* New York: Basic Books.

Bargh, J. A., Chen, M., and L. Burrows. (1996). Automaticity of social behavior: Direct effects of trait construct and stereotype activation on action. *Journal of Personality and Social Psychology, 71,* 230–244.

Bargh, J. A., Lombardi, W. J., and E. T. Higgins. (1988). Automaticity of chronically accessible constructs in person–situation effects on person perception: It's just a matter of time. *Journal of Personality and Social Psychology, 55,* 599–605.

Barry, B., and R. L. Oliver. (1996). Affect in dyadic negotiation: A model and propositions. *Organizational Behavior and Human Decision Processes, 67,* 127–144.

Bartlett, F. C. (1967/1932). *Remembering.* Cambridge: Cambridge University Press.

Bastardi, I. (1999). *Motivated responses to evidence and to concession offers: Effects of self-interest, identity, and prior beliefs.* Unpublished doctoral dissertation, Stanford University.

Bazerman, M. H. (1983). Negotiator judgment: A critical look at the rationality assumption. *American Behavioral Scientist, 27,* 618–634.

Bazerman, M. H., and M. A. Neale. (1982). Improving negotiation effectiveness under final offer arbitration: The role of selection and training. *Journal of Applied Psychology, 67,* 543–548.

———. (1983). Heuristics in negotiation: Limitations to effective dispute resolution. In M. H. Bazerman and R. J. Lewicki (Eds.), *Negotiating in organizations* (pp. 51–67). Beverly Hills, CA: Sage.

Bazerman, M. H., Magliozzi, T., and M. A. Neale. (1985). The acquisition of an integrative response in a competitive market. *Organizational Behavior and Human Decision Processes, 35,* 294–313.

Ben-Yoav, O., and D. G. Pruitt. (1984a). Accountability to constituents: A two-edged sword. *Organization Behavior and Human Processes, 34,* 282–295.

———. (1984b). Resistance to yielding and the expectation of cooperative future interaction in negotiation. *Journal of Experimental Social Psychology, 20,* 323–353.

Blount, S., and R. P. Larrick. (2000). Framing the game: Examining frame choice in bargaining. *Organizational Behavior and Human Decision Processes, 81*(1), 43–71.

Blount, S., Thomas-Hunt, M. C., and M. A. Neale. (1996). The price is right—or is it? A reference point model of two-party price negotiations. *Organizational Behavior and Human Decision Processes, 68*(1), 1–12.

Borgida, E., and R. E. Nisbett. (1977). The differential impact of abstract vs. concrete information on decisions. *Journal of Applied Social Psychology, 7,* 258–271.

Bottom, W. P., and P. Paese. (1998). False consensus, stereotypic cues, and the perception of integrative potential in negotiation. *Journal of Applied Social Psychology, 27,* 1919–1940.

Bottom, W. P., and A. Studt. (1993). Framing effects and the distributive aspect of integrative bargaining. *Organizational Behavior and Human Decision Processes, 56,* 459–474.

Bower, G. H. (1981). Mood and memory. *American Psychologist, 36*(2), 129–148.

———. (Ed.). (1991). *The psychology of learning and motivation: Advances in research and theory* (Vol. 27). San Diego, CA: Academic Press.

Carnevale, P. J., and A. Isen. (1986). The influence of positive affect and visual access on the discovery of integrative solutions in bilateral negotiations. *Organizational Behavior and Human Decision Processes, 37,* 1–13.

Carnevale, P., Pruitt, D., and S. Britton. (1979). Looking tough: The negotiator under constituent surveillance. *Personality and Social Psychology Bulletin*, 5, 118–121.

Carroll, J. S., Bazerman, M. H., and R. Maury. (1988). Negotiator cognitions: A descriptive approach to negotiators' understanding of their opponents. *Organizational Behavior and Human Decision Processes*, 41, 352–370.

Chaiken, S. (1987). The heuristic model of persuasion. In M. P. Zanna, J. M. Olson, and C. P. Herman (Eds.), *Social influence: The Ontario Symposium* (Vol. 5, pp. 3–39). Hillsdale, NJ: Erlbaum.

Dawes, R. (1988). *Rational choice in an uncertain world*. New York: Harcourt, Brace, and Jovanovich.

De Dreu, C. K. W., and T. Boles. (1998). Share and share alike or winner take all? The influence of social value orientation upon choice and recall of negotiation heuristics. *Organizational Behavior and Human Decision Processes*, 76, 253–276.

De Dreu, C. K. W., Emans, B. J. M., and E. van de Vliert. (1992). The influence of own cognitive and other's communicated gain or loss frame on negotiation behavior. *International Journal of Conflict Management*, 3(2), 115–132.

De Dreu, C. K. W., Koole, S. L., and F. L. Oldersma. (1999). On the freezing and seizing of negotiator inferences: Need for closure moderates the use of heuristics in negotiation. *Personality and Social Psychology Bulletin*, 25, 348–363.

De Dreu, C. K. W., Koole, S. L., and W. Steinel. (2000). Unfixing the Fixed Pie: A motivated information-processing approach to integrative negotiation. *Journal of Personality and Social Psychology*, 79, 975–987.

De Dreu, C. K. W., Nauta, A., and E. van de Vliert. (1995). Self-serving evaluations of conflict behavior and escalation of the dispute. *Journal of Applied Social Psychology*, 25, 2049–2066.

de Grada, E., Kruglanski, A. W., Mannetti, L., and A. Pierro. (1999). Motivated cognition and group interaction: Need for closure affects the contents and process of collective negotiations. *Journal of Experimental Social Psychology*, 35, 346–365.

Deutsch, M. (1973). *The resolution of conflict*. New Haven, CT: Yale University Press.

Dittloff, S. A., and K. L. Harris. (1996). A contingency approach to understanding negotiator behavior as a function of worldmindedness and expected future interaction. *Journal of Psychology*, 130(1), 59–70.

Druckman, D. (1968). Ethnocentrism in the inter-nation simulation. *Journal of Conflict Resolution*, 12, 45–68.

Dunning, D., Griffin, D. W., Miljokovic, J. D., and L. Ross. (1990). The overconfidence effect in social prediction. *Journal of Personality and Social Psychology*, 58, 568–581.

Evans, J. S. (1993). The cognitive psychology of reasoning: An introduction. *Quarterly Journal of Experimental Psychology: Human Experimental Psychology Special Issue: The Cognitive Psychology of Reasoni. 1*, 46, 561–567.

Fein, S., and S. J. Spencer. (1997). Prejudice as self-image maintenance: Affirming the self through derogating others. *Journal of Personality and Social Psychology*, 73, 31–44.

Fiske, S. T. (1993). Social cognition and social perception. *Annual Review of Psychology,* *44,* 155–194.

Fiske, S. T., and S. E. Taylor. (1991). *Social cognition.* New York: McGraw-Hill.

Forgas, J. P. (1998a). Asking nicely? The effects of mood on responding to more or less polite requests. *Personality and Social Psychology Bulletin, 24*(2), 173–185.

———. (1998b). On feeling good and getting your way: Mood effects on negotiator cognition and bargaining strategies. *Journal of Personality and Social Psychology, 74,* 565–577.

Galinsky, A. D. (1999). *Perspective-taking: Debiasing social thought.* Unpublished doctoral dissertation, Princeton University.

Galinsky, A. D., and G. B. Moskowitz. (2000). Perspective-taking: Decreasing stereotype expression, stereotype accessibility, and in-group favoritism. *Journal of Personality and Social Psychology, 78,* 708–724.

Galinsky, A., and T. Mussweiler. (2001). Promoting good outcomes: Effects of regulatory focus on negotiation outcomes. *Journal of Personality and Social Psychology, 81,* 657–669.

Galinsky, A., Mussweiler, T., and V. H. Medvec. (2001). *Disconnecting subjective and objective utility: The role of negotiator focus.* Working paper, Northwestern University.

Galinsky, A., Seiden, V., Kim, P. H., and V. H. Medvec. (2002). The dissatisfaction of having your first offer accepted: Counterfactual thinking in negotiations. *Personality and Social Psychology Bulletin, 28*(2), 271–283.

Gilbert, D. T., Pinel, E. C., Wilson, T. D., Blumberg, S. J., and T. P. Wheatley. (1998). Immune neglect: A source of durability bias in affective forecasting. *Journal of Personality and Social Psychology, 75,* 617–638.

Gilovich, T. (1981). Seeing the past in the present: The effect of associations to familiar events on judgments and decisions. *Journal of Personality and Social Psychology, 40,* 797–808.

Gilovich, T., Savitsky, K., and V. H. Medvec. (1998). The illusion of transparency: Biased assessments of others' ability to read one's emotional states. *Journal of Personality and Social Psychology, 75,* 332–346.

Greenwald, A. G., and M. R. Banaji. (1995). Implicit social cognition: Attitudes, self-esteem, and stereotypes. *Psychological Review, 102,* 1–27.

Gruenfeld, D. H., Mannix, E. A., Williams, K. Y., and M. A. Neale. (1996). Group composition and decision making: How member familiarity and information distribution affect process and performance. *Organizational Behavior and Human Decision Processes, 67*(1), 1–15.

Halpern, J. J. (1994). The effect of friendship on personal business transactions. *Journal of Conflict Resolution, 38,* 647–664.

———. (1996). The effect of friendship on decisions: Field studies of real estate transactions. *Human Relations, 49,* 1519–1547.

Heide, J. B., and A. Miner. (1992). The shadow of the future: Effects of anticipated interaction and frequency of contact on buyer–seller cooperation. *Academy of Management Journal, 35,* 265–291.

Heider, F. (1958). *The psychology of interpersonal relations.* New York: Wiley.

Higgins, E. T., Rholes, W. S., and C. R. Jones. (1977). Category accessibility and impression formation. *Journal of Experimental Social Psychology, 13*(2), 141–154.

Isen, A. M. (1993). Positive affect and decision making. In M. Lewis and J. Haviland (Eds.), *Handbook of emotion* (pp. 261–277). New York: Guilford.

Isen, A. M., Daubman, K. A., and G. P. Nowicki. (1987). Positive affect facilitates creative problem solving. *Journal of Personality and Social Psychology, 52,* 1122–1131.

Isen, A. M., and P. F. Levin. (1972). Effect of feeling good on helping: Cookies and kindness. *Journal of Personality and Social Psychology, 21,* 384–388.

Johnson-Laird, P. N. (1983). *Mental models.* Cambridge, MA: Harvard University Press.

Jones, E. E., and R. E. Nisbett. (1987). The actor and the observer: Divergent perceptions of the causes of behavior. In E. E. Jones (Ed.), *Attribution: Perceiving the causes of behavior* (pp. 79–94). Hillsdale, NJ: Erlbaum.

Kahneman, D., and A. Tversky. (1979). Prospect theory: An analysis of decision under risk. *Econometrica, 47,* 263–291.

Kelley, H. H. (1966). A classroom study of dilemmas in interpersonal negotiations. In K. Archibald (Ed.), *Strategic intervention and conflict* (pp. 49–73). Berkeley, CA: University of California, Institute of International Studies.

———. (1967). Attribution theory in social psychology. *Nebraska Symposium on Motivation, 15,* 192–238. Lincoln: University of Nebraska Press.

Keltner, D., and R. J. Robinson. (1993). Imagined ideological differences in conflict escalation and resolution. *International Journal of Conflict Management, 4,* 249–262.

Keysar, B., Ginzel, L. E., and M. H. Bazerman. (1995). States of affairs and states of mind: The effect of knowledge about beliefs. *Organizational Behavior and Human Decision Processes, 64,* 283–293.

Korhonen, P., Oretskin, N., Teich, J., and J. Wallenius. (1995). The impact of a biased starting position in a single negotiation text type mediation. *Group Decision and Negotiation, 4,* 357–374.

Kramer, R. M., Newton, E., and P. L. Pommerenke. (1993). Self-enhancement biases and negotiator judgment: Effects of self-esteem and mood. *Organizational Behavior and Human Decision Processes, 56,* 110–133.

Kramer, R., Pommerenke, P., and E. Newton. (1993). The social context of negotiation: Effects of social identity and accountability on negotiator judgment and decision making. *Journal of Conflict Resolution, 37,* 633–654.

Kray, L. J., Galinsky, A., and L. Thompson. (2002). Reversing the gender gap in negotiations: An exploration of stereotype regeneration. *Organizational Behavior and Human Decision Processes, 87*(2): 386–409.

Kray, L. J., Thompson, L., and A. Galinsky. (2001). Battle of the sexes: Gender stereotype confirmation and reactance in negotiations. *Journal of Personality and Social Psychology, 80,* 942–958.

Kristensen, H., and T. Gaerling. (1997a). Adoption of cognitive reference points in negotiations. *Acta Psychologica, 97,* 277–288.

————. (1997b). Determinants of buyers' aspiration and reservation price. *Journal of Economic Psychology, 18,* 487–503.

Kronzon, S., and J. Darley. (1999). Is this tactic ethical? Biased judgments of ethics in negotiation. *Basic and Applied Social Psychology, 21*(1), 49–60.

Kruglanski, A. W., and D. M. Webster. (1996). Motivated closing of the mind: "Seizing" and "freezing." *Psychological Review, 103,* 263–283.

Loewenstein, G. F., and D. Schkade. (1999). Wouldn't it be nice? Predicting future feelings. In D. Kahneman and E. Diener (Eds.), *Well-being: The foundations of hedonic psychology* (pp. 85–105). New York: Russell Sage Foundation.

Loewenstein, G., Thompson, L., and M. H. Bazerman. (1989). Social utility and decision making in interpersonal contexts. *Journal of Personality and Social Psychology, 57,* 426–441.

Mannix, E. A. (1994). Will we meet again? The effects of power, distribution norms, and the scope of future interaction in small group negotiation. *International Journal of Conflict Management, 5,* 343–368.

Morley, I., and G. M. Stephenson. (1977). *The social psychology of bargaining.* London: Allen and Unwin.

Morris, M. W., Larrick, R. P., and S. K. Su. (1999). Misperceiving negotiation counterparties: When situationally determining bargaining behaviors are attributed to personality traits. *Journal of Personality and Social Psychology, 77,* 52–67.

Mussweiler, T., and F. Strack. (1999). Hypothesis-consistent testing and semantic priming in the anchoring paradigm: A selective accessibility model. *Journal of Experimental Social Psychology, 35*(2), 136–164.

Neale, M. (1984). The effect of negotiation and arbitration cost salience on bargainer behavior: The role of arbitrator and constituency in negotiator judgment. *Organizational Behavior and Human Decision Processes, 34,* 97–111.

Neale, M. A., and M. H. Bazerman. (1983). The role of perspective taking ability in negotiating under different forms of arbitration. *Industrial and Labor Relations Review, 36,* 378–388.

————. (1985). The effects of framing and negotiator overconfidence on bargaining behaviors and outcomes. *Academy of Management Journal, 28*(1), 34–49.

————. (1991). *Cognition and rationality in negotiation.* New York: Free Press.

Neale, M. A., Huber, V. L., and G. B. Northcraft. (1987). The framing of negotiations: Contextual versus task frames. *Organizational Behavior and Human Decision Processes, 39*(2), 228–241.

Neale, M. A., and G. B. Northcraft. (1990). Experience, expertise, and decision bias in negotiation: The role of strategic conceptualization. In B. Sheppard, M. Bazerman, and R. Lewicki (Eds.), *Research on negotiation in organizations* (Vol. 2, pp. 55–76). Greenwich, CT: JAI.

Nisbett, R. E., Borgida, E., Crandall, R., and H. Reed. (1982). Popular induction: Information is not necessarily informative. In D. Kahneman, P. Slovic, and A. Tversky (Eds), *Judgment under uncertainty: Heuristics and biases* (pp. 101–116). Cambridge, England: Cambridge University Press.

Nisbett, R. E., and L. Ross. (1980). *Human inference: Strategies and shortcomings of social judgment.* Englewood Cliffs, NJ: Prentice Hall.

Northcraft, G. B., and M. A. Neale. (1986). Opportunity costs and the framing of resource allocation decisions. *Organizational Behavior and Human Decision Processes, 37,* 348–356.

Northcraft, G. B., and M. A. Neale. (1987). Experts, amateurs, and real estate: An anchoring-and-adjustment perspective on property pricing decisions. *Organizational Behavior and Human Decision Processes, 39,* 84–97.

O'Connor, K. (June, 1994). *Negotiation teams: The impact of accountability and representation structure on negotiator cognition and performance.* Paper presented at the annual meeting of the International Association of Conflict Management, Eugene, OR.

Oskamp, S. (1965). Attitudes toward U.S. and Russian actions: A double standard. *Psychological Reports, 16,* 43–46.

Phillips, K. W., Mannix, E. A., Neale, M. A., and D. H. Gruenfeld. (2001). *Who knows what? The effects of asymmetrical social and knowledge ties.* Working paper, Kellogg School of Management, Northwestern University.

Pillutla, M. M., and J. K. Murnighan. (1996). Unfairness, anger, and spite: Emotional rejections of ultimatum offers. *Organizational Behavior and Human Decision Processes, 68,* 208–224.

Pinkley, R. (1990). Dimensions of conflict frame: Disputant interpretations of conflict. *Journal of Applied Psychology, 75,* 117–126.

Pinkley, R., Griffith, T. L., and G. B. Northcraft. (1995). Fixed pie a-la-mode: Information availability, information processing, and the negotiation of suboptimal agreements. *Organizational Behavior and Human Decision Processes, 37,* 101–112.

Pinkley, R., and G. B. Northcraft. (1990). *Cognitive interpretations of conflict: Implications for disputant motives and behavior.* Working paper, Southern Methodist University.

———. (1994). Conflict frames of reference: Implications for dispute processes and outcomes. *Academy of Management Journal, 37*(1), 193–205.

Polzer, J. T., and M. A. Neale. (1995). Constraints or catalysts? Reexamining goal setting within the context of negotiation. *Human Performance, 8,* 3–26.

Pruitt, D. G. (1981). *Negotiation behavior.* New York: Academic Press.

Raiffa, H. (1982). *The art and science of negotiation.* Cambridge, MA: Belknap.

Ritov, I. (1996). Anchoring in simulated competitive market negotiation. *Organizational Behavior and Human Decision Processes, 67,* 16–25.

Robinson, R. J., Keltner, D., Ward, A., and L. Ross. (1995). Actual versus assumed differences in construal: "Naive realism" in intergroup perception and conflict. *Journal of Personality and Social Psychology, 68,* 404–417.

Robinson, R. J., and L. Kray. (2001). Status versus quo: Naive realism and the search for social change and perceived legitimacy. In J. T. Jost and B. Major (Eds.), *The psychology of legitimacy: Emerging perspectives on ideology, justice, and intergroup relations* (pp. 135–154). New York: Cambridge University Press.

Ross, L. (1977). The intuitive psychologist and his shortcomings: Distortions in the attribution process. In L. Berkowitz (Ed.), *Advances in experimental social psychology* (Vol. 10, pp. 173–220). Orlando, FL: Academic Press.

Ross, L., and R. Nisbett. (1991). *The person and the situation.* New York: McGraw-Hill.

Ross, L., and S. M. Samuels. (1993). *The predictive power of personal reputation vs. labels and construal in the prisoner's dilemma game.* Working paper, Stanford University.

Ross, L., and C. Stillinger. (1991). Barriers to conflict resolution. *Negotiation Journal, 8,* 389–404.

Rothbart, M., and W. Hallmark. (1988). In-group and out-group differences in the perceived efficacy of coercion and concilliation in resolving social conflict. *Journal of Personality and Social Psychology, 55,* 248–257.

Samuelson, W. F., and M. H. Bazerman. (1985). The winner's curse in bilateral negotiations. In V. L. Smith (Eds.), *Research in experimental economics* (pp. 105–137). Greenwich, CT: JAI.

Schwarz, N. (1990). Feelings as information: Informational and motivational functions of affective states. In E. T. Higgins and R. M. Sorrentino (Eds.), *Handbook of motivation and cognition: Foundations of social behavior* (Vol. 2, pp. 527–561). New York: Guilford Press.

Shah, P. P., and K. A. Jehn. (1993). Do friends perform better than acquaintances: The interaction of friendship, conflict, and task. *Group Decision and Negotiation, 2,* 149–166.

Siegel, S., and L. E. Fouraker. (1960). *Bargaining and group decision making.* New York: McGraw-Hill.

Simons, T. (1993). Speech patterns and the concept of utility in cognitive maps: The case of integrative bargaining. *Academy of Management Journal, 36*(1), 139–156.

Steele, C. M. (1988). The psychology of self-affirmation: Sustaining the integrity of the self. In L. Berkowitz (Ed.), *Advances in experimental social psychology: Vol. 21. Social psychological studies of the self: Perspectives and programs* (pp. 261–302). San Diego, CA: Academic Press.

Stillinger, C., Epelbaum, M., Keltner, D., and L. Ross. (1990). The *"reactive devaluation" barrier to conflict resolution.* Working paper, Stanford University.

Tabossi, P., Bell, V. A., and P. N. Johnson-Laird. (1999). Mental models in deductive, modal, and probabilistic reasoning. In G. Rickheit and C. Habel (Eds.), *Mental models in discourse processing and reasoning* (pp. 299–331). Amsterdam, the Netherlands: Elsevier.

Taylor, S. E., and J. Brown. (1988). Illusion and well-being: A social-psychological perspective. *Psychological Bulletin, 103,* 193–210.

Taylor, S. E., and S. T. Fiske. (1975). Point of view and perceptions of causality. *Journal of Personality and Social Psychology, 32,* 439–445.

Taylor, S. E., and S. C. Thompson. (1982). Stalking the elusive "vividness" effect. *Psychological Review, 89*(2), 155–181.

Tetlock, P. E. (1985). Accountability: A social check on the fundamental attribution error. *Social Psychology Quarterly, 48,* 227–236.

———. (1992). The impact of accountability on judgment and choice: Toward a social contingency model. *Advances in Experimental Social Psychology, 25,* 331–376.

Tetlock, P. E., Skitka, L., and R. Boettger. (1989). Social and cognitive strategies for coping with accountability: Conformity, complexity, and bolstering. *Journal of Personality and Social Psychology, 57,* 632–640.

Thompson, L. (1990a). An examination of naive and experienced negotiators. *Journal of Personality and Social Psychology, 59,* 82–90.

————. (1990b). The influence of experience on negotiation performance. *Journal of Experimental Social Psychology, 26,* 528–544.

Thompson, L., and T. DeHarpport. (1994). Social judgment, feedback, and interpersonal learning in negotiation. *Organizational Behavior and Human Decision Processes, 58,* 327–345.

————. (1998). Relationships, goal incompatibility, and communal orientation in negotiations. *Basic and Applied Social Psychology, 20*(1), 33–44.

Thompson, L., Gentner, D., and J. Loewenstein. (2000). Avoiding missed opportunities in managerial life: Analogical training more powerful than individual case training. *Organizational Behavior and Human Decision Processes, 82*(1), 60–75.

Thompson, L., and R. Hastie. (1990). Social perception in negotiation. *Organizational Behavior and Human Decision Processes, 47,* 98–123.

Thompson, L., and P. Kim. (2000). How the quality of third parties' settlement solutions are affected by the relationship between negotiators. *Journal of Experimental Psychology: Applied, 6*(1), 1–16.

Thompson, L., and G. Loewenstein. (1992). Egocentric interpretations of fairness and negotiation. *Organizational Behavior and Human Decision Processes, 51,* 176–197.

Thompson, L., Medvec, V. H., Seiden, V., and S. Kopelman. (2001). Poker face, smiley face, and rant and rave: Myths and realities about emotion in negotiation. In M. Hogg and S. Tindale (Eds.), *Blackwell handbook in social psychology: Vol. 3. Group processes* (pp. 139–163). Oxford, England: Blackwell.

Thompson, L., and J. Nadler. (2000). Judgmental biases in conflict resolution and how to overcome them. In M. Deutsch and P. Coleman (Eds.), *Handbook of constructive conflict resolution: Theory and practice* (pp. 213–235). San Francisco: Jossey-Bass.

Thompson, L., Nadler, J., and P. Kim. (1999). Some like it hot: The case for the emotional negotiator. In L. Thompson, J. Levine, and D. Messick (Eds.), *Shared cognition in organizations: The management of knowledge* (pp. 139–161). Hillsdale, NJ: Erlbaum.

Thompson, L., Peterson, E., and L. Kray. (1995). Social context in negotiation: An information-processing perspective. In R. Kramer and D. Messick (Eds.), *Negotiation as a social process* (pp. 5–36). Thousand Oaks, CA: Sage.

Thompson, L., Valley, K. L., and R. M. Kramer. (1995). The bittersweet feeling of success. *Journal of Experimental Social Psychology, 31,* 467–492.

Tjosvold, D. (1977). The effects of the constituent's affirmation and the opposing negotiator's self-presentation in bargaining between unequal status groups. *Organizational Behavior and Human Decision Processes, 18*(1), 146–157.

Tversky, A., and D. Kahneman. (1973). Availability: A heuristic for judging frequency and probability. *Cognitive Psychology, 5,* 207–232.

————. (1974). Judgment under uncertainty: Heuristics and biases. *Science, 185,* 1124–1131.

von Neumann, J., and O. Morgenstern. (1947). *Theory of games and economic behavior.* Princeton, NJ: Princeton University Press.

Vorauer, J. D., and S. Claude. (1998). Perceived versus actual transparency of goals in negotiation. *Personality and Social Psychology Bulletin, 24,* 371–385.

Wade-Benzoni, K. A., Tenbrunsel, A. E., and M. H. Bazerman. (1996). Egocentric interpretations of fairness in asymmetric, environmental social dilemmas: Explaining harvesting behavior and the role of communication. *Organizational Behavior and Human Decision Processes, 67,* 111–126.

————. (1997). Egocentric interpretations of fairness as an obstacle to the resolution of environmental conflict. In R. J. Lewicki, R. J. Bies, and B. H. Sheppard (Eds.), *Research on negotiation in organizations* (Vol. 6, pp. 189–206). Greenwich, CT: JAI.

Webster, D. M., and A. W. Kruglanski. (1994). Individual differences in the need for cognitive closure. *Journal of Personality and Social Psychology, 67,* 1049–1062.

Wegner, D. M. (1987). Transactive memory: A contemporary analysis of the group mind. In B. Mullen and G. R. Goethals (Eds.), *Theories of Group Behavior* (pp. 185–208). New York: Springer-Verlag.

————. (1989). *White bears and other unwanted thoughts: Suppression, obsession, and the psychology of mental control.* New York: Viking/Penguin.

————. (1995). A computer network model of human transactive memory. *Social Cognition, 13,* 319–339

Weiner, B. (1985). An attributional theory of achievement motivation and emotion. *Psychological Review, 92,* 548–573.

————. (1996). Searching for order in social motivation. *Psychological Inquiry, 7,* 197–214.

Weingart, L. R., Thompson, L. L., Bazerman, M. H., and J. S. Carroll. (1990). Tactical behavior and negotiation outcomes. *International Journal of Conflict Management, 1,* 7–31.

White, S., and M. Neale. (1994). The role of negotiator aspirations and settlement expectancies in bargaining outcomes. *Organizational Behavior and Human Decision Processes, 57,* 303–317.

White, S., Valley, K., Bazerman, M. H., Neale, M. A., and S. Peck. (1994). Alternative models of price behavior in dyadic negotiations: Market prices, reservation prices, and negotiator aspirations. *Organizational Behavior and Human Decision Processes, 57,* 430–447.

Whyte, G., and J. Sebenius. (1997). The effect of multiple anchors on anchoring in individual and group performance. *Organizational Behavior and Human Decision Processes, 69,* 75–85.

Wilson, M. G., Northcraft, G. B., and M. A. Neale. (1989). Information competition and vividness effects in on-line judgments. *Organizational Behavior and Human Decision Processes, 44,* 132–139.

Wilson, S. R. (1992). Face and facework in negotiation. In L. L. Putnam and M. E. Roof (Eds.), *Communication and negotiation* (pp. 176–205). Thousand Oaks, CA: Sage.

Wilson, T. D. (1985). Strangers to ourselves: The origins and accuracy of beliefs about one's own mental states. In J. H. Harvey and G. Weary (Eds.), *Attribution in contemporary psychology* (pp. 9–36). New York: Academic Press.

Wilson, T. D., and D. S. Dunn. (1986). Effects of introspection on attitude–behavior consistency: Analyzing reasons versus focusing on feelings. *Journal of Experimental Social Psychology, 22,* 249–263.

CHAPTER 2

Cultural Differences and Cognitive Dynamics
EXPANDING THE COGNITIVE PERSPECTIVE
ON NEGOTIATION

Michael W. Morris and Michele J. Gelfand

COGNITIVE RESEARCH focuses on the many judgments negotiators make at the bargaining table, judgments that shape negotiators' decisions, their actions and reactions, and ultimately their outcomes. As noted by Thompson, Neale, and Sinaceur in their chapter of this volume, a key contribution has been identifying biases in judgment that underlie common shortcomings in negotiators' tactical and strategic choices.[1] Biases are understood as resulting from the mental shortcuts that humans unconsciously revert to when facing otherwise overwhelming information-processing demands. In negotiations, we have to carry on a conversation while simultaneously making a series of numerical judgments (e.g., What are the risks and payoffs of the offers coming across the table?) and social judgments (e.g., Has the person across the table been consistent? Honest? Cooperative?). We just don't have the capacity to perceive and process the real facts needed to rationally answer these questions, so we make estimates or guesses by imposing preconceptions onto the stimuli we experience. Shortcuts using knowledge structures as templates for interpreting matters and reaching conclusions work most of the time, providing quick and accurate-enough answers, but they fail on certain kinds of judgment problems. In negotiation situations that pose these kinds of problems, negotiators show predictable biases that often lead to suboptimal strategic and tactical decisions. By revealing the processes underlying negotiators' mistakes, cognitive research has made both a practical and theoretical contribution.

Although the cognitive approach has flourished, it has not gone uncritiqued. In an early challenge, field researchers (e.g., Barley, 1991) questioned whether its findings, largely drawn from simulated negotiations between in-experienced and unacquainted participants, correspond to the dynamics of real-world negotiations in which industry norms and prior relationships fig-ure so prominently. This challenge spurred a broadening of the cognitive approach to include concepts from social cognition research. Researchers have investigated the micro-social context in which negotiators are embed-ded and found that factors such as prior relationships between counterparts or shared group identities change negotiators' judgment biases and strategic choices (for a review, see Kramer and Messick, 1995).

A contemporary challenge to the cognitive approach pertains to the macro-context of national culture (Smith and Bond, 1988). Although the biases and their consequences have been documented repeatedly, the evi-dence comes almost exclusively from studies in the United States and a few other culturally similar Western countries. This raises the question of cultural generalizability: Are the biases documented thus far merely local habits—characteristics of "Western" or "individualistic" negotiators—rather than invariant, fundamental aspects of human nature? Has negotiation research overlooked other biases that appear only in other cultural settings? Taking it to an extreme, is the whole approach of studying negotiator cognitions itself a culturally bound Western product, unhelpful for understanding the decisions of actions of non-Western negotiators? We submit that negotia-tion research is not well served by this extreme pole of radical relativism (the stance that human behavior differs incommensurably across cultures) nor by the opposite pole of ethnocentric universalism (the stance that Western findings suffice to characterize humans everywhere, or the stance of silence on the question of culture, which in practice amounts to the same thing). The challenge is to find theoretically graceful ways of incorporating cultural variation into models of negotiation. We focus on cognitive models in this chapter, but this statement holds for models of emotion in negotiation (see Kumar, Chapter 4, this volume), as well as for models of communication in negotiation (see Adair and Brett, Chapter 7, this volume).

In assessing this cross-cultural challenge, we begin this chapter by describ-ing several examples of negotiation biases for which compelling evidence of cultural variation has accumulated. We then delineate a theory, based on a dynamic, constructivist analysis, that explains how culture influences nego-tiators. As we shall see, this theory explains several different ways in which culture influences negotiator biases. Moreover, it not only extends our un-derstanding of biases in other cultures but also deepens our understanding of the familiar biases exhibited by Western negotiators. Far from warranting abandonment of the cognitive approach, the cross-cultural challenge is an occasion for expanding and enriching cognitive theorizing.

Let us now preview some central features of our dynamic constructivist analysis. We posit a process of cultural influence that is *constructivist* in the sense that it focuses on the role of cultural knowledge structures in guiding judgments. Our account is also *dynamic* in its emphasis in that we argue that these knowledge structures exert an influence only when they have been triggered or activated. Constructivism, by itself, is not new in theories of culture. Prominent anthropological theories, particularly those in France, have made the constructivist premise that mental structures shape culturally specific patterns of thinking (e.g., Levi-Strauss, 1966), albeit this tradition has only recently integrated psychological theories into its models (Sperber, 1996). In research on culture and negotiation, some researchers have advocated a constructivist approach (e.g., Leung, 1987). However, the personality psychology approach of positing traits such as value-orientations as the sources of cultural divergences in negotiation patterns has been far more dominant. Constructivist and value accounts can be distinguished in the domain-specificity of their predictions about cultural patterns; knowledge structures are more restricted in their applicability than values, so cultural differences produced by them should be narrower in scope than those produced by values.

The truly novel aspect of our theory is its emphasis on the dynamics of cultural knowledge. Prior constructivist theories have posited that the knowledge structures used in one culture simply do not exist in other cultures—they are not cognitively *available* to individuals in the second culture. In our view, this is part of the story about how cultures differ but not the whole story. A key point is that just because knowledge exists in one's memory, this does not mean that the knowledge will be used to make judgments. Only a limited number of our knowledge structures are *accessible* or easy to retrieve at any one point in time. Moreover, even if a given knowledge structure is accessible, that doesn't mean it will be *activated* or brought into use for a particular judgment. Hence, culture differences do not require that a knowledge structure used in one culture is completely unavailable in another culture; differences can also result from differences in accessibility or activation. Recent social cognition research has delineated numerous factors that determine accessibility and activation of knowledge structures (Higgins, 1996), and we draw on these insights about the determinants of activation to make predictions about when negotiators will and will not be dramatically influenced by their culture. In sum, culture can influence whether a knowledge structure is *available* or possible to retrieve from memory, whether it is highly *accessible* or easy to retrieve, and finally, whether it is *activated* or brought into working memory to guide one's current judgment.

Another noteworthy feature of the dynamic constructivist theory is its interlinking of public and private cultural elements. Some elements of culture are ontologically public—artifacts, institutions, and texts that exist objectively—and others are ontologically private—mental representations in the heads of cultural members. The public–private distinction has traditionally divided theories of culture. Theories in anthropology that emphasize public, objective elements of culture refer to public discourses and texts (Geertz, 1976) and to economic and ecological conditions (Harris, 1979). Private, subjective elements of culture were emphasized in the French structuralist (Levi-Strauss, 1966) and American ethnoscience programs (D'Andrade, 1995). In psychology, there has been recognition of the role of public artifacts in sustaining culture over the generations; yet models of cultural influence on behavior focus almost exclusively on subjective culture, particularly on values, as the proximal mechanism in shaping people's behavior (Triandis, 1972). Our approach gives public cultural elements a larger role in the shaping of behavior. We argue that public elements of culture—such as cultural institutions, public discourses, and social structure—affect the availability, accessibility, and activation of knowledge structures in the minds of individuals who participate in the culture.

In sum, we suggest a response to cross-cultural challenge that avoids the dangers of relativism on the one side, and universalism on the other. It is a theory of the role of culture in negotiator cognition that suggest answers to previously unaddressed questions, such as the following:

- Which negotiation biases are most culturally variable and which most invariant?
- Through what causal pathways does culture influence negotiators' thinking?
- What factors at the bargaining table trigger the influence of culture?

As we review the literature and develop the assumptions and predictions of our theory, we will suggest answers to these questions, starting with the issue of which biases are most culturally variable. As we shall see, the answer to this question turns on the nature of the knowledge that underlies the bias—whether it is an innate information processing heuristic conferred by biological evolution or a learned construct (a category, theory, or rule) conferred by cultural evolution.

Which Negotiator Biases Are Culturally Variable?

Research within the cognitive approach to negotiation has been largely silent on the question of cultural variation. Silence, we would argue, implies a position on the issue, namely, the position that culture is not a crucial variable in understanding negotiator biases. From the standpoint of cross-cultural psychology, however, it is only when psychological processes are linked to a biological substrate that the presumption of cultural universality is justified (Pepitone, 1987). Aside from hard-core evolutionary psychologists (Barkow, Cosmides, and Tooby, 1992), few would contend that all the biases identified in cognitive research on negotiation reflect hardwired mental rules and structures rather than learned ideas.

In grappling with the question of which biases might reflect hardwired rather than learned structures, a useful distinction may be between negotiators' numerical judgments and social judgments. Biases in numerical judgments, such as estimates of the risk and value, were the first major findings of the cognitive approach. For example, several studies have documented and traced the consequences of negotiators' risk aversion for offers framed as gains versus losses (Bazerman, Magliozzi, and Neale, 1985). This bias of undervaluing risky options, predicted from the convex value function in prospect theory (Kahneman and Tversky, 1979), is related to the more general tendency in human and animal perception of sensitivity to changes rather than absolute levels (Fechner, 1966). As this example suggests, biases in numerical judgments may arise from hardwired features of the perceptual system and hence may vary minimally across cultures.

Biases in social judgments—assessments of character, evaluations of fairness, expectations of others' reactions—have been a prominent topic in cognitively oriented research on negotiation. This research takes its concepts and methods from the field of social cognition, which draws together research on the inferential tendencies exhibited when people think about themselves, about other social actors, and about social situations and relationships. There are fewer bases for assumed cultural invariance in the domain of social judgment, unlike in the domain of numerical judgment. Perceivers vary in how they interpret social situations (e.g., what looks to a New Yorker like friendly teasing of one's boss may look to a Japanese observer like a grave insult); in how they categorize groups (e.g., along caste lines in Hindu contexts but along class lines in England); or in how they read meaning into relationships (e.g., one builds trust through *compadres* in Mexico and through *guanxi* in China). Moreover, recent research has identified cultural differences even in the constructs that social cognition researchers have traditionally been assumed to be natural and necessary, such as the concept of self (Heine, Lehman, Markus, and Kitayama, 1999) and the concept of other persons (Morris and Peng, 1994).

In sum, social judgment biases arise from negotiators' reliance on culturally derived knowledge structures, such as conceptions of the negotiation situation, conceptions of self, and conceptions of other people. Hence, social judgment biases should vary across cultures. Next we provide three examples of recent studies that have illustrated that social judgment biases are not universal.

EXAMPLE 1: FIXED-PIE BIAS IN JUDGMENTS OF THE COUNTERPARTS' INTERESTS

Fixed-pie bias occurs when negotiators falsely assume that there is no room for integrative bargaining—that counterparts' interests are diametrically opposed to their own (Thompson and Hastie, 1990) Studies in the

North American context suggest that the fixed-pie bias arises from the conceptions of conflict that negotiators bring to a situation; the bias occurs when negotiations are framed as a game with a winner and loser, like in sports, as opposed to a collaborative undertaking, like solving a problem jointly (Pinkley, 1990). North American negotiators apply a win–lose frame even after they have been provided full information illustrating that the interests of the parties are not diametrically opposed (Pinkley and Northcraft, 1994), which indicates that the perceiver's knowledge structure can override the evidence of perception.

With respect to cultural variability in fixed-pie biases, there seems to be no theoretical or empirical basis to assume that the conception of conflict as win–lose games is biologically rooted; hence, the readiness with which North American negotiators apply the construct may reflect the influence of North American culture. In other words, such win–lose conceptions are likely grounded in knowledge structures that are culturally based. In the United States, where most negotiation research has been conducted, negotiation is often (implicitly) mapped to the domain of sports, games, and battle—themes that pervade the larger cultural context (Gelfand and McCusker, 2002). Such meta-theories guide information processing at the individual level, where attention is directed to who is winning and losing, and to competitive scripts. This mapping may seem obvious—even inevitable—to American readers; yet it is not very marked in other cultures. Ethnographic descriptions of the scripts for negotiation conflicts in Japan, for example, such as *naniwabushi* (March, 1988), show a mapping onto coordination within the family, resulting in attention being directed to maintaining harmony between parties, keeping disagreements covert, and saving face for all involved. We will return to the question of how a cultural group comes to share certain knowledge structures; for now, it is enough to say that individuals are exposed to public representations—institutions that presuppose an idea, texts that explicate the idea, discourses that assume the idea—and the public prominence of the construct becomes mirrored in its prominence within their mental representations.

Cross-cultural studies suggest that negotiators differ in the default conceptions that are used to construe conflicts. Gelfand, Nishii, Holcombe, Dyer, Ohbuchi, and Fukuno (2001) found that Japanese construed conflicts more in terms of mutual blame and cooperation, whereas Americans interpreted the same conflict episodes in terms of a win–lose frame in which one party is right and the other wrong. These cultural differences occurred even when participants were making judgments about conflicts that took place in a cultural context other than their own. In addition, Americans focused their attention more on the nature of individual rights in the conflicts, whereas Japanese focused their attention on duties, obligations, and violations of "face." A diminished level of fixed-pie bias is not unique to Japanese culture but has been observed in other cultures where negotiators may be guided by family rather than sports metaphors. Gelfand and Christakopoulou (1999) found that American negotiators exhibited more fixed-pie bias than Greeks in intercultural negotiations (i.e., were less accurate in reporting the priorities of their counterparts), even after the same priority information was exchanged within dyads. Americans, as compared to Greeks, interestingly, were more confident that they understood their counterparts' interests. Thus, fixed-pie biases—which are often implicitly assumed to be universal—may depend on which knowledge structures are activated, which in turn depends on culture.

EXAMPLE 2: EGOCENTRIC BIAS IN FAIRNESS JUDGMENTS

Another judgment bias that is widespread among North American negotiators is egocentrism, or the tendency to view one's own behaviors as more fair than others (Thompson and Loewenstein, 1992). For example, disputants enter final-offer arbitration with overly optimistic assessments of the likelihood that their proposal will be perceived as more fair and will be favored (Neale and Bazerman, 1985). Disputants' self-serving fairness judgments also lead them to take aggressive positions, which result in costly delay that "shrinks" the pie of value to be ultimately divided (Babcock and Loewenstein, 1997; Thompson and Loewenstein, 1992). Research on egocentrism in negotiation builds theoretically on studies of egocentric judgments in other types of social interaction, such as estimates of one's proportional contribution to tasks or to conversations (see Fiske and Taylor, 1991). The origin of egocentric biases is the privileged status of the self-concept in information processing; information processed through the lens of the self is remembered better and ultimately weighted more than information that falls outside of the purview of the self. One's own valid arguments and concerns are weighted more heavily than valid arguments and concerns of the counterpart.

Yet, if the self-concept has a different structure or scope in non-Western as compared to Western cultures, then its biasing effect on one's judgment should differ accordingly. There is considerable evidence (Heine et al., 1999) that in many East Asian cultures, individuals conceive of themselves less as isolated individuals and more in terms of their relationships to others—as the spouse of their partner, the mentor of their junior partner, and so forth. Hence, at least in conflicts with close counterparts, such as a spouse or business partner, we should expect that the egocentric bias and problems it breeds in negotiation should be attenuated in East Asian cultures. This is because East Asians should process the arguments and concerns on both sides of the conflict through their interdependent self-concepts.

Cross-cultural research in negotiation provides evidence consistent with this prediction. Gelfand et al. (2002) found that Americans associated themselves with fair behaviors and others with unfair behaviors to a much greater extent than did Japanese. Gelfand et al. (2002) also found, in the domain of conflict, that American disputants believed that an "objective third party" would judge their behavior as more fair, judge offers from the counterpart as unfair, and would reject these offers more as compared to Japanese. Consistent with our argument, they found that Americans had greater independent self-construals and that these construals were related to greater egocentric bias in a negotiation simulation. In sum, egocentric bias in judging fairness varies across cultures as a function of underlying differences in self-conception.[2]

EXAMPLE 3: DISPOSITIONIST BIAS IN JUDGING COUNTERPARTS'
INTENTIONS AND TRAITS

Another set of negotiation errors resulting from bias in social judgment are misattributions of traits to one's counterpart. Negotiators often have illusory impressions of each other's characteristics (e.g., inflexibility, greed) because negotiators fail to weigh the situational influences in understanding the other's behavior. These biased judgments may lead to maladaptive decisions. For example, the decision to let a third-party arbitrator resolve a conflict rather than negotiating directly with the counterpart means giving up control and the potential for value creation through negotiation. Negotiators make these decisions based on judgments about the counterpart's traits—for example, that the other party is greedy—and thus are unlikely to engage in the search for a value-creating outcome and are more likely to try to claim all of the value in hard bargaining. Yet if these judgments are unfounded, this pattern of behavior can be a costly mistake.

Patterns of attribution to others' traits arise from our implicit theories of agency—theories about the extent to which a given actor is autonomous or is bound by external constraints (for a review, see Morris, Menon, and Ames, 2001). A great deal of Western research on interpersonal perception shows that even when a sufficient contextual force is known to be present, perceivers still tend to attribute behaviors to personality traits and other dispositions of the actor (Nisbett and Ross, 1980). Conflict is a ripe setting for this bias, because parties to a negotiation invariably exhibit disagreement. The extent to which parties disagree, however, is not necessarily due to negotiators' dispositions. Rather, it is largely determined by the party's bargaining alternatives (their best alternatives to a negotiated agreement, or BATNAs) and the zone of agreement that exists. However, dispositionist attributional errors lead negotiators to interpret disagreement as being caused by personality traits and not the situation (Morris, Larrick, and Su, 1999). Moreover, these attributions can have lingering and self-fulfilling consequences—they lead negotiators to choose to resolve future conflicts with the same person through arbitration rather than negotiation and to assign the other person to minor organizational roles that require haggling rather than to more central roles that require cooperation (Morris et al., 1999).

As with other biases reviewed, however, there is ample evidence that this bias is subject to cultural variability. The dispositionist bias, so robust among North American participants that it was designated the "fundamental attribution error," is less dramatic among East Asians, for whom the concept of the individual person as agentic is less absolute. The default conceptions of agency applied by East Asians enable them to understand the situationally contingent nature of an individual's behavior (Morris and Peng, 1994). Hence, errors such as turning an interpersonal dispute over to an arbitrator based on illusory impressions of one's counterpart's traits should be less likely among East Asians than North Americans.

Lest it seem that North Americans suffer from more biases than East Asians, we should point out that research has found that East Asians make attribution errors that North Americans do not. When the event being explained is an act by a group or organization, East Asians exhibit a stronger dispositionist bias than do North Americans (Menon, Morris, Chiu, and Hong, 1999). For example, they explain the success or failure of an organization in terms of internal dispositions, such as its discipline or harmony, rather than in terms of external factors, such as the difficulty of the task or the unpredictability of changes in its environment. Hence, in intergroup as opposed to interpersonal conflicts, East Asians may be more likely to make unwarranted judgments about negative traits of the opposing side and to make unwise strategic decisions as a consequence.

Summary

Taken together, these examples illustrate that social judgments that occur in negotiations, and the biases they exhibit, may differ across cultures. Although it would be premature to attempt a comprehensive taxonomy, we contend that social judgments are likely to diverge across cultures, to a greater extent than numerical judgments. A fruitful direction for future research would be to systematically investigate cultural variation in the biases that are linked to social knowledge structures, such as conceptions of self, of other persons, and of relationships in negotiation (the social perception biases, and some of the cognitive and motivational biases discussed in Thompson, Neale, and Sinaceur, Chapter 1, this volume). Indeed, this is the most basic contribution of the constructivist theory: it provides a basis for predicting which biases differ and which do not—a middle path between the conservative (and potentially ethnocentric) assumption that people everywhere share the biases of American negotiators and the relativist (and potentially nihilistic) stance that all negotiation biases vary across every culture. Although increased precision in our ability to document the content of

cultural variation is important, an even greater contribution of the constructivist theory is its capability to increase our understanding of the forms of
cultural influences. By form, we mean the causal pathways—in the negotiator's head and in the environment—through which the influence of culture
runs. As we shall see, it is in delineating the form or process of cultural
influence where the contributions of the constructivist theory are richest.

Distinguishing Distinct Points of Cultural Influence

The dynamic constructivist theory identifies three points at which culture
influences negotiators' judgments: the *availability, accessibility,* and *activation*
of their knowledge structures, or constructs. A software metaphor may be
helpful in illustrating these points: construct availability is akin to a software
program existing on the computer (e.g., the Powerpoint program is installed
on your PC); construct accessibility is akin to a frequently used program
being stored where it is easy to access (Powerpoint stored on your desktop
rather than deeply embedded in your files); construct activation is akin to
the program being selected as the active program (Powerpoint is currently
processing the input of commands from the keyboard). In order for a knowledge structure to be activated, it must become accessible, and before this it
must be available—a priority illustrated in Figure 2.1.

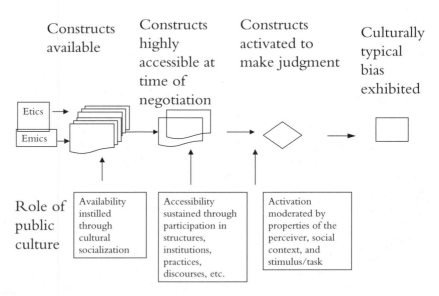

FIGURE 2.1. Culture and cognition in negotiation.

The stages in Figure 2.1 depict three points at which culture has an influence, and thus points at which cultural differences may arise. In understanding cultural differences, we must consider:

1. Which knowledge structures negotiators have internalized from their cultural socialization, or, in other words, which knowledge structures have become available in a particular culture.
2. Which knowledge structures have high accessibility as a result of frequent use, which, as discussed below, is a direct reflection of their predominance in cultural institutions, public discourse, social structures, and the like.
3. Which knowledge structures are actually triggered, or activated, at the negotiation table, which is a function of the properties of the negotiator, the conflict itself, and features of the social context.

We now discuss these three points of cultural influence, paying particular attention to the interplay of public and private culture in producing cultural differences in negotiator judgment.

INFLUENCE POINT I: CONSTRUCT AVAILABILITY

When a negotiation bias is stronger among North Americans than among members of another cultural group, it may reflect that the relevant knowledge structure is not cognitively available to members of the other group. Take, for example, the fixed-pie bias that we have linked to North American conceptions of conflict based on metaphorical mappings of negotiation to win–lose games (Gelfand and McCusker, 2002). In some cultures, the concept of win–lose games may be completely unavailable. This was the claim of some early ethnographers of Hopi and Navaho groups, in which children played collaborative string games like the cat's cradle (see Roberts, Arth, and Bush, 1959). In a culture where the public practice of win–lose games is absent, and the concept was not known from contact with other cultural groups, the construct of a win–lose game would be unavailable to cultural members.[3] Hence they could not use this construct to frame everyday conflicts and would not suffer from the resulting fixed-pie bias. The key point is that cultural differences in judgment can arise because of differences in construct availability. The chain of causal explanation for this kind of difference starts with public practices, which lead to differences in socialization, in the cultural members' knowledge structures, and ultimately in which constructs they use to make judgments.

Identifying this form of cultural influence enables us to make two further points. First, given that some cultural differences arise because a central construct in one culture has no meaningful equivalent in another culture, it follows that we cannot always rely exclusively on *etic* methods, which require that constructs be meaningful in both cultures. In this respect, ethnographic methods should play an important part in our science. Second, we should not assume that differences in construct availability are the primary source of cultural differences in behavior. The knowledge structures underlying the major negotiation biases that we have reviewed, such as independent versus interdependent self-conceptions, or conceptions of personal and group agency, are probably cognitively available in all cultures. Hence, most cultural differences in social judgment must reflect a more subtle difference than the availability versus unavailability of a knowledge structure. To understand this, we turn next to construct accessibility and activation as further mechanisms of cultural difference.

INFLUENCE POINT 2: CONSTRUCT ACCESSIBILITY

When we are diagnosing a cultural difference, and we establish that the relevant knowledge structure is cognitively available in both cultures, the next possibility is that the construct accessibility differs across the cultural groups. When we say a construct or knowledge structure is low in accessibility, we mean that it is "deeply buried" in memory rather than "on the top of the stack." Accordingly, it is less likely to be recruited as the guide to processing information and making judgments. It is useful to distinguish sources of temporary accessibility and chronic accessibility, because they are two ways cultural differences can arise through accessibility dynamics.

Temporary Accessibility

Temporary increases in accessibility occur when a knowledge structure has received stimulation from a recent experience and hence has become more likely than otherwise to be activated. Consider, for instance, the phenomenon of priming, which refers to the notion that information from a prior context can affect the interpretation of new information (Fiske and Taylor, 1991). Priming occurs through a temporary increase in the accessibility of a knowledge structure after its direct use in a recent judgment, or indirectly through its associations with other structures that have been used recently (Higgins, 1996). A priming manipulation—exposing individuals to an image or word related to the knowledge structure of interest—is a way of diagnosing the source of a cultural difference. That is, the manipulation can bring a deeply buried structure to the surface and thus increase its influence, but it can't affect a structure that is absent, that is not cognitively available. Hence cultural differences magnified by a priming manipulation reflect differences in the structure's availability, whereas differences diminished by a priming manipulation reflect differences in the structure's chronic accessibility. Hence, we can conclude that cultural differences, such as those involving the self-concept, arise from accessibility rather than availability differences from the evidence that priming different aspects of the self-concept removes the cultural difference in responding (Trafimow, Triandis, and Goto, 1991).

Priming is relevant to another dynamic that can create cultural differences. Negotiators from different cultures may experience different indirect priming effects in the same situation because their associations differ. Images, symbols, and words that are innocent of associations to some may be powerful primes to others. For example, a negotiation over the sale of a perfume called *Opium* may have no particular associations among American negotiators, but it might trigger knowledge of exploitative events among Chinese negotiators and, in turn, might trigger a win–lose frame and defensive negotiating tactics.

Priming is an event that occurs within one individual's mind involving *private elements* of culture, but similar effects occur within a society involving public elements of culture. Salient historical events act like primes at this culturally shared level. In periods following external threats to a nation, there is an increase (at least temporarily) in *public symbols* of national unity and cooperative practices. For example, in the United States, following the Pearl Harbor attacks, sacrifice and cooperation were reinforced by public culture— for example in discourse in radio and shows. Similar reactions occurred in the months following the terrorist attacks on the World Trade Center. The increase in the salience of these public elements of culture undoubtedly exists in a reciprocal causal relationship with the increased accessibility of private elements of culture, such as the ideas of patriotism and cooperative effort to help to meet the threat.

Chronic Accessibility

Theories about the dynamics of chronically accessible knowledge structures are also very helpful in understanding cultural influences. To illustrate, let's take the example of independent versus interdependent self-concepts. Evidence that both self-conceptions can be primed for American and Chinese participants suggests that both constructs are available cross-culturally; yet, the fact that cultures differ in the absence of primes indicates that the independent self-concept is chronically higher in accessibility for Americans, and the interdependent self-concept is chronically higher for Chinese (Gardner, Gabriel, and Lee, 1999). A recent paper with more specific primes found similar patterns, but also found that more specific components of the self-concept related to rights and duties could not be evoked everywhere with primes and hence may reflect differences in construct availability (Hong, Ip, Chiu, Morris, and Menton, 2001).

Elements of public culture play a role in how a knowledge structure becomes chronically accessible in one culture but not another. At the level of the individual, chronic accessibility results from the frequency with which the knowledge structure has been used to process information in the past (Higgins, 1996). For chronic accessibility of a construct to be widespread among the members of a culture, there have to be aspects of public culture that induce, if not require, cultural members to use the knowledge structure. In addition to the socialization practices that first insert knowledge into the heads of cultural members, stimuli embedded in everyday practices (e.g., independent sleeping arrangements), institutions (the media), and public discourses (win–lose speech metaphors) play a role by sustaining the heightened accessibility of particular knowledge structures in the heads of cultural members who participate in these forms of public culture (review, see Morris, Menon, and Ames, 2001). Let us illustrate a few of the ways in which public cultural elements sustain the heightened accessibility of knowledge structures relevant to negotiation biases.

Consider the discourses that surround American negotiators. When issues of disagreement are discussed—on television shows such as *Crossfire,* in newspaper stories on political elections and current events, in the courtroom, and in educational settings—they are often framed through sports (i.e., boxing, racing, tennis, etc.) or war metaphors (Gelfand and McCusker, 2002; Tannen, 1998). Indeed, in an empirical analysis of framing of negotiations in public culture, Gelfand et al. (2001) also found results similar to those found in private culture: American newspapers referenced competition and blamed one party, whereas Japanese newspapers references cooperation and mutual blame. The same methods of comparing the proportional frequency of particular content in newspaper stories has been used to establish that attribution of outcomes to personal agency is more frequent in the North American context (Morris and Peng, 1994), and attribution to group agency is more frequent in East Asian contexts (Menon et al., 1999).

The institutions and practices in which individuals are embedded also serve to activate chronically accessible knowledge structures. In particular, family, school, work, and legal and political institutions require certain roles to be played by the individuals that enter them. For example, practices within the family and schools contribute to the development and reinforcement of knowledge structures related to the self (e.g., interdependent and independent self-construals). In American schools, children are given many opportunities to identify their positive attributes, to feel special, and to think of themselves as "stars" (Markus, Kitayama, and Heiman, 1996). These socialization practices reinforce that it is important to express and affirm one's positive attributes and be different from, and better than, others, thus lending to the repeated activation of egocentric knowledge structures. In Japan, by contrast, parents and teachers teach their children that emphasizing one's uniqueness or positive attributes will invariably weaken the solidarity of the group and will lead to a disruption of group harmony. The practice of *hansei,* or critical self-reflection, is pervasive throughout Japanese schools (Heine et al., 1999). Such practices extend to Japanese work organizations, where the achievement of group harmony (*wa*) is emphasized through group activities and awards that stand in contrast to American practices of singling out individuals (Kashima and Callan, 1994).

Another form of public culture that has a very general effect on accessibility is social structure. At a macro level, there is a structure of categories or strata in society, both those constituted by ascribed categories, such as class or caste, as well as those constituted by economic factors. In American society, the relative unimportance of ascribed characteristics—which define a person in terms of group membership rather than in terms of personal preferences and achievements—most likely serves to sustain the accessibility of the conception of autonomous persons. At a micro level, people are embedded in a structure of relationships and roles, but cultures differ in the kinds of relationships that might be present in a situation requiring business negotiations (see Gelfand and Cai, Chapter 11, this volume). In Chinese culture, it is often the case that friendship connections (*guanxi*) are developed before commencing business transactions, and such relationship structures serve to reinforce activation of knowledge structures related to obligations and duty. By contrast, in American culture, business transactions often occur between parties without any prior relationship or friendship (Morris, Podolny, and Ariel, 2000). In general, the accessibility of knowledge structures tends to reflect their public prominence in the society.

In addition to these general influences, macro and micro structure determine the kinds of negotiations that will be frequent or endemic in a society. For example, the American economic structure creates opportunities for many consumer decisions, and Americans are socialized to express internal preferences. As such, conflicts are likely to be related to individual rights, autonomy, and conflicting preferences. By contrast, Chinese social structure creates opportunities for relational connections, and Chinese are socialized to fulfill obligations within their groups. As such, conflicts are likely to be related to competing obligations, such as those owed toward mothers, spouses, or colleagues (Ho, 1998). Thus, cultural variation in which kinds of conflict are endemic determines which knowledge structures are chronically accessible as a result of frequent use.

Finally, we should note that construct accessibility is not entirely passive; individuals exert some control over what is accessible in their minds. Some individuals strongly define themselves in terms of their ethnicity and have a commitment to the activities and traditions of their groups. This involves learning about one's cultural group (history, traditions, and customs), being active in social groups that involve members of one's own culture, and participating in the cultural practices of one's group (e.g., food, customs and music; Phinney, 1990). Others do not. This also, of course, occurs at the level of the actions by groups to raise ethnic consciousness and cultivate community practices. In this way, groups of people with culturally shared knowledge structures come to be constituted within larger multicultural societies through the same processes of socialization and attribution that organizational scholars have identified in organizations (Schneider, 1987).

CONSTRUCT ACTIVATION

Finally, we turn to factors present at the bargaining table that determine whether or not culturally shared knowledge structures are likely to exert an influence on negotiation. We have already mentioned some of these factors under the rubric of temporary accessibility, but we now focus on factors that determine whether chronically accessible cultural constructs become activated. We draw on social cognition research about the kinds of people and kinds of contexts that induce social perceivers to rely more on heuristic, knowledge-structure-based, "top down" processing as opposed to more deliberate, perception-based, "bottom up" processing (see Fiske and Taylor, 1991). Also, we draw on studies of the situationally induced motives that lead individuals to rely on chronically accessible knowledge structures (Kruglanski, 1990). By including these factors in our analysis, we can predict under which conditions cultural differences will be dramatic and under which conditions they will be lessened. These factors include the perceiver's social context, properties of the social stimulus or negotiation task, and properties of the individual perceiver–negotiator. We suggest how these three groups of variables interact with differences in the chronic accessibility of knowledge structures in order to produce particular patterns of cultural variation.

Properties of the Social Context

Some aspects of social context that affect negotiators are role expectations, accountability, audience, time pressure, and atmosphere (Gelfand and Dyer, 2000). The impact of these context variables on knowledge activation may vary across cultures. The moderating role of particular social context variables may help resolve inconsistencies in past findings of cultural differences. For instance, negotiators from hierarchical cultures may exhibit concerns with power only when they are in certain social roles, such the formal leader of a delegation; when in roles that do not make vertical power relationships salient, they may be just as egalitarian as anyone else. Another important variable is whether the conversation occurs privately or publicly. The proverbial Chinese concern for "face" is often confusing to Western negotiators who expect such concerns to operate uniformly in all situations. This stereotypical view fails to recognize that concern for face becomes salient only in particular social contexts, such as those involving an audience of subordinates (Chang and Holt, 1994; Ho, 1980).

Several social context factors may magnify negotiators' tendencies toward culturally normative or typical behaviors, because they increase reliance on chronically accessible knowledge structures. Consider the factor of accountability. Classic research in North American contexts shows that accountability to constituents makes negotiators more competitive because it creates concern for ones reputation of toughness (Carnevale, Pruitt, and Britton, 1979). Gelfand and Realo (1999) found that accountability magnified cultural differences in negotiation. Their results suggest that accountability increases reliance on norms and thus produces different effects in more collectivist contexts where cooperative norms are more predominant than in individualistic contexts. Future research could explore whether other factors, such as stress and time pressure, increase reliance on cultural norms (because of increased need for cognitive closure, or NFC) and thus magnify cultural differences. Past research has shown that time pressure increases competitive processes in the United States, which, in light of our theory, is not surprising given that schemas of self-interest and competition are highly accessible in this culture. Yet time pressure may enhance cooperation in cultures where schemas of collective interest are accessible.

Another way the immediate social context may affect negotiations is through primes in the atmosphere or setting. The negotiation atmosphere and setting includes the structure of the table and room, the level of formality, the persons present, the language spoken, the drinks consumed, background music, and so forth. Aspects of the setting that remind negotiators of their culture may prime culturally related knowledge structures and provoke culturally typical behaviors. Although there has been little research on atmospherics, the epic struggles in diplomatic negotiations over the shape of the table or the location of the talks may indicate its importance. It is also a variable that negotiators in international business can control in order to increase or decrease certain cultural influences on a given negotiation.

Properties of the Stimulus

Another set of factors are the stimuli or tasks presented to a negotiator by the conflict and by their counterparts. The social stimuli in negotiations are actions, statements, and emotional displays by one's counterpart. When these stimulus events are ambiguous, perceivers are more likely to engage in constructivist processing. Yet knowledge structures can only guide interpretation if they map onto the stimulus event, and this applicability constraint means that even if there are cultural differences in chronically accessible knowledge structures, such structures will not always be used to

process information if they do not match the negotiation task, thus attenu-
ating cultural differences in negotiation (Hong, Benet-Martinez, Chiu, and
Morris, 2001; Wittenbrink, Hilton, and Gist, 1998). Indeed, the applicability between stimuli and perceivers' constructs is higher when the stimuli are
behaviors by individuals from the perceiver's culture, and lower when the
stimuli are behaviors from individuals from other cultures. Contrary to the
notion that there are stable "cultural frames" that individuals use to process all
information, this analysis suggests that individuals will not necessarily apply
culturally shared knowledge to stimuli derived from other cultural contexts
(see Gelfand et al., 2001, for evidence of such frame switching).

Features of the decision or judgment task also matter. If the task requires
that individuals articulate a reason for their decision, they are more likely
to rely on culturally shared knowledge structures to make decisions. When
asked to reason, people use generic decision rules rather than the particular
details of the problem at hand, and cultural knowledge is the primary source
of these generic rules. In a series of studies on the resolution of intrapersonal
conflict, Briley, Morris, and Simonson (2000) found that decision rules in
favor of compromise were more frequent in Chinese than in American culture, as measured by their rates of occurrence in proverb dictionaries, in the
proverbs that participants endorsed, and in the reasons that participants gave.
Moreover, in an experiment, Briley et al. (2000) found that when decision
makers were required to give a reason for their decision (as opposed to no
such requirement), Chinese participants were more likely to compromise,
whereas Americans participants were less likely to compromise. Thus, the
need to give a reason or rationale for ones decision seems to be another
magnifier of cultural influence and therefore another potential lever for negotiators desiring to control the impact of culture on negotiations.

Another task property is the cognitive load placed on the negotiator. Negotiations can be extremely attentionally demanding if one is working alone
and without much preparation; they are less so when division of labor and
preparation mean that one doesn't have to multitask at the table. Top down,
constructive processing increases under high load (Macrae, Hewstone, and
Griffiths, 1993). Consistent with this, Knowles, Morris, Chiu, and Hong
(2000) found that attentional load increased differences in dispositional attributions between American and Chinese in a task that required judging
a person who gave a speech in support of an unpopular view yet did so
under pressure from an authority. In the no-load condition in which participants had ample time and attention for the task, both Americans and
Chinese attributed the speaker's act not to an attitude but to the authority's
social pressure. Yet in the load condition, Americans exhibited the familiar
dispositionist bias, unable to correct for their knowledge of the situation,
whereas Chinese attributed to the authority's social pressure. It was only

in the condition that forced participants to rely on a shortcut strategy for social judgment that the cultural biases appeared. Attentional load is thus another potential lever for increasing or decreasing the influence of one's counterpart's culture on his or her behavior.

Properties of the Perceiver

A final set of factors relates to properties of the perceiver. An important topic in the last decade of social cognition research has been people's motives about their own information processing, such as the NFC (Kruglanski, 1990). Need for closure is operationalized both as a stable individual difference and as a situational factor (e.g., time pressure induces NFC). A link to cultural differences was drawn by Chiu, Morris, Hong, and Menon (2000), who found that NFC magnifies perceivers' reliance on the implicit theories chronically accessible in their culture. Americans who are chronically high in NFC (or who are in a situation producing NFC) are more likely than otherwise to attribute a target person's action to dispositions, whereas NFC does not affect this tendency for Chinese. (Among Chinese, high NFC magnifies the dispositionist bias with regard to actions by target groups, whereas it does not affect this among Americans; Chiu et al., 2000.) Likewise, Fu and Morris (2000) found that the greater tendency of Americans compared to Chinese to have a competitive style of managing conflict is due to high-NFC Americans rather than low-NFC Americans. In another study, Fu and Morris (2000) investigated another manifestation of the difference between the American competitive style and the Chinese harmonizing style; namely, when choosing a third party to act as a mediator, Americans preferred a stranger whereas Chinese preferred a person with ties to both disputing parties. As in the study of bargaining style, the culturally typical pattern is most pronounced among high NFC respondents.

Other motives act to increase people's reliance on cultural shared knowledge structures. A series of studies support the claim that the motive to deny one's mortality leads individuals to embrace cultural symbols (Arndt, Greenberg, Solomon, Pyszcyzynski, and Simon, 1997). This suggests that in conflicts involving danger—wartime negotiations, for example—parties should be particularly likely to rely on knowledge structures associated with their own culture. This hypothesized dynamic might hinder mutual understanding across cultures in mortal conflicts such as warfare—precisely where understanding is most crucial.

Conclusion

In this chapter, we have advanced a dynamic perspective on culture and cognition in negotiation. Our theory has several notable limitations and strengths. The first limitation is that most of its empirical support at present comes from post hoc reinterpretation of findings rather than from *a priori* tests. The second limitation is that one must proceed carefully when using social cognition principles as moderators of cultural influence because these principles themselves may not have a common meaning across cultures; in other words, they may not be *etic* constructs that can be applied to both cultures. There are procedures for examining the equivalence of measuring instruments (Berry, 1980), and some social cognition constructs, such as the NFC, have been found to have parallel factor structures and convergent and discriminant validity across American and Chinese cultures. Our view is that a common meaning can be identified for properties of knowledge structures such as availability, accessibility, and applicability; for properties of the social context such as audience or accountability; and for properties of tasks such as ambiguity, the requirement of reasons, and time pressure. Yet studies will invariably need to incorporate *emic* conceptualizations of the social context given that they are, in part, derived from culture. Undoubtedly some principles that North American social cognition researchers have regarded as basic are culturally bound (for a review of possibilities, see suggestions by Markus, Kitayama, and Heiman, 1996), and so research must proceed carefully with an eye to contributing to cross-cultural research while also contributing to basic social cognition research.

Despite the forgoing limitations, there are a number of strengths of our theory. It yields predictions about the content of cultural differences, namely that social judgment biases should be more culturally variable than numerical judgment biases. It also yields predictions about the form of cultural differences. It distinguishes several different points at which cultural influence may arise, namely differences in availability, chronic accessibility, and the proximal triggers of construct activation. In sum, the dynamic constructivist theory suggests questions and provides answers that cannot be accounted for by prior models. It also delineates causal pathways involving public and private elements of culture in influencing availability, accessibility, and activation. This corrects a tendency many theorists on culture and negotiation have to locate culture inside individuals rather than in institutions and other supraindividual entities. Likewise, the theory incorporates both differences arising from culture-specific constructs (availability differences) and from culture-general structures (accessibility differences), which helps to integrate findings from *emic* and *etic* analyses. So in addition to providing better answers to empirical questions, the model allows for theoretical integration of research traditions that often remain separated.

Finally, although we have primarily discussed how individuals are affected by factors around them, the theory elucidates how individuals can control and manage cultural influences. The activation of cultural knowledge depends on properties of the judgment task, the social context, and the individual's state of mind, and individuals can exert a certain degree of control over the tasks they take on, the contexts they enter, and the state of mind they bring to negotiations. In this way, negotiators may negotiate culture—they may actively use their knowledge of their own culture and the opponent's culture to manage the behaviors enacted in the setting. In regard to themselves, negotiators may control perceiver variables (such as their recent priming), context variables (such as the presence of an audience), and stimulus variables (such as their cognitive load) in order to avoid or increase cultural tendencies. Bicultural negotiators may have particularly rich options (Francis, 1991; Hong et al., 2000). In regard to counterparts, negotiators can change the likelihood of culturally typical responses by setting the atmosphere, controlling the pace, requesting reasons, and so forth (see D'Amico and Rubinstein, 1999). Thus, our account provides a view of individuals as active—not passive—participants in creating and managing culture.

Another application of the theory is in understanding differences between intracultural and intercultural negotiations. Negotiators from the same culture, exposed to the same public cultural elements, will have a common set of chronically accessible constructs—self-conceptions, metaphors, expectations, and scripts—making for an "organized" interaction (Gelfand and McCusker; 2002). Not so in intercultural conflicts, which inherently involve two negotiations, the original conflict over resources and the meta-level negotiation over the meanings that should define the event. A challenge for future research is how successful intercultural negotiations overcome this obstacle.

In conclusion, we have reviewed numerous ways in which our cognitively rooted theory contributes to an understanding of culture. Importantly, the reverse is also true. The challenge of taking on culture is a healthy one for the cognitive research program. We gain a deeper understanding of familiar biases when we trace them back not only to knowledge structures but to the socialization practices and institutions that the knowledge structures reflect. We gain a broader understanding of biases by discovering new biases in other cultures. Moreover, the riddle of culture has brought dynamic social cognition theories into the negotiation literature (Fu and Morris, 2000), which may be useful in understanding other puzzling issues, such as gender and personality (see Gelfand, Smith, Raver, and Nishii, 2004). In closing, we can see that the cross-cultural challenge, far from having a diminishing effect on the cognitive approach to negotiation, has instead opened the door for an expansion into new phenomena and greater complexity.

Notes

1. Bias refers to a pattern of judgment that deviates from what is rationally warranted.

2. Recently, scholars have also investigated cultural differences in egocentrism in other domains, such as social dilemmas (Wade-Benzoni et al., 2002). In Wade-Benzoni et al., although there were trends that Japanese were less egocentric than Americans, the effect did not reach significance. It is possible that the lack of mutual monitoring and a strong sanctioning system within the social dilemma task attenuated the activation of the interdependent self in Japan and thus attenuated cultural differences in egocentrism (see Yamagishi, 1988). Later we will elaborate upon the notion that the match between the nature of the task and cultural knowledge structures is an important moderator of cultural differences in our dynamic constructivist theory.

3. We should note that in this discussion, we are simplifying by talking as though all cultural members have the same knowledge, whereas in reality there is not anything like complete consensus in the constructs that members of cultures possess (Martin, 1992), albeit some constructs related to social judgment are held with very high consensus (Romney and Batchelder, 1999). When we speak of a construct as available in one culture but not in another, this is shorthand for the claim that the construct is widely held among the population of one culture and that it is rarely held in another culture.

Works Cited

Arndt, J., Greenberg, J., Solomon, S., Pyzynski, T., and L. Simon. (1997). Suppression, accessibility of death-related thoughts, and cultural worldview defense: Exploring the psychodynamics of worldview defense. *Journal of Personality and Social Psychology, 73,* 5–18.

Babcock, L., and G. Loewenstein. (1997). Explaining bargaining impasse: The role of self-serving biases. *Journal of Economic Perspective, 11*(1), 109–125.

Barkow, J. H., Cosmides, L., and J. Tooby. (1992). *The adapted mind: Evolutionary psychology and the generation of culture.* New York: Oxford University Press.

Barley, S. R. (1991). Contextualizing conflict: Notes on the anthropology of disputes and negotiations. In M. H. Bazerman, R. J. Lewicki and B. H. Sheppard (Eds.) *Research on negotiation in organizations,* Vol. 3 (pp. 165–199). Greenwitch, CT: JAI Press.

Bazerman, M. H., Magliozzi, T., and M. A. Neale. (1985). The acquisition of an integrative response in a competitive market. *Organizational Behavior and Human Decision Processes, 35,* 294–313.

Berry, J. W. (1980). Acculturation as varieties of adaptation. In A. Padilla (Ed.), *Acculturation: Theory, models and some new findings* (pp. 9–25). Boulder, CO: Westview.
——(1990). Imposed etics, emics, derived etics: Their conceptual and operational status in cross-cultural psychology. In T. N. Headland, K. L. Pike, and M. Harris (Eds.), *Emics and etics: The insider/outsider debate* (pp. 28–47). Newbury Park, CA: Sage.

Briley, D. A., Morris, M. W., and I. Simonson. (2000). Reasons as carriers of culture: Dynamic versus dispositional models of cultural influence on decision making. *Journal of Consumer Research, 27,* 157–178.

Bruner, J. (1990). *Acts of meaning.* Cambridge: Cambridge University Press.

Carnevale, P. J. D., Pruitt, D. G., and S. D. Britton. (1979). Looking tough: The negotiator under constituent surveillance. *Personality and Social Psychology Bulletin, 5,* 118–121.

Chang, H-C., and G. R. Holt. (1994). A Chinese perspective on face as inter-relational concern. In S. Ting-Toomey (Ed.), *The challenge of facework: Cross-cultural and interpersonal issues* (pp. 95–132). Albany: State University of New York Press.

Chiu, C., Morris, M., Hong, Y., and T. Menon. (2000). Motivated social cognition: The impact of cultural theories on dispositional attribution varies as a function of need for closure. *Journal of Personality and Social Psychology, 78,* 247–259.

D'Amico, L. C., and R. A. Rubinstein. (1999). Cultural considerations when "setting" the negotiation table. *Negotiation Journal,* 389–395.

D'Andrade, R. G. (1995). *The development of cognitive anthropology.* Cambridge: Cambridge University Press.

Fechner, G. T. (1966/1860). *Elements of psychophysics* (Vol. 1). New York: Holt, Rinehart, and Winston.

Fiske, S. T., and S. E. Taylor. (1991). *Social cognition.* New York: McGraw-Hill.

Francis, J. N. P. (1991). When in Rome? The effects of cultural adaptation on intercultural business negotiations. *Journal of International Business Studies, 22,* 403–428.

Fu, H., and M. W. Morris. (2000). *Need for closure fosters adherence to cultural norms: Evidence from cross-cultural studies of conflict resolution choices* (Stanford Graduate School of Business Research Paper No. 1649). Palo Alto.

Gardner, W. L., Gabriel, S., and A. Y. Lee. (1999). "I" value freedom, but "we" value relationships: Self-construal priming mirrors cultural differences in judgment. *Psychological Science, 10,* 321–326.

Geertz. C. (1976). From the native's point of view: On the nature of anthropological understanding. In K. Basso and H. Selby (Eds.), *Meaning in anthropology* (pp. 221–237). Albuquerque: University of New Mexico Press.

Gelfand, M. J., and S. Christakopoulou. (1999). Culture and negotiator cognition: Judgment accuracy and negotiation processes in individualistic and collectivistic cultures. *Organizational Behavior and Human Decision Processes, 79,* 248–269.

Gelfand, M. J., and N. Dyer. (2000). A cultural perspective on negotiation: Progress, pitfalls, and prospects. *Applied Psychology: An International Review, 41*(1), 62–99.

Gelfand, M. J., Higgins, M., Nishii, L., Raver, J., Dominguez, A., Yamaguchi, S., Murakami, F., and M. Toyama. (2002). Culture and egocentric biases of fairness in conflict and negotiation. *Journal of Applied Psychology, 87,* 833–845.

Gelfand, M. J., and C. McCusker. (2002). Metaphor and the cultural construction of negotiation: A paradigm for theory and research. In M. Gannon and K. L. Newman (Eds.), *Handbook of cross-cultural management* (pp. 292–314). New York: Blackwell.

Gelfand, M. J., Nishii, L., Dyer, N., Holcombe, K., Ohbuchi, K., and M. Fukuno. (2001). Cultural influences on cognitive representations of conflict: Interpretations of conflict episodes. *Journal of Applied Psychology, 86,* 1059–1074.

Gelfand, M. J., and A. Realo. (1999). Individualism and collectivism and accountability in intergroup negotiations. *Journal of Applied Psychology, 84,* 721–736.

Gelfand, M. J., Smith, V., Raver, J. L., and L. H. Nishii. (2004). Negotiating relationally: The dynamics of the relational self in negotiation. Working paper.

Harris, M. (1979). *Cultural materialism: The struggle for a science of culture.* New York: Vintage.

Heine, S. J., Lehman, D. R., Markus, H. R., and S. Kitayama. (1999). Is there a universal need for positive self-regard? *Psychological Review, 106,* 766–794.

Higgins, E. T. (1996). Knowledge activation: Accessibility, applicability and salience. In E. T. Higgins and A. W. Kruglanski (Eds.), *Social psychology: Handbook of basic principles* (pp. 133–168). New York: Guilford.

Ho, D. Y. (1980). Face and stereotyped notions about Chinese face behavior. *Philippine Journal of Psychology, 13*(1–2), 20–33.

———. (1998). Interpersonal relationships and relationship dominance: An analysis based on methodological relationalism. *Asian Journal of Social Psychology, 1,* 1–16.

Hong, Y., Benet-Martinez, V., Chiu, C., and M. W. Morris. (2001). *From cultural boundaries to boundary conditions: Construct applicability as moderator of cultural influences.* Unpublished manuscript, Hong Kong University of Science and Technology.

Hong, Y., Ip, G., Chiu, C., Morris, M. W., and T. Menon. (2001). Cultural identity and dynamic construction of the self: Collective duties and individual rights in the Chinese and American Cultures. *Social Cognition, 19,* 251–268.

Hong, Y., Morris, M. W., Chiu, C., and V. Benet-Martinez. (2000). Multicultural minds: A dynamic constructivist approach to culture and cognition. *American Psychologist, 55,* 709–720.

Kahneman, D., and A. Tversky. (1979). Prospect theory: An analysis of decision under risk. *Econometrica, 47,* 263–291.

Kashima, Y., and V. J. Callan. (1994). The Japanese workgroup. In H. C. Triandis, M. D. Dunnette, and L. M. Hough (Eds.), *Handbook of industrial and organizational psychology* (2nd ed., Vol. 4, pp. 606–649). Palo Alto, CA: Consulting Psychologists.

Knowles, E. D., Morris, M. W., Chiu, C., and Y. Hong. (2000). Culture and the process of person perception: Evidence for automaticity among East Asians in correcting for situational influences on behavior. *Personality and Social Psychology Bulletin, 27,* 1344–1356.

Kramer, R. M., and D. M. Messick. (1995). *Negotiation as a social process.* Thousand Oaks, CA: Sage.

Kruglanski, A. W. (1990). Lay epistemic theory in social-cognitive psychology. *Psychological Inquiry, 1*(3), 181–197.

Levi-Strauss, C. (1966). *The savage mind.* Chicago: University of Chicago Press.

Leung, K. (1987). Some determinants of reactions to procedural models for conflict resolution: A cross national study. *Journal of Personality and Social Psychology, 53,* 898–908.

Macrae, C., Hewstone, M., and R. J. Griffith, (1993). Processing load and memory for stereotype-based information. *European Journal of Social Psychology,* Vol. 23(1), Jan–Feb 1993. pp. 77–87.

Markus, H. R., Kitayama, S., and R. J. Heiman. (1996). Culture and "basic" psychological principles. In E. T. Higgins and A. W. Kruglanski (Eds.), *Social psychology: Handbook of basic principles* (pp. 857–913). New York: Guilford.

Martin, J. 1992. *Cultures in organizations: Three Perspectives.* London: Oxford University Press.

Menon, T., Morris, M. W., Chiu, C., and Y. Hong. (1999). Culture and the construal of agency: Attribution to individuals versus group dispositions. *Journal of Personality and Social Psychology, 76,* 701–717.

Morris, M. W., and K. Peng. (1994). Culture and cause: American and Chinese attributions for social and physical events. *Journal of Personality and Social Psychology, 67,* 949–971.

Morris, M. W., Larrick, R. P., and S. K. Su. (1999). Misperceiving negotiation counterparts: When situationally determined behaviors are attributed to personality traits. *Journal of Personality and Social Psychology, 77*(1), 52–67.

Morris, M. W., Menon, T., and D. R. Ames. (2001). Culturally conferred conceptions of agency: A key to social perception of persons, groups, and other actors. *Personality and Social Psychology Review, 5*(2), 169–182.

Morris, M. W., Podolny, J. M., and S. Ariel. (2000). Missing relations: Incorporating relational constructs into models of culture. In P. C. Earley and H. Singh (Eds.), *Innovations in international and cross-cultural management* (pp. 52–90). Thousand Oaks, CA: Sage.

Neale, M. A., and M. H. Bazerman. (1985). The effects of framing and negotiator overconfidence on bargaining behaviors and outcomes. *Academy of Management Journal, 28*(1), 34–49.

Nisbett, R. E., and L. Ross. (1980). *Human inference: Strategies and shortcomings of social judgment.* Englewood Cliffs, NJ: Prentice Hall.

Pepitone, A., and H. C. Triandis. (1987). On the universality of social psychological theories. *Journal of Cross-Cultural Psychology, 18,* 471–498.

Phinney, J. S. (1990). Ethnic identity in adolescents and adults: Review of research. *Psychological Bulletin, 108,* 499–514.

Pinkley, R. (1990). Dimensions of conflict frame: Disputant interpretations of conflict. *Journal of Applied Psychology, 75,* 117–126.

Pinkley, R. L., and G. B. Northcraft. (1994). Cognitive interpretations of conflict: Implications for dispute processes and outcomes. *Academy of Management Journal, 37*(1), 193–205.

Roberts, J. M., Arth, M. J., and R. R. Bush. (1959). Games in culture. *American Anthropologist, 61,* 597–611.

Romney, A. K., and W. H. Batchelder. (1999). Cultural consensus theory. In R. Wilson and F. Keil (Eds.), *The MIT encyclopedia of the cognitive sciences* (pp. 208–209). Cambridge, MA.: MIT Press.

Schneider, B. (1987). The people make the place. *Personnel Psychology, 40,* 437–453.

Smith, P., and M. H. Bond. (1988). *Social psychology across cultures*. London: Prentice Hall.

Sperber, D., (1996). *Explaining culture: A naturalistic approach*. Oxford: Blackwell

Tannen, D. A. (1998). *The argument culture*. New York: Random House.

Thompson, L., and R. Hastie. (1990). Social perception in negotiation. *Organizational Behavior and Human Decision Processes, 47*, 98–123.

Thompson, L., and G. Loewenstein. (1992). Egocentric interpretations of fairness and negotiation. *Organizational Behavior and Human Decision Processes, 51*, 176–197.

Trafimow, D., Triandis, H. C., and S. G. Goto. (1991). Some tests of the distinction between the private self and the collective self. *Journal of Personality and Social Psychology, 60*, 649–655.

Triandis, H. C. (1972). *The analysis of subjective culture*. New York: John Wiley.

Wade-Benzoni, K. A., T. Okumura, J. M. Brett, D. A. Moore, A. E. Tenbrunsel, and M. H. Bazerman, (2002). Cognitions and behavior in asymmetric social dilemmas: A comparision of two cultures. *Journal of Applied Psychology*, Vol. 87(1), Feb 2002. pp. 87–95.

Wittenbrink, B., Hilton, J. L., and P. L. Gist. (1998). In search of similarity: Stereotypes as naive theories in social categorization. *Social Cognition, 16*, 31–55.

Yamagishi, T. (1988). Exit from the group as an individualistic solution to the free rider problem in the United States and Japan. *Journal of Experimental Social Psychology, 24*, 530–542.

CHAPTER 3

I Laughed, I Cried, I Settled
THE ROLE OF EMOTION IN NEGOTIATION

Bruce Barry, Ingrid Smithey Fulmer, and Gerben A. Van Kleef

THE NATURAL TEMPTATION is to open this chapter with the observation that negotiation research has emphasized cognitive aspects of joint decision making at the expense of the emotional aspects of social interaction that occurs when two or more people negotiate. But we resist doing so (even if, in fact, we just did so)—not because the assertion lacks veracity, but because it lacks originality. More than a decade has passed since Neale and Northcraft (1991), reviewing and integrating behavioral research on two-party bargaining, described affect as "one of the least studied areas of dyadic negotiation" (p. 170). In that time, a small number of conceptual papers and empirical studies directly examining the role of affect have appeared, and the study of emotion in negotiation, although still embryonic, can now be said to have passed beyond the point of conception. It is clearly still the case that the role of emotion is both theoretically and empirically underdeveloped in the social–psychological literature on conflict and negotiation, but it is (as we shall see) now attracting significant attention from negotiation researchers.

Accordingly, our aim in this chapter is to move past simply mounting an argument for the importance of affect and emotion in negotiation. This case has been made recently and effectively elsewhere (e.g., Barry and Oliver, 1996; Kumar, 1997; Morris and Keltner, 2000; Thompson, Nadler, and Kim, 1999). Our objective is to propel research on this topic into specific areas that are ripe for theoretical development and empirical investigation. The chapter is organized in the following manner. We begin with a brief discussion of issues involved in defining the terms *affect, mood,* and *emotion.* We then provide a narrative review of existing research—both conceptual and empirical—that has specifically addressed the intersection of affect and

negotiation. Two sections that follow explore specific areas of inquiry that
are ripe for research going forward: (a) how individual differences are implicated in the connection between negotiation, emotional experience, and
emotional expression; and (b) the interpersonal effects of emotion within negotiation encounters. We conclude with comments on the methodological
implications and challenges of the research agenda we have proposed.

DEFINING TERMS

The terms *emotion, mood,* and *affect* are sometimes used loosely or in-
terchangeably but carry distinct meanings in emotion research, and so we
distinguish among them here. Following Parrott (2001), we adopt the widely
accepted view that emotion and mood are differentiated by the degree to
which affective states are more or less directed toward specific situational
stimuli (which can include people, things, events, etc.). As Parrott put it,
"Emotions are about, or directed toward, something in the world. . . . In contrast, moods lack this quality of object directedness; a person in an irritable
mood is not necessarily angry about anything in particular—he or she is just
generally grumpy" (p. 3). Emotions may also be said to be more differentiated
and of shorter duration, whereas moods are more enduring and pervasive, if
generally of lower intensity (Barry, 1999; Forgas, 1992). These distinctions
notwithstanding, emotions and moods in reality are often interdependent—
they can alternate, be mutually determinative or reinforcing, or occur simultaneously (Davidson, 1994; Parrott, 2001). We use the term
affect as an umbrella concept to describe the constellation of responses that
comprise both moods and emotions, including both ephemeral responses
that are situationally driven (so-called state affect), as well as broader, stable
tendencies to experience emotion or mood states that are dispositionally
based (trait affect; e.g., Watson, Clark, and Tellegen, 1988).

Research on affect comes from a variety of intellectual and theoretical
perspectives, leading to myriad conceptualizations of the nature and structure
of human emotion. Indeed, the one thing on which emotion researchers do
seem to agree is the elusiveness of definitions that can be widely accepted. In
very general terms, Parrott (2001) described emotions from a psychological
perspective as "ongoing states of mind that are marked by mental, bodily, or
behavioral symptoms" (p. 3). Articulating a more precise definition requires
the adoption of a particular theoretical perspective. This is no easy task, given
that, according to one thorough inventory (Strongman, 1996), more than
150 theories of emotion exist.

For brevity and simplicity, we summarize emotion theories here in
four broad categories. One perspective analyzes emotions in terms of
biological consequences of arousal. This so-called psychophysiological
approach has its early origins in the writings of Darwin (1965/1872)

and James (1983/1890), and more recently is found in research on facial expressions of emotion (e.g., Ekman, 1993). A second perspective, labeled "language-analytic" by Metts and Bowers (1994), defines affect in terms of underlying dimensions that distinguish among specific emotions. Prominent examples are Russell's (1980) two-dimensional circumplex of emotion, Plutchik's (1980) three-dimensional "solid" representation of emotion, and the emotion prototypes derived through cluster analysis by Shaver, Schwartz, Kirson, and O'Connor (1987).

Given that negotiation is fundamentally a form of contextualized social interaction, the theoretical perspectives that connect intuitively to an examination of emotion's role in negotiation are those that are primarily social in nature. Psychosocial theories (e.g., Lazarus, 1991), broadly speaking, consider the interplay between affect, cognition, and social exchange as a way to understand how emotions propel interaction, contribute to individual "sense making" about social relations, and emerge as a consequence of those relations. Social constructivist models are similar, adhering to the premise that emotions are best understood in relation to social context, but moving beyond treating emotions simply as psychological responses. Constructivists (e.g., Averill, 1980) analyze emotions as interpretive phenomena that are culturally determined, shaped by language and social learning, and used to extract meaning from social contexts (Strongman, 1996).

In the next section we review existing research on affect and negotiation. We then explore individual differences and interpersonal effects as two promising avenues for future research on this topic.

Existing Research on Affect and Negotiation

In a recent review of negotiation research, Bazerman, Curhan, Moore, and Valley (2000) observed that the focus on cognitive approaches to negotiation over the last two decades "has ignored most emotion-relevant variables" (p. 285). A smattering of conceptual and empirical papers that specifically address the role of affect have appeared since the mid-1980s, with increasing frequency since the mid-1990s, and we briefly review them here.

CONCEPTUAL–THEORETICAL RESEARCH

Six published conceptual pieces (Allred, 1999; Barry and Oliver, 1996; Davidson and Greenhalgh, 1999; Lawler and Yoon, 1995; Morris and Keltner, 2000; Thompson et al., 1999) have specifically and extensively focused on theoretical development on affective processes in negotiation. All six make the case that the study of emotional aspects of negotiation is important and underexplored, and we will not reconstruct that case here. Instead, our brief review focuses on the specific conceptual approach to negotiator affect developed by each set of authors.

Lawler and Yoon (1995) proposed that affective commitment to a relationship emerges from the emotional consequences of repeated negotiations between the same parties. Starting with the assumption that interdependence between the parties creates incentives to negotiate repeatedly, Lawler and Yoon argued that frequent agreements between the same parties give rise to mild positive emotions, and consequently the development of dyadic relations. Negotiators come to "credit their relationship, at least in part, for the sense of control and related positive feeling" (Lawler and Yoon, 1995, p. 155). The result is affective commitment that sets the stage for subsequent interaction.

Barry and Oliver (1996) adopted a broader perspective, identifying emotion states that are relevant at multiple points within a negotiation encounter. First, anticipatory emotion states are theorized to result from ambient conditions for bargaining, prior intradyadic exchanges, and negotiators' levels of dispositional affect. Second, affect experienced within the negotiation is described as resulting from early offers and concessions and other tactical behaviors, inducing adjustments of aspirations and expectations, and producing modifications of tactical behavior. Third, the model examines postnegotiation affect that results from particular bargaining outcomes and from attributions the parties make about those outcomes. Postnegotiation affect is seen as influencing one's desire for future interaction and other subsequent behavior, including the alacrity with which parties implement a negotiated settlement.

Thompson et al. (1999) examined both the experience and expression of emotion. A unique contribution is their attention to emotional contagion in negotiation—the transmission of emotion from one party to another. Contagion occurs through mimicry (imitation of another's facial expressions and emotions) or through "catching" others' emotions (genuine experience of the other party's affect state). With respect to expressed emotion, Thompson et al. proposed that negotiators engage in "emotional tuning" (p. 149) when they construct messages designed to control or regulate the other party's emotional responses. Another distinctive feature of their analysis is a discussion of how negotiators may buffer or suppress emotion in situations where affect is undesirable.

Davidson and Greenhalgh (1999) focused on negative emotion, and specifically anger, arguing that emotions are a function not of conflict issues but of the meaning that parties ascribe to those issues. By giving too little attention to how parties subjectively make sense of conflict, according to Davidson and Greenhalgh, traditional (cognitive–behavioral) negotiation theory relies too heavily on positive utility functions to explain settlements. The emotions that attend real-world disputes, they argue, lead negotiators to sometimes accept outcomes in an expanded settlement space capturing negative utility—harm to self or other—that is not otherwise present when emotions are merely neutral or positive.

Allred (1999) also focused narrowly on negative emotion, proposing a model of retaliatory conflict that is driven by anger. The model sets forth interactive processes by which parties to a conflict perceive each other's harmful behavior and respond to it. It shows a series of stages, or junctures, of conflict at which parties may retaliate or defuse tensions, depending on the forms of cognitive appraisal and attribution that occur. The model is potentially prescriptive in the sense that some junctures may represent better opportunities than others for creating constructive attributional patterns that will end "destructive cycles of anger-driven retaliation" (Allred, 1999, p. 51).

Morris and Keltner's (2000) social–functional perspective grows out of a substantial research tradition in the study of affect that highlights the social functions that emotions serve in interaction (e.g., Keltner and Kring, 1998). Social functions of emotion are illuminated when one identifies how "emotion-related behavior helps the individual or the dyad respond to the problem in the interaction" (Morris and Keltner, 2000, p. 14). Their four-stage model explores how relational problems trigger particular social emotions, which in turn give rise to interaction behaviors. During the first stage—opening moves—negotiators face the relational problem of initiation, which is solved by openness and interest. In the positioning stage, negotiators face the problem of influence. The relevant emotions in this stage are anger and contempt. In the third stage, which is dedicated to problem solving, negotiators face the problem of trust. This stage is accompanied by embarrassment and empathy. Finally, during the endgame, negotiators face the problem of binding, which is accompanied by pain and exasperation. Morris and Keltner explored the implications of their functional approach for understanding two popular and important issues in negotiation research generally: the role of cultural differences and the impact of variations in communication media through which bargaining takes place.

Summary

Most of the conceptual pieces reviewed here propose formal models with testable predictions. All give some attention to emotion as an outcome of the bargaining encounter, although this is a central focus in just one (Lawler and Yoon, 1995). The others emphasize how emotion unfolds or is strategically regulated within the encounter. Taken together, the models are not so much competing as complementary frameworks that address multiple elements of the negotiation process from diverse perspectives.

EMPIRICAL STUDIES

Fewer than a dozen published empirical papers have addressed the emotional aspects of negotiation as a principal focus. We organize this literature

76 Barry, Fulmer, and Van Kleef

into categories capturing (a) the predictive role of emotion as an experienced or manipulated factor, (b) the role of emotion as an outcome of the negotiation process, and (c) the strategic role of emotion as a negotiation tactic.

Emotion as Predictor

Three studies have examined the influence of positive affect on negotiation process and performance, with generally consistent results. Carnevale and Isen (1986) manipulated prenegotiation mood by having some subjects examine humorous cartoons and receive a small gift. Positive-affect subjects participating in a mixed-motive negotiation simulation achieved higher joint gains and used fewer contentious tactics (although the latter finding held only when negotiators had visual access to each other) compared with neutral-affect negotiators who were not exposed to a mood manipulation.

Kramer, Newton, and Pommerenke (1993) also manipulated positive mood (by showing subjects either a humorous or an affect-neutral videotape before the negotiation) and replicated the finding that positive mood leads to enhanced joint outcomes in a mixed-motive negotiation task. Kramer et al. were primarily interested in the role of judgment biases—particularly self-enhancement—and found that positive-mood negotiators were more confident going into the negotiation and gave higher self-ratings of performance after the negotiation (controlling for the actual level of performance) compared with neutral-mood negotiators. Thus, positive mood may not only enhance joint gain, but also distort negotiators' perceptions of their performance.

Baron (1990) also manipulated positive mood, but using a different technique: he investigated environmentally induced affect by exposing some subjects to a pleasant odor. Positive-mood negotiators set higher prenegotiation goals and made more concessions during negotiation than did neutral-mood negotiators. Baron's subjects negotiated against a confederate behaving in a programmed way, so negotiation performance was not measured or examined.

Among studies exploring the predictive role of affect in negotiation, only one to date has focused exclusively on negative emotion. Allred, Mallozzi, Matsui, and Raia (1997) induced opponent-directed anger in some subjects by stimulating perceptions that the other party is personally responsible for actions that will affect them in negative ways. The negative emotional regard for an opponent that these subjects experienced led to less regard for opponent's interests, which in turn diminished the accuracy of judgments of the other party's interests and, ultimately, lower joint gains. Negative emotional regard also reduced negotiators' desire for future interaction with the other party. Allred et al. hypothesized that anger would help negotiators claim more value for themselves in negotiated settlements, but results did not support this prediction.

Forgas (1998) examined positive and negative moods in a three-experiment study using a false-feedback manipulation to induce good moods in some subjects and bad moods in others. Consistent with prior studies we have discussed, Forgas found that compared to those in bad moods, negotiators in good moods were more likely to plan to be cooperative before the negotiation, used more cooperative strategies during the negotiation (self-reported), achieved better outcomes, and were more inclined afterward to honor the deal they reached. The mood of the negotiator's opponent also had an effect: negotiators facing a "happy" opponent reported more cooperative behavior and a greater willingness to honor deals than those facing a "sad" opponent. Forgas found that some of these effects varied with negotiator disposition in the form of Machiavellianism and need for approval.

Additional evidence on the role of affect in negotiation came from a study that was not designed specifically around emotion. Moore, Kurtzberg, Thompson, and Morris (1999), investigating negotiation via e-mail, manipulated group affiliation (in-group vs. out-group dyads, operationalized as negotiating against a student at the same university vs. one from a competitor university) and self-disclosure (availability or not of personal information about opponent). Results point to a causal chain suggesting that the presence of the basis for a relationship (in-group status and self-disclosure) elicits expressions of positive affect within the negotiation that enhance rapport and diminish the likelihood of impasse. Conversely, in the absence of a relationship, expressions of negative affect (in the form of threats and ultimatums) are more likely to occur and to weaken rapport, increasing the likelihood of impasse.

Emotion as Consequence

A few studies have investigated the emotional reactions that negotiators experience following interaction with an opponent. O'Connor and Arnold (2001) found that negotiators who impasse experience more negative emotions in form of anger and frustration than do negotiatiors who are able to reach agreement. Individual self-efficacy buffered this relationship, however: higher self-efficacy was related to less negative emotion experienced by negotiators who failed to reach agreement. Hegtvedt and Killian (1999) explored the intersection between perceptions of justice and emotion following negotiation. Negotiators who regard the negotiation process as fair were more likely to experience positive emotion (feel pleased about how it went) and less likely to express negative feelings (agitation, anger, resentment) after the encounter. With respect to the fairness of outcomes (distributive justice), perceptions of the fairness of one's own outcome increased satisfaction but also guilt; outcome fairness was negatively associated with disappointment and resentment. However, the fairness one perceives about the outcomes received by the other party were not related to emotional reactions. Pillutla and Murnighan (1996) considered the link between fairness and emotion in an ultimatum game experiment, finding that perceptions of unfairness and anger were substantially related; this was particularly the case when individuals responding to a take-it-or-leave-it offer had access to complete and shared information about the size of the resource being divided.

Emotion as Tactic

Although the strategic use of emotion as a tactical gambit in negotiation has been frequently commented upon, we are aware of just one published study (an edited volume chapter) that has empirically examined this issue. Barry (1999) explored the extent to which individuals regard the strategic display of emotions that are not actually felt as ethically appropriate, comparing those judgments with individual assessments of the ethicality of other (cognitive or information-oriented) forms of deception. Results indicated that people are substantially more approving of and more confident in their own ability to deploy negotiation tactics involving emotional deception effectively—both positive and negatively valenced emotion—compared to other forms of misrepresentation.

Summary

The scant empirical literature on emotion in bargaining has yielded a reasonably convincing finding that positive mood helps negotiators create value and reduces contentious behavior, whereas other-directed anger, and more generally negative affect, has the opposite effect. Although the underlying mechanism here has not been directly explored in a negotiation context, this finding has been attributed to demonstrated links between positive affect and creativity in problem solving, flexible thinking, cooperative motives, information processing, confidence, and risk-taking behavior (Barry and Oliver, 1996; Forgas, 1998; Kramer et al., 1993; Kumar, 1997; Thompson et al., 1999). We also know that impasse elicits negative emotional reactions following negotiation, as do perceptions that the negotiation process is procedurally unfair. But beyond these largely intuitive findings, little is known specifically about the social psychology of emotional actions and responses in a negotiation context. We also note a dearth of research on the role of individual differences as they pertain to emotion in the negotiation process. This absence reflects both the relative newness of concerted research interest in the emotional side of negotiation and a broader tendency in negotiation research to emphasize cognitive processes over individual differences.

Emotion, Negotiation, and Individual Differences

Although we indicated earlier that "social" approaches to emotion are well suited to understanding the role of emotion in negotiation, we take the position that such approaches are considerably linked to (rather than standing apart from) the study of individual differences. Research indicates that individual differences in motivational tendencies explain effects of mood on cognitive behavior of the kind that is involved in negotiation (Forgas, 1998). Indeed, one cannot fully understand emotion's role in negotiation without understanding the cross-individual variation in emotional experience and expression that persists throughout repeated social interaction (Kumar, 1997).

A number of stable individual difference variables that have been linked with emotional experience or emotional expression are potentially relevant for an analysis of emotion in negotiation. In the interest of providing a general flavor of these individual differences as they relate to emotion (and in the interest of space), our discussion focuses on a subset of those individual difference variables that we believe to be most proximately related to emotion as it enters into the negotiation context (versus, for example, a therapeutic context). In addition, with one exception,[1] we focus on variables having substantial theoretical and empirical underpinnings. In the discussion that follows, we consider (a) emotional expressivity, self-monitoring, and the "Big Five" personality dimensions (McCrae and John, 1992); (b) the relatively new domain of emotional intelligence; and (c) emotion in relation to gender.

PERSONALITY

Expressivity

Emotional expressivity has been conceptualized as a stable dispositional trait with a number of facets: impulse strength, negative expressivity, positive expressivity, expressive confidence, and emotion masking (Gross and John, 1998). These facets are associated with both positive and negative emotionality (mood), as well as with a number of the Big Five personality dimensions (Gross and John, 1995, 1998). Gross, John, and Richards (2000) examined conditions under which emotional experience translates into emotional expression. For individuals high in expressivity, experience was related to expression for both positive and negative emotions, whereas for low-expressivity individuals only positive emotional experience translated into expression; one interpretation for this is that low-expressivity individuals engage in more emotional regulation. Emotional expressivity, and the ability to regulate it, may have bearing on negotiation via effects on tactical choice. For example, if I am relatively emotionally expressive, I might find it easier—and thus choose—to share information versus concealing it in a negotiation, or I might be more adept at using certain emotion management tactics (Barry, 1999), such as pretending to be surprised or angry when I am not. On the other hand, less expressive individuals might find it easier to choose emotion masking tactics. Conversely, given traditional thinking about the importance of rationality (versus emotionality) in negotiation, an emotionally expressive person, or a person with poor ability to regulate emotional expression, may risk being perceived as a poor negotiator, with implications for both episodic bargaining outcomes and long-term negotiator reputation.

Self-monitoring

The dispositional trait of self-monitoring further explains the role of emotional expression in negotiation. High self-monitors are better able to communicate emotion (both verbally and facially) than low self-monitors, and they are more likely to look to others for information on how to express emotion appropriately (Snyder, 1974). High self-monitors are also more inclined to conceal emotion (Friedman and Miller-Herringer, 1991). One potential side-effect of being so attuned to external cues is reduced responsiveness to one's own internal emotional cues; high self-monitors have been found to rely more on self-attribution of emotion from external cues than low self-monitors (Graziano and Bryant, 1998). Given their knack for communicating emotion, high self-monitors should have more success with emotional tactics such as emotional masking or false displays of positive or negative affect. Paradoxically, however, because self-monitors tend to look to the context for cues about their own experienced emotions, they may be more easily emotionally manipulated by a negotiating counterpart.

The Five-Factor Model

Among the Big Five personality factors, extraversion and neuroticism encompass constituent facets related to, respectively, warmth–positive emotions and negative emotions such as hostility and depression (Costa and McCrae, 1980). These dimensions have also been associated with positive and negative mood susceptibility (Larsen and Ketelaar, 1991) and with mood-congruent processing, where an individual's mood affects cognitive processes such as memory and judgment (Rusting, 2001). In one series of studies, Rusting (2001) found that extraverts were more likely to recall positive words and make positive judgments, whereas high-neuroticism individuals recalled more negative words and made more negative overall judgments. In negotiation, these effects may underpin judgments of how an encounter is evolving, yielding consequences for tactical choice and strategy. The nexus of personality and affect may also influence overall satisfaction with the bargaining process and outcomes, with implications for postsettlement compliance and attitudes toward future interaction (cf. Barry and Oliver, 1996). Finally, the study of personality and affect in groups suggests that the personality traits of individuals (e.g., trait positive and negative affect, which have been related to extraversion and neuroticism) are related to within-group affective consistency, referred to as group affective tone; for example, individual positive affect is significantly related to group-level positive affective tone or mood (George, 1990). The aggregate mood of the group has, in turn, been shown to influence the behavior of individuals within the group (George, 1990; Totterdell, 2000). Whether the negotiation involves a dyad or a larger group, there is reason to expect that the personalities of negotiators might be similarly related to negotiator performance (e.g., cooperative vs competitive behavior) through their effects on the collective mood of the group or dyad.

EMOTIONAL INTELLIGENCE

Emotional intelligence is "the ability to monitor one's own and others' feelings and emotions, to discriminate among them, and to use this information to guide one's thinking and actions" (Salovey and Mayer, 1990, p. 189). Multiple conceptualizations of emotional intelligence exist, ranging from Salovey and Mayer's relatively simple description of discrete emotional abilities to Bar-On's (1997) and Goleman's (1995) sweeping mixed models, which incorporate personality characteristics, the ability to manage stress, impulse control, and more (see Mayer, Salovey, and Caruso, 2000, for a comparative analysis). Early empirical research points to the existence of a higher-order factor for general emotional intelligence, as well as three primary factors: emotional perception, emotional understanding, and emotional management (Mayer, 2001; Mayer et al., 2000) A related, process-oriented perspective treats emotional intelligence as a dynamic phenomenon that reflects individual differences in both emotion differentiation and contextually appropriate emotion regulation (Feldman Barrett, and Gross, 2001).

In the study of negotiation, we surmise that the consideration of emotional intelligence may be potentially enlightening in a number of ways. An obvious line of inquiry is to explore specific ways in which emotional intelligence might prove beneficial to a particular negotiator. For example, where negotiations involve mixed objectives, we predict that an emotionally intelligent negotiator's ability to pick up on subtle emotional cues provides an advantage by providing insight into additional issues and opportunities for cooperation, logrolling, and other approaches. In addition, an emotionally intelligent negotiator should be in a position to use this ability to advantage by influencing or manipulating the emotions of the other party. Another line of potential research could explore the conditions under which emotional intelligence is more or less predictive of "successful" negotiator behavior (e.g., actual distributive outcomes, negotiator reputation, etc.). For example, how do the goals of the negotiation (i.e., transactional vs. relational) influence the extent to which emotional intelligence may prove to be beneficial? Last, another intriguing stream of questioning concerns how emotional intelligence might be related to conventional intelligence (i.e., cognitive ability) in a negotiation setting. Are there circumstances where it is more beneficial to be emotionally intelligent than cognitively intelligent, or vice versa? Or is emotional intelligence superior to the conventional notion of intelligence in virtually all situations, as some of its advocates have suggested?

GENDER

Empirical research suggests that although women and men do not necessarily experience emotion differently (Kring and Gordon, 1998), women are more emotionally expressive (e.g., Gross and John, 1995, 1998), a distinction that is often explained as resulting from biological and evolutionary mechanisms and/or from social influences regarding gender-appropriate behavior (see Guerrero and Reiter, 1998, for an overview). Women are observed to be more emotionally animated and are better at accurately conveying emotion to an observer; in addition, they are better at judging and decoding nonverbal emotional cues than men (Hall, 1998; Hall, Carter, and Horgan, 2000; Mufson and Nowicki, 1991). Men, on the other hand, report masking emotion more often than women (Gross and John, 1998). Women tend to use more complex language than men to describe emotion (Feldman Barrett, Lane, Sechrest, and Schwatz, 2000), an indicator of maturity in emotional awareness (Lane et al., 1990). Finally, in ability measures of emotional intelligence, women seem to have a slight edge over men—roughly half a standard deviation on average (Mayer et al., 2000).

Although a number of researchers have examined gender differences as they impact negotiation, these studies tend to focus either on differences in negotiation style, such as cooperation–competitiveness (e.g., see Walters, Stuhlmacher, and Meyer, 1998, for a review and meta-analysis) or on differences in outcomes (Gerhart and Rynes, 1991; Stuhlmacher and Walters, 1999). We know little about how gender differences in emotional expression or in ability to interpret the cues of others might impact negotiation outcomes.

Despite having what might be construed as emotional "advantages" that would be useful in interpersonal encounters, women often do not reap these benefits in the negotiation arena. In some types of distributive negotiations, such as salary negotiations, women lag behind men in their ability to claim value (e.g., Gerhart and Rynes, 1991). An unanswered research question is whether men and women of similar emotional sensitivity have similar negotiation outcomes; in other words, is it emotional sensitivity that is a detriment, or some other aspect of gender? A related question is whether emotionally sensitive people differ from others in how they process emotion-related and nonemotion-related information—to wit, does greater emotional awareness and sensitivity somehow interfere with one's ability to focus on cognitive information?

With respect to the strategic use of emotion in negotiation, Barry (1999) suggested that sex differences in emotional expressiveness might be related to sex differences in attitudes toward the use of emotion as a tactic. Future research could take this a step further by exploring the mechanisms by which gender differences in emotional expression and perception might affect selection of emotion management tactics in negotiations (with implications for performance outcomes). Another question is whether women use emotion-related information to frame their decisions in a negotiation context differently than men: Are there situations in which women are more cognizant of and reliant upon emotion-related outcomes alongside economic outcomes? If so, the risk–reward profile of a given negotiation might look different depending upon gender, with implications for negotiator behavior. For example, prospect theory suggests that individuals tend to seek risk in a perceived loss situation and to avoid risks in a perceived gain situation (Kahneman and Tversky, 1979); the decision to engage in risky behavior in a given negotiation (e.g., disclosure of information) is likely a function of how the negotiation payoffs are mentally calculated, which may vary by gender as a result of the relative weight given to emotion-related factors versus other factors.

So far, we have reviewed prior research on the role of emotion in negotiation, and we have identified a number of individual difference variables that may influence the way in which individual negotiators experience and express emotion. In the next section we take up the question of how these experienced and expressed emotions influence the negotiation process, and specifically how they influence the other negotiator's behavior.

Interpersonal Effects of Emotion

In conceptualizing the role of emotions in negotiation, it is useful to distinguish between *intra*personal and *inter*personal effects. The former refers to the effects of a negotiator's emotions on his or her own negotiation behavior, whereas the latter refers to the effects on the other negotiator's behavior. So far, research has focused mostly on the *intra*personal effects of affect and emotions, such as the making of offers and concessions (Baron, 1990; Pillutla and Murnighan, 1996), creative problem solving (Isen, Daubman, and Nowicki, 1987), preferences for cooperation (Baron, Fortin, Frei, Hauver, and Shaek, 1990), individual and joint outcomes[2] (Allred et al., 1997; Carnevale and Isen, 1986; Kramer et al., 1993), and other tactical choices (Carnevale and Isen, 1986; Forgas, 1998). In contrast to the intrapersonal effects, the *inter*personal effects of emotions in negotiations have received surprisingly little attention. This is unfortunate because emotions have important social functions and consequences (Frijda and Mesquita, 1994; Keltner and Haidt,

1999; Oatley and Jenkins, 1992), which may influence negotiation behavior and outcomes in a number of ways. First, emotions tend to evoke reciprocal or complementary emotions in others that help individuals to respond to significant social events (Keltner and Haidt, 1999). In a negotiation context, for example, a disappointed or sad opponent might elicit compassion, which might in turn lead to more cooperative behavior.

Second, emotions convey information about how one feels about things (Ekman, 1993; Scherer, 1986), about one's social intentions (Ekman, Friesen, and Ellsworth, 1972; Fridlund, 1994), and about one's orientation toward other people (Knutson, 1996). In this way, emotions can serve as incentives or deterrents for other people's behavior (Klinnert, Campos, Sorce, Emde, and Svejda, 1983), which may prevent negotiators from engaging in destructive behaviors by indicating what behaviors will be tolerated and what behaviors will not. Negative emotions play a fundamental role in regulating social interaction by serving as a call for mental or behavioral adjustment, whereas positive emotions serve as a cue to stay the course (Cacioppo and Gardner, 1999). Thus, in a negotiation, negative emotions may be used to communicate dissatisfaction with a particular state of affairs, which may be interpreted by the opponent as endangering agreement and may thereby produce more conciliatory behavior. Conversely, positive emotions may be taken to suggest that no further concessions are needed. This would suggest that it is not in the negotiator's strategic interest to express happiness, as it may cause the opponent to refrain from making any further concessions.

Particularly relevant for the effects of the interpersonal effects of emotion is Morris and Keltner's (2000) four-stage social–functional model, which we discussed earlier. Their central idea that interactions are guided by emotions was also the starting point of a study by Van Kleef, De Dreu, and Manstead (2001)—the first to empirically investigate the interpersonal effects of emotions in negotiation. In a computer-mediated distributive negotiation task with a simulated opponent, their participants were assigned the role of seller of a consignment of mobile phones and were provided with a payoff table that showed them their profits on each of nine possible levels of agreement. At three times during the negotiation, participants received standardized information about the opponent's "intentions" (i.e., what the opponent was about to offer in the next round), accompanied by a pretested emotion statement. In this way, participants were led to believe that the opponent was either angry, happy, or nonemotional. Results showed that participants with an angry opponent placed lower average demands than participants with a happy opponent; participants with a nonemotional opponent assumed an intermediate position. Furthermore, participants with an angry opponent conceded more between the first and last negotiation round than did participants with a happy opponent, with those with nonemotional opponents again falling in between. Finally, participants with a happy opponent evaluated both the opponent and the negotiation itself more favorably than did participants with an angry opponent.

The results of the study by Van Kleef et al., (2001) are consistent with the social functions perspective outlined above and show that anger elicits cooperation, whereas happiness elicits competition. These findings shed new light on the consequences of positive and negative emotions for negotiation effectiveness. So far, the prevailing view in the field has been that positive emotions improve negotiator effectiveness, whereas negative emotions decrease effectiveness (for a review, see Thompson et al., 1999; see also Parrott, 1993; Wall, 1991). However, this view is based solely on findings regarding the intrapersonal effects of emotions, and the results of the Van Kleef et al., study suggest that it needs refinement. Van Kleef et al., focused on the interpersonal effects of emotions and found that negative emotions are more effective in negotiations than are positive emotions. At first glance these findings may seem contradictory, but they need not necessarily be. Most intrapersonal effects studies employed integrative negotiation tasks, showing that positive emotions have beneficial effects and that negative emotions have adverse effects. Van Kleef et al., in contrast, used a distributive task, with anger emerging as more "effective" than happiness. Thus, anger appears to be more conducive to claiming value in distributive negotiation, whereas happiness appears to be more beneficial in integrative negotiation.

The implications of the research discussed above are straightforward. In a distributive bargaining task, anger may help a party do better for himself or herself. On the other hand, if the negotiation task has integrative potential, the experience of positive emotions such as happiness may provide a more constructive basis for collaborative problem solving. Thus, an interesting avenue for future research concerns the interplay between the intrapersonal and interpersonal effects of emotions. For example, do the positive effects of happiness at the intrapersonal level of analysis (e.g., more creative problem solving) outweigh the negative effects at the interpersonal level of analysis (e.g., risk of exploitation by one's opponent)? Are the strategic advantages gained by expressing anger offset by the negative impact of anger on the interpersonal relationship? Do the advantageous effects of anger in distributive bargaining persist, or do they wear off over time?

Another interesting question for future research concerns the potentially distinct effects of genuinely experienced and strategically faked emotions. For example, Van Kleef et al., (2001) showed that anger induces concessions. What happens, however, if the negotiator discovers that the opponent is faking his or her anger? Might the discovery of emotional deceit cause the negotiator to become intransigent? In other words, is "real" anger more effective in eliciting concessions than faked anger?

Last, we see a need for more attention to the nature of emotions that are investigated. Most research on the role of emotions in negotiation has focused on general positive and negative affect. Recently, researchers have started to investigate the effects of specific discrete emotions on negotiation behavior (e.g., Allred et al., 1997; Van Kleef et al., 2001). Although this research has increased our understanding of the role of specific emotions in negotiation, much work remains to be done in this area. We believe that the literature can be further enriched by expanding its focus from primarily anger and happiness to, for example, disappointment, contempt, fear, and anxiety. In this context, it would also be fruitful to investigate the interactions between these emotions and relevant personality variables. For example, are individuals with high compassion or concern for others' outcomes more influenced by the opposing negotiator's disappointment than individuals with an egoistic orientation? Are individuals high in emotional intelligence more susceptible to and more easily influenced by the opponent's emotions?

Implications

We conclude with brief remarks on the empirical study of affect in negotiation, giving particular attention to methodological concerns that impede research in this area. These comments are built around two principal observations.

First, the near-total reliance in negotiation research on simulations of mixed-motive bargaining leads us to wonder whether the experience of emotion is meaningfully represented within the social interaction under study. To put it simply, we question whether individuals experience an adequate range of authentic emotion in laboratory and classroom experiments. Certainly it is plausible that experimental participants experience mild positive and negative emotions: a role-playing simulation participant can presumably become annoyed by the behavior of a role opponent, or be mildly elated by or disappointed with one's own performance. The field accepts that modest incentives, combined with the intrinsically interesting nature of bargaining simulations, yields mental engagement between participant and task at a sufficient level to support claims of external validity for research on negotiator cognition.

We surmise, however, that the genuine experience of a range of moods or emotions in "live" negotiations—anger, delight, anxiety, frustration, sadness—is related to the significant personal stakes involved the contextualized social relations that are in place, or both. These are not easily reproducible in the laboratory or the classroom, where modest links are commonly drawn between negotiator performance and token payments or modest class grades. Assurances of generalizability for laboratory studies of negotiator emotion, on the other hand, seem suspect, in large part because the variety of negotiation subject matter that can be simulated in the laboratory or the classroom is limited. Real-world negotiations frequently involve important and ongoing personal relationships, large monetary outcomes (e.g., car purchase, salary negotiation), life-altering events (e.g., child custody), and the like that cannot be enacted in the lab. Yet clearly one might expect stronger emotional responses and more concerted efforts to use emotion strategically in these kinds of situations. Echoing Barley (1991), we acknowledge that experiments and simulations are certainly useful for understanding the role of information processing in negotiation. The problem is that "norms, values, morals, emotions, relationships, power structures, religious beliefs, the content of specific disagreements and conceptual frameworks may be just as important, or even more important, for understanding conflict and its course than are rational calculation, profit maximization, and universal imperfections in information processing" (Barley, 1991, p. 169).

A related concern is that classroom simulations and laboratory studies do not capture the impact of choice on the part of the negotiator on emotional responses during the negotiation. Lab studies impose the situation on the participant. In the field, individuals choose which negotiations they will enter into and often can select their negotiation counterparts. For example, one might observe less intense emotion in the field than in a corresponding lab study because the negotiator has chosen to engage a negotiation where he or she would be less likely to become emotional. Conversely, we might encounter more frequent or intense emotion in the field for individuals who choose negotiation as an interdependence strategy only when the stakes are sufficiently high. A lab study may capture what happens when a rat runs a given maze, but it does not necessarily capture the rat's real-life experience because it doesn't get at which maze the rat prefers to run, which (shifting from the analogy back to negotiation) may be particularly consequential for the experience and expression of emotion, but not so meaningful for the study of negotiator cognition.

Second, even if one accepts the (dubious) proposition that negotiator emotion is routinely and legitimately felt within the prevailing laboratory paradigm, there is still the issue of whether the full range of emotional expression and experience that occurs can be reliably detected. The most common empirical approach to negotiation process is the use of content coding of audiotapes, videotapes, or transcripts (e.g., Carnevale and Isen, 1986; O'Connor and Arnold, 2001). To be sure, emotion research in other domains (e.g., Kring and Gordon, 1998) has established that coders of these media can identify the expression of emotion with interrater consistency.

In negotiation, however, emotion may be suppressed as frequently as it is expressed, or simulated as a strategem rather than genuinely projected. These forms of emotional labor cannot readily be detected by observers engaged in content coding of process data. Another problem could be termed one of duration: the longevity of emotions and mood states varies considerably, and establishing their presence from origination to completion is difficult but perhaps necessary in order to isolate their effects on negotiation processes. As a result of these complications, it is inevitably difficult for the researcher to isolate the impact of specific affect states on particular elements of the negotiation dynamic.

Given these methodological difficulties, research that has been undertaken on affect in negotiation tends to simulate emotional responses from a programmed opponent as a behavioral stimulus (e.g., Allred et al., 1997; Van Kleef et al., 2001), induce low-level prenegotiation mood states using affect inductions (e.g., Baron, 1990; Carnevale and Isen, 1986; Forgas, 1998; Kramer et al., 1993), or simply measure postnegotiation affect via self-report (e.g., Hegtvedt and Killian, 1999; O'Connor and Arnold, 2001). These studies are limited to affect that is experimentally induced beforehand or reported after the fact. Left unexamined are the "real" emotions that negotiators experience, express, mask, and strategically deploy within the encounter.

Moving this area forward may require that researchers migrate toward more qualitative and ethnographic methods that tap rich description from participants in contextualized negotiation encounters. Emotion is arguably more socially and culturally embedded, and more contextually influenced, than cognitive processing, and so may lend itself more to qualitative methods. To glean a deeper sense of the variables that matter for quantitative research on emotion in negotiation, we see obtaining "thick" description (Geertz, 1973) about how emotion manifests itself in vivo as both necessary and useful. A hallmark of ethnography and related forms of qualitative research is the ability to collect data unconstrained by prior expectations about the information that can be required and the variables that can be examined (Becker, 2001/1996).

One specific research technique that offers intriguing possibilities for studying emotion in conflict is experience sampling methodology (ESM), which involves asking research subjects to report at certain times (randomly, episodically, or at particular time intervals) over a period of several days on the nature of their experiences—cognitive as well as emotional (Kubey, Larson, and Csikszentmihalyi, 1996). The major advantage of ESM is to "make variations in daily experience, often outside the domain of ready observation, available for analysis, replication, and falsifiability, thereby opening a broad range of phenomena to systematic observation" (Kubey et al. p. 100). Its principal limitations are its intrusiveness (halting an activity in order to self-report) and possible self-selection bias: Who would participate in this kind of study? (Alliger and Williams, 1993). It has, nevertheless, been applied successfully to a number of research topics related to communication and social behavior and represents one feasible way to tease out the mix of emotions and emotion-regulation strategies in use by negotiators.

To conclude, we are very encouraged by the expansion of scholarly attention to the emotional life of negotiators in recent years and look forward to further developments—both theoretical and empirical—as this research area moves forward. Our optimism is tempered, however, by concerns that the prevailing methods upon which negotiation researchers have grown dependent over the last two decades represent a significant obstacle to progress. Without a shift in methodological emphasis, we fear that our conceptual reach on the topic of emotion in negotiation will exceed our empirical grasp for some time to come.

Notes

1. The exception, emotional intelligence, is a relatively new concept that is currently and properly being subjected to what will likely be a long process of refinement and validation before it gains universal acceptance as a unique and important construct (e.g., Ciarrochi, Chan, and Caputi, 2000; Davies, Stankov, and Roberts, 1998; Mayer, Caruso, and Salovey, 2000). However, given the high current level of interest in emotional intelligence among both the public and researchers, and given the interesting implications that emotional intelligence might have for the study of emotion in the negotiation realm if or when it is properly validated, we explore it further here.

2. One could argue that the impact of affect on joint outcomes represents an interpersonal rather than an intrapersonal effect. Indeed, the attainment of joint outcomes can be regarded as an interpersonal phenomenon in the sense that they follow from the actions of both negotiators. However, in the studies discussed here, mood effects influence the focal negotiator, not the opponent. The focal negotiator subsequently adopts a certain negotiation style that results in (or doesn't result in) higher outcomes at both individual and dyadic levels. As such, affect directly influences the focal negotiator's behavior (intrapersonal effect) and indirectly determines joint benefits.

Works Cited

Alliger, G. M., and K. J. Williams. (1993). Using signal-contingent experience sampling methodology to study work in the field: A discussion and illustration examining task perceptions and mood. *Personnel Psychology, 46,* 525–549.

Allred, K. G. (1999). Anger and retaliation: Toward an understanding of impassioned conflict in organizations. In R. J. Bies, R. J. Lewicki, and B. H. Sheppard (Eds.), *Research on negotiation in organizations* (Vol. 7, pp. 27–58). Stamford, CT: JAI Press.

Allred, K. G., Mallozzi, J. S., Matsui, F., and C. P. Raia. (1997). The influence of anger and compassion on negotiation performance. *Organizational Behavior and Human Decision Processes, 70,* 175–187.

Averill, J. R. (1980). A constructivist view of emotion. In R. Plutchik and H. Kellerman (Eds.), *Emotion: Theory research, and experience* (Vol. 1, pp. 305–339). New York: Academic Press.

Barley, S. R. (1991). Contextualizing conflict: Notes on the anthropology of disputes and negotiations. In M. H. Bazerman, R. J. Lewicki, and B. H. Sheppard (Eds.), *Research on negotiation in organizations* (Vol. 3, pp. 165–199). Greenwich, CT: JAI Press.

Bar-On, R. (1997). *The emotional quotient inventory (EQ-i): Technical manual.* Toronto: Multi-Health Systems.

Baron, R. A. (1990). Environmentally induced positive affect: Its impact on self-efficacy, task performance, negotiation, and conflict. *Journal of Applied Social Psychology, 20,* 368–384.

Baron, R. A., Fortin, S. P., Frei, R. L., Hauver, L. A., and M. L. Shack. (1990). Reducing organizational conflict: The role of socially-induced positive affect. *International Journal of Conflict Management, 1,* 133–152.

Barry, B. (1999). The tactical use of emotion in negotiation. In R. J. Bies, R. J. Lewicki, and B. H. Sheppard (Eds.), *Research on negotiation in organizations* (Vol. 7, pp. 93–121). Stamford, CT: JAI Press.

Barry, B., and R. L. Oliver. (1996). Affect in dyadic negotiation: A model and propositions. *Organizational Behavior and Human Decision Processes, 67,* 127–143.

Bazerman, M. H., Curhan, J. R., Moore, D. A., and K. Valley. (2000). Negotiation. *Annual Review of Psychology, 51,* 279–314.

Becker, H. S. (2001). The epistemology of qualitative research. In R. Emerson (Ed.), *Contemporary field research: Perspectives and formulations* (pp. 317–330). Prospect Heights, IL: Waveland Press. Reprinted from R. Jessor, A. Colby, and R. A. Shweder (Eds.). (1996). *Ethnography and human development context and meaning in social inquiry* (pp. 53–70). Chicago: University of Chicago Press.

Cacioppo, J. T., and W. L. Gardner. (1999). Emotion. *Annual Review of Psychology, 50,* 191–214.

Carnevale, P. J. D., and A. M. Isen. (1986). The influence of positive affect and visual access on the discovery of integrative solutions in bilateral negotiation. *Organizational Behavior and Human Decision Processes, 37,* 1–13.

Ciarrochi, J. V., Chan, A. Y. C., and P. Caputi. (2000). A critical evaluation of the emotional intelligence construct. *Personality and Individual Differences, 28,* 539–561.

Costa, P. T., and R. R. McCrae. (1980). Influence of extraversion and neuroticism on subjective well-being: Happy and unhappy people. *Journal of Personality and Social Psychology, 38,* 668–678.

Darwin, C. (1965/1872). *The expression of the emotions in man and animals.* Chicago: University of Chicago Press.

Davidson, R. J. (1994). On emotion, mood, and related affective constructs. In P. Ekman and R. J. Davidson (Eds.), *The nature of emotion: Fundamental questions* (pp. 51–55). New York: Oxford University Press.

Davidson, M. N., and L. Greenhalgh. (1999). The role of emotion in negotiation: The impact of anger and race. In R. J. Bies, R. J. Lewicki, and B. H. Sheppard (Eds.), *Research on negotiation in organizations* (Vol. 7, pp. 3–26). Stamford, CT: JAI Press.

Davies, M., Stankov, L., and R. D. Roberts. (1998). Emotional intelligence: In search of an elusive construct. *Journal of Personality and Social Psychology, 75,* 989–1015.

Ekman, P. (1993). Facial expression and emotion. *American Psychologist, 48,* 384–392.

Ekman, P., Friesen, W. V., and P. Ellsworth. (1972). *Emotion in the human face: Guidelines for research and an integration of findings.* London: Pergamon.

Feldman Barrett, L., and J. J. Gross. (2001). Emotional intelligence: A process model of emotion representation and regulation. In T. J. Mayne and G. A. Bonanno (Eds.), *Emotions: Current issues and future directions* (pp. 286–310). New York: Guilford.

Feldman Barrett, L., Lane, R. D., Sechrest, L., and G. E. Schwartz. (2000). Sex differences in emotional awareness. *Personality and Social Psychology Bulletin, 26,* 1027–1035.

Forgas, J. P. (1992). Affect in social judgments and decisions: A multiprocess model. *Advances in Experimental Social Psychology, 25,* 227–275.

———. (1998). On feeling good and getting your way: Mood effects on negotiator cognition and behavior. *Journal of Personality and Social Psychology, 74,* 565–577.

Friedman, H. S., and T. Miller-Herringer. (1991). Nonverbal display of emotion in public and in private: Self-monitoring, personality, and expressive cues. *Journal of Personality and Social Psychology, 61,* 766–775.

Frijda, N. H., and B. Mesquita. (1994). The social roles and functions of emotions. In S. Kitayama and H. S. Markus (Eds.), *Emotion and culture: Empirical studies of mutual influence* (pp. 51–87). Washington, DC: American Psychological Association.

Geertz, C. (1973). *The interpretation of cultures: Selected essays.* New York: Basic Books.

George, J. M. (1990). Personality, affect and behavior in groups. *Journal of Applied Psychology, 75,* 107–116.

Gerhart, B., and S. Rynes. (1991). Determinants and consequences of salary negotiations by male and female MBA graduates. *Journal of Applied Psychology, 76,* 256–262.

Goleman, D. (1995) *Emotional intelligence.* New York: Bantam Books.

Graziano, W. G., and W. H. M. Bryant. (1998). Self-monitoring and the self-attribution of positive emotions. *Journal of Personality and Social Psychology, 74,* 250–261.

Gross, J. J., and O. P. John. (1995). Facets of emotional expressivity: Three self-report factors and their correlates. *Personality and Individual Differences, 19,* 555–568.

———. (1998). Mapping the domain of expressivity: Multimethod evidence for a hierarchical model. *Journal of Personality and Social Psychology, 74,* 170–191.

Gross, J. J., John, O. P., and J. M. Richards. (2000). The dissociation of emotion expression from emotion experience: A personality perspective. *Personality and Social Psychology Bulletin, 26,* 712–726.

Guerrero, L. K., and R. L. Reiter. (1998). Expressing emotion: Sex differences in social skills and communicative responses to anger, sadness, and jealousy. In D. J. Canary and K. Dindia (Eds.), *Sex differences and similarities in communication* (pp. 321–350). Mahwah, NJ: Erlbaum.

Hall, J. A. (1998). How big are nonverbal sex differences? The case of smiling and sensitivity to nonverbal cues. In D. J. Canary and K. Dindia (Eds.), *Sex differences and similarities in communication* (pp. 155–177). Mahwah, NJ: Erlbaum.

Hall, J. A., Carter, J. D., and T. G. Horgan. (2000). Gender differences in nonverbal communication of emotion. In A. H. Fischer (Ed.), *Gender and emotion: Social psychological perspectives* (pp. 97–117). Paris: Cambridge University Press.

Hegtvedt, K. A., and C. Killian. (1999). Fairness and emotions: Reactions to the process and outcomes of negotiations. *Social Forces, 78,* 269–303.

Isen, A. M., Daubman, K. A., and G. P. Nowicki. (1987). Positive affect facilitates creative problem solving. *Journal of Personality and Social Psychology, 52,* 1122–1131.

James, W. (1983/1890). *The principles of psychology.* Cambridge, MA: Harvard University Press.

Kahneman, D., and A. Tversky. (1979). Prospect theory: An analysis of decision-making under risk. *Econometrica, 47,* 263–291.

Keltner, D., and J. Haidt. (1999). Social functions of emotions at four levels of analysis. *Cognition and Emotion, 13,* 505–521.

Keltner, D., and A. M. Kring. (1998). Emotion, social function, and psychopathology. *Review of General Psychology, 2,* 320–342.

Klinnert, M., Campos, J., Sorce, J., Emde, R., and M. Svejda. (1983). Emotions as behavior regulators: Social referencing in infants. In R. Plutchik and H. Kellerman (Eds.), *Emotion theory, research, and experience: Vol. 2. Emotions in early development* (pp. 57–68). New York: Academic Press.

Knutson, B. (1996). Facial expressions of emotion influence interpersonal trait references. *Journal of Nonverbal Behavior, 20,* 165–182.

Kramer, R. M., Newton, E., and P. L. Pommerenke. (1993). Self-enhancement biases and negotiator judgment: Effects of self-esteem and mood. *Organizational Behavior and Human Decision Processes, 56,* 110–133.

Kring, A. M., and A. H. Gordon. (1998). Sex differences in emotion: Expression, experience, and physiology. *Journal of Personality and Social Psychology, 74,* 686–703.

Kubey, R., Larson, R., and M. Csikszentmihalyi. (1996). Experience sampling method applications to communication research questions. *Journal of Communication, 46,* 99–120.

Kumar, R. (1997). The role of affect in negotiations. *Journal of Applied Behavioral Science, 33,* 84–100.

Lane, R. D., Quinlan, D. M., Schwartz, G. E., Walker, P. A., and S. B. Zeitlin. (1990). The levels of emotional awareness scale: Cognitive-developmental measure of emotion. *Journal of Personality Assessment, 55,* 124–134.

Lawler, E. J., and J. Yoon. (1995). Structural power and emotional processes in negotiation. In R. M. Kramer and D. M. Messick (Eds.), *Negotiation as a social process* (pp. 143–165). Thousand Oaks, CA: Sage.

Lazarus, R. S. (1991). Cognition and motivation in emotion. *American Psychologist, 46,* 352–367.

Mayer, J. D. (2001). Emotion, intelligence and emotional intelligence. In J. P. Forgas (Ed.), *Handbook of affect and social cognition* (pp. 410–431). Mahwah, NJ: Erlbaum.

Mayer, J. D., Caruso, D. R., and P. Salovey. (2000). Emotional intelligence meets traditional standards for an intelligence. *Intelligence, 27,* 267–298.

Mayer, J. D., Salovey, P., and D. R. Caruso. (2000). Models of emotional intelligence. In R. Sternberg (Ed.), *Handbook of intelligence* (pp. 396–420). Cambridge: Cambridge University Press.

McCrae, R. R., and O. P. John. (1992). An introduction to the five-factor model of personality. *Journal of Personality, 60,* 175–216.

Metts, S., and J. W. Bowers. (1994). Emotion in interpersonal communication. In M. L. Knapp and G. R. Miller (Eds.), *Handbook of interpersonal communication* (pp. 508–541). Thousand Oaks, CA: Sage.

Moore, D. A., Kurtzberg, T. R., Thompson, L. L., and M. W. Morris. (1999). Long and short routes to success in electronically mediated negotiations: Group affiliations and good vibrations. *Organizational Behavior and Human Decision Processes, 77,* 22–43.

Morris, M. W., and D. Keltner. (2000). How emotions work: The social functions of emotional expression in negotiations. In B. M. Staw and R. I. Sutton (Eds.), *Research in organizational behavior* (Vol. 11, pp. 1–50). Amsterdam: JAI Press.

Mufson, L., and S. Nowicki. (1991). Factors affecting the accuracy of facial affect recognition. *The Journal of Social Psychology, 131,* 815–822.

Neale, M. A., and G. B. Northcraft. (1991). Behavioral negotiation theory: A framework for conceptualizing dyadic bargaining. In L. L. Cummings and B. M. Staw (Eds.), *Research in organizational behavior* (Vol. 13, pp. 147–190). Greenwich, CT: JAI Press.

Oatley, K., and J. M. Jenkins. (1992). Human emotions: Functions and dysfunctions. *Annual Review of Psychology, 43,* 55–85.

O'Connor, K. M., and J. A. Arnold. (2001). Distributive spirals: Negotiation impasses and the moderating role of disputant self-efficacy. *Organizational Behavior and Human Decision Processes, 84,* 148–176.

Parrott, W. G. (1993). Beyond hedonism: Motives for inhibiting good moods and for maintaining bad moods. In D. M. Wegner and J. W. Pennebaker (Eds.), *Handbook of mental control* (pp. 278–305). Upper Saddle River, NJ: Prentice Hall.

———. (2001). Emotions in social psychology: Volume overview. In W. G. Parrott (Ed.), *Emotions in social psychology* (pp. 1–19). Philadelphia: Psychology Press.

Pillutla, M. M., and J. K. Murnighan. (1996). Unfairness, anger, and spite: Emotional rejections of ultimatum offers. *Organizational Behavior and Human Decision Processes, 68,* 1208–1224.

Plutchik, R. (1980). *Emotion: A psychoevolutionary synthesis.* New York: Basic Books.

Russell, J. A. (1980). A circumplex model of affect. *Journal of Personality and Social Psychology, 39,* 345–356.

Rusting, C. L. (2001). Personality as a moderator of affective influences on cognition. In J. P. Forgas (Ed.), *Handbook of affect and social cognition* (pp. 371–391). Mahwah, NJ: Erlbaum.

Salovey, P., and D. Mayer. (1990). Emotional intelligence. *Imagination, Cognition and Personality, 9,* 185–211.

Scherer, K. R. (1986). Vocal affect expression: A review and a model for future research. *Psychological Bulletin, 99,* 143–165.

Shaver, P. R., Schwartz, J. C., Kirson, D., and C. O'Connor. (1987). Emotion knowledge: Further explorations of a prototype approach. *Journal of Personality and Social Psychology, 52,* 1061–1086.

Snyder, M. (1974). Self-monitoring of expressive behavior. *Journal of Personality and Social Psychology, 30,* 526–537.

Strongman, K. T. (1996). *The psychology of emotion* (4th ed.). Chichester, England: Wiley.

Stuhlmacher, A. F., and A. E. Walters. (1999). Gender differences in negotiation outcome: a meta-analysis. *Personnel Psychology, 52,* 653–677.

Thompson, L. L., Nadler, J., and P. H. Kim. (1999). Some like it hot: The case for the emotional negotiator. In L. L. Thompson, J. M. Levine, and D. M. Messick (Eds.), *Shared cognition in organizations: The management of knowledge* (pp. 139–161). Mahwah, NJ: Erlbaum.

Totterdell, P. (2000). Catching moods and hitting runs: Mood linkage and subjective performance in professional sports teams. *Journal of Applied Psychology, 85,* 848–859.

Van Kleef, G. A., De Dreu, C. K. W., and A. S. R. Manstead. (2001, June). *Why the happy negotiator shouldn't be so happy: The interpersonal effects of anger and happiness on negotiation behavior and outcomes.* Paper presented at the 14th conference of the International Association for Conflict Management, Cergy, France.

Wall, J. A., Jr. (1991). Impression management in negotiations. In R. A. Giacalone and P. Rosenfeld (Eds.), *Applied impression management: How image-making affects managerial decisions* (pp. 133–156). Thousand Oaks, CA: Sage.

Walters, A. E., Stuhlmacher, A. F., and L. L. Meyer. (1998). Gender and negotiator competitiveness: A meta-analysis. *Organizational Behavior and Human Decision Processes, 76,* 1–29.

Watson, D., Clark, L. A., and A. Tellegen. (1988). Development and validation of brief measures of positive and negative affect: The PANAS scales. *Journal of Personality and Social Psychology, 54,* 1063–1070.

CHAPTER 4

Culture and Emotions
in Intercultural Negotiations
AN OVERVIEW

Rajesh Kumar

INTERCULTURAL NEGOTIATIONS are increasingly common in an interdependent world and span a broad array of cooperative arrangements, including buyer–seller negotiations, licensing agreements, strategic alliances, and mergers and acquisitions. Because they are unconfined by industry or geographical borders, these negotiations bring together participants whose values and beliefs often conflict. Cultural differences can increase the time required to reach an agreement, and they can lead to a suboptimal agreement or complete breakdown of negotiations. Even if an agreement is reached, it may be very fragile if differences have not been effectively bridged. The protracted difficulties experienced by Cogentrix in negotiating and implementing an agreed-upon contract in India, cultural clashes between Daimler and Chrysler managers during the merger of their companies, and conflicts between Dutch airline KLM and American carrier Northwest all illustrate the potential pitfalls of cross-cultural negotiation.

Although academic work as well as anecdotal evidence suggests that differences in values and beliefs make intercultural negotiation problematic, the psychological processes and associated interactional dynamics of intercultural negotiations remain relatively unexplored (e.g., Gelfand and Dyer, 2000; George, Jones, and Gonzales, 1998; Kumar, 1999b). Furthermore, although a number of researchers have explored how cognitive processes shape negotiator decision making (for reviews, see Bazerman and Carroll, 1987; Bazerman and Neale, 1992), and although others have begun to recognize that schemas and scripts vary across cultures (e.g., Brett and Okumura, 1998; Gelfand, Niishi, and Holcombe, Ohbuchi, and Fukuno, 2001; Tinsley,

1998), there has been a relative neglect of the role of emotion in shaping the dynamics of intercultural negotiations.

There is a growing recognition among researchers of the close link between emotions, thinking, and behavior (Forgas, 2000), and of the need to explicate the role of emotions in the negotiating process to advance the theory and practice of negotiation (see Barry, Fulmer, and Van Kleef, Chapter 3, this volume, as well as Barry and Oliver, 1996; Kumar, 1997, 1999a, 1999b; Morris and Keltner, 2000). In an intercultural context, greater variation in cognitive content is more likely across cultures than within cultures, and cognitive content is affectively valenced (D'Andrade, 1981).

The purpose of this chapter is to provide an overview of the links between culture and emotions in an intercultural negotiating context. I begin by delineating the circumstances that generate emotions in an intercultural negotiating setting. I then assess the nature of emotions that are likely to arise in this setting and consider the implications of these emotions for negotiators from different cultures. I conclude by suggesting directions for future research with a particular focus on some of the methodological issues involved in measuring emotions in an intercultural negotiation setting.

Defining Emotion

For the purposes of this chapter, emotions can be viewed as high-intensity affective states that stem from the focal actors' ability or inability to achieve their goals (e.g., Lazarus, 1991; Oatley and Johnson-Laird, 1996). Negotiators experience positive emotions when they are able to attain their desired goals and negative emotions when thwarted from their goals. Appraisal theorists suggest that emotions reflect the presence of a discrepancy between a desired outcome and the actual outcome (e.g., Frijda, 1986; Ortony, Clore, and Collins, 1988; Roseman, 1991). Whether reflective or unconscious, the appraisal process is fundamental to the negotiator's understanding of the meaning of events.

Emotions, as Ben Ze'ev (2000) noted, "are not theoretical states; they involve a practical concern associated with a readiness to act" (p. 61). Frijda (1986) described different emotions as representing different "action tendencies." Approach, withdrawal, avoidance, rejection, help seeking, hostility, breaking contact, dominance, and submission are some examples of action tendencies that can stem from emotion (Davitz, 1969). The link between an emotion and a specific behavior is often variable (Averill, 2001; Mesquita et al., 1997); although anger creates an impulse for aggression, the impulse will not always manifest itself in an aggressive response.

As discussed in Chapter 3, emotions are both personal and social; this dual nature is likely to affect the behavior of individual negotiators as well as the relationship between them (Keltner and Haidt, 1999). Emotions are the vehicle through which individuals continuously negotiate and renegotiate the relational meaning of their interactions with their counterparts (Davidson and Greenhalgh, 1999).

Emotions vary in frequency, duration, and intensity (Kumar, 1997). The more frequently people are unable to attain their goals, the more often they will experience emotions. In addition, the greater the importance of one's goal, the greater the intensity and/or the duration of the emotion. Although emotions are always goal based, the nature of the goals that individuals pursue varies across cultures. "Core cultural ideas" lead to the salience of different goals in different cultures (Markus and Kitayama, 1994). Although individuals in different cultures use a similar set of appraisal dimensions in negotiations, such as novelty–familiarity, unpleasantness–pleasantness, uncertainty–certainty, and controllability, the frequency with which these dimensions are used is culturally variable (Mesquita, Frijda, and Scherer, 1997).

Emotions in Intercultural Negotiations

Barry and Oliver (1996) have suggested that emotions emerge at multiple stages during a negotiation interaction. Negotiators may experience emotions either just prior to the onset of negotiations, during the negotiation process, or when they are evaluating negotiating outcomes. This framework suggests that emotions may have long-term consequences on the negotiation process; individuals may not be fully cognizant of these effects, and the effects may not be fully within their control. The interdependence among the various stages in the negotiation process is well captured in Barry and Oliver's (1996) framework, which I use to assess the impact of culture on the origins of emotions in intercultural negotiations.

The dynamics of emotions in intercultural negotiations are likely to be much more complex than in intracultural negotiations. Barry and Oliver (1996) have noted that anticipatory negative emotional states are often a product of bargaining conditions, prior interactional history, and negotiators' level of dispositional affect. An understanding of the role of emotions in intercultural negotiations is likely to warrant the inclusion of additional variables to their framework. Specifically, I argue that anticipatory negative emotional states may also stem from the cultural distance between negotiators. Triandis, Kurowski, and Gelfand (1994) suggested that differences and similarities between cultures can be conceptualized in terms of objective elements, subjective elements, or both. Differences in language, religion, and political and economic systems reflect differences in objective elements, whereas differences in values and beliefs reflect differences in subjective elements. In this chapter I focus on the subjective dimension of culture, placing particular emphasis on the values and beliefs that are dominant in a culture. It is widely known that cultures vary on a number of value dimensions, including individualism versus collectivism, egalitarianism versus hierarchy, tightness versus looseness, mastery versus harmony, high context versus low context, and analytical versus holistic thinking (e.g., Brett, 2000; Gelfand and Dyer, 2000; Nisbett, Peng, Choi, and Norenzayan, 2001; Triandis, 2000). These contrasting values have also been linked to different behaviors and scripts within negotiations (e.g., Adair, Okumura, and Brett, 2001; Brodt and Tinsley, 1998; Graham and Sano, 1984; Kumar, 1999b). A script is defined as an event schema that specifies the temporal sequence by which a given activity is to be completed. I define cultural distance as the degree of divergence in cultural values and beliefs, and the consequent divergence in negotiation scripts across cultures.

Cultural distance is more likely to produce negative affective states prior to negotiation than cultural closeness for a number of reasons. First, perceived dissimilarity produces a lack of attraction that is likely to produce negative affect (e.g., Triandis, 1977; Triandis, Kurowski, and Gelfand, 1994). Dissimilarity in values and beliefs makes it difficult for individuals to find a common frame of reference and draws attention to the fact that the other individual does not belong to one's in-group. Second, cultural distance lessens negotiators' sense of control, inasmuch as they find themselves negotiating in ambiguous and difficult situations. Reis, Collins, and Berscheid (2000) noted that the emergence of negative emotions is particularly pronounced in social environments that are "ambiguous, fluid, and thus unpredictable" (p. 860). Cultural distance also lessens the opportunities for rewarding interaction in intercultural settings, as negotiators with conflicting beliefs and values may enter the negotiation expecting the situation to be difficult. This recognition may lower trust at the onset of the negotiation and, in conjunction with reliance on stereotyping, this ambiguity and dissimilarity may generate negative emotional states (George et al., 1998).

The argument has also been made that emotions often stem from the ability or inability of negotiators to attain their goals. While this proposition may be universally true, it is worth bearing in mind that (a) there are many different kinds of emotional states that may emerge from these conditions and (b) different emotional states are associated with different behavioral tendencies. Furthermore, culture influences both of these processes (Kornadt, 1990; Kumar, 1997; Mesquita et al., 1997). Thus, critical questions emerge: What emotion or emotions do negotiators from different cultures most commonly experience? What is the linkage between these emotions and behaviors? Are the action tendencies associated with different emotions universal or are they culturally specific? Finally, what is the nature of the negotiating dynamic instigated by the emergence of conflicting emotions among negotiators from different cultures? Negotiators from different cultures experience different emotions with different behavioral implications. This, in turn, leads to the emergence of behavioral incompatability, which in turn can generate even more negative emotions and possibly hinder the negotiating process even further.

CULTURAL INFLUENCES ON EXPERIENCED EMOTIONS

Theorists have categorized emotions in a number of ways, each of which can be linked to cross-cultural differences in the experience of emotions in negotiation. Higgins (2000) distinguished four types of emotions: (a) cheerfulness-related emotions like "happy," "elated," and "joyful"; (b) quiescence-related emotions like "calm," "relaxed," "serene"; (c) agitation-related emotions like "tense," "restless," and "nervous"; and (d) dejection-related emotions like "sad," "gloomy," and "disappointed." According to Higgins's theory, emotions are associated with a promotion or a prevention focus. Promotion focus implies that negotiators are very sensitive to the presence or absence of positive outcomes; a prevention focus implies that negotiators are sensitive to either the absence of or the presence of negative outcomes. Promotion focus generates cheerful emotions when the negotiators are able to attain their desired goals, and dejection and agitation when negotiators are unable to achieve their desired goals (e.g., Brockner and Higgins, 2001; Higgins, Shah, and Friedman, 1997). An interesting implication of this framework is that negotiators' ability or inability to attain goals will always produce emotions; the specific type of emotion activated is dependent on the regulatory focus of the negotiator, that is, a promotion or a prevention focus.

Recent research has shown that culture is linked to regulatory focus (Lee, Aaker, and Gardner, 2000). The authors demonstrated that individualists had a promotion focus; they were sensitive to information that had a direct bearing on their ability to realize their hopes and wishes. By contrast, collectivists were more sensitive to information that prevented them from violating their obligations. A derivative implication is that individuals from different cultures are likely to experience different emotional states. Individualists are likely to experience the dejection-related emotions associated with a promotion focus, whereas collectivists are likely to experience the agitation-related emotions associated with a prevention focus.

Another typology of emotions focuses on the distinction between ego-focused and other-focused emotions (Markus and Kitayama, 1991). Ego-focused emotions, including anger, frustration, pride, and guilt, are associated with the fulfillment or nonfulfillment of individual goals or desires. The "independent" self-construal conceives of the self as a constellation of internal attributes (traits, motives, abilities) that provide direction for individual behavior. Other-focused emotions such as shame, anxiety, and fear are associated with the ability or inability to nurture interdependence with in-group members. The "interdependent self construal" views an individual "not as separate from the social context but as more connected and less differentiated from others" (Markus and Kitayama, 1991, p. 227). Although the "interdependent self" also possesses a set of internal attributes, the linkage between these attributes and overt behavior is tenuous. Ego-focused emotions highlight the need for an individual to exhibit his or her distinctive identity; other-focused emotions stress the need to fit in. Although all emotions are goal based, the goals of the interdependent self are primarily relationship driven, whereas the goals of the independent self are driven by an individual's internal needs.

The two perspectives on emotions outlined above complement each other in different ways. Higgins (2000) focused on the emotional consequences of promotion and prevention, whereas Markus and Kitayama (1991) consider the relational or nonrelational character of emotions. Both emphasize themes that are differentially salient in individualistic and collectivistic cultures. In a collectivistic culture, the dominant emphasis is relational and preventive (i.e., preventing the relationship from deteriorating). In an individualistic culture, the dominant emphasis is nonrelational and self-promotional (i.e., the maximization of personal goals).

Although the distinction between ego- and other-focused emotions has considerable intuitive appeal and is well grounded in the existing literature, empirical studies pertaining to this distinction have been mixed. Gavazzi and Oatley (1999) found support for the distinction in their comparison of Italian (interdependent self-construal) and Canadian (independent self-construal) cultures. The authors asked respondents to indicate the intensity of the different emotions they experienced following the unsuccessful completion of a shared plan with another individual. Anger and frustration (independent emotions) appeared to be more common among Canadians than among Italians, whereas sorrow (an interdependent emotion) appeared to be the dominant emotion in Italy.

By contrast, Cookie, Stephan, Saito, and Barnett (1998) asked American and Japanese students to indicate their comfort in expressing a set of emotions in the presence of a stranger and a family member. The expectation that the Japanese would feel more comfortable expressing interdependent (other-focused) than independent (ego-focused) emotions was supported by the data. The expectation that the Japanese would experience greater discomfort in expressing negative emotions than the Americans also received empirical support. Contrary to expectations, however, the American students felt more comfortable expressing interdependent than independent emotions. Furthermore, the American students, unlike the Japanese, also felt more comfortable expressing emotions to family members than to strangers, whereas the Japanese did not make a distinction between in-group and out-group members. These findings are at odds with the independent and interdependent self-construals, perhaps due to the fact that the Japanese and American samples did not differ greatly on the individualism–collectivism dimension.

In another study, Grimm, Church, Katigbak, Alberto, and Reyes, (1999) compared moods experienced by American and Philippine students as part of a larger study of the linkages between individualism and collectivism and personality traits in these cultural groupings. Students were given a list of mood adjectives and asked to indicate the degree to which they felt a given mood during the past week on a five-point scale. The American students who scored high on individualism experienced more independent emotions, such as anger, sadness, and loneliness, than interdependent. Because the individualism score was not correlated with mood scores in the Philippine sample, it is difficult to draw any firm conclusion about the links between self-construals and emotions within this cultural grouping. Part of the problem may well be one of measurement. It has been maintained that the emotions of individuals with an interdependent self are often shaped by contextual factors (e.g., Miller, 1984); this context is missing when participants are administered a general value-orientation scale. More recently, Mesquita (2001) has argued that some emotions, such as anger, may be activated in both self-focused and other-focused ways.

Finally, there may be cultural differences in the need to experience and express emotions. Maio and Esses (2001) have proposed a new measure, "need for affect," which indicates the degree to which individuals allow their behavior to be shaped by emotions. The researchers note, "People who are high in the need for affect may be more likely to permit their emotions to influence their attitudes, behaviors, and perceptions, than people who are low in the need for affect" (2001, p. 609). In cultures where there is less need for emotions, individuals may attempt to keep emotions from shaping their behavior, either because their emotions are low in frequency or intensity, or because of cultural norms for suppressing emotions. Eid and Diener (2001) recently assessed the frequency and intensity of emotions experienced by college students in Australia, China, Taiwan, and the People's Republic of China. Notably, the frequency and intensity of emotions experienced by the Chinese students was the lowest among all of the groups studied. In the Chinese society, ". . . there is a general attitude to consider emotions as dangerous, irrelevant, or illness causing" (Eid and Diener, 2001, p. 883).

EMOTIONS AND BEHAVIOR

Because different emotions are connected with different behavioral tendencies, it is important to examine the nature of emotions that emerge in a negotiation setting. Although the link between emotions and behavior is not perfect (Averill, 2001), different types of emotions are associated with core relational themes (Lazarus, 1991). Agitation-related emotions such as fear induce individuals to escape from a situation, whereas dejection-related emotions such as anger induce individuals to either try harder to attain their goals or readjust their expectations. Similarly, whereas negative ego-focused emotions may induce an individual to try harder to redress the negative outcome, negative other-focused emotions may induce the individual to repair the damaged relationship that gave rise to this emotion.

The idea that emotions are associated with action tendencies has a number of implications for intercultural interaction. First, it highlights the importance of looking at specific negative emotional states since different negative emotional states have different motivational implications. Negotiators experiencing negative ego-focused emotions may put pressure on their counterparts to make concessions, whereas negotiators experiencing negative other-focused emotions may readjust their own aspiration levels to arrive at an agreement. Theorists also maintain that while negative ego-focused emotions have immediate behavioral–cognitive consequences, the same may not be true of negative other-focused emotions, which are generated not by oneself but by the actions of another in-group member (Matsumoto, 1996). Given the fact that other-focused negative emotions have the potential for disrupting relationships, negotiators in some cultures are likely to be much more cautious and circumspect before undertaking any strategic actions. This may explain the curious finding that Japanese negotiators do not feel pressured to undertake new initiatives when the negotiation process has hit a roadblock (March, 1988).

It is important to note that the same emotional state can lead to different behaviors in different cultures (e.g., Kornadt, 1990; Mesquita et al., 1997). Kornadt (1990) points out that in Western cultures, unjustifiably caused frustration leads to anger and a desire to punish the other party, whereas in Japan, unjustifiably caused frustration does not lead to overt aggression. The discrepancy between experienced and expressed emotion may be explained by the existence of display rules concerning emotional expression, a notion widely accepted in the literature.

Additional dynamics are likely to be present in intercultural negotiations based on cultural differences in emotions. First, in collectivistic societies as opposed to individualistic societies, there may be less individual divergence in how negotiators respond overtly to emotions. The "need to fit in," paramount in collectivistic societies, is likely to constrict the behavioral options open to negotiators. In addition, Mesquita (2001) has cogently argued that emotions in collectivistic cultures have an objective reality for the individual, such that there is a widespread belief among individuals that a given stimulus event will have a similar impact on other individuals. Mesquita (2001) noted, "Whereas in the individualist culture, a clear distinction was made between subjectivity and objectivity, allowing for interindividual differences in response, the collectivist cultures seem to endorse the principle of a subjective reality" (p. 73).

Second, I argue that the behavioral response of negotiators from collectivistic societies will be more sensitive to emotions stemming from violations of relational norms than to emotions stemming from the failure to attain desired goals (Kumar, 1999a). Theorists have drawn a distinction between agent-based emotions, which derive from the actions of another negotiator, and outcome-based emotions, which stem from the ability or inability to reach a negotiated agreement or settle on terms that may or may not be to one's liking (Ortony et al., 1988). In collectivistic societies, relationships play an important role; the ability to initiate or sustain these relationships may be threatened if the other negotiator engages in behaviors that either lead to the disintegration of the relationship or prevent harmony (Leung, 1997). This may lead a negotiator to conclude that the other party is untrustworthy and thereby prevent the interaction from deepening to the point where outcome considerations become salient. Thus, although the absence of agent-based emotions may not in itself guarantee a successful negotiated outcome, the presence of negative agent-based emotions will almost surely compromise the possibility of attaining a negotiated agreement. It is also worth noting that the specific behavioral response to the violation of relational norms by the opposing negotiator depends upon whether or not the opponent is a member of one's in-group or out-group. Collectivists may be less hesitant to respond in an aggressive manner to individuals who are not members of their in-group vis-à-vis individuals who are.

The recognition that negotiators from individualistic and collectivistic cultures have a propensity to experience different emotions has a number of implications. Its first consequence is the emergence of behavioral incompatibility, which I define as a behavioral pattern stemming from the emergence of negative emotions that draws negotiators further apart rather than closer to an agreement (Kumar, 1999a). For example, although the emergence of agitation-related emotions induces the negotiator to withdraw from the interaction, dejection-related emotions may induce the negotiator to even more forcefully attempt to reach an agreement. The resulting behavioral incompatibility (George et al., 1998; Kumar, 1997) may not be easily contained and may be further accentuated when negotiators differ in their need for emotions. In the process, negotiators' ability to attain their goals is compromised.

Finally, the fact that emotions in collectivistic cultures have an objective reality suggests that negotiators in collectivistic cultures may be more constrained in their ability to deal with goal blockage than negotiators in individualistic cultures. Given internal unanimity as to the significance of a given event, it is unlikely that negotiators from collectivistic cultures will be easily able to advocate a pattern of action to break an impasse. By contrast, within individualistic cultures there is likely to be a greater divergence in how a situation is perceived; although this in and of itself may not result in a changed strategy in dealing with impasse, the potential for such a change is clearly present. Finally, as Mesquita (2001) noted, ". . . . emotions are likely to reinforce and sustain the cultural themes that are significant in individualistic and collectivistic cultures respectively. Emotions can themselves be seen as cultural practices that promote important cultural ideas" (p. 73). The implication of this statement is that emotions reflect who we are as individuals and within relationships. Emotions may therefore make the in-group–out-group distinction salient, and in doing so may make the process of negotiation even more difficult.

EVALUATING NEGOTIATING OUTCOMES: THE LINKAGE BETWEEN
CULTURE AND EMOTIONS

The evaluation of outcomes is an intrinsic component of the negotiation process. Negotiation scholars have, therefore, given considerable attention to the conditions or circumstances under which negotiators are able to attain an integrative agreement. Negotiated outcomes are treated as desirable when integrative potential is maximized. Although negotiators are not oblivious to the need to maximize integrative potential, they are equally sensitive to the fairness of the negotiated outcome. Fairness is an essential component of the negotiation process and is closely linked to the emergence of emotions in negotiations (e.g., Kumar, 1997; Solomon, 1989). In intercultural negotiations, the ability to attain distributive fairness becomes problematic given the fact that, because distributive norms vary across cultures, people from different cultures are likely to apply different fairness rules in negotiation (e.g., Morris, Leung, Ames, and Nickel, 1999; see Leung and Tong in this volume).

In his analysis of fairness concerns, Deutsch (1975) drew a distinction between equity, equality, and need, each of which is differentially preferred in different cultures (Triandis, 1995). It has been argued that the equity norm is dominant in individualistic cultures and that the equality and the need norm are more prevalent in collectivistic societies (Triandis, 1995). When negotiators use conflicting criteria to evaluate the fairness of a given outcome, a perceived lack of fairness on the part of one or more individuals may prevent a mutually satisfactory agreement or the implementation of a negotiated agreement (Barry and Oliver, 1996). An inability to satisfactorily resolve disagreements about benefit allocation may lead negotiators to wonder if they can trust their opponent, bringing broader questions about the relationship to the fore. Thus, emotions are highly salient at the evaluative stage, with cultural differences playing an important role.

CULTURE AND EMOTION IN INTERCULTURAL NEGOTIATIONS:
POTENTIAL MODERATORS

While cultural distance, the negotiating process, and the evaluation of negotiation outcomes are the immediate precursors of emotions, their impact may be heightened or lessened by a number of potential moderators. I will highlight individual-level differences, expectations of differences, the history of the relationship, and task complexity as possible factors that may influence the link between culture and emotions.

Individual-Level Differences

George et al., (1998) highlight the importance of positive and negative affectivity in shaping negotiator behavior. Positive affectivity (PA) induces individuals to experience positive emotions, whereas negative affectivity (NA) induces negative emotions (Watson and Clark, 1984). Thus, we can expect that individuals who are high in positive affectivity will respond positively to difficulties in social interaction. That is to say, "High PA negotiators will . . . be more likely to be optimistic about the negotiation process, view their negotiating partners positively, be willing to collaborate with their partners, and feel good about their interactions" (George et al., 1998, p. 755). The crucial implication of this prediction is that if both negotiators are high in positive affectivity, behavioral incompatability may not emerge, making the task of the negotiators from different cultures much easier.

Even if individuals do not have a natural propensity to experience positive emotions, they may still possess the ability to deal with their negative emotions effectively. Salovey and Mayer (1990, pp. 189), for example, highlight the importance of "emotional intelligence" in determining how individuals deal with their affective state. They define emotional intelligence as "the ability to monitor one's own and others' feelings and emotions, to discriminate among them and to use this information to guide one's thinking and action." Individuals high in emotional intelligence will be better able to deal with the emotional dynamics stemming from behavioral incompatability. They may better anticipate their counterparts' reactions or may adjust their own behavior in a manner that does not disrupt the negotiation process. Although problems may still emerge, they may be easier to resolve than they might have been otherwise.

Expectations of Differences

The greater the cultural distance between negotiators, the greater the potential for the emergence of negative emotions and the greater the intensity of these emotions. Implicit in this reasoning is the recognition that the violation of expectations leads to the emergence of negative emotions (Mandler, 1975). The impact of cultural distance on the emergence or intensity of emotions experienced by negotiators may, however, be mitigated by negotiators' a priori expectations about the emergence of incongruence. Insofar as negotiators are prepared to expect this incongruence, they may not be surprised by the difficulties encountered during the negotiation process. For this reason, they may not experience negative emotions or may experience them at a much lower level of intensity. Indeed, one of the objectives of cross-cultural training is to enhance negotiator expectations of incongruence, thus lessening negative emotional reactions during the interaction.

History of Relationship

Intercultural negotiations involve negotiators who either have had a shared history (either positive or negative) or who are interacting with each other for the first time. Prior interaction may lead negotiators to characterize their relationship in one of the four quadrants: (a) low trust–low distrust; (b) high trust–low distrust; (c) low trust–high distrust; and (d) high trust–high distrust (Lewicki, McCallister, and Bies, 1998). When the prior relationship is characterized by low trust–high distrust, the propensity of the actors to experience negative emotions is amplified. By contrast, the high trust–low distrust condition (Lewicki et al., 1998) leads actors to heighten their interdependence by pursuing new opportunities with their partner; in the process, positive affect is amplified and emotional bonding increased (Lawler and Yoon, 1993; Oliver, Balakrishnan, and Barry, 1994). In the high trust–high distrust condition, the propensity of actors to experience both positive and negative emotions is simultaneously present, whereas in the low trust–distrust cell, emotional neutrality is likely to prevail at the onset of the interaction. In other words, prior interaction may either amplify or dampen negotiators' emotional responses.

Task Complexity

One might surmise that the complexity of the negotiation task also has a bearing on the emergence of emotions. Negotiating a merger or an acquisition across cultural boundaries or negotiating to build a power plant are tasks characterized by a high level of complexity compared to negotiating a buyer–seller contract across cultural boundaries. Task complexity is dependent on the a priori integrative potential of the situation, the nature of the task (transactional versus conflict management), and accountability pressures. The lower the a priori integrative potential of the task, the greater the cognitive demands it places on the negotiators, thus making the negotiation process a difficult and time-consuming undertaking. In transactional negotiations, negotiators meet with each other to determine whether or not they can arrive at a mutually acceptable agreement, whereas in conflict management negotiations, parties are trying to resolve a preexisting dispute (Brett, 2000). The fact that emotions are preexistent in conflict management negotiations makes these situations complex and difficult to resolve. Finally, task complexity is also dependent on the accountability pressures present in a negotiation situation. Accountability pressures arise when negotiators have to justify their actions to constituents and/or when their actions are punished or rewarded by their constituents. Gelfand and Realo (1999) have demonstrated that in individualistic cultures, accountability pressures lead to a competitive framing of the situation, whereas in collectivistic cultures, accountability pressures lead to a cooperative framing of the situation. This difference may add to the complexity of the negotiation process.

Task complexity is likely to slow down the intercultural negotiation process as negotiators encounter impediments to their goals. Emotions may be in abundant supply, and they may be high in intensity. When actors seek to determine the causes of the unexpected outcome, negative emotions may be further intensified by attributional processes (Weiner, 1985). Although unexpected outcomes invite attributional reasoning, it is worth noting that attributional processes are not as common among Asians as they are among European Americans (Markus and Kitayama Heiman, 1996). One implication of this finding is that attributional reasoning may heighten the emotional reactions of European-American negotiators but may have little impact on Asian negotiators.

Future Directions

In this chapter, I have articulated the role of emotions in intercultural negotiation encounters. Although a few theoretical pieces on this topic have begun to appear (e.g., Kumar, 1999a, 1999b; George et al., 1998), empirical studies remain rare. Much work in this field lies ahead. For example, as I have argued, a promising line of inquiry would be to empirically explore the notion that different emotions are salient in different cultural contexts and that conflicting emotional responses generate behavioral incompatability in intercultural negotiations. Another stream of research might explore the emergence of emotions at different stages in the negotiation process and their effect on subsequent interaction. The effectiveness of mediation in intercultural contexts is also likely to be influenced by the sensitivity of the mediators in understanding the emotional dynamics that unfold in intercultural negotiations. The more sensitive the mediators are to the emotional dynamics, the more effective they will be in positively reshaping the dynamics of social interaction. This proposition may be worth exploring both conceptually and empirically.

Although the study of culture and emotion in negotiation will doubtless be fruitful, researchers in this area must heed a number of possible methodological issues. For a thorough examination of the role of emotions in intercultural negotiation, emotions must be studied in the laboratory and in the field, where researchers could explore the impact of emotional cycles in shaping the intercultural negotiating process over a period of time. Other researchers have made similar recommendations (George et al., 1998). Although experimental simulations are useful and have been widely used in studying negotiator judgment and decision making, studying emotions in the laboratory is problematic for a number of reasons. First, emotional processes unfold over time, and it is often unclear when an emotional cycle begins and ends. Measures of emotion are most accurate when they are administered just after the onset of the emotional cycle (Levenson, 1988). George et al., (1998) recommended the employment of an experience-sampling methodology (e.g., Csikszentmihalyi and Larson, 1987) that would imply repeated measurement of positive and negative emotions during the negotiation process.

Second, the negotiation simulation needs to be highly involving for the participants to experience emotions of sufficient intensity or, for that matter, any emotions at all. Emotions are experienced most intensely when participants perceive a given situation to be highly realistic. Self-report methods are quite popular and widely used in the measurement of emotions, but they rest on the assumption that "... research participants are both able and willing to observe and report on their own emotions" (Larsen and Fredrickson, 1999, p. 48). Insofar as some emotional experiences occur outside of an individual's self-awareness, he or she may not be able to report emotions accurately. Intercultural comparisons of emotions become even more problematic, either because of response-set biases or because of difficulties in translation equivalence between emotion words across languages (Matsumoto, 1996). A further problem is that although individuals in some cultures may be comfortable with simulations that require individuals to take on artificial roles, this may not necessarily be true for individuals in all cultures. This further complicates the task of studying emotions within simulation environments.

Although the measurement of emotions is not problem-free, some of these difficulties can be surmounted. For example, one could use trained observers to code emotions, as in the Specific Affect Coding system developed by Gottman (1993) to study emotions in marital interaction. A variant of this system could be used to code emotions in cross-cultural interactions, necessitating reliance on a cross-cultural research team. A cross-cultural team would be essential in exploring the links between emotions and behavior in cross-cultural negotiation.

Studying the dynamics of intercultural negotiations in a field setting provides greater ecological validity than laboratory work, but it presents its own complications. In addition to the problem of obtaining unrestricted access to negotiations, there are the associated problems of time, cost, and the ability to relate the dynamics of a particular negotiation episode to the negotiation as a whole. It may also be the case that an outsider will have difficulty observing negotiations in collectivistic cultures unless they have intricate connections with the parties in question. This makes the reliance on a cross-cultural team even more essential, as it is likely that team members from collectivistic cultures may be well positioned to gain access to negotiations. On the positive side, field settings provide natural ground for exploring the impact of emotions in an unrestricted manner. The more complex the negotiation and the greater the cultural distance between the partners, the more frequently will the actors experience emotions, and the greater the intensity of the emotions. The link between emotions and behavior in all of its nuances has the potential to be well captured in the field, although the measurement of emotional cycles may be just as tricky as it is in the lab.

In sum, this chapter has reviewed the existing work on the emotional dynamics of intercultural negotiations. A number of conclusions follow from this review. First, emotions in intercultural negotiations may arise either prior to negotiation, during negotiation, or after negotiation. Second, emotional intensity may be amplified or lessened by individual difference variables, expectations of differences, the history of the relationship, and/or task complexity. Finally, different cultures have a propensity to experience different kinds of emotions. Ego-focused emotions, accompanied by a promotion regulatory focus, are more prevalent in individualistic cultures; other-focused emotions and a prevention focus are likely to be more prevalent in collectivistic cultures. Different emotions activate different action tendencies, and while the linkage between emotions and behavior is not perfect, there is a high degree of regularity between the two. Empirical studies on the impact of emotions should be undertaken in a variety of different sociocultural settings, employing alternative methodologies (experiment versus field studies), and varying the complexity of the negotiating task (possible in experimental studies) to unravel the complex dynamics of emotions. There is much work to be done, and I hope that the arguments set forth here provide the needed impetus.

Works Cited

Averill, J. R. (2001). Studies on anger and aggression: Implications for theories of emotions. In G. W. Parrott (Ed.), *Emotions in social psychology: A book of readings* (pp. 337–352). Philadelphia: Academic Psychology Press.

Barry, B., and R. L. Oliver. (1996). Affect in dyadic negotiation: A model and propositions. *Organizational Behavior and Human Decision Processes, 67,* 127–143.

Bazerman, M. H., and J. S. Carroll. (1987). Negotiator cognition. In L. L. Cummings and B. M. Staw (Eds.), *Research in organizational behavior* (pp. 247–288). Greenwich, CT: JAI Press.

Bazerman, M. H., and M. Neale. (1992). *Negotiating rationally*. New York: Free Press.

Ben- Ze'ev, A. (2000). *The subtlety of emotions*. Cambridge: MIT Press.

Brett, J. M. (2000). Culture and negotiation. *International Journal of Psychology, 35,* 97–104.

Brett, J. M., and T. Okumura. (1998). Inter- and intra-cultural negotiations: US and Japanese negotiators. *Academy of Management Journal, 41,* 495–510.

Brockner, J., and E. T. Higgins. (2001). Regulatory focus theory: Implications for the study of emotions at work. *Organizational Behavior and Human Decision Processes, 86,* 35–66.

Brodt, S. E., and C. H. Tinsley. (1998). *The roles of frames, schemas, and scripts in understanding conflict across cultures*. Unpublished manuscript.

Cookie, S. W., Stephan, W. G., Saito, I., and Barnett, S. M. (1998). Emotional expression in Japan and the United States. *Journal of Cross Cultural Psychology, 6,* 728–748.

Csikszentmihalyi, M., and R. Larson. (1987). Validity and reliability of the experience sampling method. *Journal of Nervous and Mental Disease, 175,* 526–536.

D'Andrade, R. (1981). The cultural context of cognition. *Cognitive Science, 5,* 179–185.

Davidson, M. N., and L. Greenhalgh. (1999). The role of emotion in negotiation: The impact of anger and race. In R. B. Bies, R. J. Lewicki, and B. H. Sheppard (Eds.), *Research on negotiation in organizations* (Vol. 7, pp. 3–26). Greenwich, CT: JAI Press.

Davitz, C. R. (1969). *The language of emotion*. San Diego, CA: Academic Press.

Deutsch, M. (1975). Equity, equality, and need: What determines which value will be used as the basis for distributive justice? *Journal of Social Issues, 31,* 137–149.

Eid, M., and E. Diener. (2001). Norms for experiencing emotions in different cultures: Inter- and intranational differences. *Journal of Personality and Social Psychology, 81,* 869–885.

Forgas, J. P. (2000). Introduction: Affect and social cognition. In J. P. Forgas (Ed.), *Handbook of affect and social cognition* (pp. 1–24). Mahwah, NJ: Erlbaum.

Frijda, N. H. (1986). *The emotions*. Cambridge: Cambridge University Press.

Gavazzi, I. G., and K. Oatley. (1999). The experience of emotions of interdependence and independence following interpersonal errors in Italy and Anglophone Canada. *Cognition and Emotion, 13,* 49–63.

Gelfand, M. J., and N. Dyer. (2000). A cultural perspective on negotiation: Progress, pitfalls, and prospects. *Applied Psychology: An International Review, 49,* 62–99.

Gelfand, M. J., Nishii, L. H., Holcombe, K. M., Ohbuchi, K., and M. Fukuno. (2001). Cultural influences on cognitive representations of conflict: Interpretations of conflict episodes. *Journal of Applied Psychology, 86,* 1059–1074.

Gelfand, M. J., and A. Realo. (1999). Individualism–collectivism and accountability in intergroup negotiations. *Journal of Applied Psychology, 84,* 721–736.

George, J. M., Jones, G. R., and J. A. Gonzales. (1998). The role of affect in cross cultural negotiations. *Journal of International Business Studies, 29,* 749–783.

Gottman, J. M. (1993). Studying emotion in social interaction. In M. Lewis and J. M. Haviland (Eds.), *Handbook of emotions* (pp. 475–487). New York: Guilford.

Graham, J. L., and Y. Sano. (1984). *Smart bargaining: Doing business with the Japanese.* New York: HarperBusiness.

Grimm, S. D., Church, T., Katigbak, M. S., Alberto, J., and S. Reyes. (1999). Self-described traits, values, and moods associated with individualism and collectivism. *Journal of Cross-cultural Psychology, 30,* 466–500.

Higgins, E. T. (2000). Promotion and prevention experiences: Relating emotions to non emotional motivational states. In J. P. Forgas (Ed.), *Handbook of affect and social cognition* (pp. 186–211). Mahwah, NJ: Erlbaum.

Higgins, E. T., Shah, J., and R. Friedman. (1997). Emotional responses to goal attainment: Strength of regulatory focus as a moderator. *Journal of Personality and Social Psychology, 72,* 515–525.

Keltner, D., and J. Haidt. (1999). Social functions of emotion at multiple levels of analysis. *Cognition and Emotion, 13,* 505–522.

Kornadt, H. J. (1990). Aggression motive and its developmental condition in eastern and western cultures. In N. Bleichrodt and P. J. D. Drenth (Eds.), *Contemporary issues in cross-cultural psychology.* Berwyn, PA: Swets and Zeitlinger.

Kumar, R. (1997). The role of affect in negotiations: An integrative overview. *The Journal of Applied Behavioral Science, 33,* 84–100.

Kumar, R. (1999a). Communicative conflict in intercultural negotiations: The case of American and Japanese business negotiations. *International Negotiation Journal, 4,* 63–78.

Kumar, R. (1999b). A script theoretical analysis of international negotiating behavior. In R. J. Bies, R. J. Lewicki, and B. H. Sheppard (Eds.), *Research on negotiation in organizations* (pp. 285–311). Greenwich, CT: JAI Press.

Larsen, R. J., and B. L. Fredrickson. (1999). Measurement issues in emotion research. In D. Kahneman, E. Diener, and N. Schwarz (Eds.), *Well-being: The foundations of hedonic psychology* (pp. 40–60). New York: Russell Sage Foundation.

Lawler, E. J., and J. Yoon. (1993). Power and the emergence of commitment behavior in negotiated exchange. *American Sociological Review, 58,* 465–481.

Lazarus, R. S. (1991). *Emotion and adaptation.* New York: Oxford University Press.

Lee, A. Y., Aaker, J. L., and W. L. Gardner. (2000). The pleasures and pains of distinct self-construals: The role of interdependence in regulatory focus. *Journal of Personality and Social Psychology, 78,* 1122–1134.

Leung, K. (1997). Negotiation and reward allocation across cultures. In P. C. Earley and M. Erez (Eds.), *New perspectives on international/industrial organizational psychology* (pp. 640–675). San Francisco: New Lexington.

Levenson, R. W. (1988). Emotion and the autonomic nervous system: A prospectus for research on autonomic specificity. In H. L. Wagner (Ed.), *Social psychophysiology and emotion: Theory and clinical applications* (pp. 17–42) Chichester, England: Wiley.

Lewicki, R. J., McCallister, D. J., and R. J. Bies. (1998). Trust and distrust: New relationships and realities. *Academy of Management Review, 23,* 438–458.

Maio, G. R., and V. M. Esses. (2001). The need for affect: Individual differences in the motivation to approach or avoid emotions. *Journal of Personality, 69,* 583–615.

Mandler, G. (1975). *Mind and emotion.* New York: Wiley.

Markus, H. R., Kitayama, S., and R. J. Heiman. (1996). Culture and "basic" psychological principles. In E. T. Higgins and A. W. Kruglanski (Eds.), *Social psychology: Handbook of basic principles* (pp. 57–913). New York: Guilford.

Markus, H. R., and S. Kitayama. (1991). Culture and the self: Implications for cognition, emotion, and motivation. *Psychological Bulletin, 98,* 221–253.

———. (Eds.). (1994). *Emotion and culture: Empirical studies of mutual influence.* Washington DC: American Psychological Association.

Matsumoto, D. (1996). *Unmasking Japan: Myths and realities about the emotions of the Japanese.* Stanford, CA: Stanford University Press.

Mesquita, B. (2001). Emotions in collectivist and individualist cultures. *Journal of Personality and Social Psychology, 80,* 68–74.

Mesquita, B., Frijda, N. H., and K. R. Scherer. (1997). Culture and emotion. In J. W. Berry (Ed.), *Handbook of cross cultural psychology: Vol. 2. Basic processes and human development* (pp. 254–297). Boston: Allyn and Bacon.

Miller, J. G. (1984). Culture and the development of everyday self regulation. *Journal of Personality and Social Psychology, 46,* 961–978.

Morris, M. W., and D. Keltner. (2000). How emotions work: The social functions of emotional expression in negotiations. In B. M. Staw (Eds.), *Research in Organizational Behavior,* vol. 22, (pp. 1–50), Greenwich, CT: JAI Press.

Morris, M. W., Leung, K., Ames, D., and B. Lickel. (1999). Views from inside and outside: Integrating emic and etic insights about culture and justice judgment. *Academy of Management Review, 24,* 781–796.

Nisbett, R. E., Peng, K., Choi, I., and A. Norenzayan. (2001). Culture and systems of thought: Holistic vs. analytic cognition. *Psychological Review, 108,* 291–310.

Oatley, K., and P. N. Johnson-Laird. (1996). The communicative theory of emotions. In L. L. Martin and A. Tesser (Eds.), *Striving and feeling: Interactions among goals, affect, and self-regulation* (pp. 363–366, 372–380) Mahwah, NJ: Erlbaum.

Oliver, R. L., Balakrishnan, P. V., and B. Barry. (1994). Outcome satisfaction in negotiation: A test of expectancy disconfirmation, *Organizational Behavior and Human Decision Processes, 60,* 252–275.

Ortony, A., Clore, G. L., and A. Collins. (1988). *The cognitive structure of emotions.* New York: Cambridge University Press.

Reis., H. T., Collins, A. A., and E. Berscheid. (2000). The relationship context of human behavior and development. *Psychological Bulletin, 126,* 844–872.

Roseman, I. J. (1991). Appraisal determinants of discrete emotions. *Cognition and Emotion, 5,* 161–200.

Salovey, P., and J. D. Mayer. (1990). Emotional intelligence. *Imagination, cognition, and personality, 9,* 185–211.

Solomon, R. (1989). The emotions of justice. *Social Justice Research, 3,* 345–374.

Tinsley, C. (1998). Models of conflict resolution in Japanese, German, and American cultures. *Journal of Applied Psychology, 83,* 316–323.

Triandis, H. C. (1977). *Interpersonal behavior.* Monterey, CA: Brooks/Cole.

Triandis, H. C. (1995). *Culture and social behavior.* New York: McGraw-Hill.

Triandis, H. C. (2000). Culture and conflict. *International Journal of Psychology, 35,* 145–152.

Triandis, H. C., Kurowski, L. L., and M. J. Gelfand. (1994). Workplace diversity. In H. C. Triandis, M. D. Dunnette, and L. M. Hough (Eds.), *Handbook of industrial and organizational psychology* (Vol 4), (pp. 769–827). Palo Alto, CA, Consulting Psychologists.

Watson, D., and L. A. Clark. (1984). Negative affectivity: The disposition to experience aversive emotional states. *Psychological Bulletin, 96,* 465–490.

Weiner, B. (1985). An attributional theory of achievement, motivation, and emotion. *Psychological Review, 92,* 548–573.

CHAPTER 5

Motivation in Negotiation
A SOCIAL PSYCHOLOGICAL ANALYSIS

Carsten K. W. De Dreu

STARTING WITH THE PIONEERING WORK BY, among others, Siegel and Fouraker (1960), Kelley (1966), and Deutsch (1958), social psychologists have examined a host of variables explaining individuals' suboptimal information processing, inadequate strategic choice, and difficulty in reaching integrative agreements in negotiation. Critical in many of these studies is how negotiation processes, including information processing and strategic choice, varies as a function of motivation—the focused and persistent energy that drives cognition and behavior (Mook, 2000). Motivation is indeed central to negotiation—it is difficult, if not impossible to imagine an individual entering a negotiation without some motivational goal that he or she is pursuing, implicitly or explicitly, unconsciously or consciously. It is the discrepancy between the current situation and the desired goal that motivates negotiators to engage in certain activities, including information search and processing, and strategic choice.

The purpose of this chapter is to review recent research on motivation and negotiation and to highlight areas for future research. Although there are a great variety of motivational goals that individuals in negotiation pursue, some are more central and have received more attention in research than others. Specifically, I review the influence of three broad classes of motivation and their influence on information processing and strategic choice in negotiation: (a) social motivation, or the need to attain certain distributions of outcomes between oneself and the other party; (b) epistemic motivation, or the need to develop a rich and accurate understanding of the world; and

Preparation of this manuscript was supported by a grant from the Netherlands Foundation for Scientific Research (NWO 490-22-173).

(c) impression motivation, or the need to induce and maintain a certain impression of oneself and the other party. In a fourth section, I consider possible linkages between these three classes of motivation, discuss changes in motivation that may occur during negotiation, and discuss avenues for future research.[1]

Before discussing these three broad classes of motivation, it may be useful to briefly consider what is meant by strategic choice and information processing. Although negotiators have a variety of different tactics and strategies to choose from, most researchers have considered it useful to distinguish between distributive, claiming behavior, and integrative, creating behavior (Carnevale and Pruitt, 1992; Lax and Sebenius, 1986; Pruitt and Rubin, 1986; Thompson, 1990; Walton and McKersie, 1965). Distributive behavior is concerned with the division and allocation of available resources and involves using persuasive arguments, using bluffs and threats, power play, and making positional commitments. Integrative behavior is concerned with the creation of resources and the reconciliation and integration of (seemingly) opposed interests. It involves logrolling, exchange of information about preferences and priorities, and creative problem solving.

Information processing in negotiation can be broken down into (1) the encoding, storage, and retrieval of information available before or during a negotiation; (2) the search for new information; and (3) the use of decision rules and cognitive shortcuts. Motivation affects information processing in two ways. First, it drives the encoding, storage, and retrieval of information, leading to motivational bias in what is attended to and what is recalled. For instance, someone who is motivated to save face is likely to attend to information about possibilities to save face, and to information suggesting that loss of face can be avoided. Second, motivation drives the depth of information processing, leading to the occurrence of cognitive biases including reasoning errors and the use of suboptimal decision heuristics. For instance, when stakes are very high, a negotiator may more carefully scrutinize the situation before making a concession than when the stakes are not so high. In the sections that follow, the influence of motivation on both strategic choice and information processing will be reviewed.

Social Motivation

Social motives are defined as the negotiator's preference for particular outcome distributions between him- or herself and the opponent. A variety of social motives can be distinguished, including altruistic, competitive, individualistic, and cooperative motives (McClintock, 1977). Social motives derive from the combined positive or negative concern about one's own outcomes and the positive or negative concern about the interdependent other individual's outcomes. When both one's own and the other's outcomes are valued, the individual is said to have a cooperative, or prosocial, motive. When both outcomes are positively valued and the other's outcomes are disregarded or negatively valued, one could say this person has a selfish motive.

Many studies on social dilemmas, conflict, and negotiation have relied on the more crude distinction between selfish and prosocial motivation (e.g., Carnevale and Lawler, 1986; De Dreu and Van Lange, 1995; Van Lange and Kuhlman, 1994; Weingart, Bennet, and Brett, 1993). Selfish motivation comprises both competitive and purely individualistic goals, and prosocial motivation comprises both cooperative and purely altruistic goals. In the case of selfish motivation, individuals try to maximize their own outcomes, and they have no (or negative) regard for the outcomes obtained by their opposing negotiator. Individuals with a selfish motive tend to see the negotiation as a competitive game in which power and personal success is key. Negotiators with a prosocial motive try to establish a fair distribution that maximizes both one's own and another's outcomes, and they see the negotiation as a collaborative game in which fairness, harmony, and joint welfare is key.

Social motives may be rooted in individual differences in social value orientation (De Dreu and Van Lange, 1995; McClintock, 1977; Messick and McClintock, 1968). Social value orientation can be assessed through a decomposed game methodology—a measurement technique that has been demonstrated to have good internal consistency, test–retest reliability, and construct validity (Van Lange, 1999). Using this method, usually about 50 percent of the participants are classified as prosocial, 40 percent are classified as individualistic, and 5 to 10 percent are classified as competitive. Individualistic and competitive participants are often lumped together into a selfish category.

Related to social value orientation are measures of agreeableness and need for affiliation (Langner and Winter, 2001), and also measures used to assess individual differences in allocentrism–individualism (see Brett and Kopelman, Chapter 19, this volume, for a discussion of culture and social motives). Carnevale, Probst, and Triandis (1998) found positive correlations between the measure of individualism and the measure of proself responding in the decomposed game method, and positive correlations between responses on the allocentrism scales and prosocial value orientations. Similarly, Hulbert, Correa da Silva, and Adegboyega (2001) found that allocentrism was positively associated with a tendency to minimize differences between oneself and an interdependent other (prosocial values). Individualism was negatively correlated to the tendency to minimize differences.

In addition to individual differences in social value orientation, need for affiliation, and allocentrism, social motives may be cued by instructions from superiors, reinforcement schemes, or social relationships. For example, Deutsch (1958) used instructions to induce prosocial and egoistic motives. In the prosocial motive condition, participants were instructed to be concerned about the other's feelings and welfare, and to see the other as a "partner." In the selfish motive condition, participants were instructed to disregard the other and to do as well for themselves as possible. Other research has used monetary incentives to induce social motives. Participants in prosocial motive conditions are told that payment depends on how they do as a dyad, whereas participants in the selfish motive conditions are told that payment depends on how they do personally (see, e.g., Weingart et al., 1993). Other ways to manipulate social motives are to emphasize shared (versus different) group membership, to have negotiators anticipate (or not) future interaction with their opponent, or to have them negotiate with a friend (versus stranger) (for detailed discussions, see Deutsch, 1973; Pruitt, 1998).[2]

SOCIAL MOTIVATION AND STRATEGIC CHOICE

Ample research has examined the influence of social motivation on strategic choice in conflict and negotiation settings. Two theories are particularly relevant and provided the basis for many studies. These are the theory of cooperation and competition (Deutsch, 1949, 1973) and dual concern theory (Pruitt and Rubin, 1986).

The *theory of cooperation and competition* (Deutsch, 1949, 1973) sees social motives as the key to problem-solving behavior and integrative negotiation. It argues that selfish negotiators develop distrust, hostile attitudes, and negative interpersonal perceptions. They use persuasive arguments, positional commitments, threats, bluffs, and coercive power to get their way. Prosocial individuals, by contrast, develop trust, positive attitudes, and perceptions; engage in constructive exchange of information; listen; and seek to understand one another's perspective. As a result, prosocially motivated negotiators are more likely to uncover possibilities for trade-off and to realize integrative potential (Deutsch, 1973; Tjosvold, 1998).

Several studies have found support for these tenets. For instance, De Dreu and Van Lange (1995) found that prosocial individuals made more concessions and perceived their opponent as more fair and trustworthy than selfish negotiators. Olekalns et al. (1996) examined the influence of social value orientation in a face-to-face integrative negotiation task and found that prosocial negotiators tended toward more lenient opening offers, yet obtained higher personal as well as joint gain than selfish negotiators (see also Beersma and De Dreu, 1999; Weingart et al., 1993). Finally, Gillespie,

Brett, and Weingart (2000), finally, examined satisfaction with outcomes from the negotiation. They found that relative to those with a prosocial orientation, selfish negotiators were less satisfied with the group outcome. Thus, together, these studies show support for the theory of cooperation and competition. Prosocial negotiators take a more cooperative approach, give their opponent the benefit of the doubt, and reach higher personal and joint gain, with which they are relatively also satisfied, than do selfish negotiators.

More recent work on social motives has drawn on another theoretical tradition, the dual concern theory (Pruitt and Rubin, 1986). It postulates two kinds of concern, other concern and self-concern, each ranging in strength from weak to strong. Other concern is closely related to the concept of social motive, with selfish negotiators having weak other concern and prosocial negotiators having strong other concern (Pruitt, 1998). Self-concern is closely related to "toughness," resistance to yielding (Kelley et al., 1967), and the negotiator's intransigence about concession making (Druckman, 1994).[3] As Kelley et al., (1967) noted: "This resistance is felt by each party at each point throughout the negotiation session and has implications for his concession-making propensities at each point" (p. 382). Figure 5.1 presents the dual concern theory graphically. As can be seen, the model is similar to the circumplex of social motives discussed earlier, but differs in that negative concern for one's own or other's outcomes is left out of the analysis (for a more elaborate comparison, see Van de Vliert, 1997).

Like the theory of cooperation and competition, dual concern theory predicts that when parties have a prosocial rather than a selfish motive, they are likely to develop positive interpersonal attitudes and perceptions, to seek understanding of another's point of view, and to make and reciprocate concessions. However, dual concern theory predicts differences in behavior and outcomes depending on the negotiators' level of resistance to yielding. When a prosocial motive is paired with low resistance to yielding, unilateral concession making dominates and parties either accept the other party's demands or settle on an (obvious) fifty–fifty compromise. When a prosocial motive is paired with high resistance to yielding, however, parties face the dilemma of wanting good outcomes for the other, but not at their own expense. As a result, they concede slowly and engage in various kinds of problem solving (such as exchanging information) that promotes the discovery and development of integrative solutions.

De Dreu et al., (2000b) provided a quantitative evaluation of the dual concern theory. The independent variables in this study were social motive (prosocial vs. selfish) and resistance to yielding (high vs. low vs. unknown) and the dependent variables were contentious behavior,

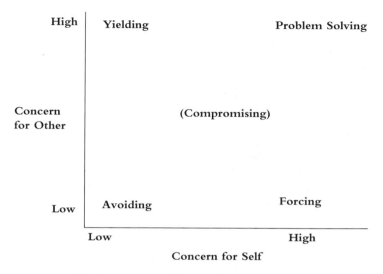

FIGURE 5.1. Dual concern model

problem-solving behavior, and joint outcomes from the negotiation. The authors concluded that with regard to negotiation outcomes, the dual concern theory makes valid predictions—social motives affect negotiation behavior and outcomes, but more when resistance to yielding is high rather than low.

SOCIAL MOTIVATION AND COGNITIVE PROCESSES

In addition to its influence on strategic choice, social motives affect cognitive processes in negotiation. For example, Camac (1992) studied how social value orientation influenced the recall of the values in a prisoner's dilemma game. Participants were classified as prosocial or selfish, and they played a prisoner's dilemma game. Afterward they were shown the dilemma again, with their own and the other's payoffs being eliminated, and they were asked to provide as good an estimate of the payoffs as possible. Results showed that accuracy of recall was consistent with social value orientation—people with a prosocial value orientation recalled the joint gain in four cells quite accurately, whereas people with a selfish orientation recalled their own gain in the four cells best. This suggests that social value orientation biases attention, encoding, and retrieval processes.

A similar conclusion derives from a negotiation study by De Dreu and Boles (1998). They measured individuals' social value orientation and classified individuals as prosocial or as selfish. Participants believed they would enter a negotiation, and they prepared for it by reading the instructions for the standard integrative negotiation task, already discussed. At the end of these instructions, a list of cooperative and competitive decision heuristics was presented. Participants subsequently engaged in a set of unrelated tasks and then were asked to recall as many decision heuristics as they could. Results showed that prosocial negotiators recalled more cooperative than competitive heuristics, while selfish negotiators recalled more competitive than cooperative heuristics.

Another indication that social motives influence individual-level cognition derives from a series of studies by Carnevale and Probst (1998). They found that expectations of conflict can result in a "freezing" of cognitive schemas. The expectation of conflict can reduce general problem-solving abilities, and it can produce rigid, black–white thinking. However, in nonconflict settings, prosocial individuals, compared to competitive and individualistic people, have greater cognitive flexibility and they are more open-minded. In conflict settings, however, competitive people were most likely to alter their thinking in response to the social context. That is, they were highly flexible in their thinking when the context was cooperative and they needed to work with the other party, and they were very rigid in their thinking when the context was competitive and they needed to win from the other. Prosocial individuals were relatively flexible in their thinking regardless of the specific context in which they were placed.

Van Kleef and De Dreu (2002) examined how social motives influence information search. In two experiments, they studied the questions negotiators ask their opponent as a function of knowledge about the opponent's personality (cooperative, competitive, unknown) and the negotiator's own social value orientation (prosocial vs. selfish). In one experiment, participants selected questions about another's cooperation or another's competition from a prewritten list. In another experiment, participants generated questions themselves and these were coded as dealing with the other's cooperative or competitive tendency. Social motives did not influence the amount of questions asked. However, negotiators engaged in confirmatory search, such that they asked about competition when the other was competitive and about cooperation when the other was cooperative. When another's goals were unknown, negotiators relied on their own orientation—selfish negotiators asked about competition and prosocial negotiators asked about cooperation.

The studies reviewed thus far strongly suggest that individuals in conflict and negotiation search, encode, and retrieve information consistent with their prosocial or selfish motivation. Also, prosocial and selfish negotiators engage in confirmatory information search likely to support their initial assumptions and beliefs. All this suggests that social motive moderates ego defensiveness—selfish negotiators fall prey to motivational biases that strengthen their egocentric tendencies, while prosocial individuals develop motivational bias geared toward equality, consensus, and joint gain.

Epistemic Motivation

To deal with their cognitively and emotionally taxing situation, negotiators can and often do use a "quick and dirty" strategy when processing information, arriving at usually reasonable approaches to the situation efficiently and effortlessly (see Thompson, Neale, and Sinaceur, Chapter 1, this volume). Alternatively, negotiators can try hard to think deeply about the situation, sometimes arriving at qualitatively different approaches than the "quick and dirty" strategy would have suggested.

Making a distinction between shallow and systematic processing of information is consistent with dual process models (Chaiken and Trope, 1999). These models assume that the extent to which individuals engage in systematic information processing depends on their epistemic motivation— the desire to develop and hold accurate and well-informed conclusions about the world. As such, it is argued that negotiators with high epistemic motivation are more likely to engage in deliberate, deep, and systematic processing of available information, and they search additional information about the task and their opponent. Negotiators with low epistemic motivation, in contrast, are more likely to engage in heuristic processing of information.

Epistemic motivation relates to (lack of) need for cognitive closure, which is central to lay-epistemic theory developed by Kruglanski and associates (Kruglanski, 1989; Kruglanski and Webster, 1996; Webster and Kruglanski, 1994). It argues that there exists a single dimension underlying the desire for different kinds of knowledge, termed need for cognitive closure. Individuals at the high need for closure end of the continuum are characterized by considerable cognitive impatience, leaping to judgment on the basis of inconclusive evidence and rigidity of thought. At the other end of the continuum, individuals with low need for closure may prefer to suspend judgment, engaging in extensive information search and generating multiple interpretations for known facts. In other words, individuals with high need for cognitive closure may be more likely to use cognitive heuristics in making judgments and decisions than individuals with low need for cognitive closure. The latter instead postpone judgment until they have processed as much information as possible, or until time and energy is depleted.

In addition to chronic preferences for cognitive closure, situational cues may affect epistemic motivation as well. Within lay epistemic theory (Kruglanski, 1989), it is assumed that epistemic motivation is lower when the individual is exposed to distracters such as noise, time pressure, or extreme temperatures. Others have suggested that epistemic motivation increases when the task becomes more involving (cf. Petty and Cacioppo, 1986), when there is process accountability (Tetlock, 1992), or when one finds oneself in a low-power position (Fiske, 1992). As to the latter, the argument is that when people depend on others they may (re)gain control over their own outcomes by paying close attention to the powerful other so as to be able to accurately predict and anticipate the other's intentions and behaviors.

Taken together, epistemic motivation is defined as the desire to acquire a full and accurate understanding of the world. Epistemic motivation is related to accuracy motivation, and to the need for cognitive closure. It has its roots in individual differences, including the need for cognition and the need for cognitive closure. Situational cues may, however, temporarily induce a particular level of epistemic motivation.

EPISTEMIC MOTIVATION AND COGNITIVE PROCESSES

In contrast to the work on social motivation, research considering epistemic motivation primarily focused on cognitive processes and ignored strategic choice. Therefore, in this section I will focus on research findings concerning information processing. Clearly, research is needed to address the effects of epistemic motivation on strategic choice.

It was argued that epistemic motivation affects information processing in negotiation such that higher levels of epistemic motivation lead to more deliberate and sophisticated information processing. Put differently, it is predicted that the negotiator's tendency to rely on simplifying decision heuristics, and to engage in erroneous reasoning, is moderated by his or her epistemic motivation. Results reported by De Dreu, Koole, and Oldersma (1999) are consistent with this general prediction. These authors examined the influence of need for cognitive closure on anchoring and adjustment (Experiment 1) and stereotyping in negotiation (Experiment 2). In Experiment 1, participants in the high (low) anchor condition were, prior to negotiation, told that some participants in earlier sessions had reached agreements that valued around 11,000 (3,000) points (with 14,000 being the maximum). Results showed that participants made more concessions in the case of low anchor values, but only when they had high need for cognitive closure. In Experiment 2, psychology students were told that their opponent majored in business or theology. Psychology students hold more competitive beliefs about business majors than about religion majors (De Dreu et al.,

1995c). Results showed, accordingly, that participants made smaller concessions when the opponent was a business student, and this tendency was stronger when participants had high rather than low need for cognitive closure.

Recent work by Galinsky and Mussweiler (2001) provided another indication that motivating negotiators to consider information carefully moderates their tendency to use heuristic cues in judgment and decision making. Across three experiments, whichever party made the first offer obtained a better outcome, suggesting that the first offer in a negotiation provides an important anchor value. In addition, first offers were a strong predictor of final settlement prices. It is interesting that when the negotiator who did not make a first offer focused on information that was inconsistent with the implications of their opponent's first offer, the advantageous effect of making the first offer was eliminated. Thinking about one's opponent's alternatives to the negotiation, one's opponent's reservation price, or one's own target, all negated the effect of first offers on outcomes. Thus, anchoring processes in negotiation are eliminated when negotiators are stimulated to think carefully before proceeding with making offers and counteroffers.

We have argued that time pressure and fatigue reduces epistemic motivation and increase reliance on heuristics and erroneous reasoning. De Dreu (2003) tested this idea. In Experiment 1, time pressure (high vs. low) was crossed with information about the opponent's group membership (business student vs. religion student). Individuals placed higher demands when they faced a business rather than a religion student, especially when time pressure was acute rather than mild. In Experiment 2, time pressure was either high or low, and prior to and immediately following the negotiation, fixed-pie perceptions were measured. Results showed more accurate perceptions (i.e., less fixed-pie error) at the end of the negotiation and more integrative agreements when time pressure was mild rather than acute.

Impression Motivation

Impression motivation is usually defined as the desire to make a good impression on the other and to get along (Snyder, 1992; Tetlock and Manstead, 1985). However, in the context of negotiation, individuals may be highly motivated to convey the impression of a tough negotiator not to be trifled with (Wall, 1991). A manager may be motivated to convey the image of a tough negotiator, only to avoid his or her employees trying to negotiate about every single task assignment or allocation decision. Likewise, a personnel officer overseeing salary negotiations may prefer the image of a tough negotiator rather than the image of a friendly and compliant person who likes to please others.

Impression motivation can be rooted in individual differences or vary as a function of the situation. For example, individuals high in self-monitoring have more impression-management concerns than individuals low in self-monitoring (e.g., Snyder, 1992). Likewise, individuals with collectivist values are more concerned with face than individuals with individualist values (Triandis, 1989). Brown (1968) showed that negotiators are willing to incur substantial cost to "save face" and impress an audience.

With regard to situational cues, negotiation research has considered accountability to constituents—the need to account to constituents the outcomes one obtained from the negotiation. Negotiators under outcome accountability tend to be more competitive with their opponent, presumably because they want to impress their constituents by winning the negotiation (e.g., Carnevale, Pruitt, and Seilheimer, 1981; but see Gelfand and Realo, 1999, and Morris and Gelfand, Chapter 2, this volume). Constituent surveillance tends to increase negotiator competitiveness, apparently because negotiators make greater effort to impress their constituents (Carnevale, Pruitt, and Britton, 1979).

IMPRESSION MOTIVATION AND STRATEGIC CHOICE

Insight into the consequences of impression management also comes from research on attribution processes in negotiation. A good example is research by Baron (1985), who examined the consequences of negotiators suggesting that their tough behavior is due to either their own decisions (an internal attribution) or to their organization's policy (i.e., the "my hands are tied ploy," an external attribution). Results showed more concession making in the internal attributions condition than in the external attributions condition. Related to this work is research on the so-called good-cop/bad-cop strategy, a strategy that involves a cooperative and a competitive stance, often assumed by two different negotiators played out sequentially (e.g., Hilty and Carnevale, 1993). The cooperative–competitive sequence elicits most concessions, perhaps because embedding a competitive strategy within a cooperative context makes the competitive strategy loom particularly tough, thus inducing the most concessions (Hilty and Carnevale, 1993). In other words, embedding a competitive stance within an otherwise cooperative strategy may evoke the impression of someone who is willing to work together yet demands important concessions in return. Such an impression appears rather effective when it comes to getting the opponent to concede.

IMPRESSION MOTIVATION AND COGNITIVE PROCESSES

Few studies on impression management in negotiation have considered cognitive processes. An exception is a study by Jordan and Roloff (1997). Negotiators were classified as being high or low in self-monitoring, and negotiators scoring high on a self-monitoring scale engaged more in planning of impression management (e.g., "Be friendly so he'll think I'm giving him a good deal"). More important, results showed positive correlations between self-monitoring and the variety of strategies and tactics negotiators thought of prior to the negotiation. It appeared that self-monitoring and concomitant impression motivation makes negotiators creative and flexible in their strategic thinking. Ohbuchi and Fukushima (1997) found self-monitoring to be associated with more integrative negotiation, albeit only when there was mild (rather than acute) time pressure. Integrative behavior can be seen as requiring substantial cognitive flexibility. Thus, it appears that impression motivation is related to cognitive and motivational biases in conflict and negotiation, but research is needed to further develop this idea.

Future Directions: On Linkages Among Motives and Changes in Motivation

The three preceding sections considered social motivation, epistemic motivation, and impression motivation in isolation, and discussed these motives as if they were static. In this section, the interrelationship between the motives as well as the way in which motives may change overtime is considered as important areas of future research.

CORRELATIONS BETWEEN MOTIVATIONS

Cognitive processes and strategic choices are influenced by more than one motivational goal. In fact, certain variables have a dual (or even triple) role, in that they affect social, epistemic, and impression motivation simultaneously. A good example is power: low-power negotiators were argued to have higher epistemic motivation and to be more concerned with impression management than were powerful negotiators. Furthermore, there is some evidence that power asymmetry makes selfish motivation more likely than power balance (Giebels et al., 2000).

That certain variables have effects on more than one motivational goal is not to say that these motivational goals are necessarily related. In fact, there is increasing evidence that the three classes of motivational goals discussed in this chapter are unrelated and that negotiators may have more or less epistemic motivation regardless their social motive or their desire to make a specific kind of impression. For example, De Dreu et al., (2000a) manipulated process accountability in a face-to-face integrative negotiation task. Manipulation checks confirmed that negotiators under process accountability had higher levels of epistemic motivation than negotiators not held accountable.

In two experiments, process accountability did not influence self-reported social motivation. Likewise, research has found no significant correlations between individual differences and epistemic and social motivation. In three different samples, De Dreu et al., (1999) examined the relationship between individual differences in the need for cognitive closure on the one hand, and social value orientation on the other. Results showed that need for cognitive closure did not differ as a function of social value orientation in either sample.

That social motives are unrelated to epistemic motivation has interesting implications for future research. For instance, it begs the questions how prosocial (selfish) negotiators differ in their strategic choices and information processing tendencies when they have high rather than low epistemic motivation. We saw that social motivation biases information search and encoding, and it might be that epistemic motivation either amplifies this tendency set forth by the negotiator's social motivation. Alternatively, it may be that epistemic motivation attenuates the biasing influence of social motivation on information processing and strategic choice, because under high levels of epistemic motivation people tend to consider the situation from multiple perspectives and rely less on cognitive heuristics.

Future research is needed also to examine the interrelations between social and epistemic motivation on the one hand, and impression motivation on the other. It may be that impression motivation is unrelated to social motives. However, it is likely that prosocial negotiators desire to convey a different image of themselves than selfish negotiators—perhaps even that selfish negotiators adopt and convey images that serve their own interests best, and thus are more flexible than prosocial negotiators when it comes to impression motivation.

SHIFTS IN MOTIVATIONAL GOALS

Negotiation is dynamic and inherently social in nature, and it cannot be excluded that in the course of the negotiation motivational goals change (Weingart et al., 2001) and new motivational concerns arise (Chaiken et al., 2001). For example, negotiators may have high epistemic motivation prior to the negotiation, when they prepare their case. Once the negotiation starts, they may switch to a state of relatively high need for cognitive closure with concomitant low epistemic motivation. Likewise, a negotiator may start the negotiation with the selfish goal of doing well for him- or herself. In the course of the negotiation, he or she may come to like the opponent and switch to a more prosocial motive. Finally, as Wall (1991) noted, negotiators may be motivated to build an image of themselves as a tough person, but simultaneously try to induce into their opponent the impression of a likeable and friendly person who can be trusted and "isn't out to get him or her."

Several studies implicitly or explicitly point to shifts in social motives. Research by Pinkley and Northcraft (1994) examined shifts in conflict frame over time. Their study showed that negotiators who start with a different representation of the conflict than their opponent converged in the course of the interaction toward one and the same conflict frame (for similar findings and extensions, see De Dreu, Carnevale, Emans, and Van de Vliert, 1994). Thus, when one party sees the negotiation as problem solving and the other sees it as a competitive game, one or the other is going to change the representation and adopt the opponent's conflict frame. Research by Weingart et al., (2001) indicated that four-person groups containing one selfish negotiator become over time as selfish as groups containing two or more selfish negotiators. This suggests that selfish motivation is more likely to dominate the negotiation than a prosocial negotiation, despite the fact that prosocial motivation facilitates the discovery of mutually beneficial, integrative agreements.

Most deep changes occur when participants (have to) take time to reflect upon current practice and modes of conduct (Carter and West, 1998). In a similar vein, Walton and McKersie (1965) observed that labor–management negotiations often begin with distributive, claiming behavior. After a while, when costly impasse looms, negotiators switch to more integrative strategies. Recent experiments have revealed similar patterns of "differentiation–before–integration" in settings other than labor–management negotiations only (Brett, Shapiro, and Lytle, 1998; Harinck, De Dreu, and Van Vianen, 2000).

Although it has not been tested, the work on ripeness and differentiation before integration suggests that the negotiators' level of epistemic motivation may change as a function of the occurrence and duration of (temporary) impasse. When the parties reach an impasse, they have the time to reflect upon their current strategies, realize current practices may lead nowhere, and face the cost of not reaching an agreement. The desire to better understand the task and one's opponent increases, and higher level of epistemic motivation translates into higher levels of problem-solving behavior, more sophisticated information processing, and, ultimately, greater probability of finding an integrative agreement.

Although the preceding paragraphs contain many reasonable hypotheses about shifts in epistemic, social, and impression motivation, very little research exists that speaks to these issues directly. We know far too little about the ways in which motivation changes in negotiation. We need to know what makes goals change and under what conditions change is more or less likely. Future research could study these issues by taking a closer look at interaction processes and communication sequences in negotiation (see Weingart and Olekalns, Chapter 6; Adair and Brett, Chapter 7, this volume).

Future research is also needed to connect and integrate the current motivational analysis with a renewed emphasis on affect and emotion. The discussion thus far, and much of the research on conflict and negotiation, has ignored the role of emotions. Emotions involve physiological reactions, action tendencies, and subjective experience (Lazarus, 1991), and they can be considered as an antecedent to, and a by-product of, motivation (Frijda, 1993). For example, fear produces the desire to leave the situation, and happiness produces the desire to preserve the situation. Also, receiving lower outcomes than one's opponent, frustrates one's desire to come out ahead and, hence, produces dissatisfaction (Gillespie et al., 2000; Thompson, Nadler, and Kim, 1999).

Studies considering affect and emotion as triggers of behavior have focused on positive versus negative moods and emotions. Although positive affect, empathy, and happiness appears to induce prosocial motivation, negative affect, anger, and frustration seems to make people more egoistic and self-centered (see Barry, Fulmer, and Van Kleef, Chapter 3, this volume, for a discussion of the influence of emotion on tactics and outcomes in negotiation). In a similar vein, it may be that fear and surprise enhance epistemic motivation in conflict and negotiation settings, but research is needed to examine this.

Perhaps one of the biggest challenges for researchers interested in motivational processes in negotiation is to examine cross-cultural differences and similarities in motivation. Although it is reasonable to assume that individuals across cultures can have prosocial or selfish motivation, that they are more or less concerned about impressions they make, and have high or low epistemic motivation, there is accumulating evidence that individuals across cultures differ in their tendencies to adopt some motivational goals. When dealing with others seen as belonging to one's ingroup, individuals from collectivist cultures appear more likely to assume prosocial goals than individuals from individualist cultures. Also, there is evidence that individuals from collectivist cultures have greater concern for "face" (see Morris and Gelfand, Chapter 2, this volume). Future research is needed to address these issues in full and should focus in particular on the question of whether it is the motivation that differs across culture, or the specific operations that people in different cultures use to pursue their motivational goals.

Summary and Conclusions

The research reviewed in this chapter reveals the importance of motivation in negotiation in several ways. Without claiming to be exhaustive, I have shown that epistemic motivation, social motivation, and impression motivation together form the motivational framework within which negotiators think and act. Based on this review, we can draw the following conclusions:

1. Negotiators with a prosocial rather than selfish motivation are more likely to engage in integrative negotiation, and unlikely to engage in contentious behavior, especially when they have high resistance to concession making.
2. Negotiators with a prosocial motivation have a preference to search, provide, and process "cooperative information"; negotiators with a selfish motivation have a preference for "competitive information." Negotiators with a prosocial motivation are not more or less likely than negotiators with a selfish motivation to engage in deep and systematic processing of new information.
3. Negotiators with high epistemic motivation are more likely to process new information in a systematic and thorough way, and they are less likely to rely on heuristic cues that have no true relevance to the negotiation situation.
4. Negotiators with high epistemic motivation are more likely to take a passive and distant approach, while the strategic choices made by negotiators with low epistemic motivation are more active and focused.

The list of conclusions contains none referring to impression motivation because research in this area is relatively scarce and not very well developed. Although some excellent writing exists on impression motivation (e.g., Wall, 1991), the concept appears in its infancy. To do justice to the fact that impression motivation has both a directional and a nondirectional element to it, I suggest considering it in terms of a matrix composed of high versus low motivation to manage an impression and a desire to induce a positive versus a negative image. Research is needed to examine the ways in which information processing and strategic choice in negotiation varies as a function of the importance attached to either a positive or negative image.

As mentioned at the outset, it is almost impossible to imagine an individual walking into a negotiation without some sort of goal or purpose, however vague or implicit. Motivation is inherent to negotiation, and we cannot understand negotiation without an understanding of basic motivational forces that drive negotiator cognition and strategic choice.

Notes

1. It is important to note that other motivational goals exist. For instance, it has been argued that disputants are motivated to attain a particular aspiration level (Siegel

and Fouraker, 1960), which induces "resistance to concession making" (Kelley, Beckman, and Fisher, 1967). It has been suggested further that negotiators are motivated to be consistent and to reduce cognitive dissonance (Ross and Ward, 1995), to protect their "face" (Brown, 1977), to develop and maintain a positive self-image (Kramer, Pommerenke, and Newton, 1993), and to avoid being taken advantage of (Coombs, 1987). Furthermore, when parties to a conflict want to be treated with respect, they strive for a fair distribution of outcomes (Tyler and Blader, Chapter 14, this volume) and they are motivated to take another's perspective (Chaiken et al., 2001; Kemp and Smith, 1994). Some of these motives can be subsumed under either epistemic, social, or impression motivation. Others (i.e., fairness goals) are discussed in Tyler and Blader (Chapter 14, this volume).

2. In a meta-analytical review of the studies on social motivation in integrative negotiation, De Dreu et al., (2000b) contrasted effects on joint outcomes of individual differences (mainly social value orientation), incentives, instructions, and implicit cues (group membership, future interaction, friend vs. stranger). All four categories yielded positive and significant effect sizes, indicating that prosocial negotiators achieved higher joint outcomes than selfish negotiators. It is important that De Dreu et al., found no significant differences in effect sizes between the four classes. This suggests that the various ways of manipulating or measuring social motives in negotiation are *functionally equivalent*—they may have different roots, but similar effects.

3. In dual concern theory, high (versus low) resistance to yielding is usually operationalized by giving negotiators high (versus low) aspirations or limits below which they should not concede (e.g., Pruitt and Lewis, 1975; Siegel and Fouraker, 1960; Yukl, 1974). A meta-analytical review by Druckman (1994) further showed higher resistance to yielding when negotiators are subject to low (rather than high) time pressure, or when they are accountable to constituents rather than to their opposing negotiator. Pruitt (1998) reviewed evidence to suggest that negotiators also have high (rather than low) resistance to yielding when prospective outcomes from the negotiation are framed as losses rather than gains.

Works Cited

Baron, R. A. (1985). Reducing organizational conflict: An incompatible response approach. *Journal of Applied Psychology, 70,* 434–441.

Beersma, B., and C. K. W. De Dreu. (1999). Negotiation processes and outcomes in prosocially and egoistically motivated groups. *International Journal of Conflict Management, 10,* 385–402.

Blake, R., and J. S. Mouton. (1964). *The managerial grid.* Houston, TX: Gulf.

Brett, J. M., Shapiro, D. L., and A. L. Lytle. (1998). Breaking the bonds of reciprocity in negotiations. *Academy of Management Journal, 41,* 410–424.

Brown, B. R. (1968). The effects of need to maintain face on interpersonal bargaining. *Journal of Experimental Social Psychology, 4,* 107–122.

———. (1977). Face-saving and face-restoration in negotiation. In D. Druckman (Ed.), *Negotiations* (pp. 275–300). Beverly Hills, CA: Sage.

Camac, C. (1992). Information preferences in a two-person social dilemma. In W. Liebrand, D. Messick, and H. Wilke (Eds.), *Social dilemmas: Theoretical issues and research findings* (pp. 147–161). Berlin: Springer-Verlag.

Carnevale, P. J., Pruitt, D. G., and S. Seilheimer. (1981). Looking and competing: Accountability and visual access in integrative bargaining. *Journal of Personality and Social Psychology, 40,* 111–120.

Carnevale, P. J., and E. J. Lawler. (1986). Time pressure and the development of integrative agreements in bilateral negotiations. *Journal of Conflict Resolution, 30,* 636–659.

Carnevale, P. J., and D. G. Pruitt. (1992). Negotiation and mediation. *Annual Review of Psychology, 43,* 531–582.

Carnevale, P. J., Probst, T. M., and H. C. Triandis. (1998). Social values and social conflict in creative problem solving and categorization. *Journal of Personality and Social Psychology, 74,* 1300–1309.

Carnevale, P. J. D., Pruitt, D. G., and S. D. Britton. (1979). Looking tough: The negotiator under constituent surveillance. *Personality and Social Psychology Bulletin, 5,* 118–121.

Carter, S., and M. A. West. (1998). Reflexivity, effectiveness, and mental health in BBC-TV production teams. *Small Group Research, 29,* 583–601.

Chaiken, S., and Y. Trope. (Eds.). (1999). *Dual-process theories in social psychology.* New York: Guilford.

Chaiken, S., Gruenfeld, D. H., and C. M. Judd. (2001). Persuasion in negotiations and conflict situations. In M. Deutsch and P. T. Coleman (Eds.), *The handbook of conflict resolution* (pp. 144–165). San Francisco: Jossey-Bass.

Coombs, C. H. (1987). The structure of conflict. *American Psychologist, 42,* 355–363.

De Dreu, C. K. W., and T. Boles. (1998). Share and share alike or winner take all? Impact of social value orientation on the choice and recall of decision heuristics in negotiation. *Organizational Behavior and Human Decision Processes, 76,* 253–267.

De Dreu, C. K. W., Carnevale, P. J., Emans, B. J. M., and E. Van de Vliert. (1994). Effects of gain-loss frames in negotiation: Loss aversion, mismatching, and frame adoption. *Organizational Behavior and Human Decision Processes, 60,* 90–107.

De Dreu, C. K. W., and P. A. M. Van Lange. (1995). The impact of social value orientations on negotiator cognition and behavior. *Personality and Social Psychology Bulletin, 21,* 1178–1188.

De Dreu, C. K. W., Yzerbyt, V., and J-Ph. Leyens. (1995c). Dilution of stereotype-based cooperation in mixed-motive interdependence. *Journal of Experimental Social Psychology, 21,* 575–593.

De Dreu, C. K. W., Koole, S., and F. L. Oldersma. (1999). On the seizing and freezing of negotiator inferences: Need for cognitive closure moderates the use of heuristics in negotiation. *Personality and Social Psychology Bulletin, 25,* 348–362.

De Dreu, C. K. W., Koole, S., and W. Steinel. (2000a). Unfixing the fixed-pie: A motivated information processing of integrative negotiation. *Journal of Personality and Social Psychology, 79,* 975–987.

De Dreu, C. K. W., Weingart, L. R., and S. Kwon. (2000b). Influence of social motives on integrative negotiation: A meta-analytical review and test of two theories. *Journal of Personality and Social Psychology, 78,* 889–905.

Deutsch, M. (1949). A theory of cooperation and competition. *Human Relations, 2,* 199–231.

———. (1958). Trust and suspicion. *Journal of Conflict Resolution, 2,* 265–279.

———. (1973). *The resolution of conflict: Constructive and destructive processes.* New Haven, CT: Yale University Press.

Druckman, D. (1994). Determinants of compromising behavior in negotiation: A meta-analysis. *Journal of Conflict Resolution, 38,* 507–556.

Fiske, S. T. (1992). Controlling other people: The impact of power on stereotyping. *American Psychologist, 48,* 621–628.

Frijda, N. H. (1993). Moods, emotion episodes, and emotions. In M. Lewis and J. M. Haviland (Eds.), *Handbook of emotions* (pp. 381–403). New York: Guilford.

Galinsky, A. D., and T. Mussweiler. (2001). First offers as anchors: The role of perspective-taking and negotiator focus. *Journal of Personality and Social Psychology, 81,* 657–669.

Gelfand, M. J., and A. Realo. (1999). Individualism-collectivism and accountability in intergroup negotiations. *Journal of Applied Psychology, 84,* 721–736.

Giebels, E., De Dreu, C. K. W., and E. Van de Vliert. (2000). Interdependence in negotiation: Impact of exit options and social motives on distributive and integrative negotiation. *European Journal of Social Psychology, 30,* 255–272.

Gillespie, J. J., Brett, J. M., and L. R. Weingart. (2000). Interdependence, social motives, and outcome satisfaction in multiparty negotiation. *European Journal of Social Psychology, 30,* 779–797.

Harinck, F., De Dreu, C. K. W., and A. E. M. Van Vianen. (2000). The impact of issue content on fixed-pie perceptions, problem solving and integrative outcomes in negotiation. *Organizational Behavior and Human Decision Processes, 81,* 329–358.

Hilty, J. A., and P. J. Carnevale. (1993). Black-hat/white-hat strategy in bilateral negotiation. *Organizational Behavior and Human Decision Processes, 55,* 444–469.

Hulbert, L. G., Correa da Silva, M. L., and G. Adegboyega. (2001). Cooperation in social dilemmas and allocentrism: A social values approach. *European Journal of Social Psychology, 31,* 641–658.

Jordan, J. M., and M. E. Roloff. (1997). Planning skills and negotiator goal accomplishment: The relationship between self-monitoring and plan generation, plan enactment, and plan consequences. *Communication Research, 24,* 31–63.

Kelley, H. H. (1966). A classroom study of the dilemmas in interpersonal negotiations. In K. Archibald (Ed.), *Strategic interaction and conflict: Original papers and discussion* (pp. 49–73). Berkeley, CA: Institute of International Studies.

Kelley, H. H., Beckman, L. L., and C. S. Fischer. (1967). Negotiation the division of reward under incomplete information. *Journal of Experimental Social Psychology, 3,* 361–389.

Kramer, R. M., Pommerenke, P., and E. Newton. (1993). The social context of negotiation. *Journal of Conflict Resolution, 37,* 633–654.

Kruglanski, A. W. (1989). The psychology of being "right": The problem of accuracy in social perception and cognition. *Psychological Bulletin, 106,* 395–409.

Kruglanski, A. W., and D. M. Webster. (1996). Motivated closing of the mind: "Seizing" and "freezing." *Psychological Review, 103,* 263–283.

Langner, C. A., and D. G. Winter. (2001). The motivational basis of concessions and compromise: Archival and laboratory studies. *Journal Of Personality And Social Psychology, 81,* 711–727.

Lax, D. A., and J. K. Sebenius. (1986). *The manager as negotiator: Bargaining for cooperation and competitive gain.* New York: Free Press.

Lazarus, R. S. (1991). *Emotion and adaptation.* Oxford, England: Oxford University Press.

McClintock, C. (1977). Social motives in settings of outcome interdependence. In D. Druckman (Ed.), *Negotiations: Social psychological perspective* (pp. 49–77). Beverly Hills, CA: Sage.

Messick, D. M., and C. McClintock. (1968). Motivational bases of choice in experimental games. *Journal of Experimental Social Psychology, 4,* 1–25.

Mook. J. (2000). *Motivation.* New York: Prentice Hall.

Ohbuchi, K.-I., and O. Fukushima. (1997). Personality and interpersonal conflict: Aggressiveness, self-monitoring, and situational variables. *International Journal of Conflict Management, 8,* 99–113.

Olekalns, M., Smith, P. L., and T. Walsh. (1996). The process of negotiating: Strategy and timing as predictors of outcomes. *Organizational Behavior and Human Decision Processes, 68,* 68–77.

Petty, R. E., and J. T. Cacioppo. (1986). The elaboration likelihood model of persuasion. In L. Berkowitz (Ed.), *Advances in Experimental Social Psychology* (Vol. 19, pp. 123–205). New York: Academic Press.

Pinkley, R. L., and G. B. Northcraft. (1994). Conflict frames of reference: Implications for dispute processes and outcomes. *Academy of Management Journal, 37,* 193–205.

Pruitt, D. G. (1998). Social conflict. In D. Gilbert, S. T. Fiske, and G. Lindzey (Eds.), *Handbook of social psychology* (4th ed., Vol. 2, pp. 89–150). New York: McGraw-Hill.

Pruitt, D. G., and S. A. Lewis. (1975). Development of integrative solutions in bilateral negotiation. *Journal of Personality and Social Psychology, 31,* 621–633.

Pruitt, D. G., and J. Z. Rubin. (1986). *Social conflict: Escalation, stalemate, and settlement.* New York: Random House.

Raiffa, H. (1982). *The art and science of negotiation.* Cambridge, MA: Belknap.

Ross, L., and A. Ward. (1995). Psychological barriers to dispute resolution. In M. Zanna (Ed.), *Advances in Experimental Social Psychology* (Vol. 27, pp. 255–304). San Diego, CA: Academic Press.

Schelling, T. C. (1960). *The strategy of conflict.* Boston: Harvard University Press.

Siegel, A. E., and L. E. Fouraker. (1960). *Bargaining and group decision making.* New York: McGraw-Hill.

Snyder, M. (1992). Motivational foundations of behavioral confirmation. *Advances in Experimental Social Psychology, 25,* 67–114.

Tetlock, P. E. (1992). The impact of accountability on judgment and choice: Toward a social contingency model. In L. Berkowitz (Ed.), *Advances in experimental social psychology* (Vol. 25, pp. 331–376). New York: Academic Press.

Tetlock, P. E., and A. S. R. Manstead. (1985). Impression management versus intrapsychic explanations in social psychology: A useful dichotomy? *Psychological Review, 92,* 59–77.

Thompson, L. L. (1990). Negotiation behavior and outcomes: Empirical evidence and theoretical issues. *Psychological Bulletin, 108,* 515–532.

———. (1995). "They saw a negotiation:" Partisanship and involvement. *Journal of Personality and Social Psychology, 68,* 839–853.

Thompson, L. L., Nadler, J., and P. H. Kim. (1999). Some like it hot: The case for the emotional negotiator. In L. L. Thompson, J. M. Levine, and D. M. Messick (Eds.), *Shared cognition in organizations: The management of knowledge* (pp. 139–161). Mahwah, NJ: Erlbaum.

Tjosvold, D. (1998). Cooperative and competitive goal approach to conflict: Accomplishments and challenges. *Applied Psychology, 46,* 285–342.

Triandis, H. C. (1989). Self and social behavior in differing cultural contexts. *Psychological Review, 96,* 269–289.

Van de Vliert, E. (1997). *Complex interpersonal conflict behavior.* London: Psychology Press.

Van Kleef, G. A., and C. K. W. De Dreu. (2002). Social value orientation and confirmatory information search in negotiation. *International Journal of Conflict Management, 13,* 59–77.

Van Lange, P. A. M. (1999). The pursuit of joint outcomes an equality in outcomes: An integrative model of social value orientations. *Journal of Personality and Social Psychology, 77,* 337–349.

Van Lange, P. A. M., and M. D. Kuhlman. (1994). Social value orientations and impressions of partner's honesty and intelligence: A test of might versus morality effect. *Journal of Personality and Social Psychology, 67,* 126–141.

Wall., J. A. (1991). Impression management in negotiations. In R. A. Giacalone and P. Rosenfeld (Eds.), *Applied impression management: How image-making affects managerial decisions* (pp. 163–187). London: Sage.

Walton, R. E., and R. McKersie. (1965). *A behavioral theory of labor negotiations: An analysis of a social interaction system.* New York: McGraw-Hill.

Webster, D., and A. W. Kruglanski. (1994). Individual differences in need for cognitive closure. *Journal of Personality and Social Psychology, 67,* 1049–1062.

Weingart, L. R., Bennett, R. J., and J. M. Brett. (1993). The impact of consideration of issues and motivational orientation on group negotiation process and outcome. *Journal of Applied Psychology, 78,* 504–517.

Weingart, L. R., Brett, J. M., and M. Olekalns. (2001, September). *Social motives in small group negotiations.* Presentation to the University of Amsterdam, Department of Psychology.

Yukl, G. A. (1974). The effects of situational variables and opponent concessions on a bargainer's perception, aspirations, and concessions. *Journal of Personality and Social Psychology, 29,* 227–236.

PART TWO

Social Processes

MOVING BEYOND basic psychological processes, the four chapters in Section 2 examine negotiation as a *social process*. Together, the chapters provide a window into the dynamics of how parties communicate and sequence their actions when managing social conflict, as well as how culture affects such social dynamics.

In Chapter 6, Weingart and Olekalns examine communication patterns through a number of lenses, including communication frequencies, sequences, and phases, showing that they each provide unique and complementary information about negotiation processes. For example, studying the frequency of communication can reveal the tactics negotiators are emphasizing and the overall effects that tactics have on negotiation outcomes. Negotiation sequences capture the social dynamics of the negotiation and reveal the cue and response pattern embedded in the negotiators' communications. Negotiation phases illuminate how negotiators' focus shifts over time as the negotiator progresses toward settlement or impasse. Throughout their chapter, Weingart and Olekalns take a contextual perspective, illustrating how different situational conditions can affect the patterns of frequencies, sequences, and phases of negotiation communication. They address such questions as: How do situational factors such as the role of negotiators, time pressure, and relationships among negotiators affect communication patterns? How do communication patterns vary as a function of task characteristics (e.g., types and number of issues) and negotiator characteristics (e.g., social motives and expertise)? All in all, their chapter urges us to take a dynamic and contextual view of communication in order to understand negotiation processes.

In Chapter 7, Adair and Brett argue that communication is cultural because people from different cultures rely on distinct signs, symbols, and norms when exchanging information. They advance a model that incorporates two cultural constructs—independent versus interdependent self-construals, and high versus low context communication—to explain how communication in negotiation varies across cultures. They point out that culture influences the nature of self-construals, and consequently, the frames and goals that individuals adopt in negotiations. They also illustrate that culture affects communication, with negotiators in the East tending to share information indirectly and making emotional appeals, and negotiators in the West tending to share information directly and making rational appeals. Following the conceptual lead of Weingart and Olekalns, the authors then develop a number of interesting propositions regarding how these two elements of culture affect the frequency, sequences, and stages of behavior in deal-making negotiations. For example, they illustrate that there are multiple paths to obtaining joint gains in negotiation and that negotiators in different cultures use different strategies to get there. U.S. negotiators achieve higher joint gain when they share information directly, whereas Japanese negotiators achieve higher joint gain when they share information indirectly. Through their cross-cultural analyses, they broaden our understanding of the social dynamics of negotiation.

In Chapter 8, Shapiro and Kulik provide a historical overview of theories of dispute resolution, discussing the dual concern model, and the interest–rights–power (IRP) theory of dispute resolution, which captures the dynamic way in which parties combine strategies to resolve disputes. Although differing in their orientations, both of these theories have made important contributions to the study of conflict management. Nevertheless, Shapiro and Kulik question their relevance to much modern-day disputing. They argue, for example, that these theories falsely assume that parties in disputes each have a "face," or, in other words, know who the "self" and "others" are in a conflict. They also point out that not only do disputants' goals and strategies differ from those delineated in classic conflict resolution theory, but disputants may have much less discretion over the types of strategies at their disposal in modern contexts. It is difficult, for example, to carry out interest-based negotiation when parties cannot talk to one another but rather must signal their intentions. The authors argue that classic dispute resolution theory also takes for granted that talking with the opponent is a more effective and power-enhancing strategy than avoiding the opponent. Rather, they contend that in modern-day disputing, parties to a conflict often use a *diffused* voice in which they express views to a generalized public and use avoidance strategies in order to gain power. All in all, the authors' analysis implores us to redefine the very notions of "conflict" and "disputing" and to broaden our theories and interventions to better capture the dynamics of disputes in the modern era.

In Chapter 9, Tinsley extends classic dispute resolution theory by adopting a cultural perspective. She advances a cultural-fit model that posits that the use of different interests, rights, and power strategies is a function of the congruence that exists between the assumptions of these strategies and the dominant value patterns that exist in the larger culture. For example, she argues that the assumptions of interest-based strategies—namely, that disputants' underlying interests take precedent over collective interests, all parties interests are equally legitimate, and parties can express their interests—are all congruent with American values of individualism, egalitarianism, and direct communication. From this perspective, it is not surprising that interest-based strategies tend to be preferred over rights or power strategies in the United States. By contrast, rights-based strategies tend to be preferred in cultures that value explicit contracting, such as Germany, wherein dominant cultural values stress the importance of adhering to abstract, generalized principles that can serve parties in the long term. Tinsley's analysis also illustrates how considerations of national culture can help to expand IRP theory. For example, she argues that there is no theoretical imperative that the interests-based strategy must be based only on individual interests; rather, this strategy may be based on group interests in collectivistic cultures. With these considerations in mind, she concludes her chapter with a cost–benefit of IRP strategies and illuminates the conditions under which each of these strategies are most likely to be effective.

CHAPTER 6

Communication Processes in Negotiation
FREQUENCIES, SEQUENCES, AND PHASES

Laurie R. Weingart and Mara Olekalns

ALTHOUGH DEFINITIONS of negotiation vary in their form and content, one thing many have in common is a focus on negotiation as a *process.* For example, Lax and Sebenius (1986) defined negotiation as "a *process* of potentially opportunistic interaction by which two or more parties, with some apparent conflict, seek to do better through jointly decided action than they could otherwise" (*p. 11*). Despite definitional attention, the process of negotiation, or the ways in which negotiators communicate in their search for an agreement, has received less research attention than have inputs (e.g., negotiator characteristics, styles, cognitions, motives, goals; contextual features, culture) and outcomes of negotiation (distribution of resources, integrativeness of agreements).

Communication behaviors in negotiation can be characterized as tactics, as they are employed in service of a goal. However, tactics are not used in isolation, but rather in combination, either consciously or unconsciously to form a strategy. The way in which tactics are combined to form a strategy or the way strategies are employed to reach a goal is reflected in the form of the communication. By form, we mean the pattern of communication, that is, how frequently distributive or integrative tactics are used, when different tactics are introduced, and the sequencing of goal-oriented communications over time. Recent research suggests that frequency, phasing, and sequencing of communications shape how settlement is reached (Donohue and Roberto, 1996).

In this chapter, we focus on the form of negotiator communication. Regardless of whether negotiation processes are modeled as frequencies, sequences, or phases, it is important to understand the influence of exogenous factors in order to predict how a negotiation process will begin and unfold over time. We consider three general categories as input factors: (1) the situational context, which includes the role of constituents, time pressure, and past and future relationship among the negotiators; (2) task characteristics, including the number and types of issues and their integrative potential; and (3) negotiator characteristics, including social motives, and expertise. In the next chapter, Adair and Brett consider how national culture influences negotiation processes.

The Emergent Nature of Negotiation Through Communication: Its Form

Negotiation processes emerge through the communication between the negotiating parties. The majority of the literature has focused on verbal behaviors—what one party says to the other. When aggregated within the individual, these messages provide information about the sender's strategy. When aggregated across parties, the messages provide information about process of the negotiation—the general approach being taken to the negotiation (often represented by *frequencies* of tactics), the influence of one party on the other (captured by the *sequences* of tactics), or the flow of the negotiation toward solution (as passing through *phases* of negotiation). Each approach differs in terms of how the negotiation process is characterized.

The first way of characterizing negotiations is to view integrative and distributive processes as separable approaches to the task (Putnam, 1990). This model is based on the assumption that, to a large extent, negotiators' goals at the start of a negotiation shape their strategic choices. Negotiators who start with the goal of maximizing joint gain use integrative tactics proportionately more frequently than negotiators who start with the goal of maximizing individual gain. These latter negotiators use proportionately more distributive tactics. As a result of these early strategic choices, negotiators establish either an integrative or a distributive dynamic for the entire negotiation. Although establishing a negotiation dynamic does not imply that negotiators will use only distributive or integrative tactics, it does imply that one of these strategic approaches will dominate the negotiation.

A second way of characterizing the negotiation process is to view integrative and distributive strategies as interdependent components of a single strategy (Putnam, 1990). This approach recognizes that most negotiations have both distributive and integrative elements, and that negotiators attempt to satisfy the dual goals of maximizing joint and personal gain (Lax and Sebenius, 1986; Walton and McKersie, 1965) or of reaching agreement and achieving high-quality outcomes (Hyder, Prietula, and Weingart, 2000).

This model focuses the level of analysis on how negotiators sequence their tactics, viewing negotiation as a series of actions and reactions where recurring patterns "constrain interaction by reducing the probability that other categories of talk will occur" (Putnam, 1983, p. 469).

The third characterization of negotiation processes also deals with the temporal component of negotiations but at a more aggregated level—in terms of negotiation phases (Douglas, 1962; Gulliver, 1979; Holmes, 1992; Morley and Stephenson, 1977). *Phase models* suggest that a negotiation progresses through an evolutionary process (Putnam, 1990) that blends integration and distribution. Two types of phase models, stage models and episodic models, differ in how phases are defined (Holmes, 1992). *Stage models* assume that negotiations pass through a series of predictable stages on the path to agreement: issue definition, problem solving, and resolution (Holmes, 1992). *Episodic models,* in comparison, look for unified periods of coherent activity, such as an uninterrupted series of offers. Using this approach, a phase is defined on the basis of a clearly identifiable pattern of tactics with an explicit beginning and ending (Baxter, 1982). Thus, a major distinction between stage and episodic models is that stage models treat phases as fixed, whereas episodic models treat phases as flexible, allowing variations in both their lengths and the order in which they occur.

In the next section we review the literature on frequencies, sequences, and phases separately and discuss their antecedents and consequences for negotiation outcomes.

Frequency of Negotiation Tactics and Strategies

Much of the research on negotiation processes reflects a frequency perspective. These studies have examined the effect of strategy and tactics on outcomes, exogenous inputs on strategy and tactics, and the interactive relationships between exogenous inputs, strategy or tactics, and outcomes.

OUTCOME EFFECTS

There is considerable evidence that the frequency with which integrative or distributive tactics are used is associated with the level of joint gain. Negotiators who engage in integrative tactics such as information exchange, concession exchange, and relationship building achieve high joint gain; those who more frequently use distributive tactics such as demands, threats, and argumentation may fail to optimize outcomes (Hyder et al., 2000; Lewis and Fry, 1977; Pruitt and Lewis, 1975; Putnam and Jones, 1982; Schulz and Pruitt, 1978; Weingart, Thompson, Bazerman, and Carroll, 1990).

Although empirical evidence points to the positive effect of integrative tactics on joint gain, findings regarding the effect of information exchange on joint gains are somewhat mixed. Exchanging information is believed to increase insight into the other party's preferences and the probability that negotiators will find integrative agreements if a zone of agreement exists (Pruitt, 1981; Putnam and Jones, 1982; Walton and McKersie, 1965). Although there is substantial empirical support for this view, a small number of studies suggest there may be a more subtle relationship between information exchange and joint gain (Putnam and Wilson, 1989; Roloff, Tutzauer, and Dailey, 1989; Tutzauer and Roloff, 1988).

Two studies differentiate information about preferences and positions from information about priorities (Olekalns, Smith, and Walsh, 1996; Weingart, Hyder, and Prietula, 1996). This distinction is important because information about positions and preferences is more distributive in that it highlights differences, whereas information about priorities is more integrative in that it identifies potential trade-offs. With this distinction in mind, a reexamination of prior research shows that the positive relationship between information exchange and joint outcomes depends on the nature of the information that negotiators give or seek. Negotiators who rely on the exchange of positional information typically reach agreements of lower joint gain, whereas those who give or seek priority information reach agreements of higher joint gain (Hyder et al., 2000; Olekalns and Smith, 2000; Olekalns et al., 1996; Thompson, 1991; Tutzauer and Roloff, 1988; Weingart et al., 1996). Some research has also looked at the impact of negotiation tactics on impasses. One study showed that impasse groups used higher levels of distributive tactics (contention and positional arguing) and lower levels of integrative tactics (including exchanging priority information and conciliation) than expected (Olekalns and Smith, 2000). Groups that reached low-joint-gain agreements used distributive and integrative tactics with relative frequencies that were similar to impasse dyads. What distinguished the low-joint-gain and impasse dyads was the type of distributive tactics they used. Impasse dyads used both positional argument and contention, whereas low-joint-gain groups did not use contention.

INPUT VARIABLES

Several input variables have been studied in the frequency literature. Two can be classified as negotiator characteristics: social motives and tactical knowledge, and one can be characterized as contextual: the frames of the other party.

First, research has shown that, compared to negotiators who start negotiations with an individualistic orientation, those who start with cooperative orientation use integrative tactics more (information exchange, reciprocal concessions, problem solving) and distributive tactics less (arguments and threats; see De Dreu, Chapter 5, this volume, for an in-depth discussion of social motives and strategic choice).

Second, research has shown that negotiators' tactical knowledge influences frequency of tactical use (Hyder et al., 2000; Thompson, 1991; Weingart et al., 1996). Negotiators who were primed with integrative tactics were more likely to use those tactics than negotiators who were not primed. Furthermore, the use of primed tactics accounted for the joint gain differences between primed and unprimed groups. This pattern of results occurred in dyads in which only one negotiator was primed with instructions to seek or provide information about the importance of issues (Thompson, 1991) and in dyads where both negotiators were primed by being presented with a more comprehensive list of both distributive and integrative tactics (Hyder et al., 2000; Weingart et al., 1996). It is interesting that distributive priming did not influence the use of distributive tactics, suggesting that naive negotiators are already aware of the relevance of distributive tactics to negotiation (Weingart et al., 1996).

Two studies examined characteristics of the other party and the influence of these characteristics on negotiator behavior. In these studies, gain-framed negotiators send different messages to gain- versus loss-framed opponents. Negotiators tend to mention losses more frequently in negotiations with a loss-framed than with a gain-framed opponent (De Dreu, Carnevale, Emans, and Van de Vliert 1994; De Dreu, Emans, and Van de Vliert, 1992).

INPUT VARIABLES AND OUTCOMES

Two studies test interactions among motivational orientation, negotiators' tactics, and joint gains. Both studies report that whereas the level of priority information exchange is positively associated with high joint gain under a cooperative orientation, it is unrelated to the level of joint gain under an individualistic orientation (O'Connor, 1997; Olekalns and Smith, 2003). Both studies conceptualize the input factor (social motive) as the moderator. An alternative interpretation of these results is that, in the absence of priority information, cooperatively oriented dyads perform no better and may perform more poorly than individualistic dyads. These findings suggest that insight into the other party's payoffs, rather than social motive, is the critical variable in determining joint gain (e.g., Thompson and Hastie, 1990; Tutzauer and Roloff, 1988). At least one study has linked insight via multi-issue offers under an individualistic social motive and insight via priority information under a cooperative social motive to joint gain (Olekalns and Smith, 2003). It appears that priority information exchange is a useful strategy for developing insight for cooperative negotiators, perhaps because they are willing to trust the information they receive. Multi-issue offer exchange, a more indirect way of sharing information, may be more useful for obtaining priority information that is less likely to be strategically manipulated by the other party.

Negotiation and Strategic Sequences

The literature on strategic sequences in negotiation identifies three different types of sequences. The first is a reciprocal sequence in which negotiators match each other's moves exactly. For example, priority information from one party elicits priority information from the other party. Researchers interpret frequent reciprocal sequences as evidence that negotiators hold a shared understanding of the negotiation (Putnam, 1990). Whether this understanding is functional or dysfunctional is determined by the nature of this reciprocity. Confirming that we share an integrative strategic perspective is likely to promote high joint gains, whereas confirming that we share a distributive strategic perspective may promote impasse.

The other two types of sequences identified in the negotiation literature are nonreciprocal in nature. These sequences pair dissimilar tactics, although this dissimilarity may occur in one of two ways. The first of these has been described as an action–reaction sequence (Putnam and Jones, 1982) and pairs two tactics drawn from opposing strategic sets. We refer to these sequences as structural sequences. An attack that is met by information giving provides one example of this type of sequence. Several authors have argued that structural sequences can be used to change the negotiating dynamic (Brett, Shapiro, and Lytle, 1998; Neale and Northcraft, 1991; Olekalns and Smith, 2000). The second type of nonreciprocal sequence pairs tactics drawn from similar but not the same strategic set. An example is when an attacking move is followed by a defensive move. Both tactics are distributive, but they are not identical. These sequences do not signal a shared perspective as clearly as reciprocal sequences and so create greater uncertainty about each party's intentions. To the extent that negotiators do not signal a clear distributive strategic orientation, these complementary sequences may help negotiators to break out of an escalating competitive spiral. Conversely, because integrative sequences are highly fragile (e.g., Weingart, Prietula, Hyder, and Genovese, 1999), the ambiguity of motive associated with integrative complementary sequences may prematurely end an integrative strategy. The analysis of strategic sequences in negotiation has received relatively less attention than the analysis of strategic frequencies. However, like the analysis of strategic frequencies, differences in strategic sequences have been linked to negotiation outcomes and input variables.

STRATEGIC SEQUENCES AND OUTCOMES

A small body of research considers the relationship between strategic sequences and negotiation outcomes. Studies comparing resolved and unresolved disputes have consistently shown that these groups are differ-entiated not by their level of integrative reciprocity, but by their level of distributive reciprocity. Not only are impasse dyads more likely to engage in distributive reciprocal sequences of defensive moves such as substantiation, commitment, and retraction, but they are also more likely to use distributive complementary sequences, pairing these defensive strategies with offensive strategies such as threats, attacks, and rejections (Putnam and Jones, 1982). Conversely, impasse dyads are less likely than agreement dyads to use struc-tural sequences (Olekalns and Smith, 2000) and thereby lose the opportunity to restructure the negotiating dynamic.

Several studies address how sequences assist (or inhibit) negotiators in obtaining high joint gain. Generally speaking, reciprocation of distributive tactics leads to more distributive outcomes (Brett et al., 1998), and reciproca-tion of integrative tactics (e.g., process management, priority information) is related to more integrative outcomes (Olekalns and Smith, 2000; Weingart et al., 1990, 1999). Despite these general trends, several differences appear in how negotiators manage information and the harmony of the negotiation relationship. In particular, high-efficiency dyads (high joint gains) manage both information exchange and the negotiating relationship more effectively than low-efficiency dyads (low joint gains). We go on to describe findings that support this argument.

In our discussion of frequencies, we identified the role of the integra-tive tactic, priority information, in increasing joint gain. An examination of how such information is sequenced further clarifies this link. Negotia-tors who obtain high efficiency outcomes differ from those who obtain low efficiency outcomes in two ways: their willingness to reciprocate priority information (Olekalns and Smith, 2000) and their willingness to continue searching for information in the face of negative reactions from the other party (Weingart et al., 1990). Rather than search for additional information in response to negative reactions, as high-efficiency dyads do, negotiators who obtain low-efficiency outcomes suggest trade-offs (Weingart et al., 1990). When faced with resistance, low efficiency dyads appear more willing to take the information available and, perhaps prematurely, suggest an oppor-tunity for trade-off.

Differences in approaches to maintaining the relationship between the parties parallel these differences in information search. If high-efficiency dyads are characterized by their willingness to engage in information search, then low-efficiency dyads are characterized by their willingness to yield to the other party, perhaps in an attempt to maintain the negotiating relationship. In comparison to low-efficiency dyads, high-efficiency dyads introduced an el-ement of distributive strategy either by responding distributively to proposed concessions (Olekalns and Smith, 2000) or by reciprocating threats (Weingart et al., 1990). A critical feature of the negotiation process of high-efficiency dyads is that distributive sequences are embedded in a more clearly integrative context, established through the use of reciprocal priority information (Olekalns and Smith, 2000), reciprocal information requests, and reciprocal trade-offs (Weingart et al., 1999). In summary, the occasional but strategic use of distributive strategy within the context of a clearly established integrative exchange relationship seems to assist negotiators to maximize their outcomes.

INPUT VARIABLES AND STRATEGIC SEQUENCES

Role effects, specifically in terms of labor–management roles, have been found to influence interaction patterns in negotiation. In general, Donohue, Diez, and Hamilton (1984) reported that labor is more likely to attack, whereas management is more likely to defend. However, research shows that when management initiates a behavior (either attacking/offensive or defensive), labor tends to respond in a reciprocal way; when labor initiates, management tends to respond in a complementary way (Donohue et al., 1984; Putnam and Jones, 1982). These findings are suggestive and identify a need to further explore role-based differences in strategic sequences. It seems plausible that differences in the norms implicit in these roles as well as differences in structural power may contribute to the emergence of stable complementary sequences.

The effects of negotiator characteristics on strategic sequences have been examined in terms of negotiators' social motives and tactical knowledge. In general, cooperative dyads (and groups) are just as likely as individualistic dyads (and groups) to reciprocate integrative and distributive behaviors (Olekalns and Smith, 1999; Weingart, Bennett, and Brett, 1993), but there are important subtle differences. A cooperative orientation can help negotiators overcome the constraints of a sequential decision-making process (i.e., discussing one issue at a time) through delayed integrative reciprocity— suggestions for using delayed reciprocity were reciprocated in cooperative, sequential decision-making groups (Weingart et al., 1993). The social motive composition of the dyad also influences how negotiators respond to proposals for restructuring the negotiation (i.e., statements that propose a new way of proceeding, open-ended statements, or request additional information from the other party). Negotiators in individualistic and cooperative dyads respond to such proposals in diametrically opposed ways: Whereas negotiators in individualistic dyads are more likely be supportive of these proposals and less likely to reject them, in cooperative dyads negotiators are more likely to reject them and less likely to express support. Negotiators in mixed-orientation dyads respond to restructuring proposals with an integrative tactic (priority information; Olekalns and Smith, 1999). Similarly, negotiators with tactical knowledge use different strategic sequences than do naïve negotiators. Reciprocity of integrative tactics is more likely (and will last longer) in dyads with integrative tactical knowledge than dyads without, but this will only happen when an integrative strategy already has been established (Weingart et al., 1999). These results suggest that an integrative strategy is a highly fragile process that is difficult to establish and maintain.

On the flip side, distributive strategy is just as difficult to break away from. Tactical knowledge did not influence the reciprocity of distributive tactics in Weingart and her colleagues' study (1999). However, three communication strategies have been identified as effective at breaking conflict spirals: (1) not reciprocating a distributive tactic, (2) reciprocating a distributive tactic in combination with an integrative tactic, and (3) labeling the process as ineffectual (Brett, Shapiro, and Lytle, 1998).

INPUT VARIABLES, STRATEGIC SEQUENCES, AND OUTCOMES

The sequences that shape outcomes differ according to negotiating dyads' social motives (Olekalns and Smith, 2003). Cooperative dyads use the following types of sequences in reaching high-efficiency outcomes: reciprocal process management, reciprocal integrative strategy, and complementary integrative strategy. Cooperative dyads that reach lower efficiency outcomes do not use these sequences. Although these dyads do provide integrative information about priorities, they do so at less appropriate times—in response to proposal modifications or process suggestions—resulting in a looser complementary structure rather than the tighter reciprocal structure used by dyads reaching highly efficient outcomes.

The reverse pattern is evident in individualistic dyads. These dyads are notable in that they do not exhibit any identifiable sequential patterns of tactics (Olekalns and Smith, 2003). Relative to cooperative dyads, high joint gain in individualistic dyads occurs in the absence of several sequences, most notably reciprocal process management, reciprocal integrative sequences (multi-issue offers), and structural sequences shifting from distributive to integrative tactics (positional to priority information exchange). Instead, the introduction of more structured communication through reciprocal distributive tactics (positional arguing) and the complementary pairing of proposal modifications with concessions (perhaps also distributive in nature) leads to low-efficiency outcomes. These findings clearly identify offer-oriented sequences as central to low efficiency outcomes in individualistic dyads. However, these findings provide no insight into the process through which individualistic dyads discover high joint gain.

In sum, the examination of strategic sequences provides insight beyond that obtained from a frequency approach. First, there seems to be one dominant path toward integrative agreements: through reciprocal information exchange and a lack of willingness to compromise. However, there appear to be two paths to inefficient agreements: either contentious reciprocity that leads to impasse or suboptimal agreements, or yielding in an attempt to reach agreement or maintain the relationship. Second, similar to frequencies of behavior, sequences are also influenced by input variables. Negotiator roles and tactical knowledge each influence the ways negotiators respond to one another. Negotiator reactions appear to be influenced by social motives, knowledge, and normative beliefs and expectations. Although cooperatives appear to benefit from the use of reciprocity and restructuring, we know little about how individualists improve joint gain. More research is needed to examine potential social motive effects on strategy sequences in negotiation.

Negotiation Phases and Other Aspects of Time

In his summary of stage models, Holmes (1992) identified three stages in negotiation: initiation, problem solving, and resolution. Several studies examine the relationship between stages and strategy use, independent of outcome. Consistent with the assumptions of a stage model, these studies demonstrate that strategy use varies across negotiation stages. The patterns that emerge, however, also suggest that the precise nature of stages is also context sensitive. When negotiations are distributive (involve a fixed resource pool), negotiators increase their messages to each other over time and also increase the number of proposals and offers immediately before their deadline (Lim and Murnighan, 1994).

In mixed-motive negotiations (i.e., negotiations in which individuals must both create and claim value), proposals increase in a linear fashion over time, with significant increases occurring during the middle (problem-solving) and ending (resolution) stages (Lytle, Brett, and Shapiro, 1999). The use of integrative strategies (interests) peaks during the third quarter of the negotiation (the problem-solving stage; Lytle et al., 1999). Negotiators working on mixed-motive negotiations also tend to cycle in and out of distributive strategies, including the use of rights, power, demands, and concessions (Lytle et al., 1999; Olekalns et al., 1996), although positional arguments occur most frequently in the middle stages of a negotiation (Olekalns et al., 1996). Moreover, increasing integrative tactics over time are associated with integrative agreements, whereas increasing distributive tactics over time are associated with distributive agreements (Olekalns and Smith, 2000; Olekalns et al., 1996; Putnam et al., 1990). Finally, negotiators' roles shape how strategies unfold over time. In a teacher–labor negotiation, teachers and administrators used the same types of arguments, but during different stages and for different purposes (Putnam, Wilson, and Turner, 1990).

In contrast to the fixed-phase approach taken by researchers studying negotiation stages, Holmes takes a more episodic approach in using flexible phase mapping[1] (Poole, 1983; Poole and Roth, 1989) to capture the emergent phases in hostage negotiations (Holmes, 1997; Holmes and Sykes, 1993). Holmes finds that hostage negotiations pass through a series of phases that loosely map onto Gulliver's (1979) phase model, which maps more generally onto the commonly identified phases of initiation, problem solving, and resolution (Holmes, 1992).[2] However, hostage negotiations that are less orderly (e.g., multiple negotiators, problems with communication channels, incoherent participants) begin to depart from the model sequence (Holmes, 1997).

The research on negotiation phases is relatively sparse. A debate exists regarding whether phases should be considered fixed or flexible (Holmes, 1992). Fixed phases, although they allow for more generalizability across studies, have been criticized as being too global to capture the true progression of any given negotiation. Flexible phases allow for the identification of emergent patterns, but limit generalizability. Given that the two approaches complement one another, we believe both approaches are worth pursuing.

Conclusion

Communication in negotiation can be analyzed at three levels: frequencies, sequences, and phases. Because each level aggregates and places structure on the preceding one, we might expect that what happens in terms of the frequency with which strategies are used underpins the structure of sequences and phases. Our review shows this is not the case. Instead, each level of analysis provides unique and complementary insights into the relationship between negotiating context, patterns of communication, and outcomes.

Studies of frequencies of tactics tell us about the strategies employed by aggregating over time. These studies highlight the importance of integrative strategy, especially the tactic of giving and receiving priority information, in reaching high joint gain. We have also learned from these studies that the critical variable for reaching high joint gain is insight into the other party's preferences, and that the strategies that create insight vary as a consequence of the negotiating context.

Sequential approaches inform us about how communication develops and how negotiators respond to one another. By examining the predictability of a tactic given the occurrence of a prior tactic, sequential analyses attempt to understand how negotiations unfold at the level of communication acts. These studies add to our understanding of information exchange in negotiation. They highlight that the type of information that is reciprocated is a central element of the strategic negotiation process (distributive or integrative) and influences levels of joint gain. Analyses of sequences also show that when contention is introduced within a negotiation that is dominated by integrative strategy, dyads improve their joint outcomes. Like frequency studies, sequential analyses show that context influences the way in which negotiators obtain high joint gain. Finally, links between sequences and outcomes show that sequences do not simply add structure to already existing patterns of communication. Instead they provide a vehicle for introducing infrequent strategies, and so restructure the negotiation.

Phase approaches provide information about how the negotiation process shifts over time by examining frequencies of tactics within temporally ordered segments of the negotiation. Our review identified this area as having received the least research attention. Findings in this area demonstrate not only that patterns of communication change over time, but also that the way in which they change affects negotiators' outcome.

When considering frequencies, sequences, and phases simultaneously, several issues arise from this review. First, the distinction between integrative and distributive strategies is useful, but the strategies should not be considered mutually exclusive. There is ample evidence that negotiators use a mix of tactics in their search for agreements. Second, the processes that lead to impasse are somewhat different from those that lead to low-quality agreements. More research is needed for a better understanding of when and why negotiation breakdowns occur. How far does a negotiation progress before the participants believe that there is no room for agreement? Does an impasse in early phases of a negotiation indicate a different process breakdown than one that occurs later in the process? Third, the exchange of priority information repeatedly arises as a central strategy to improve joint gain. This is not surprising given the heavy reliance on scorable tasks in the literature. Negotiation tasks that quantify issues and options typically include integrative issues that can best be realized by trading off. Negotiators often determine what issues to trade off through the exchange of priority information. Thus, it is not surprising that priority information exchange arises as being a central negotiation strategy. Future research needs to find ways to maintain the benefits of quantified negotiations (comparability across observations) while structuring the task to allow for alternative problem-solving strategies (such as bridging interests using creative solutions; see Pruitt, 1981, for other types of integrative agreements).

In this chapter, we have highlighted links between input factors, patterns of communication, and negotiation outcomes. However, empirical studies of these phenomena are in their infancy. Although analyses of sequences and phases show great promise in deepening our understanding of the complex relationships between communication and negotiation outcomes, there are as yet very few systematic studies of these relationships. Much of this research focuses on the strategy–outcome link, and very little addresses the role of context in this relationship. Additional research in each domain is needed to continue to pry open the black box of the negotiation process.

Notes

1. Flexible phase mapping involves the application of researcher-defined parsing rules that identify phases and boundaries between phases.

2. Gulliver's (1979) phases include: searching for an arena, identifying the agenda and issues, exploring the range, narrowing the range, preliminaries to final bargaining; final bargaining, ritualization, and execution.

Works Cited

Baxter, L. A. (1982). Conflict management: An episodic approach. *Small Group Behavior, 13,* 23–42.

Brett, J. M., Shapiro, D. L., and A. L. Lytle. (1998). Breaking the bonds of reciprocity in negotiations. *Academy of Management Journal, 41,* 410–424.

De Dreu, C. K. W., Carnevale, P. J., Emans, B. J. M., and E. Van de Vliert. (1994). Gain–loss frames in negotiation: Loss aversion, mismatching and frame adoption, *Organizational Behavior and Human Decision Processes, 60,* 90–107.

De Dreu, C. K. W., Emans, B. J. M., and E. Van de Vliert. (1992). The influence of own and other's communicated gain or loss frame on negotiation behavior. *The International Journal of Conflict Management, 3,* 115–132.

Donohue, W. A., Diez, M. E., and M. Hamilton. (1984). Coding naturalistic negotiation interaction. *Human Communication Research, 10,* 403–425.

Donohue, W. A. and A. J. Roberto. (1996). An empirical examination of three models of integrative and distributive bargaining. *The International Journal of Conflict Management, 7,* 209–229.

Douglas, A. (1962). *Industrial peacemaking.* New York: Columbia University Press.

Gulliver, P. H. (1979). *Disputes and negotiations: A cross-cultural approach.* Orlando, FL: Academic Press.

Holmes, M. E. (1992). Phase structures in negotiation. In L. L. Putnam and M. E. Roloff (Eds.). *Communication and negotiation* (pp. 83–105). Newbury Park, CA: Sage.

———. (1997). Optimal matching analysis of negotiation phase sequences in simulated and authentic hostage negotiations. *Communication Reports, 10,* 1–8.

Holmes, M. E., and R. E. Sykes. (1993). A test of the fit of Gulliver's phase model to hostage negotiations. *Communication Reports, 44,* 38–55.

Hyder, E. B., Prietula, M. J., and L. R. Weingart. (2000). Getting to best: Efficiency versus optimality in negotiation. *Cognitive Science, 24* (2), 169–204.

Lax, D. A., and J. K. Sebenius. (1986). *The manager as negotiator: Bargaining for cooperation and competitive gain.* New York: Free Press.

Lim, S. G.-S., and K. Murnighan. (1994). Phases, deadlines and the bargaining process, *Organizational Behavior and Human Decision Processes, 58,* 153–171.

Lytle, A. L., Brett, J. M., and D. L. Shapiro. (1999). The strategic use of interests, rights, and power to resolve disputes. *Negotiation Journal, 15* (1), 31–51.

Morley, I., and G. Stephenson. (1977). *The social psychology of bargaining.* London: Allen and Unwin.

Neale, M. A., and G. B. Northcraft. (1991). Dyadic negotiation, *Research on Negotiation in Organizations, 3,* 203–230.

O'Connor, K. M. (1997). Motives and cognitions in negotiation: A theoretical integration and an empirical test. *The International Journal of Conflict Management, 8,* 114–131.

Olekalns, M., and P. L. Smith. (1999). Social value orientations and strategy choices in competitive negotiations, *Personality and Social Psychology Bulletin, 25,* 657–668.

———. (2000). Negotiating optimal outcomes: The role of strategic sequences in competitive negotiations. *Human Communication Research, 24,* 528–560.

———. (2003). Testing the relationships among negotiators' motivational orientations, strategy choices, and outcomes. *Journal of Experimental Social Psychology, 39,* 101–117.

Olekalns, M., Smith, P. L., and T. Walsh. (1996). The process of negotiating: Strategies, timing and outcomes. *Organizational Behavior and Human Decision Processes, 67,* 68–77.

Poole, M. S. (1983). Decision development in small groups, II: A study of multiple sequences in decision making. *Communication Monographs, 50,* 206–232.

Poole, M. S., and J. Roth. (1989). Decision development in small groups, IV: A typology of group decision paths. *Human Communication Research, 15,* 323–356.

Pruitt, D. G. (1981). *Negotiation behavior.* New York: Academic Press.

Pruitt, D. G., and S. A. Lewis. (1975). Development of integrative solutions in bilateral negotiation. *Journal of Personality and Social Psychology, 31,* 621–633.

Putnam, L. L. (1983). Small group work climates: A lag sequential analysis of group interaction. *Small Group Behavior, 14,* 465–494.

Putnam, L. L. (1990). Reframing integrative and distributive bargaining: A process perspective. In B. H. Sheppard, M. H. Bazerman, and R. J. Lewicki, (Eds.), *Research on negotiation in organizations* (Vol. 2, pp. 3–30). Greenwich, CT: JAI Press.

Putnam, L. L., and T. S. Jones. (1982). Reciprocity in negotiations: An analysis of bargaining interaction. *Communication Monographs, 49,* 171–191.

Putnam L. L., and S. R. Wilson. (1989). Argumentation and bargaining strategies as discriminators of integrative outcomes. In M. A. Rahim (Ed.), *Managing conflict: An interdisciplinary approach* (pp. 549–599). Newbury Park, CA: Sage.

Putnam, L. L., Wilson, S. R., and D. B. Turner. (1990). The evolution of policy arguments in teachers' negotiations. *Argumentation, 4,* 129–152.

Roloff, M. E., Tutzauer, F. E., and W. O. Dailey. (1989). The role of argumentation in distributive and integrative bargaining contexts: Seeking relative advantage but at what cost? In M. A. Rahim (Ed.), *Managing conflict: An interdisciplinary approach* (pp. 109–120), New York: Praeger.

Schulz, J. W., and D. G. Pruitt. (1978). The effects of mutual concern on joint welfare. *Journal of Experimental Social Psychology, 14,* 480–492.

Thompson, L. L. (1991). Information exchange in negotiation. *Journal of Experimental Social Psychology, 27,* 161–179.

Thompson, L., and R. Hastie. (1990). Social perception in negotiation, *Organizational Behavior and Human Decision Processes, 47,* 98–123.

Tutzauer, F., and M. E. Roloff. (1988). Communication processes leading to integrative agreements: Three paths to joint benefit, *Communication Research, 15,* 360–380.

Walton, R. E., and R. B. McKersie. (1965). *A behavioral theory of labor negotiations: An analysis of a social interaction system.* New York: McGraw-Hill.

Weingart, L. R., Bennett, R. J., and J. M. Brett. (1993). The impact of consideration of issues and motivational orientation in group negotiation process and outcome. *Journal of Applied Psychology, 78,* 504–517.

Weingart, L. R., Hyder, E. B., and M. J. Prietula. (1996). Knowledge matters: The effect of tactical descriptions on negotiation behavior and outcome. *Journal of Personality and Social Psychology, 70,* 1205–1217.

Weingart, L. R., Prietula, M. J., Hyder, E., and C. Genovese. (1999). Knowledge and the sequential processes of negotiation: A markov chain analysis of response-in-kind. *Journal of Experimental Social Psychology, 35,* 366–393.

Weingart, L. R., Thompson, L. L., Bazerman, M. H., and J. S. Carroll. (1990). Tactical behavior and negotiation outcomes. *The International Journal of Conflict Management, 1,* 7–31.

CHAPTER 7

Culture and Negotiation Processes

Wendi Lyn Adair and Jeanne M. Brett

NEGOTIATION IS A COMMUNICATION PROCESS by which two or more inter-dependent parties resolve some matter over which they are in conflict. Negotiators' strategies and goals are revealed in the content and form of their communication. Communication, the process by which people exchange information through a common system of signs, symbols, and behaviors, is cultural because different social groups have distinct ways of communicating.

In this chapter we review the literature on culture and communication as it relates to negotiation. We suggest that culture affects peoples' beliefs or cognitive representations of what negotiation is all about, for example, reaching agreement about an outcome or building a long-term relationship. We suggest that culture affects the goals people have for negotiation, what they strive for in this interdependent social situation, and what they think is important. We suggest that culture affects the norms people have for negotiation, what they consider appropriate and inappropriate behavior in a negotiation setting. We argue that beliefs, goals, and norms influence communication processes such as negotiation. Following the conceptual lead of Weingart and Olekalns (Chapter 6, this volume) we frame our discussion around the frequency, sequences, and stages of different types of negotiation behavior across cultures.

Culture is a distinctly group construct. Individuals have personalities; groups have cultures. Culture consists of group members' shared beliefs, attitudes, norms, and behaviors, and the group's social, political, economic, and religious institutional structures (Lytle, Brett, Barsness, Tinsely and Janssens, 1995). Social institutions carry culture in their ideology and reinforce it by rewarding and sanctioning social interaction within the group (Brett, 2001).

The research discussed in this chapter was supported by grants from the Dispute Resolution Research Center, Northwestern University.

In this chapter we use national boundaries to identify cultures, because national boundaries define institutional boundaries, and as a result provide an objective way to distinguish cultural groups.

How Culture Affects the Process of Negotiation

CULTURE AND BELIEFS ABOUT NEGOTIATION

People in different cultures use different language to conceptualize or frame negotiation (Gelfand, Nishii, Holcombe, Dyer, Ohbuchi, and Fukuno, 2001; see Pinkley, 1990, for a general discussion of cognitive frames). In many, possibly even most, cultures negotiation is believed to be about distributing resources. Yet, at the same time, people seem to recognize that negotiation can have both a task focus and a relationship focus, that argument may be dominated by rationality or emotion, and that outcomes can be distributive, reflecting one party's interests (win–lose) or integrative, reflecting both parties' interests (win–win). People in all cultures probably have access to all of these different frames for perceiving and interpreting the negotiation process (Gardner, Gabriel, and Lee, 1999; Morris and Gelfand, Chapter 2, this volume). Cues in the context of the social interaction affect which frame dominates their thoughts and behaviors (see Gelfand and Cai, Chapter 11, this volume.) Culture is one such contextual cue.

We propose that culture may explain a negotiator's tendency to think that negotiation is primarily a process of building, reconstructing, and maintaining relationships or a process of distributing resources. This distinction is similar to Pinkley's (1990) dimension of task versus relationship focus and consistent with Wilson and Putnam's (1990) interaction goals (see also Olekalns and Weingart, 2001). These researchers recognize that negotiators have both relational goals and outcome goals. Relational goals emphasize social distance by stressing trust and/or dominance; outcome goals emphasize individual and/or joint gains. Cultural differences in negotiators' relative emphasis on relationship versus outcome may be due to cultural differences in self-construal—how people understand themselves in a social setting (Markus and Kitayama, 1991).

People from Western cultures tend to have independent, also called individualistic, self-construals. They understand themselves as independent or detached from the social groups to which they belong and view themselves as agents free to focus on personal goals to self-actualize rather than on social obligations (Marcus and Kitayama, 1991; Ting-Toomey, 1985). People from Eastern cultures tend to have interdependent, also called collectivist, self-construals. They tend to understand themselves within the context of the social groups to which they belong and view themselves as agents constrained

TABLE 7.1

Culture and Negotiation Processes: A Model

Region	East		West	
Self-construal	Interdependent		Independent	
Communication Norms	High Context		Low Context	
Beliefs	Relationship Building		Distribution of Resources	
Goals	Cooperative trust	Competitive dominance	Cooperative joint gains	Competitive individual gains
Behaviors	Indirect information sharing	Affective influence	Direct information sharing	Rational influence

by social obligations to maintain harmony and preserve "face" within their social groups (Marcus and Kitayama, 1991; Ting-Toomey, 1985).

An independent self-construal seems to be a worldview that is naturally associated with the perspective that negotiation is about distributing resources, not so much about relationships. An interdependent self-construal seems to be a worldview that is naturally associated with the perspective that negotiation is about relationships first, and then about distributing resources.[1] This is the first distinction reflected in our model of culture and negotiation processes (Table 7.1).

For example, Gelfand and Realo (1999) reported that accountability caused collectivists to frame the negotiation cooperatively (win–win), while accountability caused individualistic negotiators to frame the negotiation competitively (win–lose). In this research, the manipulation of accountability seemed to cue culturally normative differences in framing. In another study, Gelfand and Christakopoulou (1999) found that individualistic U.S. negotiators made more extreme offers, indicating they were focused on claiming, and more self-enhancing statements, indicating a focus on the self, whereas collectivist Greek negotiators were more focused on both parties. Graham (1993) also reported that Japanese negotiators (whom we would presume to be more collectivistic) were less likely to make commands and threats, which might indicate a concern with relationship management, than negotiators from several other Western cultures (whom we would presume to be more individualistic).

This leads us to predict that a relationship frame will be more salient for negotiators in Eastern cultures, while a resource distribution frame will be more salient for negotiators in Western cultures. This implies that negotiators in Eastern cultures are more likely to think about negotiation in terms of relationships and that this frame should influence their negotiation goals.

Negotiators in Western cultures are more likely to think about negotiation in terms of outcome, and this frame should influence their negotiation goals.

CULTURE AND NEGOTIATORS' GOALS

Because negotiation is a mixed-motive task (Lax and Sebenius, 1986), cooperation and competition are both central elements of negotiation in the East and the West. Cooperative goals focus negotiators on integrative outcomes or joint value creation, while competitive goals direct the distributive or value-claiming aspects of negotiation. We propose that the normative behaviors that negotiators from different cultures use to enact cooperative and competitive goals are different and can be predicted from cultural differences in goals and how negotiation is framed in Eastern and Western cultures.

If people from Eastern cultures believe negotiation is more about relationships, the interplay between cooperative and competitive goals may represent an attempt to create a long-term relationship that is not too cooperative but has enough social distance to justify claiming value. For example, the primary cooperative goal may be to build trust, and the primary competitive goal may be to establish dominance. If people from Western cultures believe negotiation is more about the distribution of resources, the interplay between cooperative and competitive goals may represent an attempt to both create joint gains and claim the largest possible portion of that gain. This is the second distinction reflected in our model of culture and negotiation processes (Table 7.1). Thus, although negotiators from Eastern and Western cultures have both cooperative and competitive goals, the meaning of those goals may be different and may be one factor affecting normative negotiation behavior.

CULTURE AND NEGOTIATORS' NORMS

Norms are standards of appropriate behavior in social interaction. As with negotiation beliefs and goals, we argue that culture affects negotiation norms and therefore the behaviors that negotiators are more or less likely to use. In addition to cooperative and competitive goals, another major difference between Eastern and Western cultures that may affect negotiation behavior is low-versus high-context communication (Gibson, 1998; Hall, 1976; Harris and Moran, 1991; Ting-Toomey, 1985). In Eastern cultures that tend to be high context (e.g., Japan and China), meaning is communicated not just by a person's words or acts, but also by the context in which those words or acts are communicated. High-context communication is indirect and requires considerable familiarity with the cultural meaning conveyed by various contexts. In Western cultures that tend to be low context (e.g., the United States and Germany), meaning is embedded in words or acts. Low-context communication is direct, and although it requires familiarity with words and acts, it does not require familiarity with contexts.

Discussions of low- and high-context communication emphasize the differences between direct and indirect communications, but the dimensions on which high- and low-context communication cultures differ go beyond directness. For example, a negotiator from a low-context culture might suggest that his company is so financially weak that without a good price, his company will not be able to buy the product at all. In the same situation, a negotiator from a high-context culture might appeal to sympathy: "We've had a bad quarter, and our acquisitions budget is extremely limited." In the first example, the negotiator's message is explicit: "If you do not give us a good price, we will not be able to buy from you." In the second example, the negotiator's message is implicit; the other negotiator has to infer that a sale depends on an especially competitive price. The appeal is different in each case, too. In the first example, the appeal is to fact: "If you do not give us a good price, we will not be able to buy." In the second example, the appeal is to a more general principle: you are stronger, and you should take care of us. Logic in low-context communication therefore tends to be linear, developed in "if–then" terms. Logic in high-context communication tends be more amorphous and may require the listener to infer the focus of the argument.

Several research studies on negotiation processes support the low- and high-context communication distinction in the East and West. In low-context cultures, persuasion makes appeals to rationality; in high-context cultures, persuasion makes appeals to emotions and affect (Glenn, Witmeyer, and Stevenson, 1977; Johnstone, 1989). For example, in a content analysis of U.S.–Taiwanese cross-cultural negotiation transcripts, Drake (1995) found that U.S. negotiators used more analytic statements, relying on logic and reasoning to persuade. In contrast, Taiwanese negotiators used more normative statements, relying on social roles and relationships to persuade. Other research has found U.S. negotiators using more commitments, a form of rational persuasion, than Chinese negotiators (Adler, Brahm, and Graham, 1992) and making more promises, a form of rational persuasion, than Soviet negotiators (Graham, Evenko, and Rajan, 1992).

In low-context cultures, information sharing is explicit and direct, whereas in high-context cultures, information sharing is implicit and indirect (Cohen, 1991; Hall, 1976). For example, Adler, Brahm, and Graham, (1992) found that U.S. negotiators used more no's, a direct form of information exchange, than Chinese negotiators (Adler et al., 1992). Our own research also reveals that negotiators from low-context cultures engage in more direct information sharing, whereas negotiators from high-context cultures favor more indirect, implicit communication (Adair, Okumura, and Brett, 2001).

These differences comprise the third distinction in our model of culture and negotiation processes (Table 7.1).

In sum, our model implies an East–West distinction in negotiation with respect to beliefs, goals, and norms (Table 7.1). Negotiators from the East tend to frame negotiation as a relationship. They have both cooperative trust goals that we propose are enacted through indirect information sharing behaviors, and competitive dominance goals that we propose are enacted through affective influence behaviors. Negotiators from the West tend to frame negotiation as a distribution of resources. They have both cooperative joint-gain goals that we propose are enacted through direct information sharing behaviors, and competitive claiming goals that we propose are enacted through rational influence behaviors. In order to understand how culture and communication norms affect negotiation processes, we turn next to a discussion of the negotiation behaviors in terms of frequencies, sequences, and stages.

Culture and Negotiation Strategy: Frequencies, Sequences, and Stages

Negotiators' strategies, the goals underlying their behaviors, are revealed by the content and form of their communications. In this chapter we focus on cross-cultural differences in the content of deal-making negotiation behavior that is revealed through frequencies, sequences, and stages.[2] And, although communications scholars parse the form of communication in terms of verbal, paraverbal, and nonverbal communication,[3] we limit our focus to the form of verbal communication.

As discussed in Weingart and Olekalns (Chapter 6, this volume), communication in negotiation can be examined at three levels: frequencies, sequences, and phases. Each level of analysis provides unique insights into the negotiation process. *Frequencies* of negotiation behavior measure what behaviors negotiators use relatively more or less. Because we assume that negotiators talk about what they care about, the analysis of frequencies provides insight into negotiators' goals and their approach to realizing those goals. By contrast, *sequences* of negotiators' behaviors are action–response sets of behavior. One negotiator's acts provide the stimulus for the other negotiator's response. The second negotiator's response provides the stimulus for the first, and so on. Prior research identifies three types of sequences in negotiation: reciprocal, complementary, and structural (also called transformational; see Weingart and Olekalns, Chapter 6, this volume, for a review). Reciprocal sequences occur when negotiators match each other's behaviors. Complementary sequences consist of congruent but not matched strategies.

Structural sequences are cycles of seemingly unmatched behavior. Finally, communication in negotiation can be analyzed in terms of phases or stages. Negotiation phases are periods of the negotiation identifiable by the content of negotiators' communications. Negotiation stages, in contrast, are periods of the negotiation identified by time. By analyzing stages, we get a picture of how a negotiation progresses and changes focus over time.

THE CONTENT OF DEAL-MAKING NEGOTIATION BEHAVIOR

Our own research explores the content of negotiation processes in terms of information and influence strategies. We focus on these strategies because they are the most common means of creating and claiming value in a transactional negotiation with integrative potential. Of course, negotiators do not just exchange information and engage in influence attempts; they may also talk about the negotiation process itself, and about things that are irrelevant to the negotiation. Our focus on information exchange and influence does not mean that other categories of negotiation behavior are unimportant. By categorizing the content of deal-making negotiations, we can separate negotiation processes from negotiation outcomes and empirically verify what behaviors lead to what outcomes.

We use multiple indicators to measure information exchange. Our three behavioral indicators of low context, direct information exchange are statements about priorities, statements about commonalities or differences between the parties' interests, and direct responses to the other party's suggestions or offers. We use three different behavioral indicators of high-context, indirect information exchange: offers, multi-issue offers, and multi-issue offers with trade-offs. The low- and high-context or direct–indirect distinction is based on the ease with which a party can infer preferences and priorities from the communication. Preferences and priorities are stated explicitly in words when a direct question is being answered. "What is more important to you, runs or financing?" is a common question used by Western negotiators in our study.[4] "Runs are more important to me, because every time I run the show I get advertising revenue" is a direct response.

With indirect communication, preferences and priorities are embedded in the configuration of multi-issue offers or a series of single-issue offers and counteroffers. "I'll give you $50,000 per episode, and pay you 50 percent up front and 25 percent in years one and two of the contract if you will allow me eight runs" is an example of a multi-issue proposal with tradeoffs. The seller might reply with a counteroffer: "I'll give you the eight runs if you give me 100 percent of the financing up front and $60,000 per episode." In this exchange, the meaning of the offer on one issue depends on the context of the other offers. Understanding requires placing each offer in the context of prior offers.

The inferential task is even greater when negotiators exchange single-issue offers, especially when neither is directly responding to the other's offer. Seller: "I want $60,000 per episode." Buyer: "I want to run each episode eight times." Seller: "I want all the payments up-front." Can we infer from this exchange that the buyer is willing to pay $60,000 per episode and the seller will allow eight runs? Probably not, but the buyer may correctly infer that up-front payments are important to the seller, and the seller may correctly infer that runs are important to the buyer since each is taking an extreme position on that issue. The level of inference determines the distinction between direct and indirect information-exchange behavior.

Influence strategies also vary in high- and low-context communication. We use two indicators of high-context influence strategy that are geared toward affective influence: appeals to legitimacy, including references to status and relationships, and appeals to sympathy. For example, a negotiator from a high-context culture might remind the other of relative status: "We are an award-winning film studio and therefore get high prices for our productions" or their long-term relationship: "We've had a long and profitable relationship and have many contracts; it would be awkward for another station in your area to be showing this series when you have been the sole source of our programming for many years."

We use three indicators of low-context, rational influence: positive and negative substantiation and references to alternative-based power. For example, a negotiator from a low-context culture might suggest that his company has alternative sources of programming or mention that "even though your studio has won awards for its film series, you've moved this series into syndication a year early, so you cannot expect a high price under those market conditions." The low- and high-context distinction applied to influence strategies captures whether the argument appeals to facts relevant to the decision task or to external, contextual factors such as emotion and relationship.

Of course, the East–West divide is not a dichotomy, but rather a continuum representing cultures that are more high-context on one side and more low-context on the other. Culturally normative behaviors occur in degrees of more or less, and contextual cues less subtle than culture may cause the frame to flip from what is culturally normative to what is not (Gardner et al., 1999). For example, even high-context culture conflict avoiders may make a direct refusal in a competitive negotiation situation (Cai and Drake, 1998).

Culture and Negotiation Process

Our research examines how culture affects negotiation processes in terms of information-sharing and influence strategies. We measure these behaviors in frequencies, sequences, and stages. This line of inquiry offers insight into culturally dominant or normative negotiation behaviors, adaptation over time in cross-cultural negotiation, and cultural variation in processes leading to joint gains. In this section we review our research in each of these areas in turn.

CULTURE AND FREQUENCIES

Recall that frequency studies report counts of particular negotiation behaviors in one group versus another. This is where we expect to see large differences between low versus high context cultures, because negotiators should use more behaviors that are culturally normative for them (Kumar, 1999). Our research on culture and frequencies aims to identify culturally normative strategies that negotiators from different cultures use when presented with the same negotiation situation.

We use the Cartoon negotiation (see endnote 4) to collect data as part of executive education programs on negotiations, so we observe managers negotiating the same set of facts given the same time constraints, using the behaviors that are most comfortable for them. We have found that U.S. managers, relative to Japanese managers, are more likely to share information directly, less likely to share information indirectly, and less likely to use influence (Adair et al., 2001). These results confirm predictions of high- and low-context communication theory (Hall, 1976; Okabe, 1983) that negotiators from low context cultures would use more direct forms of information sharing to understand priorities, and that negotiators from high-context cultures would use more indirect forms of information sharing to infer each other's priorities.

In a study comparing negotiation behaviors in six cultures (the United States, Russia, France, Brazil, Japan, and Hong Kong), we looked at behavioral differences along a low–high context culture continuum (Adair, Brett, Lempereur, Okumura, Shikhirev, Tinsley, and Lytle, 2004). U.S. negotiators used relatively more direct information sharing than negotiators from the other five cultures. Russian, Japanese, and Hong Kong Chinese negotiators were more likely to use indirect information sharing than other negotiators, and, Russian and Japanese negotiators were more likely to use both rational and affective influence than negotiators from the other four cultures. These results confirm a relatively consistent low–high context continuum, with the U.S. negotiators more low context, Japanese and Russian negotiators more high context, and French, Brazilian, and Hong Kong Chinese negotiators somewhere in the middle of the continuum.

Brett (2001) compared the relative use of negotiation strategies of the Japanese sample in Adair et al., (2001) to executive MBA students from the United States, Germany, Israel, and Hong Kong. The results are complex, suggesting different types of communications may be handled relatively differently across cultures. For example, the German negotiators appeared to be low context in their use of information but high context in their use of influence. Japanese negotiators appeared to be high context in their use of information but low context in their use of influence. Hong Kong Chinese negotiators appeared to be high context in their use of influence. U.S. negotiators appeared to be low context in their use of influence. Israeli negotiators exhibited no distinct pattern of influence or information sharing.

This series of studies only partially supports our model's predictions for the use of culturally normative negotiation strategies in the East and West. Japan and Russia offer the clearest evidence of a high-context negotiation where negotiators use a more relational approach enacted with both cooperative, trust building behavior through indirect information sharing and competitive, dominance behavior through both affective and rational influence. The U.S. offers the clearest evidence of a low-context negotiation where negotiators seem to use a more outcome-oriented approach that is enacted with cooperative, direct information sharing to generate joint gains.

CULTURE AND SEQUENCES

Sequences of negotiation behaviors tell us about strategic direction at the dyad level. If both negotiators are reciprocating informational behaviors, the dyad has a more cooperative focus; if both negotiators are reciprocating influence behaviors, the dyad has a more competitive focus (Olekalns and Smith, 2000; Weingart, Prietula, Hyder, and Genovese, 1999). Reciprocal, complementary, and structural sequences allow us to compare the degree to which negotiators have a similar strategic focus.

In a study of negotiators from four low-context cultures: the United States, Israel, Sweden, and Germany; four high-context cultures: Hong Kong, Japan, Russia, and Thailand; and two mixed-culture samples: the United States–Hong Kong and the United States–Japan, Adair (in press) reported that negotiators from high-context cultures reciprocated indirect information exchange more and direct information exchange less than negotiators from low-context cultures, evidence that is consistent with the predictions of our model. Contrary to the model's predictions, negotiators from high-context cultures reciprocated rational forms of influence more than negotiators from low-context cultures, and there were no cultural differences for reciprocal affective influence (Adair, 2000).

These results, together with the frequency results presented previously, suggest that in a same-culture context, negotiators tend to match culturally normative information-sharing behaviors. However, the picture for influence behaviors is not so clear. The results suggest that negotiators from high-context cultures use and reciprocate all forms of influence, both direct rational appeals and indirect, affective appeals more than negotiators from low context cultures.

Several results indicate that low- and high-context communication in negotiation differs not just in terms of the behaviors (direct vs. indirect) that are reciprocated, but also in terms of the scope and flexibility of communication. Adair and Brett (2002) reported that negotiators from high-context cultures used complementary sequences, cycling between direct and indirect forms of information exchange more than negotiators from low-context cultures. Adair and Brett (2002) also reported that negotiators from high-context cultures used structural sequences, cycling between indirect information exchange and affective influence more than negotiators from low-context cultures. For example, one negotiator might make an offer, indirectly revealing some information on preferences, and the other negotiator would respond with an appeal to emotion, claiming such an offer was unjust. This is further evidence that strategic flexibility is more common in high- than in low-context cultures. Negotiators from high-context cultures appear to be facile at switching between integrative and distributive strategies, and therefore may be better equipped to balance the creating and claiming aspects of negotiation than negotiators from low-context cultures. This would help explain why reciprocating distributive tactics may lead to conflict spirals in the United States (Brett et al., 1998) but not in Japan (Adair, 1999). The high-context Japanese negotiators may be more skilled at refocusing influence sequences by switching to an informational strategy than the low-context U.S. negotiators (Brett et al., 1998).

STAGES AND CULTURE

In one study (Adair and Brett, 2002), we divided negotiations into four quarters based on the number of speaking turns in a negotiation transcript. We found that regardless of culture, negotiators' focus shifted from sequences marked by influence attempts to sequences marked by information exchange in the first two quarters. The third quarter was transitional, marked by structural sequences of influence and information, and offer sequences dominated the fourth quarter. Furthermore, we found that the influence attempts in the first stage were relational, whereas the influence attempts that came later in the negotiation appealed more to logic and facts. These patterns over time did not vary by whether the negotiators were from high- versus low-context cultures. The patterns of sequences suggest that across cultures, negotiation involves interplay between cooperative and competitive motives.

Some additional evidence supporting this conclusion comes from a study by Natlandsmyr and Rognes (1995), who analyzed the content of Mexican and Norwegian negotiators' offers over time. They report that Mexican negotiators established a relatively stable pattern of single-issue win–lose offers, but that the Norwegian negotiators' offers reflected a three-phase pattern, with early offers being single issue and later offers involving more issues with trade-offs. Their results suggest that there may be emic differences in negotiation stages, as well as the etic stages suggested by the Adair and Brett (2002) study.

The limited empirical research on stages in cross-cultural negotiation suggests that across cultures, negotiators are relatively similar in using both information and influence behaviors throughout the negotiation. Where cultures may differ is in the content and sequencing of such behaviors, such as how information behaviors shift from question and answer to proposals over time, and in the flexibility of reciprocating a question with an offer or an influence attempt with information sharing. It is possible that because we have grounded our research in Western models of cultural differences, we may be limiting our ability to identify some rich emic negotiation processes. Understanding such differences should also offer insight into our work on the complex processes of adaptation that occur in cross-cultural negotiation.

CULTURE AND ADAPTATION

The communication literature offers several theories on dyadic adaptation that address how people adapt their interaction styles to one another (e.g., matching behaviors or behaving in similar ways). (See Burgoon, Stern, and Dillman, 1995, for a review.) However, there is very little empirical research that tests theories of adaptation in cross-cultural negotiation. Weiss (1994) recommended that the negotiator who is most familiar and comfortable with the other's style should adapt in a cross-cultural encounter. Yet, even if negotiators determine who has greater cultural-competency and should adapt, it may be quite challenging to use behaviors that are not culturally normative in an effective manner.

We view adaptation as an emergent process that happens as negotiators discover each other's styles, interpret each other's goals, and gradually begin to move in sync. We have used a dance metaphor to describe how two unfamiliar parties come together and begin dancing quite awkwardly at first, but eventually figure out each other's rhythm and start navigating the dance floor as a single unit (Adair and Brett, 2002). We found evidence of adaptation in the individual behaviors used by mixed U.S.–Japanese dyads in the Adair et al. (2001) study. Japanese negotiators in mixed-culture dyads exhibited levels of direct information sharing, indirect information sharing, and power that were more typical of U.S. same-culture negotiators than Japanese same-culture negotiators.

We have also looked at reciprocity for evidence of adaptation, because reciprocity in negotiation suggests that both parties have a similar strategic focus (Putnam, 1990; Putnam and Jones, 1982). In our research, reciprocal sequences of direct information exchange occurred with similar frequency in low-context dyads and mixed-context dyads, but reciprocal sequences of indirect information exchange occurred with greater frequency in high-context dyads (Adair, in press). These results offer evidence of high-context negotiators adapting low-context norms for direct information sharing in a mixed-culture context. This pattern of adaptation can be explained by Hall's (1976) theory that people from high-context cultures have flexible use of both low- and high-context communication norms, and therefore may have greater facility to adapt in a cross-cultural encounter. High-context negotiators may also be more likely to adapt than low-context negotiators because low-context communication is easier to master than high-context communication, as it only requires understanding of the meaning of words, not the meaning of contexts. Finally, high-context negotiators may also be more likely to adapt than low-context negotiators because high-context cultures are typically also interdependent cultures, where social obligations for harmony in the group may mean that negotiators are more aware of differences and more willing to adapt than low-context negotiators.

The Adair and Brett (2002) study offers a closer look at adaptation by comparing sequential behavior over time. Mixed high–low context dyads demonstrated much less patterned sequential behavior than low- or high-context dyads. This lag was particularly true with respect to reciprocity of direct and indirect information sharing. However, the frequency of reciprocal, complementary, and structural sequences increased over time for mixed-context dyads. Given that repetition of sequenced patterns represents a form of stability in interaction (Weick, 1969), the increase in patterned sequences over time suggests that mixed-context negotiators were adapting their different styles, leading to more stable negotiation processes.

The empirical research on adaptation in cross-cultural negotiations suggests that adaptation does occur and that it is beneficial for certain kinds of adaptation to occur. What we still know little about is what exactly prompts adaptation and to what degree we can manipulate or manage the process. In addition to our findings that high-context negotiators adapt by using low-context information sharing styles, we need to understand how negotiators adapt when using influence behaviors. We hope our work on adaptation will help us to understand what sort of adaptation will facilitate the negotiation of joint gains in cross-cultural negotiations.

CULTURE, NEGOTIATION, AND JOINT GAIN

Brett and Okumura (1998) reported that same-culture Japanese and U.S. negotiators achieved similar levels of joint gain. But further research shows that they achieved those gains using different negotiation behaviors (Adair et al., 2001). U.S. same-culture dyads achieved higher joint gain when they shared more information directly, and Japanese same-culture dyads achieved higher joint gain when they shared more information indirectly and used influence. The U.S. negotiators' results are consistent with Pruitt's (1981) observation that negotiators who generate joint gains share information and eschew influence tactics. However, the Japanese negotiators' results suggest an extension of Pruitt's (1981) conclusions. Pruitt (1981) talked about joint gain resulting from implicit information or heuristic trial-and-error search and power avoidance. The Japanese negotiators' behavior in this study suggests that using proposals is not a trial-and-error process, but a highly sophisticated inferential search engine that is effective in identifying joint gain. The Japanese data indicate that it is possible to realize joint gain while engaging in attempts to influence the other party to concede, so long as search for alternative outcomes is also going on.

Adair (in press) also examined the relationship between reciprocal direct and indirect information exchange and joint gains in low-context, high-context, and mixed-context dyads. She found that culture moderated the effect of reciprocal information exchange on joint gains. The impact of reciprocal direct information exchange on joint gains was greater for mixed-context dyads than for same-context dyads. However, the impact of reciprocal indirect information exchange on joint gains was greater for high-context dyads than for low-context or mixed-context dyads. These findings suggest that effective communication in mixed-culture dyads is realized best when the dyad engages in stable, consistent patterns of reciprocity of direct information that negotiators from high- and low-context cultures can understand.

In the Natlandsmyr and Rognes (1995) study, Mexican and Norwegian negotiators opened negotiations making similar single-issue offers, but Norwegian negotiators substantially increased joint gains by settlement and the Mexican negotiators did not. A content analysis of offers showed that Norwegian negotiators used more multi-issue offers and Mexican negotiators stayed with single-issue offers. It is likely to be more difficult to construct joint gains from sequences of single-issue offers because negotiators must deduce priorities from the patterns of shifts in the single-issue offers.

The research on culture, negotiation processes, and joint gains suggests that there are multiple paths to joint gains and that different cultures may use different strategies and behaviors to get there. The traditional model linking information-sharing behaviors to joint gains and influence attempts to distributive outcomes and impasse needs to be modified to address cultural differences. The research suggests that influence behaviors that lead to distributive outcomes in the low-context United States culture may motivate search that leads to integrative outcomes in the high-context Japanese culture.

Conclusion

Because researchers are just beginning to study culture and negotiation pro-cesses, the research referenced in this chapter is not yet cumulative. Thus, our model of culture's effect on negotiation behaviors and sequences is ten-tative; our understanding of how negotiators in a cross-cultural setting can most effectively adapt their behaviors to maximize effective communication is limited; and, our evidence for what patterns of adaptation lead to joint satisfaction and joint gain is restricted. This chapter attempts to summarize what we know at this point and encourage researchers to further delineate the model and test its predictions.

Our model predicting culturally normative negotiation behaviors reflects our theory that independent and interdependent self-construals and low- and high-context communications are the critical cultural dimensions ex-plaining normative behaviors in negotiation. Our model's predictions about information sharing behaviors have received stronger empirical support than the parallel predictions about influence behavior. Negotiators from inde-pendent and low-context cultures use direct forms of information sharing more than negotiators from interdependent and high-context cultures, and high–low context mixed-culture negotiators tend to use direct information sharing, although perhaps not as effectively as same-culture low-context ne-gotiators. We find that negotiators from high-context cultures use all kinds of influence behaviors more than negotiators from low-context cultures. We have explained this finding by the higher levels of hierarchy in high-context cultures, which seems to translate into stronger norms for the use of power and persuasion in negotiation (Adair et al., 2001). However, we know that U.S., Israeli, and other low-context negotiators not only cre-ate joint gains, but also claim distributive gains (Brett, 2001). The ques-tion is how low-context negotiators claim value. Are they, for example, able to use less influence because they have such open information-sharing styles that there is high trust and they can take advantage of the other side? There is a great deal more research to be done on influence behaviors across cultures.

We recognize that the behaviors we have studied are not all inclusive and that there is much to learn about culturally normative behavior and patterns of adaptation. Our own analyses have not examined the content of offers. Single-issue offers, for example, are distributive on their face but may be integrative in context, whereas multi-issue offers are both distributive and integrative. We also have not examined the differential use of questions as a direct form of information gathering or an indirect way to avoid revealing information. By expanding the type of behaviors we investigate, we may gain a better understanding of how adaptation occurs in cross-cultural encounters and what behaviors lead to joint gains in various cultural contexts.

Another important area for future research is the role of other indirect forms of information exchange, in particular nonverbal behaviors. Many cultural researchers comment that the role of nonverbal communication is particularly important in collectivist, high-context cultures where being indirect is key to maintaining harmony and saving face (Hall, 1976; Ting-Toomey, 1988). Assuming that nonverbal behaviors are an integral part of successful communication in high-context cultures, the inability of low-context negotiators to understand nonverbal behaviors could be a major obstacle to successful cross-cultural negotiations.

Finally, we hope future research will explore how situational factors other than dyad composition affect negotiation processes across cultures. For example, Gelfand and Realo (1999) found that accountability in intergroup negotiations led individualists to adopt a more competitive frame and collectivists to adopt a more cooperative frame. How culture moderates the cognitive and behavioral effects of other situational variables, for example, negotiator role, power, negotiator status, or communication medium (see Barsness and Bhappu, Chapter 17, this volume) is an interesting question for further investigation into the negotiation process.

Notes

1. Asian cultures also tend to be hierarchical (Hofstede, 1980; Schwartz, 1994). The process of establishing a relationship may also be one of establishing relative status in that relationship. In hierarchical cultures, social inferiors are expected to defer to social superiors, but they can also expect social superiors to look out for their well-being (Brett, 2001; Leung, 1997).

2. Here we focus on content relevant to deal-making negotiations where negotiators seek to reach agreement on the terms of a resource exchange relationship. Please see Tinsley, Chapter 9, this volume, for more about behavior in dispute-resolution negotiations.

3. Paraverbal communication refers to pauses, loudness, interrupts, use of non-language sounds, and so forth.

4. Our deal-making scenario is Cartoon (Brett and Okumura, 2002). It is a buyer-seller transactional negotiation between a film company with a cartoon series to sell and a TV station with a need to purchase programming. There is one distributive issue: price, and two issues to trade-off: runs (how many times each of the 100 cartoon episodes can be shown during the contract) and financing (when the money will be paid). With more runs, the buyer gains more than the seller loses and with

more payment upfront, the seller gains more than the buyer loses. There is also one compatible issue: a second cartoon series that can create value for both parties.

Works Cited

Adair, W. L. (1999). Exploring the norm of reciprocity in the global market: U.S. and Japanese intra- and inter-cultural negotiations. In S. J. Havolvic (Ed.), *59th annual meeting of the academy of management best paper proceedings*, Briar cliff Manor, NY: Academy of Management, Conflict Management Section pp A1–A6.

————. (2000). *Reciprocity in the global market: Cross-cultural negotiations.* Unpublished doctoral dissertation, Northwestern University.

————. (in press). *Reciprocal information sharing and negotiation outcome in East–West negotiations.* International Journal of Conflict Management 2003.

Adair, W. L., and J. M. Brett. (2002, Jan). *Time, culture, and behavioral sequences in negotiations* (Working Paper No. 268) Evanston, IL: Northwestern University, Dispute Resolution Research Center.

Adair, W. L., Brett, J. M., Lempereur, A., Okumura, T., Shikhirev, P., Tinsley, C., and A. Lytle. (2004). *Culture and negotiation strategy.* Negotiation Journal 20:1, 87–111.

Adair, W. L., Okumura, T., and J. M. Brett. (2001). Negotiation behavior when cultures collide: The U.S. and Japan. *Journal of Applied Psychology, 86,* 371–385.

Adler, N. J., Brahm, R., and J. L. Graham. (1992). Strategy implementations: A comparison of face-to-face negotiations in the People's Republic of China and the US. *Strategic Management Journal, 13,* 449–466.

Brett, J. M. (2001). *Negotiating globally: How to negotiate deals, resolve disputes, and make decisions across cultural boundaries.* San Francisco: Jossey-Bass.

Brett, J. M., and T. Okumura. (1998). Inter- and intracultural negotiation: U.S. and Japanese negotiators. *Academy of Management Journal, 41,* 495–510.

Brett, J. M., and T. Okumura. (2002). Cartoon. In J. M. Brett (Ed.), *Negotiation and decision making exercises, 2002 version.* Evanston IL: Dispute resolution research center, Northwestern University.

Brett, J. M., Shapiro, D. L., and A. Lytle. (1998). Breaking the bonds of reciprocity in negotiations. *Academy of Management Journal, 41,* 410–424.

Burgoon, J. K., Stern, L. A., and L. Dillman. (1995). *Interpersonal adaptation: Dyadic interaction patterns.* New York, NY: Cambridge University Press.

Cai, D. A., and L. E. Drake. (1998). The business of business negotiation: Intercultural perspectives. *Communication Yearbook, 21,* 153–189.

Cohen, R. (1991). *Negotiating across cultures: Communication obstacles in international diplomacy.* Washington, DC: United States Institute of Peace Press.

Donohue, W. A. (1981). Analyzing negotiation tactics: Development of a negotiation interact system. *Human Communication Research, 7,* 273–287.

Drake, L. (1995). Negotiation styles in intercultural communication. *International Journal of Conflict Management, 6,* 72–90.

Gardner, W. L., Gabriel, S., and A. Lee. (1999). "I" value freedom, but "we" value relationships: Self-construal priming mimics cultural differences in judgment. *Psychological Sciences, 10,* 321–326.

Gelfand, M. J., Nishii, L. H., Holcombe, K. M., Dyer, N., Ohbuchi, K. I., and M. Fukuno. (2001). Cultural influences on cognitive representations of conflict: Interpretations of conflict episodes in the U.S. and Japan. *Journal of Applied Psychology. 86,* 1059–1074.

Gelfand, M. J., and S. Christakopoulou. (1999). Culture and negotiator cognition: Judgment accuracy and negotiation processes in individualistic and collectivistic cultures. *Organization Behavior and Human Decision Processes, 79,* 248–269.

Gelfand, M. J., and A. Realo. (1999). Individualist–collectivism and accountability in intergroup negotiations. *Journal of Applied Psychology, 84,* 721–736.

Gibson, C. B. (1998). Do you hear what I hear: A model for reconciling intercultural communication difficulties arising from cognitive styles and cultural values. In P. C. Earley and M. Erez (Eds.), *New perspectives on international industrial/organizational psychology* (pp. 335–362). San Francisco: New Lexington.

Glenn, E. S., Witmeyer, D., and K. A. Stevenson. (1977). Cultural styles of persuasion. *International Journal of Intercultural Relations, 1*(3), 52–66.

Graham, J. L. (1993). The Japanese negotiation style: Characteristics of a distinct approach. *Negotiation Journal, 9*(2), 123–140.

Graham, J. L., Evenko, L. I., and M. N. Rajan. (1992). An empirical comparison of Soviet and American business negotiations. *Journal of International Business Studies,* 387–418.

Hall, E. T. (1976). *Beyond culture.* Garden City, NY: Anchor.

Harris, P. R., and R. T. Moran. (1991). *Managing cultural differences.* Houston, TX: Gulf.

Hofstede, G. (1980). *Cultures consequences: International differences in work related values.* Sage publications: Beverly Hills, CA.

Johnstone, B. (1989). Linguistic strategies and cultural styles for persuasive discourse. In S. Ting-Toomey and F. Korzenny (Eds.), *Language, communication and culture* (pp. 139–156). Newbury Park, CA: Sage.

Kopelman, S., and M. Olekalns. (1999). Process in cross-cultural negotiations. *Negotiation Journal, 15,* 373–380.

Kumar, R. (1999). A script theoretical analysis of international negotiating behavior. In R. J. Bies and R. J. Lewicki (Eds.), *Research in negotiation in organizations,* (Vol. 7, pp. 285–311). Stamford, CT: JAI Press.

Lax, D. A., and J. K. Sebenius. (1986). *The manager as negotiator: Bargaining for cooperation and competitive gain.* New York: Free Press.

Leung, K. (1997). Negotiation and reward allocation. In P. C. Earley and M. Erez (Eds.), *New directions in cross-cultural industrial/organizational psychology.* Oxford: Jossey-Bass.

Lytle, A. L., Brett, J. M., Barsness, Z. I., Tinsely, C. H., and M. Janssens. (1995). A paradigm for confirmatory cross-cultural research in organizational behavior. In L.L. Cummings and B.M. Staw (Eds.), *Research in organizational behavior* (pp. 167–214). Greenwich, CT: JAI Press.

Markus, H. R., and S. Kitayama. (1991). Culture and the self: Implications for cognition, emotion, and motivation. *Psychological Review, 98,* 224–253.

Natlandsmyr, J. H., and J. Rognes. (1995). Culture, behavior, and negotiation outcomes: A comparative and cross-cultural study of Mexican and Norwegian negotiators. *The International Journal of Conflict Management, 6*(1), 5–29.

Okabe, R. (1983). Cultural assumptions of East and West: Japan and United States. In W. B. Gudykunst (Ed.), *Intercultural communication theory: Current perspectives* (Vol. 7, pp. 21–44): Sage.

Olekalns, M., and P. L. Smith. (2000). Understanding optimal outcomes: The role of strategy sequences in competitive negotiations. *Human Communication Research, 26,* 527–557.

Olekalns, M., and L. R. Weingart. (2001). Negotiators talk: An analysis of communication processes in negotiation (Working Paper No. 2001–19.) Melbourne, Australia: Melbourne Business School.

Pinkley, R. L. (1990). Dimensions of conflict frame: Disputant interpretations of conflict. *Journal of Applied Psychology, 75,* 117–126.

Pruitt, D. G. (1981). *Negotiation behavior.* New York: Academic Press.

Putnam, L. L. (1990). Reframing integrative and distributive bargaining: A process perspective. In B. H. Sheppard, M. H. Bazerman, and R. J. Lewick (Eds.), *Research on Negotiation in Organizations, 2,* 3–30.

Putnam, L. L., and T. S. Jones. (1982). Reciprocity in negotiations: An analysis of bargaining interaction. *Communication Monographs, 49*(3), 171–191.

Schwartz, S. H. (1994). Beyond individualism/collectivism: New cultural dimensions of values. In U. Kim, H. C. Triandis, C. Kagitcibasi, S-C Choi, and G. Yoon (Eds.), *Individualism and collectivism: Theory, method, and applications* (pp. 85–122). Sage: Thousand Oaks, CA.

Ting-Toomey, S. (1985). Toward a theory of conflict and culture. In W. B. Gudykunst, L. P. Stewart, and S. Ting-Toomey (Eds.), *Communication, culture, and organizational processes* (Vol. 9, pp. 71–86). Sage: Newbury Park, CA.

Ting-Toomey, S. (1988). Intercultural conflict styles: A face-negotiation theory. In Y. Y. Kim and W. B. Gudykunst (Eds.), *Theories and intercultural communication* (pp. 213–235): Sage Publications.

Weick, K. (1969). *The social psychology of organizing.* Menlo Park, CA: Addison-Wesley.

Weingart, L. R., Prietula, M. J., Hyder, E. B., and C. R. Genovese. (1999). Knowledge and the sequential processes of negotiation: A Markov chain analysis of response-in-kind. *Journal of Experimental Social Psychology, 35,* 366–393.

Weiss, S. E. (1994). Negotiating with "Romans"—Part 1. *Sloan Management Review,* 51–99.

Wilson, S. R., and L. L. Putnam. (1990). Interaction goals in negotiation. In J. A. Anderson (Ed.), *Communication yearbook* (Vol. 13, pp. 374–406). Newbury Park, CA: Sage.

CHAPTER 8

Resolving Disputes Between Faceless Disputants
NEW CHALLENGES FOR CONFLICT
MANAGEMENT THEORY

Debra L. Shapiro and Carol T. Kulik

RESEARCHERS STUDYING CONFLICT, dispute resolution, and negotiation have long been concerned with a single, broad issue: How do disputing parties resolve conflict, and what consequences are associated with the dispute-resolution choices they make? In this chapter, we review the theoretical frameworks most often used by scholars to categorize dispute-resolution strategies and predict their effects. We suggest that these theories share assumptions that fail to capture the complexity of modern-day disputes—and therefore lead researchers to overlook important, interesting questions about dispute resolution in the real world. We explain, using examples of world events (e.g., the war against terrorism) and business practices (Web sites that enable "cyber disputing"), why we believe these common assumptions are in need of revision.

An Overview: Common Conflict Resolution Frameworks

Numerous authors (cf. Pondy, 1967; Putnam and Poole, 1987; Schmidt and Kochan, 1972; Thomas, 1992) have attempted to define *conflict*—a construct that is clearly central to a field whose primary mission is to understand people's efforts to manage and resolve disputes. These definitions converge on the fact that conflict occurs when: (1) people differ in their preferences regarding how to accomplish an objective and (2) these differing preferences impede each side's ability to get what they want (see Rahim, 2001, for a review). Based on this definition, several models have been developed that explain how the parties involved in conflict—that is, the "disputants" whose differing preferences block everyone's ability to get the outcomes they seek—will act to satisfy their interests.

THE DUAL CONCERNS MODEL

As discussed in Chapter 5 by De Dreu, the dual concerns model suggests that a disputant's strategic choices reflect his or her relative concerns for the welfare of "self" and "other" (the other side). Considering these concerns in combination yields a typology of conflict-handling styles that disputants may choose: (1) domination, (2) integration, (3) compromise, (4) suppression, and (5) avoidance. A disputant who chooses domination as a strategy is more concerned about his or her own (rather than the other side's) welfare, although the reverse is true for the disputant who chooses to suppress, or subordinate, his or her own needs. A disputant who chooses integration as a strategy tends to be highly concerned about both parties' welfare; a disputant who chooses compromise tends to be moderately concerned about both parties' welfare; and a disputant who chooses avoidance tends to be unconcerned about whether either party's needs are met (and therefore this strategy choice typically means the issue under dispute is of relatively little importance).

The avoidance strategy involves no talking among the disputants regarding their differences. All of the other dispute-handling strategies involve concession making on the part of one or both disputants. Typically, conflict scholars suggest that the strategies involving mutual concession making (integrating or compromising) are most likely to result in mutually satisfying, hence long-lasting, agreements. But of these two strategies, the integrating style is generally identified theoretically and empirically as the most appropriate or effective way to resolve disagreements, since, unlike compromise, integrating involves brainstorming ways to completely or nearly completely satisfy both parties' needs (rather than only halfway; cf. Gross and Guerrero, 2000; Pruitt, 1983; Pruitt and Carnevale, 1993; Rahim, Magner, and Shapiro, 2000).

These five strategies have a long history within the conflict and organizational literatures. For fuller descriptions of these five strategies, see Pruitt and Carnevale (1993, pp. 104–106), Rahim (2001, pp. 27–30), and Thomas (1976), as well as De Dreu (Chapter 5, this volume).

IRP THEORY

IRP theory, formulated initially by Ury, Brett, and Goldberg (1988), refers to the tendency for disputing parties to communicate, in a fluid manner, three kinds of messages: (1) *interest-oriented messages,* whose substance is integrating in nature; (2) *rights-oriented messages,* whose substance refers to rules, laws, norms, or other standards of fairness that a disputant believes ought to be used to guide the dispute's resolution; and (3) *power-oriented messages,* whose substance is dominating (e.g., threatening) in nature. The fluidity of these communications means that one type accompanies another, as would occur, for example, if someone expressed a preference for resolving a dispute in a way that satisfies everyone's needs (which is an interest-oriented remark) rather than "battling it out in court" (which is a power-oriented remark). Thus, unlike the dual concerns model, IRP focuses on the use and effects of communication strategies in combination (see elaborations of IRP theory by Brett, Shapiro, and Lytle, 1998; Lytle, Brett, and Shapiro, 1999; Ury et al., 1993). Brett and her colleagues note that the rights- and power-oriented communications are especially likely to be used in combination since the former often escalates into the latter—as would occur, for example, if someone expresses a feeling that a contract has been violated and, as a result, intends to bring about a lawsuit if the violation goes uncorrected. The escalatory nature of rights and power communications and the difficulty of deescalating heated discussions (or "conflict spirals") is why Brett and her colleagues advise disputants to refrain from expressing rights or power remarks early in their dispute-resolution dialogue. In their empirical test of IRP theory, Brett et al., (1998) found that the most effective way to stop conflict spirals was to combine a power-oriented statement with an interest-oriented one. This is illustrated by a disputant saying that hopefully there will be no need to report policy violations since both sides' interests (which the disputant would then specify) can more effectively be met if they help one another find a mutually acceptable agreement. This finding reinforces the importance of viewing the various dispute-handling strategies as a combinational rather than independent set of choices, a view expressed also by Putnam (1990) with regard to integrative and distributive communications.

Assumptions Guiding Conflict-Related Research to Date

Despite the passage of time since the dual concern model and IRP were conceived, both theories continue to be reflected in the descriptions that conflict scholars give to dispute or negotiation dynamics that they study, including cross-cultural dynamics (Tinsley, 1998; Tinsley and Brett, 2002). These theories' persistence is probably due to the fact that they share several commonly held assumptions. First, both models assume that disputants have varying concerns for the needs of a known "other." Second, both models assume that a disputant consults a mental menu of options and freely chooses a dispute resolution strategy. Third, both models assume that a disputant has the opportunity to communicate directly (and thus also privately) with the other side in an attempt to get the other to say yes to their own request. Finally, both models assume that these direct, one-on-one strategies are preferable to conflict avoidance, since the avoiding strategy leaves the conflict unresolved.

Consistent with these assumptions, communication is a central issue within negotiation theory and studies regarding dispute resolution (see Weingart and Olekalns, Chapter 6, this volume, for a review). Many negotiation scholars have emphasized the importance of sharing information, sharing priorities, discussing more than one issue at a time, or similarly "linking issues," and using "if–then" (contingent concessionary) language in order to ensure that every concession one gives is accompanied by getting one in return (cf. Kennedy, Benson, and McMillan, 1982; Weingart, 1997). These recommendations make sense when parties are disputing with a known other and have the opportunity to communicate directly and privately.

These assumptions are also reflected in empirical studies of conflict resolution. Study participants are typically asked to do one of two things: (1) verbalize preferences to others in a simulated transaction (see reviews by Neale and Northcraft, 1991; Thompson, 1990; Weingart, 1997) or (2) describe from memory a specific incident of conflict that they had with others and how they resolved it (e.g., Lovelace et al., 2001; Pinkley, Neale, and Bennett, 1994; Shapiro and Rosen, 1994).

Why New Assumptions Need to Guide Future Conflict Research

To understand the complexity of modern-day disputes, one need look no further than the morning newspaper. Coverage of the 2000 presidential election in the United States dragged on for months, as Democrats and Republicans disputed the outcome of the election and debated the fairness of voting (and vote-counting) procedures. More recently, the American public reacted with shock and horror when hijacked planes were flown into the World Trade Center and the Pentagon on September 11, 2001—and experienced a swell of patriotism when the United States mounted its "war against terrorism" in response. At the same time that these national and international events were making front-page headlines, the business press was reporting on the growth of cyber disputing. The Internet has spawned numerous chat rooms and electronic bulletin boards that give disgruntled customers, employees, and job applicants public forums to air their gripes against organizations.

Do the assumptions guiding most of the conflict-related literature capture the complexity of these modern-day disputes? We think not. Again and again, we have found that the "facts" associated with these disputes violate the taken-for-granted assumptions contained within conflict management theory. In this section, we explore the ways that these modern-day disputes differ from traditional disputes addressed by conflict management theory. These differences, in turn, point to new assumptions that perhaps ought to guide how conflict scholars and practitioners think about, and attempt to resolve, conflicts.

PARTIES DO NOT ALWAYS KNOW THE SPECIFIC OTHERS WITH WHOM THEY ARE IN CONFLICT

As we previously noted, the theories that continue to pervade much of the conflict-related literature share many assumptions, starting with the notion that the parties in conflict know who "self" and "other" are. But in many modern-day disputes, disputants do not know the specific individuals with whom they are in conflict. For example, the September 11th events that prompted the United States to declare war on terrorism were initiated by faceless hijackers. In his remarks aired on National Public Radio on September 11, 2001, U.S. Defense Secretary Donald Rumsfeld noted that the absence of a return address for those who had launched the terror attacks on the United States placed the country in a "new war" that required a "new vocabulary" if government officials were to meaningfully communicate the "unconventional strategies" by which the United States would respond to these attacks.

Similarly, the people who air their complaints in Internet chat rooms and on Internet bulletin boards often are engaged in disputes with faceless organizations. The customer who thinks store prices are too high and the employee who thinks that pay scales are set too low are both facing an anonymous "system." These grievants may not personally know the individual employee or bureaucrat who is responsible for their problem, nor the individual(s) who might be able to solve it. And it is unlikely that the right person will be able to respond to the complaint—most firms do not actively monitor Internet Web sites (Work Week, 2000), and one observer suggests that only about 4 percent of Internet gripes get a direct response from the targeted company (Chin, 1999). Further, these Internet sites frequently provide the opportunity for posters (i.e., those who electronically post their complaints) to remain anonymous. Therefore, cyber disputes frequently involve both a faceless self and a faceless other.[1]

When disputants cannot identify a specific other, they are unable to take direct action to resolve the dispute. So what motivates disputants to act, if their activity is unlikely to result in a resolution? Resolving the conflict may be secondary to other goals such as getting the gripe "off one's chest," humiliating the opponent, or harming the opponent in some way. Many consumers say that their goal in posting gripes on the Internet is not getting a refund or an apology. Instead, they say their goal is to help other consumers or hurt the company that hurt them (Chin, 1999). Future research is needed to determine how effective the strategies and communications identified by dual concerns theory and IRP theory are for managing conflict among parties whose goal may not be conflict resolution—and under such circumstances what other options may exist if the current ones are not viable.

PARTIES CANNOT ALWAYS CHOOSE THEIR DISPUTE RESOLUTION STRATEGY

Earlier, we noted that the conflict-management literature generally describes the "strategy choices" of disputants to include the various conflict-handling styles described by the dual concerns model or the various types of communications described by IRP theory. But the term *choice* connotes the ability to freely choose, and this is not always the case.

For example, after the September 11 terrorist attacks, U.S. Secretary of Defense Donald Rumsfeld expressed the belief that doing nothing was not a choice the United States could afford to make—since apparent complacency might invite more terrorist attacks. Entering into war in unknown terrain such as Afghanistan was also not a choice that U.S. leaders would have ranked highly even a day before 9/11, but it was the choice the U.S. government made due to its lack of a better way to convey its intolerance of terrorism. Cyber disputants also frequently express the belief that they were "forced" to use the Internet as a way of airing their grievances (Ward and Ostrom, 2002). They chose that option only after previous efforts to get their complaint handled had fallen on deaf ears.

It is important that we are not the first to point out that the strategies that disputants take are influenced, in part, by constraints imposed upon them by their opponents. Indeed, forced concession-making has long been identified as a common consequence to a received threat, or power communication (cf. Bacharach and Lawler, 1981; Brett et al., 1998; Ury et al., 1993). The presence of the latter communication usually means that an exchange is no longer merely transaction based; rather, it has turned into a dispute. Brett (2001) concurred that under such circumstances, participants' choices are constrained. Indeed, she says that their "wrists are tied together," and explains that this is because "just saying no in dispute resolutions does not make the claim go away. The other party can continue to press the claim, and you have to deal with it" (p. 99). One's choice to press a claim often involves obtaining legal (or other third-party) assistance—which is why "See you in court" is a common power tactic, or gambit, used by those attempting to get acquiescence (cf. Kennedy et al., 1982). The fact that this alternative to a negotiated agreement, termed BATNA (Fisher, Ury, and Patton, 1991) affects the fate of both disputing parties (since both would be required to attend courtroom proceedings) is why Brett (2001, p. 99) said disputants'

"BATNAs are linked," and thus their strategy choices are not constraint-free.

Despite these observations of Brett and others, the word *choice* generally accompanies the word *strategy* when describing disputing parties' initial communications with each other. We wish to emphasize that in situations where disputing parties do not know the face of their opponent, the degree of choice they have in initial (as well as later) strategy decisions may be less than the conflict management literature tends to suggest that disputants' level of discretion may be. This is because in situations where harm has come to people or organizations by a faceless opponent, the victims may feel a heightened need to prevent future exploitation by demonstrating, with as much immediacy as possible, the punitive capability they have if they are directly or indirectly harmed again. Therefore, the often recommended prescription of attempting to resolve disputes first with collaborative ways and then, if necessary, via punitive ways may not apply to situations where the face of self or other is uncertain. Future research is needed to examine the extent to which disputants' feelings of strategy choice, and the strategies that disputants select, are affected by their (in)ability to know the face of those whose communications block each other from reaching desired ends.

PARTIES CANNOT ALWAYS COMMUNICATE DIRECTLY OR PRIVATELY
TO RESOLVE THEIR DISPUTE

Conflict management theory frequently encourages parties to communicate directly as well as privately so that each can share preferences and goals. But in modern-day disputes, disputants may be unable (or unwilling) to do this.

For example, in the months following the 2000 U.S. presidential election, Democratic candidate Al Gore repeatedly challenged the election outcome. He publicly disputed the accuracy of the election results, vigorously objected to the legitimacy of the elected candidate, and mounted a legal campaign that delayed George Bush's ability to assume the responsibilities of the presidential office. In contrast to classic disputes in which opponents voice their positions directly (and privately) to one another, the Gore–Bush dispute was aired in a public forum. The opponents' positions, while clearly voiced, were not voiced directly to one another. The fact that Gore and Bush spoke with each other through others (i.e., via representatives) suggests that they used "indirect voice," or indirect communication channels (cf. Shapiro and Tinsley, 2001). But the latter terminology fails to acknowledge that Gore and Bush primarily spoke not to each other (even indirectly), but to the U.S. American public about how they felt about each side's dispute-related actions. That is, Gore and Bush used what we will call diffused voice. In contrast to indirect voice, which involves communicating via indirect (non-face-to-face) ways to a person or persons whose face(s) are known, diffused voice involves expressing views to a generalized public. The discontented worker who flings open an office window to yell, "Don't work here if you care about your dignity!" to faceless passersby, and the angry worker who scrawls an obscene comment about the CEO in the company restroom are also using diffused voice. Perhaps most extremely, the suicide bombers who blow themselves up (along with innocent bystanders)—which occurred in the United States on September 11 and is occurring with increasing frequency in Israel—is yet another example of this.

Using diffused voice broadens the dispute to include a large, and potentially influential, network of people. Evidence of this is seen in the pro-Palestinian marches that erupted in Egypt and in other Middle Eastern countries in late March 2002 after Israel's troops surrounded Palestinian leader Yasir Arafat's compound following a suicide bombing attack that occurred in Israel for the third time in one week. The network-effect of diffused voice was also illustrated via the protests that occurred in many U.S. cities (especially in Florida) after Democratic presidential candidate Al Gore "spoke" to the American people (via television) about why there was a need to question the accuracy (hence fairness) of the vote-counting procedures in Florida that determined the 2000 U.S. presidential election's results. It is interesting that despite the fact that the election-results-related dispute was resolved in January 2001 by the Supreme Court justices, who determined that the election's winner was George W. Bush, Jr., and despite the fact that Al Gore amicably conceded defeat in the election (again via a televised communication to the American people), expressions of anger and perceived unfairness continued long after this resolution occurred—indicated by a rally in Washington, D.C. decrying Bush on the day of his inauguration and by books such as *The Betrayal of America: How the Supreme Court Undermined the Constitution and Chose Our President* (Bugliosi, 2001). One consequence of diffused voice may therefore be that the life span (i.e., beginning and ending) of disputes expressed in this manner may be less controllable.

Importantly, the disputant who exercises diffused voice is proactively selecting his or her audience from a larger population. In recent international-related disputes, this selection was illustrated by Saudi terrorist Osama bin Laden's choice to direct his videotaped remarks to Arab Muslims (rather than to non-Muslims or to U.S. citizens) and to make this tape available to Al Jazeera, a televised network that dominates the Arab Muslim–populated parts of the world. In the business context, audience selection occurs when a disputant posts his or her grievance on a special-interest Internet bulletin board rather than sending a letter to a local newspaper. Although previous research has demonstrated that people's perceptions of fairness are influenced by the experiences of other people (Brockner et al., 1994; Lind, Kray, and

Thompson, 1998), research is needed that studies the dynamics associated with disputants' strategies for audience selection, as well as the dynamics associated with how to manage the reactions of audience members (i.e., receivers of diffused voice messages).

AVOIDANCE MAY SOMETIMES INCREASE (NOT DECREASE)
A PARTY'S POWER

During the dispute over the 2000 U.S. presidential election, Gore's activities in challenging the election outcome were consistent with the classic recommendations of conflict theory: Rather than avoiding the conflict, he clearly identified his concern for fairness in determining which presidential candidate received the most votes, and took direct steps to resolve the dispute (cf. Rahim, 2001). Unfortunately for Gore and his supporters, this strategy may have backfired. Public approval surveys following the election suggested that the American public found Gore's postelection behavior to be distasteful, and political analysts believe that Gore's activities in disputing the election results may have weakened his political power for the future (Reaves, 2000; Sullivan, 2000). In contrast to the recommendations associated with conflict theory, these analysts hint that Gore would have maintained greater political clout if he had avoided the dispute and conceded the election earlier. The recommendations of the political analysts suggest that avoiding (rather than confronting) conflict may sometimes better enable people to maintain or strengthen their power. Such a notion is contrary to the generally pejorative way that avoidance behavior in conflict situations is described in the conflict management literature (cf. Shapiro and Rosen, 1994). For the same reason, deciding to withdraw from a negotiation without an agreement (rather than making an agreement) has also generally been described as a "failed" negotiation. Such a judgment, Kesner and Shapiro (1991) explained, is consistent with the tendency (both in the real world and in empirical studies that simulate negotiations) for negotiators or interventionists (including brokers) to receive greater rewards for reaching agreements than for not reaching them. This tendency is seen also, more generally, in organizations that often reward organizational decision makers more for "seeing things through" rather than halting the flow of resources toward failing projects—which is one of the reasons cited for the "escalation of commitment" (Staw and Ross, 1987).

The fact that avoiding, or withdrawing from, conflict can sometimes increase one's power (or not decrease it) is vividly illustrated by the adage "choose your battles wisely," since this suggests that the wise choice is sometimes to *not* choose. But training materials, including textbooks used for teaching strategies for managing negotiations or increasing power, rarely speak to the issue of when to not enter a negotiation, or when to walk away after initiating one. An exception is Fisher et al., (1991), who highlighted the importance of measuring the quality of a potential agreement against one's BATNA and others who corroborate this (e.g., Brett, 2001). Empirical research is needed regarding how this comparative evaluation is actually made, and how it may be influenced by various factors such as negotiators' emotions—which in dispute situations are likely to be high. The literature regarding "escalation of commitment" (Staw and Ross, 1987) may help to inform thinking regarding when disputants ought to reverse an initial pursuit of dispute resolution. Such research promises, also, to reverse the pejorative nature by which avoiding, or withdrawing from, conflict tends to be described in the conflict management literature.

New Assumptions Influence Conflict Management Theory, How?

Earlier, we suggested that the new assumptions we presented ought to guide how conflict scholars and practitioners think about, and attempt to resolve, conflicts. Next, we elaborate on what the new ways of thinking or interventions may be.

IMPLICATIONS FOR CONCEPTUALIZING "CONFLICT" AND "DISPUTING"

A consistent bias reflected in the conflict management literature is that disputing parties want to reach agreements, and ideally mutually satisfying ones. This may not always be true. As we noted earlier, resolving the conflict may be secondary to other (more retaliatory-oriented) goals. Perhaps the current typologies of conflict-handling strategies are ill suited for managing conflict-related incidents whose purpose is not ultimately to make peace between the disputing parties. Indeed, this may explain why the peace-making strategies between Palestine and Israel have continually failed, and why after the September 11 terrorist attacks in New York and Washington, D.C., U.S. Secretary of Defense Donald Rumsfeld expressed needing a new vocabulary to deal with the international conflicts today. Refining definitions of *conflict* and *disputing* so that they reflect disputants' motives (i.e., to ultimately reach agreement or merely to express grievances) may be one way to reconceptualize these constructs in ways that may help conflict scholars identify more effective ways to manage incidents relating to them.

Another key point we have repeatedly made in this chapter is that the "face" of those involved in the dispute is not always known, contrary to the way in which dispute resolution is typically described in the conflict management and negotiation literature. Among the faceless are observers to the dispute—due to the fact that technology (e.g., television, videotapes sent by aggrieved parties such as Osama bin Laden, and internet chat rooms) has made it increasingly possible for countless numbers of people to witness disputes that are unfolding near or far. Such technology has also increased the possibility that nonparticipants may become participants (and no longer mere observers), since passions have been stirred by the visual vividness of falling skyscrapers, huge balls of fire, angry protesters, bloody victims, financially distraught laid-off employees, and other media-reported events. Consequently, it may also be time to rethink who it is that conflict management scholars presume are "participants" in a dispute and, in turn, the extent to which self and other (which tends to suggest only two parties) characterizes who it is that is disputing. The globally linked world we now live in makes not dual concerns, but a multiplicity of parties and their concerns more likely. Consistent with this, Brett (2001) suggested that "collective interests" (i.e., the well-being of individuals other than those who are directly involved in a conflict) are important data to consider when negotiating globally.

Future research is needed to determine when disputants will feel motivated to express grievances for the purpose of resolving, versus merely expressing, discontent, and how disputants' motives may be influenced by whether the face of the disputing parties is, or is not, known to them. Research regarding the effect of electronic (non-face-to-face) versus nonelectronic (face-to-face) negotiations may be helpful toward this end (e.g., see McGinn and Croson, Chapter 16, this volume); but the interpersonal focus of such studies to date falls short of the network-wide effects of disputants' "*diffused voice*" that has been our chapter's focus. Therefore, in addition to drawing on literature regarding the effect of (non)electronic forms of communication, we recommend that the very definition of "conflict" and "disputing" be refined to allow for: (1) the form of communication between disputants to be face-known as well as face-unknown in nature; and (2) the kind of motives held by disputants to be agreement-seeking as well as nonagreement-seeking (e.g., harm oriented) in nature. Such refinements promise to help conflict scholars design studies that enable them to observe dynamics that can provide the new vocabulary needed to assist governments and businesses in answering the new forms of griping that has spread to various pockets of the globally sensitive and electronic world in which we now live.

IMPLICATIONS FOR INTERVENTIONS

The fact that disputing parties do not always know the faces of those who are harming their interests, or the faces of those who may be able to address the grievances expressed, or the faces of those who are watching the dispute has implications for possible interventions as well. Under such circumstances, direct communication-driven interventions are not possible.

Since such interventions are generally emphasized in the conflict management literature, especially communications that are integrative or collaborative (win–win) in nature, there is a need for conflict management scholars to find interventions of a different nature that also help to bring about mutually satisfying outcomes. Conflict-management studies of Eastern cultures, such as Asia—rather than of Western cultures such as the United States (which dominate the conflict management literature)—may help conflict management scholars identify a typology of strategies that are more indirect than the ones suggested by the Dual Concerns Model and IRP theory (see Tinsley, Chapter 9; Adair and Brett, Chapter 7, this volume). Drawing only on current literature regarding "indirect communication styles" seems likely to be insufficient, however. This is because this literature currently describes the disputing parties' faces and physical location as known to all who are pulled in to assist in resolving the dispute; and the kind of indirect intervention yet to be studied involves one where such knowledge is either absent or uncertain.

As typologies of these indirect strategies are developed, further consideration needs to be given to the activities of participants who join the dispute after its onset. There are situations in which disputes are resolved via the activities of individuals not directly involved in the dispute. For example, gripes posted on Internet bulletin boards sometimes foster the emergence of corporate champions. A customer complaining of poor service may be rebuked by a second customer with a different company experience, or by an employee who defends the company's behavior. The battle is fought (and potentially won) in the court of public opinion, with the actual disputants playing only minor roles in the drama. Similarly, the U.S. war on terrorism has mobilized everyday citizens. Whereas airlines previously discouraged travelers from "helping" in airborne conflicts between airline personnel and unruly passengers, regulations have been eased to permit flight attendants to recruit help from among the travelers. One consequence of these activities is that disputes are now being resolved by broad networks of people (e.g., customers, employees, citizens, or even a coalition of nations, as is currently the case in fighting the war on terrorism). We need to develop theories that address how these parties choose to become involved in a dispute that is not truly "theirs" and understand how the activities of these loosely connected parties are best managed.

Conclusion

In closing, it is our hope that this chapter has convinced the reader that it may be time to reconceptualize what is meant by conflict and disputing, since the current descriptions of these activities implicitly or explicitly suggest that there is knowledge about who is involved in the dispute. Yet, as we have pointed out repeatedly in this chapter, much harm can be inflicted on others by people whose face is unknown—ranging from acts of violence by unknown terrorists to acts of undermining, including company- or personal-damaging (Internet-publicized) complaints by employees in the workplace. And as technology (e.g., television, videotapes sent by aggrieved parties such as Osama bin Laden, and Internet chat rooms) has increasingly eased people's ability to be dispute observers and dispute pacifists, those watching (and also potentially affected by) the dispute have also become increasingly faceless as well. This observation, coupled by the others we offered in this chapter, lead us to conclude that future conflict management-related theories and interventions may be more relevant to the kinds of disputes increasingly seen today if they are more sensitive than they have been to date to indirect strategies (including, but not limited to, avoidance) that may help disputing parties resolve their differing, goal-blocking preferences, and to strategies taken by disputing parties whose aim is *not* conflict-resolution.

Note

1. Some reader may question whether merely airing a gripe in a public forum, such as an Internet chat room, fits the definition of *conflict* or *disputants* that we presented at this chapter's outset. We believe that cyber disputing does indeed illustrate conflict, since the gripe's substance threatens (implicitly or explicitly) to harm the ability of the gripe's target (e.g., a business) to meet its goals, such as maintaining positive publicity. We agree that the notion of disputing is less clear, since the cyber disputant's face is unknown to the company target to which she or he may be reffering, and since the "face" of the company may even be unclear to the cyber disputant. But this is precisely the point we wish to make: the "face" of disputing parties is *not* always clear, contrary to the assumption typically made in the conflict management literature.

Works Cited

Bacharach, S. B., and E. J. Lawler. (1981). *Bargaining: Power, tactics, and outcomes.* San Francisco: Jossey-Bass.

Brett, J. M. (2001). *Negotiating globally: How to negotiate deals, resolve disputes, and make decisions across cultural boundaries.* San Francisco: Jossey-Bass.

Brett, J. M., Shapiro, D. L., and A. Lytle. (1998). Breaking the bonds of reciprocity in negotiations. *The Academy of Management Journal, 41,* 410–424.

Brockner, J., Konovsky, M., Cooper-Schneider, R., Folger, R., Martin, C., and R. J. Bies. (1994). Interactive effects of procedural justice and outcome negativity on victims and survivors of job loss. *Academy of Management Journal, 37,* 397–409.

Bugliosi, V. (2001). *The betrayal of America: How the Supreme Court undermined the constitution and chose our president.* New York: Avalon.

Chin, R. (1999, November 7). Bash the biz.com. *The Post and Courier,* Charleston: pp. E1, E6.

Fisher, R., Ury, W., and B. Patton. (1991). *Getting to yes: Negotiating agreement without giving in.* New York: Penguin.

Gross, M. A., and L. K. Guerrero. (2000). Managing conflict appropriately and effectively: An application of the competence model to Rahim's organizational conflict styles. *International Journal of Conflict Management, 11*(3), 200–226.

Kennedy, G., Benson, J., and J. McMillan. (1982). *Managing negotiations.* Engelwood Cliffs, NJ: Prentice Hall.

Kesner, I. F., and D. L. Shapiro. (1991). Did a "failed" negotiation really fail? Reflections on the Arthur Andersen–Price Waterhouse merger talks. *The Negotiation Journal, 7,* 369–377.

Lind, E. A., Kray, L., and L. Thompson. (1998). The social construction of injustice: Fairness judgments in response to won and others' unfair treatment by authorities. *Organizational Behavior and Human Decision Processes, 75,* 1–22.

Lovelace, K., Shapiro, D. L., and L. R. Weingart. (2001). Maximizing crossfunctional new product teams' innovativeness and constraint adherence: A conflict communications perspective. *The Academy of Management Journal, 44,* 479–493.

Lytle, A., Brett, J. M., and D. L. Shapiro. (1999). The strategic use of interests, rights, and power to resolve disputes. *The Negotiation Journal, 15,* 31–52.

Neale, M. A., and G. B. Northcraft. (1991). Behavioral negotiation theory: A framework for conceptualizing dyadic bargaining. In B.M. Staw and L.L. Cummings (Eds.), *Research in organizational behavior, Vol. 13,* 147–190. Greenwich, CT: JAI Press.

Pinkley, R. L., Neale, M. A., and R. J. Bennett. (1994). The impact of alternatives to settlement in dyadic negotiation. *Organizational Behavior and Human Decision Processes, 57,* 97–116.

Pondy, L. R. (1967). Organizational conflict: Concepts and models. *Administrative Science Quarterly, 12,* 296–320.

Pruitt, D. G. (1983). Achieving integrative agreements. In M. H. Bazerman and R. J. Lewicki (Eds.), *Negotiating in organizations* (pp. 35–50). Beverly Hills, CA: Sage.

Pruitt, D. G., and P. J. D. Carnevale. (1993). *Negotiation in social conflict.* Pacific Grove, CA: Brooks/Cole.

Putnam, L. L. (1990). Reframing integrative and distributive bargaining: A process perspective. In B. H. Sheppard, M. H. Bazerman, and R. J. Lewicki (Eds.),

Research on negotiation in organizations, (Vol.2, pp. 3–30). Greenwich, CT: JAI Press.

Putnam, L. L., and M. S. Poole. (1987). Conflict and negotiation. In F. M. Jablin, L. L. Putnam, K. H. Roberts, and L. W. Porter (Eds.), *Handbook of organizational communication: An interdisciplinary perspective* (pp. 549–599). Newbury Park, CA: Sage.

Rahim, M. A. (1983). A measure of styles of handling interpersonal conflict. *The Academy of Management Journal, 26,* 368–376.

———. (2001). *Managing conflict in organizations* (4th ed.). Westport, CT: Quorum.

Rahim, M. A., and T. V. Bonoma. (1979). Managing organizational conflict: A model for diagnosis and intervention. *Psychological Reports, 44,* 1323–1344.

Rahim, A., Magner, N., and D. L. Shapiro. (2000). Do fairness perceptions influence styles of handling conflict with supervisors? What fairness perceptions, precisely? *International Journal of Conflict Management, 11*(1), 9–31.

Reaves, J. (2000, December 19). Gore's pre-wilderness handshake. *Time.* Retrieved June 1, 2000 from http://www.time.com/time/nation/article/0,8599,92389,00. html

Schmidt, S. M., and T. A. Kochan. (1972). Conflict: Toward conceptual clarity. *Administrative Science Quarterly, 17,* 359–370.

Shapiro, D. L., and B. Rosen. (1994). An investigation of managerial interventions in employee disputes. *Employee Rights and Responsibilities Journal, 7*(1), 37–50.

Shapiro, D. L., and C. Tinsley. (2001). Intervening "fairly" in employee disputes among nationally-different employees: Is this possible? In S. Gilliland, D. Steiner, and D. Skarlicki (Eds.), *Research in social Issues in management: Theoretical and cultural perspectives on organizational justice* (Vol.1, 187–213). New York: Information Age.

Staw, B. M., and J. Ross. (1987). Knowing when to pull the plug. *Harvard Business Review, 65*(2), 68–74.

Sullivan, A. (2000, December 10). Counting to infinity: Gore's legal blitz betrays his principles. *The Washington Post,* p. B1.

Thomas, K. W. (1976). Conflict and conflict management. In M. D. Dunnette (Ed.), *Handbook of industrial and organizational psychology* (pp. 889–935). Chicago: Rand McNally.

Thomas, K. W. (1992). Conflict and negotiation processes in organizations. In M. Dunnette and L. M. Hough (Eds.), *Handbook of industrial and organizational psychology, 2nd edition,* pp. 651–717. Palo Alto, CA: Consulting Psychologist Press.

Thompson, L. (1990). Negotiation behavior and outcomes: Empirical evidence and theoretical issues. *Psychological Bulletin, 108,* 515–532.

Tinsley, C. H. (1998). Models of conflict resolution in Japanese, German, and American cultures. *Journal of Applied Psychology, 83,* 316–323.

Tinsley, C. H., and J. M. Brett. (2002). Managing work place conflict in the United States and Hong Kong. *Organizational Behavior and Human Decision Processes.* 85, 316–381.

Ury, W. L., Brett, J. M., and S. B. Goldberg. (1993). *Getting disputes resolved* (2nd ed.). San Francisco: Jossey-Bass.

Weingart, L. R. (1997). How did they do that? The ways and means of studying group processes. In L. L. Cummings and B. M. Staw (Eds.), *Research in Organizational Behavior* (Vol.19, 189–239). Greenwich, CT: JAI Press.

Work Week. (2000, November 7). Message boards reflect morale, some say, but employers are mum. *Wall Street Journal*, p. A1.

CHAPTER 9

Culture and Conflict

ENLARGING OUR DISPUTE
RESOLUTION FRAMEWORK

Catherine H. Tinsley

A DISPUTE IS A REJECTED CLAIM (Felsteiner, Abel, and Sarat, 1980, 1981); one party (individual, organization, or nation) claims a position and a second party refuses to honor it. Conflict is the perception of differences (Thomas, 1992), but not all conflicts manifest themselves in actual disputes. A conflict might remain latent, or, the perception of differences may not be realized in actual differences. Thus, all disputes are conflicts, but not all conflicts are disputes. This is a chapter about culture and dispute resolution, and as disputes are a type of conflict, I draw on both disputing and conflict literature, as well as cultural findings from both fields.

Disputing is likely to occur in all cultures, as the antecedent conditions for a dispute are an interdependent relationship between two parties, different preferences, and an inability to fully specify the terms of the relationship at the outset. If interdependence, differing needs, and bounded rationality are human universals, so too are disputes. Because the irresolution of disputes is an imbalanced state, unless the disputing issues are of minor consequence to at least one party, the need for social equilibrium will necessitate dispute resolution (DR). Nonetheless, DR strategies can differ as a function of culture.

Culture is the set of solutions that a society has evolved to deal with the regular problems that face it (Trompenars, 1996). Because societies face different environments, it is reasonable to expect they will develop different cultural characteristics. Each culture has a characteristic profile (individualistic, egalitarian, etc.) that is embedded in members' norms, values, assumptions, and in institutional systems. Observing cultural differences (for example, in

193

DR behavior) should provoke us to reflect on our own DR behavior and encourage us to question whether our underlying assumptions about DR are accurate and complete. It is important that although a culture (culture A) may be characteristically hierarchical, culture A's members can and will espouse egalitarian values in some situations. Thus, cultural differences tend to be a matter of proportions; culture A is relatively more hierarchical than culture B, meaning A's members espouse hierarchical values more often and under more circumstances than B's members. Drawing on Benedict's (1934) analogy, culture is society's "personality writ large," whereby cultures have both dominant and recessive characteristics. The United States, for example, is dominantly individualistic, though members may at times act in a collective manner. Therefore, looking at the dominant DR approaches of a collective culture may offer insights into approaches that are recessive (more hidden) approaches in our own culture, but which may offer valuable choice alternatives. Because culture is continuously changing as the larger environment changes, recessive alternatives may appear to have limitations currently, but may prove to be valuable dispute resolution choices in the future. So cultural knowledge not only helps us better understand our present and dominant choices, but also offers alternatives that may prove to be valuable options in the future.

This chapter offers a review of the major DR strategies, showing how they can generally be captured in a framework of interests, rights, and power (Ury, Brett, and Goldberg, 1988). I then explore how cultural findings inform this framework by adding both depth and breadth to the strategies. I conclude with a cost–benefit analysis of these resolution strategies, suggesting circumstances under which each strategy might be most useful.

Disputes and Their Resolution

Disputes occur because contracts are always imperfect. Thomas (1976) laid out the "antecedent conditions" to conflict as: goal incompatibility, differences in judgment, or a combination of the two. These conditions occur because when two players (companies, individuals, countries) enter into an agreement with each other (over who shall contribute what resources, how an allocation shall be divided, how a process will unfold), they can never fully specify the terms of that agreement. Because parties' abilities to fully specify the nature of the relationship are bounded (Simon, 1982), disputes will occur.

Furthermore, in addition to goal incompatibility, disputes usually have an emotional component, as people are hurt by rejection and tend to take it personally (Brett, 2001). Thus, disputes can be categorized much the way as conflicts (Guetzkow and Gyr, 1954; Jehn, 1995). Disputes concerning a different understanding of goals or outcomes are analogous to task conflict; disputes concerning a different understanding of how to achieve a certain goal are analogous to procedural conflict; the interpersonal tension that arises because of the rejected claim is analogous to emotional conflict. Since most disputes include both a task–procedural claim that has been rejected and an emotional reaction to the claim and rejection, DR procedures should be rich enough to deal both with settling the rejected claim and with smoothing out the emotional tension.

Prior scholarship identifies a number of different ways of resolving disputes, yet many of these strategies can be integrated into a framework of interests, rights, or power (Ury et al., 1988; see Shapiro and Kulik, Chapter 8, this volume, for a review). In brief, the interests strategy promotes resolution through joint problem solving (Graham et al., 1994). Interests are a party's true needs, concerns, or fears (Ury et al., 1988), which underlie a party's stated position (Fisher, Ury, and Patton, 1991). Parties engaged in interests-based DR share information about the interests underlying their claims and counterclaims and try to integrate those interests (see De Dreu, Chapter 5, this volume). Parties have an incentive to accept and implement an interest-based agreement because such agreements meet their individual needs (Fisher et al., 1991; Walton and McKersie, 1965). The interests-based approach also smoothes out the emotional tension by giving disputants voice into their resolution (Folger, 1977) as well as outcome control (Shapiro, Drieghe, and Brett, 1985).

The rights strategy resolves a dispute by relying on some mutually acknowledged, objective, independent standards or regulations. Rights standards can be rules, contracts, laws, principles, or normative procedures (Ury et al., 1988), and they are used to assess the legitimacy of each side's case. Parties may offer proposals and argue their worth by referencing some objective, fair, independent standard. Alternatively, parties may counter that the other side's proposal is invalid because the rights standard on which it is grounded does not apply to this particular conflict or because the situation should be interpreted differently (Fisher, Schneider, Borgwardt, and Ganson, 1997). The rights strategy settles the claim by referencing some independent principle or law that offers a resolution, and it smoothes out the emotional tension because it legitimates and thus provides a basis for parties to feel that they achieved a fair outcome.

The power strategy relies on one party having the ability to get what they want through coercion. Power is the ability to influence the behavior, thoughts, or feelings of another (Huston, 1983), and in an exchange relationship, a party's power lies in the perceived dependence of the other (Emerson, 1962). Hence power is typically thought of as a function of a party's alternatives, that which Waller (1938) called "the principle of least interest," meaning that the party who has better alternatives (and thus is less interested in getting a resolution) typically has more power. A party's alternatives are based on their resources (Emerson, 1962). These resources might enable a party to escalate the dispute by involving other people, to commit an act of violence, to undermine the other party in the eyes of others, or even to sever the relationship. The power strategy settles the dispute by drawing on each party's ability either to enforce the original claim or reject it. The power strategy generally soothes the emotions of one party, the winner, but does little to address the emotional issues of the losing party, which is one criticism of this strategy (Ury et al., 1988).

Empirically, the IRP framework has proven quite useful for categorizing the types of strategies that people use when resolving disputes (Adair et al., 2004; Tinsley, 1998, 2001). Although researchers rely on other categorizations, their typologies can fit within the IRP framework. For example, the categories of the dual concern model (Pruitt and Rubin, 1986) map into those of the IRP framework (see Shapiro and Kulik, Chapter 8, this volume, for a review). Other typologies of DR strategies can be similarly captured by the IRP framework. Lin and Germain (1998) studied how joint-venture partners resolve conflicts. Their problem-solving strategy involves "discussing openly concerns, priorities, ideas, and issues, and involves a search for solutions that satisfy both parties' needs" (p. 181), which is analogous to the interests strategy. Their legalistic strategy involves resorting to "written contracts and informal binding agreements" (p. 181), which is analogous to the rights strategy. Their compromise strategy, where managers "seek a middle ground between the initial positions of the two sides" (p. 181), is again seeking resolution based on a preestablished principle of equity, and thus analogous to the rights strategy. Finally, their forcing strategy, in which a partner makes "a unilateral attempt to dominate decision making ... [by, for example,] calling upon his or her side's equity position or technical expertise to press the other party" (p. 181) is analogous to the power strategy. Similarly, Dyer and Song (1997) showed that managers resolve conflict by either "integrating conflict handling behaviors," formalization, or centralization. Integrating, which refers to discussing and reconciling interests, is analogous to the interests strategy. Formalization, which refers to use of standard procedures, is analogous to the rights strategy. Centralization, which refers to a hierarchical structure where one party has the ability to dictate a solution, is analogous to the power strategy.[1] Finally, Kozan (1997) explained that conflicts can be resolved either through a confrontational strategy, where people directly discuss their issues and concerns, a regulative strategy in which bureaucratic means are used to address the conflict, or a harmony strategy in which "norms stressing observance of mutual obligations and status orderings" are used to address the conflict. Again, these strategies are analogous to interests, rights, and power, respectively.[2]

Finally, some dispute literature highlights the structural mechanisms for dispute resolution (e.g., two parties vs. three parties). Although third-party dispute resolution might appear to be a power strategy, note that third-party dispute resolution can be based on either interests, rights, or power. The third party can enter as a process facilitator focused on parties interests, as a judge focused on determining who is right according to principle or law, or as an authority figure who relies on coercion to force resolution on one or both parties (Karambaya and Brett, 1989; Sheppard, 1983; Wall and Blum, 1991). Hence, this literature also fits into IRP.

Uncovering Assumptions Underlying the IRP Strategies

Culture influences dispute resolution strategies by promoting one set of values and beliefs over others. A DR process that incorporates those values and interaction patterns cherished by a culture might thus be thought of as more "fit," and be preferred or used more often than a process that does not incorporate a culture's values. Note that prior research shows a multiplicity of DR strategies within each culture (cf. Adair et al., 2004; Tinsley, 1998, 2001), which is consistent the argument previously made, that cultural differences tend to be relative. Cultures that are more collective, for example, will tend to use DR strategies that fit with collective values more often than other strategies. Yet this does not imply that these cultures never use DR strategies that are consistent with individualistic values, just that these latter DR strategies are used less often. Asking why cultural differences in DR occur is to link a culture's preferred strategies to its cultural profile of values, which in turn helps to reveal the assumptions underlying the DR strategies.

Prior research has shown that the interests strategy tends to be used in the U.S. culture more than it is used in other cultures (Brett, Shapiro, and Lytle, 1998; Campbell, Graham, Jolibert, and Meissner, 1988; Elsayed-Ekhouly and Buda, 1996; Kozan, 1989; Tinsley, 1998, 2001; Tinsley and Brett, 2001). As Tinsley (2001) explained, the U.S. proclivity toward the interests strategy occurs because the assumptions of this strategy fit with the values of the U.S. culture—individualism, egalitarianism, and direct communication. To resolve disputes based on each party's underlying interests assumes that the individual interests of parties in conflict are more important than, for example, collective interests or preestablished regulations (Tinsley, 1997). Another assumption is that all parties' interests are equally legitimate as a basis for resolution. If some parties' interests are thought to be unimportant, then they are unlikely to raise them in discussion or try to incorporate them into agreements. As well, the interests strategy may work best when parties feel free to express their interests and proposals without penalty, even if their interests appear to contradict those of the other party. Therefore it is no surprise that this strategy is used relatively often by U.S. disputants who espouse values of individualism, egalitarianism, and direct communication. It also should be used relatively often by disputants from any Anglo culture where these values predominate.

The rights strategy tends to be used more when a culture values explicit (rather than implied) contracting and egalitarianism, such as in Germanic cultures (Tinsley, 2001). To explain this phenomenon, we uncover that the rights strategy assumes that rules or procedures exist, are known by the parties, and recognized as a legitimate basis for resolution (Ury et al., 1988). Unfamiliar standards may appear arbitrary and be less useful in persuading the other party (Fisher et al., 1997). Moreover, if parties cannot agree on a rule or standard's legitimacy, then it cannot offer a basis for resolving the dispute (Pruitt and Carnevale, 1993). Prior research suggests that parties will select principles in a self-interested manner, selecting a rule that supports or enhances their position (Messick and Sentis, 1985). This is why Rawles (1971), in his treatise on justice, insisted that the fairest distribution principle is one that is decided before parties know which side of the distribution they will be allotted. Thus, when members of a culture select a rights strategy over other dispute resolution approaches, they are valuing abstract, generalized principles more than their own particular interests. Disputants choosing rights strategies, as opposed to those who do not, may have a longer time horizon, recognizing that the establishment or maintenance of an important precedent will compensate for any short-term loss.

A second assumption of the rights strategy is that standards apply equally and universally to everyone. Regulations that are selectively applied to some individuals and not others are likely to appear arbitrary and offer less credibility for a disputant who is hoping to either make or reject a claim. The importance of upholding preestablished regulations that apply universally is congruent with cultural values for formalization or explicit contracting and egalitarianism—characteristics that tend to describe Germanic cultures (Galtung, 1981; Hall and Hall, 1983).

The power strategy tends to be used is East Asian cultures (more than others), where social stratification or hierarchy is more common (Tinsley, 1998, 2001; Tinsley and Brett, 2001; Tse, Francis, and Walls, 1994; Wall and Blum, 1991). Here, resources come in the form of social status that confers on one party a stronger set of alternatives and hence the ability to pronounce a resolution. For example, in a workplace dispute, a high-status party has alternatives that impose more damage to the other side in that he or she can threaten to fire, ostracize, or move the other party to another division. The lower-status party, on the other hand, has very few alternatives that impose a cost to the other side, and thus has less power. Prior research has also found that parties try to enhance their power by alluding to the support of powerful others (Tinsley, 2001). Finding that the power strategy is used more in East Asian cultures is not to imply that the power strategy is never used in egalitarian cultures. Indeed, research shows that when power differences are unclear, U.S. disputants use power (Tinsley, 2001) to posture and ascertain their relative power (Adair et al., 2004). The point is that in cultures where social stratification is accepted, power differentials between the parties tend to be clear, and thus a power strategy becomes a more salient and accepted alternative.

As noted before, in a power strategy, one party essentially acquiesces to the wishes of the other, and thus the strategy can have limited effectiveness in smoothing over emotional stresses. The accommodators may feel that their emotional issues have not been addressed, and because they have had to accept the other party's claim (or remove their own claim), they may feel additional negative emotions. Ironically, this strategy tends to be used often in cultures where harmony is important (Hu, 1944; Leung, 1997). This paradox is due to the fact that power-based resolutions of disputes may be the most expedient option, at least in the short term (Goldberg, Green, and Sander, 1985). If a culture values quick resolution to minimize the social disruption conflict can produce (Leung, 1997; Tinsley, 1997; Yang, 1993), then the power strategy might be attractive. In some cases the power strategy promotes the status quo, as existing power structures remain intact. Those with resources have the alternatives, and hence have the power to pronounce, and if necessary, monitor and enforce a resolution. It may also be important to remember that the web of social obligations inherent in socially stratified societies can constrain the powerful party from pronouncing a resolution that disregards the well-being of the lower-power party (Hu, 1944; Yang, 1993). That is, with social power often comes the responsibility to look after those with less social status.

Hence cultural findings can contribute to "basic" research by deepening our understanding of the IRP approaches as strategies for dispute resolution. Making sense of a finding that Anglo-American cultures tend to prefer an interests strategy, Germanic cultures a rights strategy, and East Asian cultures a power strategy pushes us to question the fundamental assumptions of these strategies. Cultural findings highlight the individualism, equality, and direct communication that underlie the interests strategy, the respect for explicit and uniform regulations that underlie the rights strategy, and the conformity to existing strength and resources, and sometimes respect for harmony, that underlies the power strategy.

Enlarging the Scope of Dispute Resolution

Cultural findings can also contribute to "basic" research by broadening our understanding of dispute resolution strategies. As noted, for example, the interests strategy assumes that parties share information with each other about their underlying interests (even when uncovering parties' differences), suggesting a fit with cultures that value individualism and low-context communication. However, it is possible that parties who value collectivism and high-context communication can also use the interests strategy, albeit in a slightly different form. Brett and Okumura (1998) for example, found Japanese negotiators reached integrative solutions through an indirect information exchange, although U.S. negotiators used a direct information exchange (see Adair and Brett, Chapter 7 this volume, for a review). Along these same lines, the interests strategy generally assumes that each party's individual interests should serve as the basis for the dispute's resolution. There is no theoretical imperative, however, that requires such a narrow focus. It is quite possible to broaden the interests strategy so that it includes interests of parties who are not at the table but who might be affected by the conflict or by the future resolution. In a simulation that compared how disputants from the United States and Hong Kong resolved a workplace conflict, the data showed that Hong Kong disputants were more likely to defer issues to upper management for their input than were U.S. disputants (Tinsley and Brett, 2001). This behavior might be interpreted as a power strategy, to have someone with higher status and authority simply dictate the resolution. However, it might also be interpreted as an interests strategy, wherein the parties agreed that they wanted to be sure that interests of their broader community of colleagues would be factored into the resolution. This cultural finding suggests we might broaden the interests strategy to include, for example, collective or community interests. Questioning the assumptions about a DR strategy's breadth raises of the scope of the dispute.

Matsuda and Lawrence (1997) showed how when using a rights DR strategy, the scope of a dispute differs across cultures. They noted that U.S. law encourages disputants to contain a conflict by limiting the scope to the "relevant facts," where relevance is defined quite narrowly. Tort law, for example, relies on uncovering who is at fault for an incident. If a little boy is hit by a car, the boy's family can make a claim that the driver must somehow make amends. The family's claim will be upheld if the driver is found to be at fault (he was speeding or driving while somehow impaired). When liability is less clear (perhaps the little boy runs out from behind a parked car) then more facts are needed. But these facts will pertain to the liability of the driver (Was the driver speeding? Should he or she have been able to stop in time?). Other facts, such as the number of sons of the driver and how the family of the little boy learned of the accident, would not be relevant because they do not speak to the driver's liability. These facts, however, are completely relevant in Micronesian law (Matsuda and Lawrence, 1997) because they speak to the resources of the driver (his ability to make amends) and to the sincerity of his grief (the extent to which amends are necessary).

Thus the Micronesians embed this dispute into a larger context; they ask how this dispute and its resolution will affect the larger village community. If, for example, the driver cannot make amends himself, this will affect the entire village. Thus, although the basic rights-based principle (of making amends for a harm inflicted) is the same in Micronesia as in the United States, the application of this principle (how the driver makes amends) varies. In general, a rights-based strategy has a broader focus than an interests strategy (Ury et al., 1988), as the application of consistent principles embeds the dispute into a context of laws and procedures that exist across time. Yet, again, the strategic focus of U.S. disputants when applying a rights strategy is narrower than for disputants from other cultures; the relevant scope of the conflict tends to focus on the parties at the table rather than the broader community.

The power strategy, too, tends to reflect a more narrow scope when used by U.S. disputants than disputants from other cultures. To be sure, there are times when, in trying to amass resources, a party builds a coalition, whose members' claims are then considered. Generally, however, when U.S. parties use power, their goal is to enforce their own claim, and the impact of their actions on others is discounted. For example, if a labor–management dispute escalates to a strike, the work stoppage can hurt customers and suppliers. Parties might acknowledge this cost, but are not likely to change their course of action to prevent it. Rather, this cost will be labeled collateral damage, betraying the notion that the impact on these other parties (customers, suppliers) is secondary to the importance of the focal parties' claims. When using a power strategy, U.S. parties seem to view the dispute in isolation from its broader context and to consider the focal disputants' claims rather than the claims of, and impact on, the broader collective. In East Asian cultures, on the other hand, the power strategy is often used in concert with concern for the broader collective. Disputes are rarely seen in isolation, but rather are embedded in a network of social relationships. Therefore, how a dispute is resolved concerns not only the principal parties, but also the broader community. Indeed, it is a concern for social harmony that can drive disputants to use a power strategy, whereby one (or sometimes both) party is forced to withdraw his or her claim in order to preserve a collective peace (Leung, 1997; Wall and Blum, 1991).

The relatively narrow scope in the United States both of disputes and the IRP strategies used to resolve them likely reflects U.S. cultural values, particularly those of individualism and low-context communication. Individualism is a focus on the self, separated from social context and connections. This might encourage an isolating of disputes, whereas collectivism, which focuses on social relations, might encourage an embedding of disputes into their context. Similarly, low-context communication is a focus on what is said directly and explicitly, and meaning is derived from the spoken words. In high-context communication, meaning is derived from what is implied or

TABLE 9.1

Broadening Our Understanding of Dispute Resolution

	Focus of the Dispute and Dispute Resolution	
Justification Used	Disputing Parties	Broader Collective
Interests	Disputing parties' interests	Collective interests
Rights	Disputing parties' rights	Collective rights
Power	Disputing parties' power	Collective power

suggested and listeners need to consider the situation before knowing how to interpret a certain communication. Thus, high-context communication may encourage a focus on the surrounding context of any communication and hence promote a broader scope for viewing any event (such as a dispute).

Recognizing that U.S. DR has tended to promote a rather narrow scope which isolates and abstracts the dispute from its context highlights the need for a new framework that considers both (1) the focus of the DR (focal parties vs. the collective) and (2) the strategic basis for DR (interests, rights, or power). This new framework is depicted in Table 9.1.

Cross-cultural variation in disputing thus pushes U.S. theorists to look at how a dispute is embedded in a larger context and connected to other events. This does not imply that U.S. research never considers the larger context of a dispute or conflict, only that it is not the primary focus. Yet, when we recognize the connections between a dispute, its resolution, and other activities, we might have more insight as to when and how the next dispute will occur.

A Cost–Benefit Analysis

There are many benefits of recognizing the embeddedness of a dispute, from ideas for settlement to warnings about implementation problems to ways of preventing future disputes. However, there are costs in attempting to specify how dispute resolution activities will impact those not at the table. Disputing parties' projections will always be egocentric and hence imperfectly represent the interests of those not at the table. If those missing parties are consulted, the time and energy required to incorporate their interests can be nontrivial. The complicated calculus involved in specifying and incorporating many parties' concerns and consequences may lead to paralysis (for fear of hurting some unrepresented party) and impede DR activity. Any dispute resolution is a balancing act, a way of allocating positives and negatives across a spectrum of parties, and incorporating the interests of the collective is not always the clear choice.

A similar cost–benefit analysis can be considered for each of the strategies—interests, rights, and power. The interests strategy, for example, assumes the needs of parties at the table are important; it tends to ensure that their interests are incorporated into an agreement that is satisfying (Shapiro et al., 1985), that encourages implementation (Walton and McKersie, 1965), and thus helps lower the costs of monitoring. Moreover, because parties are encouraged to directly confront their differences and brainstorm creative ways of bridging these differences, the interests strategy tends to create novel, innovative solutions (Ury et al., 1988). These are the benefits of this strategy. On the other hand, since the interests strategy also assumes parties are equal in their abilities to present and champion their interests, it may work poorly when disputants have unequal power or legitimacy. For example, divorce mediation has been criticized because it does not protect the weaker spouse. Likewise, because the interests strategy tends to focus on the interests of the parties represented (although the scope can be enlarged to the broader community), the strategy tends to ignore parties who are not at the table (unless their interests are actively championed by someone at the table; Tinsley, 1997). Similarly, because of the general novelty of interests-based agreements, they may only be appropriate to the dispute at hand and not provide a good basis for resolving other future disputes. That is, the agreement itself is non–precedent setting; however, the process used to reach the agreement can of course be applied to future conflicts.

Thus, although the interest approach has been advocated for getting to the "root causes" of a dispute between two parties (Fisher et al., 1991), and hence decreasing dispute recurrence between these parties (Ury et al., 1988), the resolutions may be limited in their ability to address other nonrelated disputes. Two final costs: the interests strategy takes time, parties need to build trust, and as a result the interests strategy does not always work. When interests are about differences in basic human values, it is very unlikely that they will be reconcilable (Nader, 1991; see also De Dreu, Chapter 5, this volume).

The rights strategy is a process of applying preestablished rules or procedures to fashion a resolution; hence the resolution will be consistent with past resolutions. Moreover, because principles are applied equally across people, this is perhaps the best strategy for protecting the weaker party, as it does not rely on the weaker party representing his or her interests or enforcing a resolution. The rights strategy is likely to get the fairest solution, meaning a solution that is consistent across time and across people. In theory, the resolution will be consistent with how prior disputes were resolved, irrespective of the players involved. Moreover, the resolution of any dispute that helps to refine a principle can be said to help resolve future disputes. Cases that help set a precedent can be used to help resolve future disputes. On the negative side, there is a "tyranny of rights" problem in that rights are universal and faceless. They do not take into account any individual information, any unique circumstances. Indeed, some scholars suggest this is why China rejected the harsh rules of the Qin dynasty in the third century B.C., opting instead for a system of moral force (which is a power strategy; Butterton, 1996). Another downside of the rights strategy is that it is only as effective as the rules are legitimate. If parties disagree as to the legitimacy of a rule or procedure being applied, then the dispute has only shifted from the original problem to a new argument as to which rule should be applied (Fisher et al., 1997; Pruitt and Carnevale, 1993; Tinsley, 2001).

Much has been written about the costs of the power strategy. When power is actually exercised (rather than the threat of power), there are costs to both parties. The costs to the weaker party occur because the resolution does not address the concerns and emotions of the weaker party (Pruitt and Rubin, 1986; Thomas, 1992). The stronger party's costs come from monitoring and enforcement (Walton and McKersie, 1965), since the weaker party will have incentive to defect. One interesting paradox is that when the weaker party is truly powerless and thus has little to lose by defecting from an agreement, this will increase the stronger party's monitoring and enforcement costs, and may entice the stronger party to make some concessions in the agreement to avoid such heavy implementation costs. Likewise, when power is exercised there can be collateral costs to society in the form of violence, destruction, or strikes.

Yet one cultural finding highlights the benefits of this strategy, particularly when it is applied with a collective focus rather than the narrow scope of the disputing parties. When power differential are clear, then resolution can be quite expedient. This reduces the costs of DR and facilitates social harmony. Moreover, this power strategy tends to offer conservative resolutions that maintain the status quo. Power-based resolutions are premised on who has more power, and those with power are likely to want to maintain it. Thus a power strategy will tend toward maintaining the status quo, or at most incremental change. This might be beneficial when continuity and tradition are important values.

Costs and benefits of various DR strategies are summarized in Table 9.2, which builds on the cost–benefit analysis presented in Ury et al.'s (1988) initial presentation of the IRP strategies. The italicized sections represent the new costs and benefits identified by integrating the cross-cultural research on DR. Note that this table suggests cultural relationships in that one could hypothesize, for example, that when a culture values expedient resolution, disputants of that culture are more likely to use a power strategy than are disputants from a culture that does not place a premium on quick resolution.

TABLE 9.2

Cost and Benefits of the IRP Strategies and Collective Rather Than Individual Focus

	Benefits	Costs
Interests strategy	• Satisfies parties' needs so they ratify and implement solution • Decreases monitoring costs • Enhances relationship between parties • Less conflict recurrence (because of satisfying any underlying "hidden" problems) • Encourages novel, creative solutions	• Does not work if interests are irreconcilable • *Tends to ignore those not at the table* • *Solutions generally unique and thus cannot be used to set a precedent* • *Offers minimal protection for the weak who cannot represent themselves*
Rights strategy	• Solutions can be used to build a precedent for future disputes • When need to clarify rights boundary within which to seek a negotiated settlement • *Consistent solutions across time and across people, giving appearance of fairness* • *Best protection for the weaker parties*	• Higher transaction costs than for interests to determine who is right • *Does not take into account unique information or special circumstances* • *Does not work if parties cannot agree as to which principles are legitimate* • *May not address the emotional concerns of parties (beyond assuring them the outcome is consistent with prior disputes)*
Power strategy	• When need to clarify who has more power • *Expedient resolution when power differentials are clear* • *Maintains stability and the status quo*	• May not address the needs or concerns of the weaker party • Harm to the weaker party (and possibly collateral damage) if power is exercised • Higher monitoring costs if weaker party not satisfied with solution • Hard on the relationship between parties
Collective focus vs. focus on individual disputing parties	• *More parties "buy into" solution to help implementation* • *Decreases monitoring costs* • *Knowledge can help to prevent future disputes*	• *Increased time and energy to delineate consequences of activities for other parties* • *Imperfect detection of other parties' consequences* • *Imperfect integration of other parties' consequences (unless they are at the table to represent themselves)*

Note: Nonitalicized portions of the table are from Ury et al. (1989), whereas italicized portions are new costs and benefits discovered by considering cross cultural findings.

TABLE 9.3
Situational Factors Beneficial to Each Strategic Focus and Justification

	Situations Favorable to a Strategy's Usage
Interests	• Interests are reconcilable. • There is no concern for setting a precedent for future conflicts. • A dispute has several unique features and circumstances. • Parties have equal power. • Concerns of parties at the table override collective issues, or parties at the table can be trusted to incorporate collective issues.
Rights	• Parties can agree on legitimate and applicable principles. • There are few special circumstances. • Fairness or the appearance of fairness is important. • Power imbalances exist, and the powerful party is likely to exploit the weaker party. • Building principles or setting precedent is important.
Power	• Power imbalances are clear and accepted. • Other obligations encourage the stronger party to protect or assist the weaker party. • Value is placed on quick resolution.
Collective focus vs. focus on individual parties	• Collective identity is strong. • One or both parties are tightly linked (structurally) to other members of collective.

However, this table need not be exclusively about cultural research. One could hypothesize, for example, that disputants in a protracted conflict with heavy costs may yearn for expedient resolution and hence be more likely to use a power strategy than disputants involved in a noncostly conflict.

Specifying these costs and benefits in turn illuminates the circumstances under which each strategy is most likely to be effective. These factors are summarized in Table 9.3. A focus on the collective rather than individual consequences would make most sense when parties are tightly connected to their respective collectivities. If a collective's members are tightly, rather than loosely, linked, then resolution activities are more likely to reverberate through the system and their impact felt strongly by other members. If, for example, one or both parties are in an organization with a tight, uniform culture, then the consequences of disputing activities for all organizational members should probably be addressed. The interests strategy might best be used when interests are reconcilable, when there is no concern about setting precedent, when parties have equal power, and when the concerns of the parties at the table are more important than collective concerns or when parties at the table can be trusted to incorporate collective concerns. The rights strategy might be best to use when there are applicable principles that both parties find to be credible and legitimate, when there are few special circumstances, when consistency or the appearance of fairness is important, when power imbalances exist and the powerful party cannot be trusted to protect the weaker party, and when building principles or setting precedent is important (as, for example, when parties have a longer term and broader focus than just the immediate relationship). The power strategy might be best when power imbalances are clear and are accepted, when other obligations will encourage the stronger party to protect the weaker party, and when value is placed on an expedient resolution.

Conclusion

Just as contracts are imperfect, leading parties to inevitable disputes, dispute resolution strategies are also imperfect, forcing parties to weigh various benefits and costs across a spectrum of players. Most important, however, is that strategic choice be conscious and informed. Incorporating cultural findings has expanded our own understanding of the costs and benefits of various strategies and augmented the number of alternative foci, thereby hopefully improving disputants' abilities to make informed disputing choices and reach more effective resolutions.

Notes

1. Dyer and Song (1997) also discuss an avoidance strategy.
2. It may seem odd to draw an analogy between the power strategy and the harmony model, yet the harmony model reduces conflict through the lower power party acquiescing to the party with higher power. This connection between a power strategy and social harmony will be further explained in the following section.

Works Cited

Adair, W., Brett, J. M., Lempereur, A., Okumura, T., Shikhirev, P., Tinsley, C. H., and A. Lytle. (2004). Culture and negotiation strategy. *Negotiation Journal, 19,* 87–111.

Benedict, R. (1934). *Patterns of culture.* Boston: Houghton Mifflin.

Brett, J. M. (2001). *Negotiating globally.* San Francisco: Wiley.

Brett, J. M., and T. Okumura. (1998). Inter- and intracultural negotiation: U.S. and Japanese negotiators, *Academy of Management Journal, 41,* 495–510.

Brett, J. M., Shapiro, D. L., and A. L. Lytle. (1998). Breaking the bonds of reciprocity in negotiations. *Academy of Management Journal, 41,* 410–424.

Butterton, G. R. (1996). Pirates, dragons, and U.S. intellectual property rights in China: Problems and prospects of Chinese enforcement. *Arizona Law Review, 1081,* 1108–1113.

Campbell, N., Graham, C. G., Jolibert, J. L., and H. G. Meissner. (1988). Marketing negotiations in France, Germany, the United Kingdom and United States. *Journal of Marketing, 52,* 49–62.

Dyer, B., and X. Song. (1997). The impact of strategy on conflict: A cross-national comparative study of U.S. and Japanese firms. *Journal of International Business Studies,* 467–493.

Elsayed-Ekhouly, S. M., and R. Buda. (1996). Organizational conflict: A comparative analysis of conflict styles across cultures. *International Journal of Conflict Management, 7,* 71–81.

Emerson, R. M. (1962). Power-dependence relations. *American Sociological Review, 27,* 31–40.

Felsteiner, W. L. F., Abel, R. L., and A. Sarat. (1980–1981). The emergence and transformation of disputes: Naming, blaming, and claiming. *Law and Society Review, 15,* 631–654.

Fisher, R., Schneider, A., Borgwardt, E., and B. Ganson. (1997). *Coping with international conflict: A systematic approach to influence in international negotiations.* Upper Saddle River, NJ: Prentice Hall.

Fisher, R., Ury, W., and B. Patton. (1991). *Getting to yes: Negotiating agreement without giving in.* New York: Penguin.

Folger, R. (1977). Distributive and procedural justice: Combined impact of voice and improvement on experienced inequity. *Journal of Personality and Social Psychology, 35,* 108–119.

Galtung, J. (1981). Structure, culture, and intellectual style: An essay comparing Saxonic, Teutonic, Gallic, and Nipponic approaches. *Social Science Information, 20,* 817–856.

Goldberg, S. B., Green, E. D., and F. E. A. Sander. (1985). *Dispute resolution.* Boston: Little, Brown.

Guetzkow, H., and J. Gyr. (1954). An analysis of conflict in decision-making groups. *Human Relations, 7,* 367–381.

Hall, E. T., and M. R. Hall. (1983). *Hidden differences: Studies in international communications, how to communicate with the Germans.* New York: Stern.

Hu, H. C. (1944). The Chinese concepts of "face." *American Anthropologist, 46–50,* 61–64.

Huston, T. L. (1983). Power. In H. H. Kelley, E. Berscheid, A. Christensen, T. Huston, J. H. Harvey, G. Levinger, E. Meclintock, L. Peplan, and D. R. Peterson (Eds.), *Close relationships,* (pp. 169–219). New York: Freeman.

Jehn, K. A. (1995). A multimethod examination of the benefits and detriments of intragroup conflict. *Administrative Sciences Quarterly, 40,* 256–282.

Karambayya, R., and J. M. Brett. (1989). Managers handling disputes: Third party roles and perceptions of fairness. *Academy of Management Journal, 32,* 687–704.

Kozan, M. K. (1989). Cultural influences on styles of handling interpersonal conflicts: Comparisons among Jordanian, Turkish, and U.S. managers. *Human Relations, 42,* 787–789.

———. (1997). Culture and conflict management: A theoretical framework. *International Journal of Conflict Management, 8,* 338–360.

Leung, K. (1997). Negotiation and reward allocations across cultures. In P. C. Earley and M. Erez (Eds.), *New perspectives on I/O psychology* (pp. 640–675). San Francisco: Jossey-Bass.

Lin, X., and R. Germain. (1998). Sustaining satisfactory joint venture relationships: The role of conflict resolution strategy. *Journal of International Business Studies. 29* (1), 179–196.

Matsuda, M. J., and C. R. Lawrence. (1997). The telltale heart: Apology, reparation, and redress. In *We won't go back: Making the case for affirmative action (pp. 231–233).* Boston: Houghton Mifflin.

Messick, D., and P. Sentis. (1985). Estimating social and nonsocial utility functions from ordinal data. *European Journal of Social Psychology, 15,* 389–399.

Nader, L. (1991). Harmony models and the construction of law. In K. Avruch, P. W. Black, and J. A. Scimeca (Eds.), *Conflict resolution: Cross-cultural perspectives* pp. 75–108. Westport, CT: Greenwood.

Pruitt, D. M., and P. Carnevale. (1993). *Negotiation in social conflict.* Pacific Grove, CA: Brooks/Cole.

Pruitt, D. M., and J. Z. Rubin. (1986). *Social conflict: Escalation, stalemate, and settlement.* New York: McGraw-Hill.

Rawles, J. (1971). *A theory of justice.* Cambridge, MA: Harvard University Press.

Shapiro, D. L., Drieghe, R. M., and J. M. Brett. (1985). Mediator behavior and the outcome of mediation. *Journal of Social Issues, 41* (2), 101–114.

Sheppard, B. H. (1983). Managers as inquisitors: Some lessons from the law. In M. Bazerman, and R. Lewicki (Eds.), *Negotiating in organizations.* Beverly Hills, CA: Sage.

Simon, H. A. (1982). *Models of bounded rationality.* Cambridge, MA: MIT Press.

Thomas, K. W. (1976). Conflict and conflict management. In M. Dunnette (Ed.), *Handbook of industrial and organizational psychology.* (pp. 889–935). Chicago: Rand McNally.

———. (1992). Conflict and negotiation processes and organizations. In M. D. Dunnette and L. M. Hough (Eds.), *Handbook of industrial and organizational psychology* (2nd ed., vol. 3, pp. v). Palo Alto, CA: Consulting Psychologists.

Tinsley, C. H. (1997). Understanding conflict in a Chinese cultural context. In R. Bies, R. J. Lewicki, and B. Sheppard (Eds.), *Research on negotiations in organizations* (pp. 209–225). Beverly Hills, CA: Sage.

———. (1998). Models of conflict resolution in Japanese, German, and American cultures. *Journal of Applied Psychology, 83,* 316–323.

———. (2001). How we get to yes: Predicting the constellation of strategies used across cultures to negotiate conflict. *Journal of Applied Psychology, 86,* 583–593.

Tinsley, C. H., and J. M. Brett. (2001). Managing workplace conflict in the United States and Hong Kong. *Organization Behavior and Human Decision Processes, 85,* 360–381.

Trompenaars, F. (1996). Resolving international conflict: culture and business strategy. *Business Strategy Review,* 7 (3), 51.

Tse, D. K., Francis, J., and J. Walls. (1994). Cultural differences in conducting intra- and inter-cultural negotiations: A Sino–Canadian comparison. *Journal of International Business Studies, 25,* 537–555.

Ury, W. L., Brett, J. M., and S. B. Goldberg. (1988). *Getting disputes resolved: Designing systems to cut the costs of conflict.* San Francisco, CA: Jossey-Bass.

Wall, J. A., Jr., and M. E. Blum. (1991). Community mediation in the People's Republic of China. *Journal of Conflict Resolution, 35,* 3–20.

Waller, W. 1938. *The family: A dynamic interpretation.* New York: Dryden.

Walton, R. E., and R. B. McKersie. (1965). *A behavioral theory of labor negotiations.* New York: McGraw-Hill.

Yang, K. S. (1993). Chinese social orientation: An integrative analysis. In L. Y. Cheng, F. M. C. Cheung, and C. N. Chen (Eds.), *Psychotherapy for the Chinese: Selected papers from the first international conference* pp. 1–25. Hong Kong: Chinese University of Hong Kong.

PART THREE

Negotiation in Context

Introduction

WHEREAS THE PREVIOUS SECTIONS focused primarily on how individual actors—generally isolated from the context in which they are embedded—attempt to resolve social conflict, the last section of this volume focuses on how the negotiation *context* shapes conflict dynamics. Included in this section are pairs of chapters that illustrate how constituencies and groups affect negotiations; how third parties affect the resolution of disputes; how justice relates to negotiation; and how communication technology context affects negotiations. The final set of chapters focus on how the context of social dilemmas affects cooperative choice. Taken together, these chapters broaden our insight into negotiation and culture by recognizing that negotiators are fundamentally affected by the contexts in which they are embedded.

In Chapter 10, Kramer illustrates the fact that real-world negotiations are often embedded in complex systems of relationships that are distributed across time and space. He focuses on the intergroup context of negotiation and analyzes how an extreme form of distrust, termed *intergroup paranoia,* affects the dynamics of intergroup negotiations. Intergroup paranoia refers to beliefs that one's own group is being harmed, wronged, tormented, and threatened by members of another group. After tracing the origins and social-cognitive processes related to intergroup paranoia, Kramer turns to an analysis of the dynamics between groups that produce self-fulfilling prophecies of intergroup paranoia. Because of extreme feelings of distrust, negotiators are often reluctant to interact with the other group; yet the failure to do so severely limits negotiators' exposure to new information that could invalidate their paranoid beliefs. Distrust also causes negotiators to focus on the negative events that transpire between groups and to discount positive events, which also contributes to a self-fulfilling prophecy. However, Kramer also urges us to consider the (perhaps counterintuitive) idea that at least in certain circumstances, intergroup paranoia may have positive consequences in negotiation. Rather than focusing on whether trust or distrust is useful in negotiations, he sets forth a more complex agenda by asking researchers to examine how much trust *and* distrust are beneficial given the particular context of the negotiation.

In Chapter 11, Gelfand and Cai build upon Kramer's chapter by considering how culture affects the social context of negotiation. Rather than being objectively defined, they argue that aspects of the social context—relationships, roles, and constituencies—are constituted through culture-specific practices and meanings. They focus on how culture affects the social context at three levels of analysis: the dyadic, network, and group level. For example, at the group level, they illustrate how culture affects the structure of relationships between representatives (agents) and their constituents and the dynamics of within-team decision making in negotiation. Whereas agents in individualistic cultures see themselves as autonomous and as relatively distinct from their constituent groups, agents in collectivistic cultures generally see themselves as connected and embedded in their constituent groups. They show that such cultural differences have wide-ranging implications in intergroup negotiations—from the nature of agents' commitment to constituents' positions—to the meaning of audiences at the negotiation table—to the nature and scope of accountability to which agents are subject. All in all, their analysis broadens the scope of research on the social context in negotiation, which has been devoid of culture, and expands research on culture and negotiation, which has been devoid of the social context.

In Chapter 12, Conlon and Meyer explore another dimension of the social context: third parties. They first synthesize research on mediation and arbitration, and then consider "hybrid" forms of these classics (med–arb and arb–med), as well as informal third-party roles that are common in organizational contexts. They identify key criteria by which third-party procedures need to be evaluated and compared, including the amount of joint benefit achieved, the permanence of the resolution, whether the procedure generates voluntary or involuntary settlements, the relationships between disputants, justice preceptions, as well as the transaction costs of procedures in terms of time and money. By systematically comparing these procedures across a number of criteria, the authors illuminate the unique strengths and weaknesses of different third-party procedures. For example, mediation often results in high disputant satisfaction and procedural justice, and is one of the least costly third-party procedures. However, it does not always produce a settlement and can prolong disputes. By contrast, settlement rates are virtually guaranteed by arbitration; however, compliance as well as the objective quality of the solutions may be compromised. Notably, Conlon and Meyer's analysis illustrates that different procedures satisfy different criteria; in other words, there is no "best" form of third-party intervention—each has costs and benefits.

In Chapter 13, Carnevale, Cha, Wan, and Fraidin examine third-party intervention from a cross-cultural perspective. They propose that although mediation is universal, operating within and between cultures, culture affects the mediation process and its outcomes. They present a theoretical framework that suggests that culture interacts with situational conditions in mediation, affecting mediators' concerns, their tactics, and the way disputants view the process. They also argue that although general categories of mediator behavior may be applicable across cultures, there are highly culture specific tactics that may be missed by our theories. For example, the "Leopard-Skin Chief" in the Neur, a group that lives in Sudan and Ethiopia, has the option of placing a curse or threatening to call upon supernatural forces if a party refuses to accept a reasonable settlement. The authors' cultural lenses reveal nuances of mediation that are not necessarily obvious until a cultural boundary is crossed.

In Chapter 14, Tyler and Blader expound upon the importance of social justice as it relates to negotiation and third-party intervention. They point out that decades of research have examined how negotiators, motivated by self-interest, obtain outcomes of high "objective quality." Yet they argue that negotiators are motivated by concerns other than maximizing their outcomes; they are also motivated by justice. The authors advance the view that justice is a positive social force that enables negotiators and third parties to resolve conflicts because it broadens the criteria by which people decide to accept potential agreements. For example, by providing opportunities for voice, maintaining a neutral and bias-free stance, and treating disputants with dignity and respect—resources that are arguably unlimited in abundance—mediators may gain acceptance of agreements even when the agreement does not maximize disputants' self-interests. In moving beyond the objective quality of agreements achieved to considerations of distributive and procedural justice, Tyler and Blader broaden the agenda for negotiation scholars and practitioners alike.

In Chapter 15, Leung and Tong compel us to consider how culture affects perceptions of justice in negotiations. Taking a functionalist view, namely that justice principles are essential in regulating cooperation and competition in any social group, they argue that justice is a universal concern. Yet even though the concern for justice is universal, there is much cultural-specificity in justice judgments. They advance a three-stage framework that illuminates the multitude of ways in which culture affects justice perceptions. First, culture can affect the preferences that individuals have for justice rules, such as distributive and procedural justice. Second, culture can influence the nature of justice criteria, which specify how justice rules should be further defined.

Third, culture can influence justice practices—the concrete ways in which people implement justice criteria. Throughout their analysis, Leung and Tong point out numerous ways that cultural differences may generate conflict over justice rules, criteria, and practices. In this respect, while Tyler and Blader show that justice can play a positive role in facilitating the resolution of disputes, Leung and Tong make us mindful of the fact that cultural differences in justice rules, criteria, and practices can cause further conflict, making the resolution of disputes in intercultural negotiations particularly difficult. Collectively, these two chapters illuminate both the positive and the negative forces of justice in negotiation.

In Chapter 16, McGinn and Croson focus on the technological context of negotiations. They provide a taxonomy of different communication media, arguing that all media can be characterized in terms of three properties: synchronicity (whether the parties communicate in real time), communication channels (whether the parties experience each other aurally, visually, or in writing), and efficacy (the ease with which the medium conveys information). They argue that these properties—and not the medium itself—form the communication context of negotiating. Drawing on research in social psychology and economics, they discuss the effects that these properties have on the social (and not just technical) aspects of communication. They show that these media properties fundamentally affect *social awareness,* or the degree of consciousness and attention to others in the interaction. They marshal considerable evidence that negotiations that occur through asynchronous, low-efficacy media with fewer channels produce less disclosure, trust, and reciprocity, and such effects are mediated by lower social awareness. However, the authors cogently argue that social awareness is not a static process that is only affected by properties of communication media. Rather, it can also be influenced by variables such as anonymity, audiences, and expected future interaction, and therefore can be manipulated. That social awareness is malleable is also important for intercultural negotiations, where sensitivity to building social awareness is likely to be particularly important. Not only do intercultural negotiations have an increased potential for differences in understanding, they are increasingly taking place through asynchronous and low-efficacy media. Thus, social awareness can help to build bridges across cultures as well as communication divides.

Barsness and Bhappu in Chapter 17 offer an integrative framework for conceptualizing how communication media and culture jointly affect negotiation. The authors draw on concepts such as media richness, or the capacity of the medium to transmit visual and verbal cues (a construct that overlaps with McGinn and Croson's discussion of communication channels and efficacy), as well as media interactivity (including synchronicity of interactions and the degree of parallel processing afforded by the medium) to deconstruct e-mail negotiations. They then advance the proposition that properties of communication media—media richness and interactivity—will influence the intensity and manner in which culturally derived negotiator schemas are enacted. For example, they suggest that negotiators from individualistic cultures, who already are likely to have self-interest schemas activated, will do particularly poorly using e-mail. In contrast, the emphasis on self-interest in e-mail negotiations may be beneficial for negotiators in collectivistic cultures, who may tend to deemphasize self-interest schemas and might otherwise accept offers before information about integrative issues has surfaced. Likewise, they argue that the parallel processing feature of electronic media that prevents one negotiator from suppressing the views of others may be particularly beneficial for low-status negotiators from hierarchical cultures, ultimately resulting in higher joint gain, yet they may have little effect on negotiators from egalitarian cultures.

In Chapter 18, Weber and Messick analyze the psychology of social dilemma contexts. The dilemma in these contexts is that self-interested behavior has a higher payoff for individuals regardless of the behaviors of others, but everyone is better off if everyone cooperates than if everyone acts selfishly (Dawes, 1980). Drawing on March's logic of appropriateness, Weber and Messick argue that when faced with a decision to cooperate or defect in a social dilemma context, individuals ask themselves, "What does a person like me do in a situation like this?" In answering this question, they focus their attention on three factors: (1) characteristics of the situation, (2) characteristics of the decision maker, and (3) the interaction of decision makers and situational characteristics. They show, for example, that both objective characteristics of the task (task structure, group size, sanctions, leadership) as well as characteristics of decision makers (social motives) are important determinants of behavior in social dilemmas. Moving beyond main effects, they then delineate how social motives interact with features of situations to predict cooperation. For example, when faced with a situation in which a social dilemma framed in terms of a loss, prosocial individuals are more likely to cooperate, while proself individuals are more likely to compete. Yet when faced with a situation that is framed in terms of gains, prosocial individuals are less likely to cooperate, and proself individuals are less likely to compete. They conclude their chapter with numerous insights, both theoretical and methodological, into how best to pursue research on person and situation interactions in social dilemma research.

In the final chapter in this section, Brett and Kopelman analyze social dilemmas from a cross-cultural perspective. Building on Weber and Messick's chapter, they show that March's (1994) logic of appropriateness can easily be extended to culture: What do people like me do in situations like this? In unpacking this logic, they first show that cultural values and norms can help explain cultural differences in cooperative choice in social dilemmas. Their cultural analysis reveals, for example, that people from collectivistic cultures are more cooperative than people from individualist cultures, at least with in-group members. Likewise, they show that norms in social dilemmas, or rules of appropriate social interaction, are affected by culture. For example, in collectivistic cultures, the commitment norm need not be articulated in explicit communication for cooperative choices to be made. Taking a macro perspective, Brett and Kopelman then turn to a discussion of culture as it affects institutional responses to social dilemmas. They point out that societies try to protect resources by regulation and privatization, and they develop monitoring systems and legal sanctions to encourage cooperation and discourage free riding and abuse. They show how institutions that emerge to manage and monitor social dilemmas reflect fundamental cultural differences in economic, social, political, and legal systems. Overall, they illustrate the importance of taking a broad perspective on culture, including values, norms, and institutions, in understanding behavior in social dilemma contexts.

CHAPTER 10

The "Dark Side" of Social Context

THE ROLE OF INTERGROUP PARANOIA IN
INTERGROUP NEGOTIATIONS

Roderick M. Kramer

NEGOTIATION HAS LONG BEEN IDENTIFIED as one of the primary mechanisms by means of which social groups cope with conflict, especially when such negotiations cross cultural divides or national borders (e.g., Brett, 2001; Kahn and Zald, 1990; Polzer, 1996; Stephan and Stephan, 1996). The efficacy of negotiation as a conflict resolution mechanism has been demonstrated across a variety of intergroup situations (Blake and Mouton, 1986; Deutsch, 1973). In the midst of an ongoing negotiation, it is easy for the parties involved—and the social scientists who might be observing them—to conceptualize such negotiation as an activity that is socially circumscribed and temporally bounded. There are, after all, clearly demarcated beginnings, discernible intermediate processes, and identifiable endings to most negotiations. Moreover, there is a readily identifiable and seemingly discrete cast of characters who participate in the negotiation. Because of these salient features, Barley (1991) commented there is a natural tendency for both lay persons and scientists to construe negotiations as essentially "bracketed" encounters into which social actors "knowingly enter and during which they employ behaviors calculated for those situations alone" (p. 166). When people negotiate, according to this perspective, they take on the negotiator "role"; when they finish negotiating, they set aside that role.

This chapter was prepared while the author was a visiting professor at the John F. Kennedy School of Government, Harvard University. I am grateful to the school for its support in the writing of this chapter. I am also grateful for the contributions of David Messick, Keith Allred, Nancy Katz, and Diane Coutu to the development of these ideas.

In some respects, this view of negotiation as a discrete, bounded role-based activity has considerable prima facie validity. After all, negotiations are usually characterized by a period of prenegotiation in which the parties involved marshal resources and plan their strategy. This prenegotiation preparation is followed by an intense and sometimes prolonged active negotiation process, which in turn culminates in some sort of resolution, anchored at one extreme by an integrative outcome that satisfies all of the parties involved in the negotiation, and at the other by a stalemate that leaves the parties empty-handed and embittered.

This portrait of negotiation as a socially circumscribed and temporally bounded activity is reinforced by both theoretical and methodological imperatives. Social scientists who study negotiation often approach the topic of negotiation from their discipline-based interests. Thus, cognitive theorists might be interested in examining how a particular cognitive process that occurs inside the head of the negotiator (e.g., decision framing or anchoring) affects judgment and decision making in a negotiation. Empiricists like to use methods that produce clean and readily interpretable results. These theoretical proclivities and empirical preferences are embodied most clearly in much of the experimental research on negotiations over the past decade. In laboratory simulations, the specific cognitive processes of interest to a researcher can be crisply operationalized in simplistic binary terms. Context can be reduced conveniently to its bare and least troublesome features (e.g., in the prototypic laboratory simulation of a negotiation, comparative strangers with little or no prior relationship come together, adopt artificially assumed preferences, negotiate over abstract resources for a short period of time, and then depart from each other never to meet again). Little is at stake, little is invested, and the outcome is quickly forgotten.

When such imperatives drive the research engine, it is easy to lose sight of the fact that real-world negotiations are always embedded in complex systems of ongoing social, political, and institutional relationships. This is especially true, of course, when it comes to intergroup negotiations embedded in protracted conflict. Moreover, they are distributed in time, so that the legacy of past negotiations always casts its shadow over the negotiators, and the fear of the future often looms large in their deliberations. Thus, the context within which a negotiation is embedded typically plays a critical causal role, influencing every facet of an intergroup negotiation, from prenegotiation anticipation through the postnegotiation residue.

Recognizing its importance, there has been increasing attention over the past decade to the role of social context by scholars interested in intergroup negotiation (e.g., Friedman, 1994; Kahn and Zald, 1990; Kramer and Messick, 1995). In this chapter, I explore one important facet of social context on the process and outcome of intergroup negotiations. Specifically,

I examine how preexisting relations of extreme distrust and suspicion between social groups influence negotiation processes and outcomes. Negotiation researchers have long recognized, of course, the central role that trust plays in the successful negotiated resolution of conflict (Pruitt and Kimmel, 1977; Ross and LaCroix, 1996; Webb and Worchel, 1986). They have noted that trust confers many benefits upon negotiation, including facilitating key processes that enhance the attainment of more integrative bargaining outcomes, such as information exchange and reciprocal concession making (Butler, 1995; Lewicki and Bunker, 1995).

Although recognizing the benefits of trust, however, they have appreciated also how a history of distrust and suspicion between groups hinders negotiators' attempts to establish and sustain such trust (e.g., Blake and Mouton, 1986; Pruitt and Rubin, 1986). Given its obvious importance, it is somewhat surprising how little systematic theory and research has explored the origins and dynamics of distrust and suspicion in intergroup negotiations (see Kramer and Carnevale, 2001, for a recent review). In this chapter, accordingly, I present an analysis of the origins and dynamics of an extreme and historically contextualized form of distrust and suspicion that I term *intergroup paranoia*. The concept of intergroup paranoia is derived from recent theory and research on the social cognitive origins of distrust and suspicion in social systems (see Kramer, 2001, for a recent review). In drawing out the implications of this work for intergroup negotiations, the present chapter has three primary aims. The first is to define more precisely what intergroup paranoia encompasses and to review theory and research regarding its role in intergroup negotiations. A second aim is to elaborate on some of the dynamics of intergroup paranoia that impede effective negotiation processes. A third aim is to identify some fruitful directions for future research in this area to take.

Intergroup Paranoia: An Overview of the Construct and Relevant Literature

I define *intergroup paranoia* as beliefs—either false or exaggerated—held by members of one group that cluster around ideas of being harassed, threatened, harmed, subjugated, persecuted, accused, mistreated, wronged, tormented, disparaged, or vilified by a malevolent out-group or out-groups. According to this definition, the perceived source of threat (an out-group or out-groups) and the object of threat (the in-group to which an individual belongs) are both defined at the social group or category level.

Because intergroup paranoia is a new construct, it may be helpful first to provide a brief overview of theory and research related to this construct. Of particular relevance is research on distrust. Over the past forty years, the subject of distrust has received a modest amount of attention from social scientists (see, e.g., Barber, 1983; Deutsch, 1973, 1986; Gambetta, 1988). Although trust theorists have differed considerably with respect to the emphasis they afford to micro- versus macro-level determinants of distrust, several points of convergence are nonetheless discernible across these diverse perspectives. First, distrust has been generally conceptualized as a psychological state that is closely linked to individuals' expectations and beliefs about other people. For example, the expectations individuals hold regarding others' intentions have been presumed to directly influence judgments regarding their trustworthiness (or, more precisely, the likelihood of trustworthy behavior). Thus, distrust has been presumed to arise when individuals attribute such things as lack of credibility to others' claims or deceptive intentions are imputed to their actions, especially in situations where uncertainty or ambiguity is present regarding the true causes of their actions (Deutsch, 1973; Lindskold, 1978).

Most conceptions of distrust have further assumed that psychological states such as the fear of exploitation, lack of confidence in others, and uncertainty regarding the benevolence of their motives are significant correlates of distrust (Deutsch, 1973). Such fears and uncertainties contribute to suspicion, which has been treated as one of the important cognitive components of distrust.

In many of the experimental social psychological studies of distrust, especially those studies grounded in game theoretic conceptions of choice behavior, the attribution processes that underlie how decision makers cope with such suspicion have been construed as fairly rational and orderly forms of inference, consistent with the idea that social perceivers resemble "intuitive scientists" trying to make sense of the social and organizational worlds they inhabit (Kelley and Stahelski, 1970). For example, Rotter (1971) and Lindskold (1978) conceptualized distrust as a generalized expectancy or belief regarding the lack of trustworthiness of other individuals that is predicated upon a specific history of interaction with them. According to this view, when people make judgments about others' trustworthiness (or lack of it), they act much like amateur Bayesians whose inferences are updated on the basis of their prior experience. According to such research, negotiators' judgments about others' trustworthiness are characteristically anchored, at least in part, on (1) their a priori expectations about others' behavior and (2) the extent to which subsequent experience supports or discredits those expectations. In its purest form, such a view implies a rather straightforward "arithmetic" to judgments regarding trust and distrust. Some actions by the other are construed as adding to the accumulation of trust ("filling the reservoir of trust"), and others subtracting from it ("depleting the reservoir of trust"). The portrait of the negotiator that emerges from this research is that of an interpersonal bookkeeper, or *intuitive social auditor*, who attempts to maintain an accurate accounting of past exchanges and transactions with the other party (Kramer, Meyerson, and Davis, 1990).

While recognizing the importance of such rational forms of distrust, a number of researchers have noted that other forms of distrust appear to be far less rational in their antecedents and origins (Barber, 1983). For example, Deutsch (1973) proposed a form of irrational distrust that he characterized in terms of an "inflexible, rigid, unaltering tendency to act in a suspicious manner, irrespective of the situation or the consequences of so acting" (p. 171). The pathology of this form of distrust, he noted, is reflected in "the indiscriminateness and incorrigibility of the behavioral tendency" (p. 171). Irrational distrust, therefore, reflects an exaggerated propensity toward distrust, which can arise even in the absence of specific experiences or interaction histories that justify or warrant it.

Drawing on this notion of irrational distrust, David Messick and I have elsewhere elaborated on a social cognitive model of paranoid cognition at the intergroup level. To understand the distinctive features of such intergroup paranoia and its possible role in intergroup negotiations, it is useful to start at the level of the individual social perceiver embedded in an intergroup negotiation context (e.g., the representative for one group involved in resolving a dispute with another group). I noted that previous models of trust and distrust have emphasized the notion that the parties engaged in a negotiation keep track of their exchanges, much like social bookkeepers or auditors. Research has shown that the calculative or arithemtic processes of this intuitive social auditor can become corrupted by several cognitive biases, including at least two social-information-processing tendencies activated by conditions of extreme suspicion (Kramer, 1994, 2001).

The first is *hypervigilant social information processing*, which entails the perseverant attending to and overprocessing of episodic social information. For example, hypervigilant negotiators tend to overprocess the meaning of each "move" by the other party, often construing it as a deliberately provocative "insult" or strategic "countermove" designed to further the other party's nefarious interests or malignant goals. The second social-information-processing tendency is *dysphoric rumination*, which refers to the tendency for the "paranoid" negotiator to obsessively reanalyze both past and future (anticipated) interactions with the other party.

Empirical research on these two processes indicates a number of reasons why hypervigilant information processing and dysphoric rumination contributes to paranoid cognition in negotiation contexts. First, hypervigilance and rumination following events that trigger paranoid episodes have been found to increase unrealistically negative and pessimistic thinking about those events and contribute to a paranoid attributional style when trying to explain them. Second, hypervigilance and rumination can increase individuals' confidence in the interpretations they generate to explain such fear or suspicion-inducing events. This latter result may seem ironic and, at first glance, even counterintuitive. After all, one might readily argue on prima facie grounds that the more negotiations pay attention to evidence and ruminate about the meaning of that evidence, the more likely they should be to generate numerous alternative, reasonable hypotheses to explain it, leading to decreased confidence in an especially implausible or paranoid account of their difficulties. However, because it is often difficult to identify the true causes of others' actions, repeated introspection may not result in better access to the actual causes. Instead, people may focus on reasons that seem plausible and prima facie valid.

Previous research on paranoid cognition also suggests that hypervigilance and dysphoric rumination can affect social information processing in at least three ways, all of which might contribute to the development and maintenance of a paranoid belief system. I characterize these as (1) the sinister attribution error, (2) the biased punctuation of conflict, and (3) the exaggerated perception of conspiracy.

The *sinister attribution error* reflects a tendency for negotiators to overattribute hostile intentions and malevolent motives to the other negotiating party (Kramer, 1994). Individuals should—at least from the standpoint of normative attribution theory models—discount the validity of any single causal explanation when multiple, competing explanations for that behavior are available. Thus, even when individuals suspect they may be the target or cause of another's behavior, they should discount this self-referential or personalistic attribution if other plausible reasons exist. However, evidence indicates that people often make overly personalistic attributions of others' actions even when more benign or reassuring explanations are readily available as competing explanations (reviewed in Kramer, 2001).

One implication is that negotiators may have diminished expectations regarding the other party's willingness to reciprocate concessions or respond in kind to unilateral trust-building initiatives. This may result in greater inhibition about initiating cooperation and may also enhance negotiators' vigilance about the failure to reciprocate. Consequently, negotiators may react strongly to the hint or even mere suspicion that the other side is not reciprocating fully (Axelrod, 1984; Brett, Shapiro, and Lytle, 1998).

The second tendency is called the *biased punctuation of intergroup history*. The notion of "biased punctuation" refers to a tendency for negotiators to organize their interactional histories (e.g., construal of "moves" and "countermoves" in a negotiation) in a self-serving fashion (Kahn and Kramer, 1990). Thus, in the case of an intergroup negotiation, the negotiator for group A is likely to construe the history of conflict in her negotiation with the representative of group B, as a sequence B–A, B–A, B–A, in which the initial hostile or aggressive move was made by B, causing A to engage in defensive and legitimate retaliatory actions. However, negotiator B punctuates the same history of interaction as A–B, A–B, A–B, reversing the roles of aggressor and defender. Since defiance is morally acceptable whereas aggression is not, each party to negotiation will frame the interaction so as to make the other party the "prime mover" who initiated the conflict.

The third process, which I term the *exaggerated perception of conspiracy*, reflects a tendency for negotiators to overestimate the extent to which the parties on the other side of the bargaining table, the constituents they represent, and/or third parties perceived as having a vested interest in a negotiation outcome are engaged in some sort of calculated and coordinated action against them. Just as the biased punctuation of interaction history entails the overperception of causal linkages between disparate events, so the exaggerated perception of conspiracy entails an overperception of social linkages among the parties representing or having an interest in the outgroup. Exaggerated perceptions of conspiracy are likely to emerge later in a conflict after issues have intensified. In these circumstances, group positions are likely to be extreme, with the resulting perception that anyone who is not on "our side" in the negotiation must be on "their" side.

There are at least two important behavioral consequences of negotiator paranoia. The first form of behavior driven by negotiator paranoia is *defensive noncooperation*. As Kramer and Brewer (1984) noted, one reason members from one group cease cooperating with members of another group is that they believe the other group is not reciprocating fully or equally. Defensively motivated competitive behavior is thus intended to minimize the risks of exploitation. It constitutes a form of preemptive, self-protective action motivated by the expectation or anticipation that the other side is unlikely or unwilling to behave in a fully trustworthy fashion.

The second form of behavior associated with intergroup paranoia is *moral aggression*. The term *moral aggression* refers to the intense negative reactions individuals sometimes experience when they feel they have been treated in an unfair, unjust, or untrustworthy fashion (Brewer, 1981). The notion of moral aggression reflects a basic intuition regarding the phenomenology of injustice, namely, that negotiators often have a very limited tolerance for behavior that suggests their counterparts are dishonest or untrustworthy. Moral aggression has been associated with strong anger and desire for retribution, retaliation, and revenge in intergroup negotiations (Kramer, Pradhan-Shad, and Woerner, 1995). Of course, as Jervis (1976) noted, to the extent that the negotiators from each group engage in such defensive noncooperation and moralistic aggression, the result is a series of reciprocal disappointments and self-justificatory acts that serve to fuel further distrust and suspicion. Put differently, these cognitive processes—and the behavioral tendencies they prompt—set in motion a self-fulfilling dynamic that resembles the sort of "vicious cycles" or "malignant spirals" described by Jervis (1976) and Deutsch (1973).

In terms of identifying basic cognitive processes that contribute to intergroup paranoia, perhaps the most extensive research to date has examined the deleterious effects of *social categorization* on social perception and judgment in intergroup situations (Brewer and Brown, 1998; Messick and Mackie, 1989). Initial evidence for the existence of irrational distrust at the intergroup level came from ethnographic and field research on the origins and dynamics of distrust between social groups (see Brewer, 1981, for a review). This early ethnographic research bias demonstrated the existence of a robust and pervasive tendency for individuals to display favoritism toward other in-group members (Brewer 1981; Brewer and Brown, 1998). Individuals tend, for example, to hold relatively positive views of their own group and its members (the ingroup) and comparatively negative views of other groups and their members (out-groups).

Subsequent laboratory experiments on in-group bias, using the minimal group paradigm, provided further evidence for it. For example, Brewer and her students (Brewer, 1979; Brewer and Silver, 1978; Kramer and Brewer, 1984) demonstrated that categorization of individuals into distinct groups, even when those group boundaries were based on completely arbitrary and transient criteria, can lead individuals to perceive out-group members as less trustworthy, less honest, and less cooperative than members of their own (in-)group. This research showed that even the process of "mere" categorization of individuals into arbitrary but distinct groupings resulted in systematic judgmental effects (Tajfel, 1970). Brewer and her associates (Brewer, 1979; Brewer and Silver, 1978), for example, demonstrated that categorization of a set of individuals into two distinct groups resulted in individuals viewing others outside the group boundary as less cooperative, honest, and trustworthy compared to members of their own group. On the basis of such evidence, Messick and Mackie (1989) concluded that there is little doubt that "the trivial or random classification of groups of people into two subgroups is sufficient to induce people in one of the subgroups to favor others in that group relative to those in the other group" (p. 59). Several recent studies provide direct support for these effects of "mere categorization" on intergroup negotiation (Kramer, Pommerenke, and Newton, 1993; Polzer, 1996; Probst, Carnevale, and Triandis, 1999; Robert and Carnevale, 1997; Thompson, Valley, and Kramer, 1995).

Research by Insko, Schopler and their associates on the *discontinuity effect* (reviewed in Insko and Schopler, 1997) converges on a similar conclusion.

Insko and Schopler have provided evidence, in particular, for the existence of a negative out-group schema that leads negotiators to be distrustful and suspicious of out-group members and also to expect competitive behavior from them. According to Brewer and Brown (1998), this outgroup schema has two important components. The first is schema-based distrust that represents "the learned belief or expectation that intergroup relations are competitive and therefore an out-group is not to be trusted and the ingroup's welfare must be protected" (p. 569). Second, this anticipated competition generates a self-fulfilling dynamic. As Brewer and Brown noted, "when one believes that the other party has competitive intent, the only reasonable action is to compete oneself in order to avoid potential loss" (p. 569).

Another manifestation of diminished expectations surrounds the negotiating parties' beliefs about the responsiveness of the other party to specific cooperative or conciliatory gestures. Rothbart and Hallmark (1988) found that one consequence of social categorization is that individuals tend to believe that ingroup members will be more responsive to conciliatory influence strategies, whereas outgroup members will be more responsive to coercive strategies. Such presumptions are likely to lead negotiators in intergroup contexts to opt for overly coercive strategies when trying to influence a presumably resistant opponent. Since the other side is judging this negotiator's motives and intentions by his or her actions, the result is a cycle of destructive action–reaction as each side responds in what it construes as a justified, defensive way to the threatening and provocative actions of the other side (Jervis, 1976; Kramer, 1989).

Up to this point, I have defined intergroup paranoia and have identified some of its cognitive components. In the next section, I elaborate on some of the psychological and social processes that contribute to the development and maintenance of such paranoia in intergroup negotiations.

Psychological and Social Processes That Enhance and Sustain Paranoia in Intergroup Negotiations

All else being equal, it might seem as if these various judgmental distortions would be difficult to sustain, especially as disconfirming evidence becomes available to negotiators. A considerable body of theory and research on history-based forms of trust suggests that, when making judgments about others' trustworthiness, people act much like intuitive Bayesian statisticians who recalibrate or update their judgments on the basis of their personal experiences. From this perspective, one might expect that such misperceptions and errors should, over time, be self-correcting. Unfortunately, there are a number of psychological dynamics that may contribute to difficulties in correcting such misperceptions, especially in intergroup negotiation. These self-sustaining characteristics of distrust and suspicion arise, arguably, from both the distrustful perceiver's difficulty in learning from trust-related experiences, as well as their difficulty in generating useful (diagnostic) experiences.

One problem that the paranoid negotiator confronts is that, because of the presumption that the other party is completely untrustworthy and that things cannot be taken at face value, the perceived diagnostic value of any particular bit of evidence regarding the others' putative trustworthiness is tainted. As Weick (1979) noted in this regard, all diagnostic cues are inherently corruptible. He cites an interesting historical example to illustrate this problem. The day before the Japanese attack on Pearl Harbor, an American naval attaché had informed Washington that he did not believe a surprise attack by the Japanese was imminent because the fleet was still stationed at its home base. As evidence for this conclusion, he noted that large crowds of sailors could be observed casually walking the streets of Tokyo. What the attaché did not know was that these "sailors" were in actuality Japanese soldiers disguised as sailors to conceal the fact that the Japanese fleet had already sailed. From the perspective of the Japanese, this ruse was a brilliant example of what military intelligence experts call *strategic disinformation*. Such strategic misrepresentations can be used in negotiation and other conflict situations to mislead an adversary about one's capabilities or intentions (Kramer, Myerson, and Davis, 1990).

In elaborating on the implications of this incident, Weick noted that the very fact that the attaché had searched for a foolproof cue made him, ironically, more vulnerable to exploitation. Quoting a passage from Goffman (1969), Weick reasoned that

the very fact that the observer finds himself looking to a particular bit of evidence as an incorruptible check on what is or might be corruptible, is the very reason he should be suspicious of this evidence; for the best evidence for him is also the best evidence for the subject to tamper with . . . when the situation seems to be exactly what it appears to be, the closest likely alternative is that the situation has been completely faked. (pp. 172–173)

For the already suspicious or distrustful negotiator, of course, the attaché's experience dramatically illustrates what happens when one is too relaxed about others' presumed trustworthiness.

In a climate in which trust is already low, even the nonexistence of diagnostic evidence can be construed by negotiators as a compelling source of "data" that the other side should not be trusted. Dawes (1988) provided a nice illustration of this possibility in his discussion of the debate over the internment of Japanese Americans at the beginning of the Second World War. When then California governor Earl Warren testified before a congressional hearing regarding this policy, one of his interrogators noted that absolutely no evidence of espionage or sabotage on the part of any Japanese Americans had been presented or was available to the committee. Warren's response about how to construe this fact is revealing: "I take the view that this lack [of evidence] is the *most ominous sign* in our whole situation. It convinces me more than perhaps any other factor that the sabotage we are to get, the Fifth Column activities we are to get, are timed just like Pearl Harbor was timed. *I believe we are just being lulled into a false sense of security*" (p. 251, emphases added).

Other research suggests additional cognitive barriers to negotiator trust that can plague intergroup negotiators. Slovic (1993) has noted, for example, that it is easier to destroy trust than create it. To explain this fragility of trust, he suggested that a variety of cognitive factors contribute to asymmetries in the trust-building versus trust-destroying process. First, he proposed that negative (trust-destroying) events are more visible and noticeable than positive (trust-building) events. Second, he proposed that trust-destroying events carry more weight in judgment than trust-building events of comparable magnitude. To provide evidence for this general *asymmetry principle*, Slovic evaluated the impact of hypothetical news events on people's trust judgments. In support of his general thesis, he found that negative events had more impact on trust judgments than positive events. Slovic noted further that asymmetries between trust and distrust may be reinforced by the fact that sources of bad (trust-destroying) news tend to be perceived as more credible than sources of good news. In the context of intergroup negotiation, and especially those in which a climate of distrust or suspicion already exists, good news (evidence of the other side's trustworthiness) is likely to be discounted, whereas bad news (confirmatory evidence that distrust is warranted) is likely to be augmented.

In addition to impairing a negotiators' ability to learn directly from their experience, situations that induce distrust may also impede their ability to generate the kind of diagnostic information needed to accurately calibrate the other party's trustworthiness. Learning about trustworthiness entails risk taking (Hardin, 1992; Pruitt, 1981). People must engage in appropriate interpersonal "experiments" if they are to generate the diagnostic data necessary to learn who among them can be trusted and how much. Such experiments require that individuals expose themselves to the prospect of misplaced trust and misplaced distrust. Any systematic bias in the generation of data samples can, of course, influence the inferences that result from these experiments. Along these lines, trust theorists such as Hardin (1992) and Gambetta (1988) have argued that asymmetries in the presumptive trust of individuals who begin with low or high trust levels may differentially impact the frequency with which they generate useful learning opportunities. These asymmetries can also affect their ability to extract reliable cues from those opportunities that they do generate. As Gambetta (1988) noted in this regard, distrust is very difficult to invalidate through experience, because it either "prevents people from engaging in the appropriate kind of social experiment, or, worse, it leads to behavior which bolsters the validity of distrust itself"

(p. 234). Similar to the differential difficulties that competitors and cooperators have when trying to learn about others' cooperativeness and competitiveness (Kelley and Stahelski, 1970), those who expect distrust tend to engender distrust. Consequently, presumptive distrust tends to become perpetual distrust.

Because of their heightened suspicion of the other party's motives and intentions, distrustful negotiators approach negotiation situations with an orientation of presumptive distrust. An instructive parallel can be drawn from research on the dynamics of hostile attribution among aggressive children (see Dodge, 1985). Such children approach social interactions prepared for the worst. They are, in a sense, almost "preoffended." They thus elicit, through their own anticipation-driven behaviors, the very outcomes they most dread. Much like the stance of these overly aggressive boys who are perceptually vigilant when it comes to detecting hostility, so the presumptively distrustful negotiator is prepared for distrust (Kramer, 1998).

In addition to these psychological factors, there are a number of social dynamics that can contribute to the development and maintenance of paranoia in intergroup negotiations. For example, several intragroup dynamics may disrupt trust development. Insko and his associates investigated the effects of in-group discussion on trust-related judgments (Insko, Schopler, Hoyle, Daris, and Graetz, 1990). They had judges code tape-recorded discussions for both explicit and implicit statements of distrust. The results showed that there were significantly more distrust statements in discussions between groups compared to discussions between individuals. There was also a strong negative correlation between the level of distrust recorded in these conversations and subsequent cooperative behavior.

Collective discussion among ingroup members and information from third parties may further exacerbate such tendencies. In an important study, Burt and Knez (1995) examined how social network structures and the social dynamics they create affect the diffusion of distrust information and its effects of trust judgments within the managers' networks. They found that, although both trust and distrust were amplified by third-party disclosures, distrust was amplified to a greater extent than trust. In explaining these findings, Burt and Knez posited that third parties are more attentive to negative information and often prefer negative gossip to positive information and gossip.

Implications of Theory on Intergroup Paranoia and Directions for Future Research

This chapter began by noting that contemporary theory and research on negotiation—especially laboratory-based research—continues to a surprising extent to present what Barley (1991) and Grannovetter (1985) have aptly characterized as an undersocialized conception of interpersonal action. Taking the assumption that social context reflects an important but neglected aspect of negotiations as a starting point, the present chapter has explored some of the ways in which one important dimension of social context—a paranoid climate between groups—can effect negotiation processes and outcomes. Research on intergroup paranoia is still in its early stages. Consequently, there are many unanswered questions about its origins and dynamics. Accordingly, it may be helpful to suggest a few ideas regarding the current state of this literature and some fruitful avenues for future research.

First, there is a need for laboratory experiments to establish the internal validity of the framework presented here and to identify additional cognitive and affective components of intergroup paranoia. Although extant research has identified a number of distinct cognitive and behavioral mechanisms that contribute to the development of intergroup paranoia, much remains to be done. Given the seeming intractability of extreme forms of distrust and suspicion in real-world intergroup conflicts, it is evident that our understanding of the central causal factors remains incomplete. To accomplish this experimental agenda, however, it will be necessary to develop new laboratory paradigms for inducing intense distrust and suspicion in relatively rapid and compelling ways. The sort of relatively pallid experimental inductions used in much intergroup relations research—such as the minimal group paradigm—are not up to this task (Kramer, 1994).

Equally important, however, there is clearly a need for more field research in organizational settings. Similarly, ethnographic research in cross-cultural settings is needed. Qualitative research that investigates paranoid cognition in real-world intergroup negotiations is essential if we are to develop deeper and more nuanced understandings of these important phenomena. "Thick" descriptions of specific conflicts (cf. Friedman, 1994) or detailed case studies using archival documents are possible methodological routes.

More research attention should be paid to the effects of intragroup dynamics on the development and maintenance of intergroup paranoia (see Kramer and Carnevale, 2001). Along similar lines, we needed more "macro" perspectives on intergroup negotiations, including systematic consideration of how the larger social, political, and institutional contexts within which intergroup negotiations are embedded play in the development and maintenance of paranoid cognition (cf. Allison, 1971; Kahn and Zald, 1990).

There is another, a need for more theory and research on the potentially beneficial effects of intergroup paranoia on negotiation. This suggestion might seem odd to advance at this point, given the arguments that have been proffered up to this point. After all, I have focused almost exclusively in this chapter on the deleterious consequences of paranoia in intergroup negotiation contexts. For the negotiator actually involved in an intergroup dispute with a long history of deep distrust and suspicion, the critical practical question becomes not simply whether or not to be paranoid, but rather how much paranoia is sufficient or prudent. Based on my research, I would argue that paranoia has a definite place in the arsenal of the negotiator. *Prudent* paranoia and *constructive* suspicion—suspicion that sustains vigilant attention and that prompts careful information search and appraisal—can be a healthy and adaptive attitude when negotiating against an adversary whose true intentions, motives, and actions are in doubt and when the costs of misplaced trust are substantial (see Kramer, 2001). In such situations, it may be better to be safe than sorry. As Shapiro (1965) aptly noted, the "suspicious thinking [of the paranoid person] is unrealistic only in some ways . . . in others, it may be sharply perceptive . . . Suspicious people are not simply people who are apprehensive and 'imagine things.' They are, in fact, extremely keen and often penetrating observers. They not only imagine, but also *search*" (pp. 55–58). And when they search, they often find. As the adage reminds us, where there's smoke, there is often fire.

At the same time, appropriate trust—trust predicated on adequate grounds and continually updated and validated—confers important benefits on those included under its umbrella. Of course, this quandary lies at the very heart of the trust dilemma confronting negotiators trying to decide on the optimal mix of trust and distrust, the real challenge is not simply deciding *whether* trust or distrust is best, but rather *how much* trust and distrust are appropriate given the circumstances. Consider the case of the great American writer Ernest Hemingway. Late in his life, and much to the dismay of his wife and friends, Hemingway began to display many of the classic symptoms of clinical paranoia. For example, when he was drinking in bars, he would often point out to his startled drinking companions various men in dark suits who, he asserted, were FBI agents sent by J. Edgar Hoover to track his movements and harass him. He claimed the FBI was intercepting his mail and had tapped his phone lines. As he lamented to one of his closest friends, "It's the worst hell. The god damnedest hell . . . They've bugged everything. That's why we're using Duke's car. Mine's bugged. Everything's bugged. Can't use the phone. What put me on to it was that phone call with you. You remember we got disconnected? That tipped their hand . . . Mail intercepted." (Hotchner, 1966, p. 231).

At the time, Hemingway's claims—and the vehemence and certitude with which they were asserted—were viewed by the psychiatrists treating him as ample evidence of a full-blown clinical paranoia. To be sure, Hemingway was suffering from a variety of mental difficulties linked to depression, the ravages of chronic alcohol abuse, and the debilitating effects of a variety of painful physical ailments on his writing. However, several decades later, we now know that many of Hemingway's perceptions were, in fact, entirely veridical. Documents released under the Freedom of Information Act have revealed that, in fact, Hemingway *was* under FBI surveillance. Moreover, at J. Edgar Hoover's instigation, the FBI *was* engaged in an intense program of surveillance and harassment. Moreover, the scope of this surveillance and harassment was even greater than Hemingway ever imagined. Hemingway's FBI file was opened on October 8, 1942 (long before he ever suspected he was under surveillance), and contained 125 pages of entries. Even his Mayo Clinic phone was bugged, although his physicians viewed Hemingway's "paranoia" about the bugging of his phone lines as proof of the validity of their diagnosis. The last entry to Hemingway's file, moreover, was dated January 25, 1974— thirteen years after his death. Thus, the saying, "Just because you're paranoid doesn't mean they aren't out to get you," often contains more than a kernel of truth.

Such ironic realizations bring us full circle back to what seemed, at the outset of this chapter, to be a fairly sharp distinction between irrational, destructive distrust and prudent paranoia. Ultimately, how much really is enough? Weick's meditation on the nature of wisdom offers a balanced perspective on how to navigate on the edge of this judgmental razor. In defining wisdom, Weick (1979) quoted Meacham, "To be wise is not to know particular facts but to know without excessive confidence or excessive cautiousness." Wisdom, Meacham goes on to argue, is better conceptualized as "an attitude taken by persons toward the beliefs, values, knowledge, information, abilities, and skills that are held, a tendency to doubt that these are necessarily true or valid and to doubt that they are an exhaustive set of those things that could be known" (p. 187). As Weick went on to elaborate regarding this theme, "Extreme confidence and extreme caution both can destroy . . . . It is this sense in which wisdom, which avoids extremes, improves adaptability" (p. 641). Thus, when it comes to adjudicating how much distrust or trust are prudent or appropriate in any given situation, rules of adaptive vigilance and appropriate risk taking—rules that affirm the value of both attitudes or orientations toward trust and distrust simultaneously—may be useful. "Trust, but verify" and "Trust, but cut the cards" are too aphorisms that former president Ronald Reagan liked to quote when talking about negotiating with the Soviet Union. There is a way in which even superpowers can trust each other, he suggested, so long as they trust with prudence. In a world of uncertain threats and dangers, a little paranoia may bring us closer to wiser trust in negotiations between groups who have much to fear and good grounds for so doing. As the events of September 11, 2001, remind us: Underestimating an adversary can prove fatal.

Works Cited

Allison, G. T. (1971). *The essence of decision: Explaining the Cuban Missile Crisis*. Boston: Little, Brown.

Axelrod, R. (1984). *The evolution of cooperation*. New York: Basic Books.

Barber, B. (1983). *The logic and limits of trust*. New Brunswick, NJ: Rutgers University Press.

Barley, S. R. (1991). Contextualizing conflict: Notes on the anthropology of disputes and negotiations. In M. H. Bazerman, R. J. Lewicki, and B. H. Sheppard (Eds.), *Research on negotiation in organizations* (Vol. 3). pp. 64–81. Greenwich, CT: JAI Press.

Blake, R. R., and J. S. Mouton. (1986). From theory to practice in interface problem solving. In S. Worchel and W. G. Austin (Eds.), *Psychology of intergroup relations* (pp. 67–82). Chicago: Nelson-Hall.

Brett, J. M. (2001). *Negotiating globally: How to negotiate deals, solve disputes, and make decisions across cultural boundaries*. San Francisco: Jossey-Bass.

Brett, J., Shapiro, D., and L. Lytle.(1998). *Academy of Management Journal, 41,* 410–424.

Brewer, M. B. (1979). Ingroup bias in the minimal intergroup situation: A cognitive motivational analysis. *Psychological Bulletin, 86,* 307–324.

Brewer, M. B. (1981). Ethnocentrism and its role in interpersonal trust. In M. B. Brewer and B. Collins (Eds.), *Scientific inquiry in the social sciences* (pp. 345–359). San Francisco: Jossey-Bass.

Brewer, M. B., and R. J. Brown. (1998). Intergroup relations. In D. Gilbert, S. Fiske, and G. Lindzey (Eds.), *Handbook of social psychology* (Vol. 2). pp. 554–594. Boston: McGraw–Hill.

Brewer, M. B., and M. Silver. (1978). Ingroup bias as a function of task characteristics. *European Journal of Social Psychology, 8,* 393–400.

Burt, R., and M. Knez. (1995). Kinds of third-party effects on trust. *Journal of Rationality and Society, 7,* 255–292.

Butler, J. K. (1995). Behaviors, trust, and goal achievement in a win–win negotiating role play. *Group and Organization Management, 20,* 486–501.

Dawes, R. (1988). *Rational choice in an uncertain world*. New York: Harcourt Brace.

Deutsch, M. (1973). *The resolution of conflict*. New Haven, CT: Yale University Press.

———. (1986). Strategies of inducing cooperation. In R. K. White (Ed.), *Psychology and the prevention of nuclear war* (pp. 86–99). New York: New York University Press.

Dodge, K. (1985). Attributional bias in aggressive children. In P. Kendall (Ed.), *Advances in cognitive-behavioral research and therapy* (Vol. 4). pp. 131–160. New York, Academic Press.

Friedman, R. A. (1994). *Front stage, backstage: The dramatic structure of labor negotiations*. Cambridge, MA: MIT Press.

Gambetta, D. (1988). Can we trust trust? In D. Gambetta (Ed.), *Trust: Making and breaking cooperative relationships* (pp. 103–122). Cambridge: Blackwell.

Goffman, E. (1969). Strategic interaction. Philadelphia: University of Pennsylvania Press.

Granovetter, M. 1985. Economic action and social structure: The problem of embeddedness. *American Journal of Sociology, 91*, 481–510.

Hardin, R. (1992). The street-level epistemology of trust. *Annals der Kritikal, 14,* 152–176.

Hotchner, A. E. (1966). Papa Hemingway. New York: Scribners.

Insko, C. A., and J. Schopler. (1997). Differential distrust of groups and individuals. In C. Sedikides, J. Schopler, and C. Insko (Eds.), *Intergroup cognition and intergroup behavior* (pp. 75–108). Mahwah, NJ: Erlbaum.

Insko, C. A., Schopler, J., Hoyle, R., Dardis, G., and K. Graetz. (1990). Individual–group discontinuity as a function of fear and greed. *Journal of Personality and Social Psychology, 58,* 68–79.

Jervis, R. (1976). *Perception and misperception in international politics.* Princeton, NJ: Princeton University Press.

Kahn, R. L., and R. M. Kramer. (1990). Untying the knot: De-escalatory processes in international conflict. In R. L. Kahn and M. N. Zald (Eds.), *Organizations and nation states: New perspectrives on conflict and cooperation* (pp. 139–180). San Francisco: Jossey-Bass.

Kahn, R. L., and M. N. Zald. (1990). *Organizations and nation states: New perspectives on conflict and cooperation.* San Francisco: Jossey-Bass.

Kelley, H. H., and A. J. Stahelski. (1970). Social interaction basis of cooperators' and competitors' beliefs about others. *Journal of Personality and Social Psychology, 16,* 190–197.

Kramer, R. M. (1989). Windows of vulnerability or cognitive illusions? Cognitive processes and the nuclear arms race. *Journal of Experimental Social Psychology, 25,* 79–100.

———. (1994). The sinister attribution error: Paranoid cognition and collective distrust in organizations. *Motivation and Emotion, 18,* 199–230.

———. (1998). Paranoid cognition in social systems: Thinking and acting in the shadow of doubt. *Personality and Social Psychology Review, 2,* 251–275.

———. (1999). Trust and distrust in organizations: Emerging perspectives, enduring questions. *Annual Review of Psychology, 50,* 569–598.

———. (2001). Organizational paranoia: Origins and dynamics. In B. M. Staw and R. I. Sutton (Eds.), *Research in organizational behavior,* (Vol. 23). pp. 1–42. New York: Elsevier.

Kramer, R. M., and M. B. Brewer. (1984). Effects of group identity on resource use in a simulated commons dilemma. *Journal of Personality and Social Psychology, 46,* 1044–1057.

Kramer, R. M., and P. G. Carnevale. (2001). Trust and distrust in intergroup negotiations. In R. Brown and S. Gaertner (Eds.), *Blackwell handbook in social psychology: Vol. 4. Intergroup Processes* (pp. 431–450). Malden, MA: Blackwell.

Kramer, R. M., and D. M. Messick. (1995). *Negotiation in its social context.* Thousand Oaks, CA: Sage.

Kramer, R. M., Meyerson, D., and G. Davis. (1990). How much is enough? *Journal of Personality and Social Psychology, 58,* 984–993.

Kramer, R. M., Pommerenke, P., and E. Newton. (1993). The social context of negotiation: Effects of social identity and interpersonal accountability on negotiator decision making. *Journal of Conflict Resolution, 37,* 633–654.

Kramer, R. M., Pradhan-Shah, P., and S. Woerner. (1995). Why ultimatums fail: Social identity and moralistic aggression in coercive bargaining. In R. M. Kramer and D. M. Messick (Eds.), *Negotiation as a social process* (pp. 114–132). Thousand Oaks, CA: Sage.

Lewicki, R., and B. Bunker. (1995). Trust in relationships: A model of trust development and decline. In B. B. Bunker and J. Z. Rubin (Eds.), *Conflict, cooperation, and justice* (pp. 131–145). San Francisco: Jossey-Bass.

Lindskold, S. (1978). Trust development, the GRIT proposal, and the effects of conciliatory acts on conflict and cooperation. *Psychological Bulletin, 85,* 772–793.

Messick, D. M., and D. M. Mackie. (1989). Intergroup relations. *Annual Review of Psychology, 40,* 45–81.

Polzer, J. T. (1996). Intergroup negotiations: The effects of negotiating teams. *Journal of Conflict Resolution, 40,* 678–698.

Probst, T., Carnevale, P. J., and H. C. Triandis. (1999). Cultural values in intergroup and single-group social dilemmas. *Organizational Behavior and Human Decision Processes, 77,* 171–191.

Pruitt, D. G. (1981). *Negotiation behavior.* New York: Academic Press.

Pruitt, D. G., and M. J. Kimmel. (1977). Twenty years of experimental gaming: Critique, synthesis, and suggestions for the future. *Annual Review of Psychology, 28,* 363–392.

Pruitt, D. G., and J. Z. Rubin. (1986). *Social conflict: Escalation, statement and settlement.* New York: Random House.

Robert, C., and P. J. Carnevale. (1997). Group choice in ultimatum bargaining. *Organizational Behavior and Human Decision Processes, 72,* 256–279.

Ross, W., and J. LaCroix. (1996). Multiple meanings of trust in negotiation theory: A literature review and integrative model. *International Journal of Conflict Management, 7,* 314–360.

Rothbart, M., and W. Hallmark. (1988). Ingroup–outgroup differences in the perceived efficacy of coercion and conciliation in resolving social conflict. *Journal of Personality and Social Psychology, 55,* 248–257.

Rotter, J. B. (1971). Generalized expectancies for interpersonal trust. *American Psychologist, 26,* 443–452.

Shapiro, D. (1965). *Neurotic styles.* New York: Basic Books.

Slovic, P. (1993). Perceived risk, trust, and democracy. *Risk Analysis, 13,* 675–682.

Stephan, W. G., and C. W. Stephan. (1996). *Intergroup relations.* Boulder, CO: Westview.

Tajfel, H. (1970). Experiments in intergroup discrimination. *Scientific American, 223,* 96–102.

Thompson, L., Valley, K. L., and R. M. Kramer. (1995). The bittersweet feeling of success: An examination of social perception in negotiation. *Journal of Experimental Social Psychology, 31*, 467–492.

Webb, W. M., and P. Worchel. (1986). Trust and distrust. In S. Worchel and W. G. Austin (Eds.), *Psychology of intergroup relations* (pp. 213–228). Chicago: Nelson-Hall.

Weick, K. (1979). *The social psychology of organizing* (2nd ed.). New York: Addison-Wesley.

CHAPTER 11

Cultural Structuring of the Social Context of Negotiation

Michele J. Gelfand and Deborah A. Cai

ALTHOUGH THE SOCIAL CONTEXT of negotiation had been largely ignored in negotiation theory for several decades—perhaps due to the tremendous success of the cognitive and motivational paradigms in the field (Kramer and Messick, 1995)—the realization that negotiators are social actors, embedded in multiple relationships, is gaining momentum (see Kramer, Chapter 10, this volume). Within this perspective, negotiators are not seen as isolated actors attempting to reach agreement; rather, negotiators' relationships, roles, constituencies, and networks are seen as critical sources of influence within negotiations. As noted by Kramer and Messick (1995), a core assumption of the social context perspective is that "to understand bargaining phenomena, one needs to take into account the impact of the social and organizational environments within which such phenomena are not occasionally, but inevitably, embedded" (p. xi).

We expand upon this growing tradition by advancing a cultural perspective on the social context in negotiation. Our central proposition is that *culture creates the social context;* the social context in negotiation is invariably culturally constituted. In this view, although relationships, roles, and group dynamics all universally affect negotiations, these aspects of the social context are structured through cultural practices and meanings, ultimately creating different dynamics in negotiations across cultures. We seek to show that a cultural perspective on the social context can expand negotiation research to be more inclusive of the social dimensions that are encountered in negotiations in other cultures. We also seek to show that this perspective has practical implications for negotiators because cultural variations in the social context often become an additional source of conflict in intercultural negotiations.

Our social-contextual perspective also enhances the dominant paradigm that exists within cross-cultural negotiation research. Much like early negotiation research, which was devoid of the social context (Kramer and Messick, 1995), cross-cultural research on negotiation has tended to examine how individual actors, who are isolated from the social context, attempt to reach agreement (generally with strangers). Implicit in this approach is the notion that particular attributes, such as values, traits, and schemas, can be ascribed to different cultural groups, and that such attributes are generally *static*, or invariant, across situations. This approach has what we would call an individualistic bias—it gives priority to individuals' psychological attributes as the most important predictor of negotiation behavior, rather than priority to the situational contexts in which negotiation takes place. Social psychological research has long recognized the power that the situation has for behavior (Lewin, 1935; Mischel, 1977). Likewise, cross-cultural research has also long recognized that the situation is an even more powerful predictor of behavior in collectivist cultures (Miller, 1984; Morris and Peng, 1994), suggesting that the neglect of the social context is particularly problematic as we try to understand negotiation dynamics in other cultures.

The exclusive focus on how individuals reach agreement in cross-cultural negotiation research also ignores the practical reality that individuals in all cultures are often embedded in ongoing dyadic relationships, in groups, and in social networks that invariably affect negotiation dynamics. Although research in negotiation has begun to shed light on how these social contextual factors affect negotiation (see Kramer, Chapter 10, this volume), these studies have been almost all conducted in Western contexts, and thus are not necessarily generalizable to negotiations in other cultures. Because culture affects the structure of social situations and social practices, a central proposition advanced in this chapter is that the same "objective" social conditions—how one negotiates with a friend versus a stranger, how individuals negotiate within and between teams, and how individuals negotiate within negotiations with others in extended social network structures—can vary considerably across cultures (Gelfand and Dyer, 2000).

Culture and the Social Context in Negotiation: A Multilevel Analysis

We explore how culture affects three levels of social context in which negotiations are embedded: the *dyadic* level, the relationship between two individual negotiators; the *group* level, or the interactions among members within and between groups; and the *network* level, or the web of extended relationships among negotiation parties. Although much of our analysis requires further empirical substantiation, we refer to existing research where possible. We also recognize that the dynamics at each of these levels of analysis are not necessarily distinct and may be overlapping in significant ways (cf. Thompson and Fox, 2001), yet we keep them separate for analytic purposes.

SOCIAL CONTEXT: THE DYADIC LEVEL

We first consider how culture affects dyadic relationships in negotiations. As discussed by Kramer (Chapter 10, this volume), at this level of analysis, a key distinction that negotiators make is whether the other party is an in-group or out-group member. Such distinctions have importance for the development of cooperation and trust, and have a dramatic effect on negotiator behavior (Pruitt and Carnevale, 1993; Valley, Neale, and Mannix, 1995). A cultural perspective on this level of the social context would ask: How are such categories socially constructed differently across cultures? Certainly in all cultures, individuals make distinctions between those with whom they have close relations and those with whom they have no relational commitment. However, these social categories may be constructed through culture-specific meanings and practices, and likely produce different dynamics in negotiation across cultures.

For example, consider findings that compare negotiation outcomes achieved among dyads of in-group members (friends) versus dyads of out-group members (strangers). Research in the United States has illustrated that negotiations among strangers achieve higher gain at the negotiation table than close friends (Fry, Firestone, and Williams, 1983; Thompson, Peterson, and Brodt, 1996; Valley, Neale, and Mannix, 1995). This phenomenon has been generally attributed to the fact that negotiators within in-groups focus extensively on preserving the relationship, which inhibits them from focusing on the task. By contrast, in negotiations among strangers, negotiators are not as concerned with the relationship and are able to focus on the task at hand, which can ultimately result in better agreements (Thompson et al., 1996).

From a cross-cultural perspective, however, the meaning of in-groups and out-groups within American society can be quite different than those in other cultural contexts, and thus can produce different negotiation dynamics. For example, in individualistic cultures, such as the United States, there is high mobility, and people are able to join and leave groups with great frequency. As a result, individuals are more adept and open to forming relations with out-group members, who conceivably could become a member of the in-group. In contrast, in collectivist cultures, individuals are born into cohesive in-groups and mobility tends to be low, resulting in stronger and more durable ties to one's ingroup, while at the same time resulting in weaker and more distant ties to out-group members. In these cultures, social interactions with ingroup members is expected to be cooperative, whereas behavior with out-group members is expected to be indifferent, competitive, or even hostile. Put in this light, it is not surprising that studies in the United States find that strangers in negotiations are able to focus on the task and to each other's needs in order to create joint value. However, the cultural structuring of relationships in collectivist cultures makes negotiating with strangers more difficult, resulting in lower joint gain (Chan, 1992; Triandis, Carnevale, Gelfand, et al., 2001).

A cultural perspective on dyadic relationships also requires that we move beyond categories of in-groups and out-groups—dichotomies that are prevalent throughout the Western literature—to better capture the complexity of relationships in other cultures. In the Western literature, in-group and out-group relationships tend to be presented as the inside and outside of a single circle. In-groups generally include family, friends, and even colleagues, whereas out-groups include strangers. By contrast, an emic view of Chinese relationships, for example, suggests that relational categories are better depicted by two *concentric circles*. The innermost circle includes family members (*jiajen*) that have an unconditional sense of interdependence. In these relations, duty, obligations, and needs coordinate behavior, yet due to the sheer amount of interdependence, conflict can be prevalent (see also Niyekawa, 1984). The outermost circle includes the out-group, which is comprised of strangers (*shengjen*). Among these individuals, there are little or no relational expectations, and equity principles are used to coordinate relations. Finally, between the inner and outer circles exists a set of mixed relations frequently overlooked, referred to as *shoujen* (Yang, 1992). This middle circle consists of relationships that have the *potential* for becoming ingroup; however, the relationships have not been sufficiently established as of yet to be considered in-group. This middle group includes friends, neighbors, classmates, and colleagues. Most important, it is within this middle range—and not the inner and outer circle—that attention to relational issues such as giving and protecting "face," avoiding conflict, and attending to the development of the relationship is particularly important (Cai, 2001).

An emic analysis of Chinese relationships helps to show how negotiation processes may vary considerably depending on which relationship is operative in negotiations. Within the inner circle, a high level of trust is inherent in the relationship; in the outer circle, low trust is assumed; and relationships that are in the middle range are in the process of establishing trust. Further, negotiation strategies will depend on the range within which the relationship operates. The use of polite forms, cooperation, and face-saving strategies are much more important in the outer and middle ranges, but the use of too many polite forms within the inner circle of the Chinese ingroup can actually create the perception of social distance (Ting-Toomey and Cocroft, 1994). Similarly, contrary to notions that communication is indirect in collectivist cultures, within the inner circle and the very outer circle, disagreements can be managed with greater directness; by contrast, it is in the middle range, where greater attention to face issues and the avoidance of conflict is required (Ting-Toomey and Oetzel, 2001). Attention to the social obligations associated with different relational categories is also critical for successful negotiations. Chinese in-group relationships carry high responsibility for meeting relational obligations; Westerners unfamiliar with these expectations may inadvertently prevent themselves from moving beyond the middle range by not fulfilling these obligations, such as being unwilling to meet the informal requests made beyond the negotiation table (Cai and Waks, 2002).

All in all, this etic perspective suggests that there are important nuances in relationship categories in the Chinese context that are relevant to negotiation. The three-tiered level of relationships connotes different dynamics and practices that may be different from those found in other cultures. Also implicit in this discussion is our premise that negotiation behavior within cultures is not invariant across situations; it is highly dependent on the dyadic relational context.

SOCIAL CONTEXT: THE GROUP LEVEL

We next consider cultural dynamics in negotiations at the group level of analysis. Negotiations often take place between groups, who rely on individual agents to represent their interests and to conduct transactions that affect the group's welfare (Rubin and Sander, 1988). Negotiations take place between those who represent departments within organizations (e.g., unions) and those who represent organizations as a whole (e.g., joint venture negotiations). Likewise, negotiations take place between diplomats and spokespersons who represent different nations.

Adams's (1976) boundary role theory was one of the first to model the complexity inherent to such intergroup negotiation contexts (see also Walton and McKersie, 1965). Within Adams's boundary role system, organizations (or nations) interact through a spokesperson, or boundary role person (BRP; see also Walton and McKersie, 1965). Within each organization, there are groups of people, or constituents who interact with each other, and who attempt to influence their respective BRPs. Further, boundary role persons from different organizations are engaged in interaction, which constitutes the boundary transaction system. Adams (1976) argued that the structure of the boundary role system creates unique pressures for BRPs. As a direct result of their position in the intergroup system, boundary role persons are subject to the influence attempts of their constituents and their opponents, often causing considerable role conflict. Adams's also posited that because BRPs are often physically and psychologically closer to the other negotiating group, they are more likely to share a relationship with the other representative,

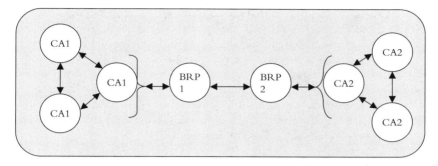

FIGURE 11.1. Within and between group negotiation dynamics (adapted from Adams 1976).

which potentially weakens their bond to their own negotiating team. This system is depicted in Figure 11.1.

These basic tenets have served as a catalyst for three decades of research focused on understanding and predicting the behavior of representatives in intergroup negotiations (see Wall and Blum, 1991). At the same time, most all of this research has focused on group negotiations within Western contexts. A critical question from a cultural point of view is how representative–constituent relations and within and between group dynamics vary across cultural contexts. Because boundary role systems are always embedded in a larger cultural context, dynamics within boundary role systems can diverge across cultures. To illustrate this point, we consider two ways in which culture is likely to impact group negotiations: (1) the nature of the relationships between the BRP and his or her constituents and (2) the nature of within-team decision making, both of which affect the between-group negotiation dynamics (Adams, 1976).

Relationships Between Constituents and BRPs

A cultural perspective on group negotiations asks the question: How is the interdependence between BRPs and his or her constitituents culturally constructed? For example, consistent with a view of the self that is independent from others (Markus and Kitayama, 1991), in individualistic cultures, BRPs are generally likely to construe themselves as separate and distinct from the groups that they represent. They are also likely to have their own set of opinions and interests, which may or may not coincide with those of their constituents. In contrast, within collectivist cultures, the self is more likely to be defined in terms of groups, and as we will argue in the next section, social network relations are likely to have high multiplicity, or have a variety of ways in which parties are interconnected (e.g., extended kinship ties). As such, we can expect that the structure of interdependence between BRPs and their constituents will vary across individualistic and collectivist cultures: BRPs in collectivist cultures are more likely to see themselves as connected to and embedded in the constituent groups, and as very distinct and separate from the opposing negotiating group, unless this group is within the in-group. In individualistic cultures, by contrast, BRPs are likely to see themselves as autonomous and distinct from their own constituent groups, yet at the same time see themselves as less distant to the other negotiating group, as compared to in collectivist cultures.

Cultural differences in the nature of interdependence between BRPs and constituents have a number of implications for intergroup negotiations. First, because the self is defined in terms of the group to a greater extent in collectivist than individualistic cultures, BRPs in collectivist cultures are likely to perceive greater role obligations and have greater commitment to their group's position as compared to BRPs in individualistic cultures. Even when they are separated from their group and their constituents are not visible, BRPs in collectivistic cultures are likely to perceive less psychological distance from their groups, resulting in greater commitment to their group's position. In this respect, BRPs in collectivist cultures may be more likely to feel that their "hands are tied" (Schelling, 1960), even when their groups are not physically present. In contrast, BRPs in individualistic cultures are likely to feel more psychological distance from their constituents and will be more likely to deviate from the group's position, especially when their behavior is not visible to their constituents (see Organ, 1971; as well as Clopton, 1984, for studies in the United States). Such cross-cultural differences in interdependence between BRPs and their constituents may ultimately cause misunderstandings in intercultural negotiations. For example, when constituents are not present, BRPs from individualistic cultures may have the expectation that their counterparts have more latitude than they actually feel they have, causing negative attributions and further conflict.

Second, because of the greater interdependence between BRPs and constituents in collectivist cultures, BRPs in these contexts are likely to have more contact with their constituents throughout negotiations. We would posit, for example, that BRPs from collectivist cultures are more likely to be accompanied by their groups to the negotiation table as compared to BRPs from individualistic cultures. They are also more likely to want to caucus with their groups during negotiations as well. In intercultural contexts, then, BRPs from individualistic cultures may be surprised to find themselves in a solo–team negotiation and may feel somewhat disadvantaged as a result (Thompson et al., 1988). At the same time, we would expect that solos facing negotiation teams would have a much easier time negotiating in individualistic cultures as compared to solos facing negotiation teams in collectivist cultures. The power of facing a group will loom much larger and will result in a much greater perception of disadvantage in collectivist as compared to individualistic cultures.

Cultural differences in the structure of interdependence between BRPs and constituents is also likely to affect the meanings that are ascribed to the presence of constituents or other audiences at the negotiation table, or what has been referred to as constituent surveillance (Pruitt and Carnevale, 1993). For BRPs in collectivist cultures, the presence of others is seen as a natural and expected part of the social order and is likely construed as a source of social support and approval. By contrast, given the emphasis on freedom of decision and autonomy in individualistic cultures, as exemplified in the previous quote, the presence of audiences is more likely to be perceived as intrusive, and as a signal of the lack of trust and the need for constituent control (Adams, 1976). In this respect, to the extent that BRPs make attributions of the presence (or lack thereof) of audiences that stems from their cultural vantage points, this may contribute to further intergroup conflict. For example, BRPs from collectivistic cultures may interpret the lack of audience presence of their counterparts as a signal of lack of constituents' support, whereas, ironically, BRPs from individualistic cultures may interpret the presence of audiences as an indication of a lack of support or distrust in the representative.

The cultural structuring of the negotiation context also has implications for the nature of accountability pressures that BRPs face in negotiation. Given the complexity and breadth of obligations that exists in collectivist cultures, BRPs are likely to be accountable to more sources of opinions— even beyond those of the immediate group—making their accountability webs much more extensive as compared to BRPs in individualistic cultures (see Gelfand, Lim, and Raver, in press, for a review). Thus, in addition to individual accountability that BRPs may have to their own groups in collectivistic cultures, one's negotiation team may also be accountable to numerous other units within the organization and groups outside of the organization (Gelfand et al., in press). For example, Chung and Lee (1989) argued that in Japan and Korea, organizations as a whole are highly accountable to the government as well as other organizations (e.g., Chaebols in Korea). Likewise, in their analysis of Chinese state-owned firms, Xin, Tsui, Wang, Zheng, and Cheng (2001) argued that Chinese organizational culture promotes the notion that employees are not only accountable to their own firm, but also to Chinese society. Such cross-level sources of accountability are consistent with Confucian philosophy, which stresses the importance of obligations that individuals have within their family, within groups, and within the nation. Applying this notion within a negotiation context, there is likely much more of a need for coordination and consultation among BRPs and multiple groups throughout the organization (and even outside of the organization) in collectivistic cultures as compared to individualistic cultures.

Some indirect support for the notion that accountability webs are more extensive in negotiations in collectivistic cultures can be found in Klineberg's (1998) ethnographic analysis of U.S.–Japanese intercultural negotiations. Consistent with the previous analysis, Klineberg (1998) found that Japanese negotiators felt they were circumscribed by numerous other units in the organization and indicated that "decision-making clearly occurs within a multiunit framework" (p. 228). By contrast, American negotiators were more accustomed to autonomous action and being accountable to fewer entities. These differences caused problems between the U.S. and Japanese negotiators. For example, Japanese negotiators were concerned about whether their American counterparts would be able to follow the rules and regulations and to understand that they operate in the "web of the larger company" (p. 233). Americans, by contrast, were concerned about the ability of their Japanese counterparts to be able to make decisions independently and had difficulty understanding their need for interunit consensus. Consistent with our premise that cross-cultural differences in the social context can become a source of conflict, this study illustrated that cross-cultural differences in the structure of accountability pressures caused misperceptions and negative attributions in intercultural negotiations.

In addition to cross-cultural differences in the structure of accountability, the content of accountability (i.e., what BRPs are answerable to) also varies across cultural contexts and can affect negotiation dynamics (Gelfand and Realo, 1999). Accountability is fundamentally a norm enforcement mechanism, and although accountability results in representatives trying to please one's constituents in all cultures, BRPs are likely to engage in behavior that is *normative* in their culture in order to ensure that they obtain a positive evaluation for their decisions. In individualistic cultures, competition is normative and, thus, is more likely to ensure positive evaluations for accountable representatives. Indeed, previous research in the United States has demonstrated that representatives who do not have any information from their constituents expect that they want them to act competitively (Benton and Druckman, 1973) and, not surprisingly, much research has shown that accountability in the United States produces competitive behavior (Benton, 1972; Carnevale, Pruitt, and Seilheimer, 1981; Klimoski and Ash, 1974; Pruitt, Kimmel, Britton, Carnevale, Magenau, Peragallo, and Engram, 1978).

By contrast, building on our previous arguments at the dyadic level of analysis, in collectivist cultures, if BRPs are negotiating with a member of the inner or middle ingroup circles (previously discussed), cooperation is normative and, thus, cooperative behavior is likely to ensure positive evaluations for accountable representatives. Support for these notions can be found in Gelfand

and Realo (1999), who found that accountability to one's constituents produced cooperation and higher outcomes among those who endorsed collectivistic values when they were negotiating with similar others. By contrast, accountability to constituents produced competition and lower outcomes among those who endorsed individualistic values. Although not empirically examined, we would also expect that when BRPs from collectivistic cultures are negotiating with a member of the outer relational circle (outgroups), competition is normative and, thus, accountability would produce competition, not cooperation. Along these lines, we would argue that negotiations with out-groups would exacerbate the intergroup paranoia processes that were discussed in Kramer's previous chapter, especially in disputing situations (as compared to deal-making situations; Brett, 2001). Thus, within collectivist cultures, accountability may precipitate either competition or cooperation in intergroup negotiations, depending on the nature of the situation.

Culture and Within-Team Processes

As compared to dyadic negotiations, the dynamics within negotiation teams also adds much complexity to the negotiations. These dynamics include, for example, the nature of within-group conflict and the degree of coordination that occurs among group members. As with the previous analysis, we expect that these internal team dynamics can vary substantially across cultures.

For example, culture is likely to affect the way in which internal conflict (or dissensus) is dealt with and manifested within negotiation teams. In collectivistic cultures, ingroup harmony and cooperation tend to be highly valued (Triandis, 1995), and achieving collective agreement regarding the negotiation issues may be an important priority *before* meeting with the other group. In this respect, teams are likely to use a consensus (i.e., a unanimous) decision rule, as compared to a majority-wins rule prior to negotiating. For example, in Japan, the practice of *nemawashi* is common in organizations, whereby individuals informally discuss ideas and solicit objections prior to a proposal being formalized. These ideas are written in a document (*ringisho*) that is circulated to all individuals involved so that modifications can be made and a consensus can be reached. This process can be highly time-consuming, especially if disagreements exist within the team. Yet as noted by March (1990), "The principle concern of a Japanese team is to clarify its own position . . . if different departments, factions, or interests persist in raising objections, there will be no decision until those objections are resolved" (p. 132). After a team decision has been reached, Japanese negotiators focus on presenting a unified front, supporting their collective decision, and maintaining a role differentiation that has been established (March, 1990). Individual members of a team rarely express different views from others—in other words, they have low minority dissent (Nemeth and Staw, 1989)—as this would disturb the harmony, or *wa,* of the group. In social psychological terms, team members have come to a private commitment or internalization of the group's decision.

The emphasis on within-team cohesion and unanimity within negotiation teams in Japan, and perhaps other collectivistic cultures, is likely to have some distinct advantages and disadvantages. On the one hand, research has shown that unanimous decision rules within groups are beneficial because they include all members' voices which can lead to greater long-term commitment to the group's position (Thompson et al., 1988). Likewise, the increase in time spent on reaching consensus can lead to social cognitive benefits in teams. It is likely to facilitate a well-developed group transactive memory system—a shared memory system in which members understand each individual's unique positions and roles—which can ultimately result in greater efficiency and coordination within the team (Brodt and Thompson, 2001). At the same time, these processes may result in much longer and more arduous between-group negotiations. After a lengthy within-team negotiation, group members are likely to have intense private and public commitment to their proposal, and there is likely to be overconfidence regarding the viability and fairness of their proposals. There is also likely little minority dissent to challenge these existing perceptions of the negotiation situation. All of these processes can result in less concession making, more deadlocks, and more time needed to come to agreement.

By contrast, negotiation teams in individualistic cultures are likely to have more dissensus and less cohesion. In these cultures, conflict is considered natural and expected; different opinions are tolerated and are often embraced. In making team decisions, majority decision rules are likely to be preferred over other decision rules (e.g., consensus or unanimous rules; Mannix, Thompson, and Bazerman, 1989; Thompson et al., 1988). Moreover, within these contexts, group members may still openly disagree with each other even at the negotiation table with the other team present. Although these team dynamics may have the benefit of increasing creativity at the bargaining table, they also have the disadvantage of having lower coordination and effectiveness within teams as compared to collectivistic cultures. Internal dissensus also enables the development of coalitions and further power struggles, which can reduce the likelihood of between-group agreements (Peterson and Thompson, 1997; see also Keenan and Carnevale, 1989).

As with other aspects of the social context, cultural differences in intrateam dynamics can also become a source of confusion and even friction within intercultural contexts. For example, team members from collectivistic cultures such as Japan are likely to interpret the lack of consensus among individualistic teams as a weakness and may view the team as less credible. On the other hand, team members from individualistic cultures are likely to perceive the unanimity and cohesion among collectivistic teams as intimidating and frustrating, especially if there is little movement from their initial position.

SOCIAL CONTEXT: THE NETWORK LEVEL

Last, we consider how culture affects social networks among negotiators and how this can affect negotiations in different cultures. We consider etic comparisons across social network characteristics and how cross-cultural differences in such characteristics create cultural differences in trust and cooperation in negotiation. We also consider emic, or culture-specific aspects of social networks that have implications for negotiation.

Social networks vary on a number of features, including density, multiplicity, and duration (Ibarra, 1993). Density refers to the number of connections among members within a social network. For example, density is high when a person's contacts all have close connections with each other (Kashima, Yamaguchi, Kim, Choi, Gelfand, and Yuki, 1995). Multiplicity refers to the number of roles that define a particular relationship (Ibarra, 1993). Individuals may interact solely on the basis of a work role—which is characteristic of a uniplex relation—or may interact on the basis of shared work, personal advice, a power dependency, and extended kinship ties—which is characteristic of a multiplex relation. Multiplex role relations in high-density networks tend to be more stable, intimate, and longer in duration than uniplex role relations in low-density networks. Put differently, if two individuals are related based on multiplex roles and are connected through their relations with multiple individuals, it is difficult to exit the relationship. By contrast, if two individuals are related through uniplex roles and are not connected through their relations to other individuals, it is much easier to exit the relationship (Morris, Polodny, and Ariel, 2000).

Cross-cultural research on social networks is in its infancy, yet there are already some important ways in which culture has been found to affect the structure of social networks. For example, individuals in collectivistic cultures tend to be embedded in multiplex social ties of a longer duration as compared to individuals in individualistic cultures (Barley, 1991; Morris et al., 2001). In Japan, multiple ties that mix both personal and professional roles are found among buyers and sellers as well as among supervisors and subordinates (Kashima and Callan, 1994). Furthermore, social networks in some collectivistic cultures, such as Israel, have been found to be more densely connected than those found in the United States (Fisher and Shavit, 1995). These results suggest that it is easier to enter and exit social networks in individualistic cultures, because relations are more likely to be uniplex and of low density.

Cultural differences in the structure of social networks will likely affect the dynamics of negotiations, including the choice of negotiation partners and the development of trust. In cultures where relationships are generally characterized by uniplex and weak ties, trust needs to be established based on attributes of individuals, such as personal reputation, or intentions to be benevolent (Cai, 2001; Cai and Hung, in press). Trust in this structure of social networks is also largely based on an instrumental calculus of costs and benefits, and not on emotional or personal connections. Indeed, given the high mobility in these cultures, trust based on close committed relationships is not necessarily desirable (Yamagishi and Yamagishi, 1994).

By contrast, in cultures with high multiplexity and durable relations, individuals are more likely to trust that others will behave in their best interest by virtue of the fact that they are within a network of long-standing committed relations—and not necessarily on the expectation of another individual's personal intentions, or personal reputation. Long-standing mutual commitments provide strong incentives for cooperation and powerful sanctions for defection, and thus trust can be assured without regard to the personal characteristics of the actors in these contexts (Yamagishi and Yamagishi, 1994). It follows from this analysis that in cultures that have multiplex and strong ties, individuals are likely to prefer, if not insist, on negotiating with individuals with whom they have connections, given that this provides assurances of cooperative behavior and helps to minimize being exploited. Yamagishi and Yamagishi (1994) found some support of this notion. As compared to Americans, Japanese were much more likely to believe that having a personal introduction prior to negotiating with another individual was very important. Graham and Sano (1989) also noted that "cold calls" are generally not made in Japan, and it is only through intermediaries who are familiar with both parties (a *shokai-sha*) that business relationships are initiated. The potential benefits of social trust that are afforded by committed relationships may be prioritized even above the potential economic benefit that could result from alliances with those outside of the social network. Put differently, in cultures characterized by multiplex and enduring ties, it isn't enough to learn that another individual has a good reputation or that there may be the possibility of high economic gain. Rather, willingness to enter into a relationship with others is based on mutual assurances that are gained by virtue of the fact that the two individuals are personally connected.

The Chinese concept of *guanxi* also illustrates the use of personal connections in order to enhance cooperation and trust in negotiation contexts in cultures with social networks of high multiplexity and duration. *Guanxi* is often described as a significant and far-reaching web of social relationships.

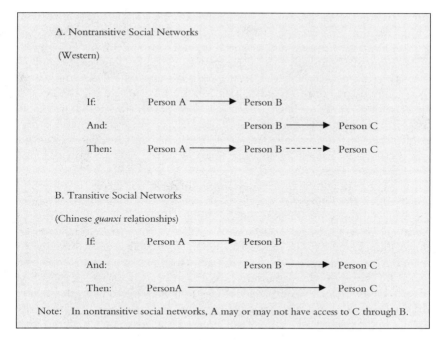

A. Nontransitive Social Networks

(Western)

If: Person A ———————▶ Person B

And: Person B ———————▶ Person C

Then: Person A ———————▶ Person B -------▶ Person C

B. Transitive Social Networks

(Chinese *guanxi* relationships)

If: Person A ———————▶ Person B

And: Person B ———————▶ Person C

Then: PersonA ————————————————————▶ Person C

Note: In nontransitive social networks, A may or may not have access to C through B.

FIGURE 11.2. An emic perspective on transitivity in relationships.

However, an emic analysis suggests that *guanxi* differs from Western social networks because *guanxi* relationships have the quality of transitivity (Massett, 1999). In particular, the transitive syllogism provides that if A = B and B = C, then A = C. Whereas such linkages are common in the Chinese context, this transitive principle does not necessarily apply to American social networks (Cai, 2001).

For example, as shown in Figure 11.2, consider that Person A has a network of relationships that includes Person B, and Person B also has a network of relationships that includes Person C. Person A needs something that Person C can provide. In Western cultures, Person B may introduce Person A to Person C and then let them decide whether they can work together; or Person B may provide Person A with Person C's phone number and have Person A contact Person C to make the request. In either case, Persons A and C are personally responsible to establish their own working relationship apart from Person B and, importantly, A and C are under no obligation to help each other. However, as can be seen in Figure 11.2, in a transitive *guanxi* relationship, Person A has access to Person C by virtue of their relationship with Person B. In other words, because Persons A and C are each directly connected to Person B, Person B provides the basis for direct connection, and, as a result, Persons A and C have distinct obligations to each other that are not present in a nontransitive social network system. In this respect, social networks in China are characterized by far-reaching links of relationships that carry distinct expectations and obligations that differ from the nature of social networks in the United States. In accordance with our analysis of Japanese preferences for negotiation partners previously discussed, it is likely that individuals in China will prefer, if not insist, on negotiating with others within their *guanxi* network, since this provides mutual assurances of trust and cooperation, even if an alternative partner outside of the network could provide higher economic value.

Apart from the theoretical importance of understanding how relationships are structured differently in negotiations across cultures, these phenomena are important to understand because cultural differences in the structure of social networks can become a source of conflict within intercultural negotiations. Take, for example, a situation wherein an American and Chinese have formed an agreement and need to contract with another company for work. Based on the principle of transitivity, Chinese negotiators may expect that that their American counterparts will give preferential treatment to those in their network, even if it is not as economical as working with a company outside of their network. From the Chinese point of view, including those in one's network is not only preferable because it provides for assurances of trust and cooperation from the company, but also because it sets the stage for future duties and obligations (*renqing*) owed from the company as well. From the American point of view, in contrast, although existing relations are important, it is generally acceptable to go to outsiders who can be trusted based on their reputation, and these outsiders may be preferred if they are of higher economic value. In sum, cultural differences in the nature of the social context can add another layer of conflict to intercultural negotiations.

Concluding Remarks

In this chapter, we advocated a cultural perspective on the social context of negotiation. Our perspective builds on mainstream negotiation research on the social context by focusing on yet another level in which the social context of negotiations are embedded: the cultural context. Our focus on how culture affects the social context at multiple levels—from the dyad to the group to the social network—also adds to cross-cultural research on negotiation, which has generally focuses on how individuals, isolated from the social context, attempt to reach agreement. From a practical point of view, we have also shown that cultural variations in the social context can add yet another source of conflict to intercultural negotiations. Negotiators in intercultural interactions are likely to face culturally constructed social conditions that are unfamiliar, causing confusion, frustration, and faulty attributions. This suggests that cross-cultural training of negotiators should focus not only on helping negotiators to understand cultural differences in values and beliefs, but should also focus on cultural differences in the structure of the social context in which negotiations are embedded in other cultures.

Our analysis was primarily limited to the cultural structuring of dyadic relationships, groups, and social networks, yet future research is needed on how culture affects other aspects of the social and nonsocial context in negotiation. For example, the temporal context of negotiation is likely to vary considerably across cultures. In cultures that have a long-term temporal perspective—in which considerations of the past are merged into the present and future (e.g., China; Gannon, 2001)—the history of the relationship is likely to loom large in negotiations. By contrast, in cultures that focus on the future, the historical context of the interaction is likely to be less influential within negotiations. Temporal entrainment processes (Ancona and Chong, 1996) are also likely to vary considerably across cultures. Geertz (1973) noted that in Bali, for example, periods of work are punctuated with periods of *sanuk,* or fun—periods where work is not allowed to interfere with enjoyment (similar to Thailand; Gannon, 2001). From a practical perspective, cultural differences in the construction of the temporal context are likely to cause intercultural negotiations to be more "out of sync" (Blount and Janicik, 2003). Other aspects of the context are equally likely subject to cultural influence. For example, preferred communication context within negotiations (i.e., face-to-face, e-mail) is likely to be culturally contingent (see Barsness and Bhappu, Chapter 17, this volume). Much research also needs to be done on the nature of coalitions and the nature of social power in negotiations across cultures. Not only may the same "objective" role have more or less power in different cultures, but also the types of rights and obligations that power begets in these roles are likely to vary across cultures. For example, high-power negotiators in collectivist cultures may behave much more benevolently in their treatment of lower-power negotiators, as compared to high power negotiators in individualistic cultures.

Finally, in order to fully capitalize on a cultural perspective on the social context in negotiation, we concur with others in this volume (Kramer, Chapter 10; Barry, Fulmer, and Van Kleef, Chapter 3; Kumar, Chapter 4) that future research will benefit from moving out of the laboratory and into the field in order to observe negotiations in their natural, culture-specific contexts. For example, techniques such as social network analysis, experiential sampling methods, participant observations, and archival analyses will complement laboratory experimentation in studies of negotiation and culture. By first examining cultural influences on the social context in the field and gathering necessary culture-specific information, we will be also be in a better position to design culturally sensitive research designs that can examine social-contextual dynamics within negotiations across cultures. Emic information will illuminate novel constructs (e.g., the structure of *guanxi* networks) that will expand the breadth and depth of negotiation theory and research.

Works Cited

Adams, J. S. (1976). The structure and dynamics of behavior in organization boundary roles. In M. D. Dunnette (Ed.), *Handbook of industrial and organizational psychology* (pp. 1175–1199). Chicago: Rand McNally.

Ancona, D., and C.-L. Chong. (1996). Entrainment: Pace, cycle, and rhythm in organizational behavior. *Research in Organizational Behavior, 18,* 251–284.

Barley, S. R. (1991). Contextualizing conflict: Notes on the anthropology of disputes and negotiations. In M. H. Bazerman, R. J. Lewicki, and B. H. Sheppard (Eds.), *Research on negotiation in organizations* (Vol. 3, pp. 165–199). Greenwich, CT: JAI Press.

Benton, A. A. (1972). Accountability and negotiations between group representatives. In *Proceedings of the 19th annual conference of the American Psychological Association* (pp. 227–228).

Benton, A. A., and D. Druckman. (1973). Salient solutions and the bargaining behavior of representatives and nonrepresentatives. *International Journal of Group Tensions, 3,* 28–39.

Blount, S., and G. Janicik. (2003). Getting and staying in-pace: The in-synch preference and its implications for work groups. In M. A. Neale, E. Mannix, and H. Sondak (Eds.), *Research on managing groups and teams in organizations* (Vol. 4, pp. 235–236). Stanford, CT: JAI Press.

Brett, J. M. (2001). *Negotiating globally: How to negotiate deals, resolve disputes, and make decisions across cultural boundaries.* San Francisco: Jossey-Bass.

Brett, J. M., and T. Okumura. (1998). Inter- and intracultural negotiations: U.S. and Japanese negotiators. *Academy of Management Journal, 41,* 495–510.

Brodt, S., and L. Thompson. (2001). Negotiating teams: A levels of analysis approach, *Group Dynamics, 5,* 208–219.

Cai, D. A. (2001). Looking below the surface: Comparing subtleties of U.S. and Chinese cultures in negotiation. In J. Weiss (Ed.), *Tigers roar: Asia's recovery and its impact* (pp. 217–237). New York: Sharpe.

Cai, D. A., and C. J. F. Hung. (in press). Whom do you trust? A cross-cultural comparison. *Organization communication: Emerging perspectives, 7.*

Cai, D. A., and L. Waks. (2002). What we know about Chinese negotiating behavior. In W. S. Jia, Lu, X., and Heisey, D. R. (Eds.), *Chinese communication theory and research: Reflections, new frontiers, and new directions* (pp. 177–193). Westport, CT: Ablex.

Carnevale, P. J., Pruitt, D. G., and S. Seilheimer. (1981). Looking and competing: Accountability and visual access in integrative bargaining. *Journal of Personality and Social Psychology, 40,* 111–120.

Chan, D. K. S. (1992). *Effects of concession pattern, relationship between negotiators, and culture on negotiation.* Unpublished master's thesis, University of Illinois, Department of Psychology.

Chung, K. H., and H. C. Lee. (Eds.). (1989). *Korean managerial dynamics.* New York: Praeger.

Clopton, S. W. (1984). Seller and buying firm factors affecting buyers' negotiation behavior and outcomes. *Journal of Marketing Research, 21, 1,* p. 39–52.

Fisher, C. S., and Y. Shavit. (1995). National differences in network density: Israel and the United States, *Social Networks, 17,* 129–145.

Fry, W. R., Firestone, I. J., and D. Williams. (1983). Negotiation process and outcome of stranger dyads and dating couples: Do lovers lose? *Basic and Applied Social Psychology, 4,* 1–16.

Gannon, M. J. (2001). *Cultural metaphors: Readings, research translations, and commentary.* Thousand Oaks, CA: Sage.

Geertz, C. (1973). *The interpretation of culture.* New York: Basic Books.

Gelfand, M. J., and N. Dyer. (2000). A cultural perspective on negotiation: Progress, pitfalls, and prospects. *Applied Psychology: An International Review, 41, 1,* 62–99.

Gelfand, M. J., and A. Realo. (1999). Individualism–collectivism and accountability in intergroup negotiations. *Journal of Applied Psychology, 84, 5,* 721–736.

Gelfand, M. J., Lim, B. C., and J. L. Raver. (in press). Culture and accountability in organizations: Variations in forms of social control across cultures. *Human Resource Management Review.*

Graham, J. L., and Y. Sano. (1989). *Smart bargaining.* New York, NY: Harper Business.

Ibarra, H. (1993). Personal networks of women and minorities in management: A conceptual framework. *Academy of Management Review, 1,* 56–87.

Kashima, Y., and V. J. Callan. (1994). The Japanese work group. In H. C. Triandis, M. Dunnette, and L. M. Hough (Eds.), *Handbook of industrial and organizational psychology* (2nd ed., Vol. 4, pp. 609–626). Palo Alto, CA: Consulting Psychologists.

Kashima, Y., Yamaguchi, S., Kim, U., Choi, S., Gelfand, M. J., and M. Yuki. (1995). Culture, gender, and self: A perspective from individualism–collectivism research. *Journal of Personality and Social Psychology, 69,* 935–937.

Keenan, P. A., and P. J. Carnevale. (1989). Positive effects of within-group cooperation on between-group negotiation. *Journal of Applied Social Psychology, 19,* 977–992.

Klimoski, R. J., and R. A. Ash. (1974). Accountability and negotiation behavior. *Organizational Behavior and Human Performance, 11,* 409–425.

Klineberg, J. (1988). An ethnographic perspective on cross-cultural negotiation and cultural production. In J. A. Wagner (Ed.), *Advances in qualitative organizational research* (Vol. 1, pp. 201–249). London: JAI Press.

Kramer, R. M., and D. M. Messick. (1995). *Negotiation as a social process.* Thousand Oaks, CA: Sage.

Lewin, K. (1935). *Dynamic theory of personality.* New York: McGraw-Hill.

Mannix, E. A., Thompson, L. L., and M. H. Bazerman. (1989). Negotiation in small group ingroups. *Journal of Applied Psychology, 74,* 508–517.

March, R. M. (1990). *The Japanese negotiator: Subtlety and strategy beyond Western logic.* Tokyo: Kadansha International.

Markus, H. R., and S. Kitayama. (1991). Culture and the self: Implications for cognition, emotion, and motivation. *Psychological Review, 98, 2,* 224–253.

Massett, H. A. (1999). *The effects of culture and other-orientation on personal communication networks and behavioral intentions: A comparison between the United States and Mexico.* Unpublished doctoral dissertation, University of Maryland, College Park, MD. (Dissertation Abstracts No. 9957185).

Miller, J. (1984). Culture and the development of everyday social explanation. *Journal of Personality and Social Psychology, 46,* 961–978.

Mischel, W. (1977). The interaction of person and situation. In E. Magnusson and N. S. Endler (Eds.), *Personality at the crossroads.* Hillsdale, NJ: Erlbaum.

Morris, M. W., and K. P. Peng. (1994). Culture and cause: American and Chinese attributions for social and physical events. *Journal of Personality and Social Psychology, 67,* 949–971.

Morris, M. W., Podolny, J. M., and S. Ariel. (2001). *Missing relations: Incorporating relational constructs into models of culture.* (Working Paper No. 1527, Stanford University, Graduate School of Business).

Nemeth, C. J., and B. M. Staw. (1989). The tradeoffs of social control and innovation in groups and organizations. In L. Berkowitz (Ed.), *Advances in experimental social psychology,* Vol. 22. San Diego, CA, US: Academic Press, Inc. pp. 175–210.

Niyekawa, A. (1984). Analysis of conflict in a television home drama. In E. S. Krauss, T. P. Rohlen, and P. G. Steinhoff (Eds.), *Conflict in Japan* (pp. 61–84). Honolulu: University of Hawaii Press.

Organ, D. W. (1971). Some variables affecting boundary role behavior. *Sociometry, 34,* 524–537.

Peterson, E., and L. L. Thompson. (1997). Negotiation teamwork: The impact of information distribution and accountability on performance depends on the relationship among team members. *Organizational Behavior and Human Decision Processes, 72,* 364–383.

Pruitt, D. G., and P. J. Carnevale. (1993). *Negotiation in social conflict.* Buckingham, England: Open University Press.

Pruitt, D. G., Kimmel, M., Britton, S., Carnevale, P. J., Magenau, J., Peragallo, J., and P. Engram. (1978). The effect of accountability and surveillance on integrative bargaining. In H. Sauermann (Ed.), *Bargaining behavior.* Tubingen, Germany: Mohr.

Rubin, J. Z., and F. E. A. Sander. (1988). When should we use agents? Direct versus representative negotiation. *Negotiation Journal, 4,* 395–401.

Schelling, T. C. (1960). *The strategy of conflict.* Cambridge, MA: Harvard University Press.

Thompson, L. L., Mannix, E. A., and M. H. Bazerman. (1988). Group negotiation: Effects of decision rule, agenda, and aspiration. *Journal of Personality and Social Psychology, 54,* 86–95.

Thompson, L., Peterson, E., and S. E. Brodt. (1996). Team negotiation: An examination of integrative and distributive bargaining. *Journal of Personality and Social Psychology, 70,* 66–78.

Ting-Toomey, S., and B. A. Cocroft. (1994). Face and facework: Theoretical and research issues. In S. Ting-Toomey (Ed.), *The challenge of facework: Cross-cultural and interpersonal issues* (pp. 307–340). New York: State University of New York Press.

Triandis, H.C. (1995). *Individualism and collectivism*. New York: Simon and Schuster.

Triandis, H. C., Carnevale, P., Gelfand, M. J., Rubert, C., Wasti, A. Probst. T. M., Kashima, E. S., Dragona, S. T., Chan, D., Chen, X. P., Kin, V., Kim, K., De Dreu, C., Van de Vlieut., E., Iwao, S., Ohbuchi, K., and P. Schmitz. (2001). Culture and deception in business negotiations: A multilevel analysis. *International Journal of Cross-cultural Management, 1,* 73–90.

Valley, K. L., Neale, M. A., and E. Mannix. (1995). Friends, lovers, colleagues, and strangers: the effects of relationships on the process and outcome of dyadic negotiations. In R. J. Lewicki, B. H. Sheppard, and R. Bies (Eds.), *Research on negotiation in organizations* (Vol. 5, pp. 65–93). Greenwich, CT: JAI Press.

Wall, J. A., and M. W. Blum. (1991). Negotiations. *Journal of Management, 17,* 273–303.

Walton, R. E., and R. McKersie. (1965). *A behavioral theory of labor negotiations: An analysis of a social interaction system.* New York: McGraw-Hill.

Xin, K. R., Tsui, A. S., Wang, H., Zhang, Z.-X., and W.-Z. Cheng. (2001, August). *Corporate culture in Chinese state-owned enterprises: An inductive analysis of dimensions and influences.* Paper presented at the annual meeting of the Academy of Management, Washington, D.C.

Yamagishi, T., and M. Yamagishi. (1994). Trust and commitment in the United States and Japan. *Motivation and Emotion, 18,* 129–166.

Yang, K. S. (1992). Do traditional and modern values coexist in a modern society? In *Proceedings of the conference on Chinese perspective on values* (pp. 117–158). Taipei, Taiwan: Center for Sinological Studies.

CHAPTER 12

Contractual and Emergent Third-Party Intervention

Donald E. Conlon and Christopher J. Meyer

HOW DO WE MAXIMIZE THE OPPORTUNITY for people in conflict to re-solve their differences? In many conflicts, the use of a third party—a person, group, government agency, or other institution—can facilitate dispute reso-lution between adversaries (Conlon and Sullivan, 1999; Kressel and Pruitt, 1989; Purdy and Gray, 1994). Generally, we presume that a third party is needed whenever two sides truly cannot reach an agreement. Thus, one might view the intervention of a third party as evidence of a negotiation "failure." However, this is not always the case. For example, parties in a dispute may be making progress toward dispute settlement, but there may be a rule governing their relationship that requires a third party to inter-vene by a certain date. In other situations, third parties may intervene even without being asked for or wanted, as when a supervisor intervenes in a dispute among two subordinates who prefer to work out their differences alone.

In this chapter, we first highlight some of the key criteria to consider when evaluating third-party procedures. We then describe a variety of third-party roles that can be implemented to help disputants achieve settlements. We begin with a consideration of the two best-known third party roles: mediation and arbitration. We then examine two "hybrid," or composite, procedures that combine elements of these procedures. After describing and evaluating these four procedures against the criteria we have developed, we discuss two additional "informal" third-party roles found in many contexts. We close with a consideration of some interesting research issues that remain to be addressed in the third-party literature.

Criteria for Evaluating the Procedures

In developing a list of criteria by which to evaluate third-party procedures, we borrowed and expanded upon prior lists of criteria developed by Sheppard (1984), Ury, Brett, and Goldberg (1988), and Lim and Carnevale (1990). We will focus on four categories and briefly discuss how each is operationalized in our analysis.

Settlement Characteristics

In considering settlements from third-party interventions, we focus on three criteria. First, we consider how effective the procedure is at getting disputants to voluntarily settle the dispute. We argue that any settlement achieved by the disputants has some inherent advantages over one imposed on them by a third party. Second, to what degree was the outcome reached one of high joint benefit? Third, to what degree is the outcome reached a permanent resolution? Does the settlement stand the test of time, or do one or both parties quickly abandon the decision and return to disputing? We argue that procedures that promote voluntary settlements of high joint benefit will be preferred over those that do not, and that such outcomes are likely to be more stable over time than other settlements.

Justice

Here, we consider four elements of fairness or justice, consistent with recent models of organizational justice (Colquitt, 2001; see also Tyler and Blader, Chapter 14, this volume). First, we are concerned with participants' subjective reactions to their outcomes, their *distributive justice* judgments. *Procedural justice* focuses on participant satisfaction with the process used to resolve the dispute and often hinges on beliefs that the procedure is free from bias, uses accurate information, and allows the disputant considerable voice or input into the procedure (Leventhal, Karuza, and Fry, 1980). *Interpersonal justice* focuses on the degree to which participants feel they were treated with politeness, dignity, and respect, whereas *informational justice* focuses on the information or explanations third parties provide about the procedure or the outcome that stems from it (Greenberg, 1993).

Effects on Relationships

We consider three criteria under this heading. First, to what degree does the procedure facilitate cooperation, or *information exchange,* between the parties as they try to resolve their dispute? Second, to what degree does the procedure bring about an improved relationship between the disputants?

Finally, how does the procedure influence the disputants' relationship with the third party?

Transaction Costs

Two final considerations when evaluating third-party procedures are the cost and timeliness of the procedure. All procedures require resources in terms of time and money, yet some require more resources than others. Below we illustrate how third-party procedures vary widely on these as well as the aforementioned criteria.

THE CLASSICS

The two best-known third-party procedures are mediation and interest arbitration. A classic organizing framework by which to differentiate these two procedures focuses on the amount of process and decision control held by the parties (Sheppard, 1984; Thibaut and Walker, 1975). Process control refers to control over the development and presentation of information to be considered in trying to resolve the dispute. Decision control reflects the degree to which any one of the participants may unilaterally determine the outcome of the dispute.

Mediation is a procedure where a third party assists disputants in achieving a voluntary settlement. In terms of process and decision control, mediation is typically viewed as a procedure that allows the third party high process control but low decision control. With no power to unilaterally impose outcomes on disputants, mediators must rely on their interpersonal skills and available resources to influence the parties and manage discussions with the disputants. The goal is to find areas of agreement, get the parties to make concessions, and ultimately help the disputants create a settlement they can both endorse. Mediation has become a very popular procedure for helping parties resolve disputes. Although originally used in the labor relations arena, it can now be found in many domains, including business, community, and marital disputes (Lewicki, Litterer, Minton, and Saunders, 1994).

Mediators can influence dispute settlement in many ways. Kressel and Pruitt (1985) and Moore (1996) suggested that mediation frequently follows several "stages" where mediators focus on different sets of activities. A mediator is free to engage in almost any behavior he or she wants in an effort to help the parties reach a settlement. However, "stage" models of mediation suggest that mediators typically (1) begin with actions designed to establish a relationship between the disputants and the mediator, followed by (2) an effort to build trust and cooperation between the disputants, and then (3) they move to consider the substantive issues under dispute.

As the parties enter the last stage and consider the issues in dispute, mediators can engage in many different tactics. Carnevale (1986) proposed that mediator behaviors fall into one of four general strategies. These are (1) pressing, or the use of assertive tactics usually intended to reduce the aspirations of one or both parties; (2) compensating, where mediators provide positive incentives in order to help the parties reach an agreement; (3) integrating, where the third party adopts a problem-solving approach to help the parties find a mutually acceptable settlement; and (4) inaction, where the third party is relatively passive and tries to allow the parties to resolve their differences with minimal intervention. The decision to use a particular strategy depends on two cognitive judgments made by a mediator, namely (1) the mediator's level of concern for the disputants' outcomes and (2) the mediator's perception of common ground, or belief that the parties will reach an agreement. Research by Carnevale and his colleagues has generally supported tenets of the model (e.g., Carnevale and Henry, 1989). For example, when time pressure was high, mediators did not reduce their concern for disputants' outcomes, but they did perceive that an agreement was less likely, leading them to rely less on integrating and inaction, and more on pressing and compensating (Carnevale and Conlon, 1988).

Interest arbitration (or, more simply, arbitration) can be defined as a procedure where a third party holds a hearing at which time the disputants state their positions on the issues (they may also call witnesses and offer supporting evidence for their respective positions). After evaluating the evidence and considering other relevant factors (e.g., legal constraints, economic conditions) the third party imposes a binding settlement on disputants (Elkouri, Elkouri, Goggin, and Volz, 1997). In terms of process and decision control, arbitration is viewed as a procedure where the third party has low process control but has high decision control. In the field of industrial relations, interest arbitration is used to determine the terms of a new collective bargaining agreement, and it stands in contrast to grievance arbitration that is concerned with the interpretation of an existing collective bargaining agreement. Arbitration is a specified (contractual) method used to resolve small-claims business disputes, consumer complaint disputes such as in the securities industry, and disputes over automobile "lemons" (cf. Kressel and Pruitt, 1989; Lewicki et al., 1994; Podd, 1997), in addition to its history of use in the labor relations field.

Arbitration usually takes one of two forms. When the third party is free to impose any settlement on the parties, the procedure is known as *conventional arbitration*. However, several problems were noticed in the implementation of conventional arbitration. First, if the disputants believe that their failure to reach an agreement will lead to conventional arbitration, *and* they believe that the third party is likely to "split the difference" between the parties' last positions, the disputants may not bargain in earnest and instead make minimal concessions, a behavior known as the chilling effect. A second concern with arbitration is that the disputants come to rely upon the third party to help them resolve their dispute, and once a particular third-party procedure is used, the probability increases that in future disputes the parties will continue to use the third-party procedure. The increased reliance upon a third-party procedure is called the narcotic effect (Graham and Perry, 1993; Kochan and Baderschneider, 1981), which is linked to the chilling effect in that, if the parties withhold concessions in bargaining because they anticipate third-party intervention, their very behavior increases the likelihood that a third party will be needed (a self-fulfilling prophecy).

Final offer arbitration (FOA) was developed to address both the chilling and narcotic effect (e.g., Feuille, 1975). In FOA, the arbitrator must select one of the two final offers made by the disputants. As the arbitrator cannot "split the difference," each party's strategy is to submit a final offer that appears slightly more reasonable to the third party than the other party's final offer (Webb, 1986).

EVALUATING THE CLASSICS

How well does mediation satisfy the criteria we have constructed? In terms of settlement characteristics, we note that mediation is successful in helping disputants reach settlements most of the time. Depending on the source, voluntary settlement rates as high as 78 percent are noted (Brett, 2001). For example, Hoh (1984) reported that over 77 percent of all public sector, collective bargaining cases in Iowa were settled during mediation. Kochan (1979) presented similar evidence from other settings. Settlements in mediation often produce considerable disputant satisfaction (Brett, Barsness, and Goldberg, 1996). This should not be surprising, for any settlement achieved in mediation is one the parties voluntarily agreed to (put differently, their retention of decision control should produce positive reactions). Presumably, if they were not satisfied with the benefit achieved, they would instead continue to dispute, either by returning to negotiation, continuing with mediation, or moving to some other dispute resolution procedure.

However, mediation cannot insure dispute resolution because it cannot guarantee that disputants will agree. In fact, the disputes most amenable to mediation may be the least difficult to resolve or have disputants who are most motivated the resolve the conflict. For example, Kressel and Pruitt (1989) cited settlement rates of 20 to 80 percent, depending on the context. Hiltrop (1989) reported settlement rates of only 46 percent for disputes involving a key issue or matters of principle. This highlights that the extent to which disputants' interests are opposed—(what Thibaut and Kelley (1959) referred to as a noncorrespondence of outcomes)—influences the success rate of mediation. Mediation is more effective when the conflict is mild (Carnevale and Pruitt, 1992). As the level of conflict increases, the probability of settlement decreases (Depner, Canata, and Ricci, 1994).

In terms of creating jointly beneficial agreements, Carnevale and Henry (1989) demonstrated that most mediators attempted to promote integrative agreements more than any other strategy, and McEwen and Maiman (1984) reported that, when compared to adjudication, mediation seldom resulted in one-sided settlements. These findings suggest that the objective quality of the agreements is often high. Finally, research suggests that a settlement reached in mediation is more likely to be complied with than a settlement reached via adjudication (Kressel and Pruitt, 1989; McEwen and Maiman, 1984; see also Tyler and Blader, Chapter 14, this volume).

Turning to the criterion of justice, mediation seems to be preferred by disputants over arbitration for many types of disputes (Brett et al., 1996; Pierce, Pruitt, and Czaja, 1993). The reason mediation is preferred to arbitration may be because disputants retain decision control and have greater perceptions of procedural justice (Brett and Goldberg, 1983; Shapiro and Brett, 1993). Whether mediation is objectively more fair than arbitration is a matter of debate. Observers (Kolb, 1983; Vidmar, 1985) have noted that in small-claims and public–labor relations disputes, mediators sometimes take heavy-handed approaches, pressuring the parties to accept particular settlements. The nascent literature on interpersonal and informational justice may one day help us understand the implications of mediator behavior on disputant outcomes. Mediation would seem to be a procedure that, because of its lack of structure, may lead to more variations in interpersonal and informational justice perceptions than might more structured third-party procedures like arbitration or adjudication. For instance, arbitration, with its opening and closing statements and opportunities for examination and cross-examination of witnesses, may not give disputants much opportunity to participate themselves, but it does provide for a balanced presentation of the case. Mediation is a much more open-ended process: mediators may separate the parties or keep them together; they may allow the disputants to participate fully in the discussion or only allow agents to speak. With no standard image such as that of a courtroom to compare the mediation procedure to, some disputants may be disappointed in the process and judge it to be unfair. Finally, distributive justice judgments are usually viewed as based on the degree to which the settlement meets disputants' expectations, which, in turn, are based upon the disputants' target and resistance points (Walton and McKersie, 1965). However, there is some research suggesting that outcomes that disputants reach on their own (e.g., a mediated settlement) are perceived as more fair than outcomes imposed by a third party, even controlling for the value of the outcome (Conlon, Moon, and Ng, 2001). This suggests that decision control, or allowing disputants to "own" the settlement, can facilitate perceptions of distributive justice.

In terms of effects on relationships, both field and experimental research indicate that mediator intervention increases cooperation, which in turn affects negotiation outcomes (e.g., Hiltrop, 1989; Ross, Conlon, and Lind, 1990). To the extent that the parties provide each other with valuable outcomes, their attraction to each other should increase, and this should have a positive effect on their relationship. Turning to disputant reaction to the third party, research suggests that this may depend strongly on the behavior of the third party during mediation. There are also questions of the role that a mediator's biases may play in shaping (a) his or her suggestions and (b) whether those suggestions are perceived by the disputants as fair (Conlon and Ross, 1993; Wittmer, Carnevale, and Walker, 1991). Research suggests that disputants are less concerned with mediators' alignment or affiliation and more concerned with what they say and do during mediation. Anecdotally, this explains why in many contexts (such as international relations) third parties can be successful in spite of national policies that might favor one nation over another (as when Henry Kissinger, a Jewish American, acted as a mediator between Israel and Egypt).

Regarding transaction costs, we note that mediation is generally considered to be the least costly and time-consuming third-party procedure (Brett et al., 1996). Champlin and Bognanno (1985) demonstrated that public-sector disputes in Minnesota were resolved faster through mediation than through arbitration. However, mediation frequently does not involve a specific time frame: disputes can continue for weeks, months, or even years with no resolution, as a mediator has no authority to force an end to the impasse, although the costs associated with an impasse may make the parties more receptive to the mediator's suggestions (Hiltrop, 1989). This highlights how timeliness of resolution can be problematic, particularly for the most intractable of disputes.

In summary, although mediation may be effective in many disputes, particularly when the level of hostility is not extreme, the obvious shortcoming is that the procedure does not always produce a settlement. This could lead to some disputes continuing indefinitely, with the disputants, and interested stakeholders, paying the price. The inability to ensure a settlement could also result in the conflict escalating with even more severe consequences for disputants and stakeholders (e.g., moving from a work slowdown to a strike produces more severe consequences for disputing parties and society as a whole).

One procedure that always produces a settlement is arbitration. The same criteria used to evaluate mediation can also be used to evaluate the effectiveness of arbitration. In terms of voluntary settlements, Farber and Katz (1979) demonstrated that the mere threat of arbitration may motivate the parties to negotiate a settlement. Final offer arbitration in particular can lead disputants to achieve voluntary settlements more frequently than can conventional arbitration (Somers, 1977). In fact, if FOA has been used in the past, the probability of using FOA in subsequent disputes decreases, reducing the "narcotic effect" (Kelly, 1985).

However, many disputes still require the arbitrator to impose a settlement, and in such cases there are a number of concerns. One relates to settlement quality: Pearson and Thoennes (1989) argued that imposed settlements from adversarial procedures like arbitration only address symptoms of the conflict and do not address the underlying core conflict. Moreover, since the parties did not voluntarily agree to the outcome, settlement permanence can be a problem. A number of scholars argue that disputants who reach agreement of their own volition will be more satisfied and committed, leading to greater adherence to such agreements, causing them to be longer lasting (McEwen and Maiman, 1984; Meagher, 1976). This suggests that compliance with arbitrated rulings may be problematic (see also Lewicki et al., 1999).

Finally, one can also question the objective quality of arbitrated settlements. Arbitrators in public-sector disputes must often consider objective criteria such as wage comparison statistics to ensure that awards are not unreasonable. Several writers have expressed concern that in such contexts third parties tend to use an "equality" heuristic, which leads the arbitrator to "split the difference" between disputing parties' positions (Farber, 1981; Notz and Starke, 1987) rather than focusing on an objectively more appropriate settlement point. In addition, one could easily surmise a final offer arbitration scenario where neither side has made a reasonable final offer, yet the arbitrator is constrained and must pick from among the two objectively poor settlements.

Turning to justice perceptions, we note that early laboratory research comparing mediation and arbitration actually found higher ratings of procedural justice for arbitration (e.g., La Tour, Houlden, Walker, and Thibaut, 1976). However, this may be because these hypothetical disputes were designed such that the disputants' interests were completely opposed to each other (making negotiation and mediation unlikely to achieve dispute resolution; cf. Lind and Tyler, 1988). In such instances, disputants are likely more willing to relinquish decision control to a third party and exert their influence with process control, often through an attorney representing and advocating their position (an adversarial model). Other studies measuring the beliefs of participants in real disputes reveal a different pattern. For instance, survey data from Brett and Goldberg (1983) and Shapiro and Brett (1993) indicated that disputants perceive that they have less process and decision control under arbitration than mediation. In reconciling these findings, it would appear that arbitration will lead to lower procedural justice judgments than mediation unless disputants perceive that the likelihood of a voluntary settlement is extremely low, in which case they may be willing to cede decision control to an arbitrator without suffering a decrement in procedural justice judgments.

We further recognize that the manner in which an arbitration procedure is enacted may have effects on disputants' procedural, interpersonal, or informational justice judgments, as has been seen in adjudication contexts (e.g., Lind and Lissak, 1985). The type of arbitration may also influence judgments of distributive fairness. For example, in an adjudication setting, Conlon, Lind, and Lissak (1989) found that "all or nothing" outcomes were seen as more fair than "compromise" outcomes. They argued that disputants in the compromise conditions viewed their third party as having considered the evidence less thoroughly. Consideration is an element in more recent theorizing that focuses on informational and interpersonal justice judgments (Shapiro, 1993). Extending this to the arbitration domain suggests that conventional arbitration outcomes, which often produce settlements between the parties positions (i.e., compromises) may be seen as less distributively fair than final offer outcomes (which give the disputant either all or nothing that they asked for).

In terms of the effects of arbitration on relationships, we can make some connections between already discussed criteria. For example, the chilling effect (Feuille, 1975), noted earlier, highlights that conventional arbitration (CA) can lead to relationship deterioration and delayed settlements. Thus, conventional arbitration may do little to promote cooperative behavior and information exchange between the parties. However, research has shown that, relative to CA, FOA reduces disputants' aspirations (Starke and Notz, 1981) and produces final positions that are closer, thus reducing the chilling effect (Ashenfelter and Bloom, 1984; Coleman, Jennings, and McLaughlin, 1993).

Turning to transaction costs, the evidence for the speed of resolution in arbitration is equivocal. For business disputes, arbitration is usually faster than using the court system, and labor arbitration can be faster than negotiations that occur during the emotional time of a strike. However, if the parties come to overrely on the procedure in lieu of negotiated or mediated settlements, arbitration can become a very expensive long-term cost.

Although arbitration always produces a settlement, it is not without problems. In particular, if we remember that a number of positive effects stem from having disputants themselves settle their problems (in terms of permanence of settlement, fairness judgments, and positive effects on relationships), then many of the side effects of arbitration become problematic.

COMBINING THE CLASSICS

Recognizing that different procedures offer different strengths, some scholars have advocated the adoption of alternative, or "hybrid," third-party procedures. Recently, Ross and Conlon (2000) provided a theoretical comparison of two such hybrid procedures by contrasting two procedures that incorporate elements of both mediation and arbitration. The two hybrid procedures they considered were *mediation–arbitration* and the relatively unknown *arbitration–mediation* procedure.

Mediation–arbitration (hereafter called med–arb) consists of (1) mediation, followed by (2) arbitration if mediation fails to secure an agreement by a predetermined deadline. The same or different third parties may serve as both mediator and arbitrator, and either conventional or final-offer arbitration may be incorporated (Kagel, 1976). The procedure is incremental: only if mediation fails to produce an agreement does the arbitration phase occur, which culminates with the third party imposing a binding settlement on the parties. The American Arbitration Association has implemented med–arb in an attempt to create a "fast track" settlement option for handling business disputes (Smith, 1999). Conceptually, the use of arbitration following mediation matches the suggestions of many scholars. For instance, Starke and Notz (1981) argued that mediation should precede arbitration because it removes less control over the ultimate outcome from the disputants; the sequencing is also consistent with Ury et al., (1988) argument that dispute resolution procedures be arranged in a "low-to-high-cost sequence" for the users (pp. 62–63). However, these scholars were envisioning the use of separate mediation and arbitration procedures (which would always involve different third parties) rather than hybrid procedures (which usually involve the same third party across the two roles).

In a field experiment comparing two forms of med–arb (differing in terms of whether the same or a different third party implemented the arbitration phase) to mediation, McGillicuddy, Welton, and Pruitt (1987) predicted that med–arb would lead disputants to be less hostile and more problem solving–oriented in their behavior because they feared the loss of control over their outcomes should the dispute go to the arbitration stage. Although these behavioral differences were found in their study, there was no difference in voluntary (mediated) settlement rates. However, the third parties in the med–arb (same third party) procedure were more assertive in their behavior toward the disputants than were the third parties in the mediation condition, which might have negative implications for interpersonal justice judgments and the future relationship between the disputants and the third party.

The other hybrid procedure, arbitration–mediation (hereafter called arb–med), consists of three phases. In phase one, the third party holds an arbitration hearing. At the end of this phase, the third party makes a decision, which is placed in a sealed envelope and is not revealed to the parties. The second phase consists of mediation. Only if mediation fails to produce a voluntary agreement by a specified deadline do the parties enter the third phase, called the ruling phase. Here, the third party removes the ruling from the envelope and reveals the binding ruling to the disputants (Coltri, L.S.). To assure that the envelope contains the original ruling and not a later ruling (e.g., a ruling created after the mediation phase), the third party can ask each side to sign the envelope across the seal at the beginning of mediation.

To date, only three empirical studies have examined arb–med, and both compared the procedure to med–arb. Conlon, Moon, and Ng (2002) found that arb–med led to more voluntary settlements (settlements in the mediation phase) than did med–arb. Settlements reached in arb–med were also of marginally greater value than those achieved under med–arb, though the arb–med procedure did take longer to resolve disputes. Arb–med also produced more voluntary settlements than did med–arb for particularly difficult disputes (in this study, defined as cases where an individual was in conflict with a three-person team, which should have led to power differentials between the disputants). Conlon et al.'s (2002) explanation for increased settlements could be summarized as a risk aversion argument: disputants are more motivated to exert their own control over the outcome than risk the unknown and potentially more negative outcome determined by the third party. Thus, if a critical goal is to create conditions that lead disputants to resolve their own disputes, arb–med may be an interesting advance. In addition, arb–med may even be well suited to handling difficult disputes, though it still needs to be tested in a field study.

Ross, Brantmeier, and Ciriacks (2002) conducted two studies where they placed students in the role of constituents who watched their bargaining representative participate in an arb–med or med–arb dispute resolution procedure. The third party imposed a settlement on all parties, as no agreements were reached in mediation. In Study 1 there were no differences between the procedures for any form of justice; however, in Study 2, they found that ratings of procedural and interpersonal justice were higher for med–arb. This contradicts other data from the Conlon et al. (2002) data set (reported in Conlon et al., 2001), which revealed no differences in disputant ratings of procedural, distributive, or interpersonal justice between the procedures, but higher ratings of informational justice for the arb–med procedure. Given the number of differences between these studies, it is easy to see why the fairness results are not consistent.

CONTEXTUALIZING THIRD PARTIES: CONTRACTUAL OR EMERGENT INTERVENTION

A number of scholars have argued that an important distinction that needs to be made when considering third-party procedures is the context in which the procedure is embedded. For example, Lewicki et al. (1999) referred to "formal" and "informal" third-party interventions. Touval (1985) referred to "political" and "apolitical" interventions. We rely on nomenclature used by Pruitt and Carnevale (1993) and characterize third-party involvement as *contractual* or *emergent*. Contractual third-party intervention occurs when a set of rules or regulations previously agreed to by parties determines the form of third-party intervention and when that intervention occurs. For example, in some collective bargaining contexts, third-party intervention is specified if an agreement is not reached by a certain point in time. Although we have elaborated on four different forms of contractual third-party intervention (even more if we discriminate between various forms of arbitration), there seem to be fewer forms of emergent third-party behavior. We will focus on two specific forms of emergent intervention, a low-power form and a high-power form. We will first describe these two different emergent third-party roles. We will then consider what makes these roles different from the contractual roles while also discussing how the emergent roles affect many of our evaluation criteria.

A Low-Power-Emergent Third Party

Take the example of an employee who becomes aware of a dispute between two coworkers at the same level of the organization's hierarchy (in other words, all three parties are peers). First, we note that this third party can only intervene with the consent of the disputants. Assuming that the disputants are receptive, this employee intervention would at many levels appear very similar to mediation. She or he can make suggestions, but certainly cannot force a settlement on the parties. However, depending on the mediator's cognitive, monetary, or nonmonetary resources, she or he may be able to engage in pressing behavior, compensation, or help the parties realize a jointly beneficial solution. However, another option available to this emergent third party that is not available to a mediator in contractual mediation is that the employee could choose not to intervene at all. Instead, the "potential mediator" could overlook the dispute and not get involved. In contractual mediation, the mediator does not have this discretion over his or her involvement.

A High-Power-Emergent Third Party

Now consider the identical situation previously described, except that the third party is the hierarchical superior of the two employees involved in the dispute. Assuming that the dispute is over something work-related, this third party would have a variety of options available in pursuing third-party intervention. Of course, as in the first example, the "boss" could choose to ignore the dispute. Or, the boss could simply tell the parties that she or he is aware of their dispute and do nothing else, something the mediator in the first story might do, but this would likely have no effect whatsoever on the parties. The high-power third party could also "act" exactly like the low-power mediator (using strategies such as those espoused by Carnevale, 1986)—though chances are that the disputants would perceive any statements and behavior made by their boss differently from the identical statements and behaviors made by a peer employee.

However, the high-power-emergent third party also has the power or authority to act like an arbitrator in the sense that she or he could impose a settlement on the disputants. In fact, one might argue that this third party is similar to a hybrid role like med–arb or arb–med, with the difference being that the third party can choose which role she or he wants to assume: something like arb–med ("I'm warning you–I already have a settlement in mind to put on you, so if you don't settle this yourselves you will have to live with it") or something like med–arb ("If you don't settle this yourselves, I'll settle it for you"). In fact, a unique option that a high-power emergent third party may have that is unavailable to all of the other third parties we have discussed is the ability to "reject" a settlement. It is entirely possible that a boss might tell disputants to "go back to the drawing board" and come up with another "more acceptable" solution. Finally, we also note that the involvement of this third party is not necessarily with the consent of the disputants—they may not desire third-party intervention at all, yet they may not be able to stop it.

NOTABLE DIFFERENCES BETWEEN EMERGENT
AND CONTRACTUAL PROCEDURES

One difference between contractual and emergent third-party intervention relates to how the procedures are invoked. Whereas contractual intervention is specified by predetermined rules or regulations that exist prior to a dispute arising, emergent TPI occurs in a more spontaneous fashion. The intervention by the third party simply "emerges" out of the social context in which all parties naturally reside. A faculty member intervening in a dispute between two other faculty members, or between two students, or between another faculty member and a student, or a parent intervening in a dispute between children or other relatives would all be examples of emergent third-party behavior. In these instances, there are no rules specifying that the parties would intervene. Thus, there is less formality in the initiation and implementation of emergent TPI than there is with contractual TPI.

A second key difference between emergent and contractual TPI concerns the "location" of the third party. Under contractual TPI, the third party is usually not a member of the same social system or organization as the disputants. For instance, in a dispute between coal miners and operators a mediator from the Federal Mediation and Conciliation Service may intervene. In the case of a dispute between an auto dealer and a customer over a new car, an arbitrator might be chosen from the American Arbitration Association. In both cases, the third party is an outsider in the sense that she or he is not someone who works at the mine or in the industry in which the dispute resides. However, Pruitt and Carnevale (1993) argued that emergent third parties usually have an ongoing or preexisting relationship with the disputants. Thus, a preexisting relationship is another characteristic differentiating emergent from contractual TPI. Of course, there may be circumstances where, over time, parties in a dispute involving contractual TPI choose to involve a third party that they have relied on before. However, this relationship differs from that in emergent TPI, as the relationship only exists in the context of intervening in multiple disputes over time.

Finally, Pruitt and Carnevale (1993) highlight that emergent third parties also tend to be *interested* third parties, meaning that (1) they may care or also be affected by the outcome that is reached by the disputants and/or (2) that they desire to make a good impression on the disputants. We would add that it is also possible that an emergent third party may seek to cultivate a bad impression on a disputant as well (for instance, a third party may desire both disputants to think that she or he is biased against them, which may lead both parties to reduce their aspirations, thereby actually increasing their likelihood of reaching an agreement). This suggests that emergent third parties may sometimes use dispute resolution as a means to further their own interests, which may or may not coincide with those of the disputants.

There have not been many studies of emergent-third-party roles. Karambayya, Brett, and Lytle (1992) contrasted high- and low-power third parties in a simulated organizational dispute by varying whether the third party was a peer or a supervisor of two employees in a dispute. Their findings revealed that high-power third parties behaved more autocratically (e.g., behaved forcefully, imposed their own settlements), but these assertive tendencies were reduced when third parties had more years of work experience. A similarly structured study by Conlon, Carnevale, and Murnighan (1994) revealed that high-power third parties were more confident, believed they were more influential, and were more satisfied with the options they had available (i.e., to mediate or impose outcomes) than low-power third parties. High-power third parties also perceived their disputants to be less cooperative. This may have served as a rationalization for their own behavior during the dispute intervention, as they engaged in the use of more assertive behavior than low-power third parties (consistent with the findings of Karambayya et al. (1992); McGillicuddy et al. (1987). Finally, those with the power to impose settlements usually did so (in two-thirds of the disputes), although they often claimed they did so in the interest of the parties (i.e., because they perceived that the disputants were uncooperative).

EMERGENT ROLES AND OUR EVALUATION CRITERIA

What are the implications of emergent third parties for our evaluation of the effectiveness of third-party intervention? The fact that emergent parties tend to be interested third parties suggests that these roles may affect our "settlement characteristics" criteria. To the degree that emergent third parties are interested in the specifics of the outcome, they may use their power or resources to push for settlements that benefit themselves. To the extent that an optimal solution for the third party is not an optimal solution for the disputants, criteria we have discussed, such as achieving a large number of voluntary settlements, or settlements of high joint benefit to the disputants, become compromised. Moreover, if the outcome favored the third party at the expense of the disputants, we would expect commitment to the settlement to be low, making the settlement a short-lived one. Perhaps a new measure of joint benefit that includes the value of the settlement to the third party might need to be constructed for emergent contexts.

Since emergent settings often provide no rules specifying when third parties might intervene, and less structure governing exactly how a third party might behave, we suspect that emergent TPI may compromise disputants justice perceptions. For example, disputants may perceive less procedural justice to the extent that the invocation of the procedure was a surprise or unwanted by one or both parties. Moreover, the behavior of an emergent third party, given the lack of formality in emergent procedures, may be more likely to create variations in ratings of interpersonal and informational justice, to the degree that the third party is intentionally or unintentionally impolite to the parties or not forthcoming with information as to why intervention occurred or why a particular decision was made. Finally, perceptions of distributive justice could be impacted because the disputants resent that the high-power third party used his or her decision control to impose a settlement on them, especially if they believed they were close to resolving the dispute on their own.

The fact that the parties have a prior and continuing history of interacting with each other makes our third set of evaluation criteria, effects on relationships, much more salient. It may be more important that the disputants learn to cooperate with each other and improve their relationship with each other in emergent contexts than in one where they are not likely to see each other again (e.g., a consumer complaint context). On the positive side, emergent contexts may also provide third parties with more opportunities to aid in information exchange. For instance, a boss intervening in a dispute between two subordinates may be privy to a higher level of information that if communicated to the disputants may influence subordinates' judgments of the value of their outcomes. In addition, the criterion evaluating the disputants' relationship with the third party may be much more important in emergent interventions, especially if the third party is a key authority figure in the disputants' lives. In fact, ensuring that the third party thinks highly of the disputants may be a more important outcome than whatever is ostensibly in dispute. Finally, disputants in an emergent context may be forced to interact with a third party they do not like. Typically in contractual interventions, either party can reject a third party if they believe that party is biased against them. But at work, if you don't like your boss and your boss chooses to intervene in a dispute, chances are there is nothing you can do about it.

Finally, transaction costs may be even more salient in emergent contexts than in contractual contexts. Consider our example of a coworker intervening with two employees in a dispute (a low-power emergent intervention). The longer the two disputants quarrel, the less likely it is that work is finished on time, and this may affect all three parties in terms of their pay or bonuses. Thus, settling disputes quickly and at a low financial burden may be even more important to disputants and third parties in emergent contexts.

Future Directions

Those interested in research on third-party intervention have many under-researched topics worthy of pursuit. In this section, we highlight some of these opportunities.

FILLING IN AND EXPANDING OUR CRITERIA

First, we note that the relative dearth of studies on hybrid and emergent roles highlights that many of the criteria we used to evaluate mediation and arbitration have not yet been applied to these other third-party roles. For example, comparing the two hybrid procedures across our four sets of criteria reveals that some of our criteria have not been investigated (e.g., permanence of settlement, improved relationship between disputants or with third party), and some that have been investigated (e.g., justice) show inconsistent results across studies. The emergent procedures also may have some unintended impact on the "settlement characteristics" and "effects on relationships" criterion sets. For instance, in an emergent context it is quite possible that a third party is more familiar with one disputant than the other. This greater understanding of one side could result in a variety of biases. For example, a third party might know that although a disputant is publicly arguing for one outcome, she or he is willing to accept less. This suggests an interesting asymmetry whereby third parties could end up selecting an outcome that favors the party they know less about because they have less insight into the underlying preferences of this party. In effect, third parties could end up punishing the disputant they know well.

In addition to our current evaluation criteria, our consideration of emergent third parties suggests that we may need to add another criterion to our list: the degree to which the procedure allows the third party to behave self-interestedly at the expense of the disputants. To the extent that procedures allow third parties latitude in shaping the outcome, procedures create the potential for third parties to attend to their interests rather than those of the disputants. Procedures that limit the third parties' abilities to unilaterally determine the outcome also limit the third parties' abilities to incorporate their own interests. Other procedures, however, offer more temptations to third parties. For instance, conventional arbitration theoretically allows the third party to fashion any agreement, not just one or the other party's position. This latitude makes it easier for the third party to incorporate self-interest into the final outcome than would final offer arbitration, where the third party is constrained to choose between two options. The hybrid procedures of med–arb and arb–med also lend themselves to self-interest to the extent that conventional or final offer arbitration is used. Self-interest concerns are particularly salient in the high power, emergent third-party role. In this situation, the third party often is a member of the same system as the disputants. Outcomes can affect the third party as well as the disputants.

SAME OR DIFFERENT THIRD PARTIES?

A central issue with regard to the hybrid procedures concerns whether the same or a different third party conducts each stage of the hybrid procedure. Having the same third party involved in both stages of med–arb or arb–med may provide an advantage on some criteria, such as those reflecting transaction costs. In fact, McGillicuddy et al., 1987, p. 110, who examined med–arb using the same and different third parties, concluded by stating, "the results of this study mostly favor the med/arb (same) procedure in contrast to straight mediation" because disputants showed less hostile behavior. However, the use of the same third party could compromise several of the other criteria.

Consider the criterion of voluntary settlements. There may be instances where the third party might be tempted to interfere with the progress disputants are making toward a voluntary settlement. A third party under med–arb might be tempted to tell one side in the mediation phase of med–arb not to voluntarily settle by telling the party, "You will do better by letting me make the arbitrated decision." Moreover, under arb–med when the same third party is used, this temptation could be even stronger because the third party knows what the arbitrated settlement is, and this information may be very compelling to the disputant. Alternatively, when the same third party works both stages of a hybrid procedure, self-interest may become an issue. The third party may know that the arbitrated settlement is better for the third party than is the settlement that the disputants are moving toward. Such interference in the progress of voluntary settlements is clearly unethical and not in the spirit of the design of these procedures.

The criterion of information exchange could also be compromised when the same third party is used in the hybrid procedures. For instance, in the med–arb procedure, there may be instances where a disputant reveals confidential information to the third party in hopes of reaching a mediated settlement during the mediation phase. However, should the dispute not be settled in mediation, the disputant may want the third party to disregard this confidential information in constructing a settlement. This may be difficult for the third party to do. Note that this problem does not occur in the arb–med procedure because the third party's arbitrated ruling is determined early in the procedure. This may allow disputants to be more willing to reveal confidential information to each other in the mediation phase of arb–med than would be the case in the mediation phase of med–arb.

The only way to guard against temptations third parties might have to interfere with voluntary settlements, or to ensure that private information revealed in the mediation phase does not somehow influence the arbitrated outcome under med–arb, would be to use a different third party (technically, a fourth party) to conduct the arbitration phase of med–arb. However, what effect this might have on the overall effectiveness of the procedure is an open question. Beyond McGillicuddy et al. (1987) study, we know of no work contrasting the use of different third parties in hybrid procedures.

OTHER HYBRID PROCEDURES

Finally, we note that research should continue to look at different forms of creative hybrid procedures and how they impact dispute resolution. The arb–med procedure effectively leverages the time between the outcome and its imposition by using mediation. This is, of course, not the only option. One could imagine a procedure such as arbitration–negotiation (arb–neg), where the parties reengage in negotiation in an attempt to settle the dispute themselves. Given the patterns observed in final offer arbitration, such a structure may prove useful: For instance, Pruitt (1981) reported that many cases are resolved by disputants after the final-offer arbitration hearing is held, but before a decision is revealed to the parties. One could design a dispute resolution system that includes combinations of hybrid procedures other than med–arb and arb–med. Parties in a dispute could begin with negotiation, then mediation, then negotiation a second time, then arb–negotiation or arb–med, or perhaps a combined three-sequence finale of arbitration–negotiation–mediation (arb–neg–med). With the addition of cooling-off periods, such a system could have many steps.

Concluding Comment

Many of the novel procedures examined here have the potential to be seen by disputants as harsh and controlling. If they are, it is unlikely that disputants will willingly adopt these procedures or perceive that they are fair if they do use them. Nevertheless, the mere existence of a harsh controlling procedure serving as the next step if parties cannot resolve a dispute at a prior step may encourage parties to settle in procedures that are less coercive. Future research may wish to evaluate hybrid procedures or systems of procedures that have this character of increasing harshness against the criteria of effectiveness that we have used in this chapter.

Works Cited

Ashenfelter, O., and D. E. Bloom. (1984). Models of arbitrator behavior: Theory and evidence. *American Economic Review, 74,* 111–124.

Brett, J. (2001). *Negotiating globally: How to negotiate deals, resolve disputes and make decisions across cultural boundaries.* San Francisco: Jossey-Bass.

Brett, J., Barsness, Z., and S. Goldberg. (1996). The effectiveness of mediation: An independent analysis of cases handled by four major service providers. *Negotiation Journal, 12,* 259–269.

Brett, J. M., and S. B. Goldberg. (1983). Grievance mediation in the coal industry: A field experiment. *Industrial and Labor Relations Review 37,* 19.

Carnevale, P. J. (1986). Strategic choice in negotiation. *Negotiation Journal, 2,* 41–56.

Carnevale, P. J., and D. E. Conlon. (1988). Time pressure and strategic choice in mediation. *Organizational Behavior and Human Decision Processes, 42,* 111–133.

Carnevale, P. J., and R. Henry. (1989). Determinants of mediator behavior: A test of the strategic choice model. *Journal of Applied Social Psychology, 19,* 469–488.

Carnevale, P. J., and D. G. Pruitt. (1992). Negotiation and mediation. In M. Rosenberg and L. Porter (Eds.), *Annual review of psychology* (Vol. 43, pp. 531–582). Palo Alto, CA: Annual Reviews.

Champlin, F. C., and M. F. Bognanno. (1985). Time spent processing interest arbitration cases: The Minnesota experience. *Journal of Collective Negotiations in the Public Sector, 14,* 53–65.

Coleman, B. J., Jennings, K. M., and F. S. McLaughlin. (1993). Convergence or divergence in final-offer arbitration in professional baseball. *Industrial Relations, 32,* 238–247.

Conlon, D., Carnevale, P. J., and K. Murnighan. (1994). Intravention: Third-party intervention with clout. *Organizational Behavior and Human Decision Processes, 57,* 387–410.

Conlon, D. E., Lind, E. A., and R. I. Lissak. (1989). Nonlinear and nonmonotonic effects of outcome on procedural and distributive fairness judgments. *Journal of Applied Social Psychology, 19,* 1085–1099.

Conlon, D. E., Moon, H., and K. Y. Ng. (2001, August). *Putting the cart before the horse: The unexpected benefits of arbitrating before mediating.* Paper presented at the 61st Annual meeting of the Academy of Management, Washington, DC.

———. (2002). Putting the cart before the horse: The benefits of arbitrating before mediating. *Journal of Applied Psychology, 87,* 978–984.

Conlon, D. E., and W. H. Ross. (1993). The effects of partisan third parties on negotiator behavior and outcome perceptions. *Journal of Applied Psychology, 78,* 280–290.

Conlon, D. E., and D. P. Sullivan. (1999). Examining the actions of organizations in conflict: Evidence from the Delaware court of chancery. *Academy of Management Journal, 42,* 319–329.

Colquitt, J. A. (2001). On the dimensionality of organizational justice: Construct validation of a measure. *Journal of Applied Psychology, 86,* 386–400.

Depner, C. E., Canata, K., and I. Ricci. (1994). Client evaluations of mediation services: The impact of case characteristics and mediation service models. *Family and Conciliation Courts Review, 32,* 306–325.

Elkouri, F., Elkouri, E. A., Goggin, E. P., and M. M. Volz. (1997). *How arbitration works* (5th ed). Washington DC: Bureau of National Affairs.

Farber, H. S. (1981, May). Role of arbitration in dispute settlement. *Monthly Labor Review, 104(5),* 34–36.

Farber, H. S., and H. Katz. (1979). Why is there disagreement in bargaining? *American Economic Review, 77,* 347–352.

Feuille, P. (1975). Final offer arbitration and the chilling effect. *Industrial Relations, 14,* 302–310.

Graham, H., and J. Perry. (1993). Interest arbitration in Ohio, the narcotic effect revisited. *Journal of Collective Negotiations in the Public Sector, 22,* 323–327.

Greenberg, J. (1993). The social side of fairness: Interpersonal and informational classes of organizational justice. In R. Cropanzano (Ed.), *Justice in the workplace* (pp. 79–103). Hillsdale, NJ: Erlbaum.

Hiltrop, J. M. (1989). Factors associated with successful labor mediation. In K. Kressel and D. G. Pruitt (Eds.), *Mediation research* (pp. 241–262). San Francisco: Jossey-Bass.

Hoh, R. (1984). The effectiveness of mediation in public-sector arbitration systems: The Iowa experience. *The Arbitration Journal, 39,* 30–40.

Kagel, J. (1976). Comment. In H. Anderson (Ed.), *New techniques in labor dispute resolution* (pp. 185–190). Washington DC: Bureau of National Affairs.

Karambayya, R., Brett, J. M., and A. L. Lytle. (1992). Effects of formal authority and experience on third-party roles, outcomes, and perceptions of fairness. *Academy of Management Journal, 35,* 426–438.

Kelly, L. (1985). FOS at the U of A. *Worklife, 4(4),* 1–3.

Kressel, K., and D. G. Pruitt. (1985). Themes in the mediation of social conflict. *Journal of Social Issues, 41,* 179–198.

———. (Eds.). (1989). *Mediation research.* San Francisco: Jossey-Bass.

Knight, F. H. (1921). *Risk, uncertainty, and profit.* London: Houghton Mifflin.

Kochan, T. A. (1979). Dynamics of dispute resolution in the public sector. In B. Aaron, J. R. Grodin, and J. L. Stern (Eds.), *Public-sector bargaining* (pp. 150–190). Washington, DC: Bureau of National Affairs.

Kochan, T. A., and J. Baderschneider. (1981). Estimating the narcotic effect: Choosing techniques that fit the problem. *Industrial and Labor Relations Review, 35,* 21–28.

Kolb, D. M. (1983). *The mediators.* Cambridge, MA: MIT Press.

La Tour, S., Houlden, P., Walker, L., and J. Thibaut. (1976). Procedure: Transnational perspectives and preferences. *Yale Law Review, 86,* 258–290.

Leventhal, G. S., Karuza, J., and W. R. Fry. (1980). Beyond fairness: A theory of allocation preferences. In G. Mikula (Ed.), *Justice and social interaction* (pp. 167–218). New York: Springer-Verlag.

Lewicki, R., Litterer, J., Minton, J., and D. Saunders. (1994). *Negotiation.* Burr Ridge, IL: Irwin.

Lewicki, R. J., Saunders, D. M., and J. W. Minton. (1999). *Negotiation* (3rd ed). New York: Irwin McGraw-Hill.

Lim, R. G., and P. J. Carnevale. (1990). Contingencies in the mediation of disputes. *Journal of Personality and Social Psychology, 58,* 259–272.

Lind, E. A., and R. I. Lissak. (1985). Apparent impropriety and procedural fairness judgments. *Journal of Experimental Social Psychology, 21,* 19–29.

Lind, E. A., and T. R. Tyler. (1988). *The social psychology of procedural justice.* New York: Plenum.

McEwen, C. A., and R. J. Maiman. (1984). Mediation in small claims court: Achieving compliance through consent. *Law and Society Review, 18,* 11–49.

McGillicuddy, N. B., Welton, G. L., and D. G. Pruitt. (1987). Third-party intervention: A field experiment comparing three different models. *Journal of Personality and Social Psychology, 53,* 104.

Meagher, W. (1976). New frontiers in dispute resolution: Skills and techniques. In H. Anderson (Ed.), *New techniques in labor dispute resolution* (pp. 166–190). Washington, DC: Bureau of National Affairs.

Moore, C. (1996). *The mediation process: Practical strategies for resolving conflict* (2nd ed.). San Francisco: Jossey-Bass.

Notz, W. W., and F. A. Starke. (1987). Arbitration and distributive justice: Equity or equality? *Journal of Applied Psychology, 72,* 359–365.

Pierce, R. S., Pruitt, D. G., and S. J. Czaja. (1993). Complaint–respondent differences in procedural choice. *International Journal of Conflict Management, 4,* 199–222.

Podd, A. (1997, January 27). NASD discloses disciplinary measures. *Wall Street Journal,* B7.

Pruitt, D. G. (1981). *Negotiation behavior.* New York: Academic Press.

Pruitt, D. G., and P. J. Carnevale. (1993). *Negotiation in social conflict.* Pacific Grove, CA: Brooks Cole.

Purdy, J., and B. Gray. (1994). Government agencies as mediators in public policy conflicts. *International Journal of Conflict Management, 5,* 158–180.

Ross, W. H., Brantmeier, C., and T. Ciriacks. (2002). The impact of hybrid dispute resolution procedures on constituent fairness judgments. *Journal of Applied Social Psychology, 32,* 1151–1188.

Ross, W. H., and D. E. Conlon. (2000). Hybrid forms of third party dispute resolution: Theoretical implications of combining mediation and arbitration. *Academy of Management Review, 25,* 416–427.

Ross, W. H., Conlon, D. E., and E. A. Lind. (1990). The mediator as leader: Effects of behavioral style and deadline certainty on negotiator behavior. *Group and Organization Studies, 15,* 105–124.

Shapiro, D. L., and J. M. Brett. (1993). Comparing three processes underlying judgments of procedural justice: a field study of mediation and arbitration. *Journal of Personality and Social Psychology, 65,* 1167–1177.

Sheppard, B. H. (1984). Third party conflict intervention: A procedural framework. In B. M. Staw and L. L. Cummings (Eds.), *Research in organizational behavior* (Vol. 6, pp. 141–190). Greenwich, CT: JAI Press.

Smith, W. C. (1999, June). Taking the fast track to 2000. *American Bar Association Journal, 85,* 80.

Somers, P. (1977). An evaluation of final-offer arbitration in Massachusetts. *Journal of Collective Negotiations in the Public Sector, 6,* 193–228.

Starke, F. A., and W. W. Notz. (1981). Pre- and postintervention effects of conventional vs. final offer arbitration. *Academy of Management Journal, 24,* 832–850.

Thibaut, J., and H. Kelley. (1959). *The social psychology of groups.* New York: Wiley.

Thibaut, J., and L. Walker. (1975). *Procedural justice: A psychological analysis.* Hillsdale, NJ: Erlbaum.

Touval, S. (1985). The context of mediation. *Negotiation Journal, 1,* 373–378.

Ury, W. L., Brett, J. M., and S. B. Goldberg. (1988). *Getting disputes resolved.* San Francisco: Jossey-Bass.

Vidmar, N. (1985). An assessment of mediation in a small claims court. *Journal of Social Issues, 41,* 127–144.

Walton, R. E., and R. McKersie. (1965). *A behavioral theory of labor negotiations: An analysis of a social interaction system.* New York: McGraw-Hill.

Webb, J. (1986, September). Third parties at work: Conflict resolution or social control? *Journal of Occupational Psychology, 59,* 247–258.

Wittmer, J. M., Carnevale, P. J., and M. E. Walker. (1991). General alignment and overt support in biased mediation. *Journal of Conflict Resolution, 35,* 594–610.

CHAPTER 13

Adaptive Third Parties in the Cultural Milieu

Peter J. Carnevale, Yeow Siah Cha, Ching Wan, and Sam Fraidin

THIRD-PARTY INTERVENTION in disputes is ubiquitous; it appears to occur even among chimpanzees: "...a female acts as catalyst by bringing male rivals together... After a fight between them... females have been observed to break the deadlock by grooming one male, then the other, until she has brought the two of them together, after which she withdraws..." (De Waal and Van Roosmalen, 1979, p. 55). This is intriguing: it may suggest that third-party intervention can occur in the absence of culture, or in the sort of relatively minimal culture that exists among chimpanzees (see Boesch and Tomasello, 1998, for relevant debate). Regardless, it does indicate that third-party intervention is a group adaptation to problems of interdependence, even if the interdependent parties are not human. When it comes to third-party intervention by humans, such as the mediation of the pope in the Beagle Channel dispute between Chile and Argentina (Princen, 1987), or acting U.N. mediator Ralph Bunche in the Middle East (Touval, 1982), or the "Leopard-Skin Chief" of the Nuer (Evans-Pritchard, 1940), or even Judge Richard Posner in the recent Microsoft antitrust dispute (MacFarquhar, 2001), third-party intervention, much like negotiation, often occurs in the context of complex social, organizational, and political systems that have legal constraints and historical underpinnings (see Touval, 1985; Touzard, 1977).

No doubt there is a long history to third-party intervention. Rubin (1981) noted the many instances of third-party intervention in the Bible, and Kramer (1963) described some of the earliest known human writings, of more than 4,000 years ago, about a Sumarian ruler who helped avert a war between neighboring groups and helped develop an agreement in a dispute over land.

The authors are grateful to Don Conlon for very helpful comments on an earlier version of this paper.

Third-party intervention appears to be universal, operating within and between cultures, groups, organizations, and nations (Bercovitch and Rubin, 1992). Third-party intervention appears to sometimes be necessary for agreements to occur (Rubin, 1981; Walton, 1969), and there is anecdotal evidence that culture can be both a help and a hindrance in the search for agreement (cf. Avruch, Black, and Scimec, 1998; Cohen, 1996; Nader and Todd, 1978; Witty, 1980).

This chapter has two aims, both stemming from the belief that more research on culture and mediation is needed. The first goal is to present a selective review of the behavioral literature on culture and third parties, with a focus on major concepts and research questions that have guided past research and that have cultural implications. We offer this review as a complement to reviews by Conlon and Meyer (Chapter 12, this volume), Rubin (1980, 1981), Bercovitch (1984), Zartman and Touval (1989), Dialdin and Wall (1999), Wall, Stark, and Standifer (2001), Carnevale and Pruitt (1992, 2004), and others. The second goal is to provide some theoretical linkages and to speculate on critical questions that might be addressed by future research.

Third-Party Cognition and Behavior

The form of third-party behavior that has received the most attention from scholars is mediation. Mediation is undertaken in a variety of forms by a wide variety of actors: private individuals, academic scholars, nongovernment organizations, government representatives, and regional and international organizations (Bercovitch, 1984; Zartman and Touval, 1989). Kressel's (1972) influential organizing framework of mediator tactics (see Kressel and Pruitt, 1989), which has some empirical support (McLaughlin, Carnevale, and Lim, 1991), places mediator behavior in three categories: (1) forceful, pressing behavior (e.g., making threats to encourage cooperation), (2) behavior that affects the context of negotiation (e.g., attempting to restructure the agenda), and (3) behavior that lays the foundation for later success (e.g., developing rapport, meeting with parties separately in a "caucus"). In an analysis of mediator strategy largely based on Schelling's (1965) notions of strategic analysis and French and Raven's (1959) analysis of social power, Carnevale (1986b) identified three basic forms of mediator strategy: pressure (the use of coercive tactics, aka "sticks"), compensation (the use of rewards, aka "carrots"), and integration, the application of information in solving the disputants' problem. As explained in the previous chapter, a series of studies provided evidence that a perceptual factor, the mediator's estimate of the likelihood of integrative agreement, and a motivational factor, the mediator's concern for the parties' aspirations, interact to predict the occurrence of these basic mediator strategies (Carnevale and Pruitt, 2004). Other factors play a role, such as the perceived feasibility of a strategy (Carnevale, 1986a).

Mediators confront a particularly difficult cognitive problem. It is not easy for a third party to come up with an efficient agreement, especially when parties are not forthcoming with their preferences and priorities. Furthermore, disputants are affected by self-serving biases that influence their judgments of the fairness and trustworthiness of the mediator (Arad and Carnevale, 1994). Mounting evidence suggests that mediators, like all people, can suffer from cognitive limitations, which become acute in situations where information is distributed across groups and individuals. For example, mediators are susceptible to framing effects; they view negotiators as more cooperative when they make a concession with a loss frame than when they make the same concession with a gain frame, and mediators tend to favor the less cooperative person in their outcome suggestions (Lim and Carnevale, 1995; see Bar-Tal and Geva, 1986; Carnevale and Probst, 1998; Devetag and Warglien, 2001; Grzelak, 1982; for discussions of cognitive effects in negotiation and social conflict). Also, many studies indicate a surprising effect (e.g., Carnevale and Conlon, 1988): the best predictor of the quality of a mediator's outcome recommendations is the quality of the disputing parties' offers. This conclusion is consistent with Thompson and Kim's (2000) finding that third-party observers made better suggestions for settlement when the parties appeared to have a positive relationship than when they seemed to have a negative one.

One clear generalization about mediator behavior is that it is *adaptive*; that is, mediators act with contingency (Carnevale, Lim, and McLaughlin, 1989; cf. Murnighan, 1986). Mediators first attempt to understand the problem they face and then use various tactics to achieve their goals. This notion of adaptation is the basis of the Carnevale (1986b) model, and it is seen in Landsberger's (1955) classic study, in which an analysis of actual session transcripts revealed that labor mediators adopted a more pressing style of intervention when the disputing parties became more intransigent. Other studies show that mediators become more forceful when time pressure increases (Carnevale and Conlon, 1988; Ross and Wieland, 1996). These findings support the proposition that mediators become more forceful when their estimate of the likelihood of success decreases (Carnevale, 1986b). For example, Carnevale and Conlon (1988) found that as time progressed toward a deadline, although parties continued to argue, mediators decreased problem-solving tactics and increased pressure tactics as well as their efforts at compensation.

Many studies also reveal that disputants adapt to mediation, which indicates that mediator behavior is contingently effective. For example, in an early important study, Pruitt and Johnson (1970) found that negotiators are especially receptive to a third party's suggestion if they simultaneously have both impression management concerns and a strong need to reach agreement. Also, negotiators appear to follow basic learning principles and react favorably to mediator rewards (Wall, 1979). Moreover, negotiators will hasten agreement if they expect punitive third-party intervention (Harris and Carnevale, 1990). An interesting question, of course, is the manner and extent to which these factors and behaviors operate across different cultural milieus.

Third Parties in the Cultural Milieu

A milieu is an environment or a setting. A cultural milieu is a gestalt: a pattern of attitudes, beliefs, categorizations, self-definitions, norms, role definitions, and values organized around a central theme, for example, the importance of the individual or the importance of the in-group (Kagitcibasi and Berry, 1989; Markus and Kitayama, 1991; Triandis, 1995). The pattern is often seen among people who speak a particular language group in a particular historical period and geographic region, and is expressed in a variety of behaviors and social forms, such as food preferences and dress. For example, Americans have burgers and Nikes, whereas Japanese have sushi and kimonos (the traditional dress worn on special occasions). Culture is ubiquitous; it is often difficult to fully characterize by focusing on one point in the pattern.

People's cognitive processes can also reflect culture. In Japanese, the word for self, *jibun,* literally means "one's portion of the shared space" (Hamaguchi, 1985), demonstrating the interdependent nature of the Japanese self. In child-rearing practice, Chinese mothers engage in more self-discipline and obedience "training" than do American mothers (Chao, 1994). In their distinction between holistic and analytic culture, Nisbett, Peng, Choi, and Norenzayan (2001) described two systems of thought. People from holistic cultures (e.g., the Far East) attend more to the entire field of human experience and make less use of formal logic. People from analytic cultures (e.g., the West) pay more attention to the primary categorization of objects and tend to apply formal logic in understanding behavior.

Cultures are often characterized in the literature by variations on certain dimensions. Individualism and collectivism (Hofstede, 2001; Triandis, 1995) correspond to the notion of the "independent" and "interdependent" self (Markus and Kitayama, 1991). Cooperation and competition are other central characterizations of culture in the conflict resolution literature. How the cooperative and competitive elements of culture affect conflict resolution remains an open question.

As noted in previous chapters, the effect of culture on people's thoughts and behavior is likely to be especially salient when people come into contact with other cultures. Culture can affect individuals' preferences and agendas (Carnevale, 1995). For example, recent research in organizational conflict resolution indicates that Japanese managers prefer a model that emphasized status power, German managers favor the application of regulations, and American managers favor the integration of interests (Tinsley, 1998).

When the cultural backgrounds of negotiators and mediators are salient, culture can play two important roles in dispute mediation. First, culture can be the reason for conflict, and differences in culture can pull negotiators even further apart. Dealing with cultural differences thus becomes an important task for the mediator (Cohen, 1996). Conversely, when cultural ties exist between the mediator and disputants, the mediator can appeal to the shared culture, which then forms an important and positive basis for mediation. Cultural ties to even just one party to the conflict can provide the basis for access, acceptability, and influence in mediation (Carnevale and Choi, 2000). Thus, mediation in culture can be both a problem and a benefit.

Culture as a Problem

When mutual understanding between negotiators and mediators does not exist, problems can arise (cf. Clarke, 1996). Huie (1987) observed a conflict between two groups of fishermen in southeast Texas—natives and recent Vietnamese émigrés. The two groups had different views on how to share the resource with others, with the natives adopting a more individualist view. Another case comes from Allred, Hong, and Kalt's (2002) study of a conflict over property rights between the Nez Perce Indian tribe and non-Indians living within their reservation: Each side misconstrued the preferences of the other side. When the third party pointed this out, the prospects for resolution increased.

Culture was a culprit in a mediation study by Bercovitch and Elgström (2001). They tested the hypothesis that cultural differences between parties reflect diversity and contradictions, and that these differences compound the difficulty of finding effective mediated outcomes. Using data from 295 international conflicts between 1945 and 1995, including 171 mediated conflicts (1,666 separate instances of mediation), the researchers measured cultural similarity on a variety of dimensions and also measured the success of mediation, which was defined as reduced conflict (e.g., a cease-fire). They found that four variables that measured culture—geographical proximity, political rights, civil rights and religion—all had a significant impact on mediation outcomes. For example, when the parties did not share the same religion, mediation was less successful than when parties shared the same religion.

Culture as a Benefit

Culture can also provide the basis for the resolution of conflicts (Carnevale and Choi, 2000). In international relations, cultural ties can qualify a third party to enter the conflict and to influence the negotiation. Mediators with cultural ties stand a better chance of understanding and interpreting messages from one side to the other, and of affecting a change in positions. In their analysis of mediation in Central America, Wehr and Lederach (1991) developed the concept of the "insider-partial"—a type of mediator who emerges from within the conflict, whose involvement stems from a positive, trust-based connection to the parties and the future relationship between disputant and mediator. In the Iran hostage crisis, Algerian mediators, compared to other groups who offered to mediate, had "the required revolutionary credentials and the necessary international connections needed for the job," according to one analyst (Slim, 1992, p. 228; see Sick, 1985). Lieb (1985) observed that Iran and Iraq agreed on mediation by the Algerian Boumedienne, a Muslim leader, in part because he was "a member of the same family" (p. 82). Could the pope have served as a mediator in this conflict? Probably not. But the pope was a mediator in the Beagle Channel dispute between Argentina and Chile from 1979 to 1985, and religious-culture ties may have provided a basis for his acceptability and even his effectiveness (Princen, 1987).

Theoretical Framework and Supporting Empirical Work

The intersection of culture and mediation can be cast in terms of the standard negotiation model presented in Carnevale and Pruitt (2004) and Carnevale (1995), and shown in Figure 13.1. Conditions that prevail at the time of negotiation (e.g., time pressure, accountability to constituents) are assumed to impact negotiators' and mediators' psychological states, including motives, emotions, perceptions, and cognitions. These states, in turn, have either a direct impact on outcomes (likelihood, quality of agreement) or an impact that is mediated by the strategies and tactics chosen by the disputants and the mediator. Culture is portrayed as both a moderator variable that can affect the impact of negotiation conditions on psychological states and a mediating variable of the relationship between conditions and psychological states. The bidirectional arrows indicate the possibility of reciprocal relationships, such as the notion that conditions can evoke certain culture variables, and that culture makes some conditions more or less likely.

Next, we use this framework to highlight areas for future research. We focus on three relationships depicted in the framework: culture and contextual features; culture, mediator tactics, and disputants' reactions to mediator tactics; and culture and mediator cognitive bias.

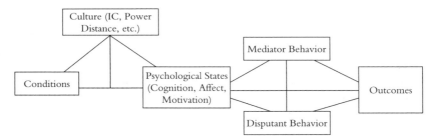

FIGURE 13.1. Model of culture and mediation of disputes.

Culture and Contextual Features

Our framework highlights the fact that culture may mediate the relationship between negotiation conditions and mediators' psychological states. One possible condition is whether the negotiation concerns property that is either individually owned or group owned (Carnevale, 1995). This condition may activate a culturally relevant variable among the parties, such as group-based self concept, which may impact loss aversion, a psychological state, and thus affect positions taken in the negotiation. A mediator might choose to pursue a "compensation" strategy or a "cost-cutting" strategy in an effort to lessen the impact of this loss aversion (Carnevale, 1986b; see Pruitt, 1981) and thus achieve agreement. This prediction is based on the assumption that felt loss may be activated by different forms of self concept, an idea expressed by William James more than one hundred years ago (James, 1890; see Carnevale, 1995).

The framework also suggests that culture will interact with contextual features of disputes to affect mediator behavior. Inasmuch as mediators vary their behaviors based on the negotiation context (Kolb, 1983), we might expect that mediators from certain cultures may be more sensitive to context than those from other cultures. Indeed, Carnevale et al. (2002) found that mediators from some collectivist cultures were more affected by the nature of the relationship between the disputing parties than were mediators from individualistic cultures.

A key question for future investigation is whether mediator tactics are universal or culture specific. Anthropologists often provide colorful descriptions of disputes mediated by third parties in disparate cultures in remote corners of the world, as in Billings's (1991) description of the mediation of disputes between the Tikana and the Lavongai, groups from adjacent islands in the Bismarck archipelago north of Papua New Guinea (cf. Avruch et al., 1998; Gulliver, 1979). Some empirical studies comparing mediation in different cultures (e.g., Wall and Blum; 1991; Wall and Callister, 1999) find remarkable similarity in behavior, such as the widespread use of caucusing. But there are hints of cultural variation, such as the effect of mediation on outcome and preferences for third-party intervention in negotiation (e.g., Kozan and Ergin, 1998), whether due to culture or to other factors such as procedural artifacts (see Schachter, Nuttin, de Monchaux, Maucorps, Osmer, Duijker, Rommetveit, and Isreal, 1954, p. 437).

Culture, Mediator Tactics, and Disputants' Reactions to Mediator Tactics

Another possible avenue for future research relates to disputant reactions to mediator behavior, which might draw on the literature on cultural effects in group behavior and negotiation (cf. Brett, 2001). People in interdependent contexts are more adaptive to the group than are those in independent contexts, suggesting that there will be greater group conformity in high-interdependence contexts. This hypothesis was supported by Bond and Smith (1996), who conducted a meta-analysis of 177 conformity studies across 17 different countries and found greater conformity in collectivist cultures than in individualistic cultures. In cultures conducive to social conformity, a mediator's suggestions, especially those that enhance norms of appropriate behavior, may carry great weight.

Several suggestive findings on power distance or verticality are relevant to mediators' tactics and disputants' reactions to them. These concepts pertain to the acceptance of hierarchies in societies and the special privileges accorded to those at the top of hierarchies (Hofstede, 2001; Triandis, 1995). In high-power-distance societies, the intervention of a high-status third party in a dispute is deemed as legitimate. James, Chen, and Cropanzano (1996) found that Taiwanese workers (a high-power-distance group) were more likely to endorse coercive power as a legitimate leadership strategy than were their U.S. counterparts. Smith, Peterson, Leung, and Dugan (1998) found that people from low-power-distance countries were less likely to involve their boss to resolve a dispute within their work group. Tyler, Lind, and Huo (2000) found that those low in power distance place greater importance on how well they are treated by authorities. Merry (1989) suggested that mediator strength operates the same way in a variety of cultural contexts, a view echoed by Carnevale (2002). But is mediator strength more effective in high-power-distance cultures? Do mediators in high-power-distance cultures and those in low-power-distance cultures rely on different forms of power? Welsh (1997, p. 68) observed that a conflict between two high-power-distance cultures, China and England, could be attributed to violations of status protocol, a finding with possible implications for the effectiveness of third-party intervention.

Culture and Mediator Cognitive Bias

Last, several lines of work suggest that judgment biases in negotiation are perpetuated by cultural values and ideals (see Morris and Gelfand, Chapter 2, this volume). The challenge of finding "perceived common ground" (Carnevale, 1986b) may be particularly acute for mediators of intercultural disputes. The study by Bercovitch and Elgström (2001) described earlier suggests that mediator-perceived common ground will be lower in interculture conflicts.

Concluding Comments

In a sense, negotiation involves joint commitment to the collection and exploration of an information set for the purpose of finding ways to maximize joint outcomes (cf. Clark, 1996). Joint commitment requires both parties to believe that the other side is able and willing to pursue a shared goal. Both parties should be accepting of the idea that the mediator is able and willing to help them produce and explore the information set. Because cultural commonalities can provide very abstract goals (e.g., "establish a positive relationship") as well as tools for communicating, cultures promote acceptance of mediators. If parties come from different cultures, it may be necessary to find a mediator who has some demonstrable familiarity with both cultures. Mediators familiar with the cultures of both parties can assist in making accurate assessments of the value of possible actions (Cohen, 1996).

Despite cultural differences in norms, roles, values, and thought processes, there do seem to be universal mediator behaviors. The *caucus*, a private meeting between the mediator and one side in the dispute, has been called the most common mediator tactic (Welton, Pruitt, and McGuillicuddy, 1988); it achieved notoriety during President Jimmy Carter's mediation of the Middle East conflict at Camp David. Israeli Prime Minister Menachem Begin and Egyptian President Anwar Sadat occupied separate cabins, and much of the mediation involved Carter shuttling back and forth between the cabins. It was also used in Llewellyn Thompson's mediation of Italy and Yugloslavia's dispute over the city of Trieste in 1954, in a hotel in London (Campbell, 1976), and it is frequently employed in labor and community mediation in the United States and elsewhere. Caucusing was the most common behavior reported by Malaysian *ketua kamungs* and imams (secular and religious leaders) in community mediation (Wall and Callister, 1999).

Some mediator behavior is less universal, at least on a literal level. Consider the Nuer, a pastoralist society of about 200,000 people that lives in a region of the upper Nile in both the Sudan and Ethiopia. When mediating disputes, the Nuer's Leopard-Skin Chief will reportedly place a curse (a threat of punishment by supernatural forces) on the party who refuses to accept a reasonable settlement (Evans-Pritchard, 1940; Haight, 1972; Merry, 1989).

On a concrete level, mediators in many other cultures might not place curses (at least publicly). However, as a form of pressure, the evoking of a higher power is common in mediation (Lovell, 1952). Consider Pope John Paul II's statement to the negotiating parties of Argentina and Chile in the Beagle Channel dispute: "Relying on this trust, the mediator, after having asked God for enlightenment, presents suggestions to the Parties with the purpose of carrying out his work of rapprochement..." (Princen, 1987, p. 350). Because the parties shared a religious culture, this appeal to God from the head of the Catholic Church was likely compelling. But the pope's message would not have been as effective on non-Catholics, just as the curse by the leopard-skin chief would not work for most negotiators in the United States. The question is, should we try to understand third-party intervention and culture at the level of abstract strategies, or should we focus on specific manifestations of strategies in everyday behaviors?

The matter of comparing third-party behavior across cultures may not be much different from comparing it across different contexts, for example, mediation done by federal mediators versus state mediators (Kolb, 1983), community mediation versus divorce mediation versus international mediation versus labor mediation, and so on (Carnevale, 1986a; Simkin, 1971; Touval, 1985). Indeed, the variation in contexts provides a real challenge for cross-cultural work on third-party intervention, since culture and context may covary. It may be that variation in context captures more of the process than variation in culture, but this, ultimately, is an empirical matter (see Touval, 1985). In building a general theory of mediation, it may be useful to not only incorporate parameters for different contexts of mediation, but also for the culture of negotiators and mediators, and to consider how these contexts interact.

Works Cited

Allred, K., Hong, K., and J. Kalt. (2002, June). *Partisan misperceptions and conflict escalation: Survey evidence from a tribal/local government conflict.* Paper presented at the annual meeting of the International Association for Conflict Management, Salt Lake City, UT.

Arad, S., and P. J. Carnevale. (1994). Partisanship effects in judgments of fairness and trust in third parties in the Palestinian–Israeli conflict. *Journal of Conflict Resolution, 38,* 423–451.

Avruch, K., Black, P. W., and J. A. Scimec. (1998). *Conflict resolution: Cross-cultural perspectives.* New York: Praeger.

Bar-Tal, D., and N. Geva. (1986). A cognitive basis of international conflicts. In S. Worchel and W. Austin (Eds.), *Psychology of intergroup relations* (pp. 118–133). Chicago: Nelson-Hall.

Bercovitch, J. (1984). *Social conflicts and third parties: Strategies of conflict resolution.* Boulder, CO: Westview.

Bercovitch, J., and O. Elgström. (2001). Culture and international mediation: Exploring theoretical and empirical linkages. *International Negotiation Journal, 6,* 3–23.

Bercovitch, J., and J. Z. Rubin. (1992). *Mediation in international relations: Multiple Approaches to conflict management.* New York: St. Martin's.

Billings, D. K. (1991). Cultural style and solutions to conflict. *Journal of Peace Research, 28,* 249–262.

Boesch, C., and M. Tomasello. (1998). Chimpanzee and human cultures. *Current Anthropology, 39,* 591–614.

Bond, R., and P. B. Smith. (1996). Culture and conformity: A meta-analysis of studies using Asch's (1952b, 1956) line judgment task. *Psychological Bulletin, 119,* 111–137.

Brett, J. M. (2001). *Negotiating globally.* San Francisco: Jossey-Bass.

Campbell, J. C. (1976). *Successful negotiation: Trieste 1954.* Princeton, NJ: Princeton University Press.

Carnevale, P. J. (1986a). Mediating disputes and decisions in organizations. In R. Lewicki, B. Sheppard, and M. Bazerman (Eds.), *Research on negotiation in organizations* (Vol. 1). Greenwich, CT: JAI Press.

———. (1986b). Strategic choice in mediation. *Negotiation Journal, 2,* 41–56.

———. (1995). Property, culture, and negotiation. In R. Kramer and D. M. Messick (Eds.), *Negotiation as a social process.* Newbury Park, CA: Sage.

———. (2002). Mediating from strength. In J. Bercovitch (Ed.), *Studies in international mediation: Essays in honor of Jeffrey Z. Rubin* (pp. 25–40). New York: St. Martin's.

Carnevale, P. J., and D. W. Choi. (2000). Culture in the mediation of international disputes. *International Journal of Psychology, 35,* 105–110.

Carnevale, P. J., and D. Conlon. (1988). Time pressure and strategic choice in mediation. *Organizational Behavior and Human Decision Processes, 42,* 111–133.

Carnevale, P. J., and K. Leung. (2001). Cultural dimensions of negotiation. In M. A. Hogg and R. S. Tindale. (Eds.), *Blackwell handbook of social psychology: Vol 3. Group processes* (pp. 482–496). Oxford, England: Blackwell.

Carnevale, P. J., Lim, R., and M. McLaughlin. (1989). Contingent mediator behavior and its effectiveness. In K. Kressel and D.G. Pruitt (Eds.), *Mediation research: The process and effectiveness of third party intervention.* San Francisco: Jossey-Bass.

Carnevale, P. J., and T. Probst. (1998). Social values and social conflict in creative problem solving and categorization. *Journal of Personality and Social Psychology, 74,* 1300–1309.

Carnevale, P. J., and D. G. Pruitt. (1992). Negotiation and mediation. *Annual Review of Psychology, 43,* 531–582.

———. (2004). *Negotiation in social conflict* (2nd ed.) Buckingham: Open University Press.

Chao, R. K. (1994). Beyond parental control and authoritarian parenting style: Understanding Chinese parenting through the cultural notion of training. *Child Development, 65,* 1111–1120.

Clark, H. H. (1996). *Using language.* Cambridge: Cambridge University Press.

Cohen, R. (1996). Cultural aspects of international mediation. In Jacob Bercovitch (Ed.), *Resolving international conflicts. The theory and practice of mediation* (pp. 107–128). Boulder, CO and London: Lynne Rienner.

Coombs, C. H. (1987). The structure of conflict. *American Psychologist, 42,* 355–363.

Devetag, G., and M. Warglien. (2001). *Representing others' preferences in mixed motive games: Was Schelling right?* Unpublished manuscript, Ca'Foscari University of Venice, Department of Business Economics and Management.

Dialdin, D. A., and J. A., Wall, Jr. (1999). Third parties and culture. *Negotiation Journal, 15,* 381–387.

De Waal, F. B. M., and A. Van Roosmalen. (1979). *Behavioral Ecology and Sociobiology, 5,* 55.

Evans-Pritchard, E. E. (1940). *The Nuer: A description of the modes of livelihood and political institutions of a Nilotic people.* London: Oxford University Press.

French, J., and B. Raven. (1959). The bases of social power. In D. Cartwright (Ed.), *Studies in social power* (pp. 150–168). Ann Arbor, MI: Institute for Social Research.

Grzelak, J. L. (1982). Preferences and cognitive processes in interdependence situations: A theoretical analysis of cooperation. In V. J. Derlega and J. Grzelak (Eds.), *Cooperation and helping behavior: Theories and research* (pp. 95–122). New York: Academic Press.

Gulliver, P. H. (1979). *Disputes and negotiations: A cross-cultural perspective.* New York: Academic Press.

Haight, B. (1972). A note on the leopard-skin chief. *American Anthropologist, 74,* 1313.

Hamaguchi, E. (1985). A contextual model of the Japanese: Toward a methodological innovation in Japanese studies. *Journal of Japanese Studies, 11,* 289–321.

Harris, K. L., and P. J. Carnevale. (1990). Chilling and hastening: The influence of third-party power and interests on negotiation. *Organizational Behavior and Human Decision Processes, 47,* 138–160.

Hofstede, G. (2001). *Culture's consequences: Comparing values, behaviors, institutions, and organizations across nations* (2nd ed.). Thousand Oaks, CA: Sage.

Huie, B. (1987). Cross-cultural conflict on the Texas Gulf Coast. *Dispute Resolution Forum,* September, 8.

James, K., Chen, D. L., and R. Cropanzano. (1996). Culture and leadership among Taiwanese and U. S. workers: Do values influence leadership ideals? In M. N. Ruderman, M. W. Hughes-James, and S. E. Jackson (Eds.), *Selected research on work team diversity* (pp. 33–52). Greensboro, NC: Center for Creative Leadership/American Psychological Association.

James, W. (1890). *The principles of psychology* (Vol. 1). New York: Holt.

Kagitcibasi, C., and J. W. Berry. (1989). Cross-cultural psychology: Current research and trends. *Annual Review of Psychology, 40,* 493–532.

Kochan, T. A., and T. A. Jick. (1978). The public sector mediation process: A theory and empirical examination. *Journal of Conflict Resolution, 22,* 209–40.

Kolb, D. M. (1983). *The mediators.* Cambridge, MA: MIT Press.

Kozan, K. M., and C. Ergin. (1998). Preference for third party help in conflict management in the United States and Turkey: An experimental study. *Journal of Cross-cultural Psychology, 29,* 525-539.

Kramer, S. (1963). *The Summarians: Their history, culture, and character.* Chicago: University of Chicago Press.

Kressel, K. (1972). *Labor mediation: An exploratory survey.* Albany, NY: Association of Labor Mediation Agencies.

Kressel, K., and D. G. Pruitt. (1989). Conclusion: A research perspective on the mediation of social conflict. In K. Kressel and D. G. Pruitt (Eds.), *Mediation research: The process and effectiveness of third-party intervention* (pp. 394–435). San Francisco: Jossey-Bass.

Landsberger, H. A. (1955). Interaction process analysis of the mediation of labor–management disputes. *Journal of Abnormal and Social Psychology, 51,* 552–559.

Leung, K. (1988). Some determinants of conflict avoidance. *Journal of Cross-cultural Psychology, 19,* 125–136.

Leung, K., and M. H. Bond. (1984). The impact of cultural collectivism on reward allocation. *Journal of Personality and Social Psychology, 47,* 793–804.

Lieb, D. (1985). Iran and Iraq at Algiers, 1975. In S. Touval and I. W. Zartman (Eds.), *International mediation in theory and practice* (pp. 67–90). Boulder, CO: Westview.

Lim, R., and P. J. Carnevale. (1990). Contingencies in the mediation of disputes. *Journal of Personality and Social Psychology, 58,* 259–272.

———. (1995). Influencing mediator perceptions through bargainer framing. *International Journal of Conflict Management, 6,* 349–368.

Lovell, H. (1952). The pressure lever in mediation. *Industrial and Labor Relations Review, 6,* 20–33.

MacFarquhar, L. (2001, December 10). The bench burner. *The New Yorker,* 78–89.

Markus, H., and S. Kitayama. (1991). Culture and self: Implications for cognition, emotion, and motivation. *Psychological Review, 98,* 224–253.

McLaughlin, M., Carnevale, P. J., and R. Lim. (1991). Professional mediators' judgments of mediation tactics: MDS and cluster analyses. *Journal of Applied Psychology, 76,* 465–472.

Merry, S. E. (1989). Mediation in nonindustrial societies. In K. Kressel and D. G. Pruitt (Eds.), *Mediation research: The process and effectiveness of third party intervention* (pp. 68–90). San Francisco: Jossey-Bass.

Murnighan, J. K. (1986). The structure of mediation and intravention: Comments on Carnevale's strategic choice model. *Negotiation Journal, 2,* 351–356.

Nader, L., and H. F., Todd, Jr. (Eds.). (1978). *The disputing process in ten societies.* New York: Columbia University Press.

Nisbett, R. E., Peng, K., Choi, I., and A. Norenzayan. (2001). Culture and systems of thought: Holistic versus analytic cognition. *Psychological Review, 108,* 291–310.

Princen, T. (1987). International mediation—The view from the Vatican: Lessons from mediating the Beagle Channel dispute. *Negotiation Journal, 3,* 347–366.

Probst, T., Carnevale, P. J., and H. C. Triandis. (1999). Cultural values in intergroup and single-group social dilemmas. *Organizational Behavior and Human Decision Processes, 77,* 171–191.

Pruitt, D. G. (1967). Reward structure and cooperation: The decomposed prisoner's dilemma. *Journal of Personality and Social Psychology, 7,* 21–27.

———. (1981). *Negotiation behavior.* Orlando, FL: Academic Press.

Pruitt, D. G., and D. F. Johnson. (1970). Mediation as an aid to face-saving in negotiation. *Journal of Personality and Social Psychology, 14,* 239–246.

Ross, W., and D. E. Conlon. (2000). Hybrid forms of third-party dispute resolution: Theoretical implications of combining mediation and arbitration. *Academy of Management Review, 25,* 416–427.

Ross, W. H., and C. Wieland. (1996). The effects of interpersonal trust and time pressure on managerial mediation strategy in a simulated organizational dispute. *Journal of Applied Psychology, 81,* 228–248.

Rubin, J. Z. (1980). Experimental research on third-party intervention in conflict: Toward some generalizations. *Psychological Bulletin, 87,* 379–391.

Rubin, J. Z. (1981). Introduction. In J. Z. Rubin (Ed.), *Dynamics of third-party intervention: Kissinger in the Middle East* (pp. 3–43). New York: Praeger.

Schachter, S. Nuttin, J., de Monchaux, C., Maucorps, P.H., Osmer, D., Duijker, H., Rommetveit, R., and J. Israel. (1954) Cross-cultural experiments on threat and rejection. *Human Relations, 7,* 403–440.

Schelling, T. C. (1960). *The strategy of conflict.* Cambridge, MA: Harvard University Press.

———. (1965). Strategic analysis and social problems. *Social Problems, 12,* 367–379.

Sick, G. (1985). The partial negotiator: Algeria and the U.S. hostages in Iran. In S. Touval and I.W. Zartman. (Eds.), *International mediation in theory and practice* (pp. 21–26) Boulder, CO: Westview.

Simkin, W. (1971). *Mediation and the dynamics of collective bargaining.* Washington, DC: Bureau of National Affairs.

Singelis, T. M., Triandis, H. C., Bhawuk, D., and M. Gelfand. (1995). Horizontal and vertical dimensions of individualism and collectivism: A theoretical and measurement refinement. *Cross-Cultural Research, 29,* 240–275.

Slim, R. (1992). Small-state mediation in international relations: The Algerian mediation of the Iranian hostage crisis. In J. Bercovitch and J. Z. Rubin (Eds.), *Mediation in international relations* (pp. 206–231). New York: St. Martin's.

Smith, P. B., Peterson, M. F., Leung, K., and Dugan, S. (1998). Individualism-collectivism, Power distance, and handling of disagreement: A cross-national study. *International Journal of Intercultural Relations, 22,* 351–367.

Thompson, L., and P. Kim. (2000). How the quality of third parties' settlement solutions are affected by the relationship between negotiators. *Journal of Experimental Psychology: Applied, 6,* 1–16.

Tinsley, C. (1998). Models of conflict resolution in Japanese, German, and American cultures. *Journal of Applied Psychology, 83,* 316–323.

Touval, S. (1982). *The peace brokers: Mediators in the Arab–Israeli conflict, 1948–1979.* Princeton, NJ: Princeton University Press.

———. (1985). The context of mediation. *Negotiation Journal, 1,* 373–378.

Touval, S., and I.W. Zartman. (1985). *International mediation in theory and practice.* Boulder, CO: Westview.

Touzard, H. (1977). *La mediation et la resolution des conflicts* [Mediation and the resolution of conflicts]. Paris: PUF.

Triandis, H. C. (1995). *Individualism and collectivism.* Boulder, CO: Westview.

Tversky, A., and D. Kahneman. (1981). The framing of decisions and the psychology of choice. *Science, 211,* 453–458.

Tyler, T. R., Lind, A. E., and Y. J. Huo. (2000). Cultural values and authority relations: The psychology of conflict resolution across cultures. *Psychology, Public Policy, and Law, 6,* 1138–1163.

Wall, J. A., Jr. (1979). The effects of mediator rewards and suggestions upon negotiations. *Journal of Personality and Social Psychology, 37,* 1554–1560.

Wall, J. A., Jr., and M. Blum. (1991). Community mediation in the People's Republic of China. *Journal of Conflict Resolution, 35,* 3–20.

Wall, J. A., Jr., and R. R. Callister. (1999). Malaysian community mediation. *Journal of Conflict Resolution, 43,* 343–365.

Wall, J. A., Jr., and A. Lynn. (1993). Mediation: A current review. *Journal of Conflict Resolution, 36,* 160–194.

Wall, J. A., Jr., Stark, J. B., and R. L. Standifer. (2001). Mediation: A current review and theory development. *Journal of Conflict Resolution, 45,* 370–391.

Walton, R. E. (1969). *Interpersonal peacemaking: Confrontations and third-party consultation.* Reading, MA: Addison-Wesley.

Wehr, P., and J. P. Lederach. (1991). Mediating conflict in Central America. *Journal of Peace Research, 28,* 85–98.

Welsh, F. (1997). *A history of Hong Kong.* London: HarperCollins.

Welton, G. L., Pruitt, D. G., and N. B. McGuillicuddy. (1988). An exploratory examination of caucusing: Its role in community mediation. *Journal of Conflict Resolution, 32,* 181–202.

Witty, C. J. (1980). *Mediation in society: Conflict management in Lebanon.* New York: Academic Press.

Zartman, I. W., and S. Touval. (1989). Mediation in international conflicts. In K. Kressel and D. G. Pruitt (Eds.), *Mediation research: The process and effectiveness of third-party intervention* (pp. 115–137). San Francisco: Jossey-Bass.

CHAPTER 14

Justice and Negotiation

Tom Tyler and Steven L. Blader

FOR THE PAST SEVERAL DECADES, the study of negotiation has been dominated by a focus on issues related to cognition and rationality (Thompson, Neale, and Sinaceur, Chapter 1, this volume). Although this focus has led to important discoveries, more recently there has been a widely expressed desire to broaden the scope of negotiation research. In this chapter, we concentrate on an issue long overlooked in negotiation research, yet central to the negotiation context: justice. Findings from justice research show great promise in contributing to our understanding of how to effectively manage bilateral and third-party negotiation processes. In this chapter, we will consider how justice judgments affect people's evaluations and reactions during negotiation and how negotiation research would benefit from increased attention to issues of social justice.

The roots of negotiation lie in the joint belief among the parties to a negotiation that they have incompatible interests at either the individual or the group level. Parties must find some method of trying to bridge their differences. Rational perspectives have elaborated the process of positional bargaining, in which parties are motivated by self-interest. The parties each make concessions, whose nature is determined by their own sense of potential gains and losses, until a mutually acceptable agreement is reached or until the negotiation comes to a standstill.

When negotiation is viewed from the perspective of rational self-interest, the various cognitive limits of individuals come to the forefront. Negotiators might fail to understand their own self-interest or be unable to optimally represent that interest in interaction with others. Accordingly, negotiation research has focused heavily on the quality of negotiated agreements and the extent to which objective outcomes are optimal given the resources available to be distributed. Researchers have sought to understand how negotiations can be structured and educated in ways that lead to the best outcomes. This perspective assumes that disputants will be satisfied with and committed to agreements that satisfy their own interests.

This perspective fails to fully consider the fact that negotiation is a social process in which issues other than immediate monetary- or resource-based self-interest are important. Indeed, researchers have long recognized that during negotiation, "irrational forces" lead people away from behaving in their own self-interest. Irrational escalation of commitment (Brockner and Rubin, 1985), for example, occurs when bidders in an auction, in their desire to "win," lose sight of the actual value of the item and bid far more than the item's worth. In this case, the social value of winning leads people away from their objective self-interest. Other "irrational" conflicts include ending a negotiation while mutually advantageous gains remain on the table and engaging in mutually destructive efforts to punish the other party through the use of coercive power (Deutsch and Krauss, 1962).

In general, discussions of negotiations have tended to treat social forces as factors that have a negative influence on negotiation because they lead people away from their objective self-interest. We argue that such social forces need not be "irrational" and, whether rational or not, can be a positive social force that facilitates the negotiation process. Rationality is based on an understanding of what a person's particular goals in a given situation are; the social forces that arise in negotiation contexts may actually help achieve those goals rather than hinder them.

We seek to show that disputants evaluate a negotiation and its outcomes according to standards other than self-interest and resources gained and given. Specifically, we will argue that justice is one social force that shapes the goals of the negotiation situation. People react to their own judgments about distributive and procedural justice, and the motivating power of justice can be valuable in encouraging the acceptance of negotiated agreements. Notably, justice is a subjective judgment that is only loosely linked to the objective quality of negotiators' outcomes (Tyler, Boeckmann, Smith, and Huo, 1997). Hence, if people feel that they are being treated justly, this becomes a distinct positive force in their dealings with others, but experiencing injustice undermines the motivation to accept agreements.

Not only is this justice-based motivation distinct from the objective or perceived quality of the outcomes of the negotiation, it can expand the elements under consideration when parties are evaluating a negotiation and its potential outcomes. Resources are obviously one of those concerns, as resources are important in judgments of distributive justice, but people also consider issues not linked to outcomes, such as politeness and explanation, many of which are more easily provided than are desirable outcomes.

DISTRIBUTIVE JUSTICE

One key problem people face in negotiations is whether or not to accept agreements in which they receive less than they desire. Is a compromise reasonable? Is the negotiator giving up too much and becoming a "sucker"? Ironically, the fear of giving away too much is one reason that people will pay more for items if they can buy them for a set price rather than negotiate for a lower price (Purohit and Sondak, 1997). It is also a reason that people are eager to take negotiation classes, which they hope will prepare them to effectively defend their interests in the future. People are very concerned about effectively representing their self-interest in negotiations and are more willing to accept agreements that they believe are in their interest than those they believe are not.

Even for a well-trained negotiator, the decision of whether or not to accept a negotiated agreement is often a difficult one—it is the bargainer's dilemma. Pushing for a better agreement means risking no agreement at all, whereas accepting a standing offer may mean agreeing to too little. The fear of taking too little and the risk of a standstill are constantly balanced against one another in the negotiator's mind. Because they define socially acceptable compromises, principles of justice are valuable in encouraging the acceptance of compromise agreements. When negotiators recognize that what they are receiving is consistent with a social principle that defines reasonable outcomes, they will feel comfortable that they are not gaining too little.

One simple type of justice judgment is equality. As Messick emphasized, people often use equality as a straightforward decision-making heuristic when dividing outcomes because it is easy to implement and widely accepted as valid (Messick, 1995). In negotiation settings, people are more typically focused on issues of equity, with outcomes distributed according to what one deserves due to merit or contribution. In either case, principles of justice legitimize compromises and thereby make them more acceptable. Principles of distributive justice facilitate social interaction, encourage settlement, and dampen conflict by assuring people that compromises are reasonable because they are fair.

Justice can supplement self-interest as an important motivation in social settings (Tyler et al., 1997). Laboratory studies of social interaction confirm that negotiators are indeed most willing to accept agreements that they believe to be fair (Walster, Walster, and Berscheid, 1978; see Leunig and Tung, Chapter 15, this volume, for a cultural perspective). In field studies, people have shown a willingness to give up valued outcomes when they believe that doing so accords with the principles of distributive justice (Tyler, 2000). For example, whites have supported the redistribution of resources to disadvantaged minorities, giving up money and other resources to make outcome distributions fairer (Smith and Tyler, 1996); western Germans have supported the redistribution of national resources to eastern Germany (Montada, 1995); and the advantaged generally support giving money to the poor (Montada and Schneider, 1989).

The finding that people react to issues of outcome fairness when in the midst of negotiation accords with an important argument from the influential text *Getting to Yes*: that negotiators can gain acceptance by framing their offers using objective standards (Fisher, Ury, and Patton, 1991). Such objective standards can persuade the other side that an offer is consistent with principles of distributive justice.

The role of distributive justice as a norm in negotiation suggests an important area of future research. Past work has relied on the activation of pre-existent norms of fairness. Future studies might focus more on the framing of the justice norms that apply in a given situation. In judicial proceedings, for example, advocates for each side try to convince the judge or jury that the norms favoring their side are those that should apply to the final decision (Ross, 1980). The process of deciding which principles of fairness are relevant applies to negotiation settings, but thus far has not studied.

Why have principles of distributive justice not received more attention in negotiation contexts? Because negotiations are typically viewed as a market transaction, in which the role of social factors is minimized. Markets are highly prized by economists as situations in which the forces of supply and demand operate more or less unrestricted by societal norms. As such, they are not an arena in which we might think of issues of social justice as being key factors shaping people's judgments and behaviors.

Yet studies of people's judgments suggest that they do feel that norms of fairness are relevant to market interactions. Kahneman, Knetsch, and Thaler (1986) made clear that the public generally regard principles of justice as important within a wide variety of situations within which market forces might be viewed as legitimate. One example is the concept of scarcity. In negotiation settings, people typically believe it is acceptable to exploit dependence and power differences. Those possessing desirable or needed resources feel justified in extracting concessions from their less powerful negotiating partners. But in the real world, the general public often regards such behavior as inappropriate. A company might reduce the wages of existing workers in order to hire new workers for lower wages; a landlord might evict existing tenants to obtain higher rents from new tenants; or a store might increase the price of snow shovels during a blizzard. Although such actions may be legal, large proportions of the public will view this behavior as inappropriate and unfair (Kahneman, Knetsch, and Thaler, 1986). Thus, when we move beyond the study of negotiation in experimental situations, we are confronted with the reality that people often apply principles of justice to settings that have typically been viewed as "market" transactions in which norms of justice are only minimally relevant. This phenomenon suggests that one reason people are unwilling to make allocation decisions based on market mechanisms alone is that issues of fairness may not receive the attention people feel they deserve.

Sondak and Tyler (2001) examined people's views about the desirability of markets for the allocation of resources in work and community settings. Their study focused on everyday allocations such as: Who should have a desirable parking space? Who should work on Christmas? Who should have additional police patrols in their neighborhood? They found that people resist the use of market mechanisms, such as negotiation, for such allocations. Instead, they seek to bring social authority into play via various forms of third-party allocation procedures. Achieving group consensus, voting, and appointing and deferring to group authorities were all regarded as more desirable procedures for allocation than was the use of a setting in which people negotiated using market norms. Yet Sondak and Tyler (2001) also found that when making allocations, people focus not only on fairness, but on self-interest. They seek a forum for making decisions that they feel best balances self-interest and fairness concerns. It is interesting that they often feel that this forum is not negotiation.

Why would people believe that their distributive justice concerns are better met by third-party mediation than by traditional negotiation? First, to encourage acceptance among parties, experienced and well-trained mediators can help to create agreements that reflect commonly held views about distributive justice. Second, mediators can provide a social justification for an agreement that confronts people's fears of being exploited. Mediators help people justify to themselves and to others that they did not "lose face," and thereby prevent these negative social forces from undermining acceptance of the agreement. Mediators therefore provide legitimacy for agreements by linking them to distributive justice.

PROCEDURAL JUSTICE

Sondak and Tyler's (2001) findings echo those of other negotiation studies (Rubin, 1980), which similarly find that third parties are often desired and brought into negotiations. Once a third party becomes involved, the principal question becomes: When and on what basis will the parties become willing to accept the mediator's decision? Studies of the acceptance of third-party decisions lead to a concern with a second type of justice, procedural justice. Although this focus on procedural justice is relatively recent, it has already amassed a sizable research literature (Tyler et al., 1997).

So far, the results of procedural justice research are optimistic about the utility of social justice as a mechanism for resolving social conflicts. Social authorities have shown an ability to bridge differences in interests and values and to make compromise decisions that parties to a dispute will accept. Further, the findings of procedural justice research suggest how authorities should act to pursue such procedural justice strategies.

Thibaut and Walker (1975) performed the first systematic set of experiments designed to show the impact of procedural justice on decision acceptance. Their studies demonstrate that people's assessments of the fairness of third-party decision-making procedures shape their satisfaction with their outcomes in third-party dispute resolution situations. This finding has been widely confirmed in subsequent laboratory studies of procedural justice (Lind and Tyler, 1988). The original hope of Thibaut and Walker was that the willingness of all of the parties to a dispute to accept decisions they viewed as fairly determined would provide a mechanism through which social conflicts could be resolved. Research strongly supports the viability of this basic psychological model.

WHAT IS A FAIR PROCEDURE?

Because procedural justice has been shown to be so critical for constructing healthy social dynamics, research has focused on defining procedural fairness. What characteristics lead people to view a third-party forum to be fair? Studies typically have found that seven, eight, or even more elements contribute to assessments of procedural fairness (Tyler, 1988). Four of these elements are the primary factors that contribute to judgments about procedural fairness: opportunities for participation (voice), the neutrality of the forum, the trustworthiness of the authorities, and the degree to which people are treated with dignity and respect.

Participation is perhaps one of the most well-documented and -researched characteristics of procedural fairness. People feel that processes that allow them to participate in the resolution of their problems or conflicts are more fair than those that do not; such opportunities are referred to as process control or voice. The positive effects of voice have been widely found, from the early work of Thibaut and Walker (1975), to studies of plea bargaining, sentencing hearings, and mediation. In all of these diverse settings, people consider themselves to be more fairly treated when they are given an opportunity to make arguments about what should be done to resolve a problem or conflict.

People are also strongly influenced by judgments about the honesty, impartiality, and objectivity of the authorities with whom they are dealing. Parties believe that authorities should not allow their personal values and biases to enter into decisions, which should be made based upon rules and facts. Basically, people seek a "level playing field" in which no one is unfairly disadvantaged. If they believe that authorities are following impartial rules and making factual, objective decisions, participants will consider procedures to be fairer. In performance appraisals, for example, people expect objective criterion to be specified in advance and to be judged according to a clear system created to determine whether they are meeting those criteria.

Third, people strongly value third parties who show respect for their rights and status within society. In the process of dealing with authorities, people become very concerned that their dignity as individuals and as members of society is recognized and acknowledged. In organizational settings, issues concerning quality of treatment, or interactional issues, often dominate the definition of procedural justice (Cropanzano et al., 2001). Because politeness and respect are essentially unrelated to the outcomes people receive when they deal with social authorities, the importance placed upon status affirmation is especially relevant to conflict resolution. Perhaps more than any other issue, treatment with dignity and respect is an infinite resource that authorities can give to everyone with whom they deal.

Another factor shaping people's views about the fairness of a procedure is their assessment of the motives of the third-party authority responsible for resolving the case. Recognizing that third parties typically have considerable discretion to implement formal procedures in varying ways, parties wonder about the motivation underlying an authority's decisions. Disputants judge whether the third party is benevolent, caring, and concerned about their situation and needs; whether he or she considers their arguments and tries to do what is right for them; and whether he or she tries to be fair. All of these elements combine to shape a general assessment of the third party's trustworthiness.

It is interesting that, these judgments about authority trustworthiness are the primary factors that shape parties' evaluations of authorities' procedural fairness (Tyler and Degoey, 1996; Tyler and Lind, 1992). Trustworthiness judgments may even shape what people think about other criteria of procedural fairness. For instance, people only value the opportunity to speak to authorities (i.e., to have voice) if they believe that the authority is sincerely considering their arguments, even if these arguments are later rejected. If they believe that authorities are soliciting their participation in an attempt to appear fair while having no intention of considering their input, people may react even more negatively than if their input had not been solicited in the first place (Greenberg, 1990; Greenberg and Folger, 1983; Harlos, 2001).

How can authorities communicate that they are trying to be fair? A key antecedent of trust is providing a justification and explanation for decisions. When authorities are presenting their decisions to parties, they need to explain how they reached their conclusions and communicate that they listened to and considered the parties' arguments. Such explanations convey to the participants that processes were fair and that the third party was concerned about making reasoned, defensible decisions (e.g., Conlon and Ross, 1997; Greenberg, 1993; Shapiro, Buttner, and Barry, 1994). Furthermore, these explicit explanations reduce the tendency to introduce biases into procedural justice judgments (Blader, 2002). People have a tendency to shape their views about the fairness of procedures in ways that lead them to feel better about themselves. If they are given clear information about the procedures used, they are less likely to do so.

Although the appearance of neutrality is crucial to assessments of procedural fairness, considerable evidence indicates that the basis of authoritativeness—the ability of authorities to gain deference to their decisions—is shifting from a neutrality base to a trust base. That is, in the past, authorities have often gained their authoritativeness through the neutral application of rules, that is, through the use of facts and formal, objective decision-making procedures that do not vary much in application among specific authority figures. Yet people link trust to judgments about particular authorities with whom they have personal connections. For example, employees may learn to trust their direct supervisors through repeated interactions and inferences about their superiors' motives and values. In sum, organizations can gain deference by having both formal rules that reflect neutrality and good personal relationships between employees and supervisors. The former approach reflects a neutrality model of procedural fairness, the latter a trust-based model.

PROCEDURAL JUSTICE IN NEGOTIATIONS

In this section, we focus on the utility of procedures aimed at bridging differences between opposing parties and building consensual agreements that maintain social harmony. Thibaut and Walker's (1975) work points to the value of using third parties to manage the negotiation process (see also Conlon and Meyer, Chapter 12, this volume; Rubin, 1980). Why do third parties provide a hopeful mechanism for resolving social conflicts through negotiation? We argue that third parties have the ability to manage the socioemotional aspects of negotiation and to gain acceptance of negotiation outcomes because they draw attention to the centrality of process-based judgments, as opposed to self-interested, outcome-based judgments and reactions. This focus alleviates competition to maximize resources and fosters compromise and mutually acceptable agreements among parties to the negotiation.

Given the utility of third parties, it becomes clear that procedural justice judgments will be critical in negotiation settings presided over by third-party mediators. The success of a mediator's ability to focus negotiation partners on process issues and to foster compromise depends almost entirely upon the negotiators' perceptions of the mediator's fairness. That is, fairness becomes absolutely critical when evaluating and predicting the role that third parties play in negotiations (although the behavior of the other negotiation party is also important). For this reason, we focus particular attention on evaluations of third parties.

Field studies of real disputes in real settings involving actual disputants have confirmed that when people judge third-party decisions to have been made fairly, they are more willing to voluntarily accept them. Lind, Kulik, Ambrose, and Vera Park (1993) conducted interviews with 179 litigants in cases arbitrated in the federal courts' mandatory nonbinding mediation program. Those interviewed were officers of private and public businesses and organizations. The amounts of money under contention varied widely—from $2,000 to $3,200,000—but were in all cases significant. This study provided an especially rich setting for examining decision acceptance, because each participant had the right to reject the mediation agreement and request a trial (thereby prolonging the procedure and increasing expenses for both parties) in an effort to gain a better settlement. The central question from a negotiation perspective was: What might encourage disputants to voluntarily settle for the mediated outcome?

The results of this study strongly support the influence of procedural justice. Lind et al. (1993) found that perceptions of the fairness of the mediation process were the dominant predictor of award acceptance ($r = 0.42$, $p < .05$), exceeding the importance of an individual's subjective evaluation of the quality of his or her own outcome ($r = 0.26$, $p < .05$) or an objective evaluation of the quality of the individual's outcome ($r = 0.21$, $p < .05$). These findings, typical of procedural justice studies, support the argument that third parties can gain immediate decision acceptance at least in part by using decision-making procedures that disputants judge to be fair.

Procedural justice judgments have been found to be equally important in generating deference to decisions made in less formal negotiation settings than those in the Lind et al. (1993) study. Tyler and Huo (2001), for example, studied deference to the police during informal encounters on the street or in people's homes. They found that people's willingness to defer to police directives was primarily a response to their judgments about the fairness of police actions. If people felt that the police were using fair procedures, they voluntarily accepted police decisions and followed directives. This was equally true of white and minority citizens and occurred in a wide variety of situations and settings. A strong procedural justice influence was found across all of these variations, supporting our argument that procedural justice-based negotiation strategies may help bridge differences in interests and values across a variety of groups. This argument is further supported by research showing only minor differences in preferences for dispute resolution procedures among members of different ethnic and gender groups (Lind, Huo, and Tyler, 1994).

Research finds that procedural justice judgments are especially important in shaping adherence to agreements over time (Pruitt, Peirce, McGillieuddy, Welton, and Castrianno, 1993; Pruitt, Pierce, Zubek, Welton, and Nochajski,

1990). Pruitt and his colleagues examined the resolution of disputes in a community mediation center; this context is especially valuable for studying long-term compliance because the structure ensuring adherence is weaker than in formal judicial proceedings. When respondents viewed a mediation session to be procedurally fair, they were more likely to comply with the mediation agreement over time ($r = .32$, $p < .01$). Those respondents who felt that the mediation session was procedurally fair also reported more positive ratings of the subsequent quality of their relationship with the complainant and were less likely to mention new problems in the relationship. These results suggest that reactions to procedural fairness judgments are not merely impulsive and emotional, but reasoned, robust responses to the social context of negotiation.

This and other research by Pruitt and colleagues (Pruitt, 1981; Pruitt and Carnevale, 1993; Pruitt and Rubin, 1986) not only demonstrates the robust influence of procedural justice judgments, but also contrasts the influence of those judgments to the influence of other factors that researchers typically regard as critical to a negotiation's long-term success. For instance, negotiation researchers often emphasize the importance of integrative, or "win–win," agreements, expecting that both parties will comply with such agreements because both receive desirable outcomes. Pruitt discusses the comparable notion of joint problem solving, which is linked to finding win–win outcomes in negotiations. To the extent that outcomes are important, joint problem solving in the mediation session ought to predict long-term compliance, as should goal achievement or satisfaction.

It is interesting that in the Pruitt et al. (1993) study, indices of the favorability or quality of the agreement do not predict long-term compliance by either the complainant or the respondent. For those who initiated mediation proceedings (complainants), there is no relationship between long-term compliance and joint problem solving ($r = -.03$, n.s.), goal achievement ($r = .18$, n.s.), or satisfaction with the agreement ($r = -.14$, n.s.). For those responding to complaints (respondents), there is also no relationship between long-term compliance and joint problem solving ($r = .11$, n.s.), goal achievement ($r = .02$, n.s.), or satisfaction with the agreement ($r = .02$, n.s.). It does not appear that people increase their compliance and their likelihood of producing a stable relationship by creating better outcomes for themselves or the other side during negotiations. As the authors note, "Contrary to the beliefs of many mediators, long-term success is not a simple function of reaching agreement or the quality of the agreement" (Pruitt et al., 1993, p. 325). These results suggest that outcomes are not the central determinant of compliance with negotiations.

Other studies confirm that procedural justice is especially important in gaining deference to third-party decisions over time. Paternoster, Brame,

Bachman, and Sherman (1997) explored how the behavior of police responding to calls about men who were abusing their wives affected subsequent compliance with the law. The researchers found that men who felt fairly treated during the initial encounter with the police were more likely to adhere to the law in the future. It is interesting that procedural justice judgments during initial encounters with the police were more powerful predictors of subsequent law-abiding behavior than were factors such as whether the police arrested the man during the initial contact, fined him, took him to the police station, or performed all of these actions (Paternoster et al., 1997).

How does procedural justice facilitate long-term adherence to agreements? One important consequence of the use of fair procedures is that they seem to change people's relationships with others, including the other parties to the dispute. We have already noted that a fair mediation procedure led to greater long-term adherence to negotiated outcomes in the Pruitt et al. study (1993). It also led to a more favorable long-term relationship with the other party to the dispute ($r = 0.29$, $p < .05$), as did the view that all of the problems came out during the session ($r = 0.44$, $p < .01$). In contrast, the long-term quality of one's relationship with the other person was unrelated to both the initial judgment that the agreement was satisfactory ($r = 0.08$, n.s.) and the immediate judgment that the agreement met one's goals ($r = 0.15$, n.s.). On the other hand, the degree of joint problem solving engaged in during mediation did shape the degree to which parties later said that they had a better long-term relationship ($r = 0.44$, $p < .01$). Hence, one way in which procedural justice may lead to long-term adherence to agreements is by improving the quality of one's relationship with the other disputant. This procedural justice influence on the relationship among disputants was also found in a study of child custody disputes (Dillon and Emery, 1996; Kitzmann and Emery, 1993).

One reason that procedural justice builds positive interpersonal relations is that it dampens the development of irrational social forces during negotiations. We have already noted that people tend to lose sight of their interests during negotiations, with social forces leading to "irrational" escalations of conflict. The use of fair procedures, like the use of objective standards advocated in *Getting to Yes*, lessens the likelihood that such forces develop. There is also a great deal of evidence to suggest that procedural justice improves a person's relationship with third parties and with the institutions represented by third parties (Tyler, Casper, and Fisher, 1989). In addition to fostering positive relationships, a second mechanism by which procedural justice promotes deference to social rules is through the promotion of the belief that authorities are legitimate (Tyler, 1990). This internal value is important because when people feel that authorities ought to be obeyed, they take on this obligation and voluntarily defer to authorities and rules. Traditionally, rational choice models of the individual have dominated the social sciences, promoting command and control, deterrence, and social-control strategies of social regulation. These strategies focus upon the individual as a calculative actor—thinking, feeling, and behaving in terms of potential rewards and costs in their immediate environment. However, in both political and legal settings, authorities have recognized that both social regulation (Tyler, 1990) and the encouragement of voluntary civic behavior (Green and Shapiro, 1994) are challenging when authorities only rely upon their ability to reward or punish citizens. Similarly, organizational theorists have begun to recognize the difficulties of managing employees using command-and-control strategies (Pfeffer, 1994). The alternative to such strategies is to focus on approaches based upon appeals to internal values. When internal values lead people to voluntarily defer to authorities and to act prosocially, authorities need not resort to promises of reward or threats of punishment. Procedural justice is therefore central to developing and maintaining judgments that authorities are legitimate and feelings of commitment and identification with groups, organizations, and societies.

These findings demonstrate that providing people with procedural justice can be an important and viable mechanism for gaining deference to decisions and compliance with agreements. This effect occurs across a variety of hierarchical and nonhierarchical situations, including political, legal, managerial, interpersonal, familial, and educational settings. It does so by promoting positive long-term relationships, internal values, and identification.

So far, we have focused on procedural justice in third-party settings. What about procedural justice in dyadic negotiations, where people view each other as adversaries? Does procedural justice matter in one-shot, competitive encounters? This crucial question needs to be addressed in future research.

Conclusions

As this review of distributive and procedural justice research makes clear, there are strong reasons for optimism concerning the viability of justice-based strategies for conflict resolution. In particular, approaches based upon an understanding of people's views about fair decision-making procedures have been very successful in gaining deference to decisions both immediately and over time. Although people care about outcomes, their feelings and behaviors also have an important procedural justice component. This aspect of people's reactions to others in social settings provides an approach to the constructive resolution of negotiation-related conflicts. Success in negotiation cannot be reduced merely to issues of distributive and procedural justice. Rather, there are two parallel tracks on which negotiation should be considered. One is the quality of the agreements reached: the degree to which they effectively capture the available resources (i.e., are optimal agreements) and provide integrative problem-solving solutions to the balancing of people's preferences. These are objective indices of outcome quality that can be separated from outcome satisfaction. Concern for outcome quality must be distinguished from satisfaction with a procedure and acceptance of its outcomes. As Pruitt's work makes clear, the quality of an agreement may not be a strong predictor of its acceptability to the people involved in the negotiation. Issues of acceptability must be treated separately from issues of outcome quality, with acceptability linked to procedural elements that may or may not produce a high-quality agreement.

This point is similar to one previously made by Tyler and Belliveau (1996) about the trade-off between the goals of increasing productivity and maintaining social harmony. It has often been suggested that the use of equity as an allocation rule leads to workplaces that are productive but marred by social disharmony, whereas the use of equality as an allocation rule leads to workplaces that are harmonious but not productive (Okun, 1975). This observation suggests the need for a trade-off to balance these two goals. However, Tyler and Belliveau (1996) suggested that managers instead might use procedural justice to create social harmony and to encourage decision acceptance, thereby freeing them to use those distributive justice principles that were most effective in enhancing productivity when allocating pay and benefits. This might initially seem to suggest paying people based upon equity, but other researchers have suggested that equality is the distribution rule that best enhances productivity (Deutsch, 1987). Whichever rule is used, managers would be building upon the finding that acceptability is linked to procedural justice, and that procedures that are viewed as fair may or may not achieve different types of desirable outcomes.

Overall, these findings support the argument that negotiators are concerned not only with maximizing their self-interest, but with socioemotional issues such as justice rules, which are central to the creation and maintenance of social groups. These justice concerns provide a mechanism that enables people to move beyond their self-interested concerns to effectively work with others in organized settings.

WHEN DOES PROCEDURAL JUSTICE MATTER?

Several streams of recent procedural justice research lend insights into when procedural justice may matter most in negotiation contexts. Fairness heuristic theory (Lind, 2001: Van den Bos and Lind, 2002) focuses on the cognitive processes underlying procedural fairness judgments. The theory emphasizes that people feel vulnerable to exploitation by authorities and decide whether to trust authorities using whatever information is available. Since procedural information is typically readily available, it is often used in making inferences about authorities' trustworthiness and judging the fairness of outcomes. In other words, procedures have *heuristic* value for making sense of outcomes and drawing inferences about authorities.

By extending the insights of fairness heuristic theory to the negotiation context, we can develop several hypotheses about factors that may moderate the importance of procedural justice. Clearly, negotiation contexts represent an atmosphere where exploitation fears may be dominant. Therefore, those negotiation contexts where exploitation concerns are strongest may promote an increased focus on procedural justice, as individuals' motivation to make sense of authorities' trustworthiness is increased. However, according to fairness heuristic theory, procedural information is valued as a substitute (or heuristic) for inferences about trustworthiness and outcomes. When more direct evidence regarding those inferences is available, or even when that information precedes procedural information, procedural justice becomes less important (Van den Bos and Lind, 2002). Thus, fairness heuristic theory suggests that those negotiation contexts in which parties have clear information about their outcomes or about the trustworthiness of other parties may demonstrate weaker influences of procedural fairness information. Empirical research is needed to examine these hypotheses.

Procedural justice matters in part because it conveys relational information to individuals about their connection with the authorities and groups represented by procedures. That relational information is most important to individuals when procedures are linked to groups they use to define themselves, that is, groups with which they identify. Thus, procedural justice effects in negotiation settings should be strongest when procedures are associated with groups that people identify with, and less strong when procedures are linked to out-groups. For instance, to the extent that the judicial system and the police are seen as representative of the U.S. government, the degree to which one defines oneself as American (i.e., the strength of one's identification with the United States) should determine the influence of procedural justice on one's reactions to negotiations with these entities. People's level of identification is a malleable concept, one that third parties may be able to use to capitalize on procedural justice strategies in negotiations. When third parties enact procedures that emphasize common group identities with the parties involved in a negotiation (i.e., if they make common superordinate group identities more salient), they will be more likely to benefit from procedural justice-based attempts to encourage deference and long-term compliance with negotiation settlements.

Finally, other procedural justice research suggests yet another important answer to the question of when procedural justice matters. Specifically, research shows that preexperience choices differ from postexperience evaluations in the emphasis they place on procedural issues (Tyler, Huo, and Lind, 1999). When people make preexperience choices, they tend to emphasize instrumental concerns. But when they are asked to judge experiences they have already encountered, the typical emphasis on procedural justice previously reviewed is replicated. This mismatch in bases of judgment has the potential to misdirect people, as they make choices using different criteria than they will later use to evaluate those choices. These results may have especially important implications for negotiation contexts, where people often have a good deal of say over the type and nature of the negotiations they enter into. If these results extend to negotiations, they suggest that while people may choose negotiation procedures based on instrumental concerns, they will react to those negotiations based on relational criteria, such as the procedural justice they experience.

THE ENACTMENT OF PROCEDURAL JUSTICE

In almost all of the research reviewed, we have emphasized how people react to the procedural justice they experience in their negotiations. However, behavior in negotiation contexts is dynamic; parties in a dispute both dispense treatment and receive others' actions. Therefore, it is important not only to study people's reactions to justice in negotiations, but to examine the influences that determine whether people treat those they are negotiating with fairly.

Research on the scope of justice addresses this issue by focusing on the boundaries people set regarding who they believe should be treated fairly (Tyler et al., 1997). That is, this research considers how people define the community toward which they should accord justice and the community they should exclude from justice considerations. Level of identification is central to this work on the scope of justice; the broader the group that people identify with, the broader the community of those deserving justice. For instance, if someone strongly identifies herself as American, she will view all those who share this identity as within her scope of justice and will concern herself with ensuring that they receive justice. Thus, this individual will be more likely to treat others in her moral community fairly. If her level of group identification is broader (e.g., the human race), then the community to which she will extend justice will likewise be more extensive. On the other hand, if she defines her scope of justice more narrowly (e.g., Caucasian Americans), then the group she is concerned about treating fairly will be smaller.

More generally, mainstream justice research can help us generate hypotheses about when people will be concerned about treating others justly in negotiations. One important determinant of fair treatment is whether people regard their negotiation partners as within the scope of their justice (or "moral") community. When they do, they will be more concerned about according fairness to those they are dealing with. Again, this suggests that emphasizing common identities among negotiation partners may have the benefit of encouraging and facilitating procedural justice-based strategies in negotiations.

Works Cited

Blader, S. L. (2002). *Procedural inference theory: Motivated reasoning and procedural justice.* Unpublished manuscript.

Brockner, J., and J. Z. Rubin. (1985). *Entrapment in escalating conflicts: A social psychological analysis.* New York: Springer-Verlag.

Conlon, D. E., and W. H. Ross. (1997). Appearances do count: The effects of outcomes and explanations on disputant fairness judgments and supervisory evaluations. *International Journal of Conflict Management, 8,* 5–31.

Cropanzano, R., Byrne, Z. S., Bobocel, D. R., and D. E. Rupp. (2001). Moral virtues, fairness heuristics, social entities and other denizens of organizational justice. *Journal of Vocational Behavior, 58,* 164–209.

Deutsch, M. (1987). *Distributive justice.* New Haven, CT: Yale University Press.

Deutsch, M., and R. Krauss. (1962). Studies of interpersonal bargaining. *Journal of Conflict Resolution, 6,* 52–76.

Dillon, P. A. and R. E. Emery. (1996). Divorce mediation and resolution of child custody disputes. *American Journal of Orthopsychiatry, 66,* 131–140.

Fisher, R., Ury, W., and B. Patton. (1991). *Getting to yes* (2nd ed.). New York: Penguin.

Green, D. P., and I. Shapiro. (1994). *Pathologies of rational choice theory.* New Haven, CT: Yale University Press.

Greenberg, J. (1990). Looking fair vs. being fair. *Research in Organizational Behavior, 12,* 111–157.

———. (1993). The social side of fairness: Interpersonal and informational classes of organizational justice. In R. Cropanzano (Ed.), *Justice in the workplace: Approaching fairness in human resource management* (pp. 79–103). Hillsdale, NJ: Erlbaum.

Greenberg, J., and R. Folger. (1983). Procedural justice, participation and the fair process effect in groups. In P. Paulus (Ed.), *Basic group processes* (pp. 235–258). New York: Springer-Verlag.

Harlos, K. P. (2001). When organizational voice systems fail: More on the deaf-ear syndrome and frustration effects. *Journal of Applied Behavioral Science, 37,* 324–342.

Kahneman, D., Knetsch, J. L., and R. H. Thaler. (1986). Fairness and the assumptions of economics. *Journal of Business, 59,* S285–S300.

Kitzmann, K. M., and R. E. Emery. (1993). Procedural justice and parents' satisfaction in a field study of child custody dispute resolution. *Law and Human Behavior, 17,* 553–567.

Lind, E. A., Kulik, C. T., Ambrose, M., and M. de Vera Park. (1993). Individual and corporate dispute resolution. *Administrative Science Quarterly, 38,* 224–251.

Lind, E. A., and T. R. Tyler. (1988). *The social psychology of procedural justice*. New York: Plenum.

Lind, E. A., Tyler, T. R., and Y. J. Huo. (1994). And justice for all: Ethnicity, gender, and preferences for dispute resolution procedures. *Law and Human Behavior, 18,* 269–290.

Lind, E. A. (2001). Fairness heuristic theory. In J. Greenberg and R. Corpanzano (Eds.), *Advances in organizational behavior* (pp. 56–88). Stanford, CA: Stanford University Press.

Messick, D. (1995). Equality, fairness, and social conflict. *Social Justice Research, 8,* 153–173.

Montada, L. (1995). Applying social psychology: The case of redistributions in united Germany. *Social justice research, 8,* 73–90.

Montada, L., and A. Schneider. (1989). Justice and emotional reactions to the disadvantaged. *Social justice research, 3,* 313–344.

Okun, A. M. (1975). *Equality and efficiency: The big tradeoff*. Washington, DC: Brookings.

Paternoster, R., Brame, R., Bachman, R., and L. W. Sherman. (1997). Do fair procedures matter? *Law and Society Review, 31,* 163–204.

Pfeffer, J. (1994). *Competitive advantage through people*. Cambridge, MA: Harvard University Press.

Pruitt, D. G. (1981). *Negotiation behavior*. New York: Academic Press.

Pruitt, D. G., and P. J. Carnevale. (1993). *Negotiation in social conflict*. Pacific Grove, CA: Brooks/Cole.

Pruitt, D. G., Peirce, R. S., McGillicuddy, N. B., Welton, G. L., and L. M. Castrianno. (1993). Long-term success in mediation. *Law and Human Behavior, 17,* 313–330.

Pruitt, D. G., Peirce, R. S., Zubek, J. M., Welton, G. L., and T. H. Nochajski. (1990). Goal achievement, procedural justice, and the success of mediation. *International Journal of Conflict Management, 1,* 33–45.

Pruitt, D. G., and J. Z. Rubin. (1986). *Social conflict*. New York: McGraw-Hill.

Purohit, D., and H. Sondak. (1997). *Fear and loathing at the car dealership: The perceived fairness of pricing policies*. Unpublished manuscript, University of Utah.

Ross, H. L. (1980). *Settled out of court: The social process of insurance claims adjustment*. New York: Aldine.

Rubin, J. Z. (1980). Experimental research on third-party intervention in conflict. *Psychological Bulletin, 87,* 379–391.

Shapiro, D. L., Buttner, E. H., and B. Barry. (1994). Explanations: What factors enhance their perceived adequacy? *Organizational Behavior and Human Decision Processes, 58,* 346–368.

Smith, H. J., and T. R. Tyler. (1996). Justice and power. *European Journal of Social Psychology, 26,* 171–200.

Sondak, H., and T. R. Tyler. (2001). *What shouldn't money buy? The psychology of preferences for market solutions to allocation problems*. Unpublished manuscript, University of Utah.

Thibaut, J., and L. Walker. (1975). *Procedural justice*. Hillsdale, NJ: Erlbaum.

Tyler, T. R. (1988). What is procedural justice? *Law and Society Review, 22,* 103–135.

———. (1990). *Why people obey the law*. New Haven: Yale University Press.

————. (2000). Social justice: Outcome and procedure. *International Journal of Psychology, 35,* 117–125.

Tyler, T. R., and M. Belliveau. (1996). Managing workforce diversity: Ethical concerns and intergroup relations. In D. Messick and A. E. Tenbrunsel (Eds.), *Behavioral research and business ethics* (pp. 171–186). New York: Russell Sage Foundation.

Tyler, T. R., and S. L. Blader. (2000). *Cooperation in groups: Procedural justice, social identity and behavioral engagement.* Philadelphia: Psychology Press.

Tyler, T. R., Boeckmann, R. J., Smith, H. J., and Y. J. Huo. (1997). *Social justice in a diverse society.* Boulder, CO: Westview.

Tyler, T. R., Casper, J., and B. Fisher. (1989). Maintaining allegiance toward political authorities. *American Journal of Political Science, 33,* 629–652.

Tyler, T. R., and P. Degoey. (1996). Trust in organizational authorities: The influence of motive attributions on willingness to accept decisions. In R. M. Kramer and T. R. Tyler (Eds.), *Trust in organizations* (pp. 331–356). Thousand Oaks, CA: Sage.

Tyler, T. R., Huo, Y. J., and E. A. Lind. (1999). The two psychologies of conflict resolution. *Group Processes and Intergroup relations, 2,* 99–118.

Tyler, T. R., and E. A. Lind. (1992). A relational model of authority in groups. In M. Zanna (Ed.), *Advances in experimental social psychology* (Vol. 25, pp. 115–191). New York: Academic Press.

Van den Bos, K., and E. A. Lind. (2002). Uncertainty management by means of fairness judgments. In M. Zanna (Ed.). *Advances in Experimental Social Psychology* (Vol. 34, pp. 1–60). NY: Academic.

Walster, E., Walster, G. W., and E. Berscheid. (1978). *Equity: Theory and research.* Boston: Allyn and Bacon.

CHAPTER 15

Justice Across Cultures

A THREE-STAGE MODEL FOR
INTERCULTURAL NEGOTIATION

Kwok Leung and Kwok-Kit Tong

JUSTICE PERCEPTIONS play a central role in conflict resolution, as Tyler and Blader have argued convincingly (Chapter 14, this volume). A sense of injustice is both a major cause of conflict and a central barrier to its successful resolution. In intercultural negotiation, cultural variations in the notion of justice add to the difficulties of successful conflict resolution (for a review, see Leung and Stephan, 1998).

To apply the justice framework to intercultural negotiation, three major concerns need to be addressed: (1) whether there is a universal concern for justice across cultures, (2) whether people conceptualize justice in the same way across cultures, and (3) whether justice concepts are operationalized similarly (i.e., manifested by similar standards and behaviors) across cultures. The major purpose of this chapter is to examine these issues in the context of intercultural negotiation. Drawing from the literature on culture and justice, we propose a three-stage, pan-cultural framework for conceptualizing differences in the enactment of justice across cultures to shed light on intercultural negotiation.

UNIVERSAL CONCERN FOR JUSTICE

In the animal kingdom, the competition for survival is merciless, but instinctual inhibitions have evolved to avoid fatal aggression within a species (e.g., de Waal, 1992). Human beings also face the problem of within-species

We thank Michael Bond for his insightful and constructive comments, which have greatly improved the chapter. The preparation of this chapter was partially supported by a research grant from the City University of Hong Kong.

competition, and in our case, social rules rather than instincts have evolved to regulate destructive conflict that may endanger the entire species (Gruter, 1992). This functionalist argument suggests that because justice principles are essential in regulating cooperation and competition, they should be recognizable in any organized social group. In line with this argument, Lind (1994) suggested that justice rules are essential to a stable social system because "by specifying power-limiting rules about how people should be treated, how decisions should be made, and how outcomes are to be allocated, rules of justice limit the potential for exploitation and allow people to invest their identity and effort in the group with confidence that they will not be badly used by the group" (p. 30). In sum, this functionalist view of justice points to its universality as a construct (for a review, see Leung and Stephan, 1998).

The Two-Stage Framework for Conceptualizing Justice

Although the concern for justice is universal, cross-cultural psychologists and anthropologists have long argued that the substance of justice varies across cultures (see Leung and Morris, 2001; Morris and Leung, 2000, for reviews). To integrate the universalistic and particularistic perspectives, Morris and Leung (2000) proposed a general framework for justice perception in which justice rules, defined as abstract principles, are distinguished from justice criteria, which specify how the justice rules are to be implemented. This two-stage framework argues that justice rules, which are essential to social functioning, should exist in all human groups and hence are pan-cultural. In contrast, the salience of these rules and the associated justice criteria are sensitive to the particularity of local ecological conditions and show substantial cross-cultural variations. In other words, although justice rules are universal, their relative salience and the way they are implemented are likely to be culture specific. It should be noted that in this framework, culture is seen as a major, but not the only, factor that affects justice perception.

To illustrate the two-stage framework, we will consider the case of distributive justice. Although people from different cultures regard a fair allocation as important, they may differ in their preference for particular allocation rules such as equity, equality, and need. For instance, Leung and Bond (1982) showed that Chinese college students showed a stronger tendency to distribute reward equally among group members than did their American counterparts. Wegener and Liebig (1995) showed that the political environment shapes people's preference for distributive rules. Young people in the former East Germany were less favorable to egalitarianism than old people, whereas the pattern was reversed in the former West Germany.

Even if similar justice rules are adopted, people in different cultures may use different justice criteria in implementing or evaluating them. Take the equity rule as an example. Many forms of input may be regarded as legitimate, such as effort and performance (Komorita and Leung, 1985). A disagreement in the definition of input could become acute in an intercultural dispute. For instance, task-irrelevant inputs such as personal attributes are more likely to be taken into account in determining compensations by Japanese than by Americans (e.g., Ouchi and Jaeger, 1978). Japanese and American coworkers negotiating about how to determine a fair salary may be trapped in a deadlock if these differences are not successfully resolved.

The Operationalization of Justice Criteria: A Three-Stage Framework

One limitation of the two-stage framework is that it is pitched at an abstract level and that justice rules and criteria, being abstract concepts, are distal from concrete actions and arrangements. Even if two cultures agree on a justice rule and its associated criteria, they may still disagree on the concrete actions that should be taken. Consistent with this view, Tyler (2000) noted that "if one person regards a jury trial as the fair way to resolve a conflict, while another person thinks that trial by combat is the fair way to resolve the same dispute, both parties may be interested in having a fair procedure, but they will not be able to agree about what such a fair procedure would look like" (p. 118). Smith, Misumi, Tayeb, Peterson, and Bond (1989) also provided a vivid illustration of this problem. Although being a considerate supervisor is regarded as important across cultures, whether a specific supervisory action is seen as considerate is influenced by culture. When an employee experienced personal difficulties, the discussion of the problems by the supervisor with other employees in the absence of this person was regarded as acceptable by Japanese and Hong Kong Chinese, but as inconsiderate by respondents from the United Kingdom and the United States.

This analysis suggests that information about justice rules and criteria is insufficient in guiding people how to act fairly in a foreign culture and in facilitating intercultural negotiation by reducing the perception of injustice. In fact, books on intercultural contact are typically pitched at a concrete level and focus on behavioral guidelines in well-defined contexts (e.g., Cushner and Brislin, 1996). To address this limitation, we propose the addition of a concrete layer, *justice practices,* to be defined, to the two-stage framework. This expanded three-stage framework is not only more comprehensive and action oriented, but also points to new directions for future research.

JUSTICE CRITERIA AND PRACTICES

In the field of communication, there has been a long tradition of scholarly work on how the meaning of a communication interacts with its context and how its social appropriateness is shaped by contextual factors, a subfield known as pragmatics. Mey (2001) provided a succinct summary of this perspective: "The language we use, and in particular the speech acts we utter, are entirely dependent on the context of the situation in which such acts are produced. All speech is situated speech; a speech act is never just an 'act of speech,' but should be considered in the total situation of activity of which it is a part" (p. 94). The contextualist approach has led to a focus on concrete speech acts, and the work on social pragmatics are highly relevant to our discussion. In this line of work, a taxonomy of sociopragmatics for interpersonal rhetoric has been developed (Leech, 1983, pp. 15–17). This taxonomy begins with a few major principles, each of which is defined by a number of maxims. Each maxim is then further defined by submaxims, and so on, with specific acts as the final level in the tree.

To illustrate this taxonomy, consider the politeness maxim, under which there are the submaxims of modesty and approbation. The submaxim of modesty is operationalized typically by the act of "minimizing praise of self," whereas the submaxim of approbation is operationalized typically by the act of "minimizing dispraise of other" (Leech, 1983). People are assumed to follow the maxim and submaxim, but cross-cultural differences are well-documented regarding the enactment of the submaxim. For instance, in contrast to the typical operational definition of the submaxim of modesty, African-Americans do not view self-praise negatively (Kochman, 1981; cited in Wierzbicka, 1991). Similarly, Mizutani and Mizutani (1987; cited in Wierzbicka, 1991) showed that, in contrast to the typical operational definition of the submaxim of approbation, praise of another was not encouraged in Japanese culture. Again, these examples suggest that although people agree on general principles, the concrete operationalization of these principles may vary across cultures.

In terms of the level of abstraction, principles, maxims and submaxims, and their operational definitions roughly correspond to justice rules, justice criteria, and justice practices, respectively. Unlike the field of communication, the taxonomy of specific acts has received little attention in organizational sciences, and the notion of justice practices that we propose is an attempt to fill this gap. A justice practice is a concrete way in which justice criteria are operationalized and implemented, and may involve concrete standards, verbal and nonverbal behaviors, and social arrangements. To put it in a different way, a justice practice is the concrete way in which people enact a justice criterion in a given situation. The three-stage framework of justice is shown in Figure 15.1.

Justice judgments and behaviors are influenced by justice rules, criteria, and practices. Justice rules, the first-level constructs, specify the rules and procedures used for decision making. Justice criteria, which are second-level

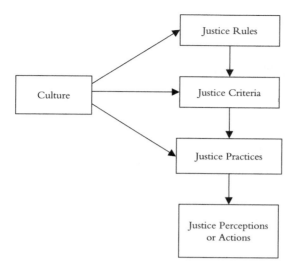

FIGURE 15.1. The three-stage model of justice.

constructs, specify the guidelines for implementing these rules and procedures. Finally, justice practices, the third-level constructs, are operational
definitions of justice criteria and provide the concrete ways with which criteria are implemented and evaluated by others to arrive at a justice judgment.
Similar to justice rules and criteria, significant variations in justice practices
may occur across situations and cultures.

One obvious concern with the notion of justice practices is that because
a large number may exist, it may not be possible to organize them into a
coherent framework. In the field of pragmatics, however, diverse speech
acts, which are also numerous, have been successfully grouped into smaller,
coherent categories. In a later section, we attempt to show that it is possible
to organize justice practices into coherent categories, which are related to
national cultures systematically.

Culture influences the preference for justice rules as well as the selection
of justice criteria (Morris and Leung, 2000). In the three-stage framework,
culture is assumed to impact all three stages (see Figure 15.1), but we will
focus on its impact on justice practices in this chapter. As an initial step, we
only consider the impact of individualism–collectivism and power distance
because of the large amount of empirical work available. In his new book,
Hofstede (2001) has provided a detailed summary of societal norms based
on these two dimensions, which provides the basis for our analysis. Societal
norms based on individualism–collectivism revolve around the extent to
which the in-group versus the individual is emphasized, and societal norms

based on power distance revolve around the importance attached to social hierarchies. Obviously, the notion of justice practices is new, and empirical work is therefore scanty. Our discussion of the relationship between culture and justice practices is conceptual and exploratory, which is guided by broad-bushed descriptions of these two cultural dimensions provided by Hofstede (2001).

Dimensions of Distributive Justice Practices

Although many distributive rules exist, three have received the most attention: equity, equality, and need, which are the focus of our discussion.

JUSTICE PRACTICES FOR EQUITY RULE

For applying the equity rule, justice criteria must be defined to measure inputs, which can be classified as task irrelevant or relevant (Komorita and Leung, 1985). Task-relevant inputs include effort and current contribution to task completion. For the criteria of effort, two categories of practices are possible, including the time spent on the task, and attention and intensity displayed as measured by some objective indicators (Hunt, 1996). With regard to current contribution, the performance management literature suggests at least six categories of justice practices: (1) quantity of output, such as the number of output per hour; (2) quality of output, as measured by some objective standards; (3) appropriateness of output as measured by being on time, within budget, and consistent with preset goals; (4) value in terms of contributing something of value to end products or services; (5) interpersonal contributions in terms of management and leadership and group functioning; and (6) lack of destructive behaviors (Borman and Brush, 1993; Hunt, 1996; Johnson, 2001; Kline and McGrath, 1998).

Task irrelevant inputs can be broadly classified into two types of criteria. The first type is group membership, which is associated with such justice practices as education level or country of origin for determining a reward. For instance, in international joint ventures, employees are sometimes paid according to their country of origin (e.g., Leung, Smith, Wang, and Sun, 1996). The second type is concerned with previous contributions that are unrelated to the present task, which may be measured by such practices as length of service or seniority. Table 15.1 summarizes the justice criteria and practices associated with the equity rule.

Justice criteria and their associated practices vary with societal norms associated with individualism–collectivism. Given the loyalty norm emphasized by collectivists, we expect that group membership characteristics that signal loyalty, such as length of service, should be used to operationalize the equity rule more often among collectivists than among individualists. This

TABLE 15.1
Equity, Equality, and Need Practices

Justice Criteria	Justice Practices
	Equity
Effort	Time spent on task
	Attention and intensity
Contribution	Quantity of output
	Quality of output
	Appropriateness of output
	Value of contribution
	Interpersonal contributions such as contributions to group cohesiveness
	Lack of destructive behaviors
Group membership	Education level
	Country of origin
Previous contribution	Seniority
	Length of service
	Equality
Objective equality	Equal usage
	Equal share after transformation to a unidimensional resource
Subjective equality	Perception of equal share of a resource
	Perception of equal share made possible by compensations
	Need
Existence	Physiological—work conditions
	Materialistic—salary and benefits
	Job security
Relatedness	Superiors
	Peers
	Subordinates
	Entire organization
	External parties
Growth	Utilization of existing capabilities
	Development of new capabilities

argument is in line with the well-known Japanese and Korean practice of placing a larger premium on length of service than their American counterparts in compensation decisions (e.g., Hundley and Kim, 1997).

With regard to justice practices for current contributions, we expect that effort exerted should be emphasized more by collectivists than by individualists, because effort may signal loyalty and commitment to the in-group. In fact, in an educational setting, Stevenson et al. (1990) have found a higher emphasis on the total time spent in attending lessons and reviewing by Chinese than by Americans. Hence, the justice practices of total working time and total output regardless of the quality achieved should be more commonly adopted by collectivists than by individualists. For performance dimensions, we expect that collectivists should emphasize contributions to interpersonal relationships, such as contributions to team cohesiveness and group harmony, more than individualists (but see Bond, Leung, and Wan, 1982). Furthermore, collectivists may put a higher emphasis on the maintenance of good internal and external relationships by leaders than by individualists. For destructive behaviors, given that deviance from norms is likely to be sanctioned more in collectivistic cultures (Yamagishi, 1988), we expect that collectivists should be more likely to consider destructive behaviors as a negative input and punish the culprits more severely than should individualists (e.g., reduction of salary for employees who break a company rule).

With regard to the influence of power distance norms, one characteristic of group membership, rank, should be emphasized more as an input for reward distribution in high- than in low-power-distance societies (Mendonca and Kanungo, 1994). Based on Hofstede (2001), high-power-distance societies should emphasize the justice practice of rank more in compensations decisions. Furthermore, destructive behaviors should be weighed more as a negative input in high-power-distance societies because these behaviors are likely to signal disobedience and challenges to authority figures. Hence, rewarding those who display no destructive behavior and punishing those who display destructive behavior should be considered fairer in high- than in low-power-distance societies.

JUSTICE PRACTICES FOR EQUALITY RULE

For the application of the equality rule, as long as the reward to be divided is quantifiable, divisible, and unidimensional, the notion of justice criteria and practices are irrelevant. In work settings, most, if not all, tangible rewards fit this description, such as salary and benefits. Complications may occur, however, if a reward is multidimensional or nondivisible, and Fiske (1991) has suggested that the solution to this problem requires "a subtle cultural understanding of what counts as 'the same.'" (p. 147). Take the example of dividing equally an office space with a nice view on one side only. Because the view is indivisible, it is controversial as to how to divide the space equally. Justice criteria are relevant for such nondivisible resources, and two types seem sensible: objective and subjective. Justice practices based on objective equality involve equal sharing of a resource, such as rotating the office with the view among participants or swap the entire office space for some other space that can be divided equally (cf. Fiske, 1991, p. 161). Justice practices based on subjective equality involve the determination of how to divide the office space into two halves that are seen as equal by giving the half without the view more space. Alternately, the office without the view may be compensated by other items, such as nicer furniture (cf. Fiske, 1991, pp. 147–148). Table 15.1 summarizes the justice rules, criteria, and practices for the equality rule.

With regard to the influence of culture, when nondivisible or multidimensional resources are involved, collectivists, who tend to value harmonious relationships with in-group members, may prefer practices that are conflict-free (e.g., turn taking among participants). With regard to the influence of power distance, subjective equality may be preferred in high-power-distance than low-power-distance societies because the subjectivity involved may provide flexibility to authority figures to decide on an allocation in a way they prefer.

JUSTICE PRACTICES FOR NEED RULE

In applying the need rule, the dynamics involved resemble those involved in the equity rule in that needs have to be defined. There is a long research tradition on needs in psychology, the most well-known of which is Maslow's (1943) hierarchy of needs: physiology, safety, belongingness, esteem, and self-actualization. Subsequently, Alderfer (1967) provided a simpler version for the work context: existence, relatedness, and growth. Existence needs refer to material needs for survival and existence; relatedness needs refer to the needs for positive interpersonal relationships; and growth needs refer to the needs for personal development. We may regard these three forms of needs as justice criteria, for each of which justice practices can be developed. For existence needs, three types of practices are possible: physiological (working conditions such as noise and temperature), materialistic (salary and benefits), and security (safety and job security). For relatedness needs, five types of practices based on the target are possible: superiors, peers, subordinates, the entire organization, and external parties, such as customers and suppliers. For growth needs, two types of practices are possible: utilization of capabilities and development of new capabilities.

The need rule is often applied in allocating benefits and training opportunities. Benefits are usually based on existence needs, but in allocating training opportunities, there may be tension between existence and growth needs. Should training be allocated based on people's need for job security, or their growth needs based on curiosity and personal interest?

With regard to the influence of culture on the justice practices for the need rule, one obvious speculation is that relatedness needs should be emphasized more in collectivist than in individualistic cultures. For instance, compared to individualists, collectivists may consider it unfair to make someone work alone for an extended period time without the opportunity to interact with coworkers. Furthermore, collectivists should be more likely to give priority to practices concerning collective well-being over individual needs. For instance, collectivists may consider it fair to reassign a room booked by an individual for his or her activities to a group that needs it for a meeting. With regard to the influence of power distance, it is likely that the needs of authority figures are given more consideration in high-power-distance than low-power-distance societies.

Dimensions of Procedural Justice Practices

In our framework, procedures for decision making and conflict resolution correspond to justice rules. Recently, Colquitt (2001) validated a taxonomy of procedural justice concepts, and three types are identified: procedural, interpersonal, and informational. Each type involves several criteria that, in the terminology of our three-stage framework, correspond to our justice criteria. Unlike distributive justice practices, we do not attempt to provide a comprehensive discussion of procedural justice practices because procedural issues are wide ranging, and current research is not of sufficient maturity to warrant such an attempt.

PRACTICES FOR PROCEDURAL JUSTICE

Seven criteria concerning procedures are identified by Colquitt (2001), which are reminiscent of the criteria proposed by Leventhal (1980) more that two decades ago: process control (opportunities for voicing one's opinions), outcome control (opportunities for influencing important outcomes), consistency, bias suppression, accuracy of information, correctability, and ethicality.

As shown in Table 15.2, each of these criteria has specific practices. Process control can be exercised directly or indirectly. Direct process control may be exercised collectively by a group or individually. Indirect process control includes written means or a third party. Likewise, outcome control may be direct or indirect, and exercised collectively or individually. Consistency may take on a universalist definition and require consistency across actors, time, and contexts (e.g., allow equal voice for employees from different levels), or a particularist definition that allows variations across different actors, time, and contexts (e.g., standards vary across rank). Bias suppression may take many forms, such as the declaration of conflict of interest and the inclusion of decision makers with diverse backgrounds, such as those who support the views of minority members. Accuracy of information can be demonstrated by expert endorsement (e.g., present expert opinion) and the disclosure of how the information is collected. Correctibility may take many forms, as reflected by a wide range of grievance and appeal procedures. One dimension is concerned with the role of the victims, with one form requiring them to actively argue for their case and another form that places the responsibility in the hands of a third party. Some grievance procedures are formal,

TABLE 15.2
Practices of Formal Procedures

Justice Criteria	Justice Practices
Process control	Direct—individual or collective
	Indirect—written or third party
Outcome control	Direct—individual or collective
	Indirect—written or third party
Consistency	Across contexts
	Across time
	Across actors
Bias suppression	Declaration of conflict of interest
	Inclusion of decision makers of diverse backgrounds
Accuracy of information	Expert endorsement
	Disclosure of mechanisms of information collection
Correctability	Active—responsibility placed in the hands of complainants
	Passive—responsibility placed in the hands of authority
	Time constraints
Ethicality	Compliance with societal norms
	Compliance with legal norms

whereas others are informal. Another dimension is whether time constraints are imposed, and a time limit may be set within which complaints will be processed. Finally, ethicality may be based on social norms (e.g., the kind of lies that are tolerated) or legal norms (e.g., equal opportunities policies).

CULTURAL DIFFERENCES IN PROCEDURAL JUSTICE PRACTICES

For formal decision-making procedures, such as management meetings in a firm, we expect that collectivists, who tend to avoid individual conflict, are more in favor of group-based process control (e.g., appointing a group representative to relay the views of a group) than are individualists, who should be more in favor of individual process control (e.g., allowing the parties to the dispute being tried and their partisan representatives to have direct process control over a dispute). Indirect process control, which may be exercised through the delegation of process control to a high-status third party, may be more acceptable to people from high-power-distance societies, because indirect means can cushion the friction with authority figures. People from low-power-distance societies are less receptive of a high-status third party to act on their behalf.

With regard to outcome control, we expect that collectivists prefer direct control, which is possible in such procedures as personal persuasion and mediated negotiation, so that compromises are possible (Leung and Stephan,

1998). In contrast, individualists may be more likely to relinquish outcome control to a neutral party, such as an arbitrator, for a win–lose verdict because of their emphasis on competition and due process (Finkel, Crystal, and Watanabe, 2001). For example, Bierbrauer (1994) found that Kurdish and Lebanese asylum seekers in Germany, who were collectivistic, preferred to use norms of religion and tradition to resolve a conflict with family members and acquaintances. On the contrary, Germans, who were individualistic, were more likely to appeal to state law and formal legal procedure. One explanation for these results is that norms of religion and tradition give Kurds direct control over the final settlement, whereas state laws place the outcome decisions in the hands of judges.

In collectivist cultures, consistency is likely to be viewed in particularistic terms because of the importance attached to group boundaries, and variations across actors, time, and contexts are more accepted. In contrast, a universal definition of consistency is likely to be normative in individualist societies, and variations across different groups of actors, time, or contexts are less accepted. With regard to the power distance norm, in low-power-distance societies, voice is likely to be granted to people regardless of their status, but in high-power-distance societies, high-ranking people may be given more voice. Bias suppression that is formal and elaborate should be preferred in lower-power-distance societies, whereas in high-power-distance societies, bias suppression is more likely to be informal and less elaborate. For instance, declaration of conflict of interest by public figures is taken seriously in low-power-distance cultures, and nondisclosures often result in serious political consequences. In Asia, where power distance is high, this justice practice tends to be more informal and ad hoc.

In demonstrating the accuracy of information, experts and authorities should be employed more frequently in high- than in low-power-distance societies. On the other hand, people from individualist societies are more likely to evaluate the accuracy of information with their own experiences and knowledge, whereas people from collectivist societies are more likely to trust information endorsed by in-group members. With regard to mechanisms that ensure correctibility, active forms that are based on the initiative of the victims should be more emphasized in lower-power-distance cultures, whereas passive forms are more prevalent in high-power-distance cultures. Because of their desire for individual control, active forms should be regarded as fairer in individualist than in collectivist societies. Finally, with regard to ethicality, individualists are more likely to view ethicality in absolute terms, basing their ethical judgments on absolute standards. In contrast, collectivists are likely to view ethicality in absolute as well as social terms, and their judgment may take into account their relationship with the target (Vasquez,

Keltner, Ebenbach, and Banaszynski, 2001). For instance, breaking a rule to help a friend is regarded as less unfair in India than in the United States (Miller and Bersoff, 1992).

Dimensions of Interpersonal Justice Practices

In interpersonal justice, two major criteria are identified: respect (being polite) and propriety (avoid inappropriate remarks and behaviors). These two criteria are highly abstract, and numerous justice practices can be identified for their implementation. For instance, the showing of respect may involve nonverbal behaviors such as eye contract, paralinguistic behaviors such as tone, and verbal remarks. Two broad categories may be distinguished for respect: compliance with norms that convey respect and social protocols. Respect for norms prescribes the verbal and nonverbal behaviors that one can enact to convey respect to a target, whereas social protocols involve social conventions that govern interpersonal interactions, such as seating arrangements.

For propriety, two broad categories are discernable: social face and respect for individual rights. Social face involves putting the target in good light and avoiding acts that embarrass or belittle them, such as derogatory and abusive remarks. Respect for individual rights involves permitting people to exercise their rights, such as privacy rights or the right to be treated as innocent before being proven guilty. See Table 15.3 for a summary.

CULTURAL DIFFERENCES IN INTERPERSONAL JUSTICE PRACTICES

With regard to interpersonal justice, it is expected that, compared with individualists, collectivists should display a higher level of respect and respectful social protocols toward in-group than out-group members. Regarding the influence of power distance, in high-power-distance cultures, it is expected that people occupying lower levels in the hierarchy would receive a lower level of respect, both in terms of paralinguistic and verbal treatments. For instance, it is rude for a boss to tell a secretary to copy something without saying the word *please* in the United States, but it is not considered rude in Japan to skip *please* (Akasu and Asao, 1993). In fact, it is considered odd if superiors use the polite form of a verb with subordinates. In high-power-distance societies, it is expected that authority figures will be subject to social protocols that are commensurate with their status. For instance, seating order should be decided on the basis of rank, authority figures should speak the most, and interruption is not expected. One can easily appreciate these differences by comparing the status-conscious protocols of the British royalties with the casual styles of the royalties in Scandinavia, a region well-known

TABLE 15.3

Practices for Interpersonal and Informational Justice

Justice Criteria	Justice Practices
	Interpersonal Justice
Respect	Compliance with social norms for showing respect, such as: restraint from interrupting
	Compliance with social protocols, such as: allow senior people to speak first
Propriety	Compliance with norms of social face maintenance, such as: restraint from abusive remarks
	Compliance with individual rights, such as: respect one's privacy
	Informational Justice
Justification	Logic
	Emotions and feelings
	Principles
	Precedents
	Cost–benefit analysis
	Norms
Truthfulness	Level of disclosure
	Forms of assurance, such as: normative, legal, third party
Reasonableness	Compliance with expectations
	Endorsement of disinterested third party
Timeliness	Norms with regard to pace of life
	Time required previously
Specificity	Level of details
	Customization based on needs

for its low-power-distance culture. Scandinavian royalties are sometimes seen in supermarkets doing their own shopping and flying with commoners in commercial airlines.

For propriety, social face is important in collectivist cultures, and it is expected that one should try to protect the face of others by not embarrassing them. For instance, Cushner and Brislin (1996, pp. 188–189) suggested that in Korea, it would be considered rude to mention subordinates' mistakes in front of their colleagues because it makes them lose face. However, a similar act in the West is usually taken more lightly. Wierzbicka (1991) noted, for example, that in Israeli culture, open confrontation is encouraged and appreciated because it reflects spontaneity, closeness, and mutual trust. With regard to rights, it is expected that individual rights, such as privacy, are taken more seriously in individualist than in collectivist cultures. For instance, discussion of the problems of coworkers in their absence was considered less acceptable in the United States and Britain than in Japan and Hong Kong (Smith et al., 1989).

Dimensions of Informational Justice Practices

In informational justice, five dimensions are identified: justification (explanations provided), truthfulness, reasonableness of explanations, timeliness (communication in a timely manner), and target specificity of communication (tailored to individuals' specific needs). For justification, many practices can be used to implement the criteria of justification, which may be based on logic, emotions, principles, or precedents. A related literature on account giving (e.g., Schönbach and Kleibaumhuter, 1989) is informative for developing of a taxonomy of justifications. This literature has suggested a number of ways to justify a negative act, such as cost–benefit arguments (benefits outweigh costs) or normative arguments (it is the typical thing to do). For truthfulness, two practices can be used: levels of disclosure and forms of assurance. In some contexts, negative information may be withheld to avoid conflicts, such as in performance appraisal situations (Larson, 1989). Forms of assurance of truthfulness also vary, some being traditional (e.g., to swear on a Bible), and some legal (a legal declaration). Endorsement of a third party may be used, as in the case of the use of an accounting firm. For reasonableness, what is seen as reasonable obviously varies drastically across contexts. One justice practice is based on the extent to which an explanation deviates from expectation. For instance, if a firm is profitable, explanations for a layoff, no matter how they are constructed, are likely to be seen as unreasonable (Kahneman, Knetsch, and Thaler, 1986) because people don't expect profitable firms to have the need to lay people off. On the other hand, the endorsement of a disinterested third party (e.g., experts and academics) may enhance the reasonableness of a decision. For timeliness, the obvious justice practice is based on the time involved. Finally, for specificity, different levels of customization may be viewed as appropriate in different settings. For instance, standard explanations should be more acceptable if people are affected by a decision uniformly, and individualized explanations are expected if people are affectedly differentially. Also, people whose self-interest is substantially affected are more likely to demand an individualized explanation. See Table 15.3 for a summary.

CULTURAL DIFFERENCES IN INFORMATIONAL JUSTICE PRACTICES

Justification is clearly connected to individualism–collectivism. It is expected that individualists would prefer cost–benefit analysis because of their emphasis on market pricing (Fiske, 1992), a tendency to rely on economic rationality in social exchanges. In contrast, collectivists would emphasize normative arguments because of their emphasis on adherence to in-group norms (Triandis, 1995, p. 155). Justifications are more likely to be strengthened by endorsements by experts and authority figures in high- than in low-power-distance cultures.

For truthfulness, full disclosure and honesty are more emphasized in individualist than in collectivist cultures. For instance, in communication, Americans regard clear messages as more appropriate than do Japanese (Gudykunst and Nishida, 1994). In fact, in collectivistic societies, honesty is sometime sacrificed for achieving more important social goals, such as the preservation of dignity (Cushner and Brislin, 1996). Triandis et al. (2001) reported that deception is more prevalent in collectivist than in individualist cultures. Finally, individualists may prefer legal forms of assurance, whereas collectivists may prefer normative forms.

For reasonableness, arguments based on individual interests and rights should appear more reasonable in individualist cultures, whereas arguments based on group interests should appear more reasonable in collectivist cultures. Bian and Keller (1999) showed that the sacrifice of individual interest to protect group interest is endorsed more by Chinese than by Americans. Finally, arguments based on status and rank should appear more reasonable in high- than in low-power-distance cultures.

For timeliness, different speeds are regarded as timely in different contexts, and there are substantial differences in the pace of life across cultures (Levine and Norenzayan, 1999). A normal service in one culture may be regarded as unreasonably slow by people from a different culture with a fast pace of life. However, it is not clear how individualism–collectivism and power distance norms may influence the justice practices for timeliness and specificity. We may speculate that for collectivists, slower and more general explanations are likely to be provided to out-groups than to in-groups, because they are less willing to invest in and provide help to out-group members. In high-power-distance cultures, faster and more specific explanations are likely to be provided to people in power than to people without power.

Justice Practices and Intercultural Negotiation

It is clear from the previous arguments that cultures vary in justice rules, criteria, and practices. In intercultural negotiation, in addition to the problem of conflict of interest, cultural mismatch in rules, criteria, and practices often cause intense feelings of injustice, trapping negotiators in deadlocks. The central tenet advanced in this chapter is that convergence in rules and criteria are insufficient: common justice practices must be used to clear cultural traps that may paralyze a negotiation. For instance, silence during negotiation does not signal passivity on the part of Japanese negotiators, and their Western counterparts often misread it as a lack of response or an indication of consent (Graham and Sano, 1984). Japanese negotiators would be upset and if their silence is interpreted erroneously. Misunderstanding in the other direction can occur when Asians misread their Western counterparts' adversarial arguments as an indication of unreasonableness and lack of respect (Morris et al., 1998). Western negotiators may find the hostile responses from their Asian counterparts uncalled for. Another example comes from cultural differences in the notion of timeliness. In a U.S.–Japan collaboration, the Aladdin and Dunes Hotel in Las Vegas, Americans found the emphasis on consensus by Japanese too slow and cumbersome in the fast-moving casino environment (Ricks, 1993). Different notions of timeliness obviously make it hard for a collaboration to function properly.

Perhaps the importance of justice practices is best illustrated by the case of the USS *Greeneville*, a U.S. submarine that accidentally sank a Japanese fisheries training ship, the *Ehime Maru*, in 2001. The captain of the ship, Scott Waddle, later issued a written statement in which he expressed his "most sincere regret" over the accident, which infuriated many Japanese. A relative of a victim told the press that Japanese refused to accept the statement as an apology, and that a real apology required him to say it to each of the victims' relatives in person. Apology in person is in fact common in Japan to show the remorse felt and the willingness to shoulder the blame. Subsequently, Commander Waddle had an opportunity to apologize in person to the captain of *Ehime Maru*, Hisao Onishi, and expressed his wish to travel to Japan to apologize in person to the relatives of the victims. President Bush and key senior officers made high-profile, public apologies, and an admiral was sent to Japan to explain to the families of the victims the results of the enquiry of the accident. In this incident, the U.S. officials understood that in Japan, a major justice practice for the decision to absolve a wrongdoer requires his or her display of a deep sense of remorse and a willingness to shoulder the responsibilities, typically expressed in the form of elaborate apologies. Despite the initial uproar generated by the incident in Japan, the handling of the event in a culturally appropriate manner led to a satisfactory settlement without harming the U.S.–Japan relationship (for details, see news stories about the incident at www.cnn.com).

Conclusion

For justice theories to be useful in real life, they must inform actions, and the practical relevance of justice theories lies in their specificity. With the introduction of the notion of justice practices, the three-stage framework proposed provides the needed specificity to formulate a concrete, yet coherent and manageable framework to put justice theories into action. Furthermore, it also provides a way to decode the myriad of cultural difference in justice phenomena and organize them into a coherent framework. We argue that a normative approach is effective in organizing otherwise numerous and unconnected justice practices, and we demonstrate how social norms based on individualism–collectivism and power distance can be used to achieve this end. Obviously, much of what we propose is speculative and calls for future empirical substantiation, but we believe that we have identified an important and productive avenue for nudging justice theories in the direction of completeness and practicability.

On the theoretical front, our three-stage framework raises many interesting conceptual questions. First, we propose that culture exerts its influence on all the three stages: justice rules, criteria, and practices. Culture is a complex variable, and its effects must be unpackaged. Different cultural elements may have different effects on these three types of justice constructs, which calls for further theoretical and empirical development. Second, we have provided a simple taxonomy of justice practices, which is obviously a starting point and is far from complete and optimal. Nonetheless, this taxonomy provides the initial step for subsequent refinement and verification. Third, we have focused on norms based on individualism–collectivism and power distance in our discussion of cultural differences. Norms based on other cultural dimensions should be explored in future work. Finally, we argue that cultural differences in justice practices may constitute significant barriers to intercultural negotiation, and we have provided some examples to illustrate this point of view. Obviously, systematic investigation into this possibility is needed in future research.

Works Cited

Alderfer, C. P. (1967). Convergent and discriminant validation of satisfaction and desire measures with and without preceding interview. *Journal of Applied Psychology, 51,* 509–520.

Akasu, K., and K. Asao. (1993). Sociolinguistic factors influencing communication in Japan and the United States. In W. B. Gudykunst (Ed.), *Communication in Japan and the United States* (pp. 88–121). Albany: State University of New York Press.

Bian, W. Q., and L. R. Keller. (1999). Chinese and Americans agree on what is fair, but disagree on what is best in societal decisions affecting health and safety risks. *Risk Analysis, 19,* 439–452.

Bierbrauer, G. (1994). Toward an understanding of legal culture: Variations in individualism and collectivism between Kurds, Lebanese, and Germans. *Law and Society Review, 28,* 243–264.

Borman, W. C., and D. H. Brush. (1993). More progress toward a taxonomy of managerial performance requirement. *Human Performance, 6* (1), 1–21.

Bond, M. H., Leung, K., and K. C. Wan. (1982). How does cultural collectivism operate? The impact of task and maintenance contributions on reward allocation. *Journal of Cross Cultural Psychology, 13,* 186–200.

Colquitt, J. A. (2001). On the dimensionality of organizational justice: A construct validation of a measure. *Journal of Applied Psychology, 86,* 386–400.

Cushner, K., and R. W. Brislin. (1996). *Intercultural interactions: A practical guide: Vol. 9. Cross-cultural research and methodology.* Thousand Oaks, CA: Sage.

De Waal, F. B. M. (1992). The chimpanzee's sense of social regularity and its relation to the human sense of justice. In R. Masters and M. Gruter (Eds.), *The sense of justice: Biological foundations of law* (pp. 241–255). Newbury Park, CA: Sage.

Finkel, N. J., Crystal, D. S., and H. Watanabe. (2001). Commonsense notions of unfairness in Japan and the United States. *Psychology, Public and Law, 7,* 345–380.

Fiske, A. P. (1991). *Structures of social life: The four elementary forms of human relations.* New York: Free Press.

————. (1992). The four elementary forms of sociality: Framework for a unified theory of social relations. *Psychological Review, 99,* 689–723.

Graham, J. L., and Y. Sano. (1984). *Smart bargaining: Doing business with the Japanese.* Cambridge, MA: Ballinger.

Gruter, M. (1992). An ethological perspective on law and biology. In R. Masters and M. Gruter (Eds.), *The sense of justice: biological foundations of law* (pp. 95–105). Newbury Park, CA: Sage.

Gudykunst, W. B., and T. Nishida. (1994). *Bridging Japanese/North American differences.* Thousand Oaks, CA: Sage.

Hofstede, G. (2001). *Culture's consequences: Comparing values, behaviors, institutions, and organizations across nations* (2nd ed.). Thousand Oaks, CA: Sage.

Hundley, G., and J. Kim. (1997). National culture and the factors affecting perceptions of pay fairness in Korea and the United States. *International Journal of Organizational Analysis, 5,* 325–341.

Hunt, S. T. (1996). Generic work behavior: An investigation into the dimensions of entry-level, hourly job performance. *Personnel Psychology, 49* (1), 51–83.

Johnson, J. W. (2001). The relative importance of task and contextual performance dimensions to supervisor judgments of overall performance. *Journal of Applied Psychology, 86,* 984–996.

Kahneman, D., Knetsch, J. L., and R. H. Thaler. (1986). Fairness as a constraint on profit seeking: Entitlements in the market. *American Economic Review, 76,* 728–741.

Kline, T. J. B., and J. McGrath. (1998). Development and validation of five criteria for evaluating team performance. *Organizational Development Journal, 16* (3), 19–27.

Kochman, Thomas (1981). Black and white style in conflict. Chicago: University of Chicago Press.

Komorita, S. S., and K. Leung. (1985). Toward a synthesis of power and justice in reward allocation. In E. J. Lawler (Ed.), *Advances in group processes* (Vol. 2, pp. 169–196). Greenwich, CT: JAI Press.

Larson, J. R. (1989). The dynamic interplay between employees' feedback-seeking strategies and supervisors' delivery of performance feedback. *Academy of management Review, 14,* 408–422.

Leech, G. N. (1983). *Principles of pragmatics.* New York: Longman.

Leung, K., and M. H. Bond. (1982). How Chinese and Americans reward task-related contributions: A preliminary study. *Psychologia: An International Journal of Psychology in the Orient, 25* (1), 32–39.

Leung, K., and M. W. Morris. (2001). Justice through the lens of culture and ethnicity. In J. Sanders and V. L. Hamilton (Eds.), *Handbook of justice research in law* (pp. 343–378). New York: Kluwer Academic/Plenum.

Leung, K., Smith, P. B., Wang, Z. M., and H. F. Sun. (1996). Job satisfaction in joint venture hotels in China: An organizational justice analysis. *Journal of International Business Studies, 27,* 947–962.

Leung, K., and W. G. Stephan. (1998). Perceptions of injustice in intercultural relations. *Applied and Preventive Psychology, 7,* 193–205.

Leventhal, G. S. (1980). What should be done with equity theory? New approaches to the study of fairness in social relationships. In K. Gergen, M. Greenberg, and R. Willis (Eds.), *Social exchange: Advances in theory and research* (pp. 27–55). New York: Plenum.

Levine, R. V., and A. Norenzayan. (1999). The pace of life in 31 countries. *Journal of Cross-Cultural Psychology, 30,* 178–205.

Lind, E. A. (1994). Procedural justice and culture: Evidence for ubiquitous process concerns. *Zeitschrift für Rechtssoziologie, 15,* 24–36.

Maslow, A. H. (1943). A theory of human motivation. *Psychological Review, 50,* 390–396.

Mendonca, M., and R. N. Kanungo. (1994). Motivation through effective reward management in developing countries. In R. N. Kanungo and M. Mendonca (Eds.), *Work motivation: Models for developing countries* (pp. 49–83). New Delhi, India: Sage.

Mey, J. L. (2001). *Pragmatics: An introduction.* Malden, MA: Blackwell.

Miller, J., and D. M. Bersoff. (1992). Culture and moral judgment: How are conflicts between justice and interpersonal responsibilities resolved? *Journal of Personality and Social Psychology, 62,* 541–554.

Morris, M. W., and K. Leung. (2000). Justice for all? Progress in research on cultural variation in the psychology of distributive and procedural justice. *Applied Psychology: An International Review, 49* (1), 100–132.

Morris, M. W., Williams, K. Y., Leung, K., Larrick, R., Mendoza, M. T., Bhatnagar, D., Li, J. F., Kondo, M., Luo J. L., and J. C. Hu. (1998). Conflict management style: accounting for cross-national differences. *Journal of International Business Studies, 29,* 729–747.

Ouchi, W. G., and A. M. Jaeger. (1978). Type Z organization: Stability in the midst of mobility. *Academy of Management Review, 3,* 305–314.

Ricks, D. A. (1993). *Blunders in international business.* Cambridge, MA: Blackwell.

Schönbach, P., and P. Kleibaumhuter. (1989). Severity of reproach and defensiveness of accounts. In M. J. Cody and M. L. McLaughlin (Eds.), *The psychology of tactical communication* (pp. 229–243). Clevedon: Multilingual Matters.

Smith, P. B., Misumi, J., Tayeb, M. H., Peterson, M. F., and M. H. Bond. (1989). On the generality of leadership style measures across cultures. *Journal of Occupational Psychology, 62,* 97–109.

Stevenson, H. W., Lee, S. Y., Chen, C. S., Stigler, J. W., Hsu, C. C., and S. Kitamura. (1990). Contexts of achievement: A study of American, Chinese, and Japanese children. *Monographs of the Society for Research in Child Development, 55* (1–2), Serial No. 221.

Triandis, H. C. (1995). *Individualism and collectivism*. Boulder, CO: Westview.

Triandis, H. C., Carnevale, P., Gelfand, M., Robert, C., Wasti, A., Probst, T., Kashima, E., Dragonas, T., Chan, D., Chen, X. P., Kim, U., De Dreu, C., Van de Vliert E., Iwao, S., Ohbuchi, K., and P. Schmidt. (2001). Culture, personality and deception: A multilevel approach. *International Journal of Cross-Cultural Management, 1,* 73–90.

Tyler, T. R. (2000). Social justice: outcome and procedure. *International Journal of Psychology, 35,* 117–125.

Vasquez, K., Keltner, D., Ebenbach, D. H., and T. L. Banaszynski. (2001). Cultural variation and similarity in moral rhetorics: Voices from the Philippines and the United States. *Journal of Cross Cultural Psychology, 32* (1), 93–120.

Wegener, B., and S. Liebig. (1995). Dominant ideologies and the variation of distributive justice norms: A comparison of East and West Germany, and the United States. In J. R. Kluegel, D. S. Mason, and B. Wegener (Eds.), *Social justice and political change: Public opinion in capitalist and post-communist states* (pp. 239–262). New York: Aldine.

Wierzbicka, A. (1991). *Cross-cultural pragmatics: The semantics of human interaction.* Berlin: de Gruyter.

Yamagishi, T. (1988). The provision of a sanctioning system in the United States and Japan. *Social Psychology Quarterly, 51,* 265–271.

CHAPTER 16

What Do Communication Media Mean for Negotiators? A Question of Social Awareness

Kathleen L. McGinn and Rachel Croson

LIFE IN THE TWENTY-FIRST CENTURY is filled with more variety and volume in communication than any century preceding it. Amidst the proliferation of media through which to communicate is a growing confusion about their usefulness in negotiations. Our goal in this chapter is to elucidate the distinctions across the options for communication, and to provide a clearer understanding of the role communication media play in negotiations.

Our analysis rests on the assumption that a negotiation is an inherently social process. In presenting past, contradictory research on media effects on negotiations, we highlight the lack of attention to the social interaction making up the negotiation. Yet, interacting with another in an interdependent fashion, as defines negotiations, is a social endeavor. We offer a categorization of media properties, and report and reflect on social psychological and economic studies of the effects of these properties on social interactions. We then review the research on social processes in negotiations, as well as our own qualitative analysis of previously unanalyzed transcript data from negotiations carried out over various media. These investigations lead us to assert that the medium in which a negotiation takes place affects outcomes by fundamentally affecting the parties' perceptions of one another and of the interaction in which they're participating. We refer to these perceptions as *social awareness*— the degree of consciousness of and attention to the other(s) in a social interaction. We conclude that an appreciation of the role of social awareness can enhance our understanding of the role communication media play in negotiations. Differences across media in the opportunities for building social awareness present an organizing explanation for the divergent results from studies of media effects in negotiations. This perspective may also provide additional insights into cross-cultural negotiation behavior and outcomes.

The role of communication media on negotiations has been a subject of investigation for over twenty-five years. The outcome measure most commonly cited in this research is the integrativeness of the agreement, the extent to which the parties at the table are able to reap the surplus available from trade. Across economic and social psychological research, face-to-face interaction has been shown to increase integrativenesss relative to text-only and audio-only interaction (Orbell, Van de Kragt, and Dawes, 1988; Raiffa, 1982; Valley, Thompson, Gibbons, and Bazerman, 2002), to decrease integrativeness relative to audio-only (Carnevale and Isen, 1986; Carnevale, Pruitt, and Seilheimer, 1981; Morley and Stephenson, 1969), and to have no effect on integrativeness relative to other media (Croson, 1999; Schweitzer, Brodt, and Croson 2001; Shell, 2001; Suh, 1999).

A second outcome measure often studied is the distribution of the surplus across the parties—the ratio of each party's payoffs relative to the other party's or parties'.[1] Face-to-face interaction has been shown to increase the differences in payoffs relative to written negotiations (Croson, 1999), to both increase (Weeks, 1976) and decrease (Morley and Stephenson, 1969; Valley, Moag, and Bazerman, 1998) differences in payoffs relative to negotiations carried out over the telephone, and to have no effect on differences in payoffs between face-to-face negotiations and those carried out over a videoconference (Schweitzer, Brodt, and Croson, 2001).

Poole, Shannon, and De Sanctis (1992), in their review of communication media in bargaining, summarize by stating that no one medium is best for negotiating. Ten years later, we look at the ever growing pile of contradictory findings and concur that conclusions regarding the impact of various communication media on negotiation outcomes are, at best, inconclusive. We turn to an exploration of the various properties of communication media and their effects on social processes and interaction as a potential explanation.

Properties of Communication Media

New technologies bring with them numerous variations in the media available for communication, and hence negotiation. To simplify and clarify the distinctions across media, we characterize all media in terms of three properties: *synchronicity* (are parties communicating together in "real time" or participating individually at different times?), *communication channels* (do the parties experience each other aurally, visually, on in other ways?), and *efficacy* (how easily does the medium convey multiple types of information, e.g., factual and emotional?). Each of these three properties is a feature of the media themselves, rather than a derivative social effect. Each also has been shown to have a significant, identifiable impact on social interaction. By attending strictly to these properties, we distinguish between the medium and the likely effect of the medium on social interaction and negotiation. In the Table 16.1, we provide examples of how various media compare in

TABLE 16.1

Properties of Communication Media

	Synchronicity	Communication Channels	Efficacy
Face-to-face	Yes	Audio, visual, tactile	High
Videoconference	Yes	Audio, limited visual	High
Telephone	Yes	Audio	Med–high
Computer chat rooms	Yes	Text only	Med–low
E-mail	No	Text only	Low
Handwritten	No	Text (+ penmanship?)	Med–low

terms of the three properties. This list is meant to be illustrative, rather than exhaustive.

Other researchers have offered related categorizations of media. For example, early research on technologically mediated interaction focused on *media richness,* said to be comprised of: the feedback potential of the given technology, dimensionality in types of messages that can be conveyed, variety in language, and personal focus (Daft and Lengel, 1986; see Barsness and Bhappu, Chapter 17, this volume, for additional discussion of this taxonomy). But this conceptualization confounds properties of the media themselves, such as the communication channels accommodated by the medium, with derivative social properties. An example of a derivative social property is personal focus (Daft and Lengel, 1986). The focus on the other may vary probabilistically with the medium, but we argue that personal focus is a feature of the social interaction rather than a property of the medium per se. For example, the presence or absence of a visual channel is not manipulable—it is either a feature of the medium (e.g., videoconference) or not (e.g., standard e-mail). In contrast, one can increase the amount of personal focus in an interaction simply by instructing participants to pay special attention to the desires and intentions of the other. Media also vary along other important dimensions that we do not include in our categorization, either because they are unlikely to affect the social aspect of negotiating or because we consider them to be derivative rather than fixed properties of the media. Anonymity and speed of transmission are examples. Anonymity certainly has an effect on the social aspect of negotiations, but this is not a fixed feature of any given medium—interactions over any medium can involve anonymous partners or known, familiar partners. Anonymity can be eliminated in any medium by simply providing identifying information and, in practice, often is. Speed of transmission is also a property of the medium—studies have shown voice to be three to ten times faster than text-only communication—but there is little evidence that the absolute quantity of information exchanged has any relationship to the quality of social interaction (Hiltz, Johnson, and Turoff, 1986; Siegel, Dubrovsky, Kiesler, and McGuire, 1986).

In contrast, previous research has demonstrated that synchronicity, communication channels, and efficacy each produce a critical and measurable influence on social interactions. *Synchronicity* increases social awareness in the sense that both parties are "present" during the interaction, regardless of their physical proximity. Empirically, synchronicity increases dynamic feedback and coordinated turn taking (Rao, 1995), as well as the perceived immediacy of the interaction (Rice, 1993). *Communication channels* control the type of paralinguistic information conveyed (any information above and beyond the words themselves, e.g., inflection, tempo, volume, body language), with audio channels allowing tone to convey more information than text alone, and visual channels allowing physical expressions to convey yet more meaning. Multiple channels provide checks for parties attempting to verify information. If words are inconsistent with tone, for example, receivers rely on tone, and if tone is inconsistent with facial expression, receivers rely on facial expression (Weeks, 1976). Paralinguistic information makes communication more "immediate" and "personal" (Mehrabian and Ksionzky, 1972). *Efficacy* governs how well the medium conveys multiple types of content, for example, objective facts, subjective information, and emotions. The efficacy of a channel affects the sense of the other experienced by both senders and receivers. High-efficacy communication results in more informal interaction, more spontaneous information exchange, and more learning about the other in the interaction (Kiesler, Zubrow, and Moses, 1985).

To study the effects of the various media, we turn first to research on media and social interaction generally, and then to the existing research on the influence of media on negotiation processes. Rather than explicitly comparing each medium to every other in these reviews, we will rely on commonalities and differences across the properties of sychronicity, communication channels, and efficacy in our propositions and conclusions. This allows us to generalize beyond the specific media used in any given study and to extend our propositions to new media such as visual-access chat rooms.

Communication Media in Social Interactions

Social psychological research assumes, almost by definition, that the social context in which an interaction takes place will have important effects on the process and outcome of the interaction. Thus the medium for interaction is a natural source of variation in social psychological studies of interaction. Throughout the late 1980s and early 1990s, much of the research on media effects concerned matching task type with technology type. The general recommendation coming out of this work was that tasks with high equivocality, high ambiguity, high interdependence, and high socioemotional content require richer media (Daft and Lengel, 1986; McGrath and Hollingshead,

1993; McLeod, 1996). McLeod's (1996) useful summary of task-technology-fit research concluded, however, that the evidence is "at best equivocal," and that the relationship between media and social interaction is much more complex than the media richness model implies (McLeod, 1996). Furthermore, parties often cannot choose the media through which they interact. Although most negotiations are high in equivocality, ambiguity, interdependence, and socioemotional content, the choice of interacting through a rich media (i.e., face-to-face) may not be available, particularly in negotiations across national boundaries.

A growing body of research in both social psychology and economics suggests that the communication medium in which social interaction takes place affects not just the mechanical aspects of communication but also the social aspects—the way people perceive information, the attributions they make about the other(s), and the behaviors they see as appropriate (Kiesler and Sproull, 1992; Orbell, Van de Kragt, and Dawes, 1988; Sally, 1995, 2000; Sproull and Kiesler, 1991). In other words, the medium used for communication affects the way people make sense of social interactions.

Short, Christie, and Williams (1976) were among the first to argue, in their theory of social presence, that social context cues vary across media, in particular that text-only communication has social psychological features distinguishing it from other communication media. Text-only media are less intimate (Argyle and Dean, 1965) and less immediate (Mehrabian and Ksionzky, 1972). Short, Christie, and Williams (1976) bundled these social properties into a variable they call social presence. They conceptualize social presence as a subjective quality of the communication medium; for example, there is less social presence in electronic communication than in face-to-face interaction. We concur that different media vary in the likelihood of felt intimacy and immediacy, but we consider these derivative properties rather than properties of the media themselves. One needn't look further than the growing number of long-term relationships initially established on-line to dispel the notion that electronic media preclude social intimacy.

In the field of economics, Sally (2000) has developed a theory and model of communication that relies on the concept of sympathy, defined as a process of identification with another within a social interaction. Sympathy depends on physical proximity and psychological proximity, and so also confounds a property of the medium with its derivative social properties. Physical proximity is approximated with bodily copresence. Sally cites philosophical and psychological research suggesting that the mutual glance, possible only with visual access, is the epitome of physical proximity. Conversation, enhanced through audio access and high-efficacy media, is the counterpart for psychological proximity. Sally reasons that sympathy affects social interaction, even holding the content of communication constant.

Underlying the theories of both social presence and sympathy is an argument that media properties affect the degree of consciousness of and attention to the other in the interaction. This overarching concept of consciousness of and attention to the other is what we refer to as *social awareness*. Social awareness, unlike social presence, is not a property of the medium. We argue, instead, that synchronicity, the number of communication channels, and efficacy are media properties, and social awareness is likely to be affected by these properties. We add an important caveat: although properties of the media used in an interaction will influence social awareness, social awareness will also reflect a myriad of other social variables such as cultural differences, anonymity, similarity, liking, expectations for future interactions, audience effects, and potentially many other factors. Anonymity provides a simple illustration: Writing a letter to an anonymous other conjures a very different level of social awareness than writing a letter to an identified, known other. In short, though it is influenced by media properties, social awareness is manipulable within any medium.

Empirical studies provide support for the idea that social awareness is augmented when communication occurs via high efficacy, synchronous, multiple-channel media. Text-only interaction reduces the awareness of and the attention to the other in the interaction relative to verbal-only interaction, and verbal-only is experienced as less intimate and immediate than interaction across multiple channels simultaneously (Kiesler, Siegel, and McGuire, 1984; Poole et al., 1992; Siegel, Dubrovsky, Kiesler, and McGuire, 1986; Sproull and Kiesler, 1986). For example, Kiesler, Zubrow, and Moses (1985) presented an experiment in which two people met and discussed preestablished questions in order to get to know one another. They found that becoming acquainted through low-efficacy, asynchronous, text-only interaction (an early version of e-mail) resulted in less informal interaction and less spontaneous information exchange than face-to-face interaction. Participants reported learning less about their partners over text than when interacting face-to-face. The text-only medium resulted in less personal interactions and explicit responsiveness to the other, and more uninhibited behavior. Relative to face-to-face, people were more impolite, swore more often, had more outbursts, and used more superlatives when communicating through the text-only medium. Kiesler and her colleagues concluded that electronic, text-only communication elicits not emotion, but decreased social awareness and, thus, more asocial behavior.

But social awareness in text-only communication can be mitigated by social context variables. Macduff (1994), taking an anthropological look at electronic communications, likens e-mail to driving a car—many people act as if nobody can see them in their car and do all sorts of weird things they would never do if they perceived themselves to be in the presence of others. He found, however, that this perception of solitude was reduced when there was a preexisting social relationship between the communicating parties. Walther (1996) concurred that computer-mediated interaction can be highly personal in actual organizational settings, when the communicators are experts with the technology and have preexisting relationships.

Numerous empirical studies delineate the mechanisms through which media properties may affect social awareness in social interactions. Krauss and Chiu (1997) asserted that face-to-face "conversation is an intrinsically cooperative endeavor" as a result of cognitively held rules dictating that contributions to face-to-face conversations should be truthful, informative, relevant, and clear (1997, p. 43). Frolich and Oppenheimer (1998) concluded that face-to-face interaction "virtually compels" cooperation in dilemma games. In contrast, asynchronous, text-only interaction is less organized and rule-oriented (Sproull and Kiesler, 1991). Politeness norms in face-to-face interactions demand that people listen to each other and refrain from explicit criticism of others and their ideas, but few such norms appear to be present in telephone or text-only communication (McLeod et al., 1997). Studies have shown that socially desirable behaviors such as cooperation (Dawes, Van de Kragt, and Orbell, 1988; Raiffa, 1982; Wichman, 1970), truth telling (Valley, Moag, and Bazerman, 1998), and rapport building (Drolet and Morris, 2000) are more likely in face-to-face interaction than in telephone or text-only communication. On the flip side, socially undesirable behaviors such as the use of pressure tactics (Crott, Kayser, and Lamm, 1980; Lewis and Fry, 1977), inappropriate language (Kiesler and Sproull, 1992; Griffith and Northcraft, 1994), and rude or impulsive responses (Dubrovsky, Kiesler, and Sethna, 1991) are more frequent in text-only communication than in face-to-face communication.

To summarize, there is solid evidence that visual access, especially when accompanied by synchronicity and high-efficacy communication, increases social awareness. Multiple channel, synchronous, high-efficacy media are more organized and rule-oriented, involve more cooperation, coordination, truth telling and rapport building, and fewer pressure tactics, inappropriate language and rude or impulsive responses than asynchronous, lower-efficacy media with fewer channels for conveying interpersonal information. In settings where social perceptions and intimacy are already established, the limitations of low efficacy, single-channel media may have less effect on behavior. But when social perceptions and intimacy are undefined, the medium used may have a significant effect on social awareness in the interaction.

Social Awareness and Negotiation Processes

Extending a social awareness lens from research on social interaction generally to negotiations, may provide new insights into media effects in negotiations.

In a negotiation, at least some of the interests of those interacting are at odds with one another. Heightened sensitivity to and immediacy of others in a negotiation my lead bargainers to work together in a way not possible, or at least less likely, than without that social awareness. We first present evidence that media properties have measurable effects on negotiation process and then propose that social awareness plays a critical role in driving these processes.

Research on media effects on negotiated outcomes has produced divergent results, as discussed earlier. But a close read of the research that analyzes both processes and outcomes suggests that there may exist systematic and robust *process* consequences of different media. These process consequences include mutual disclosure, trust, and reciprocity. Mutual disclosure is at a minimum in low-efficacy, text-only negotiations and increases with the addition of audio signals (Friedman and Currall, 2003; McGinn and Keros, 2003) and audio plus visual signals (McGinn, Thompson, and Bazerman, in press; Valley, Moag, and Bazerman, 1998). Mutual trust is similarly amplified as communication moves from text-only media to media with multiple channels, synchronicity, and high-efficacy exchange (McGinn and Keros, 2003; Valley, Moag, and Bazerman, 1998). Multiple studies also provide evidence that reciprocity is more likely in face-to-face negotiations than across other media (Fehr and Gächter, 2000; McGinn, Thompson, and Bazerman, in press). Overall, face-to-face interaction significantly increases the level of cooperation relative to negotiations using low-efficacy media lacking in multiple communication channels (telephone) and synchronous interaction (e-mail; McGinn and Keros, 2003).

Many of the studies previously cited infer these process effects from either outcome data or survey data. For direct evidence of the impact of media on negotiation processes, we examined transcripts from two-party negotiations between strangers attempting to buy or sell a commodity called Tynar.[2] The value for the Tynar was randomly and independently generated for the buyer and the seller; both had a value somewhere between $0 and $100, with all $.25 increments equally likely. The parties were given time to negotiate either in writing or face-to-face. The participants carried out similar negotiations (using different, randomly generated values for both the buyer and the seller) with six different partners—all strangers—and were paid their actual earnings for one, randomly selected round. This was as "contextless" a negotiation as one can imagine, minimizing the chance that social proprieties such as disclosure, trust, and reciprocity were demand features of the experimental setting or the social setting described in the negotiation scenario. Indeed, the percentage of negotiations involving explicitly dishonest statements was higher in these data (61 percent across communication media) than reported in other studies (e.g., 5 percent in Valley, Moag, and Bazerman, 1998). But even in this stripped-down social context, we found in the transcripts clear evidence that the medium for communication affected negotiation processes, as hypothesized in the studies cited above.

We coded the transcripts for not only *what* was conveyed, but also *how* it was conveyed.[3] In text-only negotiations, the parties often "revealed" false costs or values as soon as the interaction began: in 71 percent, at least one party lied from the onset. In contrast, lying at any point dropped to 52 percent in face-to-face negotiations, and in 77 percent of these cases the dishonest parties led themselves slowly into their lies through multiple stages of shading reality. A seller might first describe his or her costs (reservation price) as high, then later higher than a specific number, and then finally (and dishonestly) higher than another number. It was as if the face-to-face negotiators were trying to "test out" their lies by watching their partners' reactions before committing themselves. This tentativeness in face-to-face interaction preceded not just false revelation, but also honest revelation. Parties revealed their values gradually, working reciprocally with the other party to build trust before complete exposure. In 38 percent of the face-to-face negotiations, but in only 18 percent of the written negotiations, one party suggested that the other make the first offer. In written communication, negotiators boldly put forward information (true or false), process guidelines, and decision rules. This boldness in text-only negotiations supports our proposition that a lack of social awareness makes people less likely to hold to normative constraints in their behavior. In contrast, face-to-face negotiators seemed to be aware of the complexity of their partner's position and potential response to their actions, and boldness was tempered by this heightened awareness.

Our research suggests a tendency toward stable approaches to interaction within a given medium, and different approaches across media, especially with respect to disclosure, mutual trust, and reciprocity. Although we did not measure the underlying mechanism driving these different patterns of social interaction within negotiations, social awareness—the degree of consciousness of and attention to the other(s) in a social interaction—provides a parsimonious explanation.

Moore, Kurtzberg, Thompson, and Morris (1999) provided direct evidence that increased social awareness may underlie media effects in negotiations. In on-line negotiations between Stanford University and Kellogg students, all negotiators knew the school the other party attended. Half the students were given photo and bio information, along with list of "emoticons" to use when negotiating. These students were instructed to hold a "getting to know you" session before beginning their negotiation (the schmoozing treatment). In between school negotiations with schmoozing, only 6 percent of the pairs failed to reach agreement; in contrast, 29 percent of those without schmoozing reached an impasse. In within-school negotiations, schmoozing didn't matter. The authors concluded that similarity and liking are the key to solving on-line negotiation problems. We suggest that similarity and liking operate in this fashion because they create an alternative avenue for social awareness.

McGinn and Keros (2003) provided further evidence for our conclusion. In a design fully crossing personal relationship (friend, stranger) and media (face, telephone, and e-mail) in a two-party, single-issue negotiation, they found no media effects for friends but significant media effects for strangers. Note that it takes little work to be aware and receptive to a similar, liked other, even over the telephone or e-mail, but it takes considerable cognitive and emotional energy to imagine and attend to an unknown and invisible other.

De Dreu, Weingart, and Kwon's (2000) research implies that heightened social awareness increases prosocial motives in negotiations that, in turn, help people develop positive interpersonal perceptions, seek trust, and engage in reciprocity. They suggested a "motivated information processing" model, in which higher-efficacy, synchronous media increase not just cooperative behavior, but more accurate and positive attributions about the other. Negotiators who interact in a high-efficacy, multiple-channel medium are "able and motivated to process . . . information accurately and develop concomitant insights in each other's payoff structure" (p. 902). As negotiators become more socially aware of one another, they influence one another's perceptions and interpretations of the interaction.

Orcutt and Anderson (1977) provided more evidence that social awareness guides procedural consequences in negotiations across media. In their experiment, using the prisoner's dilemma game, participants were told they would be interacting with either another person or with a computer (both were actually the same programmed computer). They found that negotiators who believed they were interacting with a computer in the first fifteen rounds were more competitive and less responsive to the other in the dilemma games, and extended this "depersonalized" approach to interactions believed to be with a person in the second fifteen rounds. The authors used qualitative responses from the negotiators to differentiate between *communicative* action, which is coordinated behavior built on consensual understandings and expectations, and *instrumental* action, based on technical rules and strategies (Habermas, 1990). They concluded that negotiators come to a common definition of the situation through (1) mutual communication of intentions and (2) mutually reciprocated attributions of intent. Social awareness may work though increasing the likelihood of consensual understandings regarding intentions and attributions.

Further examination of the qualitative data from the Tynar study, discussed previously, provides textual evidence for social awareness effects on the process of negotiating. People negotiating face-to-face exuded and invoked norms of caring that revealed the deeper social embeddedness of face-to-face

344 McGinn and Croson

negotiation relative to audio-only or text-only bargaining. For example, small talk—expressing personal interest in the other party—was common in the face-to-face negotiations, but never occurred in written negotiations. The parties were simply more skilled at creating mutual understandings and expectations through face-to-face conversation than in text-only interactions. The heightened mutual awareness of the other(s) in a face-to-face negotiation appears to lead negotiators to work together to mutually construct the rules for interaction, rather than follow their own individual preferences.

Conclusion

Social awareness, enhanced by high-efficacy, synchronous, multiple-channel media, leads to shared understandings and expectations in the process of negotiating. We caution, however, that a shared construction does not necessarily have to be a positive construction. Sometimes it may be important to minimize social awareness, for example, in extremely emotionally charged negotiations (Poole et al., 1992). Similarly, when a negotiator's sole objective is to maximize individual gain in a relatively straightforward negotiation, low social awareness may be advantageous. Nevertheless, many negotiation situations require at least some cooperation, even if the driving objective is individual gain maximization, and heightened social awareness is likely to be beneficial in these common situations.

Text-only negotiations may also be preferred for reasons independent of social awareness. Electronic communication, because it is not bounded by physical constraints, makes new negotiation partners possible (see also Shapiro and Kulik, Chapter 8, this volume). eBay creates lots of value, not because an auction is a new or unique trading mechanism, but because it enables transactions that would not occur otherwise. The lack of physical constraint in electronic communication also makes new coalitions possible. In one example, Israeli academic staff members used e-mail to communicate among strikers during a strike. This "secret weapon" helped the union to communicate its message widely, to create solidarity among the strikers, to maintain community in the face of physical separation, and, ultimately, to succeed in the negotiation (Pliskin, Romm, and Markey, 1997). Perhaps face-to-face interaction among the strikers, and the accompanying increase in social awareness, could have produced even more solidarity and community, but the very feature of face-to-face that makes it valuable— the physical copresence of the parties—is what makes it untenable in many negotiations.

Even when physical copresence is possible and social awareness is desirable, face-to-face negotiations may not be necessary, especially when relationships are already established. Social awareness, unlike Short, Williams and

Christie's (1976) concept of social presence, is not a property of the medium. Initial differences between the parties may reduce social awareness, whereas similarity, liking, expectations for future interactions, audience effects, and potentially many other factors may increase social awareness. In short, social awareness may be manipulated in any medium. As we already noted, close, positive personal relationships invoke social awareness without copresence and may eliminate many of the potentially negative effects of low-efficacy, asynchronous media. It may even be that strangers can learn how to increase social awareness in negotiations over any medium. Fulk and Boyd (1991) and Walther (1996) provided evidence that technology use is more affected by the practices and norms of those using it than by the technology itself. This suggests some optimism for the possibility of creating social awareness across media. It may take new approaches to using the media, and perhaps more time, effort, and trial-and-error learning, but it appears to be possible to create new practices and norms that promote social awareness when using media with features that normally discourage it.

The lessons of social awareness take on great importance in cross-cultural negotiations. First, cross-cultural parties are likely to be especially out-of-tune with one another to start with, because of cultural differences in understandings and expectations of what a negotiation entails and how one should behave when negotiating. In addition, cross-cultural negotiations often take place across great physical space. In light of the potential for cultural differences in interaction and understanding, and the near impossibility of relying solely on face-to-face interactions in these negotiations, sensitivity to building social awareness may be particularly important. The parties in cross-cultural negotiations are doubly burdened by factors negatively affecting social awareness and the accompanying impediments to building shared understandings and expectations. Building social awareness may be a key to building shared understandings in cross-cultural negotiations. Media effects and cultural effects, precisely because they operate through social understandings, are malleable—it's not my culture or yours that matters, it's how our cultures (and the media through which we're interacting) affect our perceptions of and behavior in a negotiation (see also Barsness and Bhappu, Chapter 17, this volume).

We urge those studying media effects in negotiations to design research that directly investigates the role of social awareness in the interaction. Because our conceptualization of negotiation relies on an assumption of negotiation as a social process, research that considers the social construction of the interaction would be especially valuable. This requires a focus on the dyad or negotiating group as the unit of analysis, rather than the individual negotiator. We are optimistic that negotiation research has already begun to move in this direction.

Notes

1. Some of the research cited here refers to distribution of surplus as a proxy for fairness, implying that a more equal division of the surplus is necessarily more fair. Given distinctions across equality, equity, and need as measures of fairness, along with social contextual differences across negotiation contexts, we are agnostic about the relative fairness of equal and unequal distributions.

2. The outcome data from this experiment are reported in Valley et al. (2002).

3. Our thanks to James Evans for studying, coding and analyzing these data. The data were analyzed without any knowledge of the ideas or propositions put forward in this chapter.

Works Cited

Argyle, M., and J. Dean. (1965). Eye-contact, distance and affiliation. *Sociometry, 28,* 289–304.

Carnevale, P., and A. M. Isen. (1986). The influence of positive affect and visual access on the discovery of integrative solutions in bilateral negotiation. *Organizational Behavior and Human Decision Processes, 37,* 1–13.

Carnevale, P. J., Pruitt, D. J., and S. Seilheimer. (1981). Looking and competing: Accountability and visual access in integrative bargaining. *Journal of Personality and Social Psychology, 40,* 111–120.

Croson, R. T. (1999). Look at me when you say that: An electronic negotiation simulation. *Simulation and Gaming, 30,* 23–37.

Crott, H., Kayser, E., and H. Lamm. (1980). The effects of information exchange and communication in an asymmetrical negotiation situation. *European Journal of Social Psychology, 10,* 149–163.

Daft, R., and R. Lengel. (1986). Organizational information requirements, media richness and structural design. *Management Science, 35,* 554–571.

Dawes, R. M., Van De Kragt, A. J. C., and J. M. Orbell. (1988). Not me or thee but we: The importance of group identity in eliciting cooperation in dilemma situations: Experimental manipulations. *Acta Psychologica, 68,* 83–97.

De Dreu, C., Weingart, L., and S. Kwon. (2000). Influence of social motives on integrative negotiation: A meta-analytic review and test of two theories. *Journal of Personality and Social Psychology, 78,* 889–905.

Drolet, A. L., and M. W. Morris. (2000). Rapport in conflict resolution: Accounting for how face-to-face contact fosters mutual cooperation in mixed-motive conflicts. *Journal of Experimental Social Psychology, 36*(1), 26–50.

Dubrovsky, V. J., Kiesler, S., and B. N. Sethna. (1991). The equalization phenomenon: Status effects in computer-mediated and face-to-face decision-making groups. *Human–Computer Interaction, 6,* 119–146.

Ekman, P. (1992). *Telling lies: Clues to deceit in the marketplace, marriage, and politics.* New York: Norton.

Fehr, E., and S. Gächter. (2000). Fairness and retaliation: The economics of reciprocity. *Journal of Economic Perspectives, 14,* 159–181.

Friedman, R., and S. Currall. (2003). E-Mail escalation: Dispute exacerbating elements of electronic communication. (Working paper, Owen Graduate School of Management, Vanderbilt University.)

Frolich, N., and J. Oppenheimer. (1998). Some consequences of e-mail vs. face-to-face communication in experiments. *Journal of Economic Behavior and Organization, 35*, 389–403.

Fulk, J., and B. Boyd. (1991). Emerging theories of communication in organizations. *Journal of Management, 17*, 407–446.

Garfinkel, H. (1967). *Studies in ethnomethodology.* Englewood Cliffs, NJ: Prentice Hall.

Griffith, T., and G. Northcraft. (1994). Distinguishing between the forest and the trees—Media features and methodology in electric communication-research. *Organizational Science: 5*, 272–285.

Habermas, J. (1990). *Moral consciousness and communicative action* (C. Lenhardt & S. W. Nicholsen, Trans.). Cambridge, MA: MIT Press.

Hiltz, S., Johnson, K., and M. Turoff. (1986). Experiments in group decision-making—Communication processes and outcome in face-to-face versus computerized conferences. *Human Communication Research, 13*, 225–252.

Kiesler, S., Siegel, J., and T. W. McGuire. (1984). Social psychological aspects of computer-mediated communication. *American Psychologist, 39*, 1123–1134.

Kiesler, S., and L. Sproull. (1992). Group decision-making and communication technology. *Organizational Behavior and Human Decision Processes, 52*(1), 96–123.

Kiesler, S., D., Zubrow, and A. M. Moses. (1985). Affect in computer-mediated communication: An experiment in synchronous terminal-to-terminal discussion. *Human–Computer Interaction, 1*, 77–104.

Krauss, R., and C. Chiu. (1997). Language and social behavior. In D. Gilbert, S. Fiske, and G. Lindsey (Eds.), *Handbook of social psychology* (Vol. 2, pp. 41–88). Boston: McGraw-Hill.

Lewis, S., and W. Fry. (1997). Effects of visual access and orientation on discover of integrative bargaining. *Organizational Behavior and Human Performance, 20*(1), 75–92.

Macduff, I. (1994). Flames on the wires: Mediating from an electronic cottage. *Negotiation Journal, 10*, 5–15.

McGinn, K. L., and A. Keros. (2003). Improvisation and the logic of exchange in embedded negotiations. *Administrative Science Quarterly, 47*, 442–473.

McGinn, K. L., Thompson, L., and M. H. Bazerman. (in press). *Disclosure and reciprocity in bargaining with communication.* (HBS Working Paper No. 01–028).

McGinn, K. L., Thompson, L., and M. H. Bazerman. (2003). Dyadic processes of disclosure and reciprocity in bargaining with communication. *Journal of Behavioral Decision Making, 16*, 17–34.

McGrath, J. E., and A. B. Hollingshead. (1993). Putting the "group" back in group support systems: Some theoretical issues about dynamic processes in group with technological enhancements. In L. M. Jessup and J. S. Valacich (Eds.), *Group support systems: New perspectives* (pp. 78–96). New York: Macmillan.

McLeod, P. L. (1996). New communication technologies for group decision making. In R. Y. Hirokawa and M. S. Poole (Eds.), *Communication and group decision making* (2nd ed., pp. 426–462). Thousand Oaks, CA: Sage.

McLeod, P., Baron, R., Marti, M., and K. Yoon. (1997). The eyes have it: Minority influence in face-to-face and computer-mediated group discussion. *Journal of Applied Psychology, 85,* 706–718.

Mehrabian, A., and S. Ksionzky. (1972). Categories of social behavior. *Comparative Group Studies, 3,* 425–436.

Moore, D. A., Kurtzberg, T. R., Thompson, L. L., and M. Morris. (1999). Long and short routes to success in electronically-mediated negotiations: Group affiliations and good vibrations. *Organizational Behavior and Human Decision Processes, 77,* 22–43.

Morley, I., and G. Stephenson. (1969). Interpersonal and inter-party exchange—A laboratory simulation of an industrial negotiation at plant level. *British Journal of Psychology, 60,* 543.

Orcutt, J., and R. Anderson. (1977). Social interaction, dehumanization and computerized other. *Sociology and Social Research, 61,* 380–397.

Orbell, J., Van de Kragt, A., and R. Dawes. (1988). Explaining discussion-induced cooperation. *Journal of Personality and Social Psychology, 54,* 811–819.

Orcutt, J. D., and R. E. Anderson. (1977). Social interaction, dehumanization and the "Computerized Other." *Sociology and Social Research, 61,* 380–397.

Pliskin, N., Romm, C. T., and R. Markey. (1997). E-mail as a weapon in an industrial dispute. *New Technology, Work and Employment, 12,* 3–12.

Poole, M. S., Shannon, D. L., and G. De Sanctis. (1992). Communication media and negotiation processes. In L. L. Putnam and M. E. Roloff (Eds.), *Communication and negotiation* (pp. 46–66). Newbury Park, CA: Sage.

Raiffa, H. (1982). *The art and science of negotiation,* Cambridge, MA: Belknap/Harvard University Press.

Rao, V. S. (1995). Effects of teleconferencing technologies: An exploration of comprehension, feedback, satisfaction and role-related differences. *Group Decision and Negotiation, 4,* 251–272.

Rice, R. E. (1993). Media appropriateness: Using social presence theory to compare traditional and new organizational media. *Human Communication Research, 19,* 451–484.

Sally, D. (1995). Conversation and cooperation in social dilemmas: A meta-analysis of experiments from 1958 to 1992. *Rationality and Society, 7,* 58–92.

———. (2000). A general theory of sympathy, mind-reading, and social interaction, with an application to the prisoners' dilemma. *Social Science Information, 39,* 567–634.

Schweitzer, M., Brodt, S. E., and R. Croson. (2001). *Deception and misunderstanding in distanced negotiation: A comparison of videoconference and telephone mediated negotiations.* (Wharton School Working Paper No. 99-07-02).

Shell, G. R. (2001). Bargaining on the Internet: The perils of e-mail and other computer-assisted negotiations. In H. Kunreuther and S. Hoch (Eds.), *Wharton on making decisions* (pp. 201–222). New York: Wiley.

Short, J., Williams, E., and B. Christie. (1976). *The social psychology of telecommunications*. New York: Wiley.

Siegel, J., Dubrovsky, V., Kiesler, S., and T. McGuire. (1986). Group processes in computer-mediated communication. *Organizational Behavior and Human Decision Processes, 37,* 157–187.

Sproull, L., and S. Kiesler. (1986). Reducing social context cues: Electronic mail in organizational communication. *Management Science, 32,* 1492–1512.

Sproull, L., and S. Kiesler. (1991). Computers, networks and work. *Scientific American, 265,* 116–123.

Suh, K. (1999). Impact of communication medium on task performance and satisfaction: An examination of media-richness theory. *Information & Management, 35,* 295–312.

Valley, K. L., Moag, J., and M. H. Bazerman. (1998). "A matter of trust": Effects of communication on the efficiency and distribution of outcomes. *Journal of Economic Behavior and Organization, 34,* 211–238.

Valley, K. L., Thompson, L., Gibbons, R., and M. H. Bazerman. (2002). How communication improves efficiency in bargaining games. *Games and Economic Behavior, 38,* 127–155.

Walther, J. (1996). Computer-mediated communication: Impersonal, interpersonal, and hyperpersonal interaction. *Communication Research, 23,* 3–43.

Weeks, G. (1976). Cooperative versus conflictive problem solving in three telecommunications modes. *Perceptual and Motor Skills, 42,* 897–917.

CHAPTER 17

At the Crossroads of Culture and Technology
SOCIAL INFLUENCE AND
INFORMATION–SHARING PROCESSES
DURING NEGOTIATION

Zoe I. Barsness and Anita D. Bhappu

RECENT TRENDS IN international trade and foreign direct investment high-light the sheer size and economic importance of the global marketplace (Bartlett and Ghoshal, 1991). Whether through direct investment or collab-oration with other multinationals and local foreign firms, organizations today must develop business relationships within and across a wide variety of cul-tures. Accompanying the globalization of business have been rapid advances in information technology and telecommunications. Increasingly, organi-zations operate "virtually." Their members are geographically distributed; electronically linked; demographically, functionally, and culturally diverse; and connected via lateral rather than hierarchical relationships that span both internal and external organizational boundaries (De Sanctis and Monge, 1999). Since work in these virtual organizations is frequently distributed without regard to geography, time, or traditional organizational boundaries, members rely heavily on electronic communication to coordinate work and to negotiate transactions with each other (De Sanctis and Monge, 1999).

The resulting growth in the complexity and number of negotiated trans-actions associated with these two developments has contributed to an inten-sifying interest in culture (Brett, 2001; Gelfand and Dyer, 2000) and commu-nication media (Bazerman, Curhan, Moore, and Valley, 2000) in negotiation research. Research suggests that both culture and communication media in-fluence the type and quantity of information exchanged during negotiations as well as how parties attend to, interpret, and act upon that information. Different communication media, for example, moderate negotiation process through their effects on social context and interpersonal interaction (e.g., see McGinn and Croson, Chapter 16, this volume, for a review). Similarly, culture influences the manner in which social influence is exercised and information is elicited and integrated during negotiations (e.g., Adair et al., 1998; Adair, Okumura, and Brett, 2001; Brett, Adair, et al., 1998; Brett and Okumura, 1998).

In this chapter, we examine how culture and communication media, specifically the use of electronically mediated communication (i.e., e-mail), might interact to influence negotiator cognitions and behaviors when present together. We identify two mechanisms through which culture and communication media influence negotiations: negotiator schemas (i.e., negotiators' cognitions, beliefs, and motives) and behaviors (i.e., negotiators' acts, tactics, and multiple behaviors both organized in a normative way as scripts and in a strategic way as strategies). We also examine how these schemas and behaviors influence negotiator sense-making—that is, how negotiators attend to and interpret the other party's behavior and communication messages, and thereby the form and content of information exchange during negotiation. Although culture and communication media may influence other factors that have important effects on negotiation process and outcomes, we limit our discussion here to their effects on social influence behaviors and information-sharing strategies and tactics in intracultural negotiation, processes critical to successful information exchange and the generation of joint gains.

To begin our discussion, we briefly review the role of schemas and behaviors in negotiations. We then examine communication media characteristics that might directly constrain negotiator behavior or influence the ways in which negotiator schemas are enacted. We also examine how communication media might affect the way in which negotiators make sense of the behaviors they observe and the information they receive during negotiation, thus influencing their ability to elicit and integrate information. We follow this discussion with an examination of how culturally influenced schemas and behaviors impact negotiation in their own right. Finally, we offer an integrative framework for thinking about the joint effects of culture and communication media on negotiation processes that builds and extends on this research. We close the chapter with a discussion of our model's implications for managers and suggest some directions for future research.

The Social Context of Negotiation

Recently, researchers have directed their attention to the role of social context in negotiation (Kramer and Messick, 1995, see also Kramer, Chapter 10, this volume). Social context is critical because it determines how "players define and create the negotiation game—both psychologically and structurally"

(Bazerman et al., 2000, p. 287). The manner in which negotiators define the game determines, in large part, how they play it, their preferences and expectations, and the strategies and tactics they are likely to adopt to achieve their goals and objectives (Bazerman et al., 2000). Culture and communication media, as significant contextual variables, are likely to have important effects on negotiation processes and outcomes.

Much of the work on the social context of negotiation has focused on the role of schemas and scripts (Bazerman et al., 2000). Negotiation *schemas* are organized structures of information and expectations about negotiation that help negotiators make sense of the negotiation exchange (Thompson, 1997). Negotiation *scripts* specify sequences of appropriate negotiator actions and behaviors (Fiske and Taylor, 1991; Shank and Abelson, 1977). Thus, negotiation schemas act as implicit theories about how the negotiation might unfold. They also influence negotiators' attention to and interpretation of their surroundings (Brodt and Tinsley, 1998; Fiske and Taylor, 1991). Negotiation scripts further aid negotiators' information exchange efforts by providing a guide to appropriate negotiation behavior for themselves (Kumar, 1999) and influencing the attributions that they make about the other party's behaviors (Pruitt and Carnevale, 1993). As discussed in earlier chapters, integrative agreements are negotiated outcomes that create value for negotiators and require the communication of differentially held preferences between negotiators (Thompson, 1997). All integrative agreements encompass a distributive component; the enhanced set of resources that the parties create eventually must be divided between them. Consequently, two types of information are relevant to the creation of integrative agreements: (1) information about parties' interests and preference structures and (2) information about parties' power (e.g., their relative status or alternatives to a negotiated agreement; Fisher, Ury, and Patton, 1991). Information about the other party's interests and priorities is critical to the negotiator's ability to determine whether or not the set of resources can be further enhanced to achieve a more integrative agreement. Power serves as the basis of one party's ability to gain advantage over the other party and thus influences the distributive component of integrative negotiation (Lewicki, Saunders, and Minton, 1997). Information about power facilitates the negotiator's ability to judge (a) when to walk away from a deal, (b) when to press for additional advantage in the distribution of resources, or (c) when to accept an offer as it stands (Brett, 2001).

Researchers have identified a variety of negotiation schemas and behaviors that contribute to the generation of joint gains. Some of these schemas and behaviors may generalize across communication media and cultures, such as the schema that negotiation is distributive and the script that the process of negotiation involves reciprocal concession making between two parties (Harnett and Cummings, 1980). Other schemas and behaviors that contribute to the negotiation of joint gains, such as self-interest (Brett and Okumura, 1998), eschewal of power (Pruitt, 1981; Pruitt and Lewis, 1975), and information-sharing schema, strategies, and tactics have been shown to differ across communication media (Clark and Brennan, 1991; Kemp and Rutter, 1982; Valley, Moag, and Bazerman, 1998) and cultures (e.g., Adair et al., 1998; Adair et al., 2001; Brett et al., 1998; Brett and Okumura, 1998).

Communication Media and Negotiation

The communication media that negotiators employ influences not only what information is shared and how that information is communicated (Carnevale and Probst, 1997; Friedman and Currall, 2001; Valley et al., 1998), but also how information is attended to and interpreted, as summarized in Chapter 16. Certain information may be easy to communicate face-to-face but difficult to describe in an e-mail. Consequently, negotiators may adopt different information-sharing strategies and tactics when interacting electronically. People also pay attention to different things and are influenced by different people when interacting across different media (Bhappu et al., 1997; Kiesler and Sproull, 1992). Social status cues, for example, are less salient in computer-mediated than face-to-face communication (Bhappu, Griffith, and Northcraft, 1997; Sproull and Kiesler, 1991). As a result, negotiators may attend more closely to message content in electronic contexts (Ocker and Yaverbaum, 1999), and the messenger's social status may be less likely to influence how his or her message is interpreted. Negotiators may therefore need to adjust their social influence strategies in electronic contexts. In addition, the ways in which communication media effects alter information-sharing processes and power dynamics during negotiation may have important ramifications for information exchange and the generation of joint gains.

COMMUNICATION MEDIA DIMENSIONS

Media richness and interactivity are two dimensions of communication media that are particularly relevant to negotiation because they are likely to influence the enactment of culturally derived negotiator schemas and behaviors (see Figure 17.1).

As noted in the previous chapter, media richness is the capacity of the medium to transmit visual and verbal cues, thus supporting a variety of languages (e.g., body, paralanguage, and natural), providing more immediate feedback, and facilitating the communication of personal information (Daft and Lengel, 1984). Interactivity is the potential of the medium to sustain

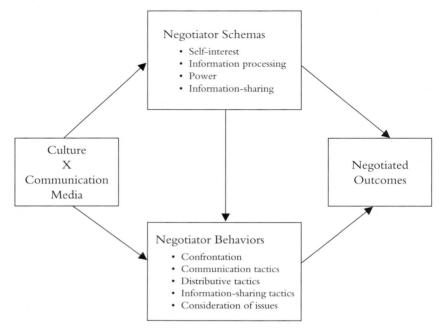

FIGURE 17.1. The influence of culture and communication media on negotiation.

a seamless flow of information between two or more negotiators (Kraut, Galegher, Fish, and Chalfonte, 1992). Both characteristics account for differences across media in the structure of information exchanged (Daft and Lengel, 1984), the number of social context cues transmitted (Sproull and Kiesler, 1986; Kiesler and Sproull, 1992), the social presence of negotiators (Short, Williams, and Christie, 1976), and the negotiation schemas and behaviors adopted (Bazerman et al., 2000). A summary of these media richness and interactivity effects can be found in Table 17.1.

Media Richness

E-mail is considered a lean medium because it transmits neither visual nor verbal cues, whereas face-to-face communication is considered a rich medium because it transmits both. Due to a lack of media richness, the social presence of others is reduced in electronic contexts (Short, Williams, and Christie, 1976; Weisband and Atwater, 1999) and the perceived social distance among negotiators who are physically separated and communicating via a machine increased (Jessup and Tansik, 1991; Sproull and Kiesler, 1986). Thus, negotiators' social awareness of each other may be seriously diminished, as described by McGinn and Croson, Chapter 16, this volume.

TABLE 17.1

The Effect of Communication Media on the Enactment and Interpretation of Negotiator Schemas and Behaviors

Media Dimensions	Negotiator Schemas	Negotiator Behavior	Information Exchange
Media richness: • Social presence • Salience of social groups and social status	Lean media: • Accentuates self-interest • Limits leveraging of power • Encourages information sharing	Lean media encourage: • More direct confrontation • More analytical–rational communication tactics • More distributive tactics • More candid information-sharing • More balanced participation • More tempered response	Lean media encourage: • Attention to self • More awareness of one's own schemas and behaviors • Focus on content vs. source of communications • Less nuanced but more diverse information exchange
Interactivity • Synchronicity • Parallel processing	Low interactivity: • Accentuates analytical–rational expression of information • Accentuates intuitive–experiential interpretation of information	Low interactivity encourages: • More direct confrontation • More analytical–rational communication tactics • More indirect information sharing • More packaging of issues (simultaneous issue consideration) • More balanced participation	Low interactivity encourages: • More intuitive–experiential interpretation of others' behavior • Less judging of others' behavior, at least initially • Feedback seeking • Information seeking

Largely because they neither see nor hear one another, and so are less aware of each other, negotiators may engage more heavily in self-interested behavior when using lean (e-mail) rather than rich media (face-to-face communication). They may also fail to elicit from the other party—or simply ignore—important information about his or her interests and priorities. The use of lean media may therefore accentuate a self-interest schema (i.e., the extent to which a negotiator emphasizes his or her own rather than collective interests) and its attendant behaviors.

Because lean media transmit fewer social cues than rich media (Kiesler and Sproull, 1992), their use also lowers the salience of social group differences and social status, potentially limiting the leverage of status-based power and encouraging more candid information sharing. Indeed, the lack of social cues in e-mail causes people to be more direct and confrontational in their communications (Kiesler and Sproull, 1992). Such confrontational behavior can be further exacerbated by the reduced social presence of others and feelings of anonymity associated with e-mail (Griffith and Northcraft, 1994; Thompson, 1997).

Finally, negotiators are more likely to focus on the content of their messages when using lean media (Ocker and Yaverbaum, 1999). Given that a significant proportion of a message's meaning comes from its associated visual and verbal cues such as facial expressions, body language, and tone of voice (De Paulo and Friedman, 1998), the inability to transmit these cues in lean media may cause negotiators to rely more heavily on logical argumentation and the presentation of facts rather than emotional or personal appeals. Research suggests, for instance, that communication styles in e-mail are more task-oriented and depersonalized than in face-to-face interactions (Kemp and Rutter, 1982). Reduced contextual information may also impede the negotiator's ability to interpret message meaning. Information exchanged in e-mail tends to be less nuanced than would be information exchanged face-to-face in the same situation (Friedman and Currall, 2001; Valley et al., 1998). Back-channel and clarifying information, such as speech acknowledgments (e.g., "mmm" or "huh?"), and reactive body language such as head nods, are reduced (Wiesband and Atwater, 1999). The significant information-processing costs associated with translating this type of information into purely textual form is sufficiently prohibitive that much of such clarifying information is simply lost.

In short, information exchange in lean media is likely to be constrained, diminishing the negotiators' ability to accurately assess differential preferences and identify potential joint gains. Indeed, one examination comparing face-to-face and computer-mediated negotiations revealed that negotiators interacting electronically were less accurate in judging the other party's interests (Arunchalam and Dilla, 1995). Interaction via lean media may also promote the use of distributive tactics exactly because it encourages direct and confrontational communications (Kiesler and Sproull, 1992), leading to conflict spirals that result in lower joint gains or even impasse. Some researchers, for example, have demonstrated a higher incidence of impasse (Croson, 1999) and less integrative outcomes (Arunchalam and Dilla, 1995; Valley et al., 1998) in lean media as opposed to rich media-based negotiations. These findings may reflect the difficulty of establishing rapport in lean media contexts where visual access to the nonverbal behavior that enables its development is limited (Drolet and Morris, 2000). The development of rapport has been shown to foster more mutually beneficial settlements (Drolet and Morris, 2000), especially in lean media contexts (Moore, Kurtzberg, Thompson, and Morris, 1999), perhaps because it engenders greater social awareness among negotiators (see McGinn and Croson, Chapter 16, this volume).

On the other hand, lean media may facilitate better processing of social conflict exactly because these media do not transmit visual and verbal cues (Bhappu, 2003; Carnevale, Pruitt, and Seilheimer, 1981). The visible presence of others can induce arousal (Zajonc, 1965) that leads to more aggressive behavioral responses. The absence of visual and verbal cues in lean media, however, may defuse such triggers. It may also reduce the salience of social group differences, which prevents coalition formation. In addition, because negotiators are physically isolated and the social presence of others is diminished, they can take time to "step out" of the discussion and thoughtfully respond rather than merely react to the other party's behavior, limiting escalation of social conflict even further (Bhappu, 2003; Harasim, 1993).

Last, lean media may promote more equal participation among negotiators. The salience of social group differences and social status is reduced in lean media because there are fewer social context cues (Sproull and Kiesler, 1991), encouraging lower-status individuals to participate more (Siegel, Dubrovsky, Kiesler, and McGuire, 1986) and reducing social influence bias among individuals (Bhappu et al., 1997). Rather than discounting or ignoring information provided by lower-status individuals, as they might in face-to-face encounters, negotiators may be influenced more by this information when using lean media. Thus, even though less nuanced information is communicated between negotiators, more diverse information may actually be received. Attention to this "new" information may subsequently enable negotiators' to identify optimal trades and create more integrative agreements.

Interactivity

Interactivity has two dimensions. The first, a temporal dimension, captures the synchronicity of interactions (see McGinn and Croson, Chapter 16, this volume). Face-to-face communication is synchronous because all negotiators are cotemporal and each party receives an utterance just as it is produced;

as a result, speaking turns tend to occur sequentially. E-mail is typically asynchronous because negotiators can read and respond to others' messages whenever they desire and not necessarily sequentially. Parallel processing, the second dimension of interactivity, describes the ability of the medium to enable two or more negotiators to simultaneously submit messages. Parallel processing is common in group-decision support systems, chat rooms, and threaded discussions such as might occur during an electronically mediated negotiation.

Asynchronous media impose high "understanding costs" on negotiators because they provide little "grounding" to participants in the communication exchange (Clark and Brennan, 1991; Friedman and Currall, 2001). Grounding is the process by which two parties in an interaction develop a shared sense of understanding about a communication and a shared sense of participation in the conversation (Clark and Brennan, 1991). Without the clues provided by shared surroundings, nonverbal behavior, tone of voice, or the timing and sequence of the information exchange, negotiators may find it challenging to accurately decode the messages that they receive electronically (Clark and Brennan, 1991). Information and context are thus parsed differently in asynchronous and synchronous media, which will certainly influence the way that negotiators construct messages as well as their ability to interpret the messages that are sent.

The use of asynchronous media, for example, may accentuate analytical–rational expression of information by negotiators. Previous research suggests that there are at least two distinct information-processing modes: an *analytical-rational mode* and an *intuitive-experiential mode* (Epstein, Pacini, Denes-Raj, and Heier, 1996). Individuals who adopt an analytical-rational mode rely more heavily on logic and deductive thinking and their associated tactics (e.g., development of positions and limits, use of logical argumentation, and the presentation of facts), although individuals who adopt an intuitive-experiential mode rely more heavily on intuition and experience and their associated tactics (e.g., appeals to emotion, the presentation of concrete personal stories, and the use of metaphors; Gelfand and Dyer, 2000). These two different information-processing styles do not necessarily lend themselves equally to the electronic context, however. Research suggests, for instance, that negotiators exchange very long comments that include multiple points all in one "bundle" when using asynchronous media like e-mail (Adair et al., 2001; Friedman and Currall, 2001; Rosette, Brett, Barsness, and Lytle, 2001). Since the receiver's opportunity to respond to or clarify points that the sender is attempting to make is reduced when using e-mail, the sender is inclined to lay out his or her arguments all in one e-mail message (Friedman and Currall, 2001; O'Connaill et al., 1993). As mentioned earlier, these messages are also likely to be more task-oriented and depersonalized (Kemp and Rutter, 1982).

Argument bundling may facilitate the identification of integrative agreements by encouraging negotiators to link issues together and consider them simultaneously rather than sequentially (Rosette et al., 2001), but such an approach can also place higher demands on the receiver's information-processing capabilities. Negotiators may therefore have more difficulty establishing meaning and managing feedback in asynchronous media (De Sanctis and Monge, 1999), further hindering their efforts to successfully elicit and integrate the information that is required to construct a mutually beneficial agreement.

Finally, although e-mail can be nearly synchronous if negotiators are all on-line simultaneously, this form of communication is less common than a punctuated series of intermittent exchanges occuring within hours or even days, or crossing paths simultaneously (Friedman and Currall, 2001). As a result, individuals may share more information when using electronic media. In contrast to face-to-face communication, which does not support parallel processing and instead constrains negotiators to sequential turn taking, electronic communication allows negotiators to voice their different perspectives simultaneously (Lam and Schaubroeck, 2000). Parallel processing can also undermine existing power dynamics and encourage direct confrontation because it prevents any one individual from suppressing the views of others by seizing control of the discussion (Nunamaker, Dennis, Valacich, and Vogel, 1991). Thus, the parallel-processing feature present in electronic communication but absent in face-to-face communication may further support the simultaneous consideration of multiple issues during negotiation. Coupled with the greater diversity of information exchange encouraged among parties by the reduction of power differentials, the side effects of parallel processing are likely to promote the search for joint gains.

Culture and Negotiation

Just as communication media influence negotiator sense-making and information exchange, so too will culture. Three dimensions of cultural variability described throughout this volume, individualism–collectivism, egalitarianism versus hierarchy, and communication context, have key implications for negotiators' social influence and information-sharing strategies and behavior (Brett, 2001; Leung, 1997). At a fundamental level, these cultural values frame and guide the interpretation of experience, influencing not only *how* negotiators share information, but also *what* information negotiators believe is relevant to the task at hand and so choose to communicate to the other party in an effort to exert influence (Adair et al., 1998; Adair et al., 2001; Brett et al., 1998; Brett and Okumura, 1998; Tinsley, 1998, 2001). They provide a system of meaning within which negotiators' interpret these messages and behaviors (Markus, Kitayama, and Heiman, 1997; Tinsley, Curhan, and

Kwak, 1999). Next we discuss the influence of these three cultural values on negotiation outcomes, as mediated by their effects on negotiator schemas and behaviors. A summary of these effects can be found in Table 17.2.

INDIVIDUALISM—COLLECTIVISM

The individualism—collectivism continuum distinguishes between cultures where either self-interest or collective interests are of primary concern (Triandis, McCusker, and Hui, 1990). Although members of individualistic cultures emphasize independence, autonomy and self-determination, members of collectivist cultures emphasize interdependence, social harmony, and concern for in-group interests (Hofstede, 1980; Schwartz, 1994).

Individualism—collectivism manifests in two schemas that have important implications for social influence processes during negotiation, the nature of information exchange, and the generation of joint gains. First, individualist values are associated with a self-interest schema that reflects the extent to which a negotiator emphasizes his or her own rather than collective interests (Brett and Okumura, 1998). Individualists, because of their strong self-interests, set high personal goals in negotiation (Brett and Okumura, 1998). Such a focus may motivate them to search for more optimal trade-offs, thereby avoiding premature closure and enhancing joint gains (Brett, 2001; Tinsley and Pillutla, 1998).

Differences in underlying values between individualists and collectivists may not only determine what motivates information search, but may also influence negotiator behaviors in substantive ways. Individualists, for instance, have been shown to prefer direct confrontation and problem solving, while collectivists have been shown to prefer indirect problem-solving approaches, such as conflict mediation, that preserve face, reduce dispantants' animosity toward each other, and thereby help to maintain relationships among the parties (Leung, 1997; Ting-Toomey, 1988). Although these behavioral differences may reflect the presence of a self-interest schema among individualists, they might also reflect the presence of different information-processing schema among negotiators.

Little research has examined whether the manifestation of analytical—rational and intuitive—experiential information-processing schema in negotiation varies across cultures. Gelfand and Dyer (2000) proposed, however, that negotiators in individualistic cultures may rely more heavily on analytical—rational thinking styles and their associated tactics (e.g., development of positions and limits, use of logical argumentation, and presentation of facts) largely because logic and deductive thinking are highly valued in individualistic cultures such as the United States. Furthermore, they suggest that negotiators in collectivist cultures such as Japan may rely more

TABLE 17.2

The Influence of Culture on Negotiation Schemas and Behaviors

Processes	Cultural Values	Negotiation Schemas	Negotiation Behaviors
Social influence	Individualism–collectivism	Self-interest	Direct *vs.* indirect confrontation
		Analytical–rational *vs.* intuitive–experiential information processing	Analytical–rational *vs.* intuitive–experiential communication tactics
	Egalitarianism *vs.* hierarchy	Power	Distributive *vs.* integrative tactics
Information sharing	Communication context	Information sharing	Direct *vs.* indirect information sharing
			Sequential *vs.* simultaneous consideration of multiple issues

heavily on intuitive–experiential thinking styles and tactics (e.g., appeals to emotions, presentation of concrete personal stories, and use of metaphors) largely because of collectivists' emphasis on maintaining relatedness (Gelfand and Dyer, 2000). Anecdotal evidence from studies of Japanese negotiators supports these researchers' assertions, finding that Japanese negotiators generally eschew the use of logic (Goldman, 1994) in favor of appealing to the feelings and goodwill of others (March, 1988).

Finally, self-interest and information processing schemas and their associated communication tactics might influence how negotiators attend to arguments made by the other party and thus not only a negotiator's ability to elicit, but also to integrate, information that is required to construct mutually beneficial agreements. Because collectivists value maintaining relatedness, cognitions in these cultures may be directed to the needs of others during negotiations (Gelfand and Christakopoulou, 1999; Markus and Kitayama, 1991). Indeed, research has shown that individualistic negotiators are less successful in their efforts to accurately identify the other party's preferences than are collectivist negotiators (Brett and Okumura, 1998; Gelfand and Christakopoulou, 1999). Individualists' ability to identify opportunities for joint gain may therefore be hampered in comparison to collectivists' same efforts and ability.

EGALITARIANISM VERSUS HIERARCHY

Egalitarianism versus hierarchy reflects the extent to which a culture's social structure is flat (egalitarian) rather than differentiated into ranks (hierarchical; Schwartz, 1994). In egalitarian societies, members' social status determines power, and social status and the social power it implies frequently hold across situations. In egalitarian societies, social boundaries are more permeable; social status, regardless of whether it is superior or inferior, is frequently short-lived and tends to vary across situations.

How power is perceived and used in negotiation differs across cultures as a result. In hierarchical cultures, lower-status individuals are expected to defer to higher-status individuals and comply with their requests; high-status individuals are likewise expected to dominate social interaction and direct the negotiation exchange (Leung, 1997). Although status differences exist in egalitarian cultures, people are less receptive to these power differences than in hierarchical cultures (Leung, 1997). Negotiation power in egalitarian cultures may be tied to negotiator skill or the best alternative to a negotiated agreement (BATNA); therefore, it tends to shift from one negotiation to another (Brett and Okumura, 1998). And, since social status in egalitarian cultures is frequently transitory, more balanced participation may be expected among parties to a negotiation exchange. In short, a power schema (i.e., the extent to which a party uses status-based power) has been shown to be more important in hierarchical cultures (Brett and Okumura, 1998).

A power schema is also associated with more pronounced use of distributive negotiation tactics (Adair et al., 2001; Brett et al., 1998; Brett and Okumura, 1998). In hierarchical Japan, negotiators not only pay more attention to social status and power than do their egalitarian U.S. counterparts, but they appear to use "hard" distributive tactics (e.g., threats and arguments) more frequently to establish leverage over the other party (Adair et al., 1998; Adair et al., 2001; Brett and Okumura, 1998; Graham and Sano, 1989). Such distributive tactics may be less appealing to egalitarian negotiators, who prefer to leave power differentials ambiguous, relying instead on more indirect distributive approaches such as persuasion and the presentation of alternative proposals (Adair et al., 1998; Adair et al., 2001).

Finally, a power schema and facility with distributive tactics may determine how negotiators respond to relative power differences. Both influence how negotiators attend to and interpret indicators of social status and therefore the other party's power, as well as their understanding of how the enhanced set of resources that they generate might be allocated between them. The role of the negotiator (e.g., buyer or seller) has consistently been shown to have a greater effect on outcomes in some cultures than in others (e.g., Adler, Brahm, and Graham, 1992; Campbell, Graham, Jolibert, and Meissner, 1988; Graham, Kim, Lin, and Robinson, 1988). In an attempt to explain these role effects, Graham, Mintu, and Rodgers (1994) demonstrated that negotiation outcomes favor the high-status role more frequently in hierarchical than egalitarian cultures. Uncertainty regarding the other party's status and the negotiator's subsequent use of distributive tactics may therefore motivate information search in hierarchical cultures (Adair et al., 2001; Brett, Adair, et al., 1998), opening up the possibility of more favorable outcomes for the low-power party, since the use of "hard" distributive tactics is neither surprising nor daunting. Negotiators in egalitarian cultures, in contrast, may interpret the use of "hard" distributive tactics such as threats when they are not normative or expected as contentious behavior (Adair et al., 2001), leading them to reciprocate in kind and launch a conflict spiral that results in low joint gains or even impasse (Brett, Shapiro, and Lytle, 1998; Pruitt, 1981; Pruitt and Lewis, 1975).

COMMUNICATION CONTEXT

Communication context is the degree to which communicated messages inherit meaning from the settings in which they are transmitted (Hall, 1976). In low-context cultures, information must be transmitted explicitly in order to compensate for a lack of shared social context (Hall, 1976). In high-context cultures, information is not only transmitted explicitly, but also indirectly and implicitly via contextual factors and the message recipient's understanding of the parties' shared social context (Hall, 1976).

Two different information-sharing strategies have been associated with these two communication contexts, respectively. Negotiators who adopt a direct information strategy share information about preferences and priorities explicitly through a series of reciprocal questions and answers (Pruitt, 1981). Negotiators who adopt an indirect information strategy employ heuristic trial-and-error search, eventually finding their way to agreement through the exchange of alternative proposals containing multiple issues that require the parties to infer each other's priorities (Adair et al., 2001). In low-context cultures (e.g., the United States, Brazil, Germany, Scandinavia, Switzerland), negotiators rely heavily on direct information-sharing strategies, although in high-context cultures (e.g., Japan, Hong Kong, China, Russia, Vietnam) negotiators rely heavily on indirect information-sharing strategies (Adair et al., 1998; Adair et al., 2001; Brett et al., 1998; Chua and Gudykunst, 1987; Tinsley, 1998, 2001). Both direct and indirect information-sharing strategies have been shown to generate joint gains by facilitating information exchange (Adair et al., 1998; Adair et al., 2001).

At the Crossroads: Culture and Communication Media

Although empirical evidence and research have demonstrated important cultural differences in schemas and behaviors when negotiators communicate face-to-face (Adair et al., 1998, 2001; Brett and Okumura, 1998), very little research has examined the influence of culture on negotiation when the negotiators communicate electronically. Gelfand and Dyer (2000, p. 84) have suggested, however, that culture is very likely "to interact with proximal conditions to predict negotiator's psychological states and tactics." We therefore suggest that not only does culture affect negotiation, but the characteristics of the communication media used to negotiate are likely to moderate the effect of culture on social influence and information-sharing processes during negotiation. Namely, media richness and interactivity are likely to influence the intensity and manner in which culturally derived negotiator schemas are enacted in negotiator behaviors. We suggest further that these two media characteristics are likely to influence negotiator sense-making efforts and the nature of information exchange through their impact on social influence and information-sharing processes during negotiation.

SELF-INTEREST SCHEMA, CULTURE, AND COMMUNICATION MEDIA

As discussed earlier, the social presence of others is lower when using e-mail than in face-to-face communication largely as a consequence of reduced visual, verbal, and other social context cues. Lean communication media, because they reduce negotiators' awareness of each other, might promote a self-interest schema and encourage negotiators to engage more heavily in self-interested behavior than they would otherwise. These effects have important and different implications for individualist and collectivist negotiators.

When using e-mail, individualists—who already exhibit a strong self-interest schema (Brett and Okumura, 1998)—may go too far, focusing so extremely on their own interests that they fail to elicit from the other party sufficient information about his or her interests and priorities to identify potential joint gains. Although a strong self-interest schema generally serves to motivate information search among individualists, helping them to avoid premature closure (Brett, 2001; Tinsley and Pillutla, 1998), the enhanced emphasis on self-interest coupled with a reduced awareness of the other party in lean media contexts may lead individualist negotiators to attend too closely to their own concerns. In such cases, even individualists' strong motivation to search for information might be unable to compensate for inaccurate perceptions of the other party, developed as a result of individualists' inattention to the other party's needs, interests, and priorities during negotiation (Brett and Okumura, 1998; Gelfand and Christakopoulou, 1999).

In contrast, the emphasis on self-interest encouraged in lean media may prove beneficial for collectivists. The risk in negotiating with someone who does not espouse a self-interest negotiation schema is that an offer will be accepted before information about integrative issues has surfaced, thus prohibiting optimal trades among issues on which negotiators' preferences differ (Brett et al., 1998). With a heightened focus on self-interest, collectivists might push harder before coming to agreement, thus enhancing joint outcomes. These additional efforts, coupled with their tendency to attend to the needs of other during negotiations (Gelfand and Christakoupoulou, 1999; Markus and Kitayama, 1991), are likely to help collectivists generate higher joint gains than would individualists when negotiating via e-mail.

POWER SCHEMA, CULTURE, AND COMMUNICATION MEDIA

In addition, reduced media richness diminishes the salience of social group differences and obscures social status, potentially lowering collectivists' reluctance to engage in direct confrontation. Diminished awareness among negotiators in regard to social status is also likely to reduce the effects of a power schema on negotiator behaviors. As we discussed previously, the use of lean media encourages lower-status individuals to participate more (Siegel et al., 1986) and reduces social influence bias among individuals (Bhappu et al., 1997). Although such effects may have limited impact in egalitarian cultures, where people expect more balanced participation among negotiators, they are likely to have significant ramifications in hierarchical cultures. Uncertainty about negotiators' relative status, and hence power, motivates information search in hierarchical cultures (Adair et al., 2001; Brett et al., 1998) and may encourage low-status negotiators to pursue their own self-interest rather than simply comply with the higher-status negotiator's requests. The parallel-processing feature of electronic media, moreover, prevents any one individual from suppressing the views of others by dominating the discussion (Nunamaker et al., 1991). Consequently, hierarchical negotiators communicating over e-mail are more likely to attend to and be influenced by information that is provided by lower-status negotiators, whereas lower status negotiators are less likely to satisfice and more likely to seek to maximize their own outcomes. Both effects should facilitate the achievement of higher joint gains among hierarchical negotiators transacting in lean media contexts. Indeed, Rosette et al. (2001) found that negotiated outcomes were highest among hierarchical Hong Kong Chinese negotiators transacting over e-mail than either Hong Kong Chinese negotiators interacting face-to-face or egalitarian U.S. negotiators transacting over either medium.

Yet, despite limiting negotiators' ability to leverage status-based power effectively, lean media may still promote the use of distributive tactics. Because the lack of social cues in e-mail causes people to be more direct and confrontational in their communications (Kiesler and Sproull, 1992), negotiators may rely more heavily on distributive tactics in e-mail than in face-to-face negotiations. The use of such distributive tactics may prove particularly problematic for egalitarian negotiators, who tend to interpret the use of these tactics when they are not normative or expected as contentious behavior (Adair et al., 2001; Brett et al., 1998). Combined with the heightened self-awareness and reduced other-awareness common to lean media contexts, egalitarian e-mail negotiators may be even more likely to respond in a highly confrontational manner to the use of distributive tactics, inevitably launching a conflict spiral that results in lower joint gains. Hierarchical negotiators, for whom the use of distributive tactics is normative, may be less likely than egalitarians to find the increased use of these tactics in lean media contexts a hindrance to the negotiation of integrative agreements (Adair et al., 2001; Brett et al., 1998).

INFORMATION-PROCESSING SCHEMA, CULTURE,
AND COMMUNICATION MEDIA

Communication media are also likely to interact with information-processing schema to influence negotiator behaviors. As mentioned before, reduced visual and verbal cues in lean media may lead negotiators to use more rational–analytical communication tactics (e.g., logical argumentation and the presentation of facts) while lowering their reliance on intuitive–experiential communication tactics (e.g., emotional or personal appeals). Such an effect is likely to favor individualists, who value logic and deductive thinking highly and who may be more adept at the use of these tactics. The depersonalized nature of e-mail in comparison to face-to-face interactions (Kemp and Rutter, 1982), on the other hand, is likely to hinder negotiators in collectivist cultures, who may rely more heavily on intuitive–experiential thinking styles and tactics (Gelfand and Dyer, 2000). By limiting the ability of collectivist negotiators to appeal to the other party's emotions and feelings or establish rapport, lean media may diminish these negotiators' ability to maintain relatedness and to exchange information in easily accessible and meaningful ways. As a result, the effectiveness of collectivists' sense-making and information exchange efforts when negotiating via e-mail may be reduced to a greater degree than it is for individualists.

INFORMATION–SHARING SCHEMA, CULTURE, AND
COMMUNICATION MEDIA

Both the synchronicity and parallel processing dimensions of interactivity have important implications for the influence of an information-sharing schema on information-sharing strategies and tactics. They influence the nature of information exchange through the manner in which multiple issues are considered and integrated during negotiation. They also influence negotiator sense-making efforts and information exchange through the absence of feedback during negotiations.

First, because the use of asynchronous media accentuates analytical–rational expression of information by negotiators, negotiators are more likely to package issues together (Adair et al., 2001; Friedman and Currall, 2001; Rosette et al., 2001). Second, the parallel-processing features present in electronic communication but absent in face-to-face communication further support the simultaneous consideration of multiple issues during negotiation. In addition, the simultaneous consideration of multiple issues favors indirect forms of information exchange. Heuristic trial-and error-search for agreement through the exchange of alternative proposals (Pruitt and Lewis, 1975; Tutzauer and Roloff, 1988) is likely to adapt well to the e-mail context since it supports issue packaging and argument bundling. The intermittent and often overlapping nature of most e-mail exchanges, however, is likely to severely inhibit direct information-sharing approaches that rely on sequential turn taking and reciprocal question-and-answer exchange. Members of low-context cultures, who generally adopt a direct information-sharing strategy (Adair et al., 1998; Brett, Adair, Lempereur, Okumura, Shikhirev, Tinsley,

Lytle, 1998), may therefore find the e-mail medium ill suited to their preferred information-sharing strategy. By contrast, members of high-context cultures, because of their preference for indirect information-sharing strategies (Adair et al., 1998; Brett, Adair et al., 1998), may find themselves more at ease in lean-media contexts. In fact, because they must regularly infer meaning both from what is said (i.e., explicit offers) and what is implied (i.e., proposals entertained), members of high-context cultures may be more skilled than members of low-context cultures at interpreting the meaning of multi-issue proposals that the use of lean media promotes, and subsequently more adept at using what they have learned to develop better integrative agreements.

Conclusion

This chapter contributes to the study of social context in negotiation by seeking to unpack the black box of process. Rather than simply associating particular cultural values or communication media with negotiation outcomes, we sought to explore several of the underlying cognitive and behavioral mechanisms that give rise to the outcome differences that have been observed across cultures and communication media. Existing cross-cultural research examines only a limited range of proximal negotiation conditions (Gelfand and Dyer, 2000). We sought to address this shortcoming by exploring how the use of different communication media might interact with culture to influence negotiation process and outcomes in substantive ways.

Managers today need to be sensitive to the effects of communication media on social influence and information-sharing processes, and thus information exchange. Moreover, the use of different communication media might both hinder and ameliorate intracultural negotiation depending on the specific negotiation schemas and behaviors enacted in that culture. By understanding more fully the differences in substance and style across cultures, and how specific characteristics of the communication media might moderate the influence of these cultural effects on negotiation processes and outcomes, managers will be better equipped to design more effective negotiation support systems in their organizations. Indeed, the first step to designing such systems will be to understand how different communication media, and not just face-to-face and e-mail communication, interact with a much wider array of culturally derived negotiation schemas and behaviors than discussed here. Only then will managers be able to identify when and in which cultural settings the use of different communication media to negotiate transactions is most appropriate, better tempered, or best assiduously avoided.

Works Cited

Adair, W., Brett, J. M., Lempereur, A., Okumura, T., Shikhirev, P., Tinsley, C., and A. Lytle. (1998, June). *Culture and negotiation strategy.* Paper presented at the annual conference of the International Association for Conflict Management, St. Louis, MO.

Adair, W., Okumura, T., and J. Brett. (2001). Negotiation behavior when cultures collide. *Journal of Applied Psychology, 86,* 372–385.

Adler, N. J., Brahm, R., and J. L. Graham. (1992). Strategy implementation: A comparison of face–face negotiations in the People's Republic of China and the United States. *Strategic Management Journal, 13,* 449–466.

Arunachalam, V., and W. N. Dilla. (1995). Judgment accuracy and outcomes in negotiations: A causal modeling analysis of decision-aiding effects. *Organizational Behavior and Human Decision Processes, 61,* 289–304.

Bartlett, C., and S. Goshal. (1991). *Managing across borders.* Boston: Harvard Business School Press.

Bazerman, M. H., Curhan, J. R., Moore, D. A., and K. L. Valley. (2000). Negotiation. *Annual Review of Psychology, 51,* 279–314.

Bhappu, A. D., Griffith, T. L., and G. B. Northcraft. (1997). Media effects and communication bias in diverse groups. *Organizational Behavior and Human Decision Processes, 70,* 199–205.

Bhappu, A. D. (2003). *Virtual democracy? The interactive effects of social group differences and communication media in decision-making teams.* Working paper, Southern Methodist University, Edwin L. Cox School of Business.

Brett, J. M. (2001). *Negotiating globally: How to negotiate deals, resolve disputes, and make decisions across cultural boundaries.* San Francisco: Jossey-Bass.

Brett, J. M., Adair, W., Lempereur, A., Okumura, T., Shikhirev, P., Tinsley, C., and A. Lytle. (1998). Culture and joint gains in negotiation. *Negotiation Journal,* 61–86.

Brett, J. M., and T. Okumura. (1998). Inter- and intracultural negotiation: U.S. and Japanese negotiators. *Academy of Management Journal, 41,* 495–510.

Brett, J. M., Shapiro, D. L., and A. L. Lytle. (1998). Breaking the bonds of reciprocity in negotiations. *Academy of Management Journal, 41,* 410–424.

Brodt, S. E., and C. H. Tinsley. (1998). *The role of frames, schemas, and scripts in understanding conflict resolution across cultures.* Manuscript under review.

Campbell, C. G., Graham, J. L., Jolibert, A., and H. G. Meissner. (1988). Marketing negotiations in France, Germany, U.K. and the U.S. *Journal of Marketing, 52*(2), 49–62.

Carnevale, P. J., and T. M. Probst. (1997). Conflict on the Internet. In S. Kiesler (Ed.), *Culture of the Internet* (pp. 233–255). Mahwah, NJ: Erlbaum.

Carnevale, P. J., Pruitt, D. G., and S. D. Seilheimer. (1981). Looking and competing: accountability and visual access in integrative bargaining. *Journal of Personality and Social Psychology, 40,* 111–120.

Chua, E., and W. B. Gudykunst. (1987). Conflict resolution styles in low- and high-context cultures. *Communication Research Reports, 4,* 32–37.

Clark, H., and S. Brennan. (1991). Grounding in communication. In L. Resnick, J. Levine, and S. Teasley (Eds.), *Perspectives on socially shared cognition* (pp. 127–149). Washington, DC: American Psychological Association.

Croson, R. (1999). "Look at me when you say that": An electronic negotiation simulation. *Simulation Gaming, 30,* 23–27.

Daft, R. L., and R. H. Lengel. (1984). Information richness: A new approach to managerial behavior and organizational design. *Research in Organizational Behavior, 6,* 191–233.

De Paulo, B. M., and H. S. Friedman. (1998). Nonverbal communication. In D. T. Gilber, S. T. Fiske, and G. Lidzey (Eds.), *The handbook of social psychology* (4th ed., pp. 3–40). Boston: McGraw-Hill.

De Sanctis, G., and P. Monge. (1999). Introduction to the special issues: Communication processes for virtual organizations. *Organization Science, 10,* 693–703.

Drolet, A. L., and M. W. Morris. (2000). Rapport in conflict resolution: Accounting for how face-to-face contact fosters mutual cooperation in mixed-motive conflicts. *Journal of Experimental Social Psychology, 36,* 26–50.

Epstein, S., Pacini, R., Denes-Raj, V., and H. Heier. (1996). Individual differences in intuitive–experimental and analytical–rational thinking styles. *Journal of Personality and Social Psychology, 71,* 390–405.

Fisher, R., Ury, W., and B. Patton. (1991). *Getting to yes: Negotiating agreement without giving in.* New York: Penguin.

Fiske, S. T., and S. E. Taylor. (1991). *Social cognition* (2nd ed.). Reading, MA: Addison-Wesley.

Friedman, R. A., and S. C. Currall. (2001, June). *E-mail escalation: Dispute exacerbating elements of electronic communication.* Paper presented at the annual meeting of the International Association for Conflict Management, Salt Lake City.

Gelfand, M. J., and S. Christakopoulou. (1999). Culture and negotiator cognition: Judgment accuracy and negotiation processes in individualistic and collectivitistic cultures. *Organizational Behavior and Human Decision Processes, 79,* 248–269.

Gelfand, M. J., and N. Dyer. (2000). A cultural perspective on negotiation: Progress, pitfalls, and prospects. *Applied Psychology: An International Review, 49,* 62–69.

Goldman, A. (1994). The centrality of "ningensei" to Japanese negotiations and interpersonal relationships: Implications for US–Japanese communication. *International Journal of Intercultural Relations, 18,* 29–54.

Graham, J. L., Kim, D. K., Lin, C.-Y., and M. Robinson. (1988). Buyer–seller negotiations around the Pacific Rim: Differences in fundamental exchange processes. *Journal of Consumer Research, 15,* 48–54.

Graham, J. L., Mintu, A. T., and W. Rodgers. (1994). Explorations of negotiation behaviors in ten foreign cultures using a model developed in the United States. *Management Science, 40,* 70–95.

Graham, J. L., and Y. Sano. (1989). *Smart bargaining: Doing business with the Japanese.* Cambridge, MA: Ballinger.

Griffith, T. L., and G. B. Northcraft. (1994). Distinguishing between the forest and the trees: Media, features, and methodology in electronic communication research. *Organization Science, 5,* 272–285.

Hall, E. T. (1976). *Beyond culture.* New York, Anchor.

Harasim, L. M. (1993). Networlds: Networks as a social space. In L. M. Harasim (Ed.), *Global networks: Computers and international communication* (pp. 15–34). Cambridge, MA: MIT Press.

Harnett, D. L., and L. L. Cummings. (1980). *Bargaining behaviors: An international study.* Houston, TX: Dame.

Hofstede, G. (1980). *Culture's consequences: International differences in work-related values.* Beverly Hills, CA, Sage.

Jessup, L. M., and D. A. Tansik. (1991). Decision making in an automated environment: The effects of anonymity and proximity with a group decision support system. *Decision Sciences, 22,* 266–279.

Kemp, N. J., and D. R. Rutter. (1982). Cuelessness and the content and style of conversation. *British Journal of Social Psychology, 21,* 43–49.

Kiesler, S., and L. Sproull. (1992). Group-decision making and communication technology. *Organizational Behavior and Human Decision Processes, 52,* 96–123.

Kramer, R. M., and D. M. Messick. (1995). *Negotiation as a social process: New trends in theory and research.* Thousand Oaks, CA: Sage.

Kraut, R., Galegher, J., Fish, R., and B. Chalfonte. (1992). Task requirements and media choice in collaborative writing. *Human Computer Interactions, 7,* 375–408.

Kumar, R. (1999). A script theoretical analysis of international negotiating behavior. *Research on Negotiation in Organizations, 7,* 285–311.

Lam, S. S. K., and J. Schaubroeck. (2000). Improving group decisions by better pooling information: A comparative advantage of group decision support systems. *Journal of Applied Psychology, 85,* 565–573.

Leung, K. (1997). Negotiation and reward allocations across cultures. In P. C. Early and M. Erez (Eds.), *New perspectives on international industrial/organizational psychology* (pp. 640–676). San Francisco: Jossey-Bass.

Lewicki, R. J., Saunders, D. M., and J. W. Minton. (1997). *Essentials of negotiation.* Chicago: Irwin.

March, R. M. (1988). *The Japanese negotiator: Subtlety and strategy beyond Western logic.* New York: Kodansha International.

Markus, H. R., and S. Kitayama. (1991). Culture and the self: Implications for cognition, emotion, and motivation. *Psychological Review, 98,* 224–253.

Markus, H. R., Kitayama, S., and R. J. Heiman. (1997). Culture and "basic" psychological principles. In E. T. Higgins and A. W. Kruglanski (Eds.), *Social psychology: Handbook of basic principles* (pp. 857–913). New York: Guilford.

Nunamaker, J. F., Dennis, A. R., Valacich, J. S., and D. R. Vogel. (1991). Information technology for negotiating groups: Generating options for mutual gain. *Management Science 37,* 1325–1346.

Ocker, R. J., and G. J. Yaverbaum. (1999). Asynchronous computer-mediated communication versus face–face collaboration: Results on student learning, quality and satisfaction. *Group Decision and Negotiations,* 427–440.

Pruitt, D. G. (1981). *Negotiation behavior.* New York, Academic Press.

Pruitt, D. G., and P. J. Carnevale. (1993). *Negotiation in social conflict.* Pacific Grove, CA: Brooks/Cole.

Pruitt, D. G., and S. Lewis. (1975). Development of integrative solutions in bilateral negotiation. *Journal of Personality and Social Psychology, 31,* 621–633.

Rosette, A. S., Brett, J. M., Barsness, Z., and A. Lytle. (2001, June). *The influence of e-mail on Hong Kong and U.S. intra-cultural negotiations.* Paper presented at the annual meeting of the International Association for Conflict Management, Paris.

Schwartz, S. H. (1994). Beyond individualism/collectivism: New cultural dimensions of values. In U. Kim, H. C. Triandis, and G. Yoon (Eds.), *Individualism and collectivism* (pp. 85–117). London: Sage.

Siegel, J., Dubrovsky, V., Kiesler, S., and T. W. McGuire. (1986). Group processes in computer-mediated communication. *Organizational Behavior and Human* Decision Processes, 37(2), 157–187.

Shank, R. C., and R. P. Abelson. (1977). *Scripts, plans, goals, and understanding: An inquiry into human knowledge structures.* Hillsdale, NJ: Erlbaum.

Short, J., Williams, E., and B. Christie. (1976). *The social psychology of telecommunications.* Chichester, England, Wiley.

Sproull, L., and S. Kiesler. (1986). Reducing social context cues: Electronic mail in organizational communication. *Management Science, 32,* 1492–1513.

———. (1991). *Connections: New ways of working in the networked organization.* Cambridge, MA: MIT Press.

Tutzauer, F., and M. E. Roloff. (1988). Communication processes leading to integrative agreements: Three paths to joint benefits. *Communication Research, 15,* 360–380.

Thompson, L. (1997). *The mind and heart of the negotiator.* Upper Saddle, NJ: Prentice Hall.

Ting-Toomey, S. (1988). Intercultural conflict styles: A face negotiation theory. In Y. Kim and W. Gudykunst (Eds.), *Theories in intercultural communication* (pp. 213–235). Newbury Park, CA: Sage.

Tinsley, C. H. (1998). Models of conflict resolution in Japanese, German, and American cultures. *Journal of Applied Psychology, 83,* 316–323.

———. (2001). How we get to yes: Predicting the constellation of strategies used across cultures to negotiate conflict. *Journal of Applied Psychology, 86,* 583–593.

Tinsley, C. H., Curhan, J. J., and R. S. Kwak. (1999). Adopting a dual lens approach for examining the dilemma of differences in international business negotiations. *International Negotiations, 4,* 1–18.

Tinsley, C. H., and M. M. Pillutla. (1998). Negotiating in the United States and Hong Kong. *Journal of International Business Studies, 29,* 711–728.

Triandis, H. C., McCusker, C., and H. C. Hui. (1990). Multimethod probes of individualism and collectivism. *Journal of Personality and Social Psychology, 59,* 1006–1020.

Valley, K. L., Moag, J., and M. H. Bazerman. (1998). "A matter of trust": Effects of communication on the efficiency and distribution of outcomes. *Journal of Economic Behavior and Organization, 34,* 211–238.

Weisband, S., and L. Atwater. (1999). Evaluating self and others in electronic and face-to-face groups. *Journal of Applied Psychology, 84,* 632–639.

Zajonc, R. B. (1965). Social facilitation. *Science, 149,* 269–274.

CHAPTER 18

Conflicting Interests in Social Life
UNDERSTANDING SOCIAL DILEMMA DYNAMICS

J. Mark Weber and David M. Messick

AT THE HEART OF MANY EXPERIENCES in social life lies a social dilemma—a fundamental conflict between the short-term interests of individuals and the longer-term interests of the groups of which they are a part. The "dilemma" is that self-interested behavior has higher payoffs for individuals in the short-run regardless of the decisions made by others, but everyone is better off in both the short and long term if everyone cooperates than if everyone acts selfishly (Dawes, 1980). Kollock (1998, p. 183) captured the essence of the problem posed by social dilemmas when he identified them as situations "in which individual rationality leads to collective irrationality. That is, individually reasonable behavior leads to a situation in which everyone is worse off than they might have been otherwise."

In this chapter we review experimental research regarding two classes of social dilemma: public goods dilemmas and common resource dilemmas (often called commons dilemmas). Public goods dilemmas are situations in which contributions are required by parties to create a good of benefit to a discrete group of stakeholders (the "public"). When two companies agree to participate in a joint venture, they are confronted with a public goods dilemma. If one party makes only a nominal contribution to the effort—and even exploits the opportunity to gather competitive intelligence about its partner—it may maximize its short-term payoffs. However, if its partner chooses to do the same, then the joint venture will yield little benefit to either party and may even have a net cost to each. The joint venture is more likely to yield continuing positive returns if both partners contribute. In this case

We are grateful for constructive suggestions and feedback from Mark Kennedy, Deepak Malhotra, and Keith Murnighan.

the "public good" would be the positive synergies and outcomes produced by the joint venture. Not-for-profit institutions like symphony orchestras and hospitals, charitable efforts like programs for street youth and famine relief, and positive environments like clean air or healthy workplaces can all be characterized as public goods.

Common resource dilemmas are the structural inverse of public goods dilemmas. Public goods dilemmas involve decisions about how much to *contribute* to a joint resource. Common resource dilemmas, on the other hand, involve decisions about how much to take, or *harvest,* from a joint resource. Fish stocks are a good example of a common resource dilemma. It is in the short-term interest of each individual fisherman to harvest as many fish as possible from the fishery. Yet communities of fishermen that collectively act in "individually" rational ways devastate fish stocks so that everyone who earns a livelihood from fishing is worse off.

The pervasive nature of social dilemmas has prompted researchers from every branch of the social sciences to invest energy and resources in trying to understand their dynamics (e.g., Agrawal, 2002; Ostrom, 1998). This chapter focuses on experimental research from the fields of social psychology, organizational behavior, and, to a lesser degree, economics.

The Early Days of Experimental Social Dilemma Research

The inspiration for experimental research related to social dilemmas can be traced to the early days of game theory and Von Neumann and Morgenstern's groundbreaking book, *Theory of Games and Economic Behavior* (1944). Game theoretic ideas were introduced into social psychology in formal modeling terms by Luce and Raiffa in their book *Games and Decisions* (1957), and into psychological theorizing by Thibaut and Kelley in *The Social Psychology of Groups* (1959). There was a subsequent explosion of interest in two-person experimental games (mostly prisoners' dilemmas) and a growth of interest in extending theory to multiperson contexts and applied problems that were seen to be analogous to "prisoners' dilemmas," like international relations during the cold war (e.g., Osgood, 1962). During this period, experimental economists and social psychologists pursued different interests. Whereas economists remained focused on rules, institutions, and formal modeling (cf. Roth, 1995), psychologists began to pursue more psychological and contextual factors like individual differences (e.g., Kelley and Stahelski, 1970; Messick and McClintock, 1968), communication (e.g., Dawes, McTavish, and Shaklee, 1977), and changes to the payoff structure of a dilemma (e.g., Kelley and Grzelak, 1972).

The breadth of this rapidly expanding field makes a comprehensive review of the literature impossible here. Interested readers are referred to several more comprehensive reviews (Dawes, 1980; Kollock, 1998; Komorita and Parks, 1996; Kopelman, Weber, and Messick, 2002; Ledyard, 1995; Messick and Brewer, 1983b; Van Lange, Liebrand, Messick, and Wilke, 1992a). In this chapter we selectively review the literature in light of March's (1994) logic of appropriateness. March suggested that, faced with a need to make a decision, people ask themselves (implicitly or explicitly), "What does a person like me do in a situation like this?" At the most basic level, this question focuses us on three important factors—two main effects and an interaction: (1) characteristics of the situation, (2) characteristics of the decision maker, and (3) the importance of the interaction between decision makers and the situations they encounter. This is, of course, consistent with classic statements of the social psychological enterprise (e.g., Ross and Nisbett, 1991). However, the additional contribution of March's logic of appropriateness framework is to hone in on the definition of the situation as the heart of the decision-making process; what is determined to be "appropriate" behavior hinges on how the situation is understood.

Though March's framework is a simple one, it offers a better fit for the accumulated social dilemma data than the traditional expected utility models of decision making that focus primarily on decision makers' predicted outcomes (cf. Messick, 1999). Consequently, we have chosen this framework to organize the literature in this chapter. We first highlight some documented main effects of important situational characteristics in dilemmas. We then turn to main effects of decision-maker characteristics, and to the more complicated area of interactions—what a person "like me" does "in a situation like this." Finally, we identify a number of opportunities for future research in light of March's interactive logic of appropriateness framework.

Characteristics of the Situation: Task Structure and Task Description

The experimental manipulation of many different situational characteristics has been found to have predictable effects on people's choices in social dilemmas. These situational characteristics fall into two broad categories: task structure and task description. Task structure variables are objective elements of a situation. In this category, we focus on communication, group size, leadership, and sanctions. Task description, on the other hand, refers to different characterizations of equivalent tasks. This category includes the effects of framing on people's behavior. In terms of March's logic of appropriateness (1994), both task structure and task description variables can influence how decision makers answer the question: What kind of situation is this?

TASK STRUCTURE

Communication

One of the most consistent main effect findings in the social dilemma literature is that allowing task-relevant communication between parties yields more cooperative behavior (e.g., Dawes et al., 1977). A number of possible explanations for this effect have been offered. By 1990, systematic programs of research had reduced the possible explanations to two: (1) letting people talk to one another enhances feelings of group identity and solidarity, and (2) when people talk to one another they elicit commitments to cooperate from their counterparts (Dawes, Van de Kragt, and Orbell, 1990). Recent studies suggest that communication derives most of its effectiveness from the latter explanation—the elicitation of commitments and individuals' internalized beliefs about the importance of following through on their commitments (Bouas and Komorita, 1996; Kerr, Garst, Lewandowski, and Harris, 1997; Kerr and Kaufman-Gilliland, 1994). Although group identification does appear to improve somewhat when communication occurs, its effect is small and not sufficient to account for the overall pattern of results (Kerr and Kaufman-Gilliland, 1994). Making a commitment seems, for most people, to define the situation as one in which follow-through is most appropriate.

Group Size

In recent years, significant advances have also been made in understanding group size effects. It was long assumed, based on much-replicated early findings, that people cooperated more in smaller groups than in larger groups (for reviews of these early findings, see Dawes, 1980; Messick and Brewer, 1983a). Recent studies suggest that this effect flows from peoples' oversimplified heuristic belief that their actions are more efficacious in small groups than in large groups (cf. Kerr, 1989; Seijts and Latham, 2000; Seijts, Latham, and Whyte, 2000). That is, compared to people in larger groups, people in smaller groups believe that their individual choices make more of a difference in their groups' outcomes. Further, people tend to adhere to this heuristic even when it is objectively not true (Kerr, 1989). Kerr calls such effects "illusions of efficacy." Smaller group size, then, seems to prime people to define their situation as one in which cooperation is reasonable because it can be effective.

Leadership

Since the very early days of social dilemma research, the appointment of leaders has been offered as a solution to the difficulties inherent in managing conflicts of interest along temporal and individual versus group dimensions (e.g., Hardin, 1968). Experimental research demonstrated that parties to a common resource dilemma were more likely to appoint leaders to manage their access to a resource when the commons was being overused (e.g., Rutte and Wilke, 1984) and when managing the common resource was seen to be particularly difficult (Samuelson, 1991).

Recent research has begun to further qualify our understanding of people's reactions to those exercising leadership by considering interactions between characteristics of both the leaders and the led. For example, Wit and Wilke (1990) demonstrated that when leaders attempt to encourage cooperation through rewards and punishments, who leaders are, and whose interests they are seen to represent, can make a difference in peoples' choices. In their study, rewards offered by government officials were counterproductive in eliciting cooperation from a group of businesspeople, while the same rewards offered by a parent company were successful in encouraging cooperation. The source of incentives made no difference to a group of undergraduates. Further, during the 1991 water shortage in California, Tyler and Degoey (1995) found a positive relationship between community members' judgments of leaders' legitimacy and the leaders' use of fair allocation and decision-making procedures. However, that relationship was moderated by community members' level of social identification with their communities; those who took pride in their community and saw procedures as fair expressed particularly great support for their municipal leaders.

Sanctions

The payoff structure of social dilemmas has been the subject of considerable study. Not surprisingly, incentives tend to encourage a target behavior and punishments tend to discourage it (see Van Lange, Liebrand, Messick, and Wilke, 1992b, for a concise review). More interesting, from a logic of appropriateness perspective, is how rewards and punishments might affect situational construal.

Tenbrunsel and Messick (1999) demonstrated that a sanctioning system intended to encourage cooperation might actually discourage it by changing how the situation is understood. Participants were assigned the role of businesspeople who had to make a decision about investing in pollution control technologies. When there were no sanctions, a substantial proportion of participants chose to invest in the public good—clean air for all—despite its implications for the bottom line. In the absence of sanctions, people viewed the dilemma as an ethical problem; investing in the technology was the "right" thing to do. However, in the presence of small sanctions, fewer decision makers made the prosocial, cooperative investment. The presence of sanctions seemed to change how decision makers understood the task from an ethical decision problem to a more calculative, cost–benefit business decision. When the sanctions were small and the probability of being caught without the technology was low, participants were more likely to act in a self-interested fashion. These results are consistent with Messick's (2000) notion that whether the situation is construed as a group problem or an individual problem is an important predictor of cooperation in social dilemmas. Arguably, in the Tenbrunsel and Messick (1999) study, sanctions focused participants on costs and benefits for their own company (i.e., an individual problem), whereas in the absence of sanctions, participants seemed to focus more on the public good of clean air (i.e., a group problem).

Each of the task characteristics reviewed—whether communication, group size, or sanctions—can be seen to affect how people define the social dilemma situation, and therefore what is construed to be appropriate or reasonable behavior. The effects of task structure on situational definition can be relatively direct (e.g., sanctions focus people on the calculus of payoffs), somewhat indirect, (e.g., communication leads to elicitation of commitments that increase cooperation by tapping into internalized personal norms), and the consequence of evoking heuristic beliefs (e.g., I can make a difference in a small group).

TASK DESCRIPTION

Peoples' answers to the question "What kind of situation is this?" can also be influenced by how the situation is described or labeled. The effects of such manipulations are called framing effects.

Framing

Since Kahneman and Tversky's (1979) introduction of "prospect theory," behavioral scientists, and decision-making researchers in particular, have examined how the framing of situations influences how people respond to them. Although prospect theory, per se, has failed to predict clear and reliable effects in social dilemmas,[1] researchers have reported a series of other intriguing framing effects and findings.

People seem to bring different assumptions to identical social dilemmas that are merely framed differently. For example, in a study of empathy and cooperation, Batson and Moran (Batson and Moran, 1999) found that participants who thought they were participating in a business transaction study cooperated less than those who thought they were participating in a "social exchange" study. It seems that being asked to make "business decisions" invoked a more competitive definition of the situation than "social exchange"—even though the underlying tasks were structurally equivalent for both groups.[2]

Batson and Moran's (1999) study is an example of how labeling a situation differently can affect behavior. How the action in a situation is labeled—its "procedural frame"—is also important. Larrick and Blount (1997) noted that the structure of a sequential social dilemma and the structure of an ultimatum bargaining game are identical; yet people cooperate more in social dilemmas than in ultimatum bargaining games. To explain this effect, Larrick and Blount (1997) pointed to how the action is labeled in each situation. In their sequential commons dilemma, the second participant was permitted to "claim" some portion of the remaining resource after the first participant had made a decision. In the ultimatum bargaining game, the second participant was entitled to "accept or reject" the first participant's offer. The researchers demonstrated experimentally that the different procedural frames led to the observed difference in cooperation between their sequential social dilemmas and ultimatum bargaining games.

van Dijk and Wilke (2000) argued that framing manipulations are effective because they focus people on particular aspects of a social dilemma's context. Like Larrick and Blount (1997), van Dijk and Wilke (2000) started with the finding that behavior in different dilemma types varies, despite other structural similarities. In this case, the researchers noted that public goods dilemmas and common resource dilemmas, two sides of the same situational coin, tend to elicit different behaviors. However, the researchers went a step further by striving to isolate the processes underlying different procedural frames, like "take" versus "leave" and "give" versus "keep." They found that the public goods frame focuses people on striving to make contributions equivalent to those of others. In other words, people seem interested in ensuring that they don't contribute more than their share to the public good. The common resource dilemma frame, on the other hand, focuses people on the achievement of equivalent final outcomes. When it comes to harvesting from a common resource, everybody wants to make sure they get their fair share. The differing foci appear to evoke different definitions of the situation and therefore elicit the application of different behavioral rules.

Framing—be it of the situation or of the required action—has proven to be an important situational characteristic. Simply changing the label given to an exercise, or the description of the decision required, is enough to elicit changes in people's responses and choices.

Characteristics of Decision Makers

Considerable research has been conducted to determine the extent to which individual differences (e.g., personality, values, etc.) can predict the outcomes of social dilemmas and the choices of individual decision makers. Many individual differences, including self-monitoring (e.g., De Cremer, Snyder, and Dewitte, 2001; Kurzban and Houser, 2001) and gender (e.g., Walters, Stuhlmacher, and Meyer, 1998), have been the subject of careful study. However, for the purposes of this review, we focus on social motives because social motives are the individual differences that have received the greatest attention in the experimental social dilemmas literature (see Chapters 5 and 6 for a discussion of social motives and negotiation).

SOCIAL MOTIVES

Social motives are also referred to as social values or social value orientations. Although there can be any number of discrete social motives (McClintock, 1978), four receive the greatest attention: individualism, competition, cooperation, and altruism (cf. McClintock, 1972). Individualism is the motive to maximize personal outcomes. Competition is the motive to maximize one's own outcomes relative to others' outcomes. Cooperation is the motive to maximize joint outcomes. Altruism is the motive to maximize others' outcomes. Typically, individualists and competitors are labeled proself, or sometimes simply competitors. Cooperators and altruists, on the other hand, are often characterized as prosocial, or simply as cooperators.

As their respective labels imply, prosocial individuals tend to behave more cooperatively in social dilemmas, whereas proself individuals tend to behave more competitively. Nobody is certain why some people have proself motives and others have prosocial motives. However, some recent research has begun to address this question. Over a series of studies, Van Lange and his colleagues found evidence that patterns of social interaction in early life and young adulthood partly predicted social motives (Van Lange, De Bruin, Otten, and Joireman, 1997). Those reporting secure attachment experiences and more siblings (particularly sisters), for example, were more likely to be prosocial. The researchers also offered some cross-sectional evidence that social motives may change over the life span; the prevalence of proself motives was lower among those in middle and late adulthood.

One of the most provocative studies in the dilemmas literature demonstrated that proself and prosocial individuals understand cooperative and competitive behavior in fundamentally different ways (Liebrand, Jansen, Rijken, and Suhre, 1986). Researchers categorized participants as having proself motives, prosocial motives, or more ambiguous motive preferences ("borderline" individuals). Participants played a series of experimental games with others who were either cooperative, altruistic, individualistic, or competitive. They were then asked to describe the choices and individuals they encountered. Factor analyses yielded two clear, uncorrelated subscales: evaluation and potency. The evaluation scale included words that connoted moral judgment (e.g., *just, fair, incorruptible, dishonest*). The potency scale, on the other hand, included descriptors that dealt with effectiveness (e.g., *weak, vigorous, purposeful, naive*). Proself individuals tended to describe the cooperative–competitive continuum of behavior in terms of potency, or power. To them, cooperative choices were weak and competitive choices powerful. Prosocial individuals, however, tended to define the cooperative–competitive dimension in evaluative—or "moral"—terms. To the prosocial individual, cooperative choices were good and competitive choices bad. This set of findings has come to be known as the might versus morality effect (Liebrand et al., 1986).

The might versus morality effect demonstrates how individual differences can have important effects on how people perceive their environments. A follow-up study found that prosocial individuals attribute cooperative behavior on the part of others to intelligence, whereas proself individuals are more likely to attribute cooperative behavior to a lack of intelligence (Van Lange, Liebrand, and Kuhlman, 1990). Liebrand et al.'s (1986) study yielded other results that demonstrate how researchers might miss important dynamics by focusing exclusively on situational factors without considering interactions with individual difference factors. Like Kelley and Stahelski (1970) before them, Liebrand and his colleagues (1986) found that prosocial individuals were behaviorally "assimilated" by their proself counterparts. That is, prosocial participants interacting with proself participants eventually acted like proself participants rather than continue to be exploited. Someone looking solely at the final outcomes, without being sensitive to relevant individual differences, could fail to identify how different people might initially understand and approach dilemmas in qualitatively different ways.

Interactions: What Does a Person Like Me Do in a Situation Like This?

As noted, the heart of March's (1994) logic of appropriateness is the definition of the situation, and under most circumstances the definition of the situation is jointly determined by the interaction between an individual's characteristics and the characteristics of the situation. Even the largest, best-known main effects in the social dilemmas literature have proven to be qualified by such interactions. For example, although Kerr and his colleagues documented that communication elicited commitments (Kerr and Kaufmann-Gilliland, 1994) and that people generally followed through on their commitments (Kerr et al., 1997), a sizable minority of their participants failed to follow through (32 percent).

Social-motive researchers have been particularly effective at demonstrating the importance of the interaction between situational characteristics and characteristics of decision makers. We demonstrate the pervasiveness of this interaction by reviewing social motive studies that reveal how motives interact with situational characteristics to affect (a) the selection of rules and procedures, (b) the effect of gain–loss frames, and (c) the impact of uncertainty on decision making.

Situation × Social Motive Interaction Elicits Different Rules

Individual differences like social motives can result not only in systematically different understandings of a situation, but also the application of different behavioral rules or heuristics—and therefore systematically different behavior. Samuelson (1993) ran a study in which proself and prosocial individuals faced situations of either moderate or extreme overuse of a common resource. The nature of the situation—moderate or extreme overuse—was defined for the individuals by the experimenter. Participants were offered an opportunity to make a structural change in how they were managing the resource—they could choose to elect a leader to oversee harvesting. More prosocial participants voted for a leader in the extreme overuse condition than in the moderate overuse condition. However, a majority of proself participants voted against the leader regardless of how poorly their group was handling the commons. Samuelson noted that prosocial participants assigned greater importance to fairness considerations when making their choices, whereas proself participants assigned greater importance to their self-interest. It appears, then, that proself and prosocial participants were using different rules to guide their behavior in identical situations.

Framing × Social Motive Interaction

As noted, prospect theory's gain–loss framing has yielded inconsistent results in social dilemmas. De Dreu and McCusker (1997) reported that they could account for inconsistent results from earlier studies of gain and loss framing in social dilemmas by taking into account the social motives of the people involved. De Dreu and McCusker found that loss frames elicited behavior consistent with their participants' social value orientations. Prosocial individuals were more likely to cooperate in loss frames than in gain frames, whereas individualists were more likely to act competitively in loss frames than in gain frames. So the frame is interpreted in individual difference–driven ways. Seeking to maximize joint outcomes, a prosocial individual sees a loss frame as identifying a situation in which cooperation is especially important. Alternatively, individualists who are watching out for their own interests see a loss frame as identifying a situation in which defensive, selfish behavior is most appropriate.

Uncertainty × Social Motive Interaction

Among the most interesting factors with respect to the decision structure of a dilemma is the degree of uncertainty about variables in the task environment. Uncertainty about the size of a common resource, or its replenishment rate, has been found to increase the amount people harvest, the amount they expect other parties to harvest, and their estimates of the size of the resource (e.g., Budescu, Rapoport, and Suleiman, 1990; Budescu, Suleiman, and Rapoport, 1995; Gustafsson, Biel, and Gaerling, 1999; Hine and Gifford, 1996). However, some recent studies have demonstrated that the "uncertainty leads to inefficient outcomes" conclusion misses some very important nuances. Roch and Samuelson (1997), for example, found that when faced with high levels of uncertainty, those with prosocial values harvested less than those with proself values and held their harvests constant, whereas those with proself values increased their harvests.

We have used a number of social motive studies to illustrate the importance of understanding interactions between characteristics of decision makers and characteristics of situations. Earlier main effect generalizations have been shown to be qualified in significant ways by such interactions. Proself and prosocial individuals apply different rules in the same situations (e.g., Samuelson and Messick, 1995). They respond in opposite ways in loss frames (De Dreu and McCusker, 1997). Similarly, high uncertainty seems to focus the attention of proself and prosocial individuals in different ways (Roch and Samuelson, 1997). However, beyond social motives, people's roles (e.g., businessperson or undergraduate; Wit and Wilke, 1990) and their experiences with similar tasks (Bettenhausen and Murnighan, 1991) lead them to respond to the same situations in different ways. The interactive nature of factors in social dilemmas is a caution to researchers and practitioners about the kinds of generalizations they might make or assume (e.g., van Dijk et al., 1999). It also reinforces the descriptive power of March's (1994) logic of appropriateness framework, with its emphasis on the interaction between characteristics of the situation and characteristics of the decision maker in defining the nature of the situation.

Opportunities for Future Research

The accumulated empirical work on social dilemmas is substantial, yet the complexities of human social behavior in such settings are far from perfectly understood. In this section we highlight five areas in which we believe additional effort would help advance the field: (1) taking into account the often shallow nature of cognitive processing, (2) thinking in terms of complex identities rather than individual differences, (3) investigating how people experience and understand dilemmas, (4) conducting field research and natural experiments, and (5) bridging the social dilemma and negotiation literatures.

RULES, HEURISTICS, AND SHALLOW PROCESSING

In recent years, social scientists have become sensitized to the significant proportion of human behavior in general (e.g., Bargh and Chartrand, 1999), and decision making in particular (e.g., Gigerenzer and Todd, 1999), that involves shallow, heuristic, or even "automatic" processing. We use the term *shallow processing* to refer to processing that does not involve significant effort or cognitive resources. When people engage in shallow processing they may adhere blindly to a heuristic (e.g., equality), make choices impulsively, or simply behave in the present situation as they have in similar situations in the past. Shallow processing can, of course, be contrasted with deep, or effortful processing—when people invest significant energy and attention in understanding the characteristics, contingencies, and dynamics of a situation.

There has been little direct investigation of such dynamics in social dilemma contexts. However, such effects seem likely given that many successful interventions (e.g., communication) appear to be disruptive of shallow processing. It would be worthwhile to explore the circumstances under which shallow processing is most likely, and whether interventions do, indeed, derive some of their efficacy from making processing more deliberate. One could imagine that this area, too, would be one in which social motives interact with characteristics of the situation to shape judgments of appropriate action. Depending on the situation, deliberate processing might affect prosocial and proself individuals differently. For example, more deliberate processing might magnify the effect of people's social motives. In other words, more deliberate processing might make prosocials more cooperative and proselves more competitive. This would be consistent with the uncertainty findings reviewed earlier; in fact, it may be that people act in particularly motive-consistent ways under conditions of uncertainty precisely because uncertainty elicits deeper, more considered processing.

A common tool for understanding such effects in other fields within psychology is the use of response time as a dependent variable. Response time is frequently used as a proxy for cognitive effort (cf. Bargh and Chartrand, 1999). Response time studies could be used, for example, to test the uncertainty–processing hypothesis. If those in "uncertain" conditions take longer to make their decisions than those in "certain" conditions, the level of processing might offer a partial explanation for the "uncertainty" effect.

INDIVIDUAL DIFFERENCES VERSUS IDENTITIES

The reality of multiple identities has long been understood in the social sciences. A single actor can simultaneously carry understandings of the self as a businessperson, a student, a parent, and a Muslim, for example. "The self is a collection of incompletely integrated identities" (March, 1994, p. 68). However, to date, experimentalists in the social dilemma literature have focused more on discrete characteristics of individuals (e.g., social motives or personality traits) than they have on these semi-integrated, more "gestalt" identities, much less multiple identities. We have learned a great deal from the individual differences (trait) approach, yet the more cohesive identities that package a set of values, assumptions, and traits—however incompletely integrated—may offer just as much insight into how people make social dilemma decisions (see Brett and Kopelman, Chapter 19, this volume, for a discussion of cultural values and social dilemmas). It seems plausible, for example, that people struggling to decide how to behave may ask themselves, as March (1994) suggested, "What does a person like me do in a situation like this?" If such a question is posed, one can imagine answers that turn on "identities" and "roles" rather than traits and characteristics. For example, what might an introverted, low-self-monitoring proself doctor do when passing an accident while rushing to a pressing engagement? His personality traits suggest he will be tempted to keep driving, whereas his sense of self as a physician and healer would dictate stopping to help. Investigating identities in situations rather than individual differences may offer a window into people's experiences of dilemma situations. Indeed, this approach might address a weakness Taylor (1998, p. 82) has identified in the field of social psychology in general: "Without an understanding of social roles, we cannot appreciate the mundane activities of daily life in which social psychological phenomena are embedded. In seeking a multifaceted and complete view of the person in social psychology, our appreciation of social roles and their contextual importance for social psychological phenomena will be essential."

INVESTIGATING PEOPLE'S UNDERSTANDINGS
AND EXPERIENCES OF SOCIAL DILEMMAS

After three decades of rigorous experimental inquiry, a great deal is known about factors that affect people's behavior in social dilemmas. Comparatively little is known about how people understand and experience the social dilemmas they encounter—about why people make the choices they make and how they feel about them. This is a consequence of how most research in the field has been conducted. Typically, situations and characteristics of participants are manipulated, and choice outcomes are the dependent variable of greatest interest. Other dependent measures are necessary to understand people's thoughts and experiences in social dilemmas.

For example, some very interesting insights have resulted from asking participants in experiments to explain their choices. In a study in which participants in a commons dilemma could buy out others' access to a resource, White (1994) found that parties who bought out others consumed more and exhausted the resource more quickly. This ran counter to her prediction that (a) a decrease in group size would yield more cooperative behavior and that (b) the cost of the buyout would make the need for conservation salient. When she asked her participants to explain their choices during debriefing, she learned that they viewed their buyout costs "not . . . as a cost of consumption but as the purchase of the right to consume more"

(p. 454). Little social dilemma research has asked such questions directly, or systematically measured people's understanding of the experimental tasks in which they participate. Though such an approach has its limitations—for example, people's limited access to why they do what they do or how they use implicit theories to construct their explanations and recollections (e.g., Ross, 1989)—it nonetheless has the potential to enrich the data upon which researchers draw their conclusions.

FIELD RESEARCH AND NATURAL EXPERIMENTS

The world is teeming with social dilemmas large and small. The ubiquity of dilemmas fuels the commitment of many social dilemma researchers; if this topic of study isn't important, what topic in the social sciences is? Yet social psychologists doing social dilemma research rarely venture outside their labs. It is more common to present participants with real-world scenarios or simulations than it is to study people in the real world (e.g., Van Vugt, Meertens, and Van Lange, 1995). Lab research is critical for a number of reasons; it is more efficient to conduct than field research, and it often allows for a measure of control that would be impossible to achieve outside a lab. However, there are merits to collecting data outside the lab—specifically with respect to external validity and the development of rich behavioral models (see also Barry, Fulmer, and Sinaceur, Chapter 3, this volume).

Although researchers in other disciplinary domains have studied social dilemmas in the field for decades, the dominant paradigm has been the case study (cf. Agrawal, 2002). A brave few social psychologists have studied dilemma behavior in the field (e.g., Tyler and Degoey, 1995), and some have even been able to take advantage of natural experiments (e.g., Van Vugt, Van Lange, Meertens, and Joireman, 1996). One alternative, creative approach involves conducting standard lab-style experiments in the field (e.g., Cardenas, 2000). Cardenas executed a lab-style dilemma experiment in several small Colombian villages. This approach has the benefits of permitting random assignment, experimental manipulation, and maintaining levels of experimental control while simultaneously strengthening claims of external validity and the generalizability of results. With the benefit of more data collected in the "real world," social psychologists studying social dilemmas might even find their contributions more welcome in public discourse and policy making.

SOCIAL DILEMMAS AND NEGOTIATION

Scholars have long treated the social dilemmas and negotiations literatures as sister domains (e.g., Bazerman and Neale, 1992; Kramer and Messick, 1995; Murnighan, 1992; Raiffa, 1982; Thompson, 1998). As fundamental conflicts of interest (short term vs. long term; individual vs. group), social dilemmas must be negotiated. Such negotiations can be explicit and involve the making and keeping of promises (Kerr et al., 1997; Kerr and Kaufman-Gilliland, 1994). However, negotiations in social dilemmas are often tacit (e.g., Larrick and Blount, 1995), relying on behavioral signaling (e.g., Isaac, Walker, and Williams, 1994) or cause-and-effect strategies meant to influence other parties' choices (e.g., Axelrod, 1984; Kramer, Wei, and Bendor, 2001) rather than explicit dialogue and agreements. Despite the close relations between research domains and researchers, relatively little has been done that explicitly applies ideas from one domain to the other. We see at least two opportunities for cross-fertilization worth considering: (1) drawing research on integrative negotiations into the social dilemmas literature and (2) drawing research on iterated dilemmas into the negotiations literature.

ENRICHING SOCIAL DILEMMA RESEARCH—DRAWING ON INTEGRATIVE NEGOTIATIONS RESEARCH

Although the stylized decision environments of much laboratory research on social dilemma behavior provides little latitude for the application of negotiation strategies, the lessons of the negotiations literature should be particularly valuable to those coping with, or studying, the complexities of real-world dilemmas. Lab-based social dilemma research tends to turn social dilemmas into iterated single-issue negotiations with limited integrative potential. This is an appropriate analogue for many important real-world dilemmas in which actual dialogue between parties is limited (e.g., recycling), but a weak one for others (e.g., international trade without bribery or corruption). The negotiations literature has acknowledged the complexity of real negotiation environments; they may have multiple differentiated parties,[3] involve coalitions, span cultural boundaries, or be steeped in emotion, for example. Although the social dilemmas literature has grappled in limited ways with richer multiple role situations (e.g., Wade-Benzoni, Tenbrunsel, and Bazerman, 1996) and the nesting of dilemmas (Polzer, Stewart, and Simmons, 1999),[4] these efforts are recent and may be further extended by considering the nature of asymmetries between parties, interests versus needs, logrolling opportunities, contingency arrangements, and the like.

Thompson and Hastie (1990), for instance, argued that people tend to have a "fixed pie" illusion when they enter negotiations. That is, they make the assumption that whatever is good for them is bad for their negotiating counterparts and vice versa (see Thompson, Neale, and Sinaceur, Chapter 1, this volume for a review). A similar phenomenon may occur in resource dilemmas when participants ignore the ability of a resource to replenish itself. If a resource were finite and fixed in size, this belief would not be an illusion, but most shared resources can grow if properly managed. To our knowledge, the impact of such a "fixed pie" assumption has not been examined in resource dilemmas.

CONSIDER THE DYNAMICS OF REPEATED NEGOTIATIONS

Two important findings with respect to the dynamics of iterated social dilemmas point to a research opportunity for negotiation scholars. First, when parties know they will interact with one another several times, they are more cooperative than when they think they are engaged in a one-shot dilemma (cf. Axelrod, 1984; Luce and Raiffa, 1957). Second, simulation data suggests that when parties can choose whom they interact with over time (i.e., known counterparts or different counterparts over repeated rounds), trusting and cooperative parties outperform those who are more self-interested (e.g., Hayashi and Yamagishi, 1998). Cooperators seem to excel under such conditions because they choose to interact with one another and enjoy the rewards of mutual cooperation, leaving competitors to languish in one another's less rewarding company. Negotiations researchers have not placed much emphasis on situations in which parties choose between negotiating with known counterparts and selecting new counterparts over repeated negotiations.[5] Such situations merit more attention since the social dilemma literature suggests that successful strategies over time may be qualitatively different (i.e., more cooperative) from successful strategies in one-off negotiations—particularly when parties have the option to exit a relationship and go in search of new counterparts. Clearly, reputation is an important factor when counterpart selection is an option.

Conclusion

The ubiquitous nature of social dilemmas, and their centrality to social life, has prompted a great deal of research in the experimental social sciences. After decades of steady incremental advances in our understanding of the "main effects" in social dilemmas (e.g., communication, uncertainty, group size), researchers have begun to study the interactions and complex contingencies that must be better specified to achieve a more complete understanding of social dilemma dynamics. Continued work in this vein is both needed and promising. Consistent with March's (1994) "logic of appropriateness," we believe a focus on the interactive dynamics of how people experience, understand, and define the dilemmas of which they are a part should be at the heart of such efforts.

Notes

1. Sonnemans, Schram, and Offerman, (1998) point out that prospect theory derives its predictive potency from a single clear reference point; social dilemmas are complex contexts with multiple reference points.

2. Those led to experience empathy for their counterparts (high-empathy condition) cooperated more than those in the low-empathy condition, regardless of the

framing condition. The task-framed differences cited were among participants in the low-empathy condition.

3. Social dilemmas have multiple parties—the distinction here is with respect to differentiation between parties' interests, roles, and so forth. In most dilemmas research, interests and payoffs are consistent across parties.

4. Social dilemmas can be nested in other social dilemmas. For example, politicians may struggle with choices to make contributions to local public goods of concern to their electors (e.g., avoiding the costs of environmental regulations), versus choices that would be supportive of broader public goods (e.g., implementing such regulations).

5. Bazerman, Magliozzi, and Neale's (1985) seminal prospect theory study in a market setting involved partner selection but did not allow negotiators to choose to continue negotiating more than a single round with the same counterpart(s). Therefore, the benefits of repeated cooperative interaction with the same party were not available.

Works Cited

Agrawal, A. (2002). Common resources and institutional sustainability. In E. Ostrom, T. Dietz, N. Dolsak, P. C. Stern, S. Stonich, and E. U. Weber (Eds.), *The drama of the commons* (pp. 41–86). Washington, DC: National Academy Press.

Axelrod, R. (1984). *The evolution of cooperation.* New York: Basic Books.

Bargh, J. A., and T. L. Chartrand. (1999). The unbearable automaticity of being. *American Psychologist, 54,* 462–479.

Batson, C. D., and T. Moran. (1999). Empathy-induced altruism in a prisoner's dilemma. *European Journal of Social Psychology, 29,* 909–924.

Bazerman, M. H., Magliozzi, T., and M. A. Neale. (1985). Integrative bargaining in a competitive market. *Organizational Behavior and Human Decision Processes, 35,* 294–313.

Bazerman, M. H., and M. A. Neale. (1992). *Negotiating rationally.* New York: Free Press.

Bettenhausen, K. L., and J. K. Murnighan. (1991). The development of an intragroup norm and the effects of interpersonal and structural challenges. *Administrative Science Quarterly, 36,* 20–35.

Bouas, K. S., and S. S. Komorita. (1996). Group discussion and cooperation in social dilemmas. *Personality & Social Psychology Bulletin, 22,* 1144–1150.

Budescu, D. V., Rapoport, A., and R. Suleiman. (1990). Resource dilemmas with environmental uncertainty and asymmetric players. *European Journal of Social Psychology, 20,* 475–487.

Budescu, D. V., Suleiman, R., and A. Rapoport. (1995). Positional and group size effects in resource dilemmas with uncertain resources. *Organizational Behavior & Human Decision Processes, 61*(3), 225–238.

Cardenas, J. C. (2000). *Real wealth and experimental cooperation: Evidence from field experiments.* Paper presented at the International Association for the Study of Common Property, June. Bloomington, IN.

Dawes, R. M. (1980). Social dilemmas. *Annual Review of Psychology, 31,* 169–193.

Dawes, R. M., McTavish, J., and H. Shaklee. (1977). Behavior, communication, and assumptions about other people's behavior in a commons dilemma situation. *Journal of Personality and Social Psychology, 35,* 1–11.

Dawes, R. M., Van de Kragt, A. J. C., and J. M. Orbell. (1990). Cooperation for the benefit of us—Not me, or my conscience. In J. J. Mansbridge (Ed.), *Beyond self-interest* (pp. 97–110). Chicago: University of Chicago Press.

De Cremer, D., Snyder, M., and S. Dewitte. (2001). 'The less I trust, the less I contribute (or not)?' The effects of trust, accountability and self-monitoring in social dilemmas. *European Journal of Social Psychology, 31*(1), 93–107.

De Dreu, C. K. W., and C. McCusker. (1997). Gain–loss frames and cooperation in two-person social dilemmas: A transformational analysis. *Journal of Personality & Social Psychology, 72,* 1093–1106.

Gigerenzer, G., and P. M. Todd. (Eds.). (1999). *Simple heuristics that make us smart:* New York: Oxford University Press.

Gustafsson, M., Biel, A., and T. Gaerling. (1999). Overharvesting of resources of unknown size. *Acta Psychologica, 103*(1–2), 47–64.

Hardin, G. (1968). The tragedy of the commons. *Science, 162,* 1243–1248.

Hayashi, N., and T. Yamagishi. (1998). Selective play: Choosing partners in an uncertain world. *Personality & Social Psychology Review, 2,* 276–289.

Hine, D. W., and R. Gifford. (1996). Individual restraint and group efficiency in commons dilemmas: The effects of two types of environmental uncertainty. *Journal of Applied Social Psychology, 26,* 993–1009.

Isaac, R. M., Walker, J. M., and A. W. Williams. (1994). Group size and the voluntary provision of public goods. *Journal of Public Economics, 54,* 1–36.

Kahneman, D., and A. Tversky. (1979). Prospect theory: An analysis of decision under risk. *Econometrica, 47,* 263–291.

Kelley, H. H., and J. Grzelak. (1972). Conflict between individual and common interest in an N-person relationship. *Journal of Personality & Social Psychology, 21*(2), 190–197.

Kelley, H. H., and A. J. Stahelski. (1970). Social interaction basis of cooperators' and competitors' beliefs about others. *Journal of Personality & Social Psychology, 16*(1), 66–91.

Kerr, N. L. (1989). Illusions of efficacy: The effects of group size on perceived efficacy in social dilemmas. *Journal of Experimental Social Psychology, 25,* 287–313.

Kerr, N. L., Garst, J., Lewandowski, D. A., and S. E. Harris. (1997). That still, small voice: Commitment to cooperate as an internalized versus a social norm. *Personality & Social Psychology Bulletin, 23,* 1300–1311.

Kerr, N. L., and C. M. Kaufman-Gilliland. (1994). Communication, commitment, and cooperation in social dilemma. *Journal of Personality & Social Psychology, 66,* 513–529.

Kollock, P. (1998). Social dilemmas: The anatomy of cooperation. *Annual Review of Sociology, 24,* 183–214.

Komorita, S. S., and C. D. Parks. (1996). *Social dilemmas.* Boulder, CO: Westview.

Kopelman, S., Weber, J. M., and D. M. Messick. (2002). Factors influencing cooperation in commons dilemmas: A review of experimental psychological research. In E. Ostrom, T. Dietz, N. Dolsak, P. C. Stern, S. Stonich, and E. U. Weber (Eds.),

The drama of the commons (pp. 113–156). Washington, DC: National Academy Press.

Kramer, R. M., and D. M. Messick. (Eds.). (1995). *Negotiation as a social process.* Thousand Oaks, CA: Sage.

Kramer, R. M., Wei, J., and J. Bendor. (2001). Golden rules and leaden worlds: Exploring the limitations of tit-for-tat as a social decision rule. In J. M. Darley, D. M. Messick, and T. R. Tyler (Eds.), *Social influences on ethical behavior in organizations* (pp. 177–200). Mahwah, NJ: Erlbaum.

Kurzban, R., and D. Houser. (2001). Individual differences in cooperation in a circular public goods game. *European Journal of Personality.* S37–S52.

Larrick, R. P., and S. Blount. (1995). Social context in tacit bargaining games: Consequences for perceptions of affinity and cooperative behavior. In R. M. Kramer and D. M. Messick (Eds.), *Negotiation as a social process* (pp. 268–284). Thousand Oaks, CA: Sage.

Larrick, R. P., and S. Blount. (1997). The claiming effect: Why players are more generous in social dilemmas than in ultimatum games. *Journal of Personality & Social Psychology, 72,* 810–825.

Ledyard, J. O. (1995). Public goods: A survey of experimental research. In J. H. Kagel and A. E. Roth (Eds.), *The handbook of experimental economics* (pp. 111–194). Princeton, NJ: Princeton University Press.

Liebrand, W. B., Jansen, R. W., Rijken, V. M., and C. J. Suhre. (1986). Might over morality: Social values and the perception of other players in experimental games. *Journal of Experimental Social Psychology, 22*(3), 203–215.

Luce, R. D., and H. Raiffa. (1957). *Games and decisions: Introduction and critical survey.* New York: Wiley.

March, J. (1994). *A primer on decision-making: How decisions happen.* New York: Free Press.

McClintock, C. G. (1972). Social motivation: A set of propositions. *Behavioral Science, 17,* 438–455.

McClintock, C. G. (1978). Social values: Their definition, measurement, and development. *Journal of Research and Development in Education*(12), 121–137.

Messick, D. M. (1999). Alternative logics for decision making in social settings. *Journal of Economic Behavior and Organization, 39*(1), 11–28.

Messick, D. M. (2000). Context, norms, and cooperation in modern society: A postscript. In M. Van Vugt, M. Snyder, T. R. Tyler, and A. Biel (Eds.), *Cooperation in modern society* (pp. 231–240). New York: Routledge.

Messick, D., and M. Brewer. (1983a). Solving social dilemmas. In Wheeler and Shaver (Eds.), *Review of Personality and Social Psychology* .

———. (1983b). Solving social dilemmas: A review. In L. Wheeler and P. Shaver (Eds.), *Review of personality and social psychology* (Vol. 4, pp. 11–44). Beverly Hills, CA: Sage.

Messick, D. M., and C. G. McClintock. (1968). Motivational bases of choice in experimental games. *Journal of Experimental Social Psychology, 4*(1), 1–25.

Murnighan, J. K. (1992). *Bargaining games.* New York: Morrow.

Osgood, C. E. (1962). *An alternative to war or surrender.* Urbana: University of Illinois Press.

Ostrom, E. (1998). A behavioral approach to the rational choice theory of collective action. *American Political Science Review, 92,* 1–22.

Polzer, J. T., Stewart, K. J., and J. L. Simmons. (1999). A social categorization explanation for framing effects in nested social dilemmas. *Organizational Behavior & Human Decision Processes, 79*(2), 154–178.

Raiffa, H. (1982). *The art and science of negotiation.* Cambridge, MA: Harvard University Press.

Roch, S. G., and C. D. Samuelson. (1997). Effects of environmental uncertainty and social value orientation in resource dilemmas. *Organizational Behavior & Human Decision Processes, 70*(3), 221–235.

Ross, L., and R. E. Nisbett. (1991). *The person and the situation: Perspectives of social psychology.* New York: McGraw-Hill.

Ross, M. (1989). Relation of implicit theories to the construction of personal histories. *Psychological Review, 96,* 341–357.

Roth, A. E. (1995). A brief history of experimental economics. In J. H. Kagel and A. E. Roth (Eds.), *The handbook of experimental economics* (pp. 3–109). Princeton, NJ: Princeton University Press.

Rutte, C. G., and H. A. Wilke. (1984). Social dilemmas and leadership. *European Journal of Social Psychology, 14*(1), 105–121.

Samuelson, C. D. (1991). Perceived task difficulty, causal attributions, and preferences for structural change in resource dilemmas. *Personality & Social Psychology Bulletin, 17*(2), 181–187.

———. (1993). A multiattribute evaluation approach to structural change in resource dilemmas. *Organizational Behavior & Human Decision Processes, 55,* 298–324.

Samuelson, C. D., and D. M. Messick. (1995). Let's make some new rules: Social factors that make freedom unattractive. In R. Kramer and D. M. Messick (Eds.), *Negotiation as a social process* (pp. 48–68). Thousand Oaks, CA: Sage.

Seijts, G. H., and G. P. Latham. (2000). The effects of goal setting and group size on performance in a social dilemma. *Canadian Journal of Behavioural Science, 32*(2), 104–116.

Seijts, G. H., Latham, G. P., and G. Whyte. (2000). Effect of self- and group efficacy on group performance in a mixed-motive situation. *Human Performance, 13,* 279–298.

Sonnemans, J., Schram, A., and T. Offerman. (1998). Public good provision and public bad prevention: The effect of framing. *Journal of Economic Behavior and Organization, 34*(1), 143–161.

Taylor, S. E. (1998). The social being in social psychology. In D. T. Gilbert, S. T. Fiske, and G. Lindzey (Eds.), *The handbook of social psychology* (Vol. 1, pp. 58–95). Boston: McGraw-Hill.

Tenbrunsel, A. E., and D. M. Messick. (1999). Sanctioning systems, decision frames, and cooperation. *Administrative Science Quarterly, 44,* 684–707.

Thibaut, J. W., and H. H. Kelley. (1959). *The social psychology of groups.* New York: Wiley.

Thompson, L. (1998). *The mind and heart of the negotiator.* Upper Saddle River, NJ: Prentice Hall.

Thompson, L., and R. Hastie. (1990). Social perception in negotiation. *Organizational Behavior and Human Decision Processes, 47,* 98–123.

Tyler, T. R., and P. Degoey. (1995). Collective restraint in social dilemmas: Procedural justice and social identification effects on support for authorities. *Journal of Personality & Social Psychology, 69,* 482–497.

van Dijk, E., Wilke, H., Wilke, M., and L. Metman. (1999). What information do we use in social dilemmas? Environmental uncertainty and the employment of coordination rules. *Journal of Experimental Social Psychology, 35*(2), 109–135.

van Dijk, E., and H. Wilke. (2000). Decision-induced focusing in social dilemmas: Give-some, keep-some, take-some, and leave-some dilemmas. *Journal of Personality & Social Psychology, 78*(1), 92–104.

Van Lange, P. A. M., de Bruin, E. M. N., Otten, W., and J. A. Joireman. (1997). Development of prosocial, individualistic, and competitive orientations: Theory and preliminary evidence. *Journal of Personality & Social Psychology, 73,* 733–746.

Van Lange, P. A., Liebrand, W. B., and D. M. Kuhlman. (1990). Causal attribution of choice behavior in three N-person prisoner's dilemmas. *Journal of Experimental Social Psychology, 26*(1), 34–48.

Van Lange, P., Liebrand, W., Messick, D., and H. Wilke. (1992a). Social dilemmas: The state of the art introduction and literature review. In W. B. G. Liebrand, D. M. Messick, and H. A. M. Wilke (Eds.), *Social dilemmas: Theoretical issues and research findings* (1st ed., pp. vii, 334). Oxford, England; New York: Pergamon.

———. (1992b). Social dilemmas: The state of the art. In W. B. G. Liebrand, D. M. Messick, and H. A. M. Wilke (Eds.), *Social dilemmas: Theoretical issues and research findings* (pp. 3–28). Oxford, England: Pergamon.

Van Vugt, M., Meertens, R. M., and P. A. M. Van Lange. (1995). Car versus public transportation? The role of social value orientations in a real-life social dilemma. *Journal of Applied Social Psychology, 25*(3), 258–278.

Van Vugt, M., Van Lange, P. A. M., Meertens, R. M., and J. A. Joireman. (1996). How a structural solution to a real-world social dilemma failed: A field experiment on the first carpool lane in Europe. *Social Psychology Quarterly, 59,* 364–374.

Von Neumann, J., and O. Morgenstern. (1944). *Theory of games and economic behavior.* New York: Wiley.

Wade-Benzoni, K. A., Tenbrunsel, A. E., and M. H. Bazerman. (1996). Egocentric interpretations of fairness in asymmetric, environmental social dilemmas: Explaining harvesting behavior and the role of communication. *Organizational Behavior & Human Decision Processes, 67*(2), 111–126.

Walters, A. E., Stuhlmacher, A. F., and L. L. Meyer. (1998). Gender and negotiator competitiveness: A meta-analysis. *Organizational Behavior & Human Decision Processes, 76*(1), 1–29.

White, S. B. (1994). Testing an economic approach to resource dilemmas. *Organizational Behavior & Human Decision Processes, 58,* 428–456.

Wit, A., and H. A. Wilke. (1990). The presentation of rewards and punishments in a simulated social dilemma. *Social Behaviour, 5,* 231–245.

CHAPTER 19

Cross-Cultural Perspectives on Cooperation in Social Dilemmas

Jeanne Brett and Shirli Kopelman

TO PRESERVE CRITICAL GLOBAL RESOURCES such as clean air and water, animal populations, and energy, decision makers from many different cultural backgrounds must forgo local self-interests and cooperate. If they do not, the aggregate harm done by noncooperative choices ultimately will deplete the environment and impact standards of living worldwide. In this chapter, we analyze how culture can affect decisions to cooperate or defect by influencing psychological factors, such as values, beliefs, and norms that have been shown to affect choice, and the social institutions that emerge to manage and contain choice.

Preserving resources is a social dilemma where self-interests in how much to take collide with collective interests. Hardin's (1968) "tragedy of the commons" metaphor is the canonical example of a resource dilemma: a number of herdsmen graze their herds on a common pasture. Each herdsman has the incentive to maximize personal profits by increasing the size of his herd, but if each does so, the pasture will deteriorate and be unable to sustain any of the herds. Because no one herdsman has an incentive to reduce the size of his own herd unilaterally, and no one herdsman has the right to exclude others from using the pasture, overuse is likely. As overuse escalates, the tragic conclusion is the destruction of the common pasture, as well as the herds.

Social dilemmas where the choice is how much to contribute are called public goods dilemmas, for example, contributing to public radio or television. Here self-interests motivate free riding—using the public good without contributing to it (Olson, 1965). The dilemma arises because once a collective good is produced and people have free access to it, they no longer have an incentive to contribute voluntarily to the provision of that good. If there are many free riders in a population relative to the number of contributors, public goods disappear, because contributors, noting they are being taken advantage of, withdraw their support (Ostrom, 2000). The research on social dilemmas shows that the decision to cooperate in the face of incentives to defect is influenced by an array of psychological and contextual factors (see Weber & Messick, Chapter 18, this volume, for a review). Psychological factors include decision makers' motives, beliefs, and norms. Institutional factors include public regulation versus privatization, and monitoring and sanctioning. The effect of culture per se on choice in social dilemmas has not been widely studied. However, if our world is to preserve critical resources, we need to understand how culture affects decisions to cooperate in social dilemmas.

Culture is both psychological, including a society's unique profile with respect to values, norms, and beliefs; and institutional, including a society's characteristic laws and social structures, such as schools and government agencies, that monitor and sanction behavior (Lytle, Brett, Barsness, Tinsley, and Janssens, 1995). Our cultural analysis of behavior in social dilemmas begins with the social psychological research that documents cultural differences in values, beliefs, and norms—all elements of subjective culture (Triandis, 1972) that the social dilemma research indicates are relevant to the choice to cooperate or defect. Then, we turn to the research describing the diverse governing institutions that different cultures develop to manage social dilemmas. Throughout our discussion we point out that culture can have a main effect on choice by influencing the psychological factors that effect choice or by influencing the types of social institutions that emerge to manage and contain choice behavior. We also point out that culture can interact with psychological or institutional factors to affect choice.

Subjective Culture and Choice in Social Dilemmas

CULTURE AND VALUES

Individualism versus collectivism is a cultural value (Hofstede, 1980; Schwartz, 1994) that may have relevance to decision making in social dilemmas. What is important in individualistic societies is self-interest. Individualists think of themselves independently of the social groups to which they belong and make decisions with little concern for social imperatives to consider the interests of others (Markus and Kitayama, 1991). Group interests are important in collective societies. People self-construe in terms of social group membership (Markus and Kitayama, 1991). They make distinctions between in-groups of which they are members and with whom they cooperate and out-groups of which they are not members and with which they compete (Triandis, 1989). The social imperatives in a collective society motivate decision makers to place group interests before individual interests.

Cultural Main Effects on Choice

Comparative cross-cultural research documents that people from collective cultures are more cooperative than individualists in social dilemmas. Parks and Vu (1994) report that Vietnamese (collectivist) are more cooperative than U.S. (individualistic) decision makers in a public goods task. Wade-Benzoni, Okumura, Brett, Moore, Tenbrunsel, and Bazerman (2002) documented that Japanese (collectivist) are more cooperative than U.S. (individualistic) decision makers in an asymmetric resource dilemma. Brett (2001) and Hemesath and Pomponio (1998) reported that Chinese (collectivist) decision makers cooperated more than U.S. decision makers. Probst, Carnevale, and Triandis (1999) reported consistent findings when studying vertical versus horizontal individualism and collectivism. Horizontal collectivists see the self as closely tied to and interdependent with others in the in-group and value equality; vertical collectivists are similar except that they accept inequality. Horizontal individualists see the self as independent of others and value equality; vertical individualists have a similar self-concept but also accept inequality. In this study, the vertical individualists made the least and the vertical collectivists the most cooperative choices.

Culture as a Moderator of Choice

Triandis's (1989) observation that collectivists distinguish between in-group and out-group members more strongly than individualists, cooperating with in-group members and competing with out-group members, leads us to expect an interaction between culture and group composition. If we are correct, decision makers from collective cultures would make fewer cooperative choices in mixed-culture than same-culture groups, but decision makers from individualistic cultures would not be affected by group composition.

Setting up an intergroup paradigm where the goal of doing the best for yourself is achieved by cooperating with your in-groups and competing with an out-group increases cooperation within the in-group. There is evidence of this effect among Israelis (e.g. Bornstein, 1992; Bornstein and Ben-Yossef, 1994), Americans (Insko et al., 1994), Dutch (Schram and Sonnemans, 1996), and Spanish (Bornstein, Gneezy, and Nagel, 2002) decision makers. Decision makers in all these different cultures are responsive to the structure of the game, competing with in-group members in the single group context and twice as likely to cooperate with them in the intergroup context (Bornstein and Ben-Yossef, 1994; Bornstein, Erev, and Goren, 1994).

Probst and her colleagues (1999) contrasted the single-group decision-making context with the intergroup context. Their findings suggested that the intergroup effect may also be moderated by culture (Probst et al., 1999). The vertical individualists in the Probst et al., study (1999) acted similarly to decision makers in the Bornstein intergroup paradigm games. They were significantly less cooperative in the single-group context than in the inter-group context where in-group cooperation served to maximize their own individual payoffs. What is fascinating about this study is that the vertical collectivists acted differently in the intergroup context. They cooperated with their three-person in-group less in the intergroup context than in the single-group context. Probst and colleagues explained that the vertical collectivists must have viewed the entire set of six people as an in-group with whom to cooperate. They saw that cooperating across intergroup boundaries maxi-mized for the six as a whole, even though such behavior would not maximize for them personally. The researchers suggested that the vertical collectivists, whose defining characteristic relates to sacrificing own interests for the in-terests of the group, redefined the "group." Probst, Carnevale, and Triandis's findings suggest an extension of Triandis's (1989) theorizing. Collectivists not only may make clearer distinctions between in- and out-groups than did individualists, but they may also define in- and out-groups differently. Both of these factors may lead collectivists to make rather different decisions in the intergroup situation.

Social motives, or people's goals for resource allocation in socially interde-pendent situations (also called social value orientations), have an important effect on cooperative choice in social dilemmas (Kramer, McClintock, and Messick, 1986; Parks, 1994; Roch and Samuelson, 1997; see also Chapter 5 and 6 for a discussion of social value orientations and negotiation). Al-though social motives are related to cultural values, they are not synonymous (Gaerling, 1999; Probst et al., 1999), possibly because cultural values are broader constructs than social motives. Prosocial decision makers (maximize joint gains) make more cooperative choices in social dilemmas than proself decision makers (maximize own or own relative to other's gain). Neverthe-less, research suggests that social motives are at least in part a function of the social environment in which decision makers grow up (Van Lange, De Bruin, Otten, and Joireman, 1997) and that social motives are unevenly dis-tributed across cultures. For example, a study of managers in an executive MBA program reported proportionately more proself decision makers from individualist cultures like the United States and Israel and more prosocial decision makers from Germany (where economic and political ideology re-flects collective values) and Hong Kong (where social values are collective; Kopelman, 1999).

When cultural values of individualism versus collectivism are narrowly defined in terms of independent and interdependent self-construal, cul-tural values and social motives may be more closely related. Thus, cultural differences in social motives may provide additional explanation for why there appears to be greater cooperation in collective than in individualistic societies. In one comparative culture study, choice was strongly related to social motives (Liebrand and Van Run, 1985) but not culture, but this may be because social motives were not differentially distributed across the two cultures. Decision makers were from the United States and the Netherlands.

Cultural norms are rules of appropriate social interaction—what one "ought" to do in a given situation. Norms are relevant to choice in social dilemmas because "they provide a means of controlling behavior without entailing the costs, uncertainties, resistances, conflicts and power losses involved in the unrestrained, ad hoc use of interpersonal power" (Thibaut and Kelley, 1959, p. 147). Yet, despite their seeming importance, researchers more often use norms to explain base rates of cooperation and to provide post hoc theoretical justifications for their findings, rather than study norms directly (Kerr, 1995; for exceptions, see Bonacich, 1972, 1976).

Kerr (1995) suggested that three categories of norms—commitment, reciprocity, and equity—might be relevant to choice in social dilemmas. Each of these norms may be affected by culture or interact with culture to affect behavior in social dilemmas.

The Commitment Norm

The commitment norm implies that one will follow through on promised actions (Kerr, 1995). Leventhal (1976) suggested the commitment norm is a requirement for social interaction, because without it mistrust and mutual exploitation would dominate and people would withdraw from interdependent social commerce. In Chapter 18, Kerr (1995) suggests that the commitment norm is the reason communication in social dilemmas generates cooperation. He explains that the opportunity to communicate cues obligations to express intentions to cooperate, and once those intentions are public, the norm of commitment and the social sanctions proscribing exploitation of others ultimately encourage cooperation.

The opportunity to communicate may interact with culture to affect cooperation in social dilemmas. In U.S. culture studies, cooperation is more likely when decision makers can communicate (for a review, see Kerr, 1995), but a study contrasting Chinese, Japanese, and U.S. decision makers reported that communication increased cooperation most among the U.S. decision makers, somewhat among the Japanese, and not at all among the Chinese (Brett, 2001). When commitment to cooperate is already high, as it was among the Chinese decision makers in this study, communication apparently does not have the same effect. These results are not inconsistent with the importance of a commitment norm in fostering cooperation in social dilemmas, but they suggest that in collective cultures the norm may be viable without communication.

The Norm of Reciprocity

The norm of reciprocity refers to the social imperative to return equivalent benefits (Gouldner, 1960). Negotiators reinforce each other's behaviors, signal their social motives (proself or prosocial), and reduce social distance by reciprocating or matching each other's behaviors (Kopelman and Olekalns, 1999; Putnam and Jones, 1982). In social dilemmas, reciprocity norms typically encourage cooperation in response to expectations of others' cooperation (see Kerr, 1995). However, reciprocity can work two ways: It can encourage cooperation when others signal such behavior or defection when others signal competitive behavior.

Although reciprocity may be a universal norm, the cultural imperative to reciprocate cooperative signals may be stronger in some cultures than others. There certainly are cultural differences in the relative frequency of what negotiation behaviors are reciprocated (see Adair & Brett, Chapter 7, this volume). Cooperative signals may be more readily reciprocated in collective than individualistic cultures, because collectivists are more attuned to the identity of others as in-group versus out-group members, and to adjusting their behavior on the basis of the others' identity. If collectivists behave contingently depending on whether they are interacting with an in-group or out-group member, it seems likely they can also behave contingently in response to a cooperative signal.

Social dilemmas provide many different ways to reciprocate, because reciprocity is defined in terms of equivalent, not equal, exchange. Equivalency in turn depends on some notion of equity in the allocation of resources. Equity norms provide for the distribution of resources according to some standard of fairness, usually in proportion to contributions, inputs, or costs (McGrath, 1984). There is evidence that decision makers in social dilemmas strive for an equitable share of rewards relative to one another, but such striving may undermine cooperation as much as enhance it (Kerr, 1995), because decision makers (at least individualists) think that what is equitable is what gives them the best outcome.

The Norm of Equity

Not only do definitions of equity differ within cultures, they are substantial across cultural differences (Leung, 1997; see Leung and Tong, Chapter 15, this volume). What is perceived to be fair in one culture may not be fair in another. When asked to make fair divisions of a good (usually money or candy) Chinese and Japanese decision makers typically distribute it more evenly than those from Australia or the United States (Kashima, Siegal, Tanaka, and Isaka, 1988; Leung and Bond, 1984; Mann, Radford, and Kanagawa, 1985). Wade–Benzoni and colleagues (2002) reported that Japanese decision makers distributed financial resources in an asymmetric social dilemma more equally than U.S. decision makers. Their prediction and interpretation was based on the normative implications of the Japanese cultural value for hierarchy and the U.S. value for egalitarianism. In hierarchical cultures, high-status parties have a responsibility to look out for the welfare of lower-status parties (doing so preserves the status quo in times of trouble); in egalitarian cultures there is no such social imperative (Brett, 2001). This implies that among the hierarchical Japanese decision makers, the high-power parties in the asymmetric social dilemma would reduce their harvesting more than egalitarian U.S. decision makers in the same roles.

Further, although somewhat conflicting, evidence of different cultural standards of fairness comes from a comparative culture study of offers in an ultimatum bargaining game (one party makes an offer, the other party can accept or reject it). Results differed not only from the game theoretic equilibrium solution, but also between national groups (Roth, Prasnikar, Okuno-Fujiwara, and Zamir, 1991). U.S. and Yugoslavian buyers made the highest offers, averaging around the midpoint of the range of 0 to 1,000 tokens (where 5 tokens was equilibrium). Japanese buyers' offers were lower, and Israeli buyers' offers still lower, around 400 tokens. The researchers ruled out the possibility that cultural "toughness" might account for the findings by showing that rejection rates were not different in the various cultural groups. They noted that the frequency of midpoint offers, found in other research as well, is explained by 50–50 fairness considerations, and implied that the amount considered fair to the buyer in Israeli and Japanese cultures may be different from the amount considered to be fair in U.S. and Yugoslavian cultures. The buyer designation may be key to the apparent contradictory results between the ultimatum game and the money or candy distribution task. The role of buyer may convey status in Japanese culture (Graham, Kim, Lin, and Robinson, 1988), where hierarchical cultural values legitimize unequal relationships between people and make acceptance and appreciation of the use of power routine in business and social relations (Johnson, Sakano, Cote, and Onzo, 1993).

Emergent Norms

There are numerous examples of emergent normative cooperative solutions to the use of common resources, ranging from forest and meadow management in mountainous areas in the Swiss Alps and in Japan, to irrigation of farmland through the use of common water canals in Spain and the Philippines (for a review, see Ostrom, 1990). The cultural differences in these emergent, normative solutions appear to be due to two factors: different cultural norms for resource allocation and ability and willingness to bar outsiders and sanction insiders from interfering with resource management.

Communities develop rather different solutions for resource allocation because of cultural variation in what groups consider fair. Experimental research shows that norm formation occurs quite rapidly in groups (Bettenhausen and Murnighan, 1985) and then settles in to sustain group behavior over time. The effect is that small differences between groups become amplified over time. This is what happened in the Roth et al. study (1991), which ran for ten sessions. Cultural differences became more pronounced over time. This appears to happen because cultural norms become elaborated. For example, definitions of who may use the resource can become refined and rights may be passed down from generation to generation (Ostrom, 1990).

Although the norms governing the common-pool resources identified by Ostrom (1990) as surviving over the centuries were not static, they did not change rapidly. The communities she identified were for the most part closed to outsiders with new ideas. These communities also monitored and socially sanctioned insiders' behavior.

CULTURE AND BELIEFS

Culture may also influence beliefs that are relevant to decision makers' own behavior in social dilemmas. Beliefs are convictions of the truth of some reality and may or may not be based on an examination of evidence (Webster, 1973). In social dilemmas, three types of beliefs seem important: beliefs about what is a dilemma, beliefs about one's own role in the dilemma, and beliefs about others' roles. Culture may affect each type of belief.

McCay (2002), who studied the emergence of self-organized cooperation in common pool resource dilemmas, pointed out that people's beliefs about resource dilemmas vary in a number of different ways. First, one should not assume a priori that all people define the same things as resources, much less agree that what they believe to be a resource is endangered. Second, she said that people will vary in the degree to which they believe that their behavior can affect conservation of the resource. In a study of Swedish recyclers (Biel, Von Borgstede, and Dahlstrand, 1999), those doing the most recycling also were the ones who believed their actions made a difference.

Prior research on social motives and cooperation in social dilemmas shows that decision makers' own social motives affect their beliefs about the situation and their expectations of others (see Weber and Messick, Chapter 18, this volume, for a review). Since social motives appear to vary at least somewhat by culture, it is reasonable to expect that there will be cultural differences in expectations of others' behavior. A comparative cross-cultural study of decision makers from Japan—a collectivist, hierarchical culture, and decision makers from the United States—an individualist, egalitarian culture, confirms this prediction (Wade-Benzoni et al., 2002). Compared to the U.S. decision makers, the Japanese expected others to be more cooperative and were more cooperative themselves. The researchers hypoth-esized that beliefs about others would be motivated by decision makers' cultural values of individualism versus collectivism. They predicted that the decision makers from the individualist culture would focus more on self-interests and personal goals and expect others to also be self-interested. In contrast, they predicted that decision makers from the collectivist culture would focus on in-group interests and expect others in their culture to sub-limate personal interests for the greater good of the group.

Culture and Institutional Responses to Social Dilemmas

Societies develop institutional responses to social dilemmas. They try to protect resources by regulation or privatization, and they develop monitoring systems and legal sanctions to encourage cooperation and discourage free riding and abuse. The institutions that emerge vary across national cultures, reflecting differences in those cultures' economic, social, political, and legal systems (e.g. Dobbin, 1994; Hall and Soskice, 2001; Hamilton and Biggart, 1988). These institutional responses raise some interesting questions about how to solve social dilemmas on a political as well as a behavioral level.

PUBLIC REGULATION AND PRIVATIZATION

Large-scale institutional solutions to social dilemmas range across a spec-trum from public regulation to private control. The Brown Bear Foundation succeeded in convincing the European Union and the government of Spain to ban hunting and set aside parkland in the Pyrenees for these endangered European bears. The Tibetan government limits access to its peaks by issuing a limited number of permits each climbing season. Government agencies cap the level of power plant emissions, water use, or fish harvesting, divide this quantity into tradable permits, or "access rights," and allocate the permits to individual abusers who then have the right to sell them or buy from others.

The classic institutional solution to the "tragedy of the commons" is privatization—demarcation of the boundaries within which an entity has the sole right to harvest the resource, because this approach internalizes the long-term sustainability to the individual owner (Demsetz, 1967; Johnson, 1972). However, privatization is not always possible or reasonable. Many natural resources are not stable, so although people may decide on international boundaries and demarcate the oceans appropriately, fish do not recognize man's boundaries. Similarly, because polluting toxins move through water, soil, and air, they are difficult to contain. Another limit on privatization is that many environmental resources are too large for individual ownership. Their very size creates the dilemma; others cannot help but be drawn into controlling the resource use because "individual uses of the resource spill out into the larger environmental arena" (Rose, 2002, p. 237).

Tradable permit regimes are an attractive alternative to privatization, because, although they do not fully privatize the resource, they do privatize the degree of access and use of the resource (Rose, 2002). Policy makers assume that if users purchase a permit they will act like owners, conserving the resource carefully and considering innovative replacements for the resource. Although tradable permits have been used by different nations to manage fisheries, water supply, and air and water pollutions successfully (for a review, see Titenberg, 2002), their use to manage resources across national boundaries may be problematic because of the difficulties in negotiating rules of use.

The meetings among industrialized and developing nations in The Hague in 2000 and Marrakech in 2001 to develop regulations to carry out the intent of the Kyoto accords on global warming illustrate the difficulty in negotiating global rules for resource use. It is interesting that the differences that lead to an impasse at The Hague meeting were not between developing and industrialized countries but between the European Union (EU) and the United States. The EU's solution to global warming was for top-down regulation that would require industrialized countries in Europe, North America, and Japan to produce less greenhouse gas emissions and the developing countries to prevent deforestation. This negotiating position is culturally consistent with European Union politics, where individual European nations have cooperated to generate regulation that affects them all. The United States rejected this singular management approach arguing for a three-pronged approach: reductions in emissions; credits for carbon "sinks," forests that absorb carbon dioxide, the main greenhouse gas; and credits for investing in cheaper pollution cleanup projects in developing countries (Revkin, 2000). The U.S. position also was also culturally consistent, because privatization and tradable permits have been effective solutions to resource dilemmas in that culture. A year later in Marrakesh, the EU led the way to acceptance of what was basically the U.S. approach (Revkin, 2001), although this time without U.S. participation. The EU's turnabout reflected a response to pressure from Japan, Russia, and Canada, and U.S. withdrawal from negotiations under President Bush. Without U.S. participation, that appeared unlikely given President Bush's positions, the EU needed Japan, Russia, and Canada, and these industrialized nations wanted credits.

Our review of the literature identifying the success of local common-pool resource solutions and the difficulty of negotiating top-down regulation makes us wonder if a more culturally astute approach to multinational, if not global, resource dilemma problems might not be some type of coordination of local solutions. The emergence of multinational social movements spurred by the formation of coalitions among nongovernmental organizations is one way that coordination could develop. For example, a coalition among environmentalists, cultural and human rights organizations from North America, and indigenous South American groups is cooperating to protect the Amazon (Schittecatte, 1999). Another small-scale example is the coalition of chefs who refuse to serve the endangered Chilean sea bass. Beginning in San Francisco, chefs are trying to save this endangered species by affecting the U.S. market price of the fish.

Coalitions like these examples may be effective because of their inherent stability due to the fact that they are formed around common interests. Coalitions among governments in contrast are formed for expediency. Governments have many interests and changing political fortunes; for example, the election of President Bush, who was opposed to the Kyoto Protocol, means that large-scale coalitions among governments are inherently instable (Botteon & Carraro, 1997).

MONITORING AND SANCTIONING

The other problem with large-scale institutional responses to commons problems is that there are no obvious third parties to monitor and sanction noncooperative behavior. Ostrom (2000), who has written extensively on common-pool resource solutions, made it clear that monitoring and sanctioning are necessary elements of effective systems. Regulation without monitoring and sanctioning is the worst of all possible worlds, because rule infractions by some set off copycat behavior on the part of others who do not wish to be suckers. The result is a downward spiral of cooperation. Thus, solutions need monitors who are accountable to the users and whose job extends beyond monitoring use to monitoring the condition of the resource. With monitoring, Ostrom (2000) advocated a system of graduated sanctions that depend on the seriousness and context of the offense, and an accessible low-cost forum to impose those sanctions. Initial, low-level sanctions are not expected to punish offenders in terms of the cost–benefit ratio of infraction to sanction. Rather, initial sanctions signal the offender and others in the community that monitoring is in place and wholesale defection is not necessary to protect self-interests. A low-cost, and we would add interest-based, forum to impose sanctions can take contextual elements of the infraction into account. A rules or rights-based forum would not have this characteristic (see Ury, Brett, and Goldberg, 1988).

The response to sanctions may depend on the strength of the culture's normative structure. In a public goods experiment, Yamagishi (1988) found that participants from the United States cooperated more than those from Japan when there was no sanctioning. In discussing this result, Yamagishi distinguishes between cultural-individualistic versus cultural-institutional explanations for cooperation in collective societies. The cultural-individualistic explanation is that collective values keep people from free riding in collective cultures. The cultural-institutional explanation is that cultural institutions—specifically systems of monitoring and sanctioning—keep people from free riding in collective cultures. The presence or absence of sanctioning systems should make no difference to cooperation if the effect is cultural-individualistic. Evidence that cooperation falters in collective societies when sanctions are not available supports the cultural-institutional perspective. Yamagishi (1988) explained that strong external systems of sanctioning destroy the basis for voluntary cooperation and therefore exacerbate the conditions that are claimed to provide their justification and for which they are supposed to be the remedy. He suggested that Japan's more collectivist culture and the culture's tendency toward mutual monitoring and sanctioning results in a decrease of trust in the absence of such control mechanisms relative to the more individualistic U.S. society, where such mutual monitoring and sanctioning systems are less dominant.

There are also cultural differences in how people react to and view appointing a leader to aid in achieving conservation goals in social dilemmas. There is greater deference to authority in hierarchical than egalitarian cultures (Brett, 2001), and this suggests that decision makers from hierarchical cultures may be more willing to turn control of the resource over to a leader even before trying self-control than would decision makers from egalitarian cultures. Decision makers from hierarchical cultures may also have more confidence that their leaders will protect the interests of the group as a whole than would decision makers from egalitarian cultures where interest groups lobby successfully for special treatment from government authorities.

There is a large literature based on studies in the United States identifying the conditions under which group members are willing to appoint leaders in social dilemmas (see Weber and Messick, Chapter 18, this volume, for a review). This research shows that groups will opt for a leader when they have failed to manage a resource efficiently and inequalities in harvesting outcomes emerge. Furthermore, followers will endorse leaders who use fair procedures while maintaining the common resource (Wilke, de Boer, and Liebrand, 1986; Wit and Wilke, 1988; Wit, Wilke, and van Dijk, 1989).

Procedural justice appears to be a culturally general phenomenon. If people judge the allocation rules as fair, they will confer legitimacy on those enforcing the rules. However, the allocation rules that people perceive as fair vary by culture (see Leung and Tong, Chapter 15, this volume), as was discussed in the previous section on norms. The question then becomes how you generate allocation rules that people will perceive to be fair. And the answer both from the procedural justice literature and the literature on common-pool resource solutions is that people will judge rules as fair if they have a hand in crafting them rather than having the rules imposed on them (Tyler and Blader, Chapter 14, this volume; Ostrom, 2000).

Conclusion

Although there has been a great deal of research on decision-making in social dilemmas, much of it has occurred in a theoretical and cultural vacuum. Messick (1999) suggested that decision making in social dilemmas could be informed by a "logic of appropriateness" (March, 1994): What does a person like me do in a situation like this? We suggest that the logic can easily be extended to culture: What do people like me do in situations like this? Unpacking the extended logic reveals cultural values and beliefs (people like me) and cultural norms and ideology (do in situations like this) that may help explain cultural differences in cooperative choice in social dilemmas.

There is much to be done studying social dilemmas across cultures and in mixed cultural settings. Culture may have a main effect on choice mediated by cultural values, norms, beliefs and institutions, or it may interact with situational features. Whether culture's effect is direct or the result of an interaction, unpacking the effect of cultural values, beliefs, norms, and social institutions relevant to choice in social dilemmas holds the most promise for effective management of global social dilemmas.

Works Cited

Bettenhausen, K., and J. K. Murnighan. (1985). The emergence of norms in competitive decision-making groups. *Administrative Science Quarterly, 30*, 350–372.

Biel, A., Von Borgstede, C., and U. Dahlstrand. (1999). Norm perception and cooperation in large scale social dilemmas. In M. S. M. Foddy (Ed.), *Resolving social dilemmas: Dynamic, structural, and intergroup aspects* (pp. 245–252). Philadelphia: Psychology Press/Taylor and Francis.

Bonacich, P. (1972). Norms and cohesion as adaptive responses to potential conflict: An experimental study. *Sociometry, 35*, 357–375.

Bonacich, P. (1976). Secrecy and solidarity. *Sociometry, 39*, 200–208.

Bornstein, G. (1992). The free-rider problem in intergroup conflicts over step-level and continuous public goods. *Journal of Personality & Social Psychology, 62*, 597–606.

Bornstein, G., and M. Ben-Yossef. (1994). Cooperation in intergroup and single-group social dilemmas. *Journal of Experimental Social Psychology, 30*(1), 52–67.

Bornstein, G., Erev, I., and H. Goren. (1994). The effect of repeated play in the IPG and IPD team games. *Journal of Conflict Resolution, 38*, 690–707.

Botteon, M., and C. Carraro. (1997). Burden sharing and coalition stability in environmental negotiations with asymmetric countries. In C. Carraro (Ed.), *International Environmental Negotiations* (pp. 26–55). Cheltenham, England: Elgar.

Brett, J. M. (2001). *Negotiating globally*. San Francisco: Jossey-Bass.

Demsetz, H. (1967). Toward a theory of property rights. *American Economic Review, 6*, 347–359.

Dobbin, F. (1994). *Forging industrial policy: The United States, Britain, and France in the railway age*. Cambridge: Cambridge University Press.

Gaerling, T. (1999). Value priorities, social value orientations and cooperation in social dilemmas. *British Journal of Social Psychology, 38,* 397–408.

Gouldner, A. W. (1960). The norm of reciprocity: A preliminary statement. *American Sociological Review, 25,* 161–179.

Graham, J. L., Kim, D. K., Lin, C., and M. Robinson. (1988). Buyer–seller negotiations around the Pacific rim: Differences in fundamental exchange processes. *Journal of Consumer Research, 15*(1), 48–54.

Hall, P. A., and D. Soskice. (2001). An introduction to varieties of capitalism. In P. A. Hall and D. Soskice (Eds.), *Varieties of capitalism: The institutional foundations of comparative advantage.* pp. 1-68. Oxford, England: Oxford University Press.

Hamilton, G. G., and N. W. Biggart. (1988). Market, culture, and authority: A comparative analysis of management and organization in the Far East. *American Journal of Sociology*(Suppl. 94), S52–S94.

Hardin, G. (1968). The tragedy of the commons. *Science, 162,* 1243–1248.

Hemesath, M., and X. Pomponio. (1998). Cooperation and culture: Students from China and the United States in a prisoner's dilemma. *Cross Cultural Research: the Journal of Comparative Social Science, 32*(2), 171–184.

Hofstede, G. (1980). *Culture's consequences: International differences in work-related values.* Newbury Park, CA: Sage.

Insko, C. A., Schopler, J., Graetz, K. A., Drigotas, S. M., Currey, D., Smith, S., Brazil, D., and G. Bornstein. (1994). Interindividual–intergroup discontinuity in the prisoner's dilemma game. *Journal of Conflict Resolution, 38*(1), 87–116.

Johnson, J. L., Sakano, T., Cote, J. A., and N. Onzo. (1993). The exercise of interfirm power and its repercussions in U.S.–Japanese channel relationships. *Journal of Marketing, 57,* 1–10.

Johnson, O. E. G. (1972). Economic analysis, the legal framework and land tenure system. *Journal of Law and Economics, 15,* 259–276.

Kashima, Y., Siegal, M., Tanaka, K., and H. Isaka. (1988). Universalism in lay conceptions of distributive justice: A cross-cultural examination. *International Journal of Psychology, 23*(1), 51–64.

Kerr, N. L. (1995). Norms in social dilemmas. In D. A. Schroeder (Ed.), *Social dilemmas: perspectives on individuals and groups* (pp. 31–47). Westport, CT: Praeger.

Kopelman, S., and M. Olekalns. (1999). Process in cross-cultural negotiations. *Negotiation Journal, 15,* 373–380.

Kramer, R. M., McClintock, C. G., and D. M. Messick. (1986). Social values and cooperative response to a simulated resource conservation crisis. *Journal of Personality, 54,* 576–592.

———. (1997). Negotiation and reward allocations across cultures. In P. C. Earley and M. Erez (Eds.), *New perspectives on international industrial/organizational psychology* (pp. 640–675). San Francisco: New Lexington.

Leung, K., and M. H. Bond. (1984). The impact of cultural collectivism on reward allocation. *Journal of Personality & Social Psychology, 47,* 793–804.

Leventhal, G. S. (1976). The distribution of rewards and resources in groups and organizations. In L. Berkowitz and E. Walster (Eds.), *Advances in experimental social psychology* (Vol. 9, pp. 92–133). San Diego, CA: Academic Press.

Liebrand, W. B., and G. J. Van Run. (1985). The effects of social motives on behavior in social dilemmas in two cultures. *Journal of Experimental Social Psychology, 21*(1), 86–102.

Lytle, A. M., Brett, J. M., Barsness, Z. I., Tinsley, C. H., and M. Janssens. (1995). A paradigm for confirmatory cross-cultural research in organizational behavior. In L. L. Cummings and F. M. Staw (Eds.), *Research in organizational behavior* (Vol. 17, pp. 167–214). Greenwich, CT: JAI Press.

Mann, L., Radford, M., and C. Kanagawa. (1985). Cross-cultural differences in children's use of decision rules: A comparison between Japan and Australia. *Journal of Personality & Social Psychology, 49*(6), 1557–1564.

March, J. (1994). *A primer on decision-making: How decisions happen.* New York: Free Press.

Markus, H. R., and S. Kitayama. (1991). Culture and the self: Implications for cognition, emotion, and motivation. *Psychological Review, 98,* 224–253.

McCay, B. J. (2002). Emergence of institutions for the commons: Contexts, situations, and events. In E. Ostrom, T. Dietz, N. Dolsak, P. C. Stern, S. Sonich, and E. U. Weber (Eds.), *The drama of the commons* (pp. 361–402). Washington DC: National Academy Press.

McGrath, J. E. (1984). *Groups: Interaction and performance.* Englewood Cliffs, NJ: Prentice Hall.

Messick, D. M. (1999). Alternative logics for decision making in social settings. *Journal of Economic Behavior and Organization, 39*(1), 11–28.

Olson, M. (1965). *The logic of collective action: Public good and the theory of groups.* Cambridge, MA: Harvard University Press.

Ostrom, E. (1990). *Governing the commons: the evolution of institutions for collective action.* New York: Cambridge University Press.

———. (2000). Collective action and the evolution of social norms. *Journal of Economic Perspectives, 14*(3), 137–58.

Parks, C. D. (1994). The predictive ability of social values in resource dilemmas and public goods games. *Personality & Social Psychology Bulletin, 20,* 431–438.

Parks, C. D., and A. D. Vu. (1994). Social dilemma behavior of individuals from highly individualist and collectivist cultures. *Journal of Conflict Resolution, 38,* 708–718.

Probst, T., Carnevale, P. J., and H. C. Triandis. (1999). Cultural values in intergroup and single-group social dilemmas. *Organizational Behavior & Human Decision Processes, 77*(3), 171–191.

Putnam, L. L., and T. S. Jones. (1982). Reciprocity in negotiations: An analysis of bargaining interaction. *Communication Monographs, 49*(3), 171–191.

Revkin, A. C. (2000, November 26). Treaty talks fail to find consensus in global warming. *The New York Times,* pp. A1, A16.

———. (2001, November 11). Global warming impasse is broken. *The New York Times,* pp. A8.

Roch, S. G., and C. D. Samuelson. (1997). Effects of environmental uncertainty and social value orientation in resource dilemmas. *Organizational Behavior & Human Decision Processes, 70*(3), 221–235.

Rose, C. M. (2002). Common property, regulatory property, and environmental protection: Comparing community based-management to tradable environmental allowances. In E. Ostrom, T. Dietz, N. Dolsak, P. C. Stern, S. Sonich, and E. U. Weber (Eds.), *The drama of the commons* (pp. 233–257). Washington DC: National Academy Press.

Roth, A. E., Prasnikar, E., Okuno-Fujiwara, M., and S. Zamir. (1991). Bargaining and market behavior in Jerusalem, Ljubljana, Pittsburgh, and Tokyo: An experimental study. *American Economic Review, 81,* 1068–1095.

Schittecatte, C. (1999). The creation of a global public good through transnational coalitions of social movements: The case of the amazon. *Canadian Journal of Development Studies, 20*(2), 203–223.

Schram, A., and J. Sonnemans. (1996). Why people vote: Experimental evidence. *Journal of Economic Psychology, 17,* 417–442.

Schwartz, S. H. (1994). Beyond individualism/collectivism: New cultural dimensions of values. In U. T. H. C. Kim (Ed.), *Individualism and collectivism: Theory, method, and applications. Cross-cultural research and methodology series* (Vol. 18, pp. 85–119). Thousand Oaks, CA: Sage.

Thibaut, J. W., and H. H. Kelley. (1959). *The social psychology of groups.* New York: Wiley.

Titenberg, T. (2002). The tradable permits approach to protecting the commons: What have we learned. In E. Ostrom, T. Dietz, N. Dolsak, P. C. Stern, S. Sonich, and E. U. Weber (Eds.), *The drama of the commons* (pp. 197–232). Washington DC: National Academy Press.

Triandis, H. C. (1972). *The analysis of subjective culture.* New York: Wiley.

———. (1989). Cross-cultural studies of individualism and collectivism. In J. Berman (Ed.), *Nebraska symposium on motivation* (pp. 41–133). Lincoln: University of Nebraska Press.

Ury, W. L., Brett, J. M., and S. B. Goldberg. (1988). *Getting disputes resolved: Designing systems to cut the costs of conflict.* San Francisco: Jossey-Bass.

Van Lange, P. A., and W. B. Liebrand. (1991). Social value orientation and intelligence: A test of the goal prescribes rationality principle. *European Journal of Social Psychology, 21,* 273–292.

Van Lange, P. A. M., de Bruin, E. M. N., Otten, W., and J. A. Joireman. (1997). Development of prosocial, individualistic, and competitive orientations: Theory and preliminary evidence. *Journal of Personality & Social Psychology, 73,* 733–746.

Wade-Benzoni, K. A., Okumura, T., Brett, J. M., Moore, D. A., Tenbrunsel, A. E., and M. H. Bazerman. (2002). Cognitions and behavior in asymmetric social dilemmas: A comparison of two cultures. *Journal of Applied Psychology, 87*(1), 87–95.

Webster, M. I. (1973). *Webster's new collegiate dictionary.* Springfield, MA: Merriam.

Wilke, H. A., de Boer, K. L., and W. B. Liebrand. (1986). Standards of justice and quality of power in a social dilemma situation. *British Journal of Social Psychology, 25*(1), 57–65.

Wit, A., and H. Wilke. (1988). Subordinates' endorsement of an allocating leader in a commons dilemma: An equity theoretical approach. *Journal of Economic Psychology*, *9*(2), 151–168.

Wit, A. P., Wilke, H. A., and E. van Dijk. (1989). Attribution of leadership in a resource management situation. *European Journal of Social Psychology*, *19*, 327–338.

Yamagishi, T. (1988). The provision of a sanctioning system in the United States and Japan. *Social Psychology Quarterly*, *51*, 265–271.

PART FOUR

Epilogue

CHAPTER 20

Integrating Negotiation and Culture Research

Michele J. Gelfand and Jeanne M. Brett

NEGOTIATION RESEARCH is flourishing. Collectively, authors in this volume have traced the breadth and depth of the field—from basic psychological processes, to social processes, to the negotiation context—and they have captured the multilevel complexity that is inherent to studying negotiation. By providing comprehensive reviews of the latest theoretical and empirical contributions, and by speculating about terrain that has yet to be explored, authors have mapped the past, present, and frontiers of negotiation research.

Throughout this volume, authors have questioned many of the fundamental assumptions of negotiation theory, leading the way for Kuhnian shifts in thinking. For example, some question the assumption that negative emotions, such as anger and paranoia (Barry, Fulmer, and Van Kleef; Kramer) and negative events, such as negotiation impasses (De Dreu), are, in fact, counterproductive in negotiation. Others question the exclusive focus on conscious processing of information in negotiations to the neglect of unconscious processing (Thompson, Neale, and Sinaceur; Weber and Messick). Still others question the criteria that are used to evaluate negotiation outcomes, showing how they need to be considerably broadened to capture everyday realities of disputing (Shapiro and Kulik; Conlon and Myer; Tyler and Blader).

Authors have also challenged the tendency for negotiation research to be artificially segmented and have presented a more dynamic view of negotiation—moving the field, for example, from a focus on cold, hardwired biases to "hot" situated cognitions and contagious emotions (Thompson et al., Barry et al.); from a focus on either contextual factors or individual differences to the complex interaction of these forces over time (De Dreu; Weingart and Olekans; Weber and Messick); from a focus on self-interest to a simultaneous consideration of how multiple motives, including social,

415

epistemic, impression management and justice, drive negotiator behavior (De Dreu; Tyler and Blader); and from a focus on the "fixed" nature of communication media to a more fluid approach where the derivative properties of such media are fully manipulable (McGinn and Croson). In addition to pushing the theoretical envelope, authors have also questioned the methodological diversity (or lack thereof) in the field (Barry et al. and Kumar), challenging that the (favored) use of laboratory experimentation is limited in its ability to capture all of the important elements of negotiation. Unearthing limiting assumptions is a difficult exercise, especially when theories and methods have proved useful for many years. Yet as Shapiro and Kulik cogently argue, as the nature of the world continues to change, it is imperative that we continue to cultivate new assumptions to capture new complexities.

One important way that the world of negotiation theory and research has changed is in the attention now being paid to culture. Virtually any topic in negotiation research—from cognitive biases, motives and emotions, to communication and disputing, to justice, mediation, and the technological and social context—can be enriched and extended by taking a cultural perspective. Negotiation, as the chapters on culture show, is always embedded in a sociocultural context. Rigorous theorizing about negotiation and culture is in its infancy, and the authors of the culture chapters have not only summarized what research has been done, they have articulated the frontier of what research needs to be done. They have raised provocative challenges for the fields of negotiation and of cultural research, and in doing so have also mapped the frontiers of the study of culture and negotiation.

BENEFITS OF CROSS-CULTURAL PERSPECTIVES TO NEGOTIATION THEORY AND RESEARCH

While editing this volume, we identified a number of benefits to negotiation research that can be traced directly to taking a cultural perspective. For example, chapter authors have pointed out that cross-cultural research expands the range of phenomena that are studied in negotiation research, and thereby *broadens* the theories, constructs, and research questions characteristic of negotiation research. Authors have also shown that cross-cultural research provides *new* explanations for old findings and thereby extends our understanding of negotiation phenomena beyond Western contexts. Cross-cultural research also plays a critical role in revealing *limiting assumptions* and identifying boundary conditions for negotiation theory and research. And finally, cross-cultural research provides *practical insights* for negotiators by revealing the conditions under which culture becomes a bridge or a barrier to successful conflict resolution. We discuss each of these benefits in turn.

Expanding the Range of Phenomena in Negotiation Research

Cross-cultural research expands negotiation theory, constructs, and research questions. Historically, psychology and organizational behavior have been highly restrictive in the human variability that they capture. Triandis (1994) estimated that 90 percent of social and organizational psychology is based on less than 30 percent of humankind. Negotiation and conflict research is no exception—it, too, has been criticized as being primarily developed in the United States, involving mostly Western research participants (Brett, 2001; Gelfand and Dyer, 2000). By confining our research to Western samples, however, we ultimately restrict the breadth of our theories, and have only a partial view of the full range of variation in negotiation phenomena. As cogently argued by Berry (1980), "It is only when all variation is present can underlying structures be detected; for with limited data, only partial structures may be discovered" (p. 5). Put differently, if scholars continue to look at negotiation only through "Western glasses," they will inevitably miss important elements of negotiation.

The chapters in this book make clear that cross-cultural research is critical to expanding core constructs so that they reflect human variation outside of the West. In their account of justice across cultures, for example, Leung and Tong show that although constructs of distributive, procedural, and interactional justice are universally applicable at an abstract level, they need to be expanded considerably at the operational level to include culture-specific practices. In the context of disputing, Tinsley demonstrates that although interests–rights–power theory travels well across cultures, the constructs need to be broadened if they are to be inclusive of individuals beyond U.S. borders. In much the same way, Adair and Brett illustrate that although cooperation and competition are universal concerns, they may be enacted in highly specific ways. And in his analysis of emotions in negotiation, Kumar shows that the same goals can produce different emotions and action tendencies, depending on the cultural context.

The chapters also show that cross-cultural research expands negotiation theories by capturing dynamics that have heretofore been unexamined. For example, Morris and Gelfand show that a cultural analysis sheds light on the dynamic nature of cognition in negotiation. They illustrate that far from being static in negotiation, cognitive biases can be activated and deactivated by features of the task, the person, and the social context. Likewise, Gelfand and Cai illustrate that cross-cultural research can illuminate new negotiation dynamics that exist at the dyadic, social network, and intergroup level of analyses. For example, classic understanding of in-groups and out-groups, the structure of social networks, and constituent and representative relationships all need to be expanded to capture the social dynamics that occur in

418 Gelfand and Brett

negotiations in other cultures. And as Carnevale, Cha, Wan, and Fraiden show, cross-cultural perspectives on negotiation ultimately give us new ideas about how to negotiate and mediate conflicts. By expanding our constructs and capturing new negotiation dynamics, cross-cultural research ultimately broadens the field of negotiation.

Deepening Our Understanding of Our Own Theories

The chapters in this volume also show that cross-cultural research provides new explanations for classic negotiation findings and thus can deepen our understanding of negotiation phenomena. For example, Tinsley uses a cultural analysis to help explain a classic finding in the U.S. literature, namely, that individuals tend to prefer interest-based strategies in dispute resolution. She shows that the assumptions that are embedded in these strategies are highly congruent with the values of American culture—individualism, egalitarianism and direct communication—providing a new explanation. In a similar fashion, Morris and Gelfand offer a new explanation for the source of classic cognitive biases, such as fixed pie biases, self-serving perceptions, and fundamental attribution errors. Although these biases have typically been linked to limited information-processing capabilities, these authors show that the biases actually may have cultural roots in recurring public practices that are embedded in the media, everyday discourses, schooling, and the like. Similarly, Gelfand and Cai show how cross-cultural research can shed new light on intergroup negotiation phenomenon such as accountability. Together these chapters illustrate that culture can make basic contributions to negotiation theory, providing new perspectives on age-old questions.

Illuminating Limiting Assumptions and Identifying Boundary Conditions

Culture, although omnipresent, is often invisible. It is only when we experience a new culture that we are able to see clearly how our own lives are constituted through cultural practices, values, and norms. Chapters show how cross-cultural research acts as a mirror that reveals hidden (Western) assumptions that pervade negotiation research.[1] Shapiro and Kulik, for example, point out that conflict avoidance is viewed as an ineffective strategy in virtually all of the dispute resolution theories that have been developed in the West, possibly because avoidance is the antithesis of the norm in the United States for direct and forthright communication. Venturing beyond our borders enables us to see the limitations inherent in assuming that avoidance is ineffective—in fact, avoidance is viewed quite positively and has important functions in other cultures. Avoidance preserves face and harmony among principals, while agents and third parties resolve the conflict in many collectivistic cultures.

Cross-cultural research also compels researchers to directly examine other assumptions—namely the (often implicit) notion that negotiation theories are universally applicable. Adair and Brett illustrate that contrary to assumptions in the literature, high joint gain is not always a function of direct information exchange. Rather, in some cultures, high joint gain is produced through indirect communication. Thus, cross-cultural research highlights the *equifinality* of negotiation outcomes—that is, that there may be different roads to the same end. In much the same way, Leung and Tong show how culture can help identify boundary conditions for our negotiation theories. For example, although voice has consistently been found to enhance perceptions of justice, cross-cultural research shows that such effects are largely limited to low-power-distance cultures—cultures, not surprisingly, where much of the research in this area has been conducted. And in the area of social dilemmas, Brett and Kopelman show that direct verbal communication, often shown to increase cooperation in the West, is not necessary for cooperation in other (Eastern) cultural contexts.

These examples notwithstanding, much more work needs to be done to examine the universality of negotiation theories. The chapters in this volume show that negotiation research has developed many rich and sophisticated theories; yet, most of the theories have been tested exclusively on Western samples. Since negotiation is ubiquitous, negotiation theory needs to be a universal science. Before making such a claim, we must examine whether our theories are laden with cultural assumptions that limit their generalizability. Surely, some theories will prove the test of universality. A critical challenge for the future, then, will be to develop theoretical accounts that clearly specify when negotiation phenomena are likely to be universal and when they are likely to be culture specific. Scholars in this volume begin to tackle this difficult question. For example, Morris and Gelfand argue that cognitive biases will be universal when they are linked to numerical processing (e.g., anchoring and adjustment biases), whereas they will be culture-specific when they are linked to social perception (e.g., self-serving biases, reactive devaluation). Much theoretical work remains to be done, however, to identify which aspects of negotiation theory are universal and which are culture-specific.

Practical Benefits: Culture as a Bridge and a Barrier

Cross-cultural research provides practical benefits by helping negotiators understand the unique difficulties and opportunities encountered in intercultural negotiations. Many chapters illustrate that cultural differences can be a source of conflict in negotiations, thereby adding another layer of complexity to the negotiation process. Cultural conflict can arise from different frames (Morris and Gelfand), different emotional experiences (Kumar), differences in communication and strategies (Adair and Brett; Tinsley), and differences in the construction of the social context (Barsness and Bhappu; Brett and Kopelman; Carnevale et al.; Gelfand and Cai). Even when parties are pursuing mutually accepted standards of fairness, differences in behavioral practices across cultures (Leung and Tong) can pose serious obstacles to reaching agreements. Thus, intercultural negotiations can involve multiple sources of conflict, all of which need to be managed if negotiations are going to be successful.

At the same time, chapters make clear that cultural differences also *benefit* negotiations. Morris and Gelfand, for example, argue that shared culture— having a common set of chronically activated constructs and symbols as a result of repeated exposure to similar public cultural elements—makes negotiation processes better organized (Gelfand and McCusker, 2000). Carnevale et al. demonstrate that shared culture can be a bridge in mediation contexts such that cultural ties help mediators' broker compromises that might otherwise not be accepted. Likewise, Brett and Kopelman emphasize the increased creative potential that arises when cross-cultural partnerships form to solve vital global environmental issues. And, as McGinn and Croson and Barsness and Bhappu discuss, technology removes the major restriction of face-to-face communication and encourages the formation of new synergistic partnerships across cultural borders. Future research must continue to understand the benefits that culture brings to negotiation, rather than citing culture merely for its negative effects, as has been typical in the past (Zartman, 1993).

KEY CHALLENGES FOR INTEGRATING CULTURE
AND NEGOTIATION RESEARCH

Although cross-cultural research has been criticized as being atheoretical, decontextualized, and prone to stereotyping national groups (Gelfand and Dyer, 2000; Zartman, 1993), the chapters in this volume show that the field is beginning to move away from the study of static group differences to provide more complex accounts of culture and negotiation. For example, Adair and Brett move us beyond studying cross-cultural differences in frequencies of negotiation behavior to a more theoretical and dynamic account of culture and communication sequences in negotiation. Another key theme of chapters is the need for a contextualized view of culture and negotiation. Morris and Gelfand show how the situation can have a profound effect on negotiator cognition across cultures. Accountability, for example, produces different construals and behaviors in collectivistic and individualistic cultures (Gelfand and Realo, 1999). Likewise, in describing the divergent effects that communication media have in different cultures, Barsness and Bhappu cogently argue that we need to look at culture by situation interactions in negotiation. These conceptual and empirical developments illustrate the increasing complexity through which culture is seen to affect negotiation.

In order to continue the trend away from an oversimplified account of cultural differences, there are a number of critical issues that we believe need attention in future theorizing and research. Future research needs to build multilevel models of culture and negotiation that examine the role of culture at multiple levels and also examine the role of culture together with other contextual factors in negotiation. Such models need to present a dynamic view of culture in negotiation, highlighting the conditions under which cultural factors become more or less relevant. Negotiation and culture research also needs to move beyond its primary focus on individualism and collectivism to incorporate other etic cultural dimensions as well as emic indigenous constructs. Finally, echoing other chapters in this volume, negotiation and culture research needs to take advantage of greater methodological diversity. Each of these issues is discussed in turn.

Toward Multilevel and Dynamic Models of Culture and Negotiation

The chapters in this volume represent culture as a multilevel phenomenon—having instantiations at the individual level, the interpersonal level, within the social context, and at the macro or institutional level. Future research must continue to study culture at different levels of analysis. Much of the culture research in negotiation still has an individualistic bias—focusing primarily on subjective culture within the minds of negotiators—and tends to ignore how cultural phenomenon at higher levels of analysis, such as cultural institutions, roles, and the nature of social networks, affect negotiation processes and outcomes (Gelfand and Cai, this volume). Cross-level theories, those that link public and private elements of culture, are only beginning to be developed and need to be considerably expanded to capture the complexity of culture in negotiation.

In developing multilevel models of negotiation, there is also a critical need to examine the role of national culture vis-à-vis other contextual and individual difference variables in negotiation. Curiously absent from most discussions in this volume, for example, is the way that the organizational culture interacts with national cultural factors. Likewise, there is little discussion in these chapters of the interaction between individual differences, for example, in personality, age, and gender, and cultural factors. Culture and negotiation research has generally ignored organizational, job, and individual differences factors, no doubt because so much of the research is experimental; yet, without an examination of the contextual complexity in which negotiations are embedded in organization, we risk developing an oversimplified picture of culture in negotiation.

Another key challenge is developing theories of culture and negotiation that are inherently dynamic—by which we mean theories about how culture is activated, communicated, challenged, and changed—and which move away from culture as a static "essence." The dominant paradigm in culture and negotiation research adopted the personality psychology approach of positing stable individual differences, such as traits, values, or styles, as the most important source of cultural difference in negotiation. More recently, however, scholars have begun to recognize that cultural knowledge structures and scripts are not always activated and do not always influence behavior in negotiation. According to this view (see Morris and Gelfand, this volume), people have a vast array of cultural knowledge structures, some of which they may seldom use unless brought out of "storage" by the occurrence of contextual factors that cue culturally consistent behavior. In other words, having cultural elements in one's negotiation tool kit does not necessarily mean that they will be used in all situations. Moreover, individuals are not necessarily passive recipients of culture; rather, they may consciously "take up" their cultural selves at their own discretion to the extent that they see it as advantageous. Thus, there are many opportunities to understand the contextual and personal "triggers" of culturally linked cognition and behavior and how they become activated in negotiation. Research is also greatly needed on the dynamics of culture change—examining, for example, the mechanisms through which negotiators' actually negotiate culture and come to a shared understanding of the negotiation process (Brannon and Salk, 2000; Gelfand and McCusker, 2000).

Beyond Individualism and Collectivism

As this volume makes clear, individualism and collectivism is currently the most favored dimension among scholars studying culture and negotiation. With few exceptions, the vast majority of chapters in this volume focus on this dimension, and it is increasingly becoming a "catch all" dimension to explain negotiation processes and outcomes in other cultures. This is perhaps not surprising given that individualism and collectivism (IC) is also the favorite heuristic in cross-cultural psychology (Segall and Kagitçibasi, 1997). Yet an exclusive focus on IC in the field of negotiation is not only an oversimplification of culture; it is also highly limiting in its scope. As an analogy, just as an exclusive reliance on one dimension of personality would result in important omissions in personality psychology, so too an exclusive reliance on individualism–collectivism highly restricts negotiation theories and research.

In order for culture to become central to the field of negotiation, future research must move beyond simple dichotomies of individualism and collectivism and must incorporate other dimensions of culture into theory and research. Lytle, Brett, Barsness, Tinsley, and Janssens (1995) identified many dimensions on which national cultures vary (see their Table 20.1) that may be relevant to negotiation and conflict. More recently, as an alternative to Hofstede's (1980) value orientations, Leung, Bond, and colleagues (2002) have advanced a taxonomy of beliefs that vary across cultures that may also be relevant to many phenomena discussed in this volume. Dimensions such as societal cynicism, or the distrust of cultural institutions and a negative view of human nature, have clear relevance to chapters in this volume on social paranoia (Kramer), justice perceptions and reactions to authorities (Tyler and Blader) and mediation (Conlon and Meyer). Leung and colleagues' dimension of fate control, or the belief that life events are predetermined, has relevance to discussion of negotiator cognition (Thompson et al.), motivation (De Dreu), and negotiation behaviors (Shapiro and Kulik). Future research also needs to consider cultural differences in time orientation (Kluckhohn and Strodtbeck, 1961), cultural differences in time urgency (Waller, Conte, Gibson, and Carpenter, 2001), and cultural differences in entrainment processes (Ancona and Chong, 1996) that may affect conflict and negotiation processes and cause intercultural negotiations to be more "out of sync" (Blount and Janicik, 2003) than intracultural negotiations. More generally, by broadening the cultural focus in negotiation theory and research, we will ultimately be better able to describe, explain, and predict negotiation phenomena.

To be sure, individualism and collectivism is also important to the study of conflict and negotiation as this volume attests, and there is much work that remains to be done on this dimension as well. Future research on this dimension needs to move beyond simple dichotomies of individualism and collectivism to further specify different types of IC and how they are relevant to negotiation. For example, Triandis and colleagues (Singelis, Triandis, Bhawuk, and Gelfand, 1995; Triandis, 1995; Triandis and Gelfand, 1998) have shown that there are important distinctions among individualistic and collectivistic cultures—termed horizontal and vertical individualism and collectivism. Although the United States is seen to be an individualistic culture, it is differentiated from other individualistic cultures (e.g., Australia, Sweden) in that it also emphasizes achieved status and competition (termed "vertical individualism," Triandis and Gelfand, 1998). Likewise, not all collectivistic cultures are alike; some emphasize ascribed status (e.g., Japan), whereas others emphasize equal status (e.g., an Israeli kibbutz). There are many further distinctions among individualism and collectivism (Triandis, 1995), and negotiation theory needs to capture this complexity so as to avoid oversimplifying this dimension.

Finally, future research on culture and negotiation will need to examine how culture is differentiated within populations. Cultural meanings, norms, and values are often treated in negotiation as uniform within national boundaries. Future research needs to model the heterogeneity that exists within nations and ethnic groups. Regional variation in cultural values and practices, for example, is area of largely unexamined territory (Nisbett and Cohen, 1996). Indeed, variance within cultures is itself a cultural construct in its own right. For example, socially shared cognition is likely to be more common in negotiation dyads in tightly structured cultures, as compared to loosely structured cultures (Gelfand, Lim, Nishii, and Raver et al., 2003). More generally, although recognizing that cultures are integrated entities, we also need to be mindful to not overlook sources of cultural differentiation as well.

Toward a Diversity of Cultural Perspectives

Although the chapters in this volume offer diverse approaches to the study of culture and negotiation, many of the authors were educated in the West and have been trained in the philosophical tradition of American cross-cultural psychology. Future research needs to capitalize on the diversity that exists in the culture and psychology movement (see debates on cultural, cross-cultural, versus indigenous psychologies in the 1998 special issue of the *Asian Journal of Social Psychology;* see also Vol. 1 of the *Handbook of Cross-Cultural Psychology*).

For example, indigenous psychologies will be important to incorporate into future research on culture and negotiation. Psychologists taking an indigenous approach argue that the study of local frames of reference and culturally derived categories—rather than Western constructs—need to be given priority in psychological research (Adair, 1992; Enriquez, 1993; Huang, 1998; Kim and Berry, 1993; Sinha, 1997). By starting with Western constructs, we may be missing important aspects of conflict resolution that are relevant in other cultures. As Azuma (1984) remarked, "When a psychologist looks at a non-Western culture through Western glasses, he may fail to notice important aspects of the non-Western culture since the schema for recognizing them are not provided by his science" (p. 49). Moreover, non-Western scientists trained in the American psychological tradition may also find that their exposure to Western cultural and philosophical ideas displaces their own indigenous values and ways of knowing. Yang (1992) noted, for example, that psychological research in China has resulted in an "Americanized Chinese psychology without a Chinese "soul" . . . which does not do much good in explaining, predicting, and understanding Chinese behavior (p. 65). Thus, in order to truly globalize the science of negotiation, we will need to go beyond Western intellectual traditions.

Fortunately, research has already begun to illuminate indigenous concepts relevant to social conflict. For example, in Japan, there is a growing psychology of *amae* (translated into indulgent interdependence) that has been implicated in conflict (Kashima and Callan, 1994). In India, psychologists have begun to investigate manifestations of ancient philosophies in modern thought and behavior (Sinha, 1997). Pande and Naidu (1992) developed the construct of *niskamakarma* ("nonattachment") from the Indian Bhagwatgita, which has implications for strategies for conflict resolution. Peng and Nisbett (1999) argued that the construct of *dialectic thinking*—or the tolerance for contradiction—which is derived from ancient Chinese philosophy, is related to cooperative conflict resolution strategies within the Chinese context. Other indigenous Chinese constructs that have clear relevance to conflict resolution are *guanxi* (relationship) as well as *mientze* (face; Huang, 1997–1998). Even within the United States, there is recognition that the local construct of *southern honor* helps to explain the escalation of violence among males in the South (Nisbett and Cohen, 1996).

Future research must give voice to intellectual traditions other than Western psychology when generating research questions and identifying and assigning meaning to constructs. We should do this not because it is culturally "correct," but because indigenous constructs are bound to provide critical insights into the psychology of social conflict in other cultures. We do not view the incorporation of indigenous constructs as leading to a splintering of our science; rather, we predict that future research will integrate aspects of indigenous psychology with aspects of traditional Western psychology to produce a science that is global in its reach (cf. Berry, 2000).

Broadening Our Methodological Scope

Finally, future research on culture and negotiation must incorporate a broader array of methods. As with mainstream negotiation research (Barry et al., this volume) cross-cultural research on negotiation is often based on laboratory experimentation. To be sure, this method has notable strengths. Yet, other methods that allow for greater contextual complexity—ethnographies, narratives, discourse analysis—are essential for modeling cultural dynamics in their multilevel complexity. Regardless of the methods we choose, we need to be mindful of whether our methods are laden with Western assumptions. For example, role-play simulations among strangers may be unnatural in cultures beyond the United States. Multiple methods are essential to guard against the numerous rival hypotheses that arise when pursuing cross-cultural research (Gelfand, Raver, and Holcombe, 2002), and ultimately provide the methodological breadth needed to match the complexity of the effects of culture.

Concluding Remarks

Negotiation, as an area of scholarly inquiry, has come of age. The chapters in this book have traced the evolution of many aspects of the field—illustrating their historical roots, their present-day discoveries, and their future possibilities. Cross-cultural perspectives will inevitably be an important aspect of future negotiation research. They will not only broaden and deepen our understanding of negotiation and conflict in other cultures, but will also help us to better understand negotiation and conflict in our own culture.

Note

1. We thank Cathy Tinsley for bringing up this metaphor at the negotiation and culture conference at Northwestern University, October 2001.

Works Cited

Adair, J. G. (1992). Empirical studies of indigenization and development of the discipline in developing countries. In S. Iwawaki, Y. Kashima, and K. Leung (Eds.), *Innovations in cross-cultural psychology* (pp. 62–74). Amsterdam: Swets & Zeitlinger.

Ancona, D., and C.-L. Chong. (1996). Entrainment: Pace, cycle, and rhythm in organizational behavior. *Research in Organizational Behavior, 18,* 251–284.

Azuma, H. (1984). Psychology in a non-Western country. *International Journal of Psychology, 19,* 45–56.

Blount, S., and G. Janicik. (2003). Getting and staying in-pace: the in-synch preference and its implications for work groups. In M. A. Neale, E. Mannix, and H. Sondak (Eds.), *Research on managing groups and teams in organizations* (Vol. 4, pp. 235–266) Stanford, CT: JAI Press.

Berry, J. W. (1980). Introduction to methodology. In H. C. Triandis and J. W. Berry (Eds.), *Handbook of cross-cultural psychology* (Vol. 2, pp. 1–28). Boston: Allyn & Bacon.

———. (2000). Cross-cultural psychology: A symbiosis of cultural and comparative approaches. *Asian Journal of Social Psychology, 3,* 197–205.

Brannon, M. Y., and J. E. Salk. (2000). Partnering across borders: Negotiating organizational culture in a German-Japanese joint venture. *Human Relations, 53,* 451–487.

Brett, J. M. (2001). *Negotiating globally: How to negotiate deals, resolve disputes, and make decisions across cultural boundaries.* San Francisco: Jossey-Bass.

Enriquez, V. G. (1993). Developing a Filipino psychology. In U. Kim and J. W. Berry (Eds.), *Indigenous psychologies: Research and experience in cultural context* (pp. 152–169). Newbury Park, CA: Sage.

Gelfand, M. J., and Dyer, N. (2000). A cultural perspective on negotiation: Progress, pitfalls, and prospects. *Applied Psychology: An International Review, 41, 1,* 62–99.

Gelfand, M. J., Lim, B. C., Nishii, L. H., and J. L. Raver. (2003, April). National culture and organizational culture strength: The system of cultural tightness-looseness. In F. Sala (Chair), *Antecedents and consequences of climate and culture strength*. Symposium to be conducted at the Society for Industrial and Organizational Psychology, Orlando FL.

Gelfand, M. J., and C. McCusker. (2002). Metaphor and the cultural construction of negotiation: A paradigm for theory and research. In M. Gannon and K. L. Newman (Eds.), *Handbook of cross-cultural management* (pp. 292–314). New York: Blackwell.

Gelfand, M. J., Raver, J. L., and K. Holcombe. (2002). Methodological issues in cross-cultural organizational research. In S. Rogelberg (Ed.), *Handbook of industrial and organizational psychology research methods* (pp. 216–246). New York: Blackwell.

Gelfand, M. J., and A. Realo. (1999). Individualism–collectivism and accountability in intergroup negotiations. *Journal of Applied Psychology, 84, 5,* 721–736.

Hofstede, G. (1980). *Culture's consequences.* Beverly Hills, CA: Sage.

Huang, K.-K. (1997–1998). *Guanxi* and *Mientze:* Conflict resolution in the Chinese society. *Intercultural communication studies, 7*(1), 17–42.

Kashima, Y., and V. J. Callan. (1994). The Japanese workgroup. In H. C. Triandis, M. D. Dunnette, and L. M. Hough (Eds.), *Handbook of industrial and organizational psychology* (2nd ed., Vol. 4, pp. 606–649). Palo Alto, CA: Consulting Psychologists.

Kim, U., and J. W. Berry. (1993). *Indigenous psychologies: Research and experience in context.* Thousand Oaks, CA: Sage.

Kluckhohn, C., and F. Strodtbeck. (1961). *Variations in value orientations.* Westport, Conn: Greenwood Press, Publishers.

Kramer, R. M., and D. Messick. (Eds.). *Negotiation as a social process.* London: Sage.

Leung, K., Bond, M. H., de Carrasquel, S. H., Munoz, C., Hernandez, M., Murakami, F., Yamaguchi, S., Bierbrauer, G., and T. Singelis. (2002). Social axioms: The search for universal dimensions of general beliefs about how the world functions. *Journal of Cross-Cultural Psychology, 33,* 286–302.

Lytle, A. L., Brett, J. M., Barsness, Z. I., Tinsley, C. H., and M. Janssens. (1995). A paradigm for confirmatory cross-cultural research in organizational behavior. *Research in Organizational Behavior, 17,* 167–214.

Miller, J. (1997). Theoretical issues in cultural psychology. In J. W. Berry, Y. Poortinga, and J. Pandey (Eds.), *Handbook of cross-cultural psychology* (2nd ed., pp. 85–128). Boston: Allyn & Bacon.

Nisbett, R. E., and D. Cohen. (1996). *Culture of honor: The psychology of violence in the south.*

Pande, N., and R. K. Naidu. (1992). *Anasakti* and health: A study of non-attachment. *Psychology and developing societies, 4,* 89–104.

Peng, K., and R. E. Nisbett. (1999). Culture, dialectics, and reasoning about contradiction, *American Psychologist, 54,* 741–754.

Segall, M. H., and C. Kagitçibasi. (Eds.). (1997). *Handbook of cross-cultural psychology: Vol. 3. Social behavior and appropriateness* (Preface). Needham Heights, MA: Allyn & Bacon.

Singelis, T. M., Triandis, H. C., Bhawuk, D. S., and M. J. Gelfand. (1995). Horizontal and vertical dimensions of individualism and collectivism: A theoretical and measurement refinement. *Cross-Cultural Research, 29, 3,* 240–275.

Sinha, D. (1997). Indigenizing psychology. In J. W. Berry, Y. Poortinga, and J. Pandey (Eds.), *Handbook of cross-cultural psychology* (2nd ed., pp. 130–169). Boston: Allyn & Bacon.

Triandis, H. C. (1994). *Culture and social behavior.* New York: McGraw-Hill.

———. (1995). *Individualism & collectivism.* Boulder, CO: Westview.

Triandis, H. C., and M. J. Gelfand. (1998). Converging measurement of horizontal and vertical individualism and collectivism. *Journal of Personality and Social Psychology, 74, 1,* 118–128.

Waller, M. J., Conte, J. M., Gibson, C. B., and M. A. Carpenter. (2001). The effect of individual perceptions of deadlines on team performance. *Academy of Management Review, 26,* 586–600.

Zartman, I. W. (1993). A skeptic's view. In G. O. Faure and J. Z. Rubin (Eds.), *Culture and negotiation* (pp. 17–21). Newbury Park, CA: Sage.

Contributors

MICHELE J. GELFAND (Ph.D., University of Illinois) is associate professor of organizational psychology at the University of Maryland. Her research focuses on cultural influences on negotiation, mediation, justice, and revenge; sexual harassment and discrimination; and basic theory and method in assessing aspects of culture. She received the Ernest J. McCormick Award for Early Career Contribution from the Society of Industrial and Organizational Psychology, and the Cummings Scholar Award from the Organizational Behavior Division of the Academy of Management.

JEANNE M. BRETT (Ph.D., University of Illinois) is the DeWitt W. Buchanan, Jr., distinguished professor of dispute resolution and organizations at the Kellogg School of Management, Northwestern University. She has contributed to theory and practice across a wide range of topics in dispute resolution and negotiation, including the interests, rights, and power theory of dispute resolution, dispute systems design, third-party procedures and procedural justice. Most recently, she has provided evidence for the effect of culture on negotiators' goals, their conception of power, their strategies for sharing information, and their cooperation. She is a coauthor of *Getting Disputes Resolved* and the author of *Negotiating Globally*.

WENDI L. ADAIR (Ph.D., Northwestern University) is assistant professor of organization behavior at the Johnson Graduate School of Business of Cornell University. Her dissertation research investigating the role of culture and communications in negotiations won the 2002 International Association of Conflict Management Award.

ZOE I. BARSNESS (Ph.D., Northwestern University) is assistant professor of business administration at the University of Washington, Tacoma. Her research focuses on teams, diversity, conflict resolution, and the impact of alternative work arrangement and technology in the workplace.

BRUCE BARRY (Ph.D., University of North Carolina) is professor of management and sociology at Vanderbilt University. His research on social processes in organizations, including negotiation, interpersonal influence, procedural justice, communication, and group dynamics, has been published in a variety of journals specializing in management, psychology and negotiation.

ANITA D. BHAPPU (Ph.D., University of Arizona) is assistant professor of management and organizations at the Cox School of Business, Southern Methodist University. She studies how the interactions and outcomes of diverse work teams are impacted by the use of computer-mediated communication technologies like e-mail and group-decision support systems.

STEVEN L. BLADER (Ph.D., New York University) is assistant professor of management at the Stern School of Business, New York University. His research investigates how people perceive and react to procedural fairness, with an emphasis on the motivations that influence those perceptions and reactions.

DEBORAH A. CAI (Ph.D., Michigan State University) is associate professor in the Department of Communication at the University of Maryland. As an international researcher with ties to China, her scholarly interests center on intercultural communication, negotiation, and conflict management, particularly the effect of contextual factors and their interaction with culture.

PETER J. CARNEVALE (Ph.D., State University of New York, Buffalo) is professor of psychology at New York University. His research interests are the social, cognitive, and cultural aspects of agreement, with a focus on negotiation, third-party intervention, and the design of dispute resolution systems. He is a recent recipient of the International Association for Conflict Management's Theory to Practice Award.

YEOW SIAH CHA (Ph.D., University of Illinois) is assistant professor of psychology at the National University of Singapore. His research focuses on the problems of cooperation in social dilemmas and negotiation.

DONALD E. CONLON (Ph.D., University of Illinois) is professor of management at Michigan State University. His research examines the dynamics of intense work groups, justice issues in organizations, negotiation and third-party dispute intervention, and decision making.

RACHEL T. A. CROSON (Ph.D., Harvard University) is associate professor at the Wharton School of the University of Pennsylvania. Her research uses experimental methods from psychology to test game-theoretic predictions from economics, and her aim is to integrate psychological concerns with mainstream economic theory.

CARSTEN K. W. DE DREU (Ph.D., University of Groningen) is professor of organizational psychology at the University of Amsterdam and research director of the Kurt Lewin Graduate School for Social Psychology. He has published award-winning papers on social influence, organizational conflict, negotiation, and interpersonal relations.

SAM FRAIDIN (Ph.D., University of Illinois and J.D., Yale University) is a postdoctoral fellow at the University of Southern California Law School. He studies group decision making, communication, and negotiation.

INGRID SMITHY FULMER (Ph.D., Vanderbilt University) is assistant professor in the Department of Management at Michigan State University. She is interested in the effects of individual differences on social processes such as negotiation and group dynamics and the impact of communication media on interpersonal influence within organizations.

SHIRLI KOPELMAN (Ph. D., Northwestern University is visiting assistant professor at the University of Michigan Business School.) She studies social motives in social dilemmas and emotion in negotiation.

RODERICK M. KRAMER (Ph.D., University of California at Los Angeles) is the William R. Kimball Professor of Organizational Behavior at the Graduate School of Business, Stanford University. His current research interests are trust and distrust in organizations, organizational paranoia, cooperation, and organizational creativity.

CAROL T. KULIK (Ph.D., University of Illinois) is professor of management at the University of Melbourne. Her research encompasses cognitive processes, demographic diversity, and procedural fairness in organizations. She is especially interested in how demographic congruence influences perceptions of fair treatment.

RAJESH KUMAR (Ph.D., New York University) is associate professor of international business at the Aarhus School of Business in Denmark. He researches cross-cultural negotiations, interorganizational collaboration, and emotional dynamics in organizations.

KWOK LEUNG (Ph.D., University of Illinois) is professor of management at the City University of Hong Kong. He publishes widely on justice, conflict, research methods, and culture.

KATHLEEN L. MCGINN (Ph.D., Northwestern University) is professor of negotiations, organizations, and markets at the Harvard Business School. Her research focuses on interpersonal improvisations and their role in decisions, conflict, and resource allocation within organizations.

DAVID M. MESSICK (Ph.D., University of North Carolina) is the Morris and Alice Kaplan Professor of Ethics and Decisions in Management at the Kellogg School of Management, Northwestern University, and director of the Ford Motor Center for Global Citizenship at Kellogg. He is interested in the ethical and social aspects of decision making and information processing, and the psychology of leadership.

CHRISTOPHER J. MEYER is a doctoral student in the Department of Management at Michigan State University. His research interests include organizational justice, conflict, and managing bad news in organizations.

MICHAEL W. MORRIS (Ph.D., University of Michigan) is a professor in the Graduate School of Business and the Department of Psychology, Columbia University. He does basic research on the role of culture in shaping social cognitive tendencies in the context of social judgment. He is also interested in the role of emotions in decision making.

MARGARET A. NEALE (Ph.D., University of Texas) is the John G. McCoy–Banc One Corporation Professor of Organizations and Dispute Resolution at the Graduate School of Management, Stanford University. She is the author of numerous articles on bargaining and negotiation, distributed work groups, and team composition, learning, and performance.

MARA OLEKALNS (Ph.D., University of Adelaide) is professor of management (negotiations) at the Melbourne Business School, University of Melbourne, Australia. Her principal interest is in studying how negotiators sequence their strategies and their ability to create value. She has investigated a range of situational and personality factors that shape the choice and sequencing of strategy.

DEBRA L. SHAPIRO (Ph.D., Northwestern University) is a professor in the Management and Organizations Department at the Robert H. Smith School of Business at the University of Maryland—College Park. She has received numerous "best paper" awards for her research on managing conflict in organizational settings.

MARWAN SINACEUR is a doctoral candidate in organizational behavior at the Graduate School of Business, Stanford University. His research focuses on interpersonal behaviors and perceptions in negotiations.

LEIGH THOMPSON (Ph.D., Northwestern University) is the J. Jay Gerber Distinguished Professor of Dispute Resolution and Organizations and director of the Kellogg Teams and Groups Center at the Kellogg School of Management, Northwestern University. She is a prolific scholar on topics of negotiation, group decision making, learning, and creativity, and the author of *The Mind and Heart of the Negotiator* and *Making the Team: A Guide for Managers.*

CATHERINE H. TINSLEY (Ph.D., Northwestern University) is an associate professor at the McDonough School of Business, Georgetown University. She studies how culture, negotiators' reputations, and perceptions of fairness influence negotiation processes and outcomes.

KWOK-KIT TONG (Ph.D., Chinese University, Hong Kong) is a research fellow in the Department of Management, City University of Hong Kong. He is particularly interested in how contextual factors affect justice judgments.

TOM TYLER (Ph.D., University of California at Los Angeles) is University Professor at New York University. His research investigates the role of justice in conflict resolution and the exercise of authority. His books include

The Social Psychology of Procedural Justice, Why People Obey the Law, Trust in Organizations, Social Justice in a Diverse Society, and *Cooperation in Groups.*

GERBEN VAN KLEEF (Ph. D., University of Amsterdam) is assistant professor of solid psychology at University of Amsterdam. He studies interpersonal effects of emotions in negotiations and is also interested in the effects of power differences on negotiators' behaviors and outcomes.

CHING WAN is a doctoral candidate in the Department of Psychology, University of Illinois. She is interested in interpersonal communication and cross-cultural psychology in the context of negotiation and dispute resolution.

J. MARK WEBER (Ph.D., Northwestern University) is an assistant professor of organizational behaviour at the Rotman School of Management, University of Toronto. Mark has a master's degree in social psychology from McGill University and a master's degree in business administration from Wilfrid Laurier University. His primary research interests include cooperation, trust, negotiations, the role of values in decision making, and social and organizational identity processes.

LAURIE R. WEINGART (Ph.D., Northwestern University) is professor of organizational behavior at the Graduate School of Industrial Administration at Carnegie Mellon University. Her research focuses on the conflict management and decision processes of integrated product development teams and the social interaction and cognitive processes of negotiating dyads and groups.

Author Index

Subject Index

Accessibility, 54
Accountability, 23t, 26; Chinese, 244; competition, 247; cross-level sources of, 245; Japan, 244, 245; Korea, 244; out-groups, 247; pressure; cross-cultural differences, 246; process, 125
Accountability webs, 246
Achieved status, 423
Activation, 54
Adaptive behavior, 282
Adaptive third parties, 280–289
Adjustment, 34
Affect, 74; consequences, 29; defined, 72; misinterpretations, 27; research, 73–75
Affective commitment, 74
Affiliation, 116
Affirmation, 23t
African-Americans; self-praise, 316
Aggression; moral, 225
Agitation-related emotions, 99, 102
Agreeableness, 116
Agreements; adherence, 303–304; process of conclusion, 239
Allocentrism individualism, 116
Alternative-based power, 165
Amae, 425
American Arbitration Association, 267
Americanized Chinese psychology, 424
American negotiators; direct information, 200
Americans, 57, 59, 62, 66; emotions, 100; moods, 101
Analogical learning, 33

Analytical-rational mode, 358
Anchoring, 10t, 13, 34
Anchoring-and-insufficient adjustment. *See* Anchoring
Anger, 28t, 30, 74
Anonymity, 336
Apology, 329
Approval; need for, 77
Arbitration, 264, 265; conventional, 261; interest, 260, 261
Arbitration hybrid procedures, 275
Arbitration-mediation procedure, 267
Arb-med procedure, 275
Arb-neg-med, 275
Arb-neg procedure, 275
Asians, 173; emotions, 107
Assumptions; illuminating limiting, 418–419; IRP strategies, 197–199
Asynchronous media, 358
Atmospherics, 61
Attention, 339
Attribution error; fundamental, 17t, 20–21, 53
Attributions, 8, 30
Authorities; beliefs, 300; reactions to, 423; trustworthiness, 301; values, 300
Autonomous action, 246
Availability, 11t, 14, 54
Avoidance; power, 185–186
Avoidance strategy, 178

Balance, 23t
Bargaining task; distributive, 85